If you're wondering why you should buy this new edition of *Cities and Urban Life,* here are six good reasons!

1. **Thorough updating.** A thorough updating of all data and information includes the most recent and relevant studies in sociology and in many other related fields as well. Data from Census 2010, incorporated into most chapters, provides new demographic information about changes to cities, suburbs, metropolitan and non-metropolitan areas, and the growing presence of minorities in all regions of the country.

2. **New maps.** Through special arrangement with Social Explorer, new maps—based on data from Census 2010—are included in Chapters 3, 10, and 11.

3. **Canadian content.** The first urban text to include the Canadian urban experience throughout the book incorporates new demographics on that country, further encouraging students to think beyond national boundaries.

4. **New terminology.** Chapter 3 now uses the preferred term *megaregion* instead of *megalopolis* to discuss areas of large population density and growth where metropolitan areas overlap with one another. A new map showing the eight U.S. megaregions helps to envision this latest urban concept. Similarly, because the term *edge cities* is a rather obsolete descriptor of these now well-established urban centers, we have opted to use the term *new cities* in Chapter 4 in our discussion of them.

5. **The Great Recession.** The collapse of the housing market, the foreclosure crisis, and the Great Recession have had wide repercussions, negatively affecting the middle class, minority home ownership, the solvency of common-interest developments (CIDs), and urban construction projects. In Chapters 5, 8, 10, 11, and 12, those effects are discussed, along with their impact on people and places.

6. **New sections.** New material on high gas prices affecting sprawl, on the greening of cities, on the role of cities in social movements like the "Arab Spring" demonstrations, on new cities and huge skyscrapers in the developing world, and on placemaking to improve urban public spaces (augmented by a photo essay) brings further insights into cities and urban life.

PEARSON

SIXTH EDITION

CITIES AND URBAN LIFE

JOHN J. MACIONIS
KENYON COLLEGE

VINCENT N. PARRILLO
WILLIAM PATERSON UNIVERSITY

PEARSON

Boston   Columbus   Indianapolis   New York   San Francisco   Upper Saddle River
Amsterdam   Cape Town   Dubai   London   Madrid   Milan   Munich   Paris   Montréal   Toronto
Delhi   Mexico City   São Paulo   Sydney   Hong Kong   Seoul   Singapore   Taipei   Tokyo

Editorial Director: Craig Campanella
Editor-in-Chief: Dickson Musslewhite
Publisher: Karen Hanson
Editorial Project Manager: Mayda Bosco
Editorial Assistant: Joseph Jantas
VP/Director of Marketing: Brandy Dawson
Senior Marketing Manager: Kelly May
Production Manager: Meghan DeMaio
Cover Art Director: Jayne Conte
Cover Designer: Bruce Kenselaar
Cover Image: © Bayda127/Dreamstime
Photo Researcher: Diahanne Lucas Dowridge
Full-Service Project Management & Composition:
    Abinaya Rajendran, Integra Software Services, Pvt. Ltd.
Printer, Binder, and Cover Printer: R. R. Donnelley & Sons
Text Font: New Baskerville

Credits and acknowledgments borrowed from other sources and reproduced, with permission, in this textbook appear on the appropriate page within text or on pages 437–438.

Many of the designations by manufacturers and seller to distinguish their products are claimed as trademarks. Where those designations appear in this book, and the publisher was aware of a trademark claim, the designations have been printed in initial caps or all caps.

Library of Congress Cataloging-in-Publication Data

Macionis, John J.
    Cities and urban life/John J. Macionis, Vincent N. Parrillo.—6th ed.
        p. cm.
    ISBN-13: 978-0-205-20637-7 (alk. paper)
    ISBN-10: 0-205-20637-9 (alk. paper)
    1. Cities and towns.   2. Cities and towns—History.   3. Sociology, Urban.   4. City and town life.
I. Parrillo, Vincent N.   II. Title.
HT151.M335 2013
307.76—dc23
                                                                    2012011084

10 9 8 7 6 5 4 3 2 1

PEARSON

ISBN 10: 0-205-20637-9
ISBN 13: 978-0-205-20637-7

To the memory of E. Digby Baltzell
mentor, friend,
and maverick sociologist
—John J. Macionis

To Donald L. Halsted
mentor, friend,
and inspiration
—Vincent N. Parrillo

CONTENTS

Special Features   xvii

Preface   xix

PART I   UNDERSTANDING THE CITY: ITS ORIGIN AND DEVELOPMENT

Chapter 1   **Exploring the City**   **1**

Why Study the City?   2

Deciding What Is "Urban"   3

The Urban Transformation   4

    Urbanization as a Process   6

    Levels of Urbanization   6

    Urbanism as a Way of Life   9

The Complexity of the City: Various Perspectives   9

    The City in History   10

    The Emergence of Urban Sociology   12

    Geography and Spatial Perspectives   12

    Critical Urban Sociology: The City and Capitalism   13

    Social Psychology: The Urban Experience   14

    Comparative Urbanism: The City and Culture   15

The Anatomy of Modern North American Cities   17

The City in Global Perspective   19

The Quality of City Life   20

Key Terms   22

Internet Activity   22

Chapter 2   **The Origins and Development of the World's Cities**   **23**

Urban Origins   24

    Archaeology: Digging the Early City   24

    The First Permanent Settlements   25

    The City Emerges   26

The First Urban Revolution: City-States and Urban Empires   30
    The Near East: Mesopotamia and Egypt   31
    The Indus Region   33
    A Glance Eastward: China   35
    A Glance Westward: The Americas   35
    Summary: Traits of Early Cities   36
    Crete and Greece   38
    Rome   38
    Decline: The Middle Ages   40
    Revival: Medieval and Renaissance Cities   40
The Second Urban Revolution: The Rise of Modern Cities   43

Case Study: London—The History of a World City   **45**

    Beginnings: 55 B.C.E.–1066 C.E.   46
    The Medieval City: 1066–1550   47
    The World City Emerges: 1550–1800   48
    Industrialization and Colonization: 1800–1900   49
    The Modern Era: 1900 to the Present   49

Summary   52
Conclusion   53
Key Terms   53
Internet Activities   54

Chapter 3   The Development of North American Cities   55

The Colonial Era: 1600–1800   56
    Characteristics of Colonial Cities   56
    The City-Instigated Revolutionary War   57
Growth and Expansion: 1800–1870   58
    The Beginnings of Industrialization   59
    Urban–Rural/North–South Tensions   60
The Era of the Great Metropolis: 1870–1950   60
    Technological Advance   60
    Suburbs and the Gilded Age   61
    The Great Migration   62
    Politics and Problems   63
    The Quality of Life in the New Metropolis   63
The North American City: 1950 to the Present   64
    Decentralization   64
    The Sunbelt Expansion   68
The Evolution of Megaregions   69
    Northeast Megaregion Assets   69
    Sunbelt Problems   71
The Postindustrial City   71
    Deterioration and Regeneration   72

The Future   74
The Human Cost of Economic Restructuring   75

Case Study: New York—The "Big Apple"   **75**

The Colonial Era   77
Growth and Expansion   77
The Great Metropolis Emerges   78
New York Today   80
Earlier Economic Problems   80
Beyond the Devastation   80
Upgrading the City   82
Changing Population   83

Summary   84
Conclusion   85
Key Terms   85
Internet Activities   85

Chapter 4   Today's Cities and Suburbs   **86**

Urban and Suburban Sprawl   87
What Is Sprawl?   87
Why Do We Have Sprawl?   90
Consequences of Sprawl   91

Smart Growth   94
Land Purchases   96
Urban Growth Boundaries   96
Revitalizing Existing Cities and Towns   96
Transit-Oriented Approaches   97
Greening Our Cities   99

Exurbs   99
The New Cities   101
Characteristics and Commonalities   102
Types of New Cities   102
Evolving Middle-Class Centers   106
Three New City Variations   106

Gated Communities   108
Types of Gated Communities   109
A Sense of Community   110

Common-Interest Developments   111

Case Study: Portland, Oregon   **113**

The Physical Setting   113
History   114
Urban Decline and Anti-Sprawl Planning   114
Portland Today   116

Summary   117
Conclusion   117
Key Terms   118
Internet Activities   118

PART II   DISCIPLINARY PERSPECTIVES

Chapter 5   Urban Sociology: Classic and Modern Statements   119

The European Tradition: 1846–1921   122
   Karl Marx and Friedrich Engels: From Barbarism to Civilization   122
   Ferdinand Tönnies: From *Gemeinschaft* to *Gesellschaft*   122
   Emile Durkheim: Mechanical and Organic Solidarity   125
   Georg Simmel: The Mental Life of the Metropolis   126
   Max Weber: The Historical and Comparative Study of Cities   129
   The European Tradition: An Evaluation   131
Urban Sociology in North America: 1915–1970   132
   Robert Park and Sociology at the University of Chicago   133
   Louis Wirth and Urban Theory   136
   Herbert Gans and the Urban Mosaic   138
   Wirth and Gans: A Comparison   139
   Claude Fischer and Subcultural Theory   140
Classic Theories and Modern Research: Myths and Realities   141
   Tolerance in the City   141
   Impersonality in the City   142
   Density and Urban Pathology   144
   Urban Malaise   145
   New Directions in Urban Sociology   146
Summary   147
Conclusion   148
Key Terms   148
Internet Activities   148

Chapter 6   Spatial Perspectives: Making Sense of Space   149

Urban Geography   150
   The Location of Cities   151
   Why Cities Are Where They Are   152
The Shape of the City   157
   The Radiocentric City   158
   The Gridiron City   159
Urban Ecology   160
   Concentric Zones   161
   Sectors   162

Multiple Nuclei   163
Limitations   165
Social Area Analysis and Mapping   166
GIS Mapping   166
Limitations   168
The Los Angeles School: Postmodernism   168
Building Blocks   169
Main Arguments   169
Limitations   170
Summary   170
Conclusion   171
Key Terms   171
Internet Activities   171

Chapter 7   Critical Urban Sociology: The City and Capitalism   172

Urban Economics: The Traditional Perspective   173
Central Place Theory   173
The General Pattern of Land Use   175
Limitations   177
Urban Political Economy   177
Henri Lefebvre: Redefining the Study of Cities   178
Urban Areas as Themed Environments   179
David Harvey: The Baltimore Study   181
Manuel Castells: Updating Marx   182
Allen Scott: Business Location and the Global Economy   183
John Logan and Harvey Molotch: Urban Growth Machines   185
The Global Economy   186
Deindustrialization   186
Economic Restructuring   187
World-Systems Analysis   187
Urban Political Economy: Four Principles   191
The Urbanization of Poverty   193
The Developing World   193
The Developed World   195
Summary   199
Conclusion   200
Key Terms   200
Internet Activities   201

Chapter 8   Social Psychology: The Urban Experience   202

The Physical Environment   203
The Image of the City   203
Cognitive Mapping   206

The Social Environment: *Gesellschaft*   208
   The Pedestrian: Watching Your Step   209
   A World of Strangers   211
   The City as *Gesellschaft:* A Reassessment   214
The Social Environment: *Gemeinschaft*   215
   Urban Networks   215
   Identifying with the City   219
   The City as *Gemeinschaft:* A Reassessment   221
The Texture of the City   221
Humanizing the City   224
Social Movements and City Life   226
Suburban Life   226
   The Stereotypes   226
   The Physical Environment   227
   The Social Environment   228
Summary   228
Conclusion   229
Key Terms   229
Internet Activities   229

Chapter 9   Comparative Urbanism: The City and Culture   230

The City and the Countryside   231
   Interdependencies   231
   Urban Dominance   233
The City and Civilization   236
   The "Soul" of the City   236
   The City as the Center of Civilization   238
   The Civic Culture of the City   238
The City and Societal Culture   240

Case Study: Ming Peking   240

   Physical Structure   241
   Symbolism   241

Case Study: Hellenic Athens   244

   The Preclassical Period   244
   The Golden Age   245
   Behind the Glory   246
Ming Peking and Athens: A Comparison   247
The Culture of Capitalism and the City   248
   The Capitalist City   249
   The Industrial Revolution   249
   Urban Life as Economics   250
   Assets and Debits   252

Case Study: Communist–Capitalist Beijing   **253**

Urban Life as Politics   253
Economic Reform and Environmental Issues   255
A Rising Consumerism   255

Summary   256
Conclusion   257
Key Terms   258
Internet Activities   258

PART III   THE STRUCTURE OF THE CITY

**Chapter 10   Stratification and Social Class: Urban
and Suburban Lifestyles**   **259**

Social Stratification   260
Social Class Distinctions   261
Income Distribution Nationwide   264
Incomes Within and Outside Cities   265
Wealth and Net Worth   265
Poverty Nationwide   266
Poverty Within and Outside Cities   267
A Cautionary Note   268

Urban Social Class Diversity   268
Upper-Class Urban Neighborhoods   270
Middle-Class Urban Neighborhoods   272
Working-Class Urban Neighborhoods   276
Mixed-Income Urban Neighborhoods   278
Low-Income Urban Neighborhoods   280
The Homeless   282

Suburban Social Class Diversity   282
Upper-Income Suburbs   283
Middle-Income Suburbs   283
Working-Class Suburbs   284
Suburban Cosmopolitan Centers   284
Minority Suburbs   284

Summary   288
Conclusion   289
Key Terms   289
Internet Activities   290

Chapter 11   Race, Ethnicity, and Gender: Urban Diversity   **291**

Cities and Immigrants   292
Ethnic Enclaves and Ethnic Identity   293
Ethnic Change   293

Racial and Ethnic Minorities   295
   Blacks   296
   Asians and Pacific Islanders   299
   Hispanics   303
   Muslims   306
   Native Peoples   307
Women and Urban Life   308
   Work   309
   Urban Space   311
   The Public Sphere   312

Case Study: Chicago, "City of the Big Shoulders"   **312**

   Early Chicago   313
   The Burning and Rebuilding of Chicago   314
   Jane Addams and Hull House   315
   Chicago in the Early Twentieth Century   316
   The Postwar Period   317
   The Chicago Machine   317
   Ordered Segmentation   317
   Chicago Today   318
Summary   321
Conclusion   321
Key Terms   321
Internet Activities   322

Chapter 12   Housing, Education, Crime: Confronting Urban Problems   323

Housing: A Place to Live   324
   Adequate Housing: Who Has It?   324
   Housing Problems: A Brief History   324
   Public Housing   326
   Deterioration and Abandonment in the Inner City 328
   The Great Recession and Foreclosures   329
   The Inner City Today: A Revival?   330
   The New Urbanism   332
Education: The Urban Challenge   336
   Meeting the "No Child Left Behind" Challenge   336
   Magnet Schools   339
   School Vouchers   339
   Charter Schools   339
Crime: Perception and Reality   341
   Public Perception of Crime   341
   Explaining High-Crime Areas   343

Effects of Crime on Everyday Life   345
What Is the Solution?   346
Summary   348
Conclusion   349
Key Terms   349
Internet Activities   350

PART IV   GLOBAL URBAN DEVELOPMENTS

Chapter 13   Cities in the Developing World   **351**

Latin American Cities   352
  Early Cities   354
  European Dominance   355
  Modern Cities   358
African Cities   359
  Early Cities   359
  European Dominance   361
  Modern Cities   362
Middle Eastern Cities   363
  Islamic Cities   363
  European Dominance   366
  Modern Cities   367
  New Cities   367
Asian Cities   368
  India   368
  China   372
  Japan   373
  Southeast Asia   375
Common Legacies   377
  Economic Legacies   377
  Political Legacies   378
Common Problems   378
  Spiraling Populations   379
  Quality of Life   379
  Environment   380
  Shantytowns   380
Summary   382
Conclusion   384
Key Terms   385
Internet Activities   385

Chapter 14	**Planning the Urban Environment**	**386**
	Visions	387
	City Planning in World History	387
	Why Plan?	389
	Planning in the Industrial Era: 1800–1900	390
	The "City Beautiful" Movement	390
	The New Towns Movement	391
	British New Towns	391
	New Towns Worldwide	392
	New Towns in North America	393
	What Makes New Towns Succeed or Fail?	397
	Architectural Visions	398
	The Radiant City	398
	Broadacre City	398
	The Arcology	399
	TRY-2004	399
	Utopia's Limitations	400
	More Focused Urban Planning	400
	Sidewalks and Neighborhoods	400
	Squares and Parks	401
	Placemaking	402
	Festival Marketplaces	405
	The Realities of Urban Planning	407
	Economics and Politics	407
	The Importance of Values	407
	Case Study: Toronto, Ontario	**408**
	The Physical Setting	408
	History	409
	Creation of a Metropolitan Government	409
	Two Phases of Urban Planning	410
	Toronto Today	411
	Summary	413
	Conclusion	414
	Key Terms	415
	Internet Activities	415
Glossary		**416**
References		**421**
Photo Credits		**437**
Index		**439**

SPECIAL FEATURES

URBAN LIVING

The Shantytowns of the Developing World	20
All New York's a Stage	76
CID Restrictions on Personal Freedom	112
Urban Apathy: Ignored Violent Attacks	128
The Shame of the Cities: Who's to Blame?	134
How City Dwellers Cope—and Cope Well	146
India: A Different Kind of Poverty	195
Latin American "Street Children": Living on the Edge	196
Living with Terrorism	206
Saigon: Learning to Cross the Street All Over Again	212
The Subway at Rush Hour	212
Clothes Make the Man	213
The Networks of Street-Corner Men	216
Great Urban Rituals	220
Mayor Fiorello La Guardia of New York	233
"Nothing but the Facts, Ma'am"—Capitalist–Industrialist Consciousness	251
The "Philadelphia Gentlemen"	262
The Bourgeois and Bohemians Merge	273
Comparing Working-Class and Middle-Class Suburbs	285
Life in a Minority Suburb	287
The Multicultural City and Food	295
Targets of Street Harassment	310
Shantytowns Throughout the World	381

CITYSCAPE

San Francisco's Massive Changes   7
Daily Life in Catal Hüyük, 6000 B.C.E.   30
Classical Rome: The Spectacle of Death   41
The East End and West End of London   50
The Northeast Megaregion (Megalopolis)   70
The Crazy-Quilt Pattern of New York, 1890   79
Atlanta's Edge Cities   100
Working-Class Manchester, 1844   120
Our Town: The Spirit of *Gemeinschaft*   124
New Orleans: Paying the Price for Its Location   154
Break-of-Bulk in Two Cities   157
Miami's Little Havana   167
The Streets of Brownsville   210
The Personality of Cities   222
The Invasion of the City Slickers   234
The Industrial City: 1844   248
Pruitt–Igoe: Symbol of a Failed National Solution   326
The Magnificent City of Tenochtitlán   354
The Islamic City   365
Toronto Plans Its Future   412

URBAN TRENDS

"As American as Apple Pie"   88
Something Is Wrong   89
If You Build It, They Will Come   180
A Bold Initiative   198
The City and Civilization   237
The Crystallization of the City   239
The New Urban Schools   338
The Evolution of Primate Cities   353
Sir Ebenezer Howard's Garden Cities of To-Morrow   388
Jane Jacobs: Planning for Vitality   401

PREFACE

In 2008, the world achieved a historic landmark: A majority of the planet's people now live in cities. Urban living is rapidly becoming the *norm* for members of our species. Surely, no more compelling reason exists for us to undertake the study of cities and urban life.

THE BASIC APPROACH

The approach of this text is multidisciplinary but fundamentally sociological. Readers will find here the enduring contributions of the classical European social thinkers, including Max Weber, Karl Marx, Ferdinand Tönnies, Georg Simmel, and Emile Durkheim, as well as those of early pioneers in North America, including Robert Park and Louis Wirth. Of course, many men and women have stood on the shoulders of these giants and extended our understanding. Thus, this text also considers the ideas of a host of contemporary urbanists, including Manuel Castells, Michael Dear, Herbert Gans, Jane Jacobs, Henri Lefebvre, Lyn Lofland, John Logan, Kevin Lynch, Harvey Molotch, Allen Scott, Edward Soja, and Michael Sorkin.

Yet, as this string of well-known names suggests, urban studies rests on research and theory developed within many disciplines. *Cities and Urban Life*, therefore, is truly a multidisciplinary text that draws together the work of historians (Chapter 2: "The Origins and Development of the World's Cities," and Chapter 3: "The Development of North American Cities"), sociologists (Chapter 4: "Today's Cities and Suburbs," Chapter 5: "Urban Sociology: Classic and Modern Statements," Chapter 10: "Stratification and Social Class: Urban and Suburban Lifestyles,"

Chapter 11: "Race, Ethnicity, and Gender: Urban Diversity," and Chapter 12: "Housing, Education, Crime: Confronting Urban Problems"), geographers and urban ecologists (Chapter 6: "Spatial Perspectives: Making Sense of Space"), political economists working within various disciplines (Chapter 7: "Critical Urban Sociology: The City and Capitalism"), social psychologists (Chapter 8: "Social Psychology: The Urban Experience"), anthropologists (Chapter 9: "Comparative Urbanism: The City and Culture," and Chapter 13: "Cities in the Developing World"), and architects as well as city planners (Chapter 14: "Planning the Urban Environment").

THE ORGANIZATION OF THIS TEXT

Part I of the text, "Understanding the City: Its Origin and Development," introduces the main concepts and themes that resonate throughout the book; surveys the historical development of cities, noting how urban life has often differed in striking ways from the contemporary patterns we take for granted (Chapters 2 and 3); and examines the current trends of sprawl, edge cities, and gated communities now shaping cities and suburbs (Chapter 4). Part II, "Disciplinary Perspectives," highlights the various disciplinary orientations that, together, have so advanced our understanding of cities (Chapters 5–9). Part III, "The Structure of the City," focuses on the social organization of today's cities in North America, highlighting how urban living reflects the importance of stratification and social class (Chapter 10) and of race, ethnicity, and gender (Chapter 11), as well as forcing us to confront vexing problems such as housing, education, and crime (Chapter 12). Part IV, "Global Urban Developments," first offers a look at urbanization in four major world regions: Latin America, Africa, the Middle East, and Asia (Chapter 13). It is in these areas of the world that urbanization is now most rapid, with cities reaching unprecedented size. Finally, Chapter 14 examines the architectural, social, and political dimensions of urban planning, and discusses approaches to help cities achieve their potential for improving everyone's lives.

FOUR KEY THEMES

This attempt to tell the urban story will lead us to consider a wide range of issues and to confront countless questions. Four main themes guide this exploration, however, and it is useful to make these explicit. Whatever else a student entering the field of urban studies might learn, he or she must pay attention to these themes:

1. *Cities and urban life vary according to time and place.* Since the idea of the city first came to our ancestors some 10,000 years ago, the urban scene has been re-created time and again, all around the world, in countless ways. The authors—informed by their own travels to some 65 of the world's nations—have labored to portray this remarkable diversity throughout this text.
2. *Cities reflect and intensify society and culture.* Although cities vary in striking ways, everywhere, they stand as physical symbols of human civilization. For example, nowhere do we perceive the inward-looking world of the Middle Ages better than in the walled cities of that era. Similarly, modern U.S. cities are powerful statements about the contemporary forces of industrial capitalism.
3. *Cities reveal the best and the worst about the human condition.* Another way to "read" cities is as testimony to the achievements and failings of a way of life. Thus, while New York boasts some spectacular architecture, exciting public parks, vital art galleries, and vibrant concert halls, it also forces us to confront chronic prejudice and wrenching poverty.
4. *Cities offer the promise—but not always the reality—of a better life.* Since at least the time of the ancient Greeks, people have recognized that the

city holds the promise of living "the good life." Yet all urban places fall short of this ideal in some ways, and in many of today's cities, people are struggling valiantly simply to survive. The great promise of urban living, coupled with the daunting problems of actual cities, provokes us to ask how we can intentionally and thoughtfully make urban places better. Although we are realistic about the problems, we remain optimistic about the possibilities.

SPECIAL FEATURES OF THE TEXT

Two special features warrant the attention of readers.

Boxes Each chapter contains several boxed inserts. These boxes are of three kinds. *Urban Trends* boxes depict a pattern, either past or present, shaping people's way of life. *Urban Living* boxes provide a picture of the city "at street level"—that is, a close-up look at how people really live. Finally, *Cityscape* boxes present a literary account or scholarly analysis of some significant dimension of urban life.

Case Studies The text includes eight case studies that offer a broad sociohistorical look at major cities in various regions of the world as they illustrate a chapter's key points. The cities profiled in these case studies are London (Chapter 2), New York (Chapter 3), Portland, Oregon (Chapter 4), Ming Peking (Chapter 9), Hellenic Athens (Chapter 9), Communist–Capitalist Beijing (Chapter 9), Chicago (Chapter 11), and Toronto (Chapter 14).

WHAT'S NEW IN THE SIXTH EDITION

This new edition reflects a number of changes. Here is a list of changes that define *Cities and Urban Life, sixth edition*:

1. **Thorough updating.** Most important is the continuance of our policy to provide a thorough updating of all data and information

and to include the most recent and relevant studies not only in sociology but in many other related fields as well.

2. **Census 2010.** Data from Census 2010 have been incorporated into most chapters, providing new demographic information about changes to cities, suburbs, metropolitan and non-metropolitan areas, and the growing presence of minorities in all regions of the country.

3. **New maps.** Through special arrangement with Social Explorer, new maps—based on data from Census 2010—are included in Chapters 3, 10, and 11.

4. **Canadian content.** The first urban text to include the Canadian urban experience throughout the book incorporates new demographics on that country, further encouraging students to think beyond national boundaries.

5. **New terminology.** Chapter 3 now uses the preferred term *megaregion* instead of *megalopolis* to discuss areas of significant population density and growth where metropolitan areas overlap with one another. A new map showing the eight U.S. megaregions helps to envision this latest urban concept. Similarly, because the term *edge cities* is a rather obsolete descriptor of these now well-established urban centers, we have opted to use the term *new cities* in Chapter 4 in our discussion of them.

6. **The Great Recession.** The collapse of the housing market, the foreclosure crisis, and the Great Recession have had wide repercussions, negatively affecting the middle class, minority home ownership, the solvency of common-interest developments (CIDs), and urban construction projects. In Chapters 5, 8, 10, 11, and 12, those effects are discussed, along with their impact on people and places.

7. **Updated case studies.** The end-of-chapter city case studies—as well as other in-text city profiles, notably those of Cleveland and Detroit—have been updated to reflect the impact of the Great Recession, the growing Asian and Hispanic presence in cities, as revealed by new census data, and renaissance of many older cities through gentrification and tourism.

8. **More on urban and suburban sprawl.** Chapter 4 contains updated and expanded discussion on the environmental consequences of urban and suburban sprawl, how higher gasoline prices affect commuter choices, and how planners seek to transform new (edge) cities such as Tysons Corner, Virginia, into more livable cities.

9. **More on environmental issues.** Livability is also examined in a new section on the greening of our cities, which informs students about efforts cities are making to reduce energy consumption and greenhouse-gas emissions.

10. **New material on common-interest developments (CIDs).** Chapter 4 also includes added material on CIDs from the differing viewpoints of rational choice theorists, new urbanists, and critical urban theorists. The spread of privately-governed CIDs to other parts of the world is also mentioned.

11. **More on urban social movements.** The discussion in Chapter 8 on social movements and city life has been expanded to include the 2011 "Arab Spring" demonstrations in Tunisia and Egypt, as well as in Libya, Syria, and Yemen.

12. **More on race and urbanism.** Chapter 12 contains an expanded discussion on the connection between racial/economic inequality and crime, including the addition of commentary on general strain theory and social disorganization theory as possible ways to understanding this relationship. A new discussion on the role of residential segregation as a contributing factor is also included, as are pro and con arguments about zero-tolerance policies.

13. **Many new issues and trends.** Chapter 13 includes dramatic changes in the developing world since the last edition: the famine in sub-Saharan Africa; the spectacular rise of new cities in the Mideast, most notably in the United Arab Emirates; and the construction of some of the world's tallest skyscrapers there and in Asia.

14. **More on improving public spaces.** Drawing from the ideas of Jane Jacobs and William H. Whyte, Chapter 14 contains a new segment on placemaking, a fairly new approach to improving public spaces. A photo essay section accompanies this material, illustrating the before and after possibilities of a sociological vision for physically improving the quality of city life.

15. **New special feature boxes.** New special features boxes have been added: on the re-branding of cities as consumerist entities ("If You Build It, They Will Come" in Chapter 7), on women in public spaces ("Targets of Street Harassment" in Chapter 11), and on school reform in Chicago ("The New Urban Schools" in Chapter 12).

Where appropriate, other boxes have been updated.

16. **A new photo program.** Finally, a new photo program, including a photo essay in Chapter 14, and a new set of supplemental materials further enhance the sixth edition, both for readers and for instructors.

SUPPLEMENTS

Instructor's Manual and Test Bank (ISBN 0205206417) The Instructor's Manual and Test Bank has been prepared to assist teachers in their efforts to prepare lectures and evaluate student learning. For each chapter of the text, the Instructor's Manual offers different types of resources, including detailed chapter summaries and outlines, learning objectives, discussion questions, classroom activities, and much more.

Also included in this manual is a test bank offering multiple-choice, true/false, fill-in-the-blank, and/or essay questions for each chapter. The Instructor's Manual and Test Bank is available to adopters at www.pearsonhighered.com.

MyTest (ISBN 0205206387) The Test Bank is also available online through Pearson's computerized testing system, MyTest. MyTest allows instructors to create their own personalized exams, to edit any of the existing test questions, and to add new questions. Other special features of this program include random generation of test questions, creation of alternative versions of the same test, scrambling question sequence, and test preview before printing. Search and sort features allow you to locate questions quickly and to arrange them in whatever order you prefer. The Test Bank can be accessed from anywhere with a free MyTest user account. There is no need to download a program or file to your computer.

PowerPoint Presentation (ISBN 0205206395) Lecture PowerPoints are available for this text. The Lecture PowerPoint slides outline each chapter to help you convey sociological principles in a visual and ex-

citing way. They are available to adopters at www.pearsonhighered.com.

MYSEARCHLAB

MySearchLab™

www.mysearchlab.com

Save TIME. Improve Results.

MySearchLab is a dynamic website that delivers proven results in helping individual students succeed. Its wealth of resources provides engaging experiences that personalize, stimulate, and measure learning for each student. Many accessible tools will encourage students to read their text, improve writing skills, and help them improve their grade in their course.

FEATURES OF MYSEARCHLAB

Writing

- Step-by-step tutorials present complete overviews of the research and writing process.

Research and citing sources

- Instructors and students receive access to the EBSCO ContentSelect database, census data from Social Explorer, Associated Press news feeds, and the Pearson bookshelf. Pearson SourceCheck helps students and instructors monitor originality and avoid plagiarism.

e-text and more

- **Pearson e-text**—An e-book version of *Cities and Urban Life, 6th Edition* is included in MySearchLab. Just like the printed text, students can highlight and add their own notes as they read their interactive text online.
- **Chapter quizzes and flashcards**—Chapter and key term reviews are available for each chapter online and offer immediate feedback.
- **Primary source documents**—A collection of documents, organized by chapter, is

available on MySearchLab. The documents include head notes and critical thinking questions.
- **Gradebook**—Automated grading of quizzes helps both instructors and students monitor their results throughout the course.

ACKNOWLEDGMENTS

The authors wish to thank the editorial team at Pearson for their efforts in making this text a reality. Particular thanks go to Nancy Roberts, publisher, for originally signing the project and helping to get the work under way; to Karen Hanson, publisher, for her support for this edition; to Mayda Bosco, editorial project manager; to Meghan DeMaio, production manager; and to Diahanne Lucas Dowridge for picture research. We also are most appreciative of the fine work by Kristin Jobe, project manager at Integra–Chicago, and Abinaya Rajendran, project manager at Integra Software Services, in guiding this new edition from its manuscript form to its actual publication.

The authors also wish to acknowledge the role played by James L. Spates, of Hobart and William Smith Colleges, in a 1980s version of this book, entitled *The Sociology of Cities*, coauthored by Spates and Macionis. Although Vince Parrillo and John Macionis have significantly revised that effort at many levels, some elements of Jim's ideas still remain.

For their efforts reviewing part or all of the manuscript and generously sharing their ideas with us, we gratefully acknowledge the reviewers for this edition and previous ones: Brian Sahd, Hunter College; Robert L. Boyd, Mississippi State University; Ivan Chompalov, Edinboro University; Patrick Donnelly, University of Dayton; Matthew Green, University of Arizona; Richard S. Muller, Monmouth University; Lee L. Williams, Edinboro University; Daniel J. Monti, Jr., Boston University; Stephanie Moller, University of North Carolina at Charlotte; Robert J. S. Ross, Clark University; Mark Abrahamson, University of Connecticut; Robert L. Boyd, Mississippi State University; Jerome Krase, Brooklyn College; Leo Pinard, California Polytechnic State University–San Luis Obispo; David Prok, Baldwin Wallace College; James D. Tasa, Eric Community College–North; Ronald S. Edari, University of Wisconsin; and Daniel J. Monti, Boston University.

John J. Macionis
Kenyon College
Gambier, Ohio 43022
E-mail: macionis@kenyon.edu
http://www.TheSociologyPage.com

Vincent N. Parrillo
William Paterson University
Wayne, New Jersey 07470
E-mail: parrillov@wpunj.edu
*http://www.wpunj.edu/cohss/departments/
sociology/faculty/vincent-n.-parrillo.dot*

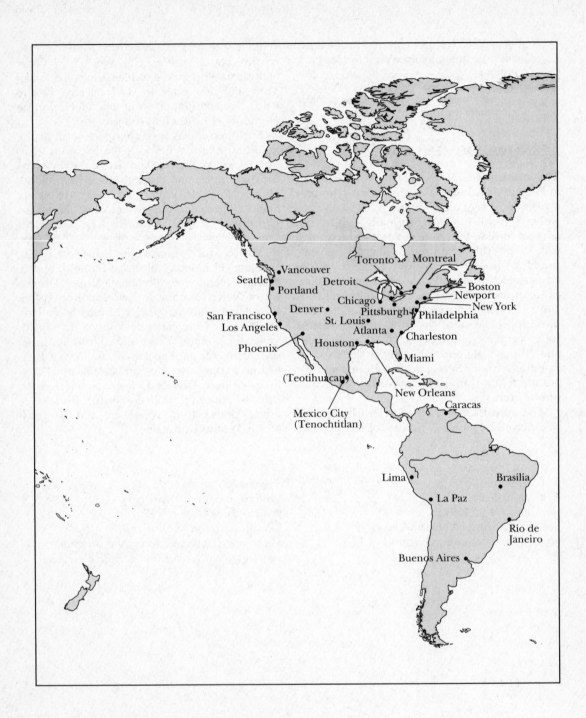

Vancouver
Seattle
Portland
Detroit
Toronto
Montreal
Boston
Newport
Chicago
New York
Denver
Pittsburgh
Philadelphia
San Francisco
St. Louis
Los Angeles
Atlanta
Charleston
Phoenix
Houston
Miami
(Teotihuacan)
New Orleans
Mexico City
(Tenochtitlan)
Caracas
Lima
Brasilia
La Paz
Rio de
Janeiro
Buenos Aires

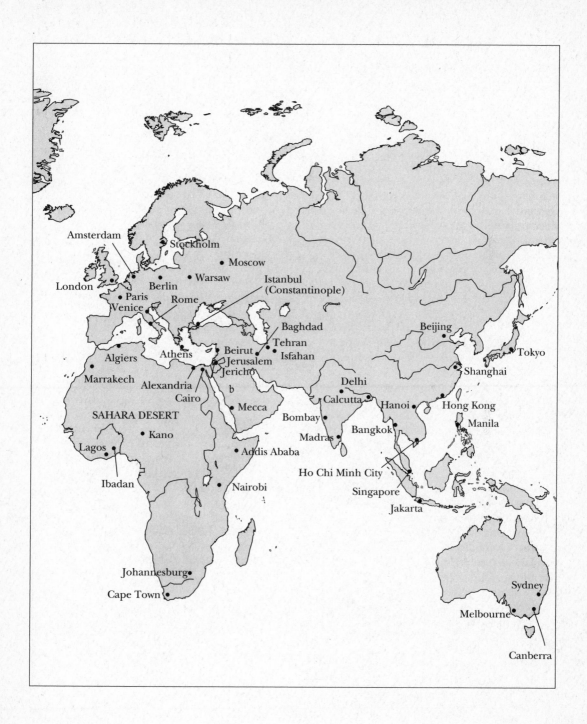

Amsterdam
Stockholm
Moscow
London
Berlin
Warsaw
Istanbul
(Constantinople)
Paris
Venice
Rome
Baghdad
Beijing
Tehran
Tokyo
Algiers
Athens
Beirut
Isfahan
Shanghai
Jerusalem
Marrakech
Jericho
Alexandria
b
Delhi
Cairo
Calcutta
Hanoi
Hong Kong
SAHARA DESERT
Mecca
Bombay
Manila
Kano
Madras
Bangkok
Lagos
Addis Ababa
Ho Chi Minh City
Ibadan
Nairobi
Singapore
Jakarta

Johannesburg
Sydney
Cape Town
Melbourne
Canberra

CHAPTER 1

EXPLORING THE CITY

WHY STUDY THE CITY?

DECIDING WHAT IS "URBAN"

THE URBAN TRANSFORMATION

Urbanization as a Process

Levels of Urbanization

Urbanism as a Way of Life

THE COMPLEXITY OF THE CITY:
VARIOUS PERSPECTIVES

The City in History

The Emergence of Urban Sociology

Geography and Spatial Perspectives

Critical Urban Sociology: The City and
Capitalism

Social Psychology: The Urban Experience

Comparative Urbanism: The City and
Culture

THE ANATOMY OF MODERN NORTH
AMERICAN CITIES

THE CITY IN GLOBAL PERSPECTIVE

THE QUALITY OF CITY LIFE

KEY TERMS

INTERNET ACTIVITY

Let us go then, you and I,
When the evening is spread out against the sky
Like a patient etherised upon a table;
Let us go, through certain half-deserted streets,
The muttering retreats
Of restless nights in one-night cheap hotels
And sawdust restaurants with oyster-shells:
Streets that follow like a tedious argument
Of insidious intent
To lead you to an overwhelming question …
Oh, do not ask, "What is it?"
Let us go and make our visit.

T. S. Eliot, "The Love Song of J. Alfred Prufrock"

WHY STUDY THE CITY?

Cities! Most of us share poet T. S. Eliot's fascination with urban places—settings of intense excitement, great mystery, and striking human diversity. With the poet, most of us probably agree that cities (London was the object of Eliot's interest) are places we would love to visit—but, of course, many of us wouldn't want to live there! Nevertheless, little compares with the excitement of visiting a major city such as New York, Toronto, Chicago, or San Francisco.

When we go into the city, we often find block after block of shops selling all kinds of things we never find at home, and we pass by every imaginable sort of person—the old and the young, the rich and the poor, the up and coming as well as the down and out. People say that virtually anything can and does happen in big cities—and it doesn't take long to realize that they're right!

Across North America, more than four out of five of us live in urban places, and even more of us build our lives around cities. We are born in cities (or near them), grow up in or near one (probably in a suburb), go to a college in or near a city (maybe one some distance away from our hometowns), and eventually settle down in or near a city that becomes "home." Across the continent, much of our favorite entertainment—including clubs, musical or sports events, and theater—is city based. We might as well admit it: We are a nation of city folks, and the urban way of life is the norm in both Canada and the United States. To study the city, therefore, is to study ourselves.

Yet the city is more than what our personal experiences reveal. A dynamic entity unto itself, the city is the most powerful drawing card in human history. The share of the world's population living in cities rose from just 9 percent in 1900 to 30 percent in 1950, and then climbed to more than 50 percent by 2009. If present trends continue, by 2030 cities will be home to 60 percent of all humans on the planet (United Nations Population Division 2012).

The city is thus the setting for all aspects of the human drama: the highest learning colliding with the grossest ignorance, unimaginable wealth juxtaposed with the most abject poverty. Historically, most people drawn to the city sought to realize their hopes of a higher standard of living and often succeeded—but will this continue to be true in the new megacities, such as Mexico City, Rio de Janeiro, Cairo, New Delhi, and Tokyo? (See the world map preceding this chapter to locate these and other prominent cities.) Such places are adding millions of new residents so rapidly that they cannot provide basic services (water, housing, and electricity) to many of their people. Unless checked soon, such growth may intensify poverty and suffering for billions, not to mention ecological disasters unparalleled in history. To study the city, therefore, is also to study a uniquely powerful form of human settlement: a physical and social environment with the potential for both satisfying and frustrating the entire spectrum of human needs.

An important theme of this book is that cities do not exist entirely by themselves. They are an inextricable part of their larger societies. For centuries, the city has been the heart, the lifeblood, of various civilizations—the center of economic, political, and artistic events. In cities, we find both the triumphs and the tragedies of the human story. For example, we associate Hellenic Athens, Renaissance Florence, and Elizabethan London with great achievements of the human spirit, while we link classical Rome and Nazi Berlin with savage human degradation. In each case, a cultural setting helped shape the city's character: During the fourth century B.C.E.,[1] the Greeks raised Athens to a pinnacle of human accomplishment, while the rise of Nazism in Germany after World War I led to Berlin's infamous decadence.

The connection between the city and a broader culture is no less evident today. In its cities exists much of what is great about the United States: intellectual excellence, political

---

[1]The authors use the designation B.C.E. ("before the common era") in place of B.C. ("before Christ") in recognition of the religious pluralism of North American society. Similarly, we use C.E. ("common era") in place of A.D. (*Anno Domini*, "in the year of our lord").

freedom, and artistic vitality. Of course, these same cities also exhibit this country's greatest failings, including grinding poverty and sometimes-savage crimes. To study the city, then, is also to examine the society in which it exists. The impact of economics can be as significant as that of culture, particularly in today's global economy, so we must also examine closely the forces of globalization in shaping a city's structure and well-being.

Understanding the city, therefore, is crucial in comprehending modern existence. But how we choose to study the city is also important. The city is a complex reality that yields few easy answers. If we look only at the facts of urban life, we will surely miss its dynamic soul. The city will appear dull and lifeless—a collection of concrete buildings, bureaucracies, and unemployment rates. But if we also ask the "how" questions, which link these factual elements to human lives, the city springs to life as a set of vital, dynamic forces.

In studying the city, then, we must not ask merely "What is it?" We must, as Eliot suggests in his poem, "go and make our visit." We must probe beyond the descriptions and the statistics to the broader and deeper reality of urban life. This book will help you do just that.

DECIDING WHAT IS "URBAN"

Urban seems like a simple enough concept to grasp, but it actually has many interpretations. Derived from the Latin word *urbanus*—meaning characteristic of, or pertaining to, the city—*urban* essentially holds that same association to most people.

Complicating that understanding, however, are the varying criteria for defining an urban area that exist among the nearly 200 countries with urban populations. These criteria include *administrative function* (a national or regional capital), *economic characteristics* (more than half the residents in non-agricultural occupations), *functional nature* (existence of paved streets, water supply, sewerage, and electrical systems), and *population size* or *population density* (the number of people living within a square mile or kilometer). Administrative function serves

as the only basis for urban designation in 89 countries, but 20 other countries apply it in combination with other criteria. Similarly, economic characteristics are one of several criteria in 27 countries, while function is one of several definition elements in 19 countries. Then again, 5 countries use only function to designate an urban area, but for 46 other countries, population size or density is the sole criterion, one that an additional 42 countries apply in combination with other criteria. No urban definition exists at all in 24 countries—while Anguilla, Bermuda, Cayman Islands, Gibraltar, Hong Kong, Macao, Monaco, Nauru, and Singapore identify their entire populations as urban.

Canada and the United States both use population density to identify an urban area, without regard to local boundaries. In Canada, an urban area must contain more than 400 people per square kilometer, with a total population exceeding 1,000 people. The United States defines an urban area as adjoining census blocks with a population density of 1,000 persons per square mile, which is equivalent to the Canadian standard. **Urban cluster** is the U.S. Census Bureau term for a combination of these adjacent urban areas that extend across city, county, or state boundaries. Sometimes social scientists use the term *conurbation* to refer to these interconnected areas of continuous built-up development. (All areas that the Census Bureau does not classify as urban—generally places of less than 2,500 persons—it defines as rural.)

Such differences worldwide make cross-national comparisons difficult. For example, the lower-range limit for population of an urban area ranges from 200 in Iceland to 10,000 in Greece. A universal standard—say, a midpoint from these two extremes of 5,000 inhabitants—would be inappropriate in populous countries such as China or India, where rural settlements—with no urban attributes at all—could easily contain such large numbers. Using each country's own criteria, the United Nations Population Division (2012) reported that 50.1 percent of the world's population was urban. Significant variations existed: Africa, 40 percent urban;

Asia, 42 percent urban; Europe, 73 percent urban; Latin America and the Caribbean, 79 percent urban; North America, 82 percent urban. The lowest urban population (11 percent) was in Burundi, while the highest (100 percent) were in the six countries previously identified.

Worldwide projections show the percentage of urban population increasing everywhere (see Table 1–1). Reporting the percentage of urban people living in the world's seven major geographical areas between the years 1975 and 2009, the table shows that urbanization is an unmistakable trend everywhere. In fact, the world's cities are growing by about 1 million people each week. This dramatic pattern means that by 2050, more than two-thirds of the planet's people will be urban dwellers.

Distinct regional patterns, however, occur within that urban growth. If we examine Table 1–1 for the percentages of growth between 1975 and 2010, we see that in the more industrialized areas of the world—North America and Europe—urban growth slowed considerably in recent years. The area of greatest urban growth is now in the developing world—Latin America, Africa, the Middle East, and Asia (see Figure 1–1, page 5). In fact, when we consult the figures on urban growth rates by country, we find that the 10 countries with the highest urban growth rates are all in these four regions. Those with the lowest rates—with the notable exceptions of Cuba, a few small island nations, and Uruguay—are all in Europe, North America, and Japan. Moreover, when we scan a list of all the world's nations ranked in order of their urban growth rates, we must look down through 87 countries before we encounter a developed country—Ireland (UN Population Division 2012).

THE URBAN TRANSFORMATION

If any one thing should astound us, it is how popular cities have become throughout the world. As a human invention, cities are scarcely 10,000 years old, but as the centuries have passed, they have become both much larger and far more numerous. For example, in 1800 only one city, Beijing, had 1 million residents; now the world contains 392 cities where a million or more people reside (UN Population Division 2012:9). The increase in world population alone cannot explain this phenomenon. Once people become aware of the advantages of cities—protection, increased material standard of living, a more stimulating mental and social life—they don't want to live anywhere else. Because this urban growth and development can occur in different ways and on several levels, however, we need to know some basic concepts about these processes and their consequences if we are to understand fully what is happening.

TABLE 1–1   Percentage of Urban Population in Major Areas of the World

Area	1975	2011	2050
Africa	25.7	39.6	57.7
Asia	25.0	45.0	64.4
Europe	65.2	72.9	82.2
Latin America and Caribbean	60.7	79.1	86.6
North America	73.8	82.2	88.6
Oceania	71.9	70.7	73.0
World	37.7	52.1	67.2
More-developed regions	68.7	77.7	85.9
Less-developed regions	27.0	46.5	64.1

Source: From *World Urbanization Prospects,* 2011 Revision. Copyright © 2012 by the United Nations, Population Division. Reprinted with permission.

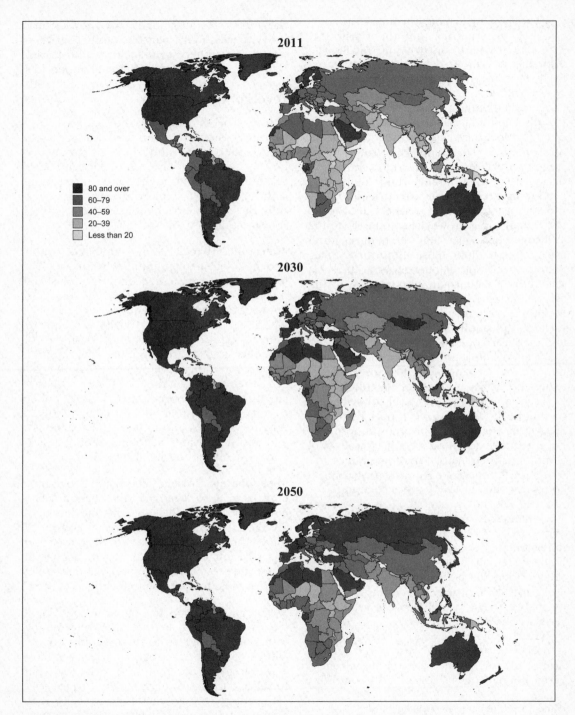

FIGURE 1–1   Percentage of Population in Urban Areas, 2011, 2030, and 2050

Source: From *World Urbanization Prospects,* 2011 Revision. Copyright © 2012 by the United Nations, Population Division. Reprinted with permission.

Urbanization as a Process

The changes resulting from people moving into cities and other densely populated areas is what we mean by **urbanization.** This process of increased population concentration can be deliberate and planned, such as in Brazil's capital, Brasilia, which was inaugurated in 1960. It can also be spontaneous and unplanned, as the rapid urban growth occurring in many developing countries. However it occurs, urbanization transforms land use from rural to urban economic activities—and often the land itself, from a porous surface absorbing rainfall, to a non-porous one of asphalt and concrete. In addition, this progression in greater population density transforms many patterns of social life, altering both the social structure and the social organization of that area. As we will discuss shortly, these changes include a more complex division of labor and social stratification, the growth of subcultures, and more formal social controls.

As an example of urbanization, consider the massive changes that San Francisco experienced. Today, it is a thoroughly modern U.S. city, famed for its hills, cable cars, fog, and natural beauty. Visitors often note its relaxed lifestyle and easygoing, pleasant atmosphere. Except during rush hour, people typically stroll along the streets, unlike midtown Manhattan or central London, where a fast-paced, push-and-shove walking style is more common.

Such was not always the case, however. The changes to San Francisco since its early existence have been profound, as historic documents attest. One such document is Richard Henry Dana's *Two Years Before the Mast* (2006, originally published in 1862), one of the greatest of nineteenth-century seagoing journals, a part of which you can read in the *Cityscape* box on page 7.[2]

What happened to San Francisco between Dana's two visits was gold, discovered in 1849. Almost overnight, the sleepy little village of Yerba Buena, the nearest port for outfitting

the Sierra Nevada mines, was transformed into a feverish city. Not for another 70 years would what others would call a sophisticated, "laid-back" San Francisco begin to appear.

Levels of Urbanization

As the process of urbanization expands into ever-increasing concentrations and areas of land, other terms and concepts are necessary to understand the complexity and scale of human organization and interaction. Although we will explore these topics more fully in subsequent chapters, here is a brief introduction to them:

Metropolitan Area.   A large population center and its adjacent communities, with which it has a high degree of economic and social integration, constitute a *metropolitan area.* Also known as an *urban agglomeration,* such a region typically has a large city (100,000 residents or more) as the hub that extends its sphere of influence into the surrounding communities. These communities may not be urban in character themselves, but they link closely with that city through transportation (roads and public transit), employment (commuters), media (city newspapers, and radio and TV stations), and leisure activities (clubbing, dining, entertainment, and professional sports).

Micropolitan   Area.   Another   geographic entity is a *micropolitan area,* which has an urban core of at least 10,000 residents but less than 50,000. Like a metropolitan area, it consists of the county containing the core urban area and any adjacent counties with a high degree of social and economic integration with that urban core, as measured by commuting there to work.

Megaregion.   When two or more metropolitan areas expand so that they intermingle with one another to form a continuous (or almost continuous) urban complex, we have a **megaregion,** the preferred term for what social scientists previously called a *megalopolis.* This merged conglomeration typically contains a population in the tens of millions, such as that along the Eastern Seaboard, although the cities therein retain their individual names

---

[2]Various kinds of boxes are included in each chapter to illustrate key points and themes. When you encounter a reference to a particular box, take a minute or two to read it before going on with the chapter.

CITYSCAPE

San Francisco's Massive Changes

Shipping from New York, Richard Henry Dana first visited San Francisco, then called Yerba Buena ("good herbs"), in 1835. Here is what he saw:

[Near the] mouth of the bay...is a high point on which the [Presidio Mexican military outpost] is built. Behind this point is the little harbor, or bight, called Yerba Buena, in which trading vessels anchor, and, near it, the Mission of Delores. There was no other habitation on this side of the Bay, except a shanty of rough boards put up by a man named Richardson, who was doing a little trading between the vessels and the Indians....We came to anchor near the mouth of the bay, under a high and beautifully sloping hill, upon which herds of hundreds and hundreds of red deer, and the stag, with his high branching of antlers, were bounding about, looking at us for a moment, and then starting off, affrighted at the noises we made at seeing the variety of their beautiful attitudes and motion.

That was not the San Francisco of the next century nor does it much resemble this description of Dana's, written in 1859 after a second visit:

We bore round the point toward the old anchoring ground of hide ships, and there, covering the sand hills and the valleys, stretching from the water's edge to the base of the great hills, and from the old Presidio to the Mission, flickering all over with lamps of its streets and houses, lay a city of one hundred thousand inhabitants....The dock into which we drew, and the streets about it, were densely crowded with express wagons and hand-carts to take luggage, coaches and cabs for passengers, and with men....Through this crowd I made my way, along the well-built and well-lighted streets, as alive as by day, where boys in high keyed voices were already crying the latest New York papers; and between one and two o'clock in the morning found myself comfortably abed in a commodious room, in the Oriental Hotel, which stood, as well as I could learn, on the filled-up cove, and not far from the spot where we used to beach our boats from the Alert.

When I awoke in the morning, and looked from my windows over the city of San Francisco, with its townhouses, towers, and steeples; its courthouses, theaters, and hospitals; its daily journals; its well-filled learned professions; its fortresses and light houses; its wharves and harbor, with their thousand-ton clipper ships, more in number than London or Liverpool sheltered that day...when I looked across the bay to the eastward, and beheld a beautiful town on the fertile wooded Shores of the Contra Costa [the area of today's Oakland and Berkeley] and steamers, large and small, the ferryboats of the Contra Costa, and capacious freighters and passenger-carriers to all parts of the great bay and its horizon—when I saw all these things, and reflected on what I once was and saw here, and what now surrounded me, I could scarcely keep my hold on reality at all, or the genuineness of anything, and seemed to myself like one who had moved in "worlds not realized."

Source: Richard Henry Dana, *Two Years Before the Mast* (New York: Library of America, 2006), pp. 196, 203, 320–22.

(Boston, New York, Philadelphia, Baltimore, and Washington, D.C.). The world's largest megaregion is perhaps Delhi–Lahore, India, home to more than 120 million (Florida 2008).

Megacity. A metropolitan area can constitute its own megalopolis if the population within its municipal boundary numbers at least 10 million people. In the past 35 years, the number of megacities has rocketed from 3 in 1975 to 23 in 2011, with an expected increase to 30 by 2025 (see Table 1–2, page 8). Today, 1 in 11 people worldwide live in a megacity (UN Population Division 2012:8).

TABLE 1-2   Population of the World's Megacities in Millions

	2011			2025	
Rank	**Urban Agglomeration**	**Population**	**Rank**	**Urban Agglomeration**	**Population**
1	Tokyo, Japan	37.2	1	Tokyo, Japan	38.7
2	Delhi, India	22.7	2	Delhi, India	32.9
3	Mexico City, Mexico	20.5	3	Shanghai, China	28.4
4	New York–Newark, USA	20.4	4	Mumbai, (Bombay), India	26.6
5	Shanghai, China	20.2	5	Mexico City, Mexico	24.6
6	São Paolo, Brazil	19.9	6	New York–Newark, USA	23.6
7	Mumbai (Bombay) India	19.7	7	São Paolo, Brazil	23.2
8	Beijing, China	15.6	8	Dhaka, Bangladesh	22.9
9	Dhaka, Bangladesh	15.4	9	Beijing, China	22.6
10	Kolkata (Calcutta) India	14.4	10	Karachi, Pakistan	20.2
11	Karachi, Pakistan	13.9	11	Lagos, Nigeria	18.9
12	Buenos Aires, Brazil	13.5	12	Kolkata (Calcutta), India	18.7
13	Los Angeles–Long Beach–Santa Ana, USA	13.4	13	Manila, Philippines	16.3
14	Rio de Janeiro, Brazil	12.0	14	Los Angeles–Long Beach–Santa Ana, USA	15.7
15	Manila, Philippines	11.9	15	Shenzhen, China	15.5
16	Moskva (Moscow), Russia	11.6	16	Buenos Aires, Argentina	15.5
17	Osaka–Kobe, Japan	11.5	17	Guangzhou, Guangdong, China	15.5
18	Istanbul, Turkey	11.3	18	Istanbul, Turkey	14.9
19	Lagos, Nigeria	11.2	19	Al-Qahirah (Cairo), Egypt	14.7
20	Al-Qahirah (Cairo), Egypt	11.2	20	Kinshasa, DR Congo	14.5
21	Guangzhou, Guangdong, China	10.9	21	Chongqing, China	13.6
22	Zhenshen, China	10.6	22	Rio de Janeiro, Brazil	13.6
23	Paris, France	10.6	23	Bangalore, India	13.2
			24	Jakarta, Indonesia	12.8
			25	Chennai (Madras), India	12.8
			26	Wuhan, China	12.7
			27	Moskva (Moscow), Russia	12.6
			28	Paris, France	12.2
			29	Osaka–Kobe, Japan	12.0
			30	Tianjin, China	11.9

Source: From *World Urbanization Prospects*, 2011 Revision. Copyright © 2012 by the United Nations, Population Division. Reprinted with permission.

Global City. Also called a *world city*, a *global city* occupies an influential position in the global economic system, attracting worldwide investments and exercising considerable economic power worldwide. London, New York, Paris, and Tokyo are at the top of the hierarchy of cities because of their role in the world system of finance and trade (Abrahamson 2004). **World-systems analysis,** an approach we will examine more closely in Chapter 7 on critical urban sociology, suggests that the economic well-being of most cities heavily depends on their placement within this world hierarchy.

Urbanism as a Way of Life

As implied earlier, the companion concept to urbanization (population growth and concentration) is **urbanism,** the culture or way of life of city dwellers. Here we are not only speaking about changes in values, attitudes, norms, and customs but also about lifestyle patterns and behavioral adaptations influenced by one's residential and/or work environment. Often, these lifestyles coincide with different geographical districts of the city. In downtown areas, for example, we are likely to see well-dressed businesspeople—many of whom live in apartments. Older residential neighborhoods may provide the sights, sounds, and even aromas of exotic cultural diversity. Still other neighborhoods contain the city's poor, who struggle every day to survive. In many suburban areas, single-family homes—replete with children and the ever-present automobile—dominate.

Lifestyles are, of course, much more than matters of individual choice. They reflect dimensions of social difference, often taking the form of social inequality. Like virtually all other societies, the United States and Canada contain marked **social stratification,** the hierarchical ranking of people in terms of valued resources. Wealth is certainly one important dimension of social stratification, and North American cities often provide striking contrasts between well-heeled urbanites who have lives of material comfort and others who must persevere just to survive.

Such differences are typically related to other dimensions of social difference: race, ethnicity, and gender. Once ignored in the urban public sphere, women are now more likely to hold public office, at least in cities with populations of 25,000 or more (Wolbrecht, Beckwith, and Baldez 2008). From both historical and contemporary viewpoints, however, women's lives and city experiences have reflected the realities of gender, interwoven with those of social class, race, and ethnicity. In a still-continuing historic pattern, North American cities attract immigrants of different races and ethnicities; on arrival, many find themselves at or near the bottom of the urban hierarchy. With time, many improve their situation, but others continue to suffer from a wide range of problems associated with poverty and/or prejudice.

Social power—the ability to achieve one's goals and to shape events—is yet another important dimension of inequality. For those with considerable wealth, urban living is often the experience of shaping their own lives (and, indeed, the lives of others). By contrast, for poorer urbanites, many of whom are members of racial and ethnic minorities, life in the city is a grim matter of trying to cope with forces that seem overwhelming.

Of course, none of these structural patterns exists exclusively in cities. Social stratification is as important in small towns in North Carolina as it is in Raleigh, the state capital; people perceive racial distinctions as keenly in rural Ohio as they do in Columbus; and "power politics" is the name of the game in rural Wyoming, just as it is in Cheyenne. Nevertheless, because these structural patterns shape our cities so strongly, we can hardly ignore them.

On another level, however, cities intensify the effects of class, race, ethnicity, gender, and power, because they concentrate everything human in a small space. If we care to look, we can find examples of wealth and poverty, of power and powerlessness, of such extremity as to be nearly incomprehensible. A walk through the poor neighborhoods of almost any major North American city will reveal numerous examples of numbing poverty. Indeed, poverty for millions continues as only one of the significant problems that beset the urban environment.

THE COMPLEXITY OF THE CITY: VARIOUS PERSPECTIVES

The city may well be the most complex of all human creations. As a result, it cannot be understood using any single point of view. While this book is fundamentally sociological in its orientation, it draws together insights, theories, and statistics from a wide variety of related disciplines, including history, archaeology, psychology, geography, economics, and political science. As we now explain, all these perspectives are vital for grasping the living entity that is the contemporary city.

The City in History

Today, cities are so much a part of our lives that they seem both natural and inevitable. You may be surprised to learn, then, that in the larger picture of human history, cities are a rather new idea. Although "modern" humans have existed on the earth for about 200,000 years, cities began to appear a scant 10,000 years ago. Moreover, it wasn't until the last 3,000 years that cities became relatively numerous and inhabited by significant numbers of people. And only in 2009 did we reach the point at which most of the world's people were urbanites.

Thus, we can see the importance of studying the city historically. Without the benefit of hindsight, we might easily fool ourselves into thinking that cities, although perhaps smaller in the past, were always more or less like those we know today.

Luckily, our understanding of past cities doesn't rely only on historical documents, such as Dana's account of early San Francisco. In recent years, urban archaeologists have made major strides in the study of urban settings about which little or no written material is available.

Abandoned cities, or cities rebuilt on earlier foundations, still contain traces of their earlier existence, providing clues for archaeologists trained in the careful excavation and analysis of artifacts. From such clues, archaeologists can piece together a picture of how a city's people lived: how they built their houses and organized their families, what they thought important enough to portray in paintings, what level of technology they employed, what they commonly drank or ate. By unearthing many such clues, archaeologists allow long-dead cities to spring back to life in our minds.

One of the most important finds during recent years was the 2001 carbon dating of Caral, an ancient, sacred city of about 160 acres located approximately 62 miles north of the Peruvian capital of Lima. Imagine the excitement of discovering that it was founded before 2600 B.C.E.—pushing back the date for the first known urban settlement in the Western Hemisphere by at least 1,000 years! This settlement predates the Incan civilization by 4,000 years, but even more astonishing is the impressive construction of its six pyramids, which are a century older than the pyramids of Giza in ancient Egypt. It appears that other nearby sites may be even older, but that Caral was the regional center for the approximately 10,000 people living in that area.

Archaeologists believe Caral contains the most important pre-Columbian ruins discovered since the 1911 discovery of Machu Picchu, also in Peru but hundreds of miles to the south. The Caral site is so old that it predates the ceramic period, which explains why archaeologists did not find any pottery shards. Caral's importance resides in its domestication of plants, especially cotton but also beans, squashes, and guava. This civilization knew how to use textiles and built many residential structures around the pyramids. Among the numerous artifacts discovered were 32 flutes made from pelican and animal bones, engraved with the figures of birds and monkeys, thus revealing that although the inhabitants lived by the Pacific coast, they were nevertheless aware of the animals of the Amazon (Isbell and Silverman 2006).

Archaeology also plays a role in contemporary cities. Most cities exist on the rubble of their own past. Take London, for example. Over the course of its 2,000-year history, this city has risen some 30 feet, building on its own refuse. In 2007, digs at the planned Olympics aquatic center in East London revealed Iron Age and Roman settlements (Reuters 2007). Ten years earlier in excavation sites in and around London Bridge unearthing Roman London—established in the first century C.E.—archaeologists found two different types of Roman buildings, one type made with timber frames and

Built by the Incas in the mid-fifteenth century, Machu Picchu remained hidden until 1911. Now a tourist attraction receiving 400,000 visitors annually, it is one of the world's most impressive archaeological sites. It is a masterpiece of urban planning, civil engineering, architecture, and stonemasonry, its many buildings still intact except for their thatch-and-reed roofs.

clay walls and floors, and the other being more substantial masonry buildings, some with mortar floors and plaster walls, both of which served as the homes of artisans, with shops or workshops in front and living quarters behind. Also uncovered were many artifacts of everyday life, including oil lamps for lighting homes and vessels for cooking and drinking (Jubilee Line Extension 1997).

Closer to home, archaeologists completed an excavation on New York's Wall Street in 1979–1980, uncovering artifacts from the original Dutch settlement of 1625. In 1991, excavation for a new federal building between Broadway and Duane Street in Lower Manhattan unearthed an eighteenth-century African American burial ground. Through such finds, we continually learn more about the past and how people lived in those times.

Two chapters of this text tell about cities in human history. Chapter 2 reviews major urban developments from the beginnings of cities some 10 millennia ago right up to the urban events of this century. We will see that the urban story is one of continuous and striking change. Chapter 3 highlights how cities have developed in the United States and Canada. Here, too, you will read about astonishing changes—changes hinted at in Dana's account of San Francisco. You will read about the alterations of North American urban life as cities grew from the small, isolated colonial centers of the seventeenth century to sprawling environments with populations often reaching into multimillions. Then, in Chapter 4, you will learn of recent urban trends shaping our urban and suburban lifestyles: sprawl, edge cities, gated communities, and common-interest developments (CIDs).

The Emergence of Urban Sociology

One key goal of this book is to help you understand how sociologists study the city. Although historians have been looking at cities for centuries, sociologists are more recent investigators. As Chapter 5 explains, early sociologists in the late nineteenth century lived during a period of dramatic urban upheaval, and naturally, they turned their attention to cities. They tried to understand just how the Industrial Revolution transformed the small villages of Europe and North America into huge, seemingly chaotic metropolises.

Many early sociologists shared a pessimistic vision of the city. Their works portray the city as a dangerous place where the traditional values of social life—a sense of community and caring for other people—were systematically torn apart. Recent sociological research, however, shows that many of these concerns about the destructiveness of urban living rested on faulty evidence. Contemporary research reveals the city as a more neutral phenomenon. Cities are neither good nor bad in and of themselves; cultural forces at work in a particular time and place push them in one direction or the other. Thus, we come to understand the horrors of nineteenth-century London as primarily a product of the massive industrialization that occurred within a capitalist society, not as a result of something inherently urban.

Geography and Spatial Perspectives

Why did people cluster together to form cities in the first place? Aristotle, an ancient Greek philosopher, provided a timeless answer: People come together in cities for security; they remain there to live the good life. For the ancient Greeks, cities satisfied a need for security, because in an age of few laws and fewer treaties, groups frequently preyed on one another. For protection, people came together in a single location, often a natural fortification, such as the Acropolis in Aristotle's Athens. Where natural defenses were not available, people built walls. But a site could become a city only with other geographical assets: water, access to transportation routes, and the ability to produce or import enough goods to meet the population's needs.

Once cities began, however, people made a remarkable discovery. Mixing together in large numbers not only afforded protection, it also generated more profitable trade and stimulated intellectual life as well. People began to hail the city as offering the potential for what Aristotle termed "the good life."

The importance of a city's physical location, and of how people come to arrange themselves within the urban area, has led urbanists to develop two related areas of study: (1) **urban geography,** which focuses on the significance of the city's location and natural resources; and (2) **urban ecology,** which analyzes how people spread out within an urban area. Let's illustrate each of these areas.

A city's geographical location has a great deal to do with how people live in that city. Take the two largest U.S. cities, New York and Los Angeles. Centered on Manhattan Island and surrounded by rivers, New York City has a land base of bedrock that is physically able to support tall buildings. By contrast, Los Angeles stretches out across a semi-arid basin that, geologically speaking, makes the building of skyscrapers a shaky business indeed. These different settings translate into very different daily routines. For example, a half-hour commute in New York may begin in the elevator, perhaps shared with another tenant. Possible encounters with a doorman, a neighbor on the street, and perhaps the news dealer on the corner precede a shared subway ride, then a stop at Starbucks for a cup of coffee and a brief conversation with the cashier, and then another elevator ride shared with fellow workers. In contrast to this series of social interactions, the worker in Los Angeles drives in the privacy of one's car, listening to the radio or a CD, moves along on the freeway, and, if traffic moves easily, can quietly get absorbed in thought. In other words, New York City's space brings people together, while the Los Angeles environment separates them (Giovannini 1983:147).

Geography is only one cause of the differing social dynamics that distinguish cities. Various categories of people stake out particular areas within the city, and particular activities come to dominate certain districts—and these categories and activities can change over time. Such shifts interest urban ecologists, who seek to understand how people choose to locate and rearrange themselves in urban space. One well-documented ecological process is **invasion–succession,** by which whole sections of a city change. A new "high-tech" area in an adjacent suburb may rather suddenly upstage an old industrial district. Or perhaps, almost overnight, the older district starts to look tawdry; secondhand stores, "gentlemen's clubs," and pornographic bookstores replace the older, more respectable businesses. Before long, income levels in the area drop and the few remaining original businesses close their doors. Where once executives and working people trod the city sidewalks, now one finds only prostitutes, drug dealers, and petty criminals. With this succession, the process of change is complete. Invasion–succession may also occur in residential areas as new categories of people enter an established neighborhood.

Many contemporary social scientists, however, no longer favor the ecological model; instead, they emphasize the critical urban sociology approach mentioned earlier. Especially influencing urban studies today is **postmodernism,** which is primarily a reaction against the assumption that rational, objective efforts can explain reality with any certainty. Why do they say that? Postmodernists insist that people have multiple interpretations based on their individual, concrete experiences, not on the abstract principles of "experts."

Therefore, urban planning should still reflect traditional visions, but only through expression of notions of community, diversity, small-scale approaches, restoration of the older urban fabric, and creation of new spaces that use modern technologies and materials (Dear 2001). Both these older and newer studies of physical arrangements, spatial perspectives, and the social dynamics for city life provide the subject matter of Chapter 6.

Critical Urban Sociology: The City and Capitalism

Just as important as a city's geographical setting and its cultural framework is its ability to generate trade—to be economically prosperous. In the fourth century B.C.E., Aristotle, as previously mentioned, said that initially, people came to cities for security. True enough, particularly at the time he was writing. But throughout history, people have flocked to the city for many reasons, most importantly, their belief that there they would significantly improve their material standard of living. For example, hope for a better life spurred millions upon millions of immigrants from rural and poor backgrounds to come to the cities of Canada and the United States during the late nineteenth and early twentieth centuries. These people, including many of our great-grandparents, settled in cities across both nations to seek their fortunes.

Comparisons of medieval and contemporary cities reveal the growing importance of the economic function of cities over the centuries. In the Middle Ages, although cities were already important centers of trade, other areas of life also were thriving. All one has to do is look at the physical layout of cities built during the Middle Ages—with their central cathedral as the tallest building—to see the importance of religion in people's lives. The Industrial Revolution, however, changed all that. Cities became ever more important as centers of wealth. To meet the economic demands of millions, skyscrapers in the new "central business district" sprang up, rising far

· The Church of Our Lady before Tyn, with its magnificent Gothic steeples, dominates the cityscape of Prague, Czech Republic. The Old Town retains many medieval qualities: visual domination by the cathedral, no central business district, narrow streets, and buildings with commercial enterprises at street level and residences on the floors above.

above the churches that once dominated old city skylines.

Looking at the decline of manufacturing in cities, the migration to the suburbs and the Sunbelt, the mushrooming cities in poor nations, and a growing world economy, a new breed of urban researchers concluded that natural processes could not explain these changes and their economic impact on cities. Instead, they argue, decision making within political and economic institutions, often thousands of miles away, affects a city economically, politically, socially, and even physically. Some, but not all, advocates of this **urban political economy,** or critical urban sociology perspective, are neo-Marxists. Regardless of their ideological orientation, they focus on investment decisions and economic trends that determine a city's fortunes.

Recent analytical thinking in this area includes postmodern theory, an emphasis on fragmented and non-traditional elements.

World-systems analysis—examining a city as one interdependent part of the global whole—is another prominent aspect of contemporary thinking. We will look at all of these structural imperatives and their ramifications on urban poverty in Chapter 7.

Social Psychology: The Urban Experience

With about four-fifths of North Americans living in cities, any student of cities needs to explore the urban experience. How and why do cities stimulate us so much? Do cities change people in one way or another?

We know that the city trips our emotions, for some in positive ways and for others in negative ways. Although these reactions are certainly personal, they are also *social* in two senses. First, it is the social environment of the city itself that generates them. Second,

Unlike the medieval Old Town section of Prague with its central cathedral and lower surrounding buildings, North American cities typically include a central business district with residences but also expressways, wider streets for cars, and a skyline dominated by tall commercial buildings, as illustrated in this view of Atlanta, Georgia.

they are social in that they are common; they resonate in one of those ways with virtually all of us.

These social dimensions of the urban experience also figure in our analysis. *Urbanism*— a concept referring to those social–psychological aspects of life, personality patterns, and behavioral adaptations influenced by the city—is the focal point of Chapter 8.

Comparative Urbanism: The City and Culture

As we have already suggested, the city does not exist in a vacuum. It is "powered" by its people, who represent a particular way of life, or culture. By the term **culture,** we mean the basic beliefs, values, and technology that characterize a city in a particular historical era. Any city reproduces and intensifies its society's culture.

Technology provides a good example. If we were to visit the London of a century and a half ago, we likely would be shocked to see how different it was from the cities of today. Yes, we would find a bustling business district and lots of people—but the similarity would end there. Rather than a sprawling metropolitan area with extensive suburbs and shopping centers, crisscrossed by superhighways and adorned with skyscrapers, we would find a relatively compact city, with all its hustle going on in narrow, winding streets of astonishing filth. Charles Dickens, who lived there, described this very scene in his novel *Bleak House.*

LONDON....Implacable November weather. As much mud in the streets as if the waters had but newly retreated from the face of the earth.... Smoke lowering down from chimney pots, making a soft black drizzle, with flakes of soot in it as big as full-grown snow-flakes—gone into

The congested, bustling activity captured in this woodcut of London in the 1870s helps us visualize the sights and sounds, the grandeur and squalor, that attracted millions of people to live, work, play, or visit the city and participate in all that it offered.

mourning, one might imagine, for the death of the sun. Dogs, undistinguishable in mire. Horses, scarcely better; splashed to their very blinkers. Foot passengers, jostling one another's umbrellas, in a general infection of ill-temper, and losing their foothold at street-corners, where tens of thousands of other foot passengers have been slipping and sliding since the day broke (if this day ever broke), adding new deposits to the crust upon crust of mud...and accumulating at compound interest. (1853:1)

Inevitable as they may seem, clean and paved streets, clean air, the skyscraper, the superhighway, and the large, sprawling suburb are very recent urban phenomena—all products of a certain level of technological development. The skyscraper only became feasible in the latter part of the nineteenth century, with the development of steel-frame buildings and electrically powered elevators. Similarly, sprawling suburbs are unthinkable without superhighways or mass public transportation linking cities and suburbs; these, in turn, are dependent on technological innovations, such as steel, railroads, electricity, and the private automobile. Finally, paved streets became common in cities only in the twentieth century, and it wasn't until the 1950s and 1960s that passage of clean air legislation in the United States curtailed exhaust excesses like those Dickens described. A given level of technology, then, has much to do with the urban experience.

At the same time, cultural beliefs play a major role in shaping city life, including certain uses of technology. Take the mobile phone, for instance. Although larger, clumsier predecessors existed in earlier decades, the 1990s were when cellular phones came into widespread use. Telephones were once a mostly private means of communication via landlines in the home, office, or enclosed phone booth, but the mobile phone today has redefined our sense of private and public space.

On the one hand, mobile phones are decidedly private. Only a limited circle of people know the user's mobile phone number, few directories list cell numbers, and the user may have fewer disruptions or eavesdropping than at home, essentially by using an "improvised open-air wireless phone booth" (Lasen 2003:1). At the same time, however, the mobile phone intrudes into the public sphere, its ringing heard by all in the vicinity, who are forced to hear only one side of a conversation—particularly if the speaker does not talk quietly.

Almost everywhere, these third parties to such calls consider them a nuisance when they occur in a theater, museum, classroom, church, waiting room, and restaurant or at social events and work. Of less annoyance, but still viewed as a nuisance, are mobile calls on a bus or train and in bars, cafés, stores, or other people's houses (Höflich 2006:63). Reaction to mobile calls in these situations is nearly universal, but cultural differences— along with such variables as education and social class—affect phone usage behavior and acceptance of that behavior.

In a comparative study of Europeans, Joachim Höflich (2006) reported that Italians are far more likely than Finns, Germans, or Spaniards to use a mobile phone to maintain communication with family members but feel more uncomfortable making a call with strangers around them. At the same time, southern Europeans (e.g., Greek, Portuguese, Spanish, and ironically even Italian) tend to speak more loudly in public than northern Europeans (e.g., Finns, Germans, and Scandinavians). Finns in particular feel a strong need for a private sphere respected by others, while use of mobile phones in public by Italians and Spaniards is extremely common.

The above is but one example of the role that cultural beliefs play in the urban setting. So central is this issue to the study of cities that we devote all of Chapter 9 to it.

THE ANATOMY OF MODERN NORTH AMERICAN CITIES

Chapters 2 through 9 provide the basic framework for a detailed analysis of the cities of the contemporary world. Next, our attention returns to North America for a detailed analysis of the cities that most of us know best. Even though urban population growth has slowed

TABLE 1–3   Population of the 30 Largest U.S. Cities, 2000 and 2010

2010 Ranking	City	2000 Population	2010 Population	2000 Ranking	Percentage Change
1	New York	8,008,278	8,175,133	1	+2.1
2	Los Angeles	3,694,820	3,792,621	2	+2.6
3	Chicago	2,896,016	2,695,598	3	−6.9
4	Houston	1,953,631	2,099,451	4	+7.5
5	Philadelphia	1,517,550	1,526,006	5	+0.6
6	Phoenix	1,321,045	1,445,632	6	+9.4
7	San Antonio	1,144,646	1,327,407	9	+16.0
8	San Diego	1,223,400	1,307,402	7	+6.9
9	Dallas	1,188,580	1,197,816	8	+0.8
10	San Jose	894,943	945,942	11	+5.7
11	Jacksonville	735,617	821,784	14	+11.7
12	Indianapolis	781,870	820,445	12	+4.9
13	San Francisco	776,773	805,235	13	+3.7
14	Austin	656,562	790,390	16	+20.4
15	Columbus	711,470	787,033	15	+10.6
16	Fort Worth	534,691	741,206	27	+38.6
17	Charlotte	540,828	731,424	26	+35.2
18	Detroit	951,270	713,777	10	−25.0
19	El Paso	563,662	649,121	22	+15.2
20	Memphis	650,100	646,889	18	−0.5
21	Baltimore	651,154	620,961	17	−4.6
22	Boston	589,141	617,594	20	+4.8
23	Seattle	563,374	608,660	23	+8.0
24	Washington, DC	572,059	601,723	21	+5.2
25	Nashville–Davidson	545,524	601,222	25	+10.2
26	Denver	554,636	600,158	24	+8.2
27	Louisville*	256,231	741,096	66	+189.2
28	Milwaukee	596,974	594,833	19	−0.4
29	Portland, Oregon	529,121	583,776	28	+10.3
30	Las Vegas	478,434	583,756	32	+22.0

*Louisville city and Jefferson County, Kentucky, became consolidated after Census 2000.
Source: U.S. Bureau of the Census.

in Canada and the United States, this by no means suggests that the situation of our cities today is stagnant and unchanging. In fact, the situation is far from it. Recent decades have been a period of enormous change for North American cities.

In the United States, the much-publicized movement to Sunbelt (southern and western) cities is one such change. As Table 1–3 indicates, with a few exceptions, Sunbelt cities have gained markedly in population during the last decade, compared to midwestern and northeastern cities. Growing significantly were the cities of Fort Worth, Charlotte, Austin, San Antonio, and Las Vegas—all in the South and West. Declining were Detroit and Baltimore, Memphis, and Chicago—most in the Midwest or Northeast. Other large northern cities not listed in this table that also lost population were Akron, Ohio; Rochester, New York; Pittsburg, Pennsylvania; Buffalo, New York; and Cleveland, Ohio. Moving against the trend were Birmingham, Alabama (down 5 percent) and New Orleans, Louisiana, which lost an astonishing 130,000 people (26 percent) in the wake of Hurricane Katrina in 2005.

A second recent development is a nationwide trend toward living in smaller cities or in areas farther away from the central cities. For instance, the census shows that the areas surrounding suburbs are growing most rapidly. Thus, just as people moved from central cities to suburbs a generation ago, now they are moving still farther from the urban core.

What accounts for these marked changes? Demographers suggest that although many older Americans prefer to remain in the community where they spent most of their adult lives ("aging in place"), retirement magnet areas attract many affluent seniors. A retirement home in such places as Dade County, Florida (Miami's home county); Austin, Texas; or Sun City, Arizona (near Phoenix) has become an attraction that millions have no desire to resist. Second, the last several decades witnessed an increasing exodus of business and industry from center cities, occasioned by a desire to escape high taxation, congestion, outmoded plants, high union wages, and excessive heating costs (the latter two factors primarily in the North). In many cases, firms moved to the South or West. If not, they typically moved to areas on the periphery of the center city. In either case, they pulled their employees with them. Employees chose to live in smaller cities, towns, and rural areas partly from their desire to be near relocated businesses or industries and partly from the long-standing desire to be free of congestion and have "living space" in affordable housing. Earlier suburbs, built primarily in the 1950s and 1960s, were the first manifestation of this cultural value, and this decentralization has continued ever since.

Whatever the final explanations for these demographic changes, their effects are profound. Those cities that lose ground to other communities, either from a declining population or a comparatively low growth rate, lose federal funding and political representation. As a result, such cities must cut budgets, services, and aid to the poor and elderly, further decreasing their attractiveness as places to live. Because of lost revenues, inner suburbs also begin to deteriorate as people move away. On the other hand, the cities and towns that gain population are likely to "get rich quick." This growth is a mixed blessing, however—many longtime residents of outlying areas, accustomed to less population density and a quieter lifestyle, now find themselves caught up in an increasingly urbanized way of life.

What is life like in these cities of ours? Who lives in them? Why do they live there? What are the problems these cities face? Such questions will be answered in three chapters (Chapters 10–12) that look at North American urban social structure.

THE CITY IN GLOBAL PERSPECTIVE

As mentioned earlier, the greatest urban growth is occurring in developing countries. Why should this concern us? Aren't growing cities generally a good thing? After all, cities produce jobs, generate better health care, and stimulate improvements in technology and the arts. The answer to this question is double-edged, however: Sometimes cities do these things, but not always; and often, they do them for only some of the city's people.

In fact, throughout most of the developing world, the urban situation is desperate—and, in some places, the situation is even getting worse. Recent decades have witnessed hundreds of millions of people, enticed by the promise of a better life, moving into the cities of Latin America, Africa, the Middle East, and Asia. Most of these cities cannot keep up with the incoming tide. The results are poverty, malnutrition, and disease for many people. The *Urban Living* box below provides tragic examples of even worse outcomes. Fortunately, these kinds of disasters do not happen often, but the conditions reported still exist in many shantytowns throughout the world.

The grave situation in these countries is common throughout the world's poor nations. Chapter 13 examines the cities of Latin America, Africa, the Middle East, and Asia and offers analysis highlighting their urban problems and successes.

THE QUALITY OF CITY LIFE

The city is a living, dynamic entity. Its capacity to concentrate human efforts means that urban places contain the greatest potential for improving the quality of human life.

For millennia, people have come to the city with hopes and dreams of living "the good life." When all is said and done, however, has the city lived up to its billing? True, many cities boast material living standards that are higher than ever before

in history, but this is not the case for everyone. Furthermore, in many cities of the developing world, material living standards are appallingly low—destitution in many cities is not the exception but the rule. Then, too, focusing on material standards alone may be a mistake. What about security, which was Aristotle's first concern? Despite a steadily declining urban crime rate during recent years, some areas in many cities are so dangerous that people cannot go out alone, especially at night, without fear of being mugged, raped, or murdered. What about strong, community-oriented neighborhoods? Once a primary element of cities, these, too, have weakened in recent decades—and, in some areas, have disappeared altogether.

We need to understand the whole range of conditions that contribute to a more stimulating, fulfilling urban life. In bits and pieces throughout this book, evidence regarding the positive and negative elements of the city will emerge. We will comment on some of this evidence as we proceed, and in

URBAN LIVING

The Shantytowns of the Developing World

Communities of squatters, so poor that they cannot pay any amount of rent, exist on the outskirts of major cities throughout Africa, Asia, the Caribbean, and Latin America. Millions of people throughout the developing world live in comparably unhealthy and dangerously situated shantytowns, most of them without indoor plumbing or electricity. Built from cast-off scraps of lumber and tin by people who often have not even heard of building codes, they sprawl either across river flood plains and low-lying coastal strips, where tidal flooding is common, or on hillsides, where deadly mudslides take their toll. The mudslides are a chronic problem. Clearing grass and shrubs from the hillsides to make way for the shantytowns causes erosion, leaving these communities vulnerable during heavy rains.

Almost every year the rainy season brings tragic stories of hundreds of deaths from these mudslides. In May 2011, for example, torrential rains deluged Rio de Janeiro, Brazil, resulting in 229 mudslide deaths among the residents living in shantytowns on the steep, unstable hillsides at the edge of the city. One month earlier, a mudslide killed

As this scene of New Year's revelers in Times Square shows, the city is a dynamic, living entity, but not just on such special occasions. A city's night life—with its excitement, bright neon lights, large digital screens, variety of activities, crowds of people, and sense of adventure—lures people of all ages and backgrounds to come and be part of one of its many simultaneous happenings.

27 shantytown residents in the Philippines, and in 2010, another mudslide killed about 200 people in a different hillside shantytown overlooking Rio. In 2007, large chunks of earth slid off the soaked hillsides into a shantytown in the Bangladeshi port city of Chittagong, killing nearly 100, while a similar number who had lived in crudely built shacks in Cairo, Egypt, also perished in a 2008 landslide.

In each of these areas, and in many others, relief agencies attempted to provide food, provisions, and emergency shelter. Governments, working in tandem with these agencies, built new housing and pledged not to allow residents to again live in dwellings on such unstable ground. This relief effort has not been enough, however, for the displaced, ever-growing population who abandon the countryside in search of better jobs and are unable to find affordable housing. Instead, they continue to occupy these shantytowns throughout the developing world. Until these countries resolve their economic problems, better housing will not be the answer, because people still won't be able to pay even a minimal amount for housing. So the shantytowns exist again, with the squatters living in houses stacked so close to one another that the edges often overlap, hoping they will be spared when the next heavy rains come.

the final chapter, we will pull together these ideas as we examine urban planning and offer some thoughtful speculation about the future of cities.

Because of the ever-increasing importance of the city to the future of human civilization, sizing up the potential of urban places for meeting human needs is clearly essential. Is the city a place of alienation, danger, dehumanization, and exploitation, as some people fear? Or can the city become the ideal suggested by historian Lewis Mumford in the following passage?

The mission of the city is to further [the human being's] conscious participation in the cosmic and historic process. Through its own complex and enduring structure, the city vastly augments [human beings'] ability to interpret these processes and take an active, formative part in them, so that every phase of the drama it stages shall have, to the highest degree possible, the illumination of consciousness, the stamp of purpose, the color of love. That magnification of all the dimensions of life, through emotional communion, rational communication, technological mastery, and above all, dramatic representation, has been the supreme office of the city in history. And it remains the chief reason for the city's continued existence.(1991:576; orig. 1961)

To find the answers to those questions, we must "go and make our visit."

KEY TERMS

culture (15)
global city (8)
invasion–succession (13)
megacity (7)
megaregion (6)
metropolitan area (6)
postmodernism (13)
social power (9)

social stratification (9)
urban cluster (3)
urban ecology (12)
urban geography (12)
urban political economy (14)
urbanism (9)
urbanization (6)
world-systems analysis (8)

INTERNET ACTIVITY

To explore New York City's Times Square area, go to *http://maps.google.com,* and in the box at the top, type in "1500 Broadway New York NY." In the balloon appearing in the middle of the map, click "Street view." When the street scene appears, click the full-screen icon in the upper right of the photo. Next, in the upper-left corner, click the left or right rotation arrows. How many different kinds of city elements can you find as you completely rotate your view?

CHAPTER 2

THE ORIGINS AND DEVELOPMENT OF THE WORLD'S CITIES

URBAN ORIGINS
   Archaeology: Digging the Early City
   The First Permanent Settlements
   The City Emerges
THE FIRST URBAN REVOLUTION:
   CITY-STATES AND URBAN EMPIRES
   The Near East: Mesopotamia and Egypt
   The Indus Region
   A Glance Eastward: China
   A Glance Westward: The Americas
   Summary: Traits of Early Cities
   Crete and Greece
   Rome
   Decline: The Middle Ages
   Revival: Medieval and Renaissance Cities

THE SECOND URBAN REVOLUTION:
   THE RISE OF MODERN CITIES

CASE STUDY: LONDON—THE HISTORY
OF A WORLD CITY

   Beginnings: 55 B.C.E.–1066 C.E.
   The Medieval City: 1066–1550
   The World City Emerges: 1550–1800
   Industrialization and Colonization:
      1800–1900
   The Modern Era: 1900 to the Present
SUMMARY
CONCLUSION
KEY TERMS
INTERNET ACTIVITIES

Can you imagine the United States without great cities such as New York, Chicago, or San Francisco? It would be like thinking about Egypt without Cairo, Japan without Tokyo, France without Paris, or England without London. Why are entire countries so closely bound up with cities? The answer, as this chapter explains, is that much of the story of human history is centered in cities. In fact, the words *city* and *civilization* are both derived from a single Latin root—*civitas*. Indeed, to be civilized is to live in or near a city.

This was not always the case, however. Most knowledgeable people today recognize the importance of cities, because in our era, the city not only is the dominant form of human association but also is becoming more so every day. In the larger picture of human history, however, the city is a "wide-eyed infant"—a very recent arrival on the human scene.

URBAN ORIGINS

When and where did the first cities develop? What were they like? How did they change over time? Here we will offer brief answers to these crucial questions. Before we can do so, however, we must look far back in time to see just how recently human beings began making history on this earth.

To get a better perspective on where we are in relation to human history, let's use astronomer Carl Sagan's concept of a **cosmic calendar.** Sagan (2005) suggested that we imagine the entire history of our planet compressed into a single calendar year. What does such a vision suggest? To begin with, for almost the entire history of the universe (beginning with the "Big Bang"—corresponding to January 1st), the human species did not exist. In fact, our species, *Homo sapiens*, appeared on earth roughly 200,000 years ago (December 31st in Sagan's year). The emergence of the first cities—and with them the way of life that we commonly call "civilization"—occurred only about 10,000 years ago (8000 B.C.E.)—in the last minute of Sagan's year! It would be several thousand years more, around 3000 B.C.E., before cities became common. Even then,

however, they contained only a small proportion of the world's population.

Only in the last several centuries (the last second in Sagan's year) did the world acquire a sizable urban population. As recently as 1950, the proportion of the world's population living in cities was only 29 percent. In 2010, this figure reached 52 percent. In other words, the existence of the city—and of the urban way of life that we so readily take for granted—is a very recent and momentous change in the history of the world.

Archaeology: Digging the Early City

Learning about the first cities has been a gradual process filled with difficulties. Urban scholars rely heavily on the work of archaeologists to gain an understanding of early settlements. Through excavation and techniques for determining the age of artifacts, we learn much about the social life of people who left behind little formal record of their existence. Often, however, simply finding the sites of early cities—frequently buried beneath the surface, hidden by dense plant growth, or even covered by a current metropolis—is a matter of hard work as well as a bit of luck. Once archaeologists find an ancient city, excavation must proceed carefully to avoid damaging the remains. Finally, even after excavating a city successfully, archaeologists do not always offer the same interpretations of findings at a given site.

Moreover, our understanding of early urban settlements is subject to continuous revision. Ongoing investigations at old sites and the discovery of new locations, such as the recent excavation of Caral in Peru, provide a steady stream of new data. In addition, techniques of analysis continually improve, often leading to a reformulation of beliefs that urbanists held with certainty only a few years before.

We still have much to learn. Nevertheless, we do know quite a bit about early cities, and this chapter summarizes a great deal of that knowledge. First, we examine cities as they took form in the ancient world, and then we consider how, as the centuries passed, cities reflected the changing character of human civilization.

The First Permanent Settlements

As already stated, humans first appeared on the earth about 200,000 years ago. For the next 190,000 years, our ancestors lived as hunters and gatherers—hunting game and gathering vegetation over large areas. Most followed the animals and moved with the seasons, without permanent settlements, in small groups ranging in size from 25 to 50 individuals. Frequently, these family bands would camp in a place for a few weeks because the hunting was good or the vegetation was plentiful. When the game left the area or the vegetation went out of season, the people moved on.

Around 10,000 years ago, near the end of the last Ice Age, a change occurred. It happened slowly and without any evident drama. Nonetheless, it was one of the most momentous changes in human history: People began to settle down in one place and to evolve more complex social structures. Civilization, as we know it, was beginning, but why did it happen?

As time passed, the number of hunter-gatherer tribes grew. Gradually, they began to deplete the natural resources that had formed the mainstay of their existence for millennia. Game became scarce, and vegetation was depleted. How could these nomads solve the food shortage problem? They could wander over larger areas, but that was difficult and threatened to place them in direct competition with other groups. They could carry extra food from areas of abundance, but this would be burdensome without the use of animals—which had not yet been domesticated. A better possibility was to settle in the most fertile areas and raise their own food. This option was the one that won out. Many experts view the domestication of plants, sometimes called the *agricultural revolution,* as the single most important event in human history (Mumford 1991:55; orig. 1961). For the first time, people could stay in one place and—once able to produce a food surplus—could allow some members of the group to pursue interests other than seeking food, such as crafts and science.

Over a period of some 5,000 years, villages began and multiplied. Humans created permanent settlements where they raised crops and learned to domesticate animals for use in the fields or as a food supply. Permanent settlements also transformed patterns of social structure. Most important, characterizing all these settlements was a more complex **division of labor.** For the first time, people began doing many different, specialized tasks to "earn a living." This was a radical shift from the social structure that prevailed in hunter-gatherer tribes. In nomadic groups, everyone knew a bit about everything; no one was a full-time specialist in anything. Only permanent settlements afforded people the opportunity to specialize, not just in food production but also in religion, military affairs, trade, and a host of other occupations.

Specialization benefited everyone: The farmer gained the protection of the military and the benefit of the priest's greater insight into religious matters, while the priest and the soldier received the fruits of the farmer's labors. In short, these early settlements provided the possibility of living a life based more on choice than on tradition. No longer did each man face the limited choice of becoming a farmer or hunter, and each woman a housekeeper and mother. Now a widening variety of options emerged that allowed personal choice instead of merely following in a parent's footsteps. Such opportunities were probably as strong an inducement thousands of years ago as they are today.

Linked to the more complex division of labor was a second major element in the social structure of these early settlements: a **hierarchical power structure.** Hunting and gathering societies tend to be egalitarian—that is, while people perform a few different tasks in daily life, all work is deemed to be equally important for the welfare of the group. For example, hunting (typically done by men) is no more important than gathering food or caring for children (usually done by women). Furthermore, with the limited productive technology possessed by hunter-gatherers, few resources are available beyond those needed for daily life; no one is able to amass much more wealth than anyone else.

Given a more complex division of labor and the development of a hierarchical power structure, a third element was necessary for cities to emerge: the development of a **productive surplus**. Earlier, we noted that many archaeologists believe that the rise of agriculture was the main reason people traded hunting and gathering for permanent settlements. A similar process was at work in the gradual transition from village to town to city. Specifically, a growing population required an increasing surplus of food. Confirming this notion of "agricultural primacy"—of food surplus supporting permanent settlements—was the discovery of the remains of domesticated plants and animals at early urban sites around the world.

To sum up, around 8000 B.C.E., hunting and gathering societies began to increase in size. As a response to population increase, people began to settle down and take up agriculture as a way of life. Characterizing these permanent settlements were increasingly complex social structures organized around a division of labor and a hierarchical power structure. Such settlements depended on a productive surplus. As these elements coalesced, they reinforced each other: The division of labor led to more efficient use of human and natural resources, which in turn led to a greater division of labor and a more intricate power structure, and so on. As this happened, villages turned into towns, and then towns became the first cities.

The City Emerges

What do we know of these earliest cities? We begin where experts believe is the first city: Jericho. The modern city of Jericho and its ancient ruins lie just to the north of the Dead Sea, in present-day Israel (see Figure 2–1 on pages 27–28).

Jericho.   With careful excavation, archaeologists found evidence to identify Jericho as the oldest city yet to be discovered anywhere in the world. We now know that Jericho was a walled city over 10,000 years ago. Put differently, it was already an ancient city when the Egyptians built the pyramids.

Research at Jericho, however, sparked a debate: At what point can we call a permanent settlement a "city"? Some archaeologists argue that given total population statistics in that period, a population of about 600 people and substantial buildings allow Jericho to be considered a city by about 8000 B.C.E. Others disagree, citing Jericho's small size by today's standards. Size, however, is not the only important factor. Population density and the complexity of social life—involving a broad range of activities and a hierarchy of power relations—add to Jericho's claim to city status.

What made Jericho different from other settlements of its time was the presence of houses made of sun-dried brick, a surrounding wall, a tower, and a large trench, all suggesting an advanced division of labor and a hierarchical social order that could oversee large-scale public works. The wall further indicates recognition of the need for defense and for protection from the elements. Even after 10,000 years of erosion, its ruins are some 12 feet high and 6 feet thick at the base. The trench, cut into solid rock, is about 27 feet across and 9 feet deep. Although archaeologists are uncertain about its use (to hold water?), certainly a complex, cooperative effort was necessary to create it.

A short account of the later history of Jericho holds an interesting lesson in the history of urban settlements. Apparently, the original settlers of Jericho did not remain after about 7000 B.C.E., when a second group took up residence. This second group was more technologically advanced than the original settlers, constructing rectangular houses of bricks and mortar with plaster walls and floors. Around this time, trade with outsiders apparently developed, adding to Jericho's cosmopolitan character. Then, about 1,000 years later—close to 6000 B.C.E.—the site was inexplicably abandoned, and it remained so for a millennium.

Resettlement began about 5000 B.C.E., providing yet another twist to Jericho's story. The later settlers were markedly less advanced in their technology, digging only primitive shelters, and no public works are traceable to this period. Then, with the coming of the Bronze Age at about 3000 B.C.E., a far more advanced culture prevailed. Artwork is evident, possibly linked to the civilization in Mesopotamia to the east or in Egypt to the southwest. By the time settlement of ancient Jericho came to an end at about 1500 B.C.E., many other groups had lived within the city.

This changing population in Jericho teaches us that we must not oversimplify the history of cities. Cities do not always grow in population and steadily advance in technical capacity. Discontinuity and unexpected events can change developmental patterns again and again, as we shall see throughout this chapter.

Catal Hüyük.   Evidence produced by excavation at Jericho places the beginning of city life between 8000 and 7000 B.C.E. By 6000 B.C.E., other well-developed sites, such as Catal Hüyük (pronounced Sha-tal Hoo-yook) in present-day Turkey, existed. Originally settled on a 32-acre site (three times larger than Jericho), Catal Hüyük eventually supported a population of some 6,000. This strange, street-less city had mud-brick dwellings clustered together like the cells of a beehive, with windowless walls facing outward. Small windows built high in the inner walls provided light, and the only entrances were on the roofs, reachable by ladders. This construction design was so secure that no evidence exists of any plunder or massacre during the city's nearly 1,000 years of existence. The *Cityscape* box on page 30 offers a portrait of life in this early city.

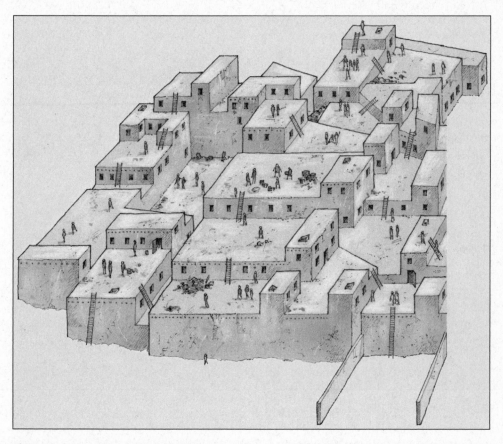

The partial excavation of the Neolithic city of Catal Hüyük has already provided archaeologists with many clues about the social life of its inhabitants. Discovered in the late 1950s, the site became internationally famous for the large size and dense occupation of the settlement, lack of ground-level doorways, spectacular wall paintings, and other art uncovered inside the houses.

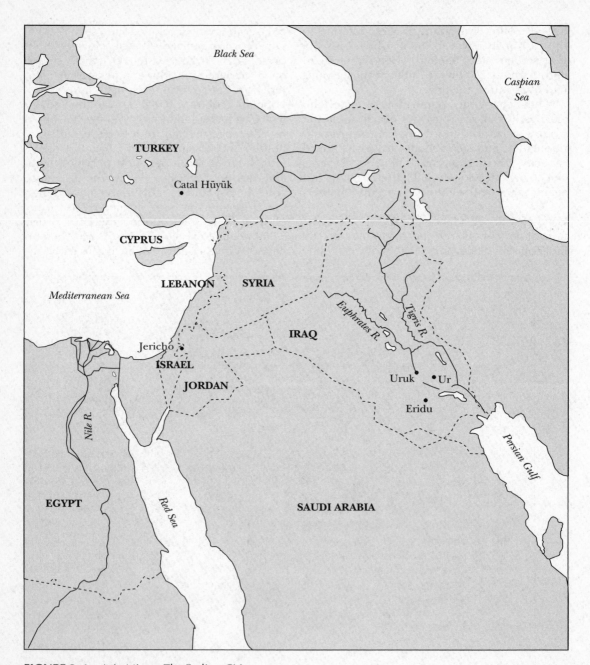

FIGURE 2–1   Asia Minor: The Earliest Cities

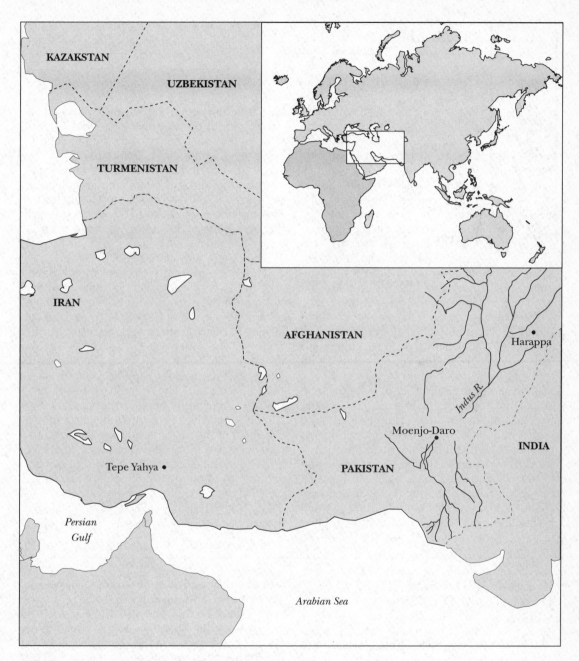

FIGURE 2–1   Asia Minor: The Earliest Cities (*continued*)

CITYSCAPE

Daily Life in Catal Hüyük, 6000 B.C.E.

When the first light of dawn struck . . . on a spring morning in the year 6000 B.C.E., it brushed lightly across the flat roofs of tightly built mud-brick houses. . . . The houses turned blank, doorless walls to the world. The household entrance was by way of the roof through either a wooden doorway or a thatch opening onto a ladder. Doors at ground level could have let in anything from floodwaters to wild animals: the roof holes and ladders provided security. . . .

Inside one of the houses the father stirred. . . . From his leather pouch he grasped a lump of yellowish, crystalline sulfur collected on his last trip to the hills, and a flint tool that he had fashioned to his needs. . . . With this prehistoric Boy Scout knife the man could make wood shavings, strike a spark, feed the spark with sulfur and produce a fire within minutes. . . . The man made a fire on the hearth while his wife went through a small doorless opening in the mud-brick wall to the family food-storage niche. In it was a bin about a yard high, made of clay and very clean. She drew some grain from a small hole at the bin's bottom: it was always filled from the top and emptied from the bottom so that the oldest grain, or that most exposed to damp, would be used first. The wife moved slowly. She was heavy with another child, and she was getting old: almost 28.

On that mythical morning the family ate a gruel of grain and milk, supplemented by bits of meat left over from a previous meal. The mother nursed the baby while she fed the next-oldest with a spoon made from a cow's rib bone. . . .

Then there was work to do. . . .

The man and the woman might have tended fields or flocks, but not many towns-folk could have been farmers—no compact community of 6,000 people could have grown enough food to support itself while doing all the other things that Catal Hüyük residents did. The city must have traded goods and services for supplies from the surrounding region. The woman of the house might conceivably have made baskets for such trade. Or the man might have spent his days as a craftsman, for although no specialized tools were found in his home, there is ample evidence in the city of skillfully woven textiles, good pottery and beautiful art work.

Source: Dora Jane Hamblin, *The First Cities: The Emergence of Man* (New York: Time–Life, 1978), pp. 43–46, excerpts.

THE FIRST URBAN REVOLUTION: CITY-STATES AND URBAN EMPIRES

Although scattered cities such as Jericho and Catal Hüyük thrived in the period between 7000 and 4000 B.C.E., it was not until about 3500 B.C.E. that urban development accelerated to a point where large numbers of cities flourished in many places.

The earliest cities, like Jericho, clearly demonstrated their ability to generate security and wealth for fairly large numbers of people. Thus, more and more people came to the city to share in these benefits. The *idea* of the city was taking hold. No longer were many people content to live the relatively backward life of the tribe, the village, or the town. They wanted the benefits of the city: more choice, better economic opportunities, and ongoing excitement.

So cities grew in number and in population, but growth also brought problems. A rising population demanded more and more goods and services, and ways to manage the needs of the city's inhabitants in some way. Some cities responded to this challenge by making their social structure even more complex by creating the state.

The central feature of the state is its ability to wield power over many people—essentially, to dictate everyone's rights and responsibilities: who must live where, who must serve in the military, and so on. With such power, the city's leaders could do pretty much what they like in order to solve (or create) the city's problems—they could reorganize production, determine who will be educated, and perhaps most important, make alliances and wage war to capture land, population, and resources.

The emergence of the state as a form of social organization generated the first **city-states**—cities that controlled the surrounding regions, including a number of other towns, villages, and rural lands. As time passed, some of these city-states conquered or made alliances with others to form the world's first urban empires—much larger regions, usually dominated by a single central city. These early urban empires emerged around the world—in Mesopotamia, Egypt, the Indus River Valley, China, Central America, and South America—and they "pushed" the city as a form of human settlement to ever-greater complexity and population size.

This, then, was the period of the *first urban revolution* (Childe 2003). From approximately 4000 B.C.E. to 500 C.E., urban sites multiplied and their populations grew to sizes previously unknown in human history (Rome at its apex, for example, surpassed a million people). In retrospect, the first urban revolution was apparently something of a mixed blessing. The city's greatest positive attributes were its ability to improve people's standard of living, provide choices in the conduct of life, and stimulate the human imagination. On the other hand, these first cities also had rigid divisions of social class that extended the city's benefits to only a small minority of the urban population. With the emergence of city-states and urban empires, human warfare and bloodshed rose to unparalleled levels as well.

With all this in mind, then, we now turn to brief descriptions of some of the first urban empires.

The Near East: Mesopotamia and Egypt

The first urban empire was in the Fertile Crescent region of the Tigris and Euphrates rivers in the southern portion of present-day Iraq. This region, known in ancient times as Mesopotamia or Sumer, began evolving significant cities as early as 4000 B.C.E. Cities such as Uruk, Eridu, and Ur (see Figure 2–1) represent a significant extension of world urbanization not only because they were larger than their earlier counterparts but also because of their more complex social structures. Wheat and barley were important domesticated crops, and city dwellers enjoyed the advantages of major technological advances, such as oxen-pulled plows and the wheel (Schomp 2005).

Rise of Mesopotamian Cities. The cities of the region reached their greatest development at about 2800 B.C.E. Uruk covered an area of approximately 1,100 acres and supported a population as high as 50,000 (Liverani 2006). All the Mesopotamian (Sumerian) cities were theocracies, ruled by a priest-king. A ruling elite, controlling and protecting the area around the city, including its outlying agricultural land, exacted a portion of the agricultural surplus as tribute and stored it in the major temple (Schomp 2005:17).

Uruk and other Mesopotamian cities had highly complex social structures, including a power hierarchy and a pronounced division of labor. Excavations affirmed the existence of monumental public buildings, including ziggurats (religious shrines); extensive trade arrangements; a system of writing (cuneiform); mathematics; and a code of law. Sumerian texts noting the concerns of everyday life still survive. These accounts reveal such activities as the counting, taxing, and exchanging of sheep, goats, and cattle; concerned parents shepherding children to school—as today, often against their will; a council of elders meeting to consider grievances against the inhabitants of an adjoining city-state; and a politician attempting to win the favor of the populace with tax reductions (Wenke 2005). Clearly, these cities had advanced to a point to enable us easily to draw parallels with cities of our own experience.

Early Mesopotamian urban life, however, centered on the temple and on religious beliefs. The populace recognized thousands of gods, and the temples, like the palaces, were large and opulently decorated. People of less favorable social position lived in irregularly organized houses along the narrow, unpaved, winding streets. The complex social structure also resulted in a strong military elite and made possible an increasing capacity to wage war. Frequently under attack, Mesopotamian cities had strong defensive walls.

After about 3500 B.C.E., the cities became organized as politically distinct city-states, each exerting its influence over a broad region. Although these city-states were independent of one another and often at war, they did represent a common civilization. They shared a common cultural heritage and saw themselves as possessors of a unique, even superior culture (Wenke 2005). By 700 B.C.E., the Assyrian Empire dominated the region, and the Persian Empire followed around 500 B.C.E.

The importance of this continual trading of urban dominance was that it spurred the development of cities and their influence throughout the Near East. To maintain control of their empires, each set of rulers tried to develop their cities as much as their culture and technology would permit. Continually renewing the cities of this region were inventions, innovations, and new ideas brought forth from trade and people of different backgrounds.

Although it would be too much to say that these cities contained all aspects of civilization in their era, they were key centers. They were "containers" in a double sense: They literally encircled their population and their valued goods with walls, and more figuratively, they served as the place where all the themes of Mesopotamian culture existed.

Egyptian Cities.   The Great Pyramids of Giza are modern reminders of another empire that flourished shortly after the rise of cities in Mesopotamia. The archaeological record of Egyptian cities dates back to 3100 B.C.E., but it is less detailed than that of their Mesopotamian counterparts. Several reasons explain why the record of the earliest Egyptian cities is less clear. First, their buildings were made of unbaked brick and other materials that crumbled over time. Second, the early Egyptians apparently built and abandoned their cities with some frequency. As a result, even though the cities were crucial centers of Egyptian civilization, none maintained its dominance long enough to reach a very large size (Kemp 2006).

Although the cities that emerged in Egypt went through what we now think is the normal process of early development—from village to town and, finally, to city—they were rather distinct from those in Mesopotamia. Egyptian civilization revolved around the ruling pharaoh, and each had his own city—a religious and political center built to reflect his power, which by 2500 B.C.E. was virtually absolute. Viewed by the populace not just as a secular leader or priest but also as a god, the pharaoh held his singular dominance over the Nile region, which thus enjoyed a relatively peaceful history.

Thus, we find little evidence of city walls in early Egypt. Each capital city became a pharaoh's administrative center, and urban artisans directed much of their activity toward construction of a palace for his pleasure in this life and an opulent tomb for his needs in the life to come. Although not as large as those of Mesopotamia, these Egyptian cities maintained distinctive urban traits, including a clear power structure and division of labor, social inequality, and an administrative organization (utilizing hieroglyphic writing, papyrus paper, and ink) to oversee public needs and maintain the pharaoh's control.

If the early Egyptian cities were peaceful, however, those that followed were not. Piercing Egypt's later history, as in Mesopotamia, is conflict both within the empire and with other empires. During the period known as the Old

Kingdom (2700–2180 B.C.E.), the pharaohs made forays into neighboring territories to procure goods. Successful in many of these adventures, they used their plundered wealth and captured slaves to build cities and palaces. Two pharaohs of this period—Cheops and his son, Cephren—were the ones who built the Great Pyramids of Giza—still the most colossal monuments ever constructed—between 2600 and 2500 B.C.E. Cephren was also responsible for the Sphinx at Giza.

Then, around 2180 B.C.E., the Old Kingdom collapsed, famine spread, and rioting in the cities was rampant. For the next 600 years, Egypt went through several alternating periods of disarray and reunification. Urban greatness once again reappeared in the New Kingdom period (1500–1100 B.C.E.). This was the time of the minor pharaoh Tutankhamun—the only pharaoh whose gravesite in the Valley of the Kings that pillaging robbers did not find—and of Ramses II, the pharaoh who conquered much of the Near East for Egypt and who may have been Moses' adversary in his attempts to free the Jews from Egyptian servitude. Ramses rebuilt many of Egypt's cities; created a new capital, Pi-Ramesse, on the Mediterranean; and constructed self-glorifying yet magnificent temples at Karnak, Luxor, and Abu Simbel.

Egypt lost its Asian territories around 1100 B.C.E., and the next 300 years saw the final decline of pharaoh-ruled Egypt. From 800 to 671 B.C.E., the African rulers of Kush—a former Egyptian outpost to the south—controlled Egypt. Near Eastern empires inflicted the final indignities. The Assyrians conquered Egypt in 671 B.C.E. and, though expelled less than 20 years later, were followed by the Persians in 525 B.C.E. The Persians more or less dominated the region until 332 B.C.E., the year that Alexander the Great arrived, became pharaoh, and built his city, Alexandria, at the head of the Nile. From then on, Egypt was at the mercy of foreign overlords.

The development of cities in the Nile region raises an interesting question as to the possible diffusion of urban influence from Mesopotamia. History records frequent contact between the two regions. Did the Egyptian cities evolve independently, or were they the result of imported ideas? Debate continues, but the currently dominant belief is that traders or nomads from early cities in Mesopotamia carried at least some urban influences toward both Egypt in the west and the Indus Valley in the east (Rice 2004). In all three regions, however, city life emerged in its own special fashion and included clearly distinct and unique aspects that revealed the stamp of the local civilization (Sjoberg 1965:49).

The Indus Region

To the east of Mesopotamia, along the Indus River of present-day India and Pakistan, was a third ecologically favorable area where early cities emerged. Trade routes linked the Indus cities with Mesopotamian cities through other outposts, such as Tepe Yahya, midway between the two areas (see Figure 2–1). Most likely, trading in such products as jade linked this area with Central Asia to the east (Magee 2005).

Excavations yielded the remains of two highly developed cities that were centers of a regional civilization beginning about 2500 B.C.E. Both were prominent in urban history until about 1500 B.C.E. Moenjo-Daro was situated on the Indus River about 175 miles from the Arabian Sea; Harappa was about 350 miles further north, on one of the Indus River's tributaries. Each had a population as high as 40,000 and represented an urban civilization distinct in many ways from those we have considered thus far. Unlike either Mesopotamia or Egypt, for example, Moenjo-Daro does not show evidence of a single, all-powerful leader or a preoccupation with temples and god-monuments, but it does show evidence of extensive "good living."

Moenjo-Daro had a physical layout similar to the same gridiron pattern common to most Western cities today. Its remarkable structures of mud-baked bricks and burnt-wood framing were up to two stories high and included an elaborate, well-built bath area with a layer of natural tar to keep it from leaking. Remarkably, it even had a building with an underground furnace, like the ancient Roman hypocausts, for heated bathing. Other city features were a central marketplace, a

The excavated site of ancient Moenjo-Daro in the Indus River Valley reveals a surprisingly modern grid pattern of two-storied brick housing and a sanitation system of brick-lined, open sewers. Not clearly visible in this photo is the uniformity of its north–south boulevard, which is 30 feet wide, and the east–west cross streets about every 200 yards.

large common well, and a citadel or administrative center, possibly with a granary for storage of food surplus.

Perhaps the most remarkable discovery about this city was its well-constructed sanitation system. Along the streets were brick-lined, open sewers that carried away house drainage. Archaeologists discovered several bathrooms with sit-down toilets, indicating the presence in 2500 B.C.E. of an urban luxury not commonly found in European cities until the nineteenth century.

Within the city, numerous craft specialists were in operation, including potters, weavers, brick makers, and copper and bronze metalworkers (Possehl 2003). In fact, the presence of extensive residential areas displaying a uniformity of mud-brick houses, streets, and drainage systems suggests the extensive existence of a comparatively high standard of living. This would make Moenjo-Daro one of the first cities to provide such a widespread state of well-being—essentially, a kind of middle-class lifestyle—among its citizenry.

Until the mid-twentieth century, archaeologists commonly thought that Mesopotamia, Egypt, and the Indus River Valley contained the cities from which all later ones took their pattern. Archaeological research since then, however, showed otherwise. Apparently, cities emerged in many places around the world independently of one another. Two other regions where this occurred were China and the Americas.

A Glance Eastward: China

Cities in China date back at least 4,300 years. A 2006 archaeological discovery suggests that the earliest was Liangzhu, in Yuhang County, Zhejiang. This city had an area of 31 million square feet, a 131-foot canal of hardened earth, and a defensive wall that was 13–20 feet thick. In its stratified society, as evidenced by jade and silk found at elite burial sites and simple pottery shards for the non-elite, religion apparently held considerable importance, given the elaborate religious structures and carefully positioned altars and piles of stones (Stark 2006)

We know much more about the second and third capital cities of the Shang Dynasty than its first (Bo). The second capital, Cheng-chou, was at its height about 1600 B.C.E. A rectangular wall 4.5 miles in length and more than 30 feet high enclosed an area of about 1.5 square miles, which contained the city's administrative and ceremonial centers. In this fortified area, the political and religious elite lived apart from the common people. Outside the enclosure lived artisans—bronze workers and craftspeople.

An-yang was the third Shang capital. Archaeological excavation uncovered remnants of its larger pattern that linked the central city to the surrounding area. As in Cheng-chou, the residences of artisans and craft workers were just outside a walled area. In the region immediately beyond, numerous villages formed a network of trade, supplying agricultural and other specialized products to the city (Thorp 2006).

What existed in China, then, was a type of urban settlement somewhat more diffused than that in the areas already considered. Rather than concentrating all their political, religious, and craft activities in a single, center-city area, the Chinese set priests and rulers apart from the remainder of the urban population. At some distance from their protected, walled enclosure, residents of satellite villages participated in the life of the urban area as a whole.

A Glance Westward: The Americas

The last major region in which early cities developed was nearer to home—in Mesoamerica, specifically the area of present-day central Mexico, the Yucatan Peninsula, and Guatemala; and in South America, particularly the western part of that continent. The history of these areas reveals, once again, several familiar patterns: A more productive agricultural technology and the formation of a complex social structure accompanied the rise of cities. The case of Mesoamerica, however, also represents several significant areas of contrast to urban development elsewhere.

People inhabited the area at least as early as 20,000 B.C.E., with the cultivation of plants achieved by 7000 B.C.E. In contrast to other parts of the world where cities arose, however, this area was not well suited to the production of large surpluses, partly because of its rocky, mountainous terrain and partly because the inhabitants lacked domesticated animals. The traditional digging stick rather than the plow remained the primary tool of cultivation for millennia, and Mesoamerica never embraced farming in the sense that other regions did. Rather, its groups developed a mixed economy in which hunting and edible wild plants continued to play a very important part. Nevertheless, one cultivated crop, maize (corn), contributed to a sturdy and nutritious diet.

By 1500 B.C.E., early villages of mud-walled houses appeared, but because hunting continued to play a major role in the economy, these village sites moved with some frequency.

In some villages, Olmec and Mayan tribes built elaborate ceremonial centers that served large populations, employing many craftspeople in their design and construction. Serving as places of permanent residence for only a small number of priests at the outset, these ceremonial centers slowly grew in size and complexity. Before the time of the birth of Christ, they had become full-fledged cities.

The same process occurred on the western coast of South America in present-day Peru and Bolivia. The ancient city of Caral, discussed in Chapter 1, is the oldest known city in the Americas, but perhaps the most famous urban empire of this region was that of the Incas, with its capital in the city of Cuzco. Less well known, but as important, was the urban empire of Chimor on the north coast of Peru. Its capital, Chan Chan, began as a city around the same time that the Incan urban centers evolved—about 800 C.E. At its height (approximately 1450 C.E.), Chan Chan ruled over a large hinterland as a major challenger to the Incas.

Chan Chan was a **regal/ritual city**—an important urban center with a population of no more than 30,000. As the term suggests, a regal/ritual city was used primarily by the ruling class: Chan Chan's rulers lived there year-round in magnificent palaces and used most of the city's buildings for their own pleasure and for the rituals of Chimor culture. Only small numbers of artisans, servants, and peasants could share in that part of the urban environment. All the rest of the empire's people were forced to live in the surrounding towns or rural areas and do the bidding of the ruling class, including producing food, paying taxes, and laboring on city projects.

In 1470, Chan Chan's challenge provoked the Incas to conquer the Chimor Empire and subjugate its inhabitants, but even this dominance was not to last. By the end of the century, Columbus would land in the New World. Under the subsequent onslaught of the Spanish and, later, the Portuguese, these proud urban empires would fall like dominoes, and a new type of city would arise—a process described in Chapter 13.

Despite conditions that were unique to the hemisphere, cities arose indigenously in the Americas and were as highly sophisticated and equal in complexity to those found elsewhere. For example, a thousand years before the Aztecs, Teotihuacan was the religious capital of Mexico. An urban center of massive structures that was at its peak around 600 C.E., it supported a population of perhaps 200,000 in a city physically larger than imperial Rome itself (Austin and Lujan 2006:106). Its 8 square miles were laid out in a specific grid plan, its north–south avenues containing palaces and pyramid temples with impressive sculptures. The city's housing complexes were large and contained a number of rooms, all opening onto patios. Some were built, like the pyramid temples, of a red volcanic rock that was mined locally. Towering over the city was the Pyramid of the Sun, rising at a sharp angle from its 720- by 760-foot base to a height of 216 feet. Probably constructed in the first century C.E., it would have taken, according to expert estimates, thousands of laborers 50 years to build (Braswell 2004).

Summary: Traits of Early Cities

Human beings first devised cities about 10,000 years ago. As shown in Figure 2–2, they appeared in the Middle East by 4000 B.C.E., in the Americas by 2600 B.C.E., in the Indus River Valley by 2500 B.C.E., and in China soon thereafter.

Some combination of favorable ecological conditions, some sort of trade or food surplus, and a complex social structure (a fairly sophisticated division of labor and a power hierarchy) characterized all early cities. Beyond these important characteristics, we can also mention some other similarities and a few differences.

First, early cities do not show any smooth progression of growth. On the one hand, the transition from the first permanent settlements to full-fledged cities took a long time—from about 8000 to 3000 B.C.E. On the other hand, city histories the world over reflect discontinuity and change, rise and fall. Sometimes, as in Teotihuacan, one group

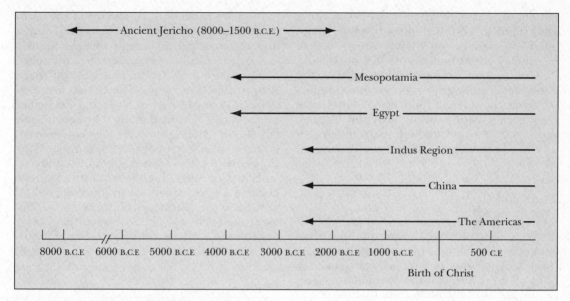

FIGURE 2–2   The Chronology of the First Cities

occupied a city for its entire duration; sometimes, as in Jericho, many groups came and went.

Second, as population centers, early cities were small. Most were mere towns by today's standards. A population of about 10,000 was usual, and even the largest settlements never went much beyond the quarter-million mark.

Third, many early cities had a theocratic power structure—a fused religious and political elite in which kings were also priests and, not infrequently, "gods." This fusion allowed a type of double control over the city's population and its problems. Royalty could, in the name of heaven, impose taxes and even servitude. Of course, the character of this elite structure varied. It was sharply evident in Egypt, China, and Teotihuacan but was more subdued in the Indus city of Moenjo-Daro. Characterizing the first cities everywhere, however, were inequalities in power and benefits: Usually, the few prospered, and the many got by as best they could.

Finally, what of the quality of life in early cities? In comparison with modern Western cities, it was probably not very high—life was usually hard, relatively short, and subject to considerable uncertainty. Yet substantial

variation occurred as well. Moenjo-Daro appears to have afforded a higher standard of living to more residents than was the case in other cities more sharply divided by class.

Other factors, such as war and slavery, also must have had a powerful effect on the quality of life experienced by many early city dwellers. The city, particularly after it reached the state and empire stage, was often an instrument of death and destruction as one urban center tried to conquer another. To some extent, cities as such are not to blame for this increase in bloodshed. Rather, the use of systematic warfare seems more coincident with primitive agriculture and the coming of the first permanent settlements around 8000 B.C.E. Apparently, agricultural techniques produced a productive surplus for the first time, and this surplus, in turn, attracted people to settlements and induced some of them to conquer other groups in an effort to procure even more surplus. When urban areas became common around 4000 B.C.E., however, the human appetite for conquest rose to a level unknown before in history.

In short, the development of the city was a most decisive event in human history. The early city magnified human activity in all its dimensions. People knew more, did more, and found more possibilities open to them. Such has always been the city's promise: to provide a better life. Early Western cities, discussed next, also held out the promise of "the good life." Although certainly some progress occurred along that road, these cities, like their earlier counterparts, also had a tragic capacity for harboring the human indignities of coercive inequality, militaristic expansion, and war.

Crete and Greece

Western cities—those of Europe and North America—are relative latecomers in the urban story. Cities had been in existence for many thousands of years before urbanization took hold in the northern Mediterranean region on the island of Crete.

About 1800 B.C.E., settlements were established in Crete, possibly by traders or migrants from the urban settlements of Mesopotamia. Little is known of these early cities, yet by all accounts, they were thriving overseas trade centers. Stone-paved roads, made from blocks cut by bronze saws, connected the cities. Lining the paved city streets that had drainage capabilities were two- to three-story buildings with flat-tiled roofs held up by ceiling timbers. Their court buildings contained inverted columns, wider at the top than the bottom. For some reason, these cities came to an end about 1400 B.C.E. (Castleden 2005). What caused the destruction of the cities of Crete remains unknown, though perhaps it was from some natural catastrophe or by invaders. Not until seven centuries later would urban development appear again in Europe, this time in Greece.

The early Greek *polis*, or city-state, did not follow the pattern of the cities of Mesopotamia and Egypt, which magnified the power of the elite at the expense of their other citizens. The fiercely independent Greek city-states— among them Athens, Corinth, and Sparta— experienced war as well as peaceful rivalry, as symbolized by the Olympic Games. Compared with earlier cities of the Near East with powerful rulers, Greek cities were more egalitarian,

though few matched Athens in having most of its free citizenry (the Greeks had slaves) directly participating in legislative decisions.

Classes whose commercial influence reached outward from Sicily to northern Africa ruled these cities. The Greeks founded such cities as Messina in Sicily and Marseilles in France. Unfortunately, however, the Greek city-states eventually turned on each other in the destructive Peloponnesian War (431–404 B.C.E.), leaving behind a remarkable legacy that highlighted the positive possibilities of urban civilization, including outstanding painting, sculpture, and architecture as well as a political system and body of philosophy that influence the world to this day (Waterfield 2006).

Rome

As Greek culture slipped into decline, another great civilization to the west gathered strength. This cultural system, perhaps more than any other before or since, focused on a single city; indeed, the city's name is synonymous with the culture itself. In his oft-cited oration *To Rome*, written in the mid-second century B.C.E., Aelius Aristides claimed, "Rome! Everything is found here. All the skills which exist or have existed, anything that can be made or grown. If something can't be found here, then it simply doesn't exist!"

Aristides was right. By the final centuries of the pre-Christian era, Rome was the dominant power of the Western world. By the time of Christ, the city that was the base of the Roman Empire was gargantuan by all previous urban standards, possibly containing a population of more than 1 million.

Rome displayed the same characteristics as the earliest cities: a favorable ecological setting, the ability to produce an economic surplus, and a complex social structure. Also, as in the Greek cities, the arts and sciences flourished and public monuments and buildings were integral parts of the cityscape. Yet Rome was an urban civilization almost exclusively based on the expression of militaristic power. For the several centuries during which the city thrived, Rome explored and revealed

At its height, Imperial Rome was the center of a vast, militaristic empire. The city, a mixture of magnificent buildings and squalid slums, contained carefully planned, broad thoroughfares and an impressive water supply and drainage system. Here, the Roman Forum—the heart of the city's ceremonial life—was crowded with temples, arches, statues, and public buildings.

for all history the consequences of concentrating a city's resources almost entirely on the accumulation of power and wealth.

If the Greek conception of the good life was a city founded on the principles of moderation, balance, and human participation, the Roman conception rested on the celebration of sheer excess and unremitting domination. At its height, the empire extended south from Rome across the Mediterranean to northern Africa, north to present-day Germany and to the border between England and Scotland (Hadrian's Wall), and east to Mesopotamia. It included almost half the world's population, and Rome ruled this territory mostly in its entirety for an amazing 450 years (Heather 2007:13–14).

What can we say of the city that served as the center of this vast empire? In physical design, Rome was similar to the cities discussed earlier. At its center were a market, a forum, and a complex of monumental buildings. Radiating outward in orderly fashion across the breadth of the city—some 7 square miles overall—were

major, broad thoroughfares constructed according to a careful plan. Indeed, roads were one of Rome's greatest achievements. In all, the Roman work force constructed more than 50,000 miles of roads. Extremely well built, these roads served as links between Rome and the empire's vast hinterland, from which the city drew tribute. Many of the major cities of Europe today—including London, York, Vienna, Bordeaux, Paris, and Cologne—were once provincial outposts of Rome.

Perhaps most striking was the city's aqueduct system, considered to be among the greatest engineering feats of the ancient world. Between 312 B.C.E. and 222 C.E., the Romans built 11 separate aqueducts, which together could deliver up to 264 gallons per person to its 1 million residents—more than the capability of most cities today. Benefiting from such a generous water supply, Rome had large public baths, fountains, hydrants along main streets, and a system of water drainage begun as early as the sixth century B.C.E. In addition, the Romans constructed aqueducts for about 200 provincial cities they founded throughout Europe (Carcopino 2008). These spillways—some of which are still in use today—brought freshwater from as far away as 59 miles, just as today's aqueduct systems bring water from as far away as 120 miles to New York City or from many hundreds of miles away in California.

The motive for Rome's impressive engineering was ultimately to serve the interests of the ruling military and political elite. While the elite enjoyed incredible riches, Rome's poorer residents, living in largely unplanned and squalid tenements, benefited little from the wealth that was brought continuously to the city. Like their modern counterparts, these tenement districts were typically overcrowded, stifling, foul smelling, disease ridden, and filled with brutal actions that desensitized its people and cheapened the value of life. This underside of Roman life had a further dimension—one that could hardly find a sharper contrast with the Greek ideal of human dignity. The enduring, if horrible, example of Rome's descent into sadistic escapism was the Circus, as described in the *Cityscape* box on page 41.

Taken as a whole, Rome was a parade of contrasts: engineering excellence and technical achievement juxtaposed with human debasement and militaristic cruelty. Eventually, its empire extended so far that it could no longer control its home base, and rotting from within, Rome sank into decline. It fell in 476 C.E. under the onslaught of northern invasion, and by the sixth century, it had become a mere town of 20,000.

Decline: The Middle Ages

As Rome collapsed, so did the empire that sustained urban life throughout much of Europe. With this eclipse came a period of about 600 years during which European cities either fell into a pattern of minimal survival or ceased to exist entirely. Commercial trade, once the source of life to the empire and its cities, plunged dramatically. Once-great cities, boasting populations in excess of 100,000, became virtually isolated hamlets. The danger of pillaging by barbarians increased, creating an almost singular concern for security. People left in surviving cities fortified them with surrounding great walls, a revival of an ancient urban feature rendered unnecessary when the Romans controlled nearly the entire continent.

The pattern of settlement typical of the fifth through the eleventh centuries was a mosaic of local manors, villages, and small towns that in many ways were reminiscent of the earliest urban settlements we considered at the beginning of this chapter. The dominance over a large hinterland so characteristic of Greek and Roman cities all but vanished. So too did the flourishing of the arts and sciences. This is, of course, the essence of the image conveyed by the phrase "Dark Ages."

During this period, a feudal system arose in which a local lord provided security in exchange for service on his lands. In most cases, however, the manors were in the countryside, weakening urban influence even further. A few highly fortified small cities and manor towns survived, but given the state of medieval technology, only a limited population received protection from them. A small population made a low level of production inevitable, however, and this, in turn, caused the city to stagnate.

Revival: Medieval and Renaissance Cities

The low point of urban life in Europe was reached in the ninth century (Holmes 2002). Then, around the eleventh century, a general "awakening" began. The reasons for this change, which occurred gradually over several centuries, are numerous and complex, but a general development of urban trade and crafts was a key factor.

The Crusades—armed marches by Christian European groups against the Islamic possessors of "The Holy Land," where more often than not the Europeans found ultimate defeat—took place between 1096 and 1291. Even so, the Crusades contributed to a rebirth of trade routes linking Europe and the Near East, as did the growth of local trade, both of which began stimulating the long-dormant urban division of labor.

CITYSCAPE

Classical Rome: The Spectacle of Death

Over the centuries, not only did Rome's political system change significantly from that which existed in the early Republic, but so too did the lifestyle for the average Roman worker. At first, demanding but worthwhile activities were an ongoing daily effort. Leisure activities were certainly also a part of life, but primarily one's time and energy were devoted to making a living.

As the Roman Empire expanded and a parasitic economy evolved, feeding off the labor of enslaved peoples, Roman workers—typically up at daybreak—finished working by noon. With their afternoons and evenings free, the citizenry soon found spectator sports to be a desired way to spend their leisure time, and their rulers gradually provided ever more lavish spectacles to entertain them. What emerged was an urban institution that; soon became an all-consuming brutal form of entertainment. The people lived for little else.

Chariot races were one of the first staged events, and these could be bloody. In time, bloodshed itself as entertainment became the norm. Added were spectacular naval battles in arenas flooded to create an artificial lake; animal hunts; gladiatorial combat; and ritualized executions through crucifixion, burning, death by wild beasts, or staged battle re-enactments. All were eagerly anticipated and enjoyed by people of all social classes. By the thousands people flocked to the arenas to see these spectacles of death. In the reign of Emperor Claudius (41–54 C.E.), so many days were set aside for these events that they totaled one-fourth of an entire year.

Public punishment of criminals, perhaps intended as a warning to others, became an "amusing" spectator sport. Public demand was so strong that an insufficient supply of criminals and prisoners led to the decision to bring conquered peoples—soldiers and civilians alike—to the arena to be tortured, maimed, and killed—by animals, horrendous devices, or professional fighters, all for the entertainment of the population.

Wild beast spectacles, in which large numbers of animals were killed, provided a meat meal for Roman citizens in attendance, many of whom—especially the poor—rarely had protein in their diet. These spectacles and entertainment enabled the emperor to interact with his people to gain and maintain their support, thus providing a practical reason for their continuance. Another function was that the "bread and circus" events effectively masked the otherwise emptiness and meaninglessness in the parasitic existence of so many, thereby helping to maintain the status quo of imperial rule.

Despite other significant contributions to civilization, this combination of blood sport games, executions, and mass slaying of animals has left a vivid image of the Roman Empire as one of brutality and violence.

The emergence of a complex and competitive commercial class at the center of this trade, dominated from the eleventh century onward by craft guilds, contributed to a newly vibrant city life. Merchants alone did not dominate these cities, however. Many groups—including the church, the landed gentry, and the feudal royalty—vied for position. Small and self-contained, medieval cities allowed no single focus to dominate urban life in the way the military and political elements had dominated Rome (Nicholas 2003).

As for their populations, medieval cities were small—both in relation to Roman cities (many of which supported more than 100,000 people) and in comparison with the industrial cities that would follow. Although a few cities, such as Paris and Venice, were much larger in area, the physical dimensions of most medieval cities also were modest. Cities typically occupied a few hundred acres, or the size of a small town of about 5,000 people today. A moat often supplemented the walls surrounding the cities, as shown in Figure 2–3. Major roads within the city connected its gated entrances to the center—typically to the cathedral, the marketplace, or major buildings, such as the guilds or town halls.

Of greatest importance, usually, was the cathedral, which often towered over the rest of the city. Indeed, the importance of the church to the social life of medieval Europe is difficult to exaggerate. All members of mainstream medieval society—both urban and rural—were Roman Catholics. The Catholic Church was an unchallenged dominant force, and exclusion from it—whether through excommunication or as a member of a religious minority (particularly Jews)—relegated one to the status of a social outcast on the fringe of society.

The medieval city did not produce the sense of awe and massive scale that mark the modern Western city. Other than the cathedral, and perhaps a palace, no tall buildings existed, and streets were narrow and winding rather than wide and straight as they are today. Paving of streets, done on a large scale in Rome during its empire, did not become common in medieval European cities until the twelfth and thirteenth centuries. Houses, typically built together in row house fashion, often had open space for growing some food in the rear. Despite the lack of such conveniences as indoor plumbing, the small population and relatively low density of these cities allowed life to proceed under conditions far more healthful than those of many cities in the developing world today.

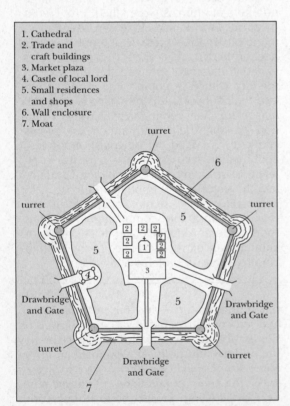

1. Cathedral
2. Trade and
   craft buildings
3. Market plaza
4. Castle of local lord
5. Small residences
   and shops
6. Wall enclosure
7. Moat

FIGURE 2–3 The medieval city, circa 1350, developed on a new site in response to the needs and patterns of the new trading system and for defense. The site was chosen at the intersection of rivers and roads, a natural route center that offered plentiful water, natural defenses, and an ample food supply from the surrounding agrarian area of the valley. The city was a trading and commercial center; craft industries produced goods for trade and for exchange with farmers of the surrounding area who supplied food as well as many of the items involved in long-distance trade. Movement within the city was mainly pedestrian, so narrow streets with many angles were not constricting. Some wider, more open streets allowed passage of horse traffic involved in long-distance trade.

The city of Carcassonne in France remains an outstanding example of a medieval walled city. Compare this picture to Figure 2–3. The local lord's fortress is on the right, and the cathedral is slightly to the left and above it. Such cities were characteristic of Europe for nearly 1,000 years after the fall of Rome (479 C.E.).

These European cities gradually grew in population size and density. First, the rear yards yielded to building extensions, and then, when unbuilt space was gone, they built upward, with floor added to floor (Pounds 2005). The period from the twelfth century until about the sixteenth century was an age of general urban rebirth, or renaissance. First evident in Italian city-states such as Venice, Florence, Palermo, and Milan, this rebirth reconnected people to the humanistic conception of city life that flourished some 1,500 years earlier in Athens. During the Renaissance, the city gradually recaptured an interest in art, literature, and architecture.

Although once again the city generated the ideal of full human development, the real contradiction of the era was that it was an ideal the great bulk of its citizens had little chance to realize, as wealth remained highly concentrated. For example, in 1545, more than half the wealth in the French city of Lyon belonged to a mere 10 percent of the population (Hohenberg and Lees 1996:147).

THE SECOND URBAN REVOLUTION: THE RISE OF MODERN CITIES

Within the walls of the Renaissance city, another type of city altogether began to emerge. The old feudal power structure was breaking down, giving people more freedom to live their lives where they chose. Trade was becoming more important, increasing the available wealth, and cities were gaining rapidly in prominence.

Throughout Europe, commerce slowly began to replace agriculture as the dominant mode of making a living. A new middle class began to rise to power. This class—the **bourgeoisie** (the French word means, literally, "of the town")—consisted of shopkeepers, traders, bureaucrats, government officials, and people engaged in commercial ventures of all sorts. As wealth increased in the cities, they began to attract ever more people who hoped to share in the obvious material benefits of this process.

By the mid-seventeenth century, feudalism was all but dead, and with it went the last remnants of the rural-centered life of the Middle Ages. In its place stood capitalism, a city mode of life fundamentally grounded in the possibilities for trade. By the eighteenth century, the Industrial Revolution began a process that fueled even more strongly the dominance of the city-based market economy. The change was striking: City populations everywhere exploded (see Table 2–1). If the first urban revolution took place when cities first appeared some 10,000 years before, the second urban revolution occurred from about 1650 on, as Europe became a continent of cities.

Characterizing the preindustrial and early industrial eras was low-efficiency technology, primitive health care, and high birth and death rates. In other words, people typically had many children, but only some lived to become adults. Even for those who did, life expectancy was much lower than today (usually less than 40 years). As a result, natural population growth (the difference between the birth and death rates) was slow and frequently checked by massive numbers of deaths occasioned by outbreaks of plague. From the 1340s to the early 1350s, for example, the Black Plague raced across Europe, killing one-third of the population overall and up to 60 percent in the continent's cities (Kelly 2005).

Fortunately, plague did not wreak its vengeance forever. In time, a larger portion of the urban population enjoyed more wealth, more efficient means of production, and better health and sanitation conditions. Death rates fell dramatically, while birth rates remained high: What population experts call a *demographic transition* was underway. A major population explosion began throughout Europe, primarily centered in the cities. Although migration caused much urban growth—that is, from people coming to the city from the countryside—natural population growth was also extremely high. Together, both forces began to produce cities with population sizes undreamed of in antiquity. Recall that Rome, at its peak, contained around a million people. By contrast, the population of London by 1900 reached 6.5 million and would increase still further.

In European and North American countries, this urban demographic transition continued well into the twentieth century. Then, the third and last phase of demographic transition took place. A rising standard of living—making more children for "productive purposes" unnecessary—and effective means of contraception led to a lowered birth rate. In most industrial nations, population growth not only slowed but today actually faces a decline in many European countries and Japan. Although the birth rate also has dropped in much of the developing world, it still remains high, leading to burgeoning growth and problems of overpopulation (see Figure 2–4).

TABLE 2–1   Population of Selected European Cities, 1700–2010, in Thousands

City	1700	1800	1900	2010
Amsterdam	172	201	510	780
Berlin	—	172	2,424	3,460
Hamburg	70	130	895	1,786
Lisbon	188	237	363	490
London	550	861	6,480	7,620
Madrid	110	169	539	3,265
Naples	207	430	563	948
Paris	530	547	3,330	2,234
Rome	149	153	487	2,612
Vienna	105	231	1,662	1,724

Source: Adapted from Tertius Chandler, *4000 Years of Urban Growth: An Historical Census*, rev. ed. (Lewiston, NY: Edwin Mellen Press, 1988); "City Population: Europe," accessed online at http://www.citypopulation.de/Europe.html on May 11, 2012.

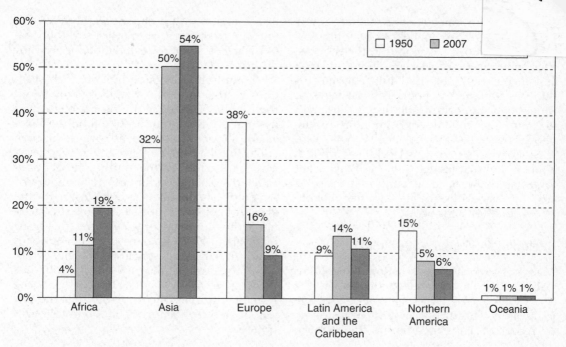

FIGURE 2–4   Distribution of the World Urban Population by Major Area, 1950, 2007, 2050
Source: United Nations Population Division.

To conclude this chapter, we turn to a case study focusing on London, a city that many consider, perhaps with Paris and Rome, to be the greatest of European urban centers. As we examine this city of kings, queens, Shakespeare, Dickens, and Churchill, we shall see reflected all the stages of urban development we have just discussed.

CASE STUDY
London—The History of a World City

When a man is tired of London, he is tired of life; for there is in London all that life can afford.

Dr. Samuel Johnson (1709–1784)

Certain great cities, suggests Saskia Sassen (2006:50), conduct a disproportionate part of the world's most important business. These are the "world cities," such as London.

For approximately 1,000 years, London has been a focus of European urban life and remains one of the four or five most important economic centers of the world. Its metropolitan area has a population of approximately 7.6 million people, and it is one of the world's leading destinations for tourists (14.6 million in 2010). Even though tourism provides employment for up to 13 percent of London's work force and brings in more than $14 billion annually, the time-honored image of a relatively sedate, typically English city no longer holds (London and Partners 2011a).

Old-timers lament the changes in London's quality of life, as its fleeing middle class and growing racial/ethnic diversity alter the city's texture. As an example, nearly two out of five workers in London in 2011 were foreign born, filling one-third of all higher-skilled job positions in the city and nearly two-thirds in the low-skilled category (Bentham 2011a). More seriously, the city lost more than 1 million jobs in recent decades. Even so, in 2010, London secured more investments in projects from overseas companies than any other European city, partly in anticipation of its hosting the

2012 Olympic Games (London and Partners 2011b). A large percentage of London's middle class, however, has moved to the suburbs, leaving the city bereft of its traditional tax base and increasingly polarized into a home for the very rich and the poor. Tension between whites and minorities still exists, although not with the violent confrontations of the mid-1980s.

So London remains, as Dr. Johnson put it, a mix of "all that life can afford." Why? What forces are at work in making a city a world city? To answer this question, we first need to look at London's history.

Beginnings: 55 B.C.E.–1066 C.E.

London's story begins with Rome and Julius Caesar. After his conquest of Gaul in the first century B.C.E., Caesar learned of a large island to the north that had important natural resources. His expedition to the island in 55 B.C.E. met with little success, however. He encountered fierce resistance from the local Celtic tribes, so he retreated to Rome to enjoy his other victories.

A hundred years later, in 43 C.E., the fifth Caesar, the emperor Claudius, conquered the island. Claudius set up his main encampment at the first point upstream on the River Thames (pronounced "tems") where his men could build a bridge to give the troops access across the river to the south. The Romans called the place "Londinium" (meaning "wild" or "bold" place), after the Celtic name for the area. A deep-water port, London's site facilitated the shipment of goods into the heart of England. The Romans built major roads in all directions and enclosed the city within a wall for protection. By 60 C.E., London was thriving: In *The Annals* (110–120 C.E.), the Roman historian Tacitus wrote that the city was "famed for commerce and crowded with traders."

Ancient Rome's domination of Europe had a profound influence on the continent's urban development, both physically and culturally. In many European cities today, we can find the remains of vast building projects, roads, bridges, enormous baths and aqueducts, temples, and theaters, such as this Roman wall remnant built in 200 B.C.E.

The Romans remained for nearly 400 years. By the beginning of the fifth century, remnants of the Celtic tribes (long ago forced by the Romans into the outer regions of Cornwall, Wales, and Scotland) continually challenged Roman rule, as did invading tribes from northern Europe. Eventually, the cost of maintaining the British Isles, combined with the necessity of protecting the parts of the empire closer to Rome itself, became too great, and Romans abandoned the islands in 410 C.E. The reemergent tribes then took great delight in destroying virtually all remnants of the Roman occupation, including the Roman remains in London. Nevertheless, the Romans left two legacies that would be crucial to London's later history: the established city and a superior road system that linked it with the hinterland.

From the time of the Roman retreat until the Norman Conquest in 1066, Britain came under a variety of political overlords. Different tribes—the original Celts, Danes, Angles, Saxons, and Vikings—vied for control of the island, gaining and losing it numerous times. To give but one example, in 1013 the Danes conquered the city, driving out the Saxon king, Ethelred. Ethelred formed an alliance with King Olaf of Norway, and together, they quickly attacked the city again. Knowing that London Bridge was the key to London's southern supply route, they attached ropes to its huge pilings and sailed downstream, pulling the bridge in their wake (hence the origin of the eleventh-century song "London Bridge Is Falling Down"). Following the Saxon–Norwegian takeover, the Danes returned in 1016, and again, they took the city. This seesaw pattern was typical.

Despite changing political fortunes, London thrived. Eager to maintain their success, its merchants usually threw in with whoever was in power, thus maintaining and strengthening London's importance as the economic center of England.

The Medieval City: 1066–1550

The year 1066 brought political stability. The Norman invader, William the Conqueror, defeated the Saxon king, Harold, at the Battle of Hastings and then marched on London. Finding the city well fortified and recognizing the vital importance of the trade connections it maintained elsewhere, William attacked the community of Southwark (pronounced "sutherk") at the opposite end of London Bridge. Leaving a standing army, he took the remainder of his forces to the smaller, less protected cities in the west and north. These he systematically destroyed (*ravaged* might be a better word), always sending back news of his conquests. The message to Londoners was all too clear: Surrender or face utter devastation. Londoners opened the gates of the city and welcomed William as their king. Without any fighting there, William gained his prize. And by not sacking the city, William not only gained access to virtually all its wealth but also ensured that the city would be able to produce more wealth in the future. Slaughtered merchants, after all, trade with no one.

Twenty-five years before William's conquest, the Saxon king, Edward the Confessor, a devout Christian, decided to build a great abbey west of the original City of London, around a sharp bend in the Thames. (Technically, and still true today, the "City of London" is the original 1-square-mile area encompassed by the Roman walls.) It was in this abbey, called Westminster (literally, "the church in the west"), where William chose to have himself crowned king of all England. William then took up residence in the nearby palace that Edward had constructed earlier.

The site of William's coronation and residence was critical to the history of London for three reasons. First, an important political residence situated in the immediate vicinity of the financial capital gave London the power of a "double magnet"—with both a financial center and a political center. Second, the establishment of the City of Westminster to the west of the City of London meant that incoming people would fill the land between, thus "dragging" greater London in a westward sprawl out of the original walled, Roman city. Third, the establishment of the royal residence in London inextricably tied London's local history to the nation's history. Henceforth, the history of London would be, to a large degree, part of the history of England.

For five and a half centuries, medieval London grew steadily. Nevertheless, it was an out-of-the-way place—an important, but not major, European city. This changed radically, however, with the onset of world exploration. By 1550, London had become a world city.

The World City Emerges: 1550–1800

Three reasons explain the transformation of London. First, with the discovery of the Americas, London suddenly became a stop "on the way" for most northern European expeditions heading west to the Americas. It thus became a place where goods could be unloaded conveniently and transferred to the ships of other nations or processed in some manner for reshipment.

Second, because of its geographical isolation from the rest of Europe and paucity of natural resources, England became a seafaring nation, with the world's most efficient sailing fleet.

Third, there was wool. Isolated from war-ravaged Europe for centuries, England was able to produce more of this precious material than any other country. With wool in ever-increasing demand, London quickly became the port for trading the largest proportion by far of the world's wool. In fact, London merchants established a virtual monopoly.

As a result of all these factors, London exploded in population, wealth, power, and influence. By the mid-1500s, the English Renaissance—comparable to those of Florence and Venice—had begun. Not only did commerce thrive, so did art, literature, music, and drama. It was the era of Henry VIII, Sir Thomas More, Elizabeth I, Roger Bacon, Sir Walter Raleigh, and of course, Shakespeare.

Shakespeare, in fact, is a marvelous example of a city's nourishing effect on human creativity. In the late 1500s, Shakespeare arrived in London—the only place where serious dramatists could have their work produced. There, he found patrons and competitors who pushed him to his peak. He wrote all of his greatest works in London. As Oscar Wilde, the great nineteenth-century poet and playwright, put it, "Town life nourishes and perfects all the more civilized elements in man—Shakespeare wrote nothing but doggerel lampoon before he came to London and never penned a line after he left" (Keyes 1999:126).

An important link exists between a thriving city and the advance of cultural ideas. First, a dynamic city attracts people from different backgrounds. As the population grows, the possibilities for transformations and combinations of ideas and lifestyles multiply. Second, an intimate historical link has long existed between wealth found in a thriving city and the development of cultural ideas. Simply put, wealth supports leisure. Creative artists with wealthy patrons or buyers for their work can literally afford to develop their art in ways that would be impossible if leisure time were not available. In addition, affluent people enjoy theater, architecture, and music, thereby enhancing the creative arts in another way.

People came to Renaissance London in droves. In 1500, the city was home to 75,000 people. By 1600, its population nearly tripled to 220,000, and by 1650, it doubled again to more than 450,000. London, however, had no plan for accommodating these huge numbers of people. Housing became scarce and overcrowded, and the streets virtually impassable. The water became polluted, and not surprisingly, so did the streets themselves. As one historian notes,

> A whole network of officials, from the mayor down to the four [officials] attached to each ward, were continuously battling with the problems of street cleaning. People like William Ward, who caused great nuisance and discomfort to his neighbors by throwing out horrible filth onto the highway, the stench of which was so odious that none of his neighbors could remain in their shops, were prosecuted as public menaces. Many people defied regulations and simply emptied their slops into the street, or, like one ingenious fellow, piped them into the cellar of a neighbor. (Gray 1997:133–34)

Then, in a single year, catastrophe hit the city twice, the first directly connected with the unsanitary conditions we just described. The Great Plague of 1665–1666 claimed as many as 100,000 city residents within the space of eight months. A major contributor to ending the bubonic plague (by killing the infected fleas and rats who transmitted it) was the Great Fire that began the evening of September 2, 1666. By the end of the fire four days later, some four-fifths of the City of London was destroyed—approximately 13,200 houses, 87 churches, and 50 Livery Halls over an area of 436 acres. But, like the mythical phoenix, London rose from its own flames. Less than 40 years later, in 1700, the London area had a population of more than half a million people, and the city—entirely, even spectacularly, rebuilt—was more powerful than ever. By 1750, the population reached more than 675,000, and by 1800, it was 851,000, 1.5 times the population size of Paris.

Industrialization and Colonization: 1800–1900

The onset of the Industrial Revolution in the late 1700s spurred the growth of London as never before. London was already the center of British trade: What the city did not produce, it shipped; what it did not ship was simply not available for human consumption. To fuel its voracious industrial machine, England needed cheap raw materials in huge portions. Unable to supply all these materials itself, England, like many European nations of the period, colonized much of the globe as quickly as possible. Thus grew the British Empire, on which the sun never set and which, from its center in London, controlled the destinies of a quarter of the earth's population.

To accommodate the burgeoning empire and its industry, the city grew immensely. The docks expanded and provided huge numbers of jobs in the East End; the government civil service expanded to oversee the empire; growing industry provided still more jobs. London became like a huge, expanding mouth, swallowing up people by the millions. By 1861, the population of London totaled nearly 3 million. By 1901, the figure was approximately 6.5 million, thus increasing by more than 3 million in just 40 years.

The Industrial Revolution brought migrants by the millions to cities such as London. Misery and despair, a life of squalor in unbelievable slum conditions, were the lot of many, as poignantly shown in this picture of London's Harrow Alley, drawn by French artist Gustav Doré in the 1870s.

The city also developed a level of poverty among millions of its residents that was unlike anything experienced before. Many—including Charles Dickens, Karl Marx, and Friedrich Engels—described the suffering of the poor in nineteenth-century London, but few captured it as well as the French illustrator Gustave Doré, whose drawing accompanies this discussion.

The Modern Era: 1900 to the Present

After 1900, life improved. World War I united the country against a common enemy, and ironically, the Great Depression of the 1930s helped equalize the suffering by cutting the economic bottom out from under the country's middle

CITYSCAPE

The East End and West End of London

These two ends of central London appear to have little in common. The West End and its neighbours, Whitehall and Westminster, are linked together by centuries of state power and by the wealth of its royal, aristocratic, and (more recently) bourgeois residents. They contain most of the principal contemporary tourist sites, as well as monuments and buildings redolent of empire and pre-colonial, medieval elites. The East End, on the other hand, has long been a poor suburb of the City of London. During the nineteenth century it rapidly expanded into a vast working-class area containing substantial pockets of intense poverty. Its residents were excluded from the centers of political and social power until the early twentieth century. Here the struggle for survival operated over a terrain sharply divided by occupational, ethnic, racial, and gender distinctions.

While Soho shares many of the characteristics associated with the East End, it is nevertheless a small enclave contained within a generally prosperous area of central London. Soho became a central London locality where middle- and upper-class visitors could easily find "low life" entertainment. In the East End the scale of its social and economic problems, and its overwhelmingly working-class population, has deterred all but the most determined visitors from the West End and other more prosperous areas of London.

The terms "West End" and "East End," therefore, conjure up two sharply different images of London—images shaped by the realities of social and economic inequality. Yet the gap between these two ends of central London has recently narrowed as the dockland neighbourhoods have been redeveloped.

Source: John Eade, *Placing London: From Imperial Capital to Global City* (London: Berghahn Books, 2000), p. 123.

and upper-middle classes. Then, in 1940, Adolf Hitler's *Luftwaffe*, through continuous bombings, destroyed much of the city once again.

After World War II, the city regenerated itself once more. Rebuilt offices in the devastated city boomed, and tourists came by the millions. Yet London lost population, partly because of the policy of shifting people out of the slums and into new towns and partly because of the decline in heavy industries. The docklands—an 8.5-square-mile area in the East End that housed the world's largest complex of enclosed docks and warehouses—went into rapid decline as the advent of container ships and other technological changes rendered the docks obsolete (see *Cityscape* box on this page). As England's colonies became independent states, the empire disappeared

as well—and with it the immense wealth that enabled growth.

Long-term unemployment was virtually unknown in London until the 1960s and 1970s, when massive Commonwealth immigration brought racial and ethnic minorities (primarily Indians, Pakistanis, and Bangladeshis) into the city's decaying and dangerous inner districts. An outcast group emerged, whose unemployment remained two to three times above the city average. Race riots in 1981 and 1985 demonstrated that the city's social fabric was unraveling. Londoners began to fear that the city had lost its ability to integrate diverse elements of society and survive social upheaval without shattering into fragments.

A dramatic change to London's economic structure then followed. Until the 1980s, the

London effectively blends its past and present, its modern buildings serving as a backdrop to the eleventh-century Tower of London and complex along the River Thames. The city continues successfully modernizing to remain competitive, but its rich traditions and charm of bygone years remain an important part of London and are major attractions for millions of visitors annually.

finance and business services sector employed only about a tenth of the labor force, with manufacturing employing about one-third. By 2001, as the nature of work and the workplace changed, those numbers completely reversed. Offices replaced factories to meet the expansion of such occupational areas as banking, consultancy, law, and marketing. As construction of new office buildings in redeveloped areas like Canary Wharf and King's Cross met the new needs, housing demand intensified for accommodations close to where the jobs were. This renewed interest in living in the city center resulted in large-scale gentrification. Decaying rental housing units and public housing in the inner city yielded to clearance and redevelopment of owner-occupied housing. Developers (1) converted multi-occupied rented houses into single-family housing; (2) converted old warehouses and factories into loft or luxury apartments; and (3) built new residences along the river frontage and old docklands areas (Hamnett 2003; O'Hanlon and Hamnett 2009).

As property prices increased for formerly cheap property in older inner-city neighborhoods, gentrification spread outward from the city. A new group of wealthy professionals, the "international rich," took up residence in London and imposed its mark on the inner-city housing market. Unlike traditional gentrifiers or traditional urban upper classes, however, they expressed little interest in civic engagement or community bonding (Butler and Lees 2006; Butler 2007; Hamnett 2009). Moreover, rapidly growing differences in earnings and income between these highly paid professional and managerial workers and those in semi-skilled and unskilled jobs led London to become a far more unequal city than in much of the twentieth century (O'Hanlon and Hamnett 2009:212).

In addition to social class distinctions, London also contains a larger-than-ever ethnic minority population as a result of international migration. Numbering only a few hundred thousand in the 1960s, its minorities now are 2.5 million, or 29 percent of Greater London's total population. In Inner London, ethnic minorities, primarily Afro-Caribbean, Black African, Indian, Pakistani, and Bangladeshi, now account for 34 percent of the total population, and in three boroughs the ethnic minority population exceeds 50 percent. Once predominantly white and homogeneous, London is now a multiethnic, multiracial city.

Today, mixed trends still are evident. Despite the current setbacks, Canary Wharf remains one of the busiest and most important areas of commerce. This thriving community is in the docklands area, at the famous "U" bend in the River Thames, with its blend of restored warehouses and historic buildings as well as contemporary housing complexes and office developments, many with award-winning glass-and-steel designs. In two decades, this area has undergone a massive, landscape-changing development, with towering skyscrapers, including Britain's tallest building, the 50-story Canary Wharf Tower, and the uniquely designed, 41-story Swiss Re building, known to Londoners as "the Gherkin." Nearby is the popular promenade on the south bank of the Thames, with its new attraction, the London Eye, the world's largest observation wheel, standing at about 443 feet and attracting approximately 10,000 visitors daily.

Meanwhile, the influx of immigrants has placed a serious strain on public services and resulted in more children with a poor command of English in the schools. As Londoners flee the congestion and higher cost of living, the city has become more foreign and diverse than the rest of Britain. London has also become more economically polarized, with its high cost of living making it difficult for those struggling to find economic security and a home of their own. Thus, even as London improves, not everyone is necessarily better off.

Perhaps Dr. Johnson was right after all. With several trends occurring simultaneously, no one portrait of this city is possible. London in the modern era is still as it was in Johnson's day: a world city that inevitably contains "all that life can afford."

SUMMARY

Cities have been with us for 10,000 years. They began after the last Ice Age in favorable ecological settings in many areas of the world. Slowly and tentatively, they established themselves, fueled by a surplus of goods and materials, whether developed by agriculture, trade, or military dominance. As they grew, they evolved a complex social structure—most particularly, a specialized division of labor and a hierarchical power structure. All these elements allowed cities, over time, to increase their dominance in human affairs. Thus began the first urban revolution.

The earliest cities, such as Jericho and Catal Hüyük, were scattered, independent units, often linked by trade but not much more. Sometime after 4000 B.C.E., however, the first urban empires began to appear. First in Mesopotamia and then in Egypt, China, the Indus River Valley, and the Americas, systems of cities emerged. These became not only centers of culture but also centers of regional domination. This link between city and empire was a central factor in the development of civilization for nearly 5,000 years. Urban empires pulled into their sphere diverse peoples, ideas, and great wealth and power. This was as true of Teotihuacan in North America as it was of Egypt in the Middle East.

Early Western civilization also centered on its cities—first those of Greece and then those of the Roman Empire. When the latter finally crumbled in the late fifth century C.E., most of the other cities of Europe—outposts in the Roman chain—lost their reason for being. The next 500 years—roughly from 500 to 1000 C.E.—were a decidedly anti-urban period. Many cities disappeared entirely, and the few that managed to survive limped along as shadows of what they had been.

In the first few centuries of the second millennium C.E., a halting urban revival began. Slowly, trade began to revive, and the old feudal system began to break down as a new merchant class gained power. This revival reached its peak between 1400 and 1600, with the evolution of the Renaissance cities—most effectively symbolized by the Italian city-states of Florence, Venice, and Milan.

Then, around 1600, a turning point occurred, with the weakening beyond repair of the old feudal social order. The merchant class, generating greater wealth through increasingly successful business ventures, began to control urban life throughout Europe. Seeing new possibilities for a better life in material terms, people streamed into cities all over the continent. This influx, coupled with technological improvement and advances in health and sanitation services, created a demographic transition. Europe in general, but cities in particular, exploded in population as death rates plummeted, birth rates stayed high, and migrants arrived by the millions. From 1650 on, cities—many huge in population and dominance—began sprouting all over Europe and in North America. This was the second urban revolution, spurred on primarily by the twin engines of capitalism and industrialization.

Today, cities exist in the farthest reaches of the globe. In many cases, the growth of cities created immense problems and widespread suffering amid successes. Now, in areas of the world where the urban demographic transition first occurred (notably Europe and North America), urban growth has slowed dramatically. Unhappily, in other areas—as Chapter 13 explains— urban growth has not.

Our case study of London illustrates, in the life of a single city, nearly all of these processes. London began as an outpost of the Roman Empire, achieved initial success, and then, with the Roman retreat in 410, fell into its own dark age—unheard of for centuries and the object of multiple invasions. It began to recover after the victory of William the Conqueror in 1066. For five centuries, it built its prominence as the center of British

life and, around 1600, blossomed into one of the greatest Renaissance cities in history. Its success was linked primarily to international trade. Through the next two centuries, London grew and gained even greater control of world markets. Then, with the Industrial Revolution and intensive British colonization during the nineteenth and early twentieth centuries, the city exploded in population, undergoing a major demographic transition. Despite its incredible wealth-generating capacity, London also encountered massive problems that it has not yet fully resolved. It now faces, as do many Western industrial cities, a future of changing demographics and a transformation of its economic activities.

CONCLUSION

The emergence of cities as a dominant force in human affairs is one of the crucial events of history. In many instances, cities were the driving wheel behind the development of civilization. They combined ideas in new ways, produced great wealth, wielded incredible power (often injudiciously and inhumanely), and became home to an increasing proportion of the world's population.

Yet throughout history, cities have not always had the same character. As we suggested at the opening of this chapter, the city is largely synonymous with civilization itself. Each chapter in the story of human civilization has thus produced distinctive cities: cities of the early empires, the medieval city, the Renaissance city, and most recently, the industrial–capitalist city.

Thus, both constancy and flux coexist in the history of cities. Together, these processes create urban living. Both shall be clearly evident again as we consider the development of North American cities in the next chapter.

KEY TERMS

bourgeoisie (44)
city-states (31)
cosmic calendar (24)
division of labor (25)

hierarchical power structure (25)
productive surplus (26)
regal/ritual city (36)

INTERNET ACTIVITIES

1. You can learn much about ancient cities and structures if you go to *http://www .goldenageproject.org.uk/294jericho.php*. The first page will show you photos of the ruins of Jericho. At the bottom of the page, you will find an index to click that takes you to illustrations of many other ancient locales throughout the world.

2. You can explore the archaeological ruins at Moenjo-Daro if you go to *http://www.world-heritage-tour.org/asia/south-asia/pakistan/ moenjodaro/map.html*. Once there, if you click on any small photo, you can get a 360° view of each part of the site.

CHAPTER 3

THE DEVELOPMENT OF NORTH AMERICAN CITIES

THE COLONIAL ERA: 1600–1800
    Characteristics of Colonial Cities
    The City-Instigated Revolutionary War
GROWTH AND EXPANSION: 1800–1870
    The Beginnings of Industrialization
    Urban–Rural/North–South
        Tensions
THE ERA OF THE GREAT
    METROPOLIS: 1870–1950
    Technological Advance
    Suburbs and the Gilded Age
    The Great Migration
    Politics and Problems
    The Quality of Life in the
        New Metropolis
THE NORTH AMERICAN CITY TODAY:
    1950 TO THE PRESENT
    Decentralization
    The Sunbelt Expansion

THE EVOLUTION OF MEGAREGIONS
    Northeast Megaregion Assets
    Sunbelt Problems
THE POSTINDUSTRIAL CITY
    Deterioration and Regeneration
    The Future
    The Human Cost of Economic
        Restructuring

CASE STUDY: NEW YORK—
THE "BIG APPLE"

    The Colonial Era
    Growth and Expansion
    The Great Metropolis Emerges
    New York Today
SUMMARY
CONCLUSION
KEY TERMS
INTERNET ACTIVITIES

Come hither, and I will show you an admirable Spectacle! 'Tis a
Heavenly CITY. . . . A CITY to be inhabited by an Innumerable
Company of Angels, and by the Spirits of Just Men. . . .
Put on thy beautiful garments, O America, the Holy City!

Cotton Mather, Seventeenth-century preacher

American urban history began with the
small town—five villages hacked out of the
wilderness . . . each an "upstart" town with
no past, an uncertain future, and a host of
confounding and novel problems.

Alexander B. Callow, Jr. (1982:37)

To the visitor from London, the cities of North
America may seem to lack the rich texture that
accumulates over centuries of history. In no city
of North America, for example, does a single
building rival in age the Tower of London—
the foundations of which were erected in the
eleventh century during the reign of William
the Conqueror. Even the current Houses of
Parliament and Buckingham Palace—relative
newcomers on the London scene, dating from
the mid-nineteenth century—are older than all
but a few urban structures in the United States
and Canada. Indeed, throughout Europe and
much of the non-Western world, one can find
abundant examples of exquisite, old architecture that suggests a vibrant, urban past that
long predates the founding of Canada and the
United States.

If the cities of North America are rather
recent developments in the course of world
urban history, however, they have a fascinating
history of their own, spanning five centuries.
Europeans founded the first settlements in
North America in the early seventeenth century,
at the time when industrialization was transforming the medieval cities in Europe. Perhaps
not surprisingly, the New World cities began
specifically as trade- and wealth-generating centers to fuel the growth of European cities. The
forces of postmedieval culture—commercial
trade and, shortly thereafter, industrial production—were the primary shapers of these urban
settlements. These new cities, like the new nations themselves, began with the greatest of
hopes. Cotton Mather was so enamored of the
idea of the city that he saw its growth as fulfilling the biblical promise of a heavenly setting
here on earth. Has that promise been realized?
To find out, this chapter examines the development of urban North America in terms of four
phases: the colonial, growth and expansion,
metropolitan, and modern eras.

THE COLONIAL ERA: 1600–1800

The potential of a good river or seaport
and a strategic location for trade were principal reasons for the founding of the early
cities of Boston, Charles Town (Charleston),
New Amsterdam (New York), Newport,
Philadelphia, and Quebec City. With the
exception of Newport (eclipsed in prominence by Providence during the nineteenth
century), all of these settlements became
important North American cities.

Characteristics of Colonial Cities

Colonial cities were exceptionally small,
both in physical size and in population. New
Amsterdam, for example, occupied only
the southernmost tip of Manhattan Island,
a far cry from the huge, five-borough City
of New York incorporated in 1898. Until the
eighteenth century, neither New Amsterdam
nor any other North American urban settlement had a population approaching
even 10,000. Not until after the American
Revolution did any of these places begin to
develop the population sizes we associate
with a city today.

The lack of regular street patterns and
stone houses in early Boston, Montreal,
New York, and Quebec City gave these settlements the look of medieval towns. Even
today, we can observe that original pattern
of narrow, irregular streets in these historic
neighborhoods. Furthermore, hard-surfaced
streets were not common until many years
later. Only Philadelphia, settled half a century later than the others, was built from the
beginning on the more familiar grid system
now found in many North American cities
(see Chapter 6, Figure 6–3).

The underlying concept of all these cities
was that they would serve as export centers
for raw materials going to the European
home country. Boston, for example,
supplied lumber for the ships of the British
Royal Navy, and for its part, Charles Town
(Charleston) shipped rice and indigo
back to the British Isles. New Amsterdam

BROADWAY. NEW-YORK.

North American preindustrial cities were bustling ports of commerce. Their concentrations of people and busy activity impressed visitors, but they contained only about 5 percent of the total population. Not until the nineteenth century did any reach today's minimum standard of 100,000 for large cities, as this 1830s view of New York's Broadway suggests.

(New York) and Montreal served as bases for the lucrative fur trade.

As time wore on, however, these cities, geographically distant from Europe, prospered and became more and more independent. Colonial merchants began to compete with the British (who gained control of Quebec in 1760) and established separate trade agreements with the West Indies and even with Europe.

Many newer arrivals soon moved inland, leading to the founding of numerous secondary cities, such as New Haven and Baltimore. Although only a small fraction of the population lived in towns, an urban society emerged along the eastern shore of what soon would become a new nation. By the late 1760s, the 13 colonies had at least 12 major cities and a total population (city and hinterland) of 2 million English, half a million people of other European backgrounds, and nearly 400,000 slaves, almost all of whom were in the South (Parrillo 2009:45–49).

The City-Instigated Revolutionary War

Although the struggle for U.S. independence did not take place entirely in cities, it was in many ways a war instigated by the cities, where most of the colonial economic trade occurred. Merchants and colonists wanted freedom to pursue their life's interests as they saw fit, and economic interests were typically uppermost in their minds. The growth and development of the northern seaport towns generated numerous changes that affected labor relations, the distribution of wealth, the restructuring of social groups, and the emergence of the laboring class into the political arena (Carp 2009).

After the Revolutionary War, leadership of the new nation continued to be urban centered. New York became the first capital in 1789, and Philadelphia took over the title in 1790. Despite this urban dominance, however, most of the population was not urban at this point. The first census in 1790 identified only 5 percent residing in urban places (places with 2,500 or more persons). Only 24 such places existed, Philadelphia being the largest settlement, with a population of only 42,000.

GROWTH AND EXPANSION: 1800–1870

At the outbreak of the Revolutionary War, the western frontier of the northern colonies extended barely past the Hudson River, and the southern colonies reached outward only to the Appalachian Mountains. Soon, however, the territory of the United States extended roughly to the Mississippi River. The tremendous economic potential of this new region captured the interest of business leaders in established cities, and by the early decades of the nineteenth century, plans were under way to link the new territories with cities in the East.

The first of these links westward occurred in 1818, when the National Road (now Interstate 40) pushed through the Appalachian Mountains from the city of Baltimore. This trade route, along with Baltimore's large shipbuilding industry, caused that city to grow in size and wealth. Philadelphia attempted to keep pace, opening both canal and turnpike routes west, although with more modest success. Not to be outdone, in 1825, New York opened the Erie Canal, which soon became

the key to New York's increasing dominance over East Coast urban trade in the mid-nineteenth century. By cutting across upstate New York from the Hudson River, the canal opened a water route to the entire Great Lakes region and much of Canada. Undaunted, Baltimore began another round in this interurban rivalry by opening a railroad line to Ohio in 1828. Other cities followed suit, and soon, many railroad lines stretched westward, linking coastal cities to the hinterland.

By 1830, New York, Philadelphia, and fast-growing Baltimore had emerged as the main coastal cities, largely because of their control over the lion's share of commerce with the Ohio Valley. Table 3–1 reveals the remarkable rate of growth for these cities in comparison with Charleston, an original East Coast city still focused on tobacco and cotton production. As westward expansion proceeded, many new cities were incorporated, particularly between 1821 and 1880, the height of the westward expansion movement (see Table 3–2).

Canadian cities also benefited from new transportation links, especially in the 1850s. Toronto experienced rapid development with the coming of the Grand Trunk and Great Western railways and the signing of a trade treaty with the United States. From a population of only 9,000 in the 1830s, Toronto ballooned to 45,000 by 1861. Similarly, Montreal's railroad linkage to Toronto and initiation of shipping

TABLE 3–1   Population Growth of Selected East Coast Cities, 1790–1870

	1790	1810	1830	1850	1870
New York	33,131	100,775	214,995	515,500	942,292
Philadelphia	44,096	87,303	161,271	340,000	674,022
Boston	18,320	38,746	61,392	136,881	250,526
Baltimore	13,503	46,555	80,620	169,054	267,354
Charleston	16,359	24,711	30,289	42,985	48,956
Total U.S. urban dwellers	202,000	525,000	1,127,000	3,543,700	9,902,000
Total percentage urban	5.1	7.3	8.8	15.3	25.7

Source: Statistics derived from U.S. Censuses in 1850, 1860, and 1910 (Washington, D.C.: U.S. Government Printing Office).

TABLE 3–2   Incorporation Dates of the Largest North American Cities by Historical Period

Pre-1776 (4)	1776–1820 (7)	1821–1860 (28)	1861–1880 (8)	1881–1910 (10)
Quebec (1608)	Nashville (1784)	Boston (1822)	Denver (1861)	Calgary (1884)
New York (1685)	Baltimore (1797)	St. Louis (1822)	Tucson (1864)	Vancouver (1886)
Philadelphia (1701)	Dayton (1805)	Detroit (1824)	Minneapolis (1867)	Virginia Beach (1887)
Charlotte (1774)	New Orleans (1805)	Memphis (1826)	Seattle (1869)	Long Beach (1888)
	San Antonio (1809)	Jacksonville (1832)	Phoenix (1871)	Oklahoma City (1890)
	Pittsburgh (1816)	Montreal (1832)	Fort Worth (1873)	Miami (1896)
	Cincinnati (1819)	Columbus (1834)	Fresno (1874)	Tulsa (1898)
		Toronto (1834)	Indianapolis (1874)	Edmonton (1905)
		Cleveland (1836)		Honolulu (1909)
		Chicago (1837)		Las Vegas (1909)
		Houston (1837)		
		Toledo (1837)		
		Austin (1840)		
		Milwaukee (1846)		
		Atlanta (1847)		
		Albuquerque (1847)		
		Kansas City (1850)		
		Los Angeles (1850)		
		El Paso (1850)		
		Sacramento (1850)		
		San Diego (1850)		
		San Francisco (1850)		
		San Jose (1850)		
		Portland (1851)		
		Oakland (1854)		
		Ottawa (1855)		
		Dallas (1856)		
		Omaha (1857)		

Source: Based on data from Statistics Canada and the U.S. Census Bureau.

service with Europe brought its population to 270,000 by the end of the nineteenth century. Quebec City and its surrounding region numbered about 1 million by 1850, mostly because of rapid natural growth. Thereafter, lack of additional fertile lands in a favorable climate for this mostly agrarian economy prompted many French Canadians to migrate to work in the new industries of the United States.

The Beginnings of Industrialization

In 1792, shortly before the North American Industrial Revolution firmly took root, Secretary of the Treasury Alexander Hamilton played a major role in the founding of Paterson, New Jersey, at the site of the Great Falls—second only to Niagara Falls in width and height. Pierre L'Enfant, the French-born engineer who also planned Washington, D.C., designed a water raceway system to harness this water power for mills. As the first planned industrial city, Paterson quickly emerged as *the* cotton town of the United States and then as a locomotive-building center. Soon, with new inland cities developing, New England emerged as the leader in textiles. By the 1830s around Boston, factory towns "were rising on every hand, in Eastern Massachusetts and New Hampshire—Lawrence, Lowell, Fitchberg,

Manchester, Lynn. Every village with a waterfall set up a textile mill or a paper mill, a shoe factory or an iron foundry" (Brooks 2005:4; orig. 1936). Slowly, industrialization supported by private investment transformed the developing continent, particularly in the North, but as it did, new tensions began to mount.

Urban–Rural/North–South Tensions

The culture of the United States has always contained a streak of anti-urbanism. As long as the early North American settlements remained small and kept their relatively homogeneous character, few tensions existed between urban and rural sections. Yet some of the nation's founders worried greatly about how growing cities might transform the new nation. Thomas Jefferson, nurtured in the rural aristocratic tradition of Virginia, condemned cities as "ulcers on the body politic" and saw their growth as an invitation to all the corruption and evil found in the Old World across the Atlantic. Commenting on an outbreak of yellow fever, Jefferson wrote to Benjamin Rush in 1800,

> When great evils happen I am in the habit of looking out for what good may arise from them as consolations to us, and Providence has in fact so established the order to things, as that most evils are the means of producing some good. The yellow fever will discourage the growth of great cities in our nation, and I view great cities as pestilential to the morals, the health and the liberties of man. (University of Virginia Library 2011)

Despite Jefferson's wishes, the cities grew in size and prominence, and the westward movement enabled new ones to appear, bringing with them the more mechanized existence of the Industrial Age. By 1850, with many rural residents deeply alarmed about these developments, agrarian periodicals regularly touted the superiority of country life over the deceitful ways of city life.

The debate on the pros and cons of city life soon took on a new and powerful dimension on the regional level—namely, hostility between the North and the South. Contributing to this conflict was the unparalleled growth between 1820 and 1860 of U.S. cities, mostly in the North. Cities such as New York, Philadelphia, and Baltimore simply outdistanced the conservative, slowly growing cities like Charleston and Savannah. The northern cities had canal routes and the bulk of the railroad lines to the West, thereby significantly increasing their wealth and population. Moreover, they dominated ever-greater shares of regional and national markets, outstripping the South in overall production as industrialization spread.

The Civil War broke out in 1861. Although its causes were numerous (including slavery), many historians believe that it was, in a fundamental sense, a confrontation between urban and rural, between industrial and agricultural values. The North's victory was a symbolic turning point. The world of Jefferson was dying, thus leaving America's commitment to urban industrial expansion unchallenged. The stage was set for an urban explosion comparable to the one that had shaken Europe a century earlier.

THE ERA OF THE GREAT METROPOLIS: 1870–1950

The record number of small cities incorporated in North America during the 50-year period that ended in 1870 had not yet acquired many of the now-familiar urban characteristics: towering buildings, populations in the millions, and blazing lights downtown. Two historical events would provide the impetus for this transformation: the technological advance of industrialization and the migration of millions of people to urban North America.

Technological Advance

Industrialization was more than a proliferation of factories in and around the enlarging urban areas. Several inventions changed the face of the North American city. The construction of buildings with iron, and then with steel, pushed the city skyward. In 1848, a five-story factory built with an iron frame made news in New York; by 1884, a 10-story steel structure in Chicago ushered in the era of urban skyscrapers. Further ensuring the success of these taller buildings was another invention, the Otis elevator (devised in the 1850s), which became widespread in the 1880s. By the end of the nineteenth century, some buildings reached 30 stories; by 1910, a few were as high as 50. By 1913, New York had 61 buildings taller than 20 stories, and the famous city skyline was beginning to take form (Still 1999:206–207).

As cities grew upward, they also pushed outward, aided by a new technology in street-level transportation. Before the Civil War, pedestrians only had to contend with horse-drawn vehicles. By the 1870s, however, steam-powered trains were running on elevated tracks in New York and soon in other large cities as well.

In the 1880s, the electric street trolley increased mobility both within the city and just beyond its boundaries, leading to the creation of "streetcar suburbs" and a new population of daily commuters to work in the city. Today, streetcars still operate in such cities as Boston, Little Rock, Memphis, New Orleans, Philadelphia, Portland, San Diego, San Francisco, Seattle, and Toronto. Numerous other cities operate electric trolleybuses—electric buses that draw electricity from overhead wires using spring-loaded trolley poles (Webb and Tee 2011).

Suburbs and the Gilded Age

Trains and trolleys allowed fast and inexpensive transportation beyond the city limits. Quick to see the possibilities of development, real-estate speculators built housing tracts by the dozens. For example, from 1850 to 1900, the suburbs of Roxbury, Dorchester, and West Roxbury to the south of central Boston increased in population from 60,000 to about 227,000 (Warner 1978:35). For the burgeoning middle class, an escape from the city's dirt and din was at last possible. Here they could

relocate in a safe, clean environment in their own homes within neighborhoods of people like themselves. Those unable to afford these single-family houses found inspiration of one-day living in such comfort and style if they worked hard and earned enough money for a down payment.

The key to increased outmigration from the central cities was the previously mentioned streetcar, which carried people beyond the bounds of the old "walking city" of Boston, making frequent stops at stations that soon became centers of suburban housing. Suburban living and streetcar service, Warner (1978:49) concluded, "moved together"—the more there was of one, the more there was of the other. Later, cross-town service filled in the area between the original suburbs and downtown. By 1900, the old "walking city" was surrounded by a mosaic of "streetcar suburbs," which contained about half of the population of greater Boston (Warner 1978:3).

This process repeated itself across North America. Wherever urban subway and elevated systems extended ever farther during the early twentieth century, there did the suburbs appear. Technology thus spawned the suburban dream, enabling the middle class to move out of the city, separating their place of work from their place of residence. Unlike the more mixed pattern of the earlier walking city, the new housing tracts created homogeneous economic and social communities that usually excluded the poor. This pattern of social class segregation and the attempt by many to escape to the suburbs remain two powerful aspects of urban history.

Nothing, however, did more to encourage people to move outward than the automobile. Before cars were common, suburbs were long corridors, stretching out along the streetcar tracks that led from the city core. However, increased car ownership resulted in greater residential mobility, as commuters could live in homes built on vacant land away from main roads and railway lines. With the paving of more and more roads, the percentage of people living in suburbs moved ever upward. Even so, from 1900 to 1940, growth was moderate. "Suburban fever" did not manifest itself until the 1950s.

The Great Migration

Between 1870 and 1920, the U.S. urban population increased from less than 10 million to more than 54 million, while Canada's urban population grew from 3.9 to 8.8 million. By 1920, both countries were predominantly urban nations, with more than 50 percent of their populations living in urban areas. The rate of growth for many of the largest cities was nothing short of astonishing. By 1920, Chicago had more than 12 times its 1870 population and was fast approaching the 3 million mark. New York, not yet a city of 1 million in 1870, was by 1920 approaching the 6 million mark. Toronto grew nearly 10-fold, from 56,000 in 1871 to 522,000 by 1921, and Montreal nearly quintupled, from 133,000 to 618,000.

Perhaps nothing epitomizes immigrant city neighborhoods during the Great Migration more than New York City's Lower East Side. As this 1907 photograph shows, framing the streets filled with vehicles, children, pushcarts, and sidewalk vendors were the overcrowded tenements, where immigrants lived in such squalid conditions that sickness, disease, and death were constant companions.

One main reason for this striking increase was depopulation of rural areas as people moved into cities. Prompting this movement was automation—as machinery made old forms of hand-powered labor obsolete—and the promise of greater wealth in the city. Unable to survive in the country and lured by the cities, tens of thousands abandoned their farms to seek their fortunes elsewhere.

The number of foreign immigrants—20 million to the United States and 5.3 million to Canada—was a bit smaller than the number who left rural areas for the cities during this period, but the changes wrought by immigrants from abroad were far greater. Representing dozens of nationalities and ethnicities, they introduced staggering cultural diversity to the large cities. Glaab and Brown give some hint of that transformation in the United States:

> In 1890, New York . . . contained more foreign born residents than any city in the world. The city had half as many Italians as Naples, as many Germans as Hamburg, twice as many Irish as Dublin, and two and a half times the number of Jews in Warsaw. In 1893, Chicago contained the third largest Bohemian [Czech] community in the world; by the time of the First World War, Chicago ranked only behind Warsaw and Lodz as a city of Poles. (1983:138–39)

Clustering together in distinctive city districts, the great variety of these groups gave the cities a degree of diversity and excitement that was quite new—and that would thereafter affect the character of the city. To travel the breadth of Chicago, Cleveland, New York, Pittsburgh, or Toronto was—and still is—to experience a succession of differing worlds, each characterized by its own shops and products, its own sounds and smells, and its own language. Besides upward and outward expansion and raw population growth, cultural heterogeneity became a third major characteristic of the new metropolis.

When U.S. immigration laws in 1921 and 1924 curtailed immigration, the still-developing industrial machine simply looked elsewhere for cheap labor and found African

Americans in the South all too eager to find a better way of life. Between 1920 and 1929, more than 600,000 southern African Americans migrated to northern cities. By the end of the decade, Chicago's South Side and New York's Harlem had the largest concentrations of black populations anywhere in the world. In Hartford, Baltimore, Washington, Philadelphia, Cincinnati, and Detroit, the black population grew enormously. Soon, racial tensions developed in many northern cities, sometimes leading to riots.

Many cities also grew through annexation. The independent suburbs of Dorchester, Roxbury, and West Roxbury, for example, became part of Boston. In Canada, between 1883 and 1900, Toronto annexed adjacent villages and towns and doubled its area, and then again doubled its size by 1920 through further annexation. In 1930, Toronto's metropolitan area included the central city, four towns (Leaside, Mimico, New Toronto, and Weston), three villages (Forest Hill, Long Branch, and Swansea), and five townships (Etobicoke, East York, North York, Scarborough, and York). Montreal also annexed several cities, towns, and villages on its outskirts, thereby significantly expanding its municipal boundary as well.

Politics and Problems

Such enormous changes reshaping cities caused equally enormous problems. Only the city government was empowered to provide these incoming millions with water, electricity, jobs, and protection against unscrupulous exploitation. However, the pressures against fairly representing the public interest were great. Utility companies required street franchises—water and gas companies to lay pipes, electric companies to erect poles, and transit companies to lay iron rails. Local or out-of-town entrepreneurs offered to pay large sums for these lucrative franchises, and their bribes sometimes corrupted city officials.

Powerful political figures—known as "bosses"—took control of many city governments. They got the job done, but in the process, they usually lined their pockets with graft and kickbacks. By the start of the twentieth century, many city officials were as corrupt as any organized crime figure.

Another problem was that large-scale immigration sparked an increasingly bitter reaction against newcomers. It was not just their numbers, however. By 1900, immigrants were more often from southern and eastern Europe, more likely to be Roman Catholic or Jewish than Protestant, and more likely to have darker eyes, hair, and skin tone than whites of northern and western European descent. Moreover, these newcomers often had manners and clothing that made them stand out as "different." These "less desirable" immigrants added significantly to anti-city sentiment, because even more than earlier arrivals, they were overwhelmingly urban settlers. By 1910, in fact, more than one-third of the inhabitants of the eight largest U.S. cities were foreign born; another one-third were second-generation Americans. In sharp contrast, fewer than 1 in 10 non-urban Americans were foreign born. As a result, the towns often had a decided anti-ethnic and racist tinge (Muller 1994).

The Quality of Life in the New Metropolis

Some profited greatly in this age of great economic expansion, making remarkable fortunes and establishing industrial empires. Yet even as the enormous mansion-retreats of the "robber-baron" industrialists rose across the urban fringe, the blight of the inner-city tenements became more and more conspicuous. With a steady stream of people entering the large cities of the North, property owners responded to the rising demand for housing by making the most profitable use of building space. New York tenements, denounced as "hideous" by Charles Dickens (2010:135; orig. 1842), became even more overcrowded by 1900. By the turn of the century, perhaps 35 percent of New York City's population lived in such quarters. In most other industrial cities, the situation was only slightly improved.

Quality-of-life problems in the rapidly expanding industrial cities, unfortunately, were not limited to housing. Health hazards were greatest in high-density living areas with inadequate sewerage and generally unsanitary conditions. The frequency of typhoid epidemics was high in all cities. The *Chicago Times* summed up the problem with appropriate bluntness:

> The [Chicago] river stinks. The air stinks. Peoples' clothing, permeated by the foul atmosphere, stinks. . . . No other word expresses it so well as stink. A stench means something finite. Stink reaches the infinite and becomes sublime in the magnitude of odiousness. (quoted in Morris 2008:36)

Urban activists did attempt to help the situation of immigrants and improve living conditions, but for decades, the battle was uphill. Cities were growing uncontrollably, a trend that ended with World War II (1941–1945) and the suburban housing boom that followed.

THE NORTH AMERICAN CITY: 1950 TO THE PRESENT

Today's cities continue to experience three major changes. First, people and businesses are still abandoning many central cities,

continuing the suburbanization trend that began about 100 years ago—a process aptly called **decentralization.** Second, major population growth is occurring in areas with considerable environmental stresses, whether in U.S. cities in the South and West (the so-called **Sunbelt expansion**) or in Canadian cities, particularly around Toronto and Vancouver. Third, the work typically performed in the central city is mostly oriented toward white-collar jobs, high technology, and services, as Canadian and U.S. cities adjust to the postindustrial era of **globalization.**

Decentralization

Previously characterized by **urban implosion**—that is, ever-greater numbers of people converging on the central city itself—cities since the 1950s have been experiencing **urban explosion**—that is, people moving out from the core to the surrounding regions. Table 3–3 illustrates this decentralization with census data for major northern U.S. cities between 1910 and 2010. These cities became large metropolises by 1910, and each grew rapidly in the following few decades. By 1950, however, growth slowed, followed with a decline in central-city populations by 1970. A decade later, a full-scale central-city retreat appeared under way, although by 2010, a few cities had reversed this trend.

Those moving are not leaving the metropolitan region, however, but rather are relocating

TABLE 3–3   Population of Selected Northern U.S. Cities, 1910–2010 (in thousands)

	1910	1930	1950	1970	1990	2010
Baltimore	588	805	950	906	736	621
Boston	671	781	801	641	574	618
Chicago	2,185	3,376	3,621	3,367	2,784	2,696
Cleveland	561	900	915	751	506	397
Detroit	466	1,569	1,850	1,511	1,028	714
New York	4,767	6,930	7,892	7,895	7,323	8,175
Philadelphia	1,549	1,951	2,072	1,949	1,586	1,526

Source: U.S. Census Bureau.

TABLE 3–4   Population of Selected Metropolitan Areas, 2000–2010

	2010 Population (in thousands)	2000 Population (in thousands)	Percentage Change Since 2000
Canadian Metropolitan Areas			
Calgary	1,243	951	+30.7
Edmonton	1,176	938	+24.7
Hamilton	743	662	+12.2
Montreal	3,870	3,426	+13.0
Ottawa–Gatineau	1,238	1,064	+16.4
Quebec City	753	683	+10.2
Toronto	5,742	4,683	+22.6
Vancouver	2,389	1,987	+20.2
Northern Metropolitan Areas			
Baltimore–Towson	2,710	2,553	+6.1
Boston–Cambridge–Quincy	4,552	4,392	+3.6
Chicago–Naperville–Joliet	9,461	9,099	+4.0
Cleveland–Elyria–Mentor	2,077	2,148	−3.3
Detroit–Warren–Livonia	4,296	4,453	−3.5
New York–Northern NJ–Long Island	18,897	18,323	+3.1
Philadelphia–Camden–Wilmington	5,965	5,687	+4.9
Southern Metropolitan Areas			
Atlanta–Sandy Springs–Marietta	5,269	4,248	+24.0
Birmingham–Hoover	1,128	1,051	+7.3
Charlotte–Gastonia–Concord	1,758	1,499	+17.3
Dallas–Fort Worth–Arlington	6,372	5,162	+23.4
Houston–Sugar Land–Baytown	5,947	4,715	+26.1
Miami–Fort Lauderdale–Miami Beach	5,565	5,008	+11.1
New Orleans–Metairie–Kenner	1,168	1,317	−11.3
Orlando–Kissimmee	2,134	1,645	+29.7
Tampa–St. Petersburg–Clearwater	2,783	2,386	+16.6
Western Metropolitan Areas			
Los Angeles–Long Beach–Santa Ana	12,829	12,366	+3.7
Phoenix–Mesa–Scottsdale	4,193	3,252	+28.9
Portland–Vancouver–Beaverton	2,226	1,928	+15.5
Salt Lake City	1,124	969	+16.0
San Francisco–Oakland–Fremont	4,435	4,124	+7.5
Seattle–Tacoma–Bellevue	3,440	3,044	+13.0

Source: Statistics Canada and the U.S. Census Bureau.

in suburbs near the cities. Table 3–4 makes this clear by examining metropolitan area populations for selected cities across the continent, including those examined in Table 3–3. With few exceptions, suburbs are growing everywhere—and have been doing so for more than 50 years.

Economic Considerations. By the 1960s, many industries and manufacturing businesses were moving away from urban industrial districts. High rents and inadequate older buildings unsuitable for expansion had reduced the attraction of a city location. Furthermore, newer production procedures required large, low-level structures rather than the older, once suitable, multistory buildings. Concerns over rising crime rates, taxes, and traffic congestion also contributed to the proliferation of new **industrial parks**

outside the city. Workers often moved from the central city to be near their relocated jobs, resulting in a growth in suburban population and a decline in central-city population.

Technology.   As noted earlier, technological changes in energy (steam power) and building techniques (steel-frame skyscrapers, elevators) were important in the creation of a centralized metropolis during the nineteenth century. Since then, the development of interstate highways, the telephone, computers, and telecommunications have been equally important in the decentralization of the urban area.

Technology also changed the meaning of urban space. Because we move more easily across space—in minutes by car or public transit, or in milliseconds by telecommunications—physical proximity is no longer as necessary to tie together all the activities within the urban area. In fact, most

of us routinely think in terms of time ("We live about 40 minutes from the airport.") rather than distance; we may not even know how many miles away the airport is.

The Postwar Era: 1945–1970.   In the post–World War II era, North America's suburbs grew dramatically. Millions of GIs returned home, starting new families and the baby boom. With the resultant city housing shortage, these new families sought the suburban dream—a place of one's own out of the congested city, with more room to raise kids in clean air and send them to good schools, without fear of crime and other urban ills. All across North America, new housing developments appeared. None, however, illustrates "suburban fever" better than Levittown on New York's Long Island.

Some 30 miles east of Manhattan, Levittown rose from spinach and potato fields. Begun in 1947 by developer Abraham Levitt and

From the 1890s until the mid-twentieth century, streetcar travel was the best means of transportation within or between cities. Acting in collusion through their partnership in a holding company, General Motors, Firestone Tire, and several oil companies bought the streetcar companies, dismantled their systems, and replaced them with buses. An actual streetcar was used in the 2008 film *The Changeling*, set in 1920s Los Angeles.

his sons, the project escalated within a year from a planned 2,000 to 6,000 units, and with construction of the last house in 1951, Levittown contained 17,447 homes. Each ranch house was small (32 by 25 feet) and strikingly uniform in appearance. It sold for $7,990, with a $90 deposit and $58 monthly payment, and came in five different models, which differed only by exterior color, roofline, and the placement of windows. Built on a concrete slab with radiant heating coils, it had no garage and came with an expandable attic (Matarrese 2005). Soon, developers built similar housing developments elsewhere.

Retail businesses quickly followed the flow of population into these bedroom communities, and local shopping malls increasingly became part of suburban living. Although a suburban shopping center broke ground as early as 1907 in Baltimore and another shortly afterward in the Country Club district of Kansas City, in 1946 only eight such centers existed in the entire United States. By 1960, however, the number had soared to 3,800, and then tripled again to 13,000 "malls" by 1970. No wonder that by 1970, as many people worked in the suburbs as worked in the central cities (Kowinski 2002).

As the white middle class moved out, the cities lost even more of the tax base that departing industry already was eroding. Left behind were minorities and the poor, who were often unable to find jobs. The city faced an increasing demand for services and a shrinking ability to provide them. By the mid-1960s, a true urban crisis—largely created by the phenomenon of decentralization—existed on a national level. Urban poverty was increasing, minorities were justifiably angry over their standard of living, services got worse, and many cities faced bankruptcy.

The Metropolitan Statistical Area. With decentralization well under way, urbanization expanded as workers, unable to find adequate housing in the central city, spilled over into the surrounding towns and small cities. For example, Boston's workers began settling in Wakefield and Lynn to the north, in Wellesley and Natick to the west, and in

Quincy and Braintree to the south. While technically residents of their newly adopted local communities, on another level they were still linked to Boston for jobs and under its sphere of influence.

Noticing this trend, the U.S. Census Bureau realized the need to measure more accurately the way that cities were growing. If it merely counted the residents of the central city—in this case, Boston—it would get a relatively small population count that ignored the reality of how many people residing in Braintree and Wakefield were fundamentally tied to Boston. Consequently, the Census Bureau decided to count in its surveys both the central-city population and the population of surrounding towns and cities interdependent with that central city. Thus was born the idea of the metropolitan area.

From 1959 until 1983, the Census Bureau used the term *standard metropolitan statistical area* (SMSA), and thereafter, it used the term **metropolitan statistical area (MSA).** An MSA is at least one city with 50,000 or more inhabitants, the county or counties containing the city, and any surrounding counties with a high population density and a large proportion of inhabitants commuting to and from the central city. In 2010, the Census Bureau recognized 366 MSAs, containing roughly four-fifths of the total U.S. population. Another Census Bureau term, **combined statistical area (CSA),** refers to adjacent metro-metro or metro-micro areas. By 2010, 128 official CSAs were part of the urban landscape in the United States and Puerto Rico.

The Toronto Metropolitan Area. In 1953, Toronto created a federated form of government unique to North America in order to deal with the metropolitan phenomenon. Going beyond merely labeling a metropolitan area as such, this action created a consolidated governance system. City leaders then established a common property assessment and tax rate to deal with such regional problems as water supply, sewage disposal, mass transit, construction of school buildings, housing for the elderly, park maintenance, and urban development. This approach to metropolitan governance exists in many European countries, but it is virtually non-existent in the United States. The case study at the end of Chapter 14 will detail the Toronto metropolitan system.

Non-Metropolitan Growth.   The decentralization of the urban population dispersed people outward from central cities not just to nearby suburbs but also to the outlying, rural hinterland. Areas previously considered rural yielded territory with the expansion of metropolitan areas, which grew by 11 percent in the 2000s, more than double the rate for areas outside metro areas (Mather, et al. 2011:14). More than two-thirds of Canadians (69 percent) now live in metropolitan areas, with Calgary's population growing at a much faster rate than the other 31 percent. In non-metropolitan areas rates of growth are weaker (Statistics Canada 2011a).

No doubt improved transportation and communications are an important foundation of this change, as is the desire for a greater sense of security and a less hectic pace. Still, the newcomers are in no way traditionally rural. Most are well educated, have cosmopolitan tastes, and work in nearby cities. Local stores often spring up that supply such items as gourmet wines and sophisticated books.

The Sunbelt Expansion

A glance back at Table 3–4 (see page 65) reveals the other current trend affecting cities. Although suburban population is growing everywhere, it is growing fastest in western Canada and in the American South and West. Figure 3–1 (on this page) makes the point even more effectively, showing the considerable increases of population in virtually every U.S. state below the Mason–Dixon Line and west of the Rocky Mountains between 2000 and 2010.

The Northeast and Midwest regions and their cities once dominated national affairs,

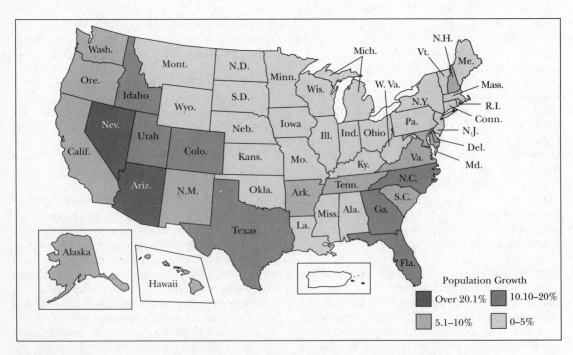

FIGURE 3–1   Change in State Populations as a Percentage, 2000–2010
Source: U.S. Census Bureau

TABLE 3–5   Ten Largest U.S. Cities in 2010 Compared to 1950 (population in thousands)

	2010		1950	
	Population	Rank	Population	Rank
New York	8,175	1	7,892	1
Los Angeles	3,793	2	1,970	4
Chicago	2,696	3	3,621	2
Houston	2,099	4	596	14
Philadelphia	1,526	5	2,072	3
Phoenix	1,445	6	107	99
San Antonio	1,327	7	408	25
San Diego	1,307	8	334	31
Dallas	1,198	9	434	22
San Jose	946	10	99	—

Note: Center city data only.

Source: U.S. Census Bureau.

but an immense power shift has occurred. Table 3–5 above illustrates the dramatic change by comparing the raw population figures and national rankings for the 10 largest U.S. cities in 2010 with those in 1950. New York, Chicago, and Philadelphia still remain in the "Top 10," but the latter two are not as populated as they were in 1950. If present trends continue, only New York and Los Angeles may appear on the next list. In addition, seemingly from nowhere, Houston, Dallas, San Antonio, San Diego, San Jose, and especially, Phoenix have leaped onto the list.

THE EVOLUTION OF MEGAREGIONS

Throughout the second half of the twentieth century, as metropolitan regions kept expanding, the distinctiveness of their boundaries blurred. Population centers became linked together through shared ecosystems and natural resources, interconnected transportation systems, and interwoven economic systems. French geographer Jean Gottmann (1966) was one of the first urbanists to note the linkages between many independent urban municipalities in sprawling urban regions. The first such area, which he called a **megalopolis,** was the unbroken urban region that emerged along the eastern seaboard of the United States, which he dubbed the "BosWash corridor." In the *Cityscape* box on page 70, he describes this development.

The BosWash corridor, now called the Northeast megaregion, was the first North American megalopolis. In Canada, the Quebec City–Windsor corridor (which includes Montreal, Ottawa, and Toronto) is quite comparable. Today, demographers and urbanists favor the term **megaregion** to describe this large-scale population growth phenomenon. Others in the United States are the Cascadia, Northern California, Southern California, Arizona Sun Corridor, Front Range, Texas Triangle, Gulf Coast, Florida, Piedmont, and Great Lakes megaregions (see Figure 3–1).

Among the criteria used to identify counties as part of a megaregion are (1) a population density exceeding 200 persons per square mile; (2) a projected population growth rate exceeding 15 percent by 2025, involving a minimum of 1,000 new residents; (3) an increase of 50 or more people per square mile between 2000 and 2025; and (4) a projected employment growth rate exceeding 15 percent with a total growth in jobs exceeding 20,000 by 2025 (Hagler 2009).

Northeast Megaregion Assets

Despite the Sunbelt expansion, the Northeast megaregion (also called the "Northeast Corridor") remains a major part of U.S. urban life. It is a region of 50 million people—almost one in five Americans—with a projected increase of 9 million by 2025. Constituting 18 percent of the total U.S. population, it accounts for 21 percent of the nation's Gross Domestic Product (*America 2050* 2011). Home to 40 of the *Fortune* Global 500 companies, it contains nearly one-half of all available global hedge fund investment capital (*Fortune* 2011).

Why does this region still attract job-creating investments? With nearly one-fifth of

CITYSCAPE

The Northeast Megaregion (Megalopolis)

The Northeastern seaboard of the United States is today the site of a remarkable development— an almost continuous stretch of urban and suburban areas from southern New Hampshire to northern Virginia and from the Atlantic shore to the Appalachian foothills. . . .

. . . As one follows the main highways or railroads between Boston and Washington, D.C., one hardly loses sight of built-up areas, tightly woven residential communities, or powerful concentrations of manufacturing plants. Flying this same route one discovers, on the other hand, that behind the ribbons of densely occupied land along the principal arteries of traffic, and in between the clusters of suburbs around the old urban centers, there still remain large areas covered with woods and brush alternating with some carefully cultivated patches of farmland. These green spaces, however, when inspected at closer range, appear stuffed with a loose but immense scattering of buildings, most of them residential but some of industrial character. That is, many of these sections that look rural actually function largely as suburbs in the orbit of some city's downtown. . . .

Thus the old distinctions between rural and urban do not apply here any more. Even a quick look at the vast area of Megalopolis reveals a revolution in land use. Most of the people living in the so-called rural areas, and still classified as "rural population" by recent censuses, have very little, if anything, to do

with agriculture. In terms of their interests and work they are what used to be classified as "city folks," but their way of life and the landscapes around their residences do not fit the old meaning of urban.

In this area, then, we must abandon the idea of the city as a tightly settled and organized unit in which people, activities, and riches are crowded into a very small area clearly separated from its non-urban surroundings. Every city in this region spreads out far and wide around its original nucleus; it grows amidst an irregularly colloidal mixture of rural and suburban landscapes; it melts on broad fronts with other mixtures, of somewhat similar though different texture, belonging to the suburban neighborhoods of other cities. Such coalescence can be observed, for example, along the main lines of traffic that link New York City and Philadelphia. Here there are many communities that might be classified as belonging to more than one orbit. It is hard to say whether they are suburbs, or "satellites," of Philadelphia or New York, Newark, New Brunswick, or Trenton. The latter three cities themselves have been reduced to the role of suburbs of New York City in many respects, although Trenton belongs also to the orbit of Philadelphia. . . .

This region indeed reminds one of Aristotle's saying that cities such as Babylon had "the compass of a nation rather than a city. . . ."

Source: Jean Gottmann, *Megalopolis: The Urbanized Northeastern Seaboard of the United States* (New York: Twentieth Century Fund, 1964), pp. 3, 5–7.

the U.S. population on 2 percent of the land mass, it is the nation's most concentrated market region. Manufacturers can reach more than half of the U.S. and Canadian industrial firms and retail sales outlets within 24 hours by

truck. Also, the corridor states are, by air and sea, close to the nearly 500 million people in the European Union countries. In addition, this 11-state megaregion has the highest concentration of higher-education institutions,

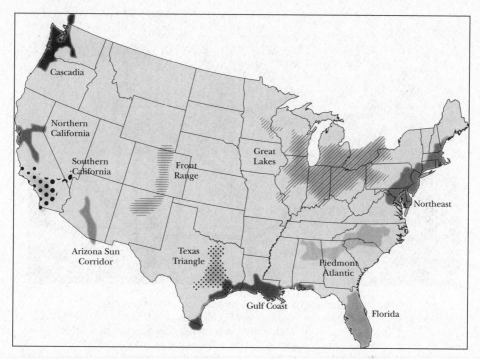

FIGURE 3–2   U.S. Megaregions

sending about 3 million students annually to 875 colleges and universities. Proximity to top colleges also has influenced location choices by high-technology firms. Massachusetts's famous Route 128 (now called "America's Technology Highway") is near Massachusetts Institute of Technology (MIT) and Harvard. New Jersey—the third smallest state, with less than 3 percent of the nation's population—is sixth in the country in the amount of venture capital invested to create new, fast-growing companies and second nationally in terms of the most workers who are IT professionals (Innovation NJ 2011).

Sunbelt Problems

Just as all is not negative in the Snowbelt, all is not rosy in the Sunbelt. The Federal Bureau of Investigation reported that violent crime in the Sunbelt region constituted 65 percent of the U.S. total (42 percent in the South and 23 percent in the West), compared with 20 percent in the Midwest and only 15 percent in the Northeast (FBI 2010). Eight of the 12 worst cities for air

pollution are in the Sunbelt (American Lung Association 2011). Pollution is increasing, water is running short (particularly in the Southwest), and in many areas, population growth is just too great to absorb. Many of the fast-growth cities face high costs in developing an adequate infrastructure (roads, bridges, water and sewage systems).

THE POSTINDUSTRIAL CITY

In the 1960s, U.S. central cities seemed to be in an irreversible process of self-destruction, with dozens of major riots occurring and middle-class whites leaving for the suburbs. Industry was close behind as old factories became obsolete. Left in the decay were those who had little choice—the trapped and the poor, many of them minorities. It looked like the end of the city as we knew it, and many doubted that U.S. cities would ever rise again. In stark contrast, Canadian cities dealt with their problems more effectively, such as Toronto—a cosmopolitan city with a distinct

Unlike Sunbelt cities, Snowbelt cities such as Minneapolis–St. Paul have high-density land use. The tight clustering of buildings—and, therefore, the closer proximity of shops, offices, and restaurants, not to mention apartment residences—places more activities within walking distance and results in more crowds, congestion, and reliance on mass transit.

racial/ethnic mix—which U.S. urbanist Jane Jacobs called "a city that works."

Deterioration and Regeneration

In the late 1960s, as central cities deteriorated—or, worse, went up in smoke—scholars, politicians, and nearly everyone else wondered what could be done. One voice suggested that we need do nothing: With time, the city would save itself. That voice belonged to Edward C. Banfield (1970), whose controversial book *The Unheavenly City* (an obvious reference to Cotton Mather's wish for a "heavenly city" quoted at the beginning of this chapter) created an enormous stir. His thesis was that the city was too powerful an economic machine to remain down and out for long. Allow enough time, he argued, and new businesses and people would see that they could return to the central city and enjoy its great communicative advantages cheaply. They could buy up land; renovate deteriorated factories, houses, and apartment complexes; and thus avail themselves of the city's many benefits.

To Banfield's critics, his "do-nothing" approach toward urban destitution seemed callous and mean-spirited. And yet, four decades later, many of his predictions have come true. Cities across the nation are in the midst of rejuvenation—and all with limited help from the federal government. The *postindustrial city* has arrived and, although slowed considerably by the economic recession of recent years, research suggests that a general economic revitalization and reformulation of cities are still continuing (Teaford 2006).

In many cities today, the contrast with the earlier picture of older U.S. cities in disrepair is nothing short of amazing. All over the United States—from Pittsburgh to Seattle, from New York to Phoenix—new urban construction is in progress. Office towers multiply almost as fast as contractors can build them. Many residential areas of the city are being totally transformed as young urban professionals—"yuppies"—move in, renovate old buildings, or settle into new apartment complexes. Although many older cities, particularly smaller ones, are still hurting, the urban

This night mosaic photographed from space illustrates the urban concentrations of people in North America more dramatically than could any artist or cartographer. The electric lights easily reveal where to find a megalopolis or metropolis and how much of the land is non-urban.

economy is alive once again. In most areas of the country, a true urban renaissance is under way as U.S. cities complete a shift to a postindustrial economy.

The reasons for this turnaround are (1) the growth of white-collar businesses tied to new computer technology and (2) a major shift in the way many industries do business. Regarding the first change, high-tech businesses were more than happy to take over, renovate, or rebuild the structures left by departing heavy industry. They needed the central-city location to maximize their efficiency. Second, many corporations went through a radical transformation, changing both their structure and their operations. In the nineteenth century, major industries believed in a "beginning-to-end" process; that is, they oversaw and controlled their product from raw material to finished, marketable item. This was true of most of the "giants," such as the Carnegie Corporation (steel) and the Ford Motor Company (which went so far as to raise sheep to produce the wool for its cars' upholstery fabric!).

Big industries divested themselves of parts of their operations that were no longer profitable and they outsourced to other firms or foreign companies. Thus, General Electric no longer makes microwave ovens or the icemakers that go into its refrigerators; instead, other firms in the United States, Korea, Japan, and elsewhere supply them. Taking a more flexible approach, firms decide which components they can produce profitably themselves and which they can produce more efficiently through outsourcing (Duesterberg and Preeg 2004:45; Whitford 2006).

Such changes, which happened all over North America, had important implications for the city. On the one hand, companies no longer required as many blue-collar workers or as many buildings geared to heavy industrial production. On the other hand, these corporations, which play so large a role in our urban scene, created more white-collar jobs—jobs that depend on regular contact with other corporations, whether in North America or abroad.

Naturally, those employed by postindustrial, high-tech industries want to live near their work, and while some (particularly those with families) commute from the suburbs, many opt to live in the central city. Illustrating this trend during the past several decades has been the process of *gentrification*, in which white-collar professionals move into and transform older, decaying neighborhoods of many cities. We will return to this topic later in the book.

The Future

The postindustrial city will likely dominate North America's future, but what form will it take? One significant worldwide trend is globalization, a subject we will explore in Chapter 7. Two other trends on this continent are occurring simultaneously, and it is uncertain whether or not both can prevail in the future. One trend is the appearance of *edge cities* (discussed more fully in Chapter 4). The evolution of new cities on the fringe of older urban areas helps explain the population increase in non-metropolitan areas. Joel Garreau (1992) suggested that North Americans have reinvented the city and that these new urban agglomerations are now the future. Numbering more than 200 in Canada and the United States, these new cities, with their malls and office parks, now dominate the nation's retail trade, office facilities, and cinemas.

The second trend is the revitalization of older cities, a significant process that shows no sign of stopping. More, not fewer, people are taking on the cosmopolitan lifestyle. Because edge cities do not offer the residential ambience that young adults can find in a central city's brownstone houses, loft apartments, cozy restaurants, and shops, the upgrading of many older city neighborhoods continues. Although office-building construction continued in many cities in 2011, the lagging economy and vacancy rate slowed it down considerably (Downs 2011).

Cleveland is a good example. During the 1960s and 1970s, this Ohio city was a symbol of urban despair. Severe social problems exploded into race riots in 1966 and 1968. Pollution was thick in the air, and in 1969, the Cuyahoga River actually burned for days because of the pollutants it contained. Cleveland's heavy industry was dying, its middle class was fleeing to the suburbs, and by 1979, the city was on the verge of financial collapse.

A public–private partnership, forged by city government and business leaders during the early 1980s, attempted to breathe new life into the city. Its linchpin for revitalization was restoration of Cleveland's famous, but abandoned, landmark—the Terminal Tower commercial complex—into a rail transit station, a multilevel shopping center with upscale national stores, an 11-screen movie theater, a Ritz-Carlton hotel, and several high-rise office buildings. The Tower City Center complex created more than 3,000 jobs and in the 1990s it appealed to many because of such stores as Banana Republic, Express, Gap, and J. Crew. Sadly, those stores are gone now, no major anchor store is on the premises, and one-time shoppers complain about its deterioration (Yelp 2011).

Tourist attractions built in the 1990s include the six-story Rock and Roll Hall of Fame and Museum, two stadiums, and capital improvements at nearby Cedar Point amusement park, with its 17 roller coasters, more than any other park in the world. Yuppies turned abandoned warehouses into lofts and apartments, and city residents enjoy a lakefront park and trendy restaurants along the Cuyahoga River, where one can sit on the patios while barges and pleasure boats navigate the river.

Nevertheless, downtown Cleveland failed to become rejuvenated, partly because the stand-alone new projects were isolated from one another. This lack of connectivity ignored one of the attractions of any city: the clustering of activities. The expansive Cleveland CBD lacks the walking distance charm and appeal of those in Boston and Philadelphia. However, new projects in the pipeline (the Medical Mart and casino) and action on the recommendations of the Downtown Cleveland Alliance (a pedestrian bridge, bike lanes, redesigning streets and closing unnecessary ones, and improving Public Square) could enhance that connectivity and make the center city more attractive to residents and visitors alike (Piiparinen 2011).

Clearly, Cleveland needs to do something to bounce back. It lost more than one-fifth of its population between 1990 and 2010, dropping from 505,615 to 396,815 people. The nation's poorest big city in 2006, Cleveland has since ranked as the fourth poorest (behind Detroit, Buffalo, and Cincinnati). To offset the city's loss of its former industrial base, Cleveland's leaders have made renovation and land-use integration important parts of their economic strategy. *Strategy* is exactly the right word. As the nation's central cities regenerate, many are engaging in a type of competition reminiscent of the interurban competition of the mid-1800s, when North American cities were growing by leaps and bounds. An increasing number of urban governments are hiring marketing professionals to spiff up the city's image so that it can attract more businesses and tourists.

The Human Cost of Economic Restructuring

The postindustrial process, unfortunately, does not benefit all city residents. As gentrification progresses, it displaces the poorer residents of many city neighborhoods. Unable to pay the rising rents, they must find somewhere else to live. Similarly, even though a few areas within a city become havens for the affluent, the postindustrial economy worsens the plight of the city's poor and unskilled.

This occupational restructuring creates a "skills mismatch" as our cities' economies become more and more white collar. Their gradual shift away from manufacturing and goods processing eliminates many unskilled jobs, once the first step up for millions of less-educated migrants and immigrants. The rising skill requirements of today's urban job market, which demands educated employees to work with words and numbers in information-processing jobs, puts these new jobs out of reach for the poor as well. Thus, even as

some urban neighborhoods improve, unemployment rates and welfare dependency among the unskilled remain high (Samuelson 2011). Gentrification is all well and good as far as it goes, but the changes do not benefit everyone.

Characterizing the postindustrial city are two labor markets that foster dramatically unequal lifestyles—that of the well-paid, white-collar professional and that of the low-paid service worker. Immigrants, not native-born blacks, are now filling the niches left vacant by whites moving out of cities (Waldinger and Lichter 2003).

The dynamic process engaging North American cities extends from its origins—those five communities "hacked out of the wilderness" in the seventeenth century—to the present configuration—much larger and still embroiled in rapid and significant change, as decentralization, Sunbelt growth, and postindustrialization unfold. Exemplifying this process is the case study that closes this chapter, that of North America's world city, New York.

CASE STUDY
New York—The "Big Apple"

New York has long been the Great U.S. City. It symbolizes the United States to the world and, in many ways, reveals the rest of the world to the United States. New York not only represents the distinctive course of North American urban history, it is a timeless display of what urban life is all about. Here are just a few of the features that make it so outstanding.

First, New York is huge, an enormous concentration of population. About 8.2 million people live within the city limits, and almost three times that many reside in the urban region that sprawls outward around the city. Second, the city is a major center for finance, insurance, real estate, media, and the arts. It has 46 of the *Fortune* 500 corporations, contains a large number of foreign corporations (1 in 10 private-sector jobs is with a foreign company), and its television and film industry is second only to Hollywood. Third, it is

URBAN LIVING

All New York's a Stage

I'll tell you an old joke that will sum up Radio City Music Hall for you. It seems a man and his wife went to the Music Hall one Sunday afternoon, arriving toward the end of the film. When it ended, the house lights came up for a few minutes before the stage show and the man rose, murmuring to his wife: "I'm going to the men's room."

He located an exit on his floor—orchestra, loge, mezzanine, balcony or second balcony—but he couldn't find a men's room on it. He descended a staircase and looked on the next floor and couldn't find a men's room and descended another staircase. He walked along corridors and pushed open doors, he went along dark passages and up and down steps, getting more and more lost and more and more frantic. Just as his need became intolerably urgent, he pushed open a heavy door and found himself on a small street lined with houses, trees and shrubs. There was no one in sight and the man relieved himself in the bushes.

All this had taken time, and it took him additional time to work his way back up to his own floor and locate his own aisle and section. By the time he finally reached his seat, the stage show had ended and the movie had begun again. The man slid into his seat whispering to his wife: "How was the stage show?" To which his wife replied: "You ought to know. You were in it."

Source: Helene Hanff, *Apple of My Eye* (New York: Moyer Bell, 1995), p. 129.

the third busiest U.S. port (in import volume, after South Louisiana and Houston). Fourth, it is a mosaic of virtually every race and ethnic group in the world, with nearly 200 languages spoken daily and more than one-third of its residents foreign born. The city contains more Chinese than any city outside of Asia, more West Indians than any city outside of the Caribbean, and more Hispanics than any other city in the United States. Fifth, many New York districts are world famous: Wall Street (finance), Madison Avenue (advertising), the garment district (center of the nation's clothing industry), Central Park (arguably the greatest urban park in the world), Fifth Avenue (for fashionable shopping and living), Greenwich Village (a longtime bohemian, student, and counterculture enclave), and Broadway (center of the most vibrant theater district in the world). Sixth, New York is also a key center of the arts, music, and publishing.

At street level, New York abounds with crowds, traffic, musicians, and vendors—multiple sights and sounds that bombard the senses. Indeed, the first experience of New York City is one that many carry with them all their lives. On another level, the city is deceptive. Its very size tricks us into thinking things are other than they are—something that the *Urban Living* box above reveals about that grandest of illusion makers, Radio City Music Hall.

One cannot escape the great contradictions, contrasts, and inconsistencies of New York life. The city is home to the richest and poorest of North Americans. Some of the worst social problems stand, literally, in the shadow of the proudest cultural achievements. In short, if something is to be found at all, it is to be found in New York. It is a world city par excellence. And since September 11, 2001, Americans elsewhere have expressed a special bond with New York as the symbol of an America united and defiant against terrorism.

New York, always at the center of U.S. life, has a varied history. Because its changes illustrate the themes of North American urban history generally, we shall look briefly at its development during each of the four phases discussed in this chapter.

The Colonial Era

New York was the earliest of the five major colonial settlements, beginning in 1624 with a small Dutch settlement, based primarily on the fur trade, in place on the southern tip of Manhattan Island. New Amsterdam, the center of the Dutch New Netherlands, prospered in the decades that followed: Houses were built, and farmland was cultivated. A vertical row of logs, put in place for protection along the northern edge of the settlement, later became known as Wall Street. In 1638, a ferry service to Breukelen (later known as Brooklyn) began, and the first settlers reached Staten Island.

The first survey, completed in 1656, revealed that the "city" had about 1,000 people living in 120 houses on 17 irregularly shaped streets. Within a few years, some of the streets were stone covered, and a town-watch (the earliest direct ancestor of New York's police force) provided security. To the north were farms the Dutch called "boweries." This area, the point at which the irregular streets end (at about Houston Street today), was long known as "The Bowery." In 1658, the Dutch established a farming village, which they called Haarlem, much farther north at the end of a long dirt road known as "Broadway."

The first Jews arrived in the 1650s, establishing a long tradition that would influence the city's history, and the first Quakers settled in 1657. The English in 1664 gained control of the town, and renamed it New York in honor of Charles II's brother, James, the Duke of York. The English thereafter continued a policy of religious freedom for all groups, reaffirming the tradition of religious tolerance initiated by the Dutch.

In 1680, New York City began its climb to economic preeminence when it gained a monopoly on the sifting of flour for export. Docks multiplied, trade prospered, and support businesses of all sorts followed. The population grew steadily as well; from 4,000 in 1703, New York grew to 7,000 in 1723 and passed the 10,000 mark in 1737. The first newspaper appeared in 1725; a stagecoach link to Philadelphia started in 1730; and the New York Public Library opened in 1731.

As this growth occurred, New York, like the other colonies, began resenting ever more sharply the British impositions on trade. In 1765, the English government instituted the Stamp Act, which placed a levy on all transactions. The colonists bitterly opposed it. Swayed, Parliament repealed the act in 1766, causing a New York group dubbed the "Sons of Liberty" to build a triumphant "Liberty Pole" in the city. The British took strong offense. An altercation followed, and some of the Sons of Liberty were killed, spilling the first blood of the American Revolution.

When the Revolutionary War began, the British occupied New York for seven years. The war drove many New Yorkers temporarily out of the city, reducing its population by several thousand from a peak of 21,500. With the end of the war, however, the city leapt once more to life. George Washington was inaugurated as the first president of the United States in Federal Hall at the corner of Wall Street and Nassau Street, and for a year thereafter (1790), New York served as the U.S. capital.

Growth and Expansion

By 1800, the city's population surpassed 60,000, and spectacular growth continued. The population exceeded 96,000 by 1810 and 202,000 by 1830. Yet this was only a hint of things to come. Earlier, in 1792, a group of traders had met in the Wall Street area and planned what became the New York Stock Exchange. In 1811, the city implemented its famous grid plan for street development. In 1825, the completed Erie Canal linked the Hudson River with the Great Lakes, giving New York a long-sought trade advantage over its East Coast urban competitors. With direct access to the North American heartland, the city quickly became the economic center of the United States.

Beginning in 1838, overseas steamships established a connection with Europe that truly opened the United States to immigration. In 1840, for example, more than 50,000 people arrived in New York Harbor from abroad, and most settled in the city. In 1846, the first telegraph line between New York and Philadelphia began operation. In 1848, a five-story factory (also a sign of things to come) opened its doors. Urban transportation improved with introduction of the rail-mounted horsecar in 1850. This made "suburbanization" of the upper island more feasible; for the fare of a nickel, this area was within reach of most New Yorkers. In 1853, New York hosted the nation's first "expo," symbolic of the grand optimism that by now was part of the city's character. In 1858, the plan for one of the greatest of urban landmarks—Central Park—was approved (the park itself was not substantially completed until after the Civil War). In 1860, although still officially consisting of only Manhattan Island, the city boasted a population of 814,000, with another 250,000 nearby in Brooklyn, Staten Island, and Jersey City.

The Great Metropolis Emerges

After the Civil War, New York matured as a great metropolis. An unprecedented surge in the city's population occurred between 1870 and 1930, dwarfing all previous gains. Table 3–6 shows that New York City as a whole quintupled its population in the six decades after 1870. However, until January 1898, the five boroughs remained legally separate municipalities.

The period between 1870 and 1920 was an era of extensive foreign immigration to the United States, and New York was the major port of disembarkation. Chinatown began to take form in 1884; Italian immigration intensified after 1885; and Jews began to make their way through the Ellis Island immigration facility to the Lower East Side in large numbers after 1890. Many of these new urbanites went directly to work in many fields, most notably the clothing industry.

As amazing as it sounds, by 1890 four out of five people living in the New York area were either born abroad or had foreign-born parents (Claghorn 2011). New York, like other U.S. metropolises, took on a characteristic "ethnic mosaic" pattern of settlement, as described by social reformer Jacob Riis in the *Cityscape* box Although citywide residential density in 1900 was about 90,000 people per square mile, in immigrant areas the densities could be as much as five times greater (Demographia 2011). Today, the density of New York City has fallen to about 27,000 persons per square mile (Census Bureau 2011c).

Sometimes, when immigrants mixed, the results were explosive. One midtown area, from about West 15th Street to West 50th Street along Eighth, Ninth, and Tenth

TABLE 3–6 Population of New York City by Borough, 1870–2010 (in thousands)

	1870	1900	1930	1960	2000	2010
New York City	1,476	3,437	6,929	7,782	8,008	8,175
Borough						
Manhattan	942	1,850	1,867	1,695	1,537	1,586
Bronx	37	201	1,265	1,425	1,333	1,385
Brooklyn	419	1,167	2,560	2,627	2,465	2,504
Queens	45	153	1,079	1,810	2,229	2,231
Staten Island	33	67	158	222	444	469

Note: The five boroughs were not officially incorporated as New York City until 1898.
Source: U.S. Census Bureau.

CITYSCAPE

The Crazy-Quilt Pattern of New York, 1890

A map of [New York], colored to designate nationalities, would show more stripes than the skin of a zebra, and more colors than any rainbow.... [G]reen for the Irish prevailing in the West Side tenement districts, and blue for the Germans on the East Side.... [I]ntermingled ... would be an odd variety of tints that would give the whole the appearance of an extraordinary crazy-quilt. From down in the Sixth Ward . . . the red of the Italian would be seen forcing its way northward along the line of Mulberry Street to the quarter of the French purple on Bleecker Street and South Fifth Avenue.... On the West Side, the red would be seen overrunning the old Africa of Thompson Street pushing the black of the negro rapidly uptown.

...[T]he Russian and Polish Jew, having overrun the district between Rivington and Division Streets, east of the Bowery, to the point of suffocation, is filling the tenements of the old Seventh Ward to the river front.... Between the dull gray of the Jew, his favorite color, and the Italian red, would be seen squeezed in on the map a sharp streak of yellow, marking the narrow boundaries of Chinatown.... Dots and dashes of color here and there would show...the Finnish sailors...the Greek pedlars...and the Swiss. . . . And so on to the end of the long register, all toiling together in the galling fetters of the tenement.

Source: Jacob Riis, *How the Other Half Lives*, 2nd ed. (New York: Bedford/St. Martin's, 2010), pp. 76–77. Originally published in 1890.

Avenues, was home to blacks and whites of different ethnic groups. During the workweek, trouble was minimal, but on weekends in the summer, when much drinking and carousing occurred, violent fighting often broke out between groups. So intense were the confrontations that police nicknamed the area "Hell's Kitchen," a name it still retains.

Governing this incredible and growing mass of people was difficult at best. City Hall became increasingly corrupt as interest groups vied with one another for contracts, favors, and patronage. The greatest symbol of political corruption was William "Boss" Tweed. In 1870, by means of $1 million in bribes to state legislators and others, Tweed and his gang gained complete political control over the city. They stole an estimated $200 million in funds from the city treasury and garnered even more from kickbacks and payoffs. Finally exposed by the *New York Times* in 1871, Tweed was arrested and brought to trial. So confident that he would be acquitted, he haughtily said in response to an allegation about his thefts, "What are ya gonna do about it?" His confidence was misplaced, however, and he went to jail in 1872. Nevertheless, extensive graft in city government continued to plague the city until well into the twentieth century.

Physical changes linked to technology contributed to the growth of the city. In 1881, the Brooklyn Bridge opened, and along with the Golden Gate Bridge in San Francisco, it remains one of the world's most beautiful. The Williamsburg Bridge (1903) offered another route to Brooklyn and, in 1904, the first tunnel under the Hudson River connected the city to New Jersey. In 1906, the Pennsylvania Railroad also tunneled under the Hudson River, establishing major rail transport in the heart of Manhattan at Penn Station. Subways soon followed. People now could live far from midtown and still get there cheaply and quickly.

At the lower end of Manhattan, the dazzling New York skyline began to take shape, capped by construction of the ill-fated twin towers of the World Trade Center between 1966 and 1972. Today, it is difficult to imagine New York without a forest of skyscrapers. Yet before 1890, Manhattan below Central Park was almost completely covered by structures of less than five stories. The first steel structure in New York appeared in 1889 and reached a "towering" 11 stories. From this point, New York grew upward as if the clouds had become great magnets. The number of buildings with 20 or more floors increased from 61 in 1913 to 188 in 1929. Indeed, half of all such buildings in the country were in New York (Douglas 2004).

Before the Great Depression stalled construction of office buildings, New York witnessed the completion of three famous architectural innovations that survive to this day. The Chrysler Building, opened in 1930, is a marvelous, 77-story example of Art Deco architecture—topped with six stories of magnificent stainless-steel arches. The following year marked the opening of the Empire State Building, which at 102 floors has symbolized New York ever since. Rockefeller Center was begun in the same year. It was designed to include "everything" in one place, as a large-scale urban complex of office buildings, stores, cafes, plazas, and sculpture to attract people in its mix of business and culture. With its huge success, Rockefeller Center served as the inspiration of similar downtown developments in many U.S. cities, including Atlanta's Peachtree Center, Hartford's Constitution Center, and San Francisco's Embarcadero Center.

New York Today

By the 1950s, New York had grown from being a metropolis to being the center of the vast Northeast megaregion. The 2010 census placed the city at the heart of an enormous MSA covering some 4,000 square miles with more than 50 million people. About 1 in 14 Americans lived in the New York

metropolitan region. Since 1980, the city has steadily grown in population, mainly due to an influx of immigrants. Demographers forecast that New York will increase from its current 8.2 million residents to 9.1 million by 2030 (NYC Department of City Planning 2006: 1–2).

Earlier Economic Problems

The recession ending in the early 1990s took its toll on the New York region, as it regained only about a third of the 770,000 jobs it lost. Then, the 2001 destruction of the World Trade Center and its immediate surroundings dealt a severe blow to the corporate and neighborhood economies of lower Manhattan. The loss of or severe damage to 20 million square feet of office space, as well as the loss of tens of thousands of jobs, was more than that of the entire central business district of a small city. Furthermore, the damage directly affected 14,000 nearby small businesses because of the resulting reduction in the number of pedestrians and customers (Ploeger 2002).

Beyond the Devastation

On that infamous day of September 11, 2001, New York City suffered the worst tragedy in its history. In addition to the heartbreaking loss of so many innocent lives were the severe economic losses. These losses included billions of dollars of damaged or destroyed private capital and public infrastructure, thousands of dislocated workers, millions of dollars in lost sales as a result of business interruption, and significant disruption to the financial services industry that makes New York the capital of the global securities and banking markets.

A decade later, downtown Manhattan has risen from the ashes. The 43-story global headquarters of the investment banking and securities firm, Goldman Sachs, opened in 2009, across from the World Trade Center site, where the national memorial is open. Two new skyscrapers—1 and 4 World Trade Center—are rising at Ground Zero and will open in 2013. In 2014, the PATH transit hub will come online. The residential population in the area has doubled and a more diverse array of businesses—including media companies, law firms, and non-profit organizations—now call this area home (Bagli 2011).

Major cities like New York are constantly changing. Just as immigration repeatedly remade the city throughout its history, so, too, have its economic fortunes rebounded

In February 2012, construction of One World Trade Tower, formerly known as the Freedom Tower, already loomed above most other office buildings. The first of four high-rise office buildings on the site of the 9/11 tragedy, when completed in 2013, will soar 1,776 feet into the sky, making it the tallest building in the Western Hemisphere.

despite the "gloom and doom" experts who sounded the city's death knell. New York and the other cities survived, and—despite the recession—they have been working their way back to financial solvency. New York City is back for many of the same reasons that Boston, Baltimore, and other cities are coming back: The postindustrial economy is remaking New York. New positions for highly trained professional workers, particularly in the information-processing and financial sectors, are available, along with lower-paying jobs in the service sectors of food, delivery, and tourism. Parts of the city, such as midtown, thrive as white-collar service centers where business professionals can remain in close contact with one another, have lunch, and socialize after work at a wide variety of places catering to their tastes.

As in other cities, the proportion of people who work in postindustrial jobs is small—perhaps less than 10 percent. Many people are working in the service sector (restaurants, hotels, and retail stores) or as public employees (education, police, fire, transit, sanitation, and social services). Although the city lost more than half of its manufacturing companies between 1990 and 2010, its food manufacturing businesses grew by 14 percent between 2007 and 2010 (NYC Economic Development Council 2011a). In 2006, the city established 16 industrial business zones, creating tax credits and other incentives to encourage long-term investment in manufacturing, warehousing, and other industrial businesses throughout the five boroughs (NYC Economic Development Council 2011b).

In 2010, tourism soared to a record-breaking 48.8 million visitors, generating $31.5 billion in revenue, with its foreign visitors setting a new record of 9.8 million. Air passenger arrivals; hotel occupancy; attendance at Broadway shows; ticket sales at tourist attractions like the Empire State Building, Ellis Island, and the Statue of Liberty; and retail sales all improved (City of New York 2011). Its 2010 total crime index for violent and property crimes put New York among the lowest for U.S. cities with a population of 100,000 or more—and the safest city among those with 1 million or more inhabitants (Federal Bureau of Investigation 2011). More feature films and television series are now shot in the city than at any time since the 1950s, and New York hosts the second-largest concentration of motion picture activity.

Throughout the city, one can find clubs, coffee bars, chic shops, and trendy restaurants springing up, and attendance at concerts, museums, theaters, sports contests, and special events has risen as well. Rental housing is scarce and expensive, especially in Manhattan, where a month's rent for a two-bedroom apartment averages $3,750 (MNS 2011).

Upgrading the City

Construction is omnipresent. In 2010, the Department of Buildings reviewed and approved 457,000 construction plans submitted by architects and engineers (NYC Office of the Mayor 2011). In mid-2011, Manhattan developers planned the biggest decade of office construction since the 1980s. The prime area for urban development may be the Far West Side, the land between Pennsylvania Station and the Hudson River. These brand-new, state-of-the-art office buildings in great locations will meet corporate needs for the latest in comfort, energy efficiency, and technological capability in an area where more than 60 percent of the buildings are at least half a century old (Levitt 2011).

Battery Park City, a $1.5-billion, 92-acre commercial and residential complex, is home to the New York Mercantile Exchange, the Commodity Exchange, and American Express. There are also 2,000 apartments in eight buildings, a Ritz-Carlton hotel, four ferry slips, and a 15-screen multiplex theater. The site also includes a museum, parks, plazas, playgrounds, public arts, and schools.

Time Warner's new world headquarters at Columbus Circle, completed in 2004, is one of the largest projects ever built in New York City. Besides its office space, the complex, with its two towers, includes one of the largest malls in the city (four floors of retail space), a screening theater, five restaurants, and a cafe with a marvelous view of Central Park.

Harlem, once the personification of black urban America, has undergone a dramatic transition. Blacks are no longer the majority, as other young families have moved in, lured to fix-up Victorian brownstones and sleek new apartment buildings. Gone are the 99-cent stores and Laundromats. In their place are large delis, stores selling imported beer, upscale shops, and restaurants. In East Harlem, a $300 million shopping mall and glass-walled $1 million condominiums adjacent to six-story tenements give testimony to the gentrification occurring (Williams 2008). East New York, a once-devastated area in Brooklyn dubbed the "murder capital of New York City," is being transformed into a livable area of rehabilitated homes and 2,300 new ones in Gateway Estates, built around the new Gateway Mall that employs about 1,500 people (Hevesi 2005).

Another dramatic symbol of New York's revival is construction in the South Bronx. Its image as a lawless, burned-out, drug-infested area whose rampant crime rate inspired the 1981 movie *Fort Apache, the Bronx* is no longer true, after one of the nation's largest urban rebuilding efforts. With more than $1 billion in public dollars trained on the South Bronx since 1986, 19,000 apartments were refurbished and more than 4,500 new houses built for working-class home buyers. More than 50 abandoned buildings that once stood like rotten teeth along major arteries like the Cross Bronx and Major Deegan expressways were reclaimed as midrise apartment houses.

Other signs of an urban renaissance are everywhere. They range in scale from massive residential enclaves like Queens West and Riverside South, both loosely modeled after Battery Park City, to the Starbucks-style cafes that have sprouted up all over. The transformation of 42nd Street, once a center of sex and sleaze, into a family entertainment center with Disney as the linchpin is simply amazing, and the renovation of Grand Central Terminal with an upscale restaurant and shops is another positive sign.

Creation or restoration of parks offers another example of the improvement in the quality of life in New York. Indoor and outdoor recreation areas now exist at Pier 25 in TriBeCa, at Pier 45 at Christopher Street, and at Pier 64 in Chelsea. Hudson River Park, the second largest after Central Park, stretches for 5 miles from Battery Park to 59th Street, with esplanades, waterfront activities, biking and rollerblading paths, dog runs, athletic facilities, gardens, and sculptures. Bryant Park—once an unsafe, sequestered area overrun by drug dealers—is one of New York's busiest public spaces, where thousands go day and night for lunch, concerts, and outdoor movies, or simply to mingle. Directly behind the New York Public Library and North America's first wireless zone park, it is a hot spot for young adults, serving—in an odd manifestation of a small-town tradition—as Manhattan's town square. High Line is an innovative and successful park converted from an elevated freight railway, into an aerial greenway, with an integrated landscape connecting three neighborhoods along the West Side. Presently 19 blocks in length, when finished it will be 1.5 miles long (High Line 2011).

On another front, 64 Business Improvement Districts (BIDs) exist in virtually every section of the city, from Harlem to Brighton Beach. More than 1,200 BIDs exist in cities across North America (including 71 in Toronto), but their greatest impact has been in cleaning up New York (particularly Times Square and Union Square). The BIDs are self-taxing districts set up to clean, patrol, and upgrade their neighborhoods, providing services once the sole responsibility of city government. Faced with budget problems, cities welcomed this privatization of municipal services. Once a majority of owners in a designated area agree, they work out a plan for services. After City Council approval, the city collects an annual assessment (above the property taxes) from all property owners and turns the money over to the district. The resulting services and improvements—new sidewalks, signs, street lights, planters, wastebaskets, flags and banners, street sweepers, and unarmed, uniformed security patrols—have reduced crime, cleaned up streets, and restored a sense of pride among merchants and the public (Gould, et al. 2007).

One of the best examples of urban renaissance occurring in many North American cities is New York City's Times Square. Once the locale of sleazy porn stores and theaters and other seedy enterprises, it has undergone a facelift that is more than cosmetic. New hotels, theaters, family-oriented businesses, pedestrian streets, and even outdoor seating now dominate the area.

Changing Population

In 1950, the population of the five boroughs was 87 percent white, 9 percent black, and 3 percent Hispanic. By 2010, the city's profile had shifted to 33 percent non-Hispanic white, 23 percent non-Hispanic black, 29 percent Hispanic, and 13 percent Asian (Census Bureau 2011c). Although these are dramatic contrasts, the change between 2000 and 2010 is far less so. Both Brooklyn and Manhattan showed an increase in the number of white young adults and children, most notably in gentrifying neighborhoods (Roberts 2011).

Although many minorities work in the information-processing and service sectors, unemployment and poverty are high within the city's African American and Hispanic American communities. The U.S. Census Bureau reported that about one in five of New York City residents (19 percent) lived in poverty in 2009. Yet the city also has the nation's widest income gap among all large U.S. cities. The Bronx is the nation's poorest urban county and Manhattan contains the three wealthiest zip codes in terms of salary (Mongabay 2011; Roberts 2010a).

And so New York goes on, with its successes and failures, its ability to symbolize simultaneously all that is great and tragic about all cities. To many, New York is the quintessential city. If New York fails, in some sense cities everywhere fail, but if it succeeds, it offers hope for all.

SUMMARY

The development of North American cities has been, in its own way, as dynamic and varied as that of European cities. Neither Canada nor the United States began as an urban nation. In fact, that idea would have been anathema to many of either country's founders. Nevertheless, that is what both have become.

After beginning as places of religious and political freedom, the new colonies rapidly established themselves as major trading centers. By 1700, coastal villages were becoming bustling towns. By the late eighteenth century, these small cities had developed into major urban areas. They traded up and down the coast and with Europe and became rich by establishing links with the vast heartland of the country. Inland cities also appeared. By the mid-nineteenth century, industrialization was transforming the northern cities of the United States and, to some degree, their Canadian and newer, midwestern counterparts into manufacturing centers. The South, still operating on the "small city" pattern

associated with agriculture, fell behind. With victory for the North, the Civil War effectively ended the small- versus large-city "debate" in the United States.

After 1870, North American cities, particularly in the North and the Midwest of the United States and in Lower Canada, exploded into metropolises of millions. Trade and industry were the driving forces behind this development. More and more jobs generated more and more wealth. Drawn to this opportunity, millions came from abroad, resulting in the ethnic–racial–religious mosaic that characterizes so many North American cities. With this influx came great problems, particularly in the United States. Quality of life began to deteriorate, and poverty and exploitation became rampant. New technological advances enabled many to escape to streetcar suburbs. Consequently, cities began to spread over the countryside. Losing revenue because of this exodus and seriously hampered by the Great Depression, cities began to depend on federal assistance.

After World War II, decentralization accelerated. People and businesses departed the central cities, leaving the innermost areas increasingly populated by the poor and minorities and by service-oriented or professional businesses. Huge metropolitan regions became the norm, replacing earlier central-city cores.

In the older Snowbelt cities of the United States, decentralization had particularly disastrous results. When the cities lost people and businesses, billions in tax and sales revenues and hundreds of thousands of jobs were lost as well. Many cities faced a continual threat of bankruptcy. The South and West, however, experienced an urban boom. Sunbelt cities were the direct beneficiaries of the northern cities' problems (old industrial systems, poor inner-city transportation for products, and deteriorating services). The Sunbelt cities built new plants, surrounded by efficient superhighways; provided good or brand-new service systems; and offered lower costs—particularly for energy and labor. Some Sunbelt cities expanded their physical boundaries; for example, in Texas, one of the states with the greatest urban expansion, suburbs were annexed almost as fast as they appeared, thus keeping the tax and business base within the city's jurisdiction.

Today, North American cities are rapidly developing a postindustrial economy based on high technology, white-collar jobs, and services. They are also rebuilding the deteriorating office and housing stock left from earlier decades and improving many other amenities that define the quality of urban life. Older large cities, once in the throes of economic disaster, are now rebounding, although problems clearly remain, particularly affecting the poorer residents. Serving as white-collar service centers, these cities have attracted young, relatively affluent professionals whose presence has had great impact. Another trend is the formation of new cities on the fringes of established metropolitan areas.

The evidence suggests that all three trends—decentralization, the move to the Sunbelt, and the growth of a postindustrial economy—will continue. As a result, northern cities such as New York will continue to adapt to a changing economic structure and a new population. Meanwhile, the Sunbelt picture is not as rosy as it once was. The population boom in many

instances has generated infrastructure problems; crime rates are high; and racial tensions are on the rise as Hispanics move up from Mexico and Latin America and African Americans move back to the South. Furthermore, even in cities where postindustrialization is in full sway, the newfound wealth of the few who are participating in a cosmopolitan lifestyle does not extend to all city dwellers. On the contrary, the gap between the urban rich and the urban poor appears to be widening, not narrowing.

CONCLUSION

In the three centuries since urbanization took hold in the New World, North Americans have not really built Cotton Mather's hoped-for "heavenly city." Nevertheless, indicators show that cities are improving. Experts are uncertain about how long this revitalization will persist. If we continue to see the city as something to "use," but not as something warranting our concern, then the outlook probably is not very bright. If, on the other hand, we see the city as a human creation and, thus, subject to understanding and human control, then we might be justified in being more optimistic about the outcome.

KEY TERMS

combined statistical area (CSA) (67)
decentralization (64)
globalization (64)
industrial parks (65)
megalopolis (69)

megaregion (69)
metropolitan statistical area (MSA) (67)
Sunbelt expansion (64)
urban explosion (64)
urban implosion (64)

INTERNET ACTIVITIES

1. You can view different parts of the historic district of Old Québec by going to *http://www.world-heritage-tour.org/america/canada/eastern-provinces/quebec/map.html*. Once there, if you click on any small photo and then click and drag inside that enlarged image, you can get a 360° view of each site.

2. You can see satellite images of many Canadian, U.S. and world cities if you go to *http://geology.com/satellite/*. Click on "Beginner's Guide to Landsat Images" to understand the color coding, so that you can enjoy the images more fully.

CHAPTER 4

TODAY'S CITIES AND SUBURBS

URBAN AND SUBURBAN SPRAWL
    What Is Sprawl?
    Why Do We Have Sprawl?
    Consequences of Sprawl
SMART GROWTH
    Land Purchases
    Urban Growth Boundaries
    Revitalizing Existing Cities and Towns
    Transit-Oriented Approaches
    Greening Our Cities
EXURBS
THE NEW CITIES
    Characteristics and Commonalities
    Types of New Cities
    Evolving Middle-Class Centers
    Three New City Variations

GATED COMMUNITIES
    Types of Gated Communities
    A Sense of Community
COMMON-INTEREST DEVELOPMENTS

CASE STUDY: PORTLAND, OREGON

    The Physical Setting
    History
    Urban Decline and Anti-Sprawl Planning
    Portland Today
SUMMARY
CONCLUSION
KEY TERMS
INTERNET ACTIVITIES

We can't always predict the future, but we do invent it. Today's decisions affect tomorrow's realities, just as we are living out the decisions made by preceding generations. For example, the change in public preference from urban to suburban living owes much to federal legislation in the late 1940s and 1950s that provided low-cost builder and buyer loans, as well as to a massive highway-building program begun in the 1930s that made it easier to live away from city jobs and activities. That growth in middle-class suburban housing, and the subsequent exodus of many businesses to suburban campuses or shopping malls, eroded the cities' economic vitality and tax base, which, in turn, worsened the quality of urban schools and the quality of life for many remaining city dwellers. The suburban lifestyles that most North Americans favor today, as well as the problems besetting many U.S. cities, are the result of social forces unleashed two generations ago. So, too, will recent decisions affect urban and suburban lifestyles for decades to come. In this regard, four current patterns—sprawl, new cities, gated communities, and common-interest developments—merit our attention.

URBAN AND SUBURBAN SPRAWL

We must make a distinction between *growth* and *sprawl*. As Canada and the United States increase in population, additional space is necessary for the construction of residences and businesses to meet the needs of a larger populace. Moreover, the days when most people lived in cities are gone. Now, most people prefer to have their own home on their own plot of land in suburbia. Therefore, the development of vacant land is a necessity, but it becomes problematic when a lack of regional planning leads to inefficient land-use management that has a negative impact on the environment and increases costs for everyone (see the *Urban Trends* box on page 88).

What Is Sprawl?

Sprawl is a term referring to spread-out or low-density residential development beyond the edge of service and employment areas. It separates where people live from where they work, shop, and pursue leisure or an education, thereby requiring them to use cars to move between these zones. This type of development results from unplanned, rapid growth and poor land-use management. Sprawl thus identifies the cumulative effects of development that is automobile-dependent, inefficient, and wasteful of natural resources.

As people move farther from core cities and into outlying regions, so do all the trappings of urban life: stores, offices, factories, hospitals, congestion, and pollution. Developments claim more and more open land as the population increases and disperses. One town looks like another; stores on the highways erect signs that shout out their wares to the fast-moving traffic going by; and every activity requires a separate trip by car.

Sprawl occurs everywhere. It is most obvious and grows most spectacularly, however, in the rapid growth areas of the South and West. Stretching across North America—from the West Coast to the East Coast, from Toronto to Miami, from Vancouver to Tucson—are large metropolitan areas fused into a series of megaregions. Gobbling up the land are strip malls and large suburban tracts with cookie-cutter housing of such striking similarity that they are creating an unvarying sameness everywhere, blurring traditional regional differences. Within this vast, homogeneous panorama, one could be almost anywhere on the continent and find few visual clues as to locale (see the *Urban Trends* box on page 89).

Three striking examples of suburban sprawl development patterns consuming far more land than urban development patterns are in Pennsylvania, Arizona, and Georgia. Between 1982 and 1997, Pennsylvania developed 1,800 square miles of open space and natural land, a 47 percent increase in an urbanized footprint when its population grew just 2.5 percent (Brookings Institution

URBAN TRENDS

"As American as Apple Pie"

Critics of suburban sprawl maintain that…sprawl—the spread-out development of separated subdivisions, office parks, malls, and strip shopping centers growing beyond existing cities and towns—has thwarted public transit development, separated rich and poor, caused unnecessary travel, consumed fragile land, and generated excessive public expenditures. On the other side of the discussion, some believe that sprawl is as American as apple pie and that citizens are getting what they want: single-family homes on large lots, safe communities with good school systems, unrestricted automobile use, and metropolitan locations far from the pace and problems of urban areas. These, and other benefits of sprawl, they argue, mean life is good.…

In fact, sprawl has been so well accepted by the public that the prime-rated locations for both residential and non-residential development are located increasingly farther out than closer in and are more rather than less segregated by type of land use. Gated communities, farmettes, research parks, law offices, medical groups, mega-hardware and home improvement stores, theatrical and comedy clubs, new and used car lots, and restaurants all now seek peripheral locations in pursuit of their markets. The move to the far reaches of the metropolitan area began with single-family subdivisions; shopping centers and garden apartments sprang up next, then research and industrial parks, followed by restaurants and entertainment facilities, and finally, discounters of every form.

The unique aspect of all this development is that few entities have ever failed because their decisions to move outward were in the wrong direction. Occasionally, a retailer or a residential development has gone under because an exit on the interstate or beltway was not developed as planned, but rarely has an economic entity failed in the United States because it was developed too far out.

If sprawl is so desirable, why should the citizens of the United States accept anything else? The answer is that they can no longer pay for the infrastructure necessary to develop farther and farther out in metropolitan areas. The cost to provide public infrastructure and services in new sprawling development is higher than the cost to service that same population in a more compact development form. Sprawling, "leapfrog" developments require longer public roads and water and sewer lines to provide service.…

Sprawl creates a never-ending upward spiral of costs. Increased usage of city roads due to the increased population makes immediate improvement necessary. The city then has to provide services to the new area. Sprawling developments also impose higher costs on police and fire departments and schools. Not as readily apparent are the costs that a new development will impose on the municipality in years to come. In all likelihood, it will not generate enough property taxes to pay for the services it requires. Farther down the road, all of the new infrastructure, originally paid for by the developer, will need maintenance and repair.

URBAN TRENDS

Something Is Wrong

Americans *sense that something is wrong* with the places where we live and work and go about our daily business. We hear this unhappiness expressed in phrases like "no sense of place" and "the loss of community." We drive up and down the gruesome, tragic suburban boulevards of commerce, and we're overwhelmed at the fantastic, awesome, stupefying ugliness of absolutely everything in sight—the fry pits, the big-box stores, the office units, the lube joints, the carpet warehouses, the parking lagoons, the jive plastic townhouse clusters, the uproar of signs, the highway itself clogged with cars—as though the whole thing had been designed by some diabolical force bent on making human beings miserable. And naturally, this experience can make us feel glum about the nature and future of our civilization.

When we drive around and look at all this cartoon architecture and other junk that we've smeared all over the landscape, we register it as ugliness. This ugliness is the surface expression of deeper problems—problems that relate to the issue of our national character. The highway strip is not just a sequence of eyesores. The pattern it represents is also economically catastrophic, an environmental calamity, socially devastating, and spiritually degrading.

... We reject the past and the future, and this repudiation is manifest in our graceless constructions. Our residential, commercial, and civic buildings are constructed with the fully conscious expectation that they will disintegrate in a few decades. This condition even has a name: "design life." Strip malls and elementary schools have short design lives. They are expected to fall apart in less than 50 years. Since these things are not expected to speak to any era but our own, we seem unwilling to put money or effort into their embellishment. Nor do we care about traditional solutions to the problems of weather and light, because we have technology to mitigate these problems—namely, central heating and electricity. Thus in many new office buildings the windows don't open. In especially bad buildings, like the average Wal-Mart, windows are dispensed with nearly altogether. This process of disconnection from the past and the future, and from the organic patterns of weather and light, done for the sake of expedience, ends up diminishing us spiritually, impoverishing us socially, and degrading the aggregate set of cultural patterns that we call civilization.

Source: James Howard Kunstler, "Home from Nowhere," *The Atlantic Monthly* 278 (September 1996), 46–66. Reprinted by permission of the author.

2003:47). The city of Phoenix now covers 520 square miles—half the land area of the state of Rhode Island. In 2008, the 13-county Atlanta region, one of the fastest-growing U.S. metropolitan areas, yielded more than 1 million acres of undeveloped land to development Three million more residents will call the Atlanta region home in 2014 than did in 2011, so Atlanta—already larger in area than Dallas and Houston but with lower population—faces challenges in its land-use development (Atlanta Regional Council 2012). Even when a city loses population, its metropolitan area population usually increases through land development. For example, Cincinnati city lost 10 percent of its population between 2000 and 2010 but its metropolitan area increased by 6 percent (U.S. Census Bureau 2011a).

Why Do We Have Sprawl?

Sprawl is like that cartoon snowball rolling down the hill, growing in size and momentum until it becomes practically unstoppable. For the past two generations, government policies on taxation, transportation, and housing—nurtured by society's embrace of *laissez faire* development—subsidized virtually unlimited low-density development. And the more this development occurred, the more people clamored for it.

For many, a house in the suburbs represents the ideal lifestyle. Massive road-building projects and community planning designed around the car encouraged people to abandon cities for the greener pastures of suburbia. As these non-metropolitan areas grew in population, a new phenomenon—the shopping center—came into existence, with large department stores from the city serving as anchors for the variety of retail enterprises along the indoor corridors. Office and industrial parks followed, either lured by tax incentives, induced by management preferences, or prompted by the relocation of competitors. Whatever the reason, the snowball effect generated more and more growth farther and farther into outlying regions, transforming much of the natural landscape around cities in Canada and the United States.

One factor in sprawl is **political fragmentation**, the splintered governance structure of numerous local municipalities in a metropolitan region, resulting in an inability to control regional growth with a comprehensive land-use plan. This situation, a springboard for postmodernist analysis, results in each town reacting individually to a developer's proposal in terms of its own zoning regulations and gains of new tax ratable properties. Little to no thought goes into how the ever-expanding settlement pattern furthers reliance on the automobile for ever-increasing distances and impacts on the environment.

This aerial view of Las Vegas shows the spread-city phenomenon occurring in the U.S. Sunbelt area. Like other Sunbelt cities, in which climate and work opportunities attract many, the rapid growth of Las Vegas strains the existing infrastructure and water supply and gobbles up the land, and its sprawling development patterns increase dependence on the automobile.

Consequences of Sprawl

The preferred lifestyle of owning a house on a large lot and enjoying the convenience of one-stop, mega-mall shopping has negative side effects. By spreading residences, medical and commercial offices, and industries throughout a region on large tracts of land, we increase residents' dependence on automobiles for transportation. Everything—and everyone—is too spread out to make public transportation economically feasible. Low-density development patterns now cause the average American household to drive 4,400 more miles per year than they otherwise would drive. Even more, the annual mileage of the average American driver grew three times faster over the past 25 years than the growth of the U.S. population. In Colorado, for example, drivers averaged 14,300 miles in 2005, up from 10,900 in 1980, a 31 percent increase per driver (Levy 2008). Longer commutes thus take time away from families, increase gasoline consumption as well as wear and tear on cars, cause traffic congestion, and increase instances of road rage.

Nor can everyone get around by car: A lifestyle that requires a car discriminates against poor families, the elderly, the disabled, and the young. Suburban teenagers, for instance, usually lack sufficient activities in their town but are unable to travel to locations where such diversions exist. Suburban parents thus spend a large part of their time chauffeuring their children to stores, cinemas, juvenile activities, and other events, or just to the mall, where they can "hang out."

Environmentalists once stood alone in their opposition to sprawl. More recently, however, other individuals, groups, and organizations have suggested that the costs and consequences of sprawl may outweigh the benefits. Those seeking to curb sprawl often base their concerns around its impact on the environment, the traffic problems it creates, its harm to cities, and the financial burden it poses on everyone.

Environmental Damage. As new construction emerges in scattered fashion across the countryside, it often disrupts wildlife habitats and fragments rural regions once abounding in farmland, fields, forests, lakes, and ponds. An example of the latter is the runoff from streets, parking lots, lawns, and farms that empties pollutants and sediment into waterways, degrading water quality and smothering habitat. In Seattle, for example, experts blame surface runoff around Puget Sound for the polluted water and habitat destruction of clams and oysters and the listing of the Chinook salmon as an endangered species (Le 2011; Stiffler 2011).

Another example is the Chesapeake Bay area, where sprawl is quickly gobbling up open space, farmlands, and forest lands. According to the Chesapeake Bay Foundation (2011), four to five times more land is used per person compared with 40 years ago. With more man-made surfaces (houses, roads, shopping centers, and parking lots), these hard (impervious) surfaces prevent the rain from soaking in. As a result, this stormwater, or urban runoff, either directly through streams or through urban storm drain systems, sends toxins and sediments into the Chesapeake Bay in increasing amounts, upsetting the delicate balance of the watershed's ecosystem. Attempts to clean up Chesapeake Bay through cooperative best management practices have had only limited success: Its health remains in moderate-to-poor condition, and the overall grade in 2010 for the Bay's health status was a C- (Chesapeake EcoCheck 2011).

Sprawl has also had disastrous consequences involving the destruction of wetlands and building on flood plains. Wetlands act as natural sponges that soak up and store rain and runoff. When they are lost to agricultural, commercial, or residential development, water—not otherwise absorbed or slowed—is free to flood. With few exceptions, floods are most frequent, and loss of life and property are greatest, in counties that have lost the most wetlands—especially during the past 40 years. Since the 1970s, the most extensive losses have occurred in Louisiana, Mississippi, Arkansas, Florida, South Carolina, and North Carolina (U.S. Environmental Protection Agency 2001).

Although such natural processes as heavy rains and snowmelt can cause floods, as can the failure of dams and levees, so, too, can inadequate drainage in urbanized areas. Scientists at the U.S. Geological Survey believe that a principal cause of flooding is poor planning and unwise development that destroy the wetlands and open spaces that protect communities. On average, U.S. floods kill 140 people each year and cause $6 billion in damage. The remarkable flooding in 2005 caused by Hurricane Katrina cost more than $200 billion in losses in New Orleans and other Gulf Coast towns, making it the costliest natural disaster in U.S. history (U.S. Geological Survey 2006).

Sometimes, the consequence of sprawl is too little water, not too much. For example, Las Vegas is one of the fastest-growing cities in the United States. This midsized city increased its population by 22 percent between 2000 and 2010, gaining another 105,322 residents. Growing at the rate of about 8,800 new residents every month, the city had such a serious water-supply problem that it began paying residents $1.50 for each square foot of lawn they ripped out to conserve water. That removal of about 6 square miles of grass saved 18 billion gallons of water. Despite these efforts, the water level at Lake Mead dropped 100 feet in the past decade to a near-precipitous level. Although the spring 2011 melting of a substantial snowpack in the Rocky Mountains restored 30 feet of the water level, the low snowpack in 2012 led to projections of a 13-foot drop by January 2013 (Brean 2012).

Three environmental groups—the National Wildlife Federation, Smart Growth America, and NatureServe—forecast that over the next 25 years, more than 22,000 acres of natural resources and habitat will be lost to development in 35 of the largest and most rapidly growing metropolitan areas. They also call attention to the fact that as many as 553 of the nearly 1,200 at-risk species live only in those areas (Heilprin 2005).

Traffic Problems. Because sprawl, by definition, is low-density, automobile-dependent development on the edge of service and employment areas, it generates longer commutes and greater traffic congestion. Cars zipping along highways—or, worse, cars stuck in traffic jams—spew millions of tons of carbon dioxide and other greenhouse gases into our atmosphere each year.

The 2011 Urban Mobility Report identified worsening traffic congestion in all 439 U.S. urban areas, costing each traveler an annual average of 34 hours extra travel time and 14 gallons of fuel wastage. In areas with 1 million persons or more, the congestion effects were even greater: 44 extra hours and 20 wasted gallons. For everyone, trips are taking longer, and congestion affects a greater portion of the day. The term *rush hour* is actually no longer accurate. Once, the rush hour was exactly that—typically, an hour between 7 and 8 A.M. and another between 4 and 5 P.M.—but today, the peak traffic periods last from 6 through 10 A.M. and from 3 until 7 P.M. (Schrank, et al. 2011).

The problem is most acute in Southern California, where traffic delays have tripled during the past 20 years. The congestion will only increase as this region of 18 million absorbs a projected 6 million new residents over the next 20 years—the equivalent of twice the population of Chicago. If population growth and transportation demands continue at their current pace, the daily delay from congestion will get far worse (Southern California Association of Governments 2008:67). Elsewhere, the story is similar. For example, the typical worker in Atlanta drives 37 miles round trip to work, while those in Dallas drive 30 miles. In Los Angeles, the daily drive is 21 miles.

Americans on average commute farther to work than Canadians do. According to the Bureau of Transportation Statistics, U.S. workers average a 16-mile, one-way commute, while 22 percent traveled between 16 and 30 miles, and 11 percent traveled more than 30 miles. By contrast, Canadian workers travel only 4 to 5 miles commuting to work (Statistics Canada 2011a).

Higher gasoline prices may well change this pattern, as they did temporarily in 2008 and 2011, when the price per gallon passed four dollars. Then, tens of thousands of

Atlanta's afternoon rush-hour traffic snarls at what commuters refer to as "spaghetti junction"—the intersection of Interstates 85 and 285. Many of these drivers are heading from their jobs to homes in suburban Gwinnett County. In three decades, Gwinnett County's population has nearly quintupled, to exceed 805,000. Atlanta's phenomenal growth and lack of adequate mass transit are the main reasons why the area suffers from traffic congestion, air pollution, and urban sprawl.

commuters nationwide abandoned their cars and took a bus or a train instead, with the biggest increases occurring in the South and West, where the driving culture is strongest. Other factors pushing people to take mass transit include expensive parking fees and technology, as wireless computers enable commuters to turn travel time into productive work time (Hargreaves 2011; Krauss 2008). Fuel prices, however, are the single biggest factor accounting for increased reliance on public transportation, and if these costs escalate again, mass transit ridership will also likely increase, possibly affecting future residential patterns.

Harm to Cities. Sprawl may be primarily a suburban phenomenon, but it has a powerful urban counterpart. The centrifugal shift of businesses and residences into outlying areas takes people away from the older, established central cities, downtowns, and neighborhoods, where so much of the heritage of both Canada and the United States is concentrated. This outward migration erodes the tax base, forcing cities to raise taxes on their remaining taxpayers to continue funding city services.

Sprawl destroys downtown commerce by pulling shoppers from once-thriving, locally owned stores and restaurants to large regional malls. These areas then lose their economic health, and the buildings and other historical reminders that define these once-bustling places fall into disrepair. Sprawl thus robs cities of character, as abandoned factories, boarded-up homes, and decaying retail centers dominate the urban landscape.

Smaller, older cities in the northeastern United States are especially vulnerable to this process. A good example is Greensboro, North Carolina, the anchor point to Guilford County, which has been experiencing extensive development. Its population density declined by more than half after 1950, even as its boundaries more than doubled outside the old city limits:

> Sprawl in Greensboro has also been associated with the movement of shopping and entertainment to the periphery and the decline of the city's once lively downtown.... [D]owntown Greensboro in the 1960s...was still a center for shopping, recreation, and many businesses. In subsequent decades, retailers, employers, and entertainment facilities followed residents to the periphery, leaving a downtown full of empty and underutilized buildings. Empty buildings pay little tax; instead they swallow large amounts of taxpayer money devoted to downtown redevelopment plans. Recent years have seen a gradual upward trend in downtown activity, but the problems of empty buildings and storefronts are far from solved. (Doss and Markham 2004:7–10)

By contrast, historic Spokane, Washington, once called "The City Beautiful," is reeling under the pressures of growth, with 50,000 newcomers expected in the next 20 years. Many city residents—believing that sprawl and automobile dependency were taking over and crushing the city's charm—banded together to form the Spokane Horizons project to develop a comprehensive plan addressing issues like parking, new roads, and infrastructure capacity while calling for a healthy downtown and surrounding neighborhoods. Adopted in 2001, the 20-year plan designates 21 mixed-use centers and corridors both within and adjacent to the city limits while maintaining the downtown as the heart of the city and the region's cultural and economic center (City of Spokane Planning Services Department 2011).

Financial Costs.   Conventional wisdom says that development strengthens the municipal tax base. Although possibly true a few decades ago, this is no longer the case: The increases in tax revenues seldom make up for the increased costs of delivering new services (water and sewer lines, schools, police and fire protection, and roads) to people who live far away from the existing infrastructure.

A Maryland planning study predicted that sprawl in the first two decades of the twenty-first century would cost state residents about $10 billion more for new roads, schools, sewers, and water than necessary if growth were more concentrated. Yet, Maryland citizens have spent 20 years fighting a $1 billion proposal to build a new Potomac River bridge and highway, despite a study showing such a bridge would encourage sprawl development (Schultz 2011). Similar studies in California, Florida, and elsewhere also demonstrated a direct relationship between sprawl and the spiraling costs of government.

In contrast, a master plan for New Jersey, the most densely populated of the 50 U.S. states, evaluated the costs of conventional sprawl growth patterns against a mix of concentrated, higher-density "infill" development, and found significant differences in cost. Infill and higher-density growth would result in a savings of $1.18 billion in roads, water, and sanitary sewer construction (or more than $12,000 per new home) and $400 million in direct annual savings to local governments. The total savings over 15 years would be $7.8 billion. This does not take into account reductions in the cost of other public infrastructure that result from infill growth—decreased spending on storm drainage, less need for school busing (and parent taxi service), fewer fire stations, and less travel time for police, ambulance, garbage collection, and other services (ANJEC 2011).

SMART GROWTH

The alternative to sprawl, partially illustrated by the New Jersey Master Plan, is **smart growth,** comprehensive land-use planning to revitalize and build compact, environmentally sensitive communities, ones that are transit and pedestrian oriented and contain a mix of residential, commercial, and retail spaces. Its focus is on regional growth within already urbanized areas as well as on newly urbanizing land (Duany, et al. 2009).

Another growing trend is an insistence on assessing the ramifications of large-scale construction projects on the environment. **Social impact analysis** is an interdisciplinary effort to determine the likely consequences of a project before its construction. This approach includes the new field of **environmental sociology,** which examines the reciprocal interactions between the physical environment, social organization, and behavior (Sydenstricker-Neto 2011).

Population growth and continued land development are ongoing realities. For several decades now, the United States has added 5 million new housing units every five years for an additional 10 to 12 million people. Over the next 30 years, it may add another 90 million new people, most of them in metropolitan areas. That means not only additional residential space but also additional work and commercial space. Clearly, the question of how the nation grows is critical (Burchell, et al. 2005:6).

Here's one example of compact growth versus sprawl. According to the Regional Plan Association—a non-profit organization dedicated to improving the quality of life in the New York metropolitan region—if the office space needed for each population increase of 5 million were built only in suburban office parks, it would cut a swath a half-mile wide and 54 miles long. In a large city with skyscrapers, however, 200 acres would fulfill the same need. The reason is that each million square feet of suburban office space requires, on average, 80 acres (25 of those acres for parking lots) as compared with only a single acre in a large city, half of which is for an office plaza. In smaller cities, the same million square feet would take up about 6 acres, involving the construction of 25-story buildings with landscaping and parking lots (Regional Plan Association 2011).

Sprawl, by definition, is a regional problem, and solving the problem requires convincing people that comprehensive, rational planning and strategies to combat it are in their self-interest. "Smart growth" public policies seek ways to stop the bulldozing of forests and farms and, instead, encourage reinvestment in cities and urbanized towns through sustainability, denser development, mass transit, and pedestrian-friendly areas. An increasing number of community leaders, concerned citizens, environmental groups, and government officials are exploring approaches to growth and development that will provide alternatives to sprawl, and some of their efforts are gaining momentum (see Table 4–1).

TABLE 4–1   Sprawl Versus Smart Growth

Definition	Sprawl is uncontrollable, unplanned, and unaccountable low-density development on an urban periphery beyond the edge of service and employment areas.	Smart growth is resource efficient; supports economic development and jobs; creates healthy, safe communities, and neighborhoods; and protects green space and farmlands.
Characteristics	Wide roads are designed to move automobiles rapidly, not to move people.	Pedestrian- and transit-friendly roads are designed to move people safely and allow interaction of neighbors.
	Single-use land isolates where people live from where they work, shop, enjoy recreation, and go to school.	Mixed-use land allows shops, schools, and jobs to be reached without using an automobile.
	Emphasis is on the private realm: yards, cars, and gated communities.	Emphasis is on the public realm: public facilities, parks, and pedestrian-friendly environments.
Effects	Decreases the quality of life, because it harms the environment and can cause health problems.	Preserves environmentally sensitive areas and farmlands, and reduces air pollution.
	Is costly to taxpayers because of the need for expensive infrastructure.	Provides an opportunity for community members and stakeholders to collaborate on development decisions.

Source: From *The Dark Side of the American Dream,* Copyright © 1998 Sierra Club™ Books. Reprinted by permission.

Land Purchases

In the 1960s, the federal government began setting aside a percentage of its royalties from offshore oil drilling to acquire or expand recreational land and open space. Today, through referendums and local or state government initiatives, efforts to protect open space and slow suburban sprawl are growing. In 1998, New Jersey voters approved a $1 billion referendum that raised the gasoline tax to pay for setting aside half the state's remaining 2 million acres of open space over a 10-year period. Similarly, voters in Monroe County, Pennsylvania, approved a $25 million bond referendum to purchase undeveloped land over a 10-year period. Voters in Austin, Texas, approved an increase in water rates to protect thousands of acres of environmentally sensitive land around the city. Through its Smart Growth and Neighborhood Conservation Program, Maryland spent $302 million to buy agricultural, forest, or natural areas that were in danger of development. Elsewhere, Pennsylvania spent $206 million and Virginia spent $232 million in the same two-year period in purchasing land to prevent development (Kobell 2011). In all, between 1998 and 2006, voters approved more than 75 percent of the 1,550 referenda setting aside open space (Banzhaf, et al. 2010).

Urban Growth Boundaries

Oregon and Washington require cities to designate official boundaries in order to separate urban areas from their surrounding greenbelt of open lands, including farms, watersheds, and parks. The intent is to funnel growth into areas with existing infrastructure while protecting the wide diversity of natural resources wrapped around these population centers. Portland, Oregon—featured in this chapter's case study—has had an urban growth boundary in place since 1975. Although the Portland metro region has grown 50 percent in population since then, it has consumed only 2 percent more land. Builders support the growth boundaries, because there is less red tape and more flexible

zoning within the designated growth areas. As a result, Portland is one of the healthiest and most livable cities in the United States (Tammemagi 2008). Other cities that have been successful with this approach are Boulder, Colorado; Lexington, Kentucky; Virginia Beach, Virginia; and San Jose, California. In Canada, the cities of Ottawa, Toronto, Vancouver, and Waterloo have green space and restrictive growth boundaries but Calgary, Edmonton, and Winnipeg—all lying on flat plains—do not and are steadily expanding outward onto farmland.

Revitalizing Existing Cities and Towns

The rejuvenation of once-thriving cities and towns—where mass transit, existing infrastructure, and high-density living can support growth—will attract new residents and limit urban flight. Many communities preserve their unique architecture through restoration and utilize good planning to restore a sense of community, improve livability, and enhance economic vitality. Through innovative public–private redevelopment strategies, they are creating vibrant urban environments that reconnect to their histories and cultural identities. Chattanooga, Tennessee, cleaned up its once seriously polluted river, the Tennessee, and created a riverfront park and promenade that now attract both wildlife and people. Suisun, California, in the San Francisco Bay area, converted an area containing a polluted waterway, decaying warehouses, and a high-crime neighborhood of dilapidated houses into a charming place filled with shops, affordable homes, and a canal for boating. As part of its smart growth plan to encourage revitalization by drawing people to the inner city, Maryland offered a financial incentive of at least $3,000 to people who buy a home in areas closer to their places of work.

A controversial approach to urban redevelopment is local or state government use of **eminent domain** to seize private property for public use, provided that the owner receives compensation at fair market value. This legal action, rooted in the Fifth Amendment of

An excellent example of revitalizing an urban environment to reconnect to the city's history is the San Antonio River Walk, one of the world's great urban linear parks and a tourist's delight. Shops, restaurants, and hotels line the San Antonio River, as people take advantage of sightseeing boats or paddleboats, walkways, footbridges, or stairs to street level to tour historic sites.

the U.S. Constitution, generated widespread attention in 2005 with a highly criticized, 5-4 decision by the U.S. Supreme Court in the case of *Kelo* v. *City of New London*. This small Connecticut city of about 25,000 had fallen on hard economic times, losing industry, population, and some of its tax base. In an effort to rejuvenate the city by spurring economic development, city officials offered to purchase 115 residential and commercial lots in the old Fort Trumbull neighborhood.

When 15 owners refused to sell, however, and the city acted to condemn their property, the owners sued and argued that the city had misused its power of eminent domain. The Supreme Court ruled against them, saying that governmental taking of private property for economic development constituted a permissible "public use." Critics charged the decision misinterpreted the Fifth Amendment and was a gross violation of property rights. Politicians, the general public, and numerous advocacy groups charged that a dangerous

precedent had been set, allowing large corporations to benefit at the expense of individual homeowners, often minorities.

Since the *Kelo* ruling, almost all states improved their laws to provide strong protection against eminent domain abuse. Meanwhile, in New London, the property owners received extra compensation, but as of 2012, the lots remained vacant, generating no tax revenues. The city's redevelopment project fell apart because of the developer's problems with financing. Nationwide, eminent domain continues to have vigorous advocates and opponents, but the widespread impact of the *Kelo* ruling lies in the 43 states that passed reform legislation to limit eminent domain powers.

Transit-Oriented Approaches

Some proposed solutions for relieving traffic congestion focus on (1) building more highway lanes, using "smart corridors" with synchronized traffic lights to move vehicles through congested areas; (2) adding car pool or high-occupancy vehicle (HOV) lanes; or (3) building more rail lines alongside the highways that connect cities and suburbs. While these proposals may alleviate traffic congestion somewhat, they do nothing to slow sprawl. Indeed, they may even intensify it. So, instead, planners seek to strengthen ridership on public transit by encouraging or requiring more compact, mixed-use development around transit stops. Some companies—worried that congested roads and long commutes hurt their ability to hire and retain workers—took other steps. Bell South consolidated 75 scattered work sites (with 13,000 workers) into three near the Atlanta rapid transit system. Safeco in Seattle offered a multifaceted approach and commuting concierges to aid its employees that resulted in 90 percent of its workers no longer taking cars to work. Microsoft provides plush, WIFI equipped buses that are widely popular (Conlin 2008).

In Vancouver, British Columbia, sprawl spread eastward and carpeted the Fraser River Valley with dozens of suburbs; as a result, rush-hour traffic headed out of the city over Lion's Gate Bridge was routinely backed up for 3 miles. Unable to stop the sprawl, planners instead sought to reduce the traffic congestion. Determined to avoid further "Los Angelization," regional leaders rejected the idea of building more highways as the backbone of their local transportation network. Instead, they set up an extensive transit system—utilizing trains and ferries, but anchored by 1,000 buses (20 times the number in the Atlanta region).

Significantly, as more suburbanites and commuters converged on the Vancouver metropolitan region, area planners opted to spread the population around by creating self-sustaining job centers in the suburbs to the east. They did so through SkyTrain, an automated light-rail train system along the

In December 2008, Phoenix ended its position as the largest metropolitan area with only bus transportation by launching an initial 20-mile light-rail system, with 28 stations located adjacent to sidewalks and vehicle lanes. Running every 12 minutes during peak hours and every 20 minutes off-peak, hopes are that this mass transit system will greatly reduce traffic congestion and air pollution.

Expo and Millennium lines that technically moves up to 30,000 people per hour in both directions. Its elevated electric cars zip along into the suburbs, taking passengers to and from their homes or work in far less time than would be needed on the clogged highways. Metrotown, once a declining suburban warehouse district, has become SkyTrain's busiest stop, as office buildings, apartments, movie theaters, and a mall now ring the station (Wolinsky 2004).

These four approaches—land purchases, growth boundaries, revitalization, transit solutions—and other grassroots efforts at comprehensive land-use planning are essential to revitalizing urban cores and protecting open space and outdoor lifestyles. When public policy directs investment of money, effort, and vision into communities rather than into sprawl by subsidizing new roads, utilities, and development at the expense of urban centers, the public has more options to make environmentally responsible lifestyle choices.

Greening Our Cities

Transit-oriented approaches are one in a series of environmental initiatives that many cities have taken to reduce energy consumption and greenhouse-gas emissions. In addition to the above-mentioned transit measures, others include replacing diesel fuel buses with hybrid models, switching to hybrid or electric taxis, and improving cycling and walking infrastructures. To reduce the "heat island" effect where cities are hotter in summer than surrounding areas, cities such as Chicago and New York encourage green roofs instead of black-tar ones atop skyscrapers, where grass, shrubs, even small trees reduce the amount of energy needed to cool buildings and capture rainwater, thereby reducing the amount flowing into overtaxed sewers. More efficient street lights, retrofitting commercial buildings to be more energy efficient, recycling to reduce the rubbish going to landfills, and repaving alleyways with light-colored, porous surfaces to avoid retention of the sun's heat and reduce water runoff into sewers are other measures.

Other cities actively involved in such environmentally friendly efforts are Austin, Houston, Los Angeles, New Orleans, Philadelphia, Portland, San Francisco, and Seattle (Economist 2011).

A new measurement tool, *The U.S. and Canada Green Cities Index,* examined 27 cities in 2011 and scored them on carbon dioxide emissions, energy, land use, buildings, transport, water, waste, air and environmental governance. Leading the list of best cities was San Francisco, followed by Vancouver, New York City, Seattle, and Denver. At the bottom were Pittsburg, Phoenix, Cleveland, St. Louis, and Detroit (Siemens 2011).

EXURBS

A. C. Spectorsky coined the term **exurb** (for "extra-urban") to describe the appearance of new residential areas developing on the metropolitan fringe. His was an observational but not-too-systematic account of prosperous residential communities on the fringes of the New York City metropolitan area. He noted that the lifestyle of these exurbanites was an intriguing mix of high tech, high culture, and rustic charm. Although they lived in a rural locale, they (1) commuted to jobs in the central business district, (2) combined their love for old things with attraction to new electronic gadgets, and (3) maintained a strong interest in books, theater, and art.

The small trend that Spectorsky noted in *The Exurbanites* (1957) has since morphed into a stampede. Then, the exurbanites settled heavily in counties such as Fairfield (Connecticut), Rockland and Westchester (New York), and Bucks (Pennsylvania). Today, exurban counties surround every major city, from Marin near San Francisco to Dacula near Atlanta (see *Cityscape* box on page 100). New exurbanites also now are more likely to be moving from a suburb, not from a central city, and are less likely to work in a central city (Eiesland 2000).

The development of shopping malls, office towers, and sit-down restaurants within the past 20 years has expanded metropolitan areas far beyond central business districts

CITYSCAPE

Atlanta's Edge Cities

He looked away from the buildings and out over the ocean of trees. Since Atlanta was not a port city and was, in fact, far inland, the trees stretched on in every direction. They were Atlanta's greatest natural resource, those trees were. People loved to live beneath them. Fewer than 400,000 people lived within the Atlanta city limits, and almost three quarters of them were black; if anything, over the past decade Atlanta's population had declined slightly. But for the past 30 years all sorts of people, most of them white, had been moving in beneath those trees, into all those delightful, leafy, rolling rural communities that surrounded the city proper. By the hundreds of thousands they had come, from all over Georgia, all over the South, all over America, all over the world, into those subdivided hills and downs and glens and glades beneath the trees, until the population of Greater Atlanta was now more than 3.5 million, and they were still pouring in. How fabulous the building booms had been!! As the G-5 banked, Charlie looked down.... There was Spaghetti Junction, as it was known, where Highways 85 and 285 came together in a tangle of 14 gigantic curving concrete-and-asphalt ramps and twelve overpasses.... And now he could see Perimeter Center, where Georgia 400 crossed 285. Mack Taylor and Harvey Mathis had built an office park called Perimeter Center out among all those trees, which had been considered a very risky venture at the time, because it was so far from Downtown; and now Perimeter Center was the nucleus around which an entire edge city, known by that very name, Perimeter Center, had grown....

Edge city...Charlie closed his eyes and wished he'd never heard of the damn term. He wasn't much of a reader, but back in 1991 Lucky Putney, another developer, had given him a copy of a book called *Edge City* by somebody named Joel Garreau. He had opened it and glanced at it—and couldn't put it down, even though it was 500 pages long. He had experienced the *Aha!* phenomenon. The book put into words something he and other developers had felt, instinctively, for quite a while: namely, that from now on, the growth of American cities was going to take place not in the heart of the metropolis, not in the old Downtown or Midtown, but out on the edges, in vast commercial clusters served by highways.

Source: Excerpt from "Atlanta's Edge Cities," in *A Man in Full*, Copyright © 1998 by Tom Wolfe. Reprinted by permission of Farrar, Straus & Giroux LLC.

and traditional suburbia (Teaford 2006). A diverse mixture of inner suburbs, large suburban edge cities, office parks, retail centers, "captured" small towns, and even low-density rural territory now comprises the metropolitan fringe:

> Businesses were drawn to the less crowded metropolitan periphery where—developers promised—their operations would be free from traffic congestion and would gain access to an underutilized rural population. Whether they were termed "edge cities," "techno-burbs," "outer cities," or "transformed suburbs," these relatively recent formations changed the patterns of metropolitan life as well as of small towns and rural areas now within the metropolitan orbit. (Eiesland 2000:5)

Once viewed by their residents as physically and socially distant from the city, small towns now often merge into the sprawling metropolitan region; outsiders view them as historic "subdivisions" adjacent and economically linked to the newly developing cities with their high-density housing, offices, shopping, and service centers (Eiesland 2000:6). The process of unfolding exurbanization and small-town absorption within metropolises comes at a cost. The small-town traditions and values that first attracted the newcomers transform into more cosmopolitan ones, resulting in social tensions between old and new residents (Siskind 2006). In addition, these once-rural areas and small towns become more expensive places to live as land values, taxes, and the overall cost of living increase.

Small towns thus become new suburbs to new cities, dramatically altering the region. An expansive pattern of urban/rural restructuring, both spatially and socially, results in significant changes in the demographics, social organization, and lifestyle (Eisland 2000:6). We will now examine this social phenomenon of the new cities that so impact on small towns.

THE NEW CITIES

Not since the expansion of small cities into huge metropolises a century ago have we seen as profound a change in our urban world. **Edge cities**—sprawling, middle-class, automobile-dependent centers typically located at the fringe of an older urban area—have emerged at the intersection of major highways, where little except villages or farmland existed a few decades earlier. Today, most edge cities are less of an "edge" and more of a new center. Although this term is still somewhat popular, in this edition we will use the term **new cities** to discuss them more fully. A good starting point is to recognize that the growth of new cities in recent decades helps explain the increases in the population of non-metropolitan areas discussed in the previous chapter.

Tysons Corner, Virginia—long the critics' model of what they say is wrong with edge cities—has no defined borders and no recognizable center, and its various buildings are not conveniently near one another. It has all the commercial activities but none of the charm of a city (pedestrians, interesting architecture, and cultural attractions). To reduce the necessity of a car and terrible traffic congestion, a four-station light-rail system will open in 2013.

During the second half of the twentieth century, North Americans went through three waves of centrifugal movement away from the older cities. First came suburbanization, most notably after World War II, as people moved into new homes beyond city boundaries. Next came the malling of North America, particularly in the 1960s and 1970s, when merchants moved their stores out to where many potential shoppers lived. Subsequently, companies moved their means of creating wealth, the essence of urbanism—jobs—out to where most people now lived and shopped. This led to the rise of the new cities, causing profound changes in the ways we live, work, and play. Numbering well over 200 in the United States and Canada, these new cities, with their malls and office parks, now dominate the nations' retail trade and office facilities.

New cities appeared in Canada and the United States for different reasons. Unlike the United States, the Canadian government does not provide suburb-enhancing tax deductions for home mortgages, and it has greater control over planning and development. Canada also has a greater emphasis on mass transit; a relative lack of freeways; vibrant, bustling urban centers; and a relative lack of racial problems. Nevertheless, new cities are flourishing, such as Markham, Mississauga, and Vaughan. Through expansion, Toronto absorbed others—Eglington–Don Mills, Etobicoke, North York, and Scarborough—dissolved municipalities now incorporated into Greater Toronto.

Characteristics and Commonalities

The new cities possess many of the same characteristics of older cities: extensive office and retail space, a large-scale influx of workers each weekday morning, and a mixed use of work, shopping, and entertainment (Garreau 1991:425). What one seldom finds, however, is a clearly defined territorial boundary; no map boundaries define where they begin and end. Unlike their older counterparts, new cities are spread out, requiring the use of a car; they lack the compactness of closely adjacent buildings and high pedestrian traffic. Further, many do not have a mayor, city council, or civic codes; their lack of political organization and elected officials usually means the only unifying element is a jointly shared security patrol.

A common feature of new cities is that they have sprouted far from the old downtowns, in locales where little existed a few decades ago except villages and farmland. They typically evolve adjacent to two or more major highways, usually with shopping malls serving as anchor points. Figures 4–1 and 4–2 show two of the more densely concentrated New City regions—the Los Angeles and New York areas, respectively.

Types of New Cities

New cities fall into one of three major categories: (1) **uptowns,** built on top of preautomobile settlements, such as Pasadena, California, or Arlington, Virginia; (2) **boomers,** the typical new city located at the intersection of two major highways and almost always centered on a mall, such as most of those in Figure 4-1; and (3) **greenfields,** a master-planned city by one developer on thousands of farmland acres, such as Irvine, California, and Las Colinas, Texas, near the Dallas–Fort Worth airport. Boomers are the most common new city type and the ones most likely to have political organization. They typically fall into three subcategories (see Figure 4–3 on page 105).

The strip boomer city is usually only a few hundred yards wide but extends for miles along a major highway. Most representative are the strips along Route 1 in Princeton, Route 128 near the Mass Pike outside Boston, and I-270 in Montgomery County, Maryland, in the Washington, D.C. region. All three suffer severe traffic congestion because of their extended shapes. The node boomer city is relatively dense and contained, such as The Galleria area near Houston, Tysons Corner in Virginia, and the Midtown–Yorkville and North York–North Yonge areas in Toronto. The pig-in-the-python boomer city is a cross between the previous two types. It is a strip that develops one or several nodes along it, such as the Lodge Freeway in Southfield, northwest of Detroit, or King of Prussia, Pennsylvania, northwest of Philadelphia. (Garreau 1991:115)

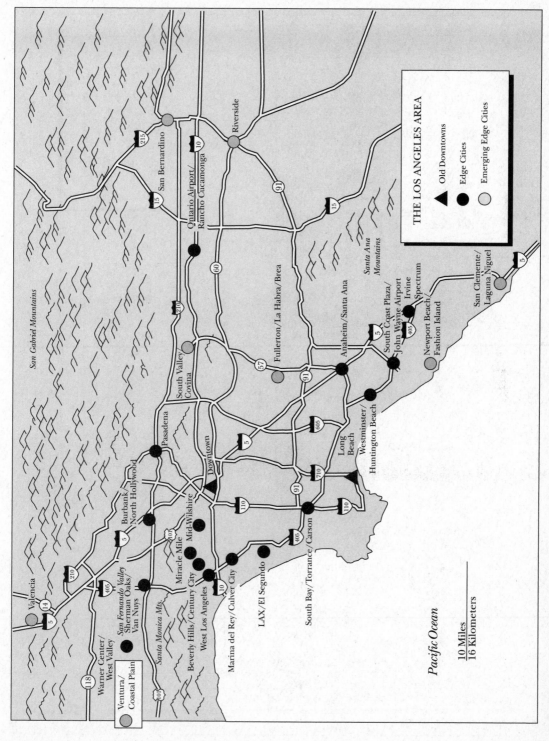

FIGURE 4-1 The Los Angeles Area

THE LOS ANGELES AREA

▲ Old Downtowns
● Edge Cities
○ Emerging Edge Cities

Pacific Ocean

10 Miles
16 Kilometers

San Gabriel Mountains

Santa Ana Mountains

Riverside

San Bernardino

Ontario Airport/
Rancho Cucamonga

Fullerton/La Habra/Brea

Anaheim/Santa Ana

South Valley/
Covina

Pasadena

Downtown

Burbank/
North Hollywood

Valencia

San Fernando Valley/
Sherman Oaks/
Van Nuys

Warner Center/
West Valley

Santa Monica Mts.

Miracle Mile

Mid-Wilshire

Beverly Hills/Century City
West Los Angeles

Marina del Rey/Culver City

LAX/El Segundo

South Bay/Torrance/Carson

Long Beach

Westminster/
Huntington Beach

South Coast Plaza/
John Wayne Airport/
Irvine Spectrum

Newport Beach/
Fashion Island

San Clemente/
Laguna Niguel

Ventura/
Coastal Plain

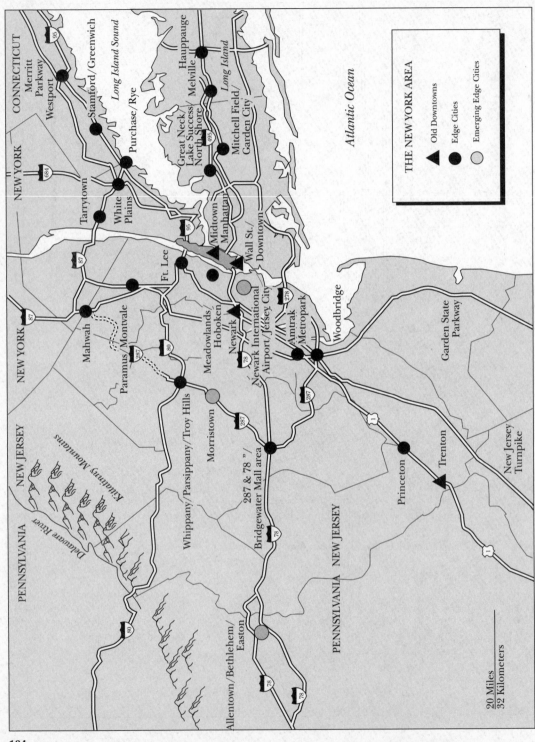

FIGURE 4–2 The New York Area

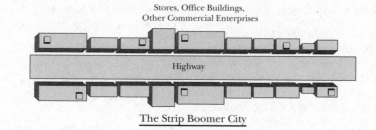

Stores, Office Buildings,
Other Commercial Enterprises

Highway

The Strip Boomer City

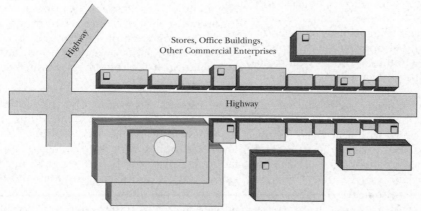

Highway

Stores, Office Buildings,
Other Commercial Enterprises

Highway

Shopping Mall, Plus Other Stores, Office Buildings, Other Commercial Enterprises

The Node Boomer City

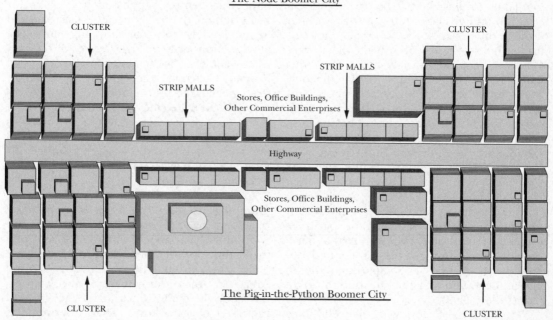

CLUSTER

CLUSTER

STRIP MALLS

STRIP MALLS

Stores, Office Buildings,
Other Commercial Enterprises

Highway

Stores, Office Buildings,
Other Commercial Enterprises

The Pig-in-the-Python Boomer City

CLUSTER

CLUSTER

FIGURE 4–3   Types of New (Edge) Cities

Evolving Middle-Class Centers

The majority of metropolitan North Americans now work, shop, and live in and around these 200-plus "new hearths of our civilization" (Garreau 1991:3). Shopping malls function as the village squares for these new urban centers. Adjacent are the hotels, office buildings, and corporate headquarters. These tall buildings are not side by side as in a downtown, but instead sit on campus-like settings of grass and trees, gazing at one another from a respectful distance. Surrounding this broad center of employment and shopping are the single-family suburban homes, whose occupants now outnumber those living next to the old downtowns.

The rise of new cities is essentially a function of social class, not race. They are evolving in metropolitan areas with low black populations (Denver, Minneapolis, Seattle, and Toronto) as well as in metropolitan areas with high black populations (Atlanta, Chicago, New York, and Washington). In the latter areas, middle-class African Americans (presently about one-third of the total U.S. black population) are as likely to be part of new cities as are middle-class whites. Just as the skin of the middle-class North American comes in various hues—shades of brown, black, tan, and white—so, too, do new cities reflect this reality. Critics often complain that the new cities, despite racial diversity, are "plastic and sterile, lacking in liveabilty, civilization, community, neighborhood—in short, having little 'urban soul' " (Garreau 1991:8).

Perhaps though, their unfinished city form is evolving further, since leading planners now speak of turning new cities into "real cities" (Barnett 2002). Some locales—such as Addison, Texas, for example—have taken steps to transform at least parts in spaces resembling a real city, with streets that have sidewalks and frontages with stores and restaurants on ground level, apartment buildings, and creation of a hub at Addison Circle Park (Dillon 2003).

New cities exist worldwide as well. They now mark the fringes of Bangkok, Beijing, London, Melbourne, Mexico City, Paris, Seoul, and Sydney. Increased affluence, the desire for more individual transportation, greater use of computers and telecommunications, and the existence of world financial centers are some of the important elements shaping the growth of new cities in urban areas throughout the world.

Three New City Variations

Not all new cities are alike, nor does their evolution occur for the same reasons everywhere. The following examples illustrate how a new city can serve as its own motivation, emerge as a solution to a problem, or simply become the problem.

New City as Motivator. By 1990, Oshawa Centre, one of the oldest shopping malls in Ontario, Canada, was showing its age. Originally built for the town's blue-collar population, the place was dark and ugly. Some of its stores had outdoor-facing windows and doors plastered with newspaper and cardboard, and its sales and rental value were declining. Not anymore. The Toronto-based Cambridge Shopping Centres purchased it in 1991 for $145 million. It did so because Garreau had written in *Edge City* that shopping malls usually function as the village squares of the new urban centers. "So, taking that theory," said Ronald Charbon, Cambridge's director of strategic market information, "we said, 'Where are the next edge cities going to occur? Where is the next wave of growth going to occur in the greater metropolitan Toronto area? And are any of our shopping centers sufficiently located to capitalize on that growth?' " (quoted in Berman 1997:74).

Using census tracts and surveys, Cambridge Shopping Centres amassed a population profile of the area, discovering that areas surrounding Oshawa were white collar and that projections of the area's growth rate were almost three times that in the Greater Toronto Area. So, the company took the gamble, invested $40 million in a major facelift, and recruited upscale stores. That, however, was only one part of a sophisticated strategy to turn Oshawa Centre into the village square that Garreau described. Cambridge secured government approval to construct six modest-sized office towers over a 25-year period. The Oshawa Centre thus underwent a massive transformation from a slapdash suburban mall into a mixed-use development that includes more than 200 retail stores as well as government and community services, all inspired by Garreau's book.

New City as the Solution.   Since incorporating in 1956, Schaumburg, Illinois, had been "the ultimate faceless postwar suburb" (Pasternak 1998). Located 26 miles northwest of Chicago, the town grew from nearly 19,000 in 1970 to more than 74,000 people by 2010, with most living in townhouses and subdivisions and shopping in one or more of the 65 stores that lined its streets. Along its expressway, glassy office towers provided a solid employment base. Home to the world headquarters of Motorola and one of Illinois' top tourist destinations, the 285-store Woodfield Mall, Schaumburg prospered with a low unemployment rate. The one thing lacking in Schaumburg was that it had no center, no downtown, and no place to walk to or for people to gather. In fact, Schaumburg hadn't had a town center since 1875.

That has now changed. The local government tore down a faded strip mall on a 30-acre site to make way for a downtown center called "Town Square." This place, however, is no small-town core like the downtowns of older suburbs that developed around train depots generations ago, even though its late nineteenth–early twentieth century architecture pays homage to the historic character of the old town center. Its design and park-like setting are intended to encourage pedestrians and shoppers, but no retail stores line Main Street. In fact, there is no Main Street. Instead, a coffee shop and a cluster of retail stores border a large parking lot, giving this area the look of a shopping center. Nearby are a new library, a chain restaurant, a brick clock tower, a green wrought-iron gazebo, a pond, curved benches, and a public amphitheater. Three miles away, a hotel/convention center complex on a 45-acre parcel of land opened in 2006, with hopes of further increasing Schaumburg's commerce and tourism.

New City as the Problem.   The more that Tysons Corner, Virginia—located 8 miles west of Washington, D.C., and one of Garreau's prime examples—continues to grow and thrive economically, the more it remains an object of derisive commentary by architects, city planners, design critics, and urban scholars. Indeed, finding a way to "fix" Tysons Corner has been the goal of several planning studies sponsored by academic institutions, professional groups, and Fairfax County, Virginia.

Home to a massive shopping mall and two shopping centers, as well as an impressive array of high-tech firms and major corporations, Tysons Corner today is larger, both in geographical size and in employment, than many U.S. central cities. It is, essentially, the central business district of Fairfax County, with the U.S. Census Bureau reporting its daytime population exceeding 100,000, about five times greater than its nighttime population of less than 20,000 residents.

Incredibly, only road transit presently exists, and during weekday rush hours and weekend shopping times, backups are horrendous. However, the Dulles Corridor Metrorail Project, scheduled for completion in 2013, will serve Tysons Corner, Virginia's largest employment center, with four stations, and should greatly alleviate traffic congestion by offering a viable alternative to automobile travel (Metropolitan Washington Airports Authority 2011).

Even if traffic congestion can be reduced and pedestrian traffic encouraged, the aesthetic and visual deficiencies, the visual chaos and formlessness, would still remain. In the interest of bringing a bit of visual order to Tysons Corner, a county task force developed a plan to address streetscapes, pedestrian walkways, site planning of buildings, and open space. Still, Tysons Corner has no civic focus, or heart, and so planners have proposed a dense urban center to eliminate the soullessness often mentioned by critics as the problem with Tysons Corner. "The Tysons Vision," a plan calling for walkable, mixed-use centers around mass transit, offers promise generating a diversity of lifestyles and mobility choices (*Washington Post* 2009). The daunting and expensive task will be to transform Tysons Corner from its car-dominated tangle of offices, malls, and auto dealers into a livable city. Proposals include building densely packed high-rises, miles of new streets, and enough parks, schools, police stations, and firehouses to serve an entirely new place (Gardner 2008).

Until then, Tysons Corner will continue to be emblematic of how poorly we have planned, zoned, and developed much of the landscape girdling our cities since the end of World War II.

GATED COMMUNITIES

Gated communities in the United States can be traced back to the first planned gated community in 1853 at Llewellyn Park in West Orange, New Jersey, and others blooming in the late 1800s, when upper-income gated developments in New York's Tuxedo Park and private streets in St. Louis sprang up as wealthy citizens sought to "insulate themselves from the troublesome aspects of rapidly industrializing cities" (Blakely and Snyder 1999:4). These communities, however, and the fenced compounds built in the twentieth century by members of the East Coast and Hollywood aristocracies, were different from today's gated communities. They were unique places for unique people. Although a few other such exclusive communities began to appear—such as Sea Pines on Hilton Head Island, South Carolina, in 1957—they remained rare until the late 1960s and 1970s, when master-planned retirement developments first appeared. These developments were the first places where average Americans could wall themselves off from the rest of society.

Gated communities are a rapidly growing phenomenon. Segregated from the outside world by walls, fences, electronically operated gates, and/or 24-hour guards, residents essentially live barricaded lives. Such communities typically cater to a housing market emphasizing prestige, lifestyle, or security-zone neighborhoods that promise a sense of community, exclusion, private control of public services, and the stability of homogenization.

Beginning in the 1980s, gated communities increased rapidly—not only in retirement villages but also in resort and country club developments, and then in middle-class suburban subdivisions, setting off a quiet but important trend that continues today. In the mid-1980s, gated communities were rare on Long Island, New York, but by the mid-1990s, they had become common, with a gatehouse included in almost every condominium of more than 50 units. Elsewhere, separately incorporated municipalities exist that feature guarded entrances; one example is Canyon Lake, 60 miles east of Orange County in California.

About 10.8 million U.S. households are in developments surrounded by fences or walls. More than 60 percent of those households are in communities that also have controlled-entry systems, such as guards and electric gates (U.S. Department of Housing and Urban Development 2011:25). Hispanics are more likely to live in rental gated communities than other minorities. Their largest concentration within gated communities is in the West and Southwest, where a large Hispanic population lives (Sanchez, et al. 2005).

Although most of these developments are in suburban areas, older, inner-city neighborhoods are also experiencing this phenomenon. Many gated communities have been built in metropolitan areas across the country, including Los Angeles, Phoenix, Dallas, Houston, Chicago, New York, and Miami. Such urban refuges exist in Canada as well. In Toronto, three older gated areas—Palmerston Avenue, Fairview Boulevard, and Wychwood Park—are city jewels that enjoy high real-estate values.

What makes these secured communities different from typical modern suburbs, which usually also have economic and social segregation? As previously stated, gated communities are actually defended by walls, with access controlled either by electronically operated gates or by 24-hour guards and grounds patrolled by private security forces. While there are a variety of approaches to living barricaded lives, the reasons why residents choose gated communities usually center on fear of crime and attempts to produce economic and physical security, free from the problems of traffic and noise. Residents enjoy their own pay-as-you-go services. They share responsibility for common areas and for enforcing the numerous rules and regulations, often through homeowners' associations, rather than relying on conventional elected local governments for many common services.

Gated communities, however, separate the people living within their walls from others even more profoundly than the most exclusive suburban jurisdiction can, and they thus accentuate patterns of segregation. Such a lifestyle reduces opportunities for positive interactions and shared experiences among people of diverse backgrounds, and it contributes to the fragmentation of the greater community (Vesselinov 2008).

Types of Gated Communities

Secured communities fall into one of three categories: (1) **lifestyle communities,** (2) **prestige communities,** and (3) **security-zone communities** (Blakely and Snyder 1999). Although these categories are helpful for analysis and understanding, much overlap exists, with some elements in one found in the others. Still, each category caters to a different housing market and has a different approach to developing a sense of community within its walls. Moreover, each promotes a particular combination of four social values: (1) a *sense of community* (preservation and strengthening of neighborhood bonds), (2) *exclusion* (separation and protection from the outside), (3) *privatization* (the desire to privatize and internally control public services), and (4) *stability* (homogeneity and predictability).

> Where sense of community is a primary value motivating the residents of gated communities, it reflects all five aspects of community: shared territory, shared values, a shared public realm, support structure, and a shared destiny. Exclusion helps define shared territory by separating community members from outsiders. Privatization reflects a desire to protect a shared destiny through increased local control. Stability suggests shared values and support structures, and retaining stability is also a way of predicting shared destiny. (Blakely and Snyder 1999:122)

Lifestyle Communities. Lifestyle communities are an expression of conspicuous consumption and a new leisure class. They emphasize amenities and include retirement communities, such as the nationwide chain of Leisure Worlds, all of which offer senior citizens the chance to engage in a wide variety of activities close to their homes. Another type is golf and leisure communities, where the gates cordon off the leisure resources for the exclusive use of community residents. Blackhawk Country Club near San Francisco and Rancho Mirage in California's Coachella Valley cater to people with special interests, like golf or tennis. Lifestyle communities attract those who want separate, private services and amenities within a homogeneous, predictable environment.

Prestige Communities. Prestige communities are status-oriented enclaves, such as those in affluent Pacific Palisades in San Clemente, and Conyers Farm in Greenwich, Connecticut, primarily containing the rich and famous, the affluent, the top one-fifth of Americans. These communities emphasize exclusion and image, and the gates symbolize the eminent status of their residents. Prestige communities attract those seeking a stable neighborhood of similar people where property values will be protected. For these residents, concerns about separation and privatization of services are secondary (Gregor 2012; Romig 2005).

Security-Zone Communities. Security-zone communities are "enclaves of fear" primarily concerned with protection. They are a defensive measure reflecting a fortress mentality, with walls, gates, closed streets, and various security systems. In these enclaves—often located in inner-city and lower-income neighborhoods—residents band together to shut out their neighbors, hoping that the gates will protect them from crime, traffic, and outsiders. Security-zone communities seek to strengthen and protect a sense of community, but their primary goal is to exclude those people their residents perceive as threats to their safety and quality of life.

A Sense of Community

For several decades, social observers have noted a loss of community in modern life, or "the great emptiness" (MacIver 2011, orig. 1962). Unlike traditional communities in small towns, where individuals have lifelong emotional bonds, today's relationships often rest on such superficial similarities as consumption style or leisure interests (Bellah, et al. 1985). Instead of interacting with different kinds of people, who nevertheless are still a part of one's community, living today in segregated and isolated enclaves diminishes social life, claim these authors. All residents can do is compare their own material gains with those of their neighbors to piece together some idea of "how they are doing." As the well-to-do wall themselves into privately policed, fortress communities, they are effectively seceding from the rest of society, creating a fragmented, polarized society.

> The fabric of civitas, communal commitment to civic and public life, has begun to rip.... The borders of the gated communities are emblematic of the proliferation of boundaries being set and hardened as communities fragment, looking inward. (Blakely and Snyder 1999:176)

As communities turn inward, motivated by security and other social needs, do the residents find what they seek? Critics charge that they do not—that gated communities reflect the social fragmentation and civic atrophy currently plaguing society. Because these barricaded neighborhoods exclude the lower classes not only from living there (through prohibitive housing costs) but also from even casually passing by, they effectively limit social contact among different members and groups of society. Such class separation is often *de facto* racial segregation, and this social distance can weaken further the civic bonds among societal members. These private, self-governing gated communities have redefined the grassroots level of the boundary between public and private realms (Stark 2002).

Despite their promise, the quality of community does not improve in gated developments. Even though residents move to such places in the belief that they will find their nostalgic idea of community, often they do not. In fact, these communities promote privacy within privacy: With no front porches to induce interaction, residents tend to stay in their own backyards and not visit one another. As a result, gating often does not provide what people are seeking. Particularly in high-income gated communities, residents report a significant lower sense of community. In comparison with non-residents, members of gated communities do not find stronger ties with one another (Wilson-Doenges 2000).

Community, however, appears to be of less importance than security. Availability of shared community recreational facilities (clubhouse, pool, tennis courts) may enhance the gated lifestyle, but the perception of safety is a more significant factor in neighborhood satisfaction, whether in gated or non-gated communities. Gates and entry-controlled access, by design, provide both a physical and a psychological crime deterrent in the minds of gated residents. The effectiveness of gates and fencing may depend on the nature of the property and the people living behind them, but for higher-income—especially older residents—the inferred safety is sufficient cause for positive feelings about living in such sheltered enclaves (Chapman and Lombard 2006).

COMMON-INTEREST DEVELOPMENTS

Gated communities are often called **common-interest developments (CIDs).** Not all CIDs, however, are segregated communities (although many are), and not all gated areas are CIDs (although most are). A close relationship exists between the two phenomena, but they are not the same thing. CIDs—which require membership in a self-governing homeowners' association—include suburban planned-unit developments of single-family homes, urban condominiums, and housing cooperatives, and they have become familiar sights throughout North America. Moreover, the rapid spread of CID housing is the largest and most dramatic privatization of local

government functions in North American history. Currently, more than 314,000 of these developments exist in the United States, housing 62.3 million people in 25.1 million housing units (Community Associations Institute 2011).

Builders find CID housing profitable, because it is a mass-produced commodity and enables them to concentrate more people on less land. Buyers are willing to accept smaller lots and narrower streets, because the development contains open spaces and desirable amenities, including facilities owned in common by all residents—such as swimming pools, gyms, parks, golf courses, social centers, and often even exclusive access to shopping centers and their own schools. Public officials are willing to issue building permits for these high-density, designed communities, with their private infrastructure, because they add taxpayers at minimal public cost.

Residents must belong to homeowners' associations, pay monthly fees, and live under the rule of residential private governments. These governments perform functions for their residents that were once the province of local government—for example, police protection, trash collection, and street maintenance and lighting. In one sense, this community design is a logical, evolutionary step in the suburban ideology of territorial control (housing-market segmentation, single-use zoning, inaccessibility to mass transit, and cul-de-sacs). For those who examine social phenomena from a rational choice perspective, CIDs are more democratic, efficient, and a preferred option over municipalities (Nelson 2005).

New urbanists favor the development of these private communities as the antidote to sprawl, in that their planning and architectural approach is environment friendly (Duany, et al. 2000). Some critics, however, think that this new civic culture undermines the diversity and vitality of cities. Because CIDs contain relatively homogeneous groupings, they argue that such planned developments promote racial and economic segregation (Putnam 2001). Critical urban theorists go further, asserting that such private governance enables

URBAN LIVING

CID Restrictions on Personal Freedom

The stories below do not merely reflect isolated neighborhood conflicts. They are examples of the control that is exerted in walled, private, urban and suburban enclaves called common-interest developments (CIDs). Although many willingly trade some privacy and personal freedoms for the CID lifestyle, some find themselves fighting for their rights against the few residents who enforce the rules with a degree of personal power over their neighbors that the Constitution denies to public officials.

- In Monroe, New Jersey, a homeowners' association sued a married couple, because the wife, at age 45, was three years younger than the association's age-48 minimum for residency. The judge ruled in favor of the association, ordering the 60-year-old husband to sell or rent the unit—or else live there without his wife.
- In Ashland, Massachusetts, a CID board informed a Vietnam veteran that he could not fly the U.S. flag on Flag Day. He called the press, the story appeared on the front page of a local newspaper, and under public pressure, the board backed down.
- In Boca Raton, Florida, an association sued a homeowner for having a dog weighing more than 30 pounds, in violation of its rules. A court-ordered weighing revealed that the dog was just an ounce over the weight limit. The association persisted nonetheless—determined to pay an attorney and use the courts to exclude

the dog from the development for even that infraction.
- In a development near Philadelphia, Pennsylvania, a couple bought a home and brought their sons' metal swing set with them. A year later, the association told them to take it down, despite the absence of any written rules about swing sets. When the couple challenged this order, the association passed a rule prescribing that all swing sets must be made of wood, in keeping "with what the overall community should look like." The family then submitted a petition from three-fourths of the homeowners supporting their swing set, along with data from the U.S. Environmental Protection Agency warning against the danger to children (theirs were aged two and four) from the poisonous chemicals found in pressure-treated wood used for outdoor swing sets. The association's response was to impose a daily fine of $10 until the set was removed—and to refuse offers to compromise, such as painting the swing set in earth tones.
- In Fort Lauderdale, Florida, condominium managers ordered a couple to stop entering and leaving their unit through their back door, claiming that they were wearing an unsightly path in the lawn by taking a short cut to the parking lot. The couple retained an attorney, who filed a lawsuit seeking a court's permission for the couple to use their own back door.

Source: Evan McKenzie, "Trouble in Privatopia," *The Progressive* 57 (October 1993), 30–36. Reprinted by permission from *The Progressive*, 409 E. Main St. Madison, WI 53709, www.progressive.com.

the affluent to create a private domain, separate from the rest of society and thus beyond normal political overview, and where they can control their neighborhood and its resources. By contrast, many officials welcome this separation because residents pay full property taxes without the local government obliged to provide the same level of services provided elsewhere within the municipal boundaries. Residents were pleased because of the promise of security, better services, and a stable neighborhood.

In gaining this form of independence, however, CID residents pay a heavy price, because they surrender much of their other freedoms and privacy. They live under the rule of their corporate board of directors, an elected group of neighbors enforcing a set of restrictions created by the developer to ensure that the master plan never changes. The board can dictate such things as barring holiday decorations in windows, the size and contents of your garden, even the color of paint on your front door, and it can legally impose daily fines until you comply. This private government operates outside the constitutional limits that bind local authorities, because court rulings have held that CID restrictions are private, voluntary arrangements among individuals, even though they are non-negotiable regulations drafted by the developer's lawyers and imposed on all residents, as illustrated in the *Urban Living* box on page 112.

Moreover, the collapse of the housing and job markets, beginning in 2008, has had a significant impact on CIDs, given their heavy reliance on the resources of homeowners to fund the provided maintenance and services. Coupled with budget cutbacks from local governments, many CIDs are struggling to remain solvent. Any that fail to survive will make them an additional burden to the larger communities instead of windfall they once were, by compelling local governments to provide basic services (such as maintenance of the tree-lined streets) previously handled by the CIDs (McKenzie 2011).

The U.S. idea of privately-governed communities has spread to other parts of the world. In Africa, Asia (including 250 million people in China), Europe, and Latin America, one can find millions of people now living in CIDs (Atkinson and Blandy 2006). As communities expand and evolve, they can have positive or negative consequences. Planners, sprawl opponents, and urban sociologists often cite Portland, Oregon, as a city that successfully controls its growth and development. Portland thus serves as an appropriate case study for the various themes and problems discussed in this chapter.

CASE STUDY
Portland, Oregon

Virtually all cities in western North America have undergone boom periods that gobbled up the land, strained the infrastructure, and resulted in congestion, dirty air, and tax-strained school systems. Yet Portland is a healthy, vibrant city displaying few of the problems found in other urban places. Years ago, the city determined to defy the boom mentality and consciously planned its future, an effort that reflected Portland's long history of concern for urban quality of life and commitment to the common good (Abbott and Margheim 2008).

The Physical Setting

Portland stands in a choice location, surrounded by natural beauty and resources that greatly impressed its founders. Situated about 100 miles from the Pacific Ocean at the confluence of the Columbia and Willamette rivers, Portland is surrounded by a combination of water and lush greenery rarely found in urban settings. Snow-capped Mount Hood, Oregon's highest point (11,235 feet), is 48 miles away, and Mount Rainier, Mount St. Helens, and Mount Adams in Washington are all visible from the city. Also nearby are the spectacular Columbia Gorge and Multnomah Falls (850 feet). The city thus offers cosmopolitan living coupled with a variety of nearby outdoor activities, such as camping, canoeing, fishing, hiking, hunting, mountain climbing, and skiing.

Portland includes some of this outlying natural beauty within the city limits. Also known as "The City of Roses" for its large International Rose Test Gardens and the second-largest, all-floral parade in the United States (after the Tournament of Roses Parade in Pasadena), Portland has a magnificent park system, including some 200 green spaces. The city boasts the largest forested municipal park in the nation (5,000 acres) and the world's smallest dedicated park, Mills End Park (24 inches). Three other important areas are the elm-shaded South Park blocks in the downtown area, McCall Waterfront Park, and Washington Park—home of the Rose Test Gardens, where more than 500 varieties of roses bloom, as well as of the Oregon Zoo (known for its re-created African rain forest) and the Japanese Garden. Portland is also the only U.S. city to have an extinct volcano, Mount Tabor, within the city limits.

History

Several gold rushes drew immigrants along the Oregon Trail, stimulating Portland's early growth. Deep water and abundant natural resources soon made the settlement a popular and prosperous port and commercial center, handling the farm and forest produce of the Cascade Range, Willamette Valley, and Columbia Basin.

Like many Old West centers, Portland had its seamy side, with vice and violence figuring into its nineteenth-century scene. By the start of the twentieth century, however, Portland had become a tamer place, with the city eliminating most of the seedy activities of its busy waterfront. About this time, Simon Benson, a teetotaling lumber baron, walked through one of his mills and noticed the smell of alcohol on his workers' breath. When he asked why they drank in the middle of the day, they replied that there was no fresh drinking water to be found downtown. To resolve this situation, Benson built 20 freshwater drinking fountains in the downtown area. Beer consumption reportedly fell by 25 percent after the fountains were installed. Those water fountains—now known as Benson's Bubblers—still bubble for

locals and visitors alike along Portland's downtown streets. Yet Portlanders also still love their beer: The microbrewery was practically invented here, long before the concept gained popularity in other cities, and today, Portland boasts 40 breweries, more than any other city in the world (Oregon Brewers Guild 2011).

Urban Decline and Anti-Sprawl Planning

In the 1960s, Portland fell victim to the same ills afflicting other U.S. cities. Its economy nose-dived as industries closed. Shuttered mills and empty warehouses dotted the waterfront. People began moving away; unemployment rose; and those who remained found their standard of living sliding downward. One after another, downtown stores went belly up as the central business district slipped into a serious economic decline. The bus system lost so much business that it, too, went bankrupt.

The stage was set for Portland's revival, however, when Governor Tom McCall signed a new state law in 1973 requiring all of Oregon's cities to devise plans to limit urban sprawl and to protect farms, forests, and open space. Portland responded with the strictest laws in the nation. Ignoring lawsuits and pressures from commercial and development interests, Portland's leaders drew a line around their metropolitan area, banning any development beyond that point (much as London had done during its post–World War II reconstruction). The intent of this Urban Growth Boundary (UGB) was to force jobs, homes, and stores into a relatively compact area served by light rail, buses, and cars.

Automobiles, of course, are a major factor in the urban sprawl besetting most cities. Portland bucked the trend by tearing up its downtown riverfront freeway, and then converting the area, along with abandoned warehouse sites, into one of the city's most-used parks, named for Governor McCall. It also limited downtown parking spaces and created an award-winning mass transit system with North America's first modern streetcar system, the MAX light rail and the TriMet bus system.

Portland's popular Tom McCall Waterfront Park attracts pedestrians at all hours of the day and is the site of numerous special events, such as the Rose Festival, Dragon Boat Races, and annual carnival. Many U.S. cities have rediscovered and revitalized their waterfronts, attracting residents and tourists alike, thereby enhancing the quality of life and ambience of the city.

These systems are fully intermodal, meaning that passengers can easily switch from one to the other. In the 330-square-block area of downtown ("Fareless Square"), rides are free all day, every day.

An average of 315,500 riders commuted daily on buses or trains in 2010—making the city eighth per capita in ridership among U.S. cities. No Portlander is forced to ride buses, MAX trains, or WES trains, but 81 percent of those who own cars choose a public transit option instead. The MAX has been so successful that it keeps expanding. With a 52-mile MAX light-rail system, 14.7-mile WES commuter rail, and 79 bus lines, Portland is a national leader in transit ridership, its numbers increasing annually for all but one in the past 22 years (TriMet 2011). The city also encourages bike travel, placing brightly colored bikes and bike racks throughout the city for anyone to use; furthermore, its buses and trains are bike accessible.

Portland also enacted in 1972 its Downtown Plan inspired by the ideas of Jane Jacobs,

August Heckscher, William H. Whyte, and James Rouse (all of whom will be discussed in Chapter 14). Together with the 1988 Central City Plan, which updated and expanded the original goals, the city embarked on a still-continuing effort to maintain and enhance Portland's special identity and vitality. All new buildings, including garages, must be people friendly at street level. Blank walls are banned in favor of stores, offices, and eating establishments. Further, Portland set aside 1 percent of public construction funds to enhance the physical attractiveness of the area through outdoor public art.

In 1996, Portland enacted an even stricter plan for its three-county metropolitan area to handle an anticipated 500,000 new residents—in essence, another Portland—within the existing urban boundaries of its now 369-square-mile metropolitan borders over 20 years, including conversion to more apartment buildings and townhouses in previously single-family neighborhoods. To keep "big box" stores from springing up in industrial areas, Portland's plan also limited retail outlets to 60,000 square feet and, in a further effort to encourage use of mass transit, restricted the number of parking spaces a new store may have. With the greater Portland area's population now projected to reach 3.85 million by 2060, planners and officials are establishing rural reserves to preserve farmland and urban reserves to expand the UGB to control the anticipated population growth (Holman 2008).

In becoming the model for growth management in the United States, the city continues to follow the visionary guide that Lewis Mumford set for the Portland City Club in 1938, when he said, "I have seen a lot of scenery in my life, but I have seen nothing so tempting as a home for man than this Oregon country....You have the basis here for civilization on its highest scale....Have you got enough intelligence, imagination and co-operation among you to make the best use of these opportunities?" (quoted in City of Portland 2011:1).

Portland Today

In its transition from a timber town to a modern city with diverse specializations—such as wholesale trade, corporate management, high-tech firms, insurance, transportation, and wholesale trade—Portland also has become a model city, one that magazines often cite as one of the best cities in which to live. It has one of the best job markets in the country, even in recent recession years. It is home to more than 1,500 companies, from Intel—the largest private-sector employer, with 15,000 workers—to Nike, Providence Health Systems, Wells Fargo Bank, and dozens of small software firms (Portland Development Commission 2010).

Portland has a dense downtown, one that now contains about twice the work force it had three decades ago. Yet, despite its growth, Portland has retained its nineteenth-century, small-sized block design, which yields a pedestrian-friendly city core. The central business district is virtually a walker's paradise,

beckoning strollers to pass along the tree-lined streets on brick walkways and stop to enjoy fountains, benches, and small parks along the way. Pedestrians may shop at more than 1,100 retail stores, enjoy many outstanding coffee houses and restaurants, visit one of the city's microbreweries, or browse in any one of the numerous bookstores—including Powell's City of Books, the world's largest independent bookstore, which occupies an entire city block.

The city's economy is healthy, helped in large measure by the silicon forest of high-tech office campuses and factories—such as Intel and Hewlett-Packard—that grew inside the metro area. Major department stores—Nordstrom's and Saks Fifth Avenue—enhance the central business district. Recreational activities include comedy clubs, ballet, opera, symphonies, modern dance, theater, a planetarium, hockey and baseball teams, and the Portland Trail Blazers professional basketball team.

In terms of aesthetics, amenities, economy, land use, and planning, most people applaud Portland as "a city that works," a label once applied only to Toronto. Another reason that Portland works is its effective, efficient, and rider-friendly transit system that has encouraged residents to make it part of their preferred mode of transportation. In fact, many Portland areas developed *after* mass transit. A good example is the Lloyd district, where housing, office towers, and businesses sprouted up after light rail began running through it. Lloyd is a community with a balanced offering of jobs and housing, a place where people conveniently walk or bike around the area.

Will Portland, with a 2010 metropolitan population of 2.2 million, control its urban growth to protect the surrounding countryside? So far, the results are mixed. The city did increase its urban density within the UGB, but the amount of urbanized land within the entire metropolitan area also increased by 36 percent between 1980 and 2000, from 349 to 474 square miles—the ninth highest increase among 32 metropolitan areas (Jun 2004:1337). Much of the effect of Portland's

UGB was in the further suburbanization of adjoining counties, particularly in Clark County, Washington. The population projections for this region will surely test both Portland's resolve and its ability to balance big-city excitement and small-town charm.

SUMMARY

By the end of the twentieth century, four patterns of land development—sprawl, new cities, gated communities, and CIDs—became so widespread that they will most likely affect both urban and suburban lifestyles for at least several generations.

Sprawl refers to low-density land development beyond the edge of service and employment areas. Sprawl uses up large tracts of land (even when cities decline in population), increases the dependence of residents on automobiles, creates traffic congestion and pollution, and wastes natural resources. Solutions to sprawl include purchasing and preserving open space, adopting smart growth approaches, setting boundaries for urban growth, revitalizing existing cities and towns, and pursuing transit-oriented approaches.

The past three decades have seen the evolution of more than 200 new cities, located at the fringes of older cities, in North America and elsewhere. Their sprawling land use and auto dependency stand in marked contrast to the compact land use of older "walking" cities. Not clearly marked by territorial boundaries but usually situated near two major highways, new cities fall into three categories: uptown, boomer, and greenfield. Boomer cities are by far the most numerous and have three subcategories: strip, node, and pig-in-a-python. Essentially middle-class entities that cut across racial lines, edge cities have a shopping mall as their anchor point and provide more jobs, shops, and entertainment than older cities do.

Although gated communities first appeared in the United States during the late 1800s and a few other such exclusive locales during the 1950s, it was only in the late 1960s and 1970s that average Americans began to wall themselves off from society. The 1980s marked a rapid increase in gated communities, both in urban and suburban locales, and today, they contain about 11 million households. Categories of gated communities are lifestyle, prestige, and security zone. Critics charge that this residence pattern contributes to social fragmentation, does not really deter crime, and does not provide any greater sense of community.

CIDs may or may not include gated communities. These master-planned developments require monthly fees for shared amenities and membership in a homeowners' association with broad regulatory powers over residents—powers that critics charge invade both the privacy and the constitutional rights of individuals.

CONCLUSION

Although Canada has stronger central government controls over land use compared to the United States, both countries experienced sprawl, the development of new cities, and an increase in exclusive communities. Some areas have more successfully contained these growth patterns than others, but they predominate nonetheless. What do these popular choices bode for the future of older cities and for the social cohesiveness of Canadian and U.S. societies?

Generations ago, zoning and planning boards throughout Canada and the United States generated building and density code variances, so economic and social segregation are by no means new social phenomena. Gated communities go much further in their exclusivity, however, because they create physical barriers to entry. Moreover, they privatize not only individual space but also community space. The CIDs do even more: They privatize civic responsibilities (police protection) and communal services (street maintenance, entertainment, and recreation). This new development creates a private world that requires residents to share little with their neighbors outside the barricades—or even with the larger political system. The evolution of new cities and exclusive communities continues, and the dominance of these urban forms in North America is easily evident.

The evolution of new cities and exclusive communities continues, and the dominance of these urban forms in North America is easily evident. This, however, is only part of the urban picture. The next five chapters will examine how social scientists—sociologists, geographers, political economists, psychologists, and anthropologists—analyze cities as living entities. Reading these chapters, you will discover that the urban story gets even more interesting.

KEY TERMS

boomers (102)
common-interest developments (CIDs) (111)
edge cities (101)
eminent domain (96)
environmental sociology (95)
exurb (99)
gated communities (108)
greenfields (102)

lifestyle communities (109)
new cities (101)
political fragmentation (90)
prestige communities (109)
security-zone communities (109)
smart growth (94)
social impact analysis (94)
sprawl (87)
uptowns (102)

INTERNET ACTIVITIES

1. Go to *http://mobility.tamu.edu/ums/congestion-data/* to access the congestion data for any U.S. city.

2. Go to *http://www.commutesolutions.org/commute/cost-calculator/* to calculate how much it really costs you to drive your car.

CHAPTER 5

URBAN SOCIOLOGY
Classic and Modern Statements

THE EUROPEAN TRADITION: 1846–1921

Karl Marx and Friedrich Engels: From Barbarism to Civilization

Ferdinand Tönnies: From *Gemeinschaft* to *Gesellschaft*

Emile Durkheim: Mechanical and Organic Solidarity

Georg Simmel: The Mental Life of the Metropolis

Max Weber: The Historical and Comparative Study of Cities

The European Tradition: An Evaluation

URBAN SOCIOLOGY IN NORTH AMERICA: 1915–1970

Robert Park and Sociology at the University of Chicago

Louis Wirth and Urban Theory

Herbert Gans and the Urban Mosaic

Wirth and Gans: A Comparison

Claude Fischer and Subcultural Theory

CLASSIC THEORIES AND MODERN RESEARCH: MYTHS AND REALITIES

Tolerance in the City

Impersonality in the City

Density and Urban Pathology

Urban Malaise

New Directions in Urban Sociology

SUMMARY

CONCLUSION

KEY TERMS

INTERNET ACTIVITIES

Once humans learned to harness the machine, the resulting social upheaval dramatically changed virtually everything. Nowhere were these changes more pronounced than in European cities. The emerging factory system drew in unheard-of numbers of people, and the cities exploded in population. In 1816, for example, Germany had barely 2.5 million

CITYSCAPE

Working-Class Manchester, 1844

Friedrich Engels, the son of a wealthy German manufacturer, went to Manchester, England, in 1842 to learn the textile business. During his early years there, he gathered material for his first book, *The Condition of the Working Class in England*, first published in 1844. This excerpt from that work vividly describes Manchester's appalling slum conditions:

Here one is in an almost undisguised workingmen's quarter, for even the shops and beerhouses hardly take the trouble to exhibit a trifling degree of cleanliness. But all this is nothing in comparison with the courts and lanes which lie behind, to which access can be gained only through covered passages, in which no two human beings can pass at the same time. Of the irregular cramming together of dwellings in ways which defy all rational plan, of the tangle in which they are crowded literally one upon the other, it is impossible to convey an idea. And it is not the buildings surviving from the old times of Manchester which are to blame for this; the confusion has only recently reached its height when every scrap of space left by the old way of building has been filled up and patched over until not a foot of land is left to be further occupied.

...Right and left a multitude of covered passages lead from the main street into numerous courts, and he who turns in thither gets into a filth and disgusting grime, the equal of which is not to be found...and which contain unqualifiedly the most horrible dwellings which I have yet beheld. In these courts there stands directly at the entrance, at the end of the covered passage, a privy without a door, so dirty that the inhabitants can pass into and out of the court only by passing through foul pools of stagnant urine and excrement.... Below it on the river there are several tanneries which fill the whole neighborhood with the stench of animal putrefaction. Below Ducie Bridge the only entrance to most of the houses is by means of narrow, dirty stairs and over heaps of refuse and filth....

The view from [Ducie] Bridge... is characteristic for the whole district. At the bottom flows, or rather stagnates, the Irk, a narrow, coal-black, foul-smelling stream, full of debris and refuse, which it deposits on the shallower right bank. In dry weather, a long string of the most disgusting blackish-green slime pools are left standing on this bank, from the depths of which bubbles of miasmatic gas constantly arise and give forth a stench unendurable even on the bridge 40 or 50 feet above the surface of the stream....

Passing along a rough bank, among stakes and washing-lines, one penetrates into this chaos of small one-storied, one-roomed huts, in most of which there is no artificial floor; kitchen, living and sleeping-room all in one. In such a hole, scarcely five feet long by six broad, I found two beds—and such bedsteads and beds!—which, with a staircase and chimney-place, exactly filled the room. In several others I found absolutely nothing, while the door stood open, and the inhabitants leaned against it. Everywhere before the doors refuse and offal; that any sort of pavement lay underneath could not be seen but only felt, here and there, with the feet....

Enough! The whole side of the Irk is built in this way, a planless, knotted chaos of houses, more or less on the verge of uninhabitableness, whose unclean interiors fully correspond with their filthy external surroundings. And

urbanites; by 1895, that number had passed 13 million. During the nineteenth century, London grew from 861,000 to a monumental 6.5 million.

Imagine such radical change: Overwhelmed by incoming migrants, cities could not provide adequate food, safe housing, sanitary facilities, medical care, or enough jobs. Not surprisingly, poverty, disease, malnutrition, and crime increased. The city streets no doubt seemed chaotic, and this was the context in which urban sociology emerged. In the *Cityscape* box on

---

how could the people be clean with no proper opportunity for satisfying the most natural and ordinary wants? Privies are so rare here that they are either filled up every day, or are too remote for most of the inhabitants to use. How can people wash when they have only the dirty Irk water at hand, while pumps and water pipes can be found in decent parts of the city alone? In truth, it cannot be charged to the account of these helots of modern society if their dwellings are not more clean than the pig sties which are here and there to be seen among them. The landlords are not ashamed to let dwellings like the six or seven cellars on the quay directly below Scotland Bridge, the floors of which stand at least two feet below the low-water level of the Irk that flows not six feet away from them; or like the upper floor of the corner-house on the opposite shore directly above the bridge, where the ground-floor, utterly uninhabitable, stands deprived of all fittings for doors and windows, a case by no means rare in this region, when this open ground-floor is used as a privy by the whole neighbourhood for want of other facilities!

As for the rest, the filth, debris, and offal heaps, and the pools in the streets are common... [and] another feature most injurious to the cleanliness of the inhabitants, is the multitude of pigs walking about in all the alleys, rooting into the offal heaps, or kept imprisoned in small pens. Here, as in most of the working-men's quarters of Manchester, the pork-raisers rent the courts and build pig-pens in them. In almost every court one or even several such pens may be found, into which the inhabitants of the court throw all refuse and offal, whence the swine grow fat; and the atmosphere, confined on all four sides, is utterly corrupted by putrefying animal and vegetable substances....

Such is the Old Town of Manchester, and on re-reading my description, I am forced to admit that instead of being exaggerated, it is far from black enough to convey a true impression of the filth, ruin, and uninhabitableness, the defiance of all considerations of cleanliness, ventilation, and health which characterise the construction of this single district, containing at least 20 to 30 thousand inhabitants. And such a district exists in the heart of the second city of England, the first manufacturing city in the world. If any one wishes to see in how little space a human being can move, how little air—and such air!—he can breathe, how little of civilisation he may share and yet live, it is only necessary to travel hither....

The couple of hundred houses, which belong to old Manchester, have been long since abandoned by their original inhabitants; the industrial epoch alone has crammed into them the swarms of workers whom they now shelter; the industrial epoch alone has built up every spot between these old houses to win a covering for the masses whom it has conjured hither from the agricultural districts and from Ireland; the industrial epoch alone enables the owners of these cattle sheds to rent them for high prices to human beings, to plunder the poverty of the workers, to undermine the health of thousands, in order that they alone, the owners, may grow rich. In the industrial epoch alone has it become possible that the worker scarcely freed from feudal servitude could be used as mere material, a mere chattel; that he must let himself be crowded into a dwelling too bad for every other, which he for his hard-earned wages buys the right to let go utterly to ruin. This manufacture has achieved, which, without these workers, this poverty, this slavery could not have lived.

Source: Friedrich Engels, *The Condition of the Working Class in England*, trans. by Florence Kelly Wischenewetsky (Springfield, MA: Seven Treasures Publications, 2009), pp. 43–47. Originally published in 1844.

pages 120–121, Friedrich Engels (1820–1895) vividly describes the appalling slum conditions that industrialization brought to Manchester, England, that also existed elsewhere.

THE EUROPEAN TRADITION: 1846–1921

Sociology was born in Europe, a child of the Industrial Revolution. Given its start by August Comte (1798–1857), others who followed—including Karl Marx, Friedrich Engels, Ferdinand Tönnies, Emile Durkheim, Georg Simmel, and Max Weber—sought to explain the great transformation wrought by urbanization and industrialization.

Karl Marx and Friedrich Engels: From Barbarism to Civilization

Karl Marx (1818–1883) spent most of his adult life in England during the heyday of the Industrial Revolution, and he was among the first of the classical sociologists to analyze the transformation of European society.

Marx argued passionately that the economic structure of society is the foundation upon which rests the nature of the social, political, and spiritual aspects of life. By this, he meant that the economic system serves as the base on which the social institutions of family, religion, and the political system take form. Although he conceded many causes of social change, such as technological advances, Marx contended that societal transformation primarily results from *conflict* between those who control the process of economic production (capitalists) and those who supply the necessary labor (proletariat). Thus, to argue that social problems, such as poverty and unemployment, are the fault of individuals is a form of **false consciousness** because, as Marx saw it, the flaws of capitalism are the real causes of these and other problems.

Marx and his colleague Engels, however, held that the city has special importance. People, they said, live as "generic, tribal beings" in preindustrial, traditional societies. Only with the rise of the city does productive specialization begin to free individuals to act

on their own. It is in cities, then, that the state emerges so that people take on a political role as citizens, deliberately planning their own environment and using new scientific skills. Thus, to Marx and Engels, the rise of the city amounted to nothing less than a transition from barbarism to civilization:

> The greatest division of material and mental labour is the separation of town and country. The antagonism between town and country begins with the transition from barbarism to civilization, from tribe to State, from locality to nation, and runs through the whole history of civilization to the present day.... (1976:143; orig. 1846)

Even so, Marx and Engels made it clear that not every city was liberating in this way. Under what they called "Asiatic modes of production," some cities remained chained to the bonds of the primitive community—with its limited division of labor, common property, and lack of individualism. As a result, these cities depended entirely on the agricultural surplus, and the functions of these cities—whether military, religious, or bureaucratic—lacked the dynamic drive of a commercial economy.

Even in industrial cities, however, Marx and Engels held that the social evolution of humans was not yet complete, because a capitalist elite controlled the economy. Seeing firsthand the destructive aspects of early industrial capitalism, Marx and Engels believed that the historical process would further evolve, with a worldwide, anticapitalist revolution that would usher in socialism. Only in this final evolutionary phase would workers become aware of the real cause of their problems, unite, and act together to transform society into a new and just order.

Ferdinand Tönnies: From *Gemeinschaft* to *Gesellschaft*

In his masterwork, *Gemeinschaft and Gesellschaft* (2003; orig. 1887), the German sociologist Ferdinand Tönnies (1855–1936) described two contrasting types of human social life: ***gemeinschaft,*** or "community," which characterized

the small country village; and *gesellschaft,* or "association," which characterized the large city. Within the village, Tönnies maintained, social life forms a "living organism," in which people have an essential unity of purpose, work together for the common good, and are united by ties of family and neighborhood. Such is not the case in the city, in which social life is a "mechanical aggregate" characterized by disunity, rampant individualism, and selfishness—even hostility. Among city dwellers, he argued, a belief in the common good is rare, and ties of family and neighborhood have little significance.

The typology of *gemeinschaft* and *gesellschaft* has had a lasting influence on urban sociology because it was one of the first theories to understand human settlements by means of a continuum, as each "pole" of the continuum was a specific, "pure" type of settlement. Using such a formulation, one could classify any actual settlement at some point along the continuum as having a certain measure of *gemeinschaft* and a certain degree of *gesellschaft.*

In Tönnies's conceptions of *gemeinschaft* and *gesellschaft,* we can observe the influence of Karl Marx, a fact Tönnies openly acknowledged. In fact, Tönnies's idea of community finds its counterpart in the "primitive community" and "primitive mode of production" that Marx and Engels had written about 40 years earlier.

Gemeinschaft. Tönnies used the concept of *gemeinschaft* to characterize the rural village and surrounding land that its inhabitants worked communally. Characterizing their social life was an "intimate, private, and exclusive living together," sharing a common language and traditions. They recognized "common goods–common evils; common friends–common

Small-town America—such as here in Camden, Maine—is often idealized as today's closest approximation to a *gemeinschaft* society. In such locales, Main Street is exactly that—a place where most of the area's commercial activity, such as banking and retail sales, occurs and where people are likely to encounter known others with whom they can easily engage in personal conversations.

enemies" and carried within them a sense of "we-ness" and "our-ness." Thornton Wilder eloquently expressed an American version of "village togetherness" in his play *Our Town* (see the *Cityscape* box below).

Gesellschaft.   In the character of the modern city, Tönnies saw a wholly different style of life, in which the meaning of existence shifted from the group to the individual. Whereas *gemeinschaft* expresses a sense of "we-ness," *gesellschaft*

CITYSCAPE

Our Town: The Spirit of *Gemeinschaft*

Thornton Wilder's play *Our Town* is an acclaimed classic for many reasons, including its poignant portrayal of ordinary life-cycle events. To many people, however, its real charm lies in the insights it provides about life in a typical small town, where people live in what we may appropriately call a *gemeinschaft* community.

The play opens with the "Stage Manager" telling the audience about "our town," Grover's Corners, a small village in New Hampshire. He asks the audience to imagine the layout of the town and the life of its inhabitants.

To orient us, he points out what first appear to be differences—where, for example, the Polish immigrants live. They migrated to Grover's Corners to work in the mill, he tells us, as did a few "Canuck" families. Next, he tells us where the various churches are: Catholic, Congregationalist, Presbyterian, Methodist, Unitarian, and Baptist, in that order. He does not tell us that such differences may separate people's lives somewhat, but they by no means isolate them from one another. Almost intuitively, however, we know this—and it is reaffirmed through our learning that everyone here knows quite a bit about almost everyone else. They don't necessarily like everyone, or always approve of certain people's behavior—such as excessive drinking, for example—but there is nevertheless a closeness, an intimacy, among the people. This is how it also was

in the medieval city—Weber's ideal form of *gemeinschaft*—where class differences, disagreements, and even conflict existed within a close-knit community dominated by traditional values and continuity.

To help us understand some of this tradition and continuity, the Stage Manager informs us that the town's earliest tombstones—dating back to 1670—are engraved with names such as Grover, Cartright, Gibbs, and Hersey. These are the same family names as exist among the townspeople in 1901, the year during which the play takes place. Emphasizing this theme of stable relationships in daily life, he tells us, "On the whole, things don't change much around here." He also offers bits of other information—the non-existence of burglars and the daily visits by nearly everyone to the grocery store and the drug store on Main Street. These manifestations of mutual trust, daily routine, familiarity, and regular social interaction suggest a cohesiveness of community that is the essence of *gemeinschaft*.

As the play unfolds about this ordinary small town, one where "nobody remarkable ever come out of it, s'far as we know," we learn about more than just some events in the lives of George Gibbs and Emily Webb, or in the lives of their families, friends, and neighbors, alive or deceased. We witness the way that life once was in simpler times in North American small towns—a way of life that no doubt still exists in whatever small towns still remain. For most of us—living in a *gesellschaft* environment—it is a bygone reality, however. It is not ours.

is more rational, more calculating. By its very nature, *gesellschaft* conditions people to be concerned primarily with their own self-interest, to "look out for Number One" in contemporary terms. In *gemeinschaft*, the "natural" social institutions of kinship, neighborhood, and friendship are predominant; in *gesellschaft*, these forms of association tend to decline.

One way to distinguish easily the difference between *gemeinschaft* and *gesellschaft* is to consider the question, "When people ask, 'How are you?' do they really want to know?" Tönnies's communal relation—*gemeinschaft*—rests on broad concern for the other as a person, and such a question has significance beyond convention, beyond politeness. In the contrasting case—*gesellschaft*—we relate to each person in terms of a particular role and service provided, such as teacher, computer programmer, or sales clerk. In the city, we usually ask the question, "How are you?" only out of politeness: We don't know other people well, and what's more, we usually don't want to know them well.

Gemeinschaft **and** *Gesellschaft* **in History.** Tönnies believed that the study of European history revealed a gradual, and generally irreversible, displacement of *gemeinschaft* by *gesellschaft*. He saw the rapid rise of cities in Europe during the nineteenth century as the inevitable emergence of *gesellschaft* as the dominant form of social life. Although he did think it to be inevitable, Tönnies obviously did not think this transformation was altogether good: For him, the unity and human concern of *gemeinschaft* were gradually lost in *gesellschaft*.

Tönnies's ideas contain the beginning of a sociology of the city. He was among the first to see urban life as distinctive and worthy of study. Moreover, his use of contrasting, pure types is a pattern that numerous other urban sociologists followed.

Emile Durkheim: Mechanical and Organic Solidarity

Like Tönnies, the French sociologist Emile Durkheim (1858–1917) witnessed the urban revolution of the nineteenth century. He, too, developed a model of contrasting types: Mechanical solidarity and organic solidarity are analogous to Tönnies's *gemeinschaft* and *gesellschaft*, respectively.

Mechanical solidarity refers to social bonds based on likeness, on common belief and custom, common ritual and symbol. Such solidarity is "mechanical," because the people who participate in it—people living in family units, tribes, or small towns—are almost identical in major respects and so are united almost automatically, without thinking. Each family, tribe, or town is relatively self-sufficient and able to meet all of life's needs without dependence on other groups.

By contrast, **organic solidarity** describes a social order based on individual differences. Characteristic of modern societies, especially cities, organic solidarity rests on a complex division of labor, in which many different people specialize in many different occupations. Like the organs of the human body, people depend more on one another to meet various needs. A lawyer depends on other people—say, restaurant owners and grocers—to supply food and, therefore, is able to specialize in legal activity. Similarly, of course, the restaurant owner and the grocer need not study law, for the same reason.

In this complex division of labor, Durkheim saw the possibility of greater freedom and choice for all of society's inhabitants. Although Durkheim acknowledged the problems that cities might create—impersonality, alienation, disagreement, and conflict—he argued for the ultimate superiority of organic over mechanical solidarity: "[The] burden that we bear [in modern society] is in a different way less heavy than when the whole of society completely bears down upon us [as it does in rural society], and this leaves much more room for the free play of our initiative" (1997:85; orig. 1893).

Durkheim and Tönnies: A Comparison. While Durkheim agreed with Tönnies's conclusion that history was characterized by a movement from an emphasis on one type of social order to another—from mechanical solidarity (or *gemeinschaft*) to organic solidarity (or *gesellschaft*)—their ideas have important differences. For instance, Durkheim took exception to labeling only the tribal or rural environment alone as "natural." Rather, he asserted that life within the larger society is just as natural as that within small groupings.

This assertion reveals that Durkheim did not share Tönnies's negative view of modern society. In fact, Durkheim reversed Tönnies's terminology and labeled *gemeinschaft* "mechanical" and *gesellschaft* "organic." Although Tönnies saw little hope for truly humane life in the city, Durkheim was more optimistic. He saw the increasing division of labor characteristic of modern urban societies as undermining traditional social integration and creating a new form of social cohesion based on mutual interdependence. Contractual agreements among individuals or groups clearly express this interdependence. Still, Durkheim cautioned, no society can exist entirely on the basis of contract: At the very least, a moral foundation must exist that allows agreement on how to enter into and execute all contracts fairly.

Durkheim thus provides an important counterpoint to Tönnies. Although both theorists recognized that cities were associated with the growth of social differentiation and individuality, Tönnies feared the disintegration of the necessary bonds of social life, whereas Durkheim saw the possibility of continuing social cohesion and greater human development. The effects of the city on individuals, however, extend beyond these two visions.

Georg Simmel: The Mental Life of the Metropolis

Both Tönnies and Durkheim described the broad societal processes that produced the modern city. Although they made passing reference to the mental characteristics of city dwellers—the city dweller was more impersonal, more rational, and freer—they did not look systematically at the social psychology of city life. Another German, Georg Simmel (1858–1918), undertook that task.

Like his contemporaries, Simmel saw, in the rise of the modern world, a cause for concern: How was the individual to maintain a spirit of freedom and creativity in the midst of the city's "overwhelming social forces"? In his famous essay "The Metropolis and Mental Life" (1905), Simmel suggested that the personality would learn to "accommodate itself" to the urban scene.

The City's Characteristics. To Simmel, the unique trait of the modern city is the intensification of nervous stimuli with which the city dweller must cope. Unlike the rural setting, where "the rhythm of life and sensory imagery flows more slowly, more habitually, more evenly" (quoted in Farganis 2007:130), the city constantly bombards the individual with an enormous kaleidoscope of sights, sounds, and smells. To avoid being overwhelmed, the individual learns to discriminate such stimuli carefully—to tune in what is important and tune out what is irrelevant. In time, urbanites become more sophisticated and intellectual, more rational and calculating, than their rural counterparts.

Such rationality means that urbanites are highly attuned to time. Cities, Simmel observed, are marked by the ever-present clock and wristwatch. "If," he continued, "all the clocks and watches in Berlin would suddenly go wrong in different ways, even if only by 1 hour, all economic life and communication of the city would be disrupted for a long time" (quoted in Farganis 2007:131). In addition to the rational organization of time, Simmel saw the rationality of the city expressed in its advanced economic division of labor (here, he echoed Durkheim). Social life in the city is the interplay of specialists.

Perhaps the most powerful means of conveying the message of urban rationality, however, was Simmel's discussion about the importance of money. "The metropolis," he stated, "has always been the seat of a money economy" (quoted in Farganis 2007:130). Why is money so important in urban life? One reason is that the advanced division of labor requires a universal means of exchange. Money performs this critical function. As Simmel (1964:414) wrote, "Money is concerned only with what is common to all: It asks for the exchange value, it reduces all quality and individuality to the question: How much?"

Whenever we walk along a city street, we encounter an abundance of stimuli, far more than we can absorb. This intensification of nervous stimuli—from the many signs, sounds, movements, and crowds of people—forces us, says Simmel, to discriminate carefully, to tune in what is important and tune out what is not.

The Individual's Response.   How, asks Simmel, is the urbanite to behave in the midst of such powerful stimulation and unending demand for rational response? Or, on a more practical level, can you really stop to help everyone you see on the street who is in some sort of trouble? Simmel believed not. Consequently, he reasoned, the urbanite adapts to city life by developing what he called a "blasé" attitude, a social reserve or detachment. Put simply, in the city, we respond with our head rather than our heart. We learn to adopt a matter-of-fact attitude about the world around us. We simply don't care. We don't want to "get involved," as shown dramatically by the examples in the *Urban Living* box on page 128.

Even worse, Simmel speculated that the cultivated indifference necessary for living in the city may harden into a measured antagonism. "Indeed, if I do not deceive myself," he wrote, "the inner aspect of this outer reserve is not only indifference, but,

more often than we are aware, it is a slight aversion, a mutual strangeness and repulsion, which will break into hatred and fight at the moment of a closer contact, however caused" (quoted in Farganis 2007:133). Perhaps you can recall feeling some anger about the way someone unknown to you behaved in a city—someone who broke into a line ahead of you, for example, or who approached you and demanded spare change.

Like Durkheim, Simmel could see freedom in the separateness fostered by city living. The urbanite, he thought, could transcend the pettiness of daily routine and reach a new height of personal and spiritual development. Simmel also detected in the city's freedom, however, a haunting specter. "It is obviously only the obverse of this freedom," he wrote, "if, under certain circumstances, one nowhere feels as lonely and lost as in the metropolitan crowd" (quoted in Farganis 2007:134).

URBAN LIVING

Urban Apathy: Ignored Violent Attacks

In 1964, the murder of Kitty Genovese near her home in the Kew Gardens section of New York's Borough of Queens exploded into a major controversy when the *New York Times* reported that dozens of Ms. Genovese's "neighbors" had observed the attacker stab her repeatedly during a period of half an hour without coming to her aid—or even calling the police until after she was dead! In an editorial the following day, the *Times* posed a frightening question: "Does residence in a great city destroy all sense of personal responsibility for one's neighbors?" The death of Kitty Genovese thus became symbolic of the argument that the city was an unhealthy setting, lacking even a rudimentary sense of human community.

A 2007 *American Psychologist* article claimed that the media exaggerated about the number of eyewitnesses, some of whom did not actually see the attack, and at least one call went to the police during the attack. Nevertheless, sad intermingling of urban violence and apathy didn't stop with Kitty Genovese. In 1984, the same thing happened in Brooklyn. A woman was attacked in the Gowanus Apartments, a New York City housing project. As she was beaten, she began screaming and continued her cries for 20 minutes. Many heard her—no one came to her rescue. Finally, her assailants dragged her into the lobby of a building and shot her dead. It was only then that someone deigned to call the police (*New York Times*, December 3, 1984).

In 1983, similar indifference to victims of urban crime had surfaced in St. Louis. In one case, a man was robbed at gunpoint while dozens of people watched. When the man approached the onlookers afterward and asked why they hadn't helped him, they replied that they just "didn't want to get involved." In another incident three men attacked a woman at Busch Memorial Stadium during a Cardinals baseball game. She screamed for help. No one responded. Later, she said, "I was shocked more than hurt. I just sat there and screamed and not one soul stopped. I saw all these legs going by, and I thought about reaching out and grabbing somebody" (*New York Times*, August 18, 1983). Said Sgt. Frank Baricevic of the St. Louis Police about these disturbing incidents, "Police departments are only as good as the people they protect. If [people] don't want to get involved, if they don't want to cooperate, then we're in trouble" (*New York Times*, August 18, 1983).

Such incidents still happen from time to time. In October 2009, a 15-year-old girl leaving a high school homecoming dance in San Francisco was accosted by a group of teenagers, beaten, and gang raped. During the more than 2 hours of this attack, word spread and others at the dance came to see; some laughed and others took footage on their mobile phones. The girl was hospitalized and four teenagers subsequently arrested. So why didn't anyone come forward?

Many criminologists and psychologists suggest that such attacks as these—as well as college riots, lynchings, and white-collar crimes—aren't reported due to a problematic social phenomenon known as the bystander effect. Essentially, this theory holds that the larger the number of people involved in a situation, the more responsibility among the group becomes diffused. Witnesses will be less likely to report a crime because they reinforce each other with the notion that reporting the crime isn't necessary or else think another person in the crowd already reported the incident.

If you encountered this stranger lying unconscious on your campus or in the parking lot of a suburban mall, the probability is high that you would either help him or get help. In the city, however, where sleeping vagrants, drunks, and addicts often abound, you might well ignore him and avoid getting involved, as several people here are doing.

Feeling like a cog in a giant machine, some people maintain their sense of individuality in a city by doing something "odd," by "being different" and, thereby, standing out. This sense of alienation is what Simmel would use to explain the motivation for the graffiti craze in so many cities, a process that has defaced buildings, signs, subway trains, and public monuments. For many of these vandals, their "tags" raise them out of their anonymity and shout "I'm not just another face among a million others. I exist. I am here!"

In the end, then, Simmel appears to side more with Tönnies than with Durkheim in his evaluation of the city. Although Simmel depicted the city as the setting where the great historical contest between true human liberation and alienation would occur, his analysis left little doubt that he believed the second option would likely be victorious.

Max Weber: The Historical and Comparative Study of Cities

Tönnies, Durkheim, and Simmel all analyzed a single type of city. In other words, they developed their theories by "reading" the main trends of European urban history and the main elements of life in the cities they knew.

German sociologist Max Weber (1864–1920), however, believed any theory that took account of cities in only one part of the world and at one point in time was of limited value. This concern proved to be his major methodological contribution to urban sociology.

Die Stadt. Weber demonstrated his approach in his famous essay "*Die Stadt*" ("The City") (1968; orig. 1921). Surveying cities of Europe, the Middle East, India, and China,

Weber developed a definition of what he called the "full urban community":

> To constitute a full urban community, a settlement must display a relative predominance of trade–commercial relations, with the settlement as a whole displaying the following features: (1) a fortification; (2) a market; (3); a court of its own and at least partially autonomous law; (4) a related form of association; and (5) at least partial political autonomy. (1968:80–81)

This definition illustrates what Weber called an **ideal type,** a model constructed from real-world observation that highlights the crucial elements of some social phenomenon. Weber was well aware that many cities would not contain all the elements in his definition. In such cases, the city simply would not be a "full urban community" in his sense.

Let's examine the characteristics of such a community in more detail. First, Weber's urban community depends upon trade or commercial relations. In rural areas, people are more or less self-sufficient—growing their own food, providing their own clothing, and so on. Trade and commerce are of limited importance there, but not so in the city. Weber clearly agreed with Tönnies, Durkheim, and Simmel that economic self-sufficiency is nearly impossible in cities, where people are economically interdependent, linked by Durkheim's organic solidarity. Indeed, the economic aspects of city life are so important that a distinct mechanism of exchange—the market—evolved to facilitate them.

Second, an urban community is relatively autonomous. Weber specified that a true city has a court and law of its own and at least partial political autonomy. It also must be militarily self-sufficient, having a fortification system and army for self-defense if and when necessary. Such autonomy is essential if urban dwellers are to identify the city as theirs, as a place demanding their allegiance in the way that a small town receives the allegiance of its inhabitants.

Third, Weber said that the urban community must have "a related form of association." By this, he meant that city living must involve social relationships and organizations through which urbanites gain a sense of meaningful participation in the life of their city.

The "Full Urban Community" in History. Like Durkheim, Weber believed that cities could be positive and liberating forces in human life. Unlike Durkheim, Weber did not see much hope for twentieth-century cities. In fact, he thought only the fortified, self-sufficient cities of the medieval period deserved the title of "full urban community." Only in these cities did the commercial relations, autonomy, and social participation exist that he believed were the defining characteristics of urbanism.

With the rise of the nation to preeminence as a political entity during the seventeenth, eighteenth, and nineteenth centuries, Weber claimed that cities had lost their military and, to a large extent, their legal and political autonomy—necessary elements for identifying with the city as a psychological "home." People came to identify with other units of society—the nation, country, or business, or as recognized by Tönnies and Simmel, with themselves alone.

By recognizing medieval cities as examples of the full urban community, Weber hoped to show that "the good life" had existed in cities and might flourish again. Yet, by suggesting that a pinnacle of urban culture had been realized before in history, Weber implied that history might not necessarily be progressive.

The City and Culture. Weber stood apart from his colleagues, who tended to see the city itself as the cause for the distinguishing qualities of urban life. In contrast, Weber's analysis, fueled by his broad understanding of cities in other cultures and at different points in history, suggested that cities are intimately linked to larger processes—for example, to particular economic or political orientations. If a society's character is different, then the nature of its cities will be different. Thus, feudal or Chinese societies would not produce the same type of urban life that European industrial capitalism produces.

The European Tradition: An Evaluation

The ideas of Marx, Engels, Tönnies, Durkheim, Simmel, and Weber form the core of classical urban sociology and have had an enormous impact on the field ever since. It is important, however, to balance their contributions with their limitations.

Contributions. Perhaps the most important contribution of the classical theorists was their insistence that the city is an important object of sociological study. Marx, Engels, Tönnies, and Durkheim all clearly analyzed the contrasts between rural life and urban life. Simmel and Weber went a step further, by actually developing theories of how cities worked.

In addition, all six theorists recognized that *something distinctive exists about the city and the way of life it creates*. All saw the city as increasing human choice, emphasizing rationality, utilizing a complex division of labor, and creating a unique experience for its inhabitants. This concern with the city's

unique qualities has been a major focus of the discipline ever since, as the next section will demonstrate.

Taken together, these theorists also suggested the main concerns of the discipline. Marx and Engels emphasized economics and the problems of inequality and conflict. Tönnies, Durkheim, and Weber considered the social structure of the city. Simmel suggested the importance of the urban experience.

Finally, all six Europeans made the evaluation of cities a fundamental element in their work. Each made quite clear what he thought beneficial, and what he considered detrimental, in the city's ability to produce a humane life for its population (see Table 5–1).

Limitations. Four generations later, we can easily see how the central ideas of these theorists were an outgrowth of the times and the cities in which they lived. Cities were quickly replacing villages and countryside as the main arena of life. For all their excitement, however, one could hardly argue that these rapidly growing cities provided a good life for many of their

TABLE 5–1   Views of Theorists About the City

Theorist	Main Concept	Attitude
Marx and Engels	The city can free individuals to act on their own, but workers will need to overcome their exploitation.	Mostly optimistic
Tönnies	The inevitable emergence of *gesellschaft* will result in a loss of communal relationships.	Pessimistic
Durkheim	The *organic solidarity* found in a complex division of labor in the city can provide greater freedom and choice in life.	Optimistic
Simmel	City can be liberating but also alienating. Abundance of stimuli promotes a detached approach.	Mixed, mostly negative
Weber	Cities are linked to the larger societal context; medieval, not modern, cities better exemplified the full urban community.	Mixed
Park	Cities have potential to enhance the human experience; need to do on-site investigation of the city and its people.	Optimistic
Wirth	Size, density, and heterogeneity lead to segmented and depersonalized relationships, possible antisocial behavior.	Negative
Gans	City is actually a complex mosaic of many lifestyles and so individuals' urban experience varies accordingly.	Mixed, mostly positive
Fischer	Large cities have capacity to support many subcultures and thus strengthen in-group relationships.	Optimistic

inhabitants. Little wonder, then, that three of these theorists—Tönnies, Simmel, and Weber—saw the cities of their day as threats to long-cherished human values. Durkheim, Marx, and Engels, however, had mixed responses to the changing cities. Durkheim acknowledged the problems of alienation and conflict in the cities, but he also saw the ultimate superiority of the new industrial age. Marx and Engels saw not the city, but the capitalist economy, as a social evil.

Of course, one can only speculate how the theories of these men might have changed had they been able to witness the growth of suburbs, major efforts at urban planning, reforms in many of the most overtly exploitative practices of turn-of-the-century cities (such as child labor), the rise of labor unions, the civil rights movement, and the collapse a few decades ago of communism in an economically bankrupt Soviet Union and a fettered Eastern Europe.

Also, the theorists show some disagreement in their interpretations. The contrast between Tönnies and Durkheim is most instructive. Tönnies saw *gemeinschaft* as humane and *gesellschaft* as brutal. Using his terms of mechanical and organic solidarity, Durkheim reversed the interpretation: The tribal or country life was overpowering and undeveloped, but the life of the city was liberating and full of potential for development.

On another level, Simmel thought the social–psychological adaptations he studied were a product of the great city itself. He implied that all metropolises would produce similar mental processes. Weber, however, disagreed. He argued that only certain historical and cultural conditions produced the type of city that Simmel observed, most particularly the modern capitalist cities, and that other historical and cultural conditions would produce very different types of urban social–psychological adaptation.

Similarly, Marx and Engels maintained that the human condition in cities was the result of the economic structure. Therefore, a different economic system would produce a different city, with different patterns of social interaction.

With the evidence available at the time, it was impossible to judge such contradictory claims. Later chapters in this book, however, will show that Weber's position on this issue was closer to the truth.

URBAN SOCIOLOGY IN NORTH AMERICA: 1915–1970

About the time of World War I, urban sociology began to develop in the United States. From the outset, the discipline's character on this side of the Atlantic was somewhat different from that in Europe, with U.S. researchers showing greater concern with actually going out and exploring the city. At the same time, many of the themes in the European tradition reappeared in North American sociology.

The era in which sociology in this hemisphere developed is noteworthy. The early twentieth century in North America, as in Europe, was a period of industrialization and rapid urban growth. A mounting flow of immigrants—who settled mostly in cities—ensured that by 1920, the United States would become a predominantly urban society. In short, the Grover's Corners of North America (as described in the *Cityscape* box on page 124) were rapidly giving way to the expanding industrial metropolis.

No city typified this explosive growth better than Chicago. A crude outpost in 1830, Chicago was approaching a population of 2 million by 1900, and it was expanding both upward and outward. The first steel-frame building—a marvel of the age—opened its doors in Chicago in 1884, towering an incredible 10 stories above the ground! By the close of World War I, Chicago boasted a population of almost 3 million. Immigrants from Europe and migrants from the countryside were everywhere. Like hundreds of exploding North American cities, Chicago factories were belching the black, smoky "flag" of prosperity, creating their share of severe problems along the way. And it was in Chicago that the main elements of U.S. urban sociology took form.

Robert Park and Sociology at the University of Chicago

Although U.S. universities had offered courses in "social science" as early as 1865, sociology first gained intellectual respectability when the University of Chicago invited Albion W. Small (then president of Colby College) to found a sociology department in 1892 (Calhoun 2007). Within the next 30 years, the department attracted several notable scholars. One of the most outstanding was Robert Ezra Park (1864–1944).

Leaving a newspaper job in 1915 to join the department, Park established the first urban studies center in the United States. His interest in urban matters had both European and North American roots. During his early years, Park had studied with the Russian sociologist Bogdan Kistiakowski, who held much the same view of social change as Tönnies, and with Georg Simmel. Park was also deeply influenced by *The Shame of the Cities*, a book by U.S. journalist Lincoln Steffens (2009; orig. 1904) that suggested serious urban problems were everyone's responsibility. An excerpt from this critique appears in the *Urban Living* box on page 134.

Although Park was aware of both the bad and the good, without question, he had an almost unbounded fascination with the city. Not only did Park guide several generations of students in explorations of all aspects of Chicago, he also served as the first president of the Chicago Urban League. Dedicating his life to relentless personal exploration of the city, Park later wrote,

> I expect that I have actually covered more ground, tramping about in cities in different parts of the world, than any other living man. Out of all this I gained, among other things, a conception of the city, the community, and the region, not as geographical phenomenon [sic] merely, but as a kind of social organism. (2005, orig. published 1964, p. viii)

A Systematic Urban Sociology. Park presented the program he used to guide urban sociology at the University of Chicago in his classic article "The City: Suggestions for the Investigation of Human Behavior in the Urban Environment" (1984; orig. 1916). First, he argued that urban research must be conducted by disciplined observation—in much the same way that anthropologists studied other cultures. Second, he conceived of the city as a social organism, with distinct parts bound together by internal processes. Urban life was not chaos and disorder (stereotypes of Chicago during the Roaring Twenties notwithstanding) but, rather, tended toward an "orderly and typical grouping of its population and institutions" (1984:1). He wrote,

> Every great city has its racial colonies, like the Chinatowns of San Francisco and New York, the Little Sicily of Chicago, and the various other less pronounced types. In addition to these, most cities have their segregated vice districts... their rendezvous for criminals of various sorts. Every large city has its occupational suburbs, like the stockyards in Chicago, and its residential enclaves, like Brookline in Boston, the so-called "Gold Coast" in Chicago, Greenwich Village in New York, each of which has a size and character of a complete separate town, village, or city, except that its population is a select one. (1984:10)

This notion of the city's orderliness led Park to urge his students to develop detailed studies of all segments of the city's population—industrial workers, real-estate officials, and VIPs but also migrants, hobos, musicians, prostitutes, and dance hall workers. The conviction of linkage among all "parts and processes" of the city was at the heart of Park's new social science, which he termed "human, as distinguished from plant and animal, ecology" (1984:2). Finally, Park also saw the city as a "moral as well as a physical organization" (1984:4), and he carried evaluative judgments of urban living deep into his sociology.

Park's Image of the City. What was it about the city that so fascinated Park? First, like Weber, Park saw in the modern city a commercial structure that owed "its existence to the market place around which it sprang up" (1984:12). And like Marx, Weber, and Durkheim, he saw in modern city life a complex division of labor driven by industrial competition. Along with Tönnies, Park believed that this market

URBAN LIVING

The Shame of the Cities: Who's to Blame?

When I set out on my travels, an honest New Yorker told me honestly that I would find that the Irish, the Catholic Irish, were at the bottom of it all everywhere. The first city I went to was St. Louis, a German city. The next was Minneapolis, a Scandinavian city, with a leadership of New Englanders. Then came Pittsburgh, Scotch Presbyterian, and that was what my New York friend was. "Ah, but they are all foreign populations," I heard. The next city was Philadelphia, the purest American community of all, and the most hopeless. And after that came Chicago and New York, both mongrelbred, but the one a triumph of reform, the other the best example of good government that I had seen. The "foreign element" excuse is one of the hypocritical lies that save us from the clear sight of ourselves....

When I set out to describe the corrupt systems of certain typical cities, I meant to show simply how the people were deceived and betrayed. But in the very first study—St. Louis—the startling truth lay bare that corruption was not merely political; it was financial, commercial, social; the ramifications of boodle were so complex, various,

and far-reaching that one mind could hardly grasp them....

And it's all a moral weakness; a weakness right where we think we are strongest. Oh, we are good—on Sunday, and we are "fearfully patriotic" on the Fourth of July. But the bribe we pay to the janitor to prefer our interests to the landlord's, is the little brother of the bribe passed to the alderman to sell a city street, and the father of the air-brake stock assigned to the president of the railroad to have this life-saving invention adopted on his road. We are pathetically proud of our democratic institutions and our republican form of government, of our grand Constitution and our just laws. We are a free and sovereign people, we govern ourselves and the government is ours. But that is the point. We are responsible, not our leaders, since we follow them. We let them divert our loyalty from the United States to some "party"; we let them boss the party and turn our municipal democracies into autocracies and our republican nation into a plutocracy. We cheat our government and we let our leaders loot it, and we let them wheedle and bribe our sovereignty from us....The people are not innocent.

Source: Lincoln Steffens, *The Shame of the Cities* (Charleston, SC: BiblioBazaar, 2009), pp. 11–12, 14. Originally published in 1904.

dominance would result in the steady erosion of traditional ways of life. The past emphasis on "family ties, local associations...caste, and status" would yield inevitably to a *gesellschaft*-like system "based on occupation and vocational interests" (1984:13–14).

Second, Park perceived the city as increasingly characterized by *formal social structures* best exemplified by large-scale bureaucracies, such as police departments, courts, and welfare agencies. In time, he reasoned, these

would replace the more "informal" means, such as neighborhood interaction, by which people historically had organized their everyday lives. Similarly, politics would develop a more formalized tone. Park contended that

the form of government which had its origin in the town meetings and was well suited to the needs of the small community based on primary relations is not suitable to the government of the changing and heterogeneous populations of cities of three or four millions. (1984:33)

The city dweller, unable to take account of all the issues at stake in the operation of a complex city, would have to rely on either political or civic organizations run by party bosses or concerned citizens for information and action.

As an ex-newspaperman, Park was not likely to omit the media from his description of the formalization of city life. Replacing the face-to-face oral network by which information flowed in the village—*gossip* is the more precise, if less scholarly, term—was reliance on impersonal mass media. Such was the significance of the city newspaper, and soon after that, radio, television, and eventually, the Internet.

The third dimension of Park's image of the city, showing the effects of his studies with Simmel, was his emphasis on the psychosocial dimension of urban life. Park suggested that life within the city would become *less sentimental* and *more rational.* Deep-seated sentiments and prejudices would give way to calculation based on self-interest. At the same time, however, Park was aware that the erosion of traditional sentimental ties in the city might give rise to new social bonds in the form of interest groups. In this, Park's argument has a clear Durkheimian quality: Ties based on likenesses (mechanical solidarity) give way to bonds based on the interdependence of differentiated parts (organic solidarity).

Freedom and Tolerance in the City.   As a social reformer, Park recognized that the modern city revealed problem upon problem, but like Durkheim, Park was fascinated with what he saw to be the possibilities for freedom and tolerance in the city. He wrote,

> The attraction of the metropolis is due in part to the fact that in the long run every individual finds somewhere among the varied manifestations of city life the sort of environment in which he expands and feels at ease; he finds, in short, the moral climate in which his peculiar nature obtains the stimulations that bring his innate dispositions to full and free expression. It is, I suspect, motives of this kind which have their basis, not in interest or even in sentiment, but in something more fundamental and primitive which drove many, if not most, of the young men and young women from the security of their homes in the country into the big, booming confusion and excitement of city life. (1984:41)

In short, what Tönnies saw as a steady disorganization, Park saw as the potential for greater human experience. He continued,

> In a small community it is the normal man, the man without eccentricity or genius who seems most likely to succeed. The small community often tolerates eccentricity. The city rewards it. Neither the criminal, the defective, nor the genius has the same opportunity to develop his innate disposition in a small town that he invariably finds in a great city. (1984:41)

As Park suggested, urbanites typically respond to people's eccentricities with great tolerance if not amusement, sometimes even to the point of ignoring them. The "Naked Cowboy," as he bills himself, is a frequent sight in New York's Times Square area. Regardless of the weather, he appears just as you see him, posing, singing, and playing his guitar.

Summing up, we see in the ideas of Robert Park a new emphasis on doing urban research and on-site investigation of the city, quite unlike the more abstract theorizing of Tönnies, Durkheim, and Simmel and the historical work of Marx, Engels, and Weber. Park's main contribution was his demand that we get out there and see how the city actually works.

Louis Wirth and Urban Theory

If the European theorists produced much theory but conducted little actual research, early Chicago sociologists did just the opposite. During the 20 years following the publication of Park's urban studies program in 1916, Chicago sociologists produced a wealth of primarily descriptive studies. Not until 1938 was this imbalance rectified, when Louis Wirth (1897–1952) published his famous essay, "Urbanism as a Way of Life," in which he identified **urbanism** as that "distinctive...mode of life which is associated with the growth of cities" (p. 1). To Wirth, the city worked its magic by forcing people to encounter one another in a special way: In the city, large numbers of heterogeneous people come into contact within dense settings, generating a new type of behavior and awareness—an urban way of life. City dwellers become rational, self-interested, specialized, somewhat reserved, and highly tolerant.

Wirth's great contribution to urban sociology was taking the insights by previous urban sociologists and then organizing them, patiently and systematically, into the first truly sociological theory of the city. By a *theory* of the city, we mean that Wirth began his analysis by isolating several factors he argued were *universal social characteristics* of the city. He then proceeded to deduce systematically the consequences of these factors for the character of urban social life. He said, in effect, as all good theorists do, that if this condition is present, then that condition will result.

Wirth began with a definition of the city as a (1) large, (2) dense, permanent settlement with (3) socially and culturally heterogeneous people. Let's examine what conditions of urban social life follow from each of these elements.

Population Size or Scale. Wirth believed, first, that large population size by itself produces great diversity in the cultural and occupational characteristics of a city. This diversity partly results from (1) the simple fact that larger numbers of people coming together logically increase the potential differentiation among themselves and (2) the migration of diverse groups to the city (as in Chicago, where Wirth was writing). Second, the condition of cultural diversity produced by a large population has the additional effect of creating a need for formal control structures, such as a legal system. Third, a large, differentiated population supports the proliferation of specialization, and an occupational structure based on differing occupations, such as artist, politician, and cabdriver, emerges. Fourth, specialization organizes human relationships more on an "interest-specific" basis, which Wirth described as "social segmentalization":

> Characteristically, urbanites meet one another in highly segmental roles. They are, to be sure, dependent on more people for the satisfactions of their life needs than are rural people...but they are less dependent upon particular persons, and their dependence upon others is confined to a highly fractionalized aspect of the other's round of activity. This is essentially what is meant by saying that the city is characterized by secondary rather than primary contacts. The contacts of the city may indeed be face-to-face, but they are nevertheless impersonal, superficial, transitory, and segmental. (Wirth and Reiss 1981:71)

In other words, rather than understanding others in terms of who they are, the urbanite typically conceives of others in terms of what they do—in terms of their roles and what they can do to advance one's own ends. The qualities of rationality and sophistication are simply additional ways of suggesting that urban ties become, in essence, relationships of utility. Lastly, even with the stabilizing constraint provided by formal controls and professional codes of conduct, Wirth could not escape the conclusion that large population size carried with it the possibility of disorganization and disintegration, a fear shared by all the European theorists.

Population Density. The consequence of population density is to *intensify* the effects of large population size on social life. Rather than manifesting the quality of sameness that one might associate with the countryside, the city separates into a mosaic of readily identifiable regions or districts. (Here, we can see the direct influence of Wirth's teacher, Park.) Both economic forces, such as differing land values, and social processes, such as attraction and avoidance based on race and ethnicity, tend to produce fairly distinct neighborhoods and districts.

For example, many U.S. cities have a predominantly Italian area, such as Boston's North End; a Chinatown, such as San Francisco's; and a high-income area, such as Chicago's North Shore. Similarly, major cities frequently have a garment district and a financial district, such as New York's Wall Street. Wirth called this process of separating the city into districts "ecological specialization." The more common term today is **natural areas,** revealing that such places evolve as unplanned clusters.

Density also operates on the social–psychological level. Exposed to "glaring contrasts… splendor and squalor…riches and poverty," Wirth (1938:14) argued, city dwellers develop mental shorthand—a mental mapping of the city, its regions, and its inhabitants. This insight (drawn from Simmel) helps us understand the urbanite's tendency toward stereotypical and categorical thinking, as well as his or her reliance on grasping the city through visible symbols and uniforms, such as clothing, cars, and fashionable street addresses. The implication is clear—population density fosters a loss of sensitivity to the "more personal aspects" of others—and suggests why people in the city sometimes seem to be "cold and heartless."

As suggested earlier by Durkheim and Simmel, Wirth (1938:15) contended that the "juxtaposition of divergent personalities and modes of life" results in a *greater toleration of differences.* In addition, physical closeness tends to *increase social distance* among urbanites. Forced into physical proximity, city dwellers characteristically close off or tune out those

In a city, we are almost never alone, but we may well be lonely. Most face-to-face contacts are impersonal, superficial, and segmental. Research, however, shows that although city dwellers have far more of these secondary relationships, they also have just as many meaningful primary relationships as non-urbanites.

around them. (On a small scale, this happens when people, busily chatting, enter a crowded elevator and abruptly become silent, staring at the numbers on the floor indicator.)

Again echoing Simmel, Wirth suggested that high density might cause an increase in antisocial behavior. Wirth (1938:16) posited, "The necessary movement of great numbers of individuals in a congested habitat causes friction and irritation."

Heterogeneity. In completing his theory of urbanism, Wirth suggested several consequences of social difference or heterogeneity.

First, "social interaction among such a variety of personality types in the urban milieu tends to break down the rigidity of caste lines and to complicate the class structure" (p. 16). Consequently, a heightened social mobility tends to exist in the city, because the inertia of family background weakens under the force of personal achievement.

Second, physical movement typically accompanies social mobility. "Overwhelmingly the city dweller is not a homeowner and since a transitory habitat does not generate binding traditions and sentiments, only rarely is he a true neighbor" (p. 17). (Remember Kitty Genovese in the *Urban Living* box on page 128.)

Finally, the concentration of diverse people leads inevitably to further depersonalization. Against a background of commercial mass production and consumption, an emphasis on money erodes personal relations, thus echoing a similar view of the city by Simmel.

These three dimensions of Wirth's theory—size, density, and heterogeneity of population—interact to produce the unique way of life that he termed *urbanism*. Clearly, Wirth was pessimistic about urbanism as a way of life. He saw the city as an acid that, over time, dissolved traditional values and undermined the formation of institutions and meaningful relationships. Like Park, he touted the possibilities for greater freedom in the city, but he also worried that urbanism's positive aspects would inevitably be compromised by the disorganization he saw in turbulent Chicago. Only by massive efforts at urban planning, Wirth imagined, could people create a humane urban environment.

As Wirth understood it, the essence of urban living was being *cosmopolitan*—literally, "belonging to all the world." Robert Merton (1968:447–53) drew a useful distinction between "localite" and "cosmopolitan" lifestyles. The life of the localite centers in the immediate area. Typically born in the area where they live, localites are bound up within social relations and life commitments encapsulated within that specific territory. Cosmopolites, on the other hand, are more rootless and think in terms of wider possibilities. They are more likely to move on (perhaps to new jobs

or a better home). Whether rich or poor, cosmopolites display a certain degree of detachment, have a somewhat blasé attitude toward their immediate surroundings, and show a sophistication in matters of taste and friendship not typical of localites. Although Merton acknowledged that cosmopolites and localites could exist anywhere, the cosmopolitan attitude exists more frequently among city dwellers and the localite attitude is more typical in small towns or rural areas.

Are cosmopolitanism and localism, however, set off as clearly as Merton thought they were? For one thing, cosmopolitanism is found in many small college towns, such as Gambier, Ohio. Then, too, Chicago, Toronto, and most other large cities contain residential enclaves where localism abounds—Hispanic neighborhoods, Vietnamese communities, perhaps a Chinatown, or maybe an old upper-class area. If this is the case, then possibly the city doesn't produce a distinctive way of life at all. Or so argues Herbert Gans, the most outspoken critic of the Wirthian position.

Herbert Gans and the Urban Mosaic

Herbert Gans (1991) contended that the city is a mosaic of many lifestyles, only some of which resemble the cosmopolitanism described by Wirth. Furthermore, he argued that Wirth's key variables—size of population, density, and social heterogeneity—cannot account for most of these lifestyles, and that his macrosocial analysis does not explain how most city dwellers see their own lives.

Exploring lifestyle diversity in North American cities, Gans identified four types of urban lifestyles: (1) the cosmopolites, (2) the unmarried or childless, (3) the ethnic villagers, and (4) the deprived or trapped. **Cosmopolites** are highly educated, urban sophisticates who choose to live in the city because of its wide range of activities, experiences, and social contacts. They include intellectuals, artists, musicians, writers, and students. The second urban lifestyle, the unmarried or childless, frequently overlaps with the cosmopolite category. It includes single adults or couples without children and/or people whose children are grown up and now on their own. The **ethnic villagers,** often first- and second-generation, working-class residents, show almost none of the so-called typical urban characteristics noted by Wirth. Instead, they sustain many rural life patterns in the city by claiming a local area, emphasizing traditional religious beliefs and family ties, and displaying suspicion of outsiders. Gans's remaining category—the deprived or trapped—includes the poor, the handicapped, those in broken family situations, and those of non-white racial backgrounds who wish to move from deteriorating neighborhoods but lack the financial means to do so.

Wirth and Gans: A Comparison

We must not be too quick to accept the negative judgments from Wirth and other Chicago sociologists. Like their European colleagues, Chicago sociologists were responding to one kind of city—namely, a North American city moving into the high gear of industrialization. Neglecting historical or cross-cultural comparisons limited the significance of their work. How would their evaluation of the urban environment have changed had they, like Weber, looked at other cities in history or in a cross-cultural perspective?

Chicago sociology may be skewed for yet another reason. Park's insistence regarding on-site study, coupled with his interest in urban disorganization and problems, led him and his colleagues to concentrate on the "seamy side" of city life. A glance at the group's classic publications, brilliant though many of them are, reveals this bias: Nels Anderson, *The Hobo* (1923); Ernest Mowner, *Family Disorganization* (1927); Harvey Zorbaugh, *The Gold Coast and the Slum* (1928); Frederich Thrasher, *The Gang* (1929); Clifford Shaw and Henry McKay, *Social Factors in Juvenile Delinquency* (1931); Paul Cressey, *The Taxi Dance Hall* (1932); Norman Hayner, *Hotel Life* (1936); and Edwin H. Sutherland, *The Professional Thief* (1937). Although many other aspects of city urban life exist for possible exploration, Wirth based his theory heavily on the evidence supplied by such studies.

Limitations notwithstanding, the Chicago group made great contributions. Park deserves lasting credit for his rejection of armchair theorizing in favor of studying the city firsthand, and Wirth deserves credit for the first true urban theory, which became a persuasive document that dominated the field for the next 20 years. All in all, Chicago sociologists were almost solely responsible for the early growth of urban sociology in the United States (Bulmer 1986).

Gans's contribution, on the other hand, was to call our attention to the complexities of urban life. Our previous discussion of prominent urban "types" as discerned by Gans is only a partial list. Obviously, there are countless variations of all these lifestyles—and that is the point. So many urban lifestyles exist that it makes little sense to claim, as Wirth did, that the city produces a relatively uniform type of human being.

The rather hard-nosed, calculating person who Wirth conceptualized as the typical urban dweller does appear—most frequently in the cosmopolite and unmarried or childless categories. Even among these people, however, Wirth's variables of population size, density, and heterogeneity appear to have limited effect. For instance, many cosmopolites can buy the space they need to fend off what they believe is excessive density, just as many ethnic villagers positively thrive in high-density neighborhoods. Population size or scale may indeed increase the number of secondary or segmented relationships, said Gans, but most individuals maintain as many primary relationships as non-city dwellers. Moreover, since their social focus is on their neighborhood, family, co-workers, and co-religionists, no increased social distance occurs because of population density or increased depersonalization because of heterogeneity, as Wirth maintained. Instead, Gans noted, city residents function in smaller social worlds at home, work, and play, enjoying the same life satisfactions as others of their social class in other environments.

Thus, while cities may act on us in much the way that Wirth claimed, we need to keep several limitations in mind. First, few lifestyles found in cities exist only there, and second, the determinants of these lifestyles are largely people's general social class characteristics rather than the city itself (an area we will explore more fully in Chapter 10). That is, cosmopolites live as they do because they are affluent and highly educated; likewise, the lives of the deprived and the trapped reflect poverty, a lack of skills and schooling, and often enough, racial or ethnic discrimination. We can make a similar argument for any other lifestyle on the list.

Wirth's mistake was in generalizing too much from the urban conditions of the time during which he lived. Observing the incredibly rapid growth of North American and European cities early in the twentieth century, Wirth became convinced the city was a powerful force that would come to dominate human life. A generation later, Gans and others could see that this simply wasn't happening: Urban diversity continued to flourish. Today, we can conclude that *urbanization*—the clustering of population in some areas—does not necessarily generate *urbanism*—a single, distinctive way of life.

Claude Fischer and Subcultural Theory

A third approach both accepts and rejects various elements offered by Wirth and Gans. While agreeing with Wirth that something *is* different about the city and its people, Claude S. Fischer (1975, 1995), in what he called a *subcultural theory of urbanism,* rejected Wirth's main point by insisting that the urban milieu strengthens, not destroys, group relationships. Fischer also disagrees with Gans that the different urban lifestyles are incidental, because particular groups of people—for example, ethnic minorities, artistic avant-garde, and professionals—choose to live in the cities and, consequently, their lifestyles typify cities (1995:544).

Fischer—in arguing against the determinist view of Wirth—suggested that the size, density, and heterogeneity of cities are positive factors that promote cohesion, and they are not negative elements causing alienation,

disorganization, or depersonalization. Once in a city, people with similar, even unconventional, interests, values, or behaviors seek out each other for their own meeting places and habitats. As they gather in sufficient size and density, they attain **critical mass,** that level needed to generate self-sustaining momentum. These subcultures, based on shared traits, flourish in large cities and attract still more like-minded people (Fischer 1995:545). Examples include the entertainment community in Hollywood, the country music people in Nashville, and the gay community in Philadelphia. Such specialized places rarely exist in non-urban areas, because the critical mass of people of any one type simply isn't there (often because they have moved to a city in order to benefit from precisely the critical mass that Fischer describes).

Since cities are both more heterogeneous and more populous than other places, these subcultures will develop there more frequently, and with greater intensity, than in less urban areas. A large city magnifies these effects in a special way. Its diversity brings urban residents into far more contact with people from different subcultures than can occur in a smaller municipality. Unable to achieve a critical mass, people in non-urban areas with unconventional interests are more likely to remain fragmented, unable to form subcultures, and thus experience the negative consequences that Wirth envisioned happening in cities.

Interestingly, says Fischer, increased contact also leads to a mutual influence through cultural diffusion—for example, hip hop and rap music moving out of urban black culture and into mainstream urban culture. As elements of the atypical subculture infiltrate the wider urban society, the city develops an unconventionality in comparison to other settings (Fischer 1995: 545–46).

In short, Fischer's theory maintains that Wirth's size, density, and heterogeneity of cities are what generate the social dynamics to produce intense subcultures, as characterized by Gans, leading, in turn, to diffusion into the general characteristics of urban dwellers.

For city residents, the streets are the "rivers of life," where people-watching and social interaction are the everyday norm. This privatization of public space—setting up crates or chairs on the sidewalk, sitting on front stoops or a bench, playing games, or holding a street fair—is the urban equivalent to the suburbanites' front and back yards combined, and it is often much more interesting.

CLASSIC THEORIES AND MODERN RESEARCH: MYTHS AND REALITIES

Is the city a heaven or a hell? Is it a place where the best attributes of human life emerge or where people inevitably "go bad"? The seventeenth-century English poet Abraham Cowley thought he knew the answer when he wrote, "God the first garden made, and the first city, Cain." Was he right? The weight of the classic tradition—European and North American—is on Cowley's side; despite qualifiers and hopeful asides, only a rare few were mostly optimistic. Wirth's theory symbolizes this verdict. On the one hand, he suggested that people in the city are more tolerant, but on the other hand, he asserted that city people are impersonal and detached from meaningful relationships. Wirth concluded that the city tends toward social pathology (crime, violence, and mental illness), a tendency only made worse as urban density increases.

Are these observations correct? More than seven decades have passed since the publication of Wirth's urban theory. Since then, a great many other social scientists have investigated cities and urban life and gathered additional evidence.

Tolerance in the City

Early urban theory contended that the characteristic aloofness and social diversity of the city produced an atmosphere of tolerance, in contrast to the jealous parochialism of the village and small town. Most researchers who looked closely at the relationship between urban life and tolerance concluded that a greater tolerance of others' lifestyles and attitudes is, in fact, more prevalent in cities than in rural areas. These findings persist both across time and across different measures of tolerance, even when taking into account such related factors as education and income (Carter, et al. 2005).

One factor that may lend itself to greater tolerance in the city is migration. One research study found that tolerance increased among those moving to a city, regardless of the size of the destination community (Wilson 1991). Perhaps geographical mobility—moving to a more heterogeneous locale—also enhances one's mental mobility in relating to strangers.

Impersonality in the City

The dominant characteristics of urban relationships, concluded most of the classical theorists, would be loneliness, indifference, and anonymity. At its most basic level, this argument is built on numerical logic. As the number of people interacting increases, attention becomes distributed more broadly, and so impersonality inevitably must rise. Wirth summarized this argument by saying, "Increase in the number of inhabitants of a community beyond a few hundred is bound to limit the possibility of each member of the community knowing all the others personally" (1964:70).

Yet the "urban anonymity" thesis fails to recognize that many urbanites are not the lonely lot that Wirth and others implied. For example, as early as the 1940s, William F. Whyte's *Street Corner Society* (1993; orig. 1943), a study of an Italian immigrant area in a slum district of Boston, revealed the existence of strong family, neighborhood, and friendship ties. Soon after, other studies (Bell and Boat 1957; Bruce 1970; Greer 1998) confirmed that primary ties were not incompatible with city living. Indeed, in some areas of the city— ethnic neighborhoods, for example—such ties appear to be as intense and intimate as any in rural areas. These self-segregated but close-knit communities enable residents, often with limited proficiency in English, to rely on one another and avoid whatever interethnic prejudice may exist against them (Bouma-Doff 2007).

Ethnicity is not the only bond among urban dwellers. Kinship, occupation, lifestyle, and other personal attributes also form the basis for group ties. For example, many cities contain districts of college students, elderly people, homosexuals, artists and musicians, and wealthy socialites. More broadly, people with interests in common, wherever they may live, may remain in close contact with one another through an interactional network, using the Internet, telephone, restaurants and bars, and special meeting places.

Perhaps, however, these are the exceptions. What of the lonely crowd living in all those high-rises, the people who don't know any of their neighbors? Doesn't Wirth's theory accurately describe them? Recent research suggests that this notion, too, may be exaggerated. The fact that one does not necessarily know (or want to know) one's urban neighbors does not mean that the urban dweller has no personal relationships. Indeed, what seems to be significant about the urban environment is not the lack of ties of attachment but, rather, how these ties vary. That is, cities seem to encourage alternative types of relationships more than other environments do. Also, it is important to understand that the neighborhood context affects the neighboring ties (Guest, et al. 2006). For example, residents in a luxury high-rise who engage in similar activities—for example, dog walking, health club, or patronizing the arts—may develop closer relationships with neighbors more easily compared with those in a low-income high-rise who may be less likely to engage in shared activities.

In the city, however, meaningful personal relationships are not dependent on a limited geographic area like a small town; a sense of community may evolve through social networks that integrate or separate, include or exclude, others in meaningful personal relations, communication, and exchanges (Piselli 2007). Think of urban people you know. Most have friends and relatives, but not always in the same building or even the same neighborhood. Strong informal ties can result from ongoing face-to-face connections with friends and relatives anywhere, and so no real difference in a sense of well-being typically exists among urban, suburban, and rural residents (Mair and Thivierge-Rikard 2010).

Without question, the proliferation of cell phones has had a dramatic impact on our social interactions. By providing more frequent personal conversations without the constraints of access to a landline phone, cell phones enable greater connectivity among people. Such an enhancement of social networking is an important factor in negating the potential impersonality of the city.

Urban neighboring, however, can vary markedly—from active and intense relationships to impersonal nods, because of the diversity of neighborhood types (Talen 2006a). Working-class people, for example, usually live in "tighter" neighborhoods, whereas upper-middle-class people typically have networks of friends dispersed over a wide area. Similarly, people with children tend to be more "localized" in their orientation compared with single people "on the move." Such differing interaction patterns reinforce the view of Herbert Gans (1962), who, in a stinging critique, concluded that the "impersonality" Wirth saw in the city *as a whole* characterized, at best, only the most poverty-stricken and down-and-out of the city's residents. Neighborhood context or environment—including residential stability, levels of affluence, mixed land use, and degree of upkeep in the area—is an important

consideration for the type of neighbor ties that prevail in urban life (Guest, et al. 2006).

Other means for urban connectedness abound. The telephone and the Internet make possible extensive contact without face-to-face interaction. Consider, too, the proliferation in cities of voluntary associations, such as film societies, singles bars, health and natural food centers, karate clubs, meditation and yoga centers, and physical fitness centers. Participants living throughout the urban area often establish primary relationships with one another in such organizations. Urbanization can thus encourage all kinds of non-kin social ties, possibly segmented by activity but nonetheless developed through choice and shared interests (Curtis, et al. 2003).

Wirth's mistake, and that of other classical theorists, was to allow the most visible aspects of city life, its *public* demeanor, to become the basis of his theory about urban living in general. Although, following Park, he did acknowledge the neighborhood element in city life, he tended to focus his attention on "street behavior," where he saw the hustling, competing, and apparently lonely crowd. By not examining more closely the *private* lives of the city's citizens, however, he inadvertently distorted urban life into a stereotype of impersonality.

We come, then, to the conclusion that the early analysts took abstract constructions, such as *gemeinschaft* and *gesellschaft*, or mechanical and organic solidarity, as comparable to such real, concrete settings as actual villages and cities. The overall social order of the city may place greater emphasis on *gesellschaft*, and the village more toward *gemeinschaft*, but it is incorrect to assume that either *gemeinschaft* or *gesellschaft* exists in any absolute, concrete sense. An important difference exists between the statement that one commonly sees more strangers in cities and the statement that cities are impersonal. In some ways, they are; in other ways, they most certainly are not.

Density and Urban Pathology

Perhaps the most provocative idea put forth by the classical theorists—particularly Simmel, Park, and Wirth—was that human beings react to increasing population density with psychological disorder, such as mental illness, or antisocial behavior, such as crime or aggression.

One source of support for this hypothesis is our own common sense. Probably all of us have experienced some measure of frustration and aggression in crowded settings—trying to push our way through the turnstile at a stadium, or fuming as hundreds of cars coalesce in a massive traffic jam. It is easy to assume that the place where this occurs—the city—is responsible for our feelings. But are we reacting to the condition of urban crowding, or are we merely experiencing the same sense of frustration that we might feel if our car broke down along a lonely country road?

A second source of the alleged linkage between density and pathology is research that appears to have some bearing on the quality of urban life. For example, John B. Calhoun (1962; Ramsden 2011) found that in rat populations, overcrowding produced a reaction he termed a "behavioral sink"—an environment in which aborted pregnancies, higher infant mortality, homosexuality, and cannibalism abounded. Calhoun made no attempt to suggest that human beings would respond in a similar fashion to conditions of crowding, but Edward Hall argued that such a connection was not only conceivable but also accurately described urban life. "The implosion of the world population into cities everywhere," Hall wrote, "is creating a series of destructive behavioral sinks more lethal than the hydrogen bomb" (1990:165; orig. 1966).

Hall realized that different groups of people—whites and blacks, for example—might have different cultural expectations about spatial behavior. Yet he appeared to believe that all these different reactions have a biological basis, and that the human species, like rats, has a genetically determined need for a certain amount of space. He asserted that any transgression of this built-in barrier—for example, a crowded apartment or a dense city block—would likely result in abnormal behavior.

One problem with this argument is that no one has been able to locate any genetic code for spatial behavior in humans. Without evidence of such linkage, projecting onto human beings who are living in cities what we know about animal pathology and overcrowding is highly questionable. It may well be, for example, that people's perceived needs for space are entirely *learned*, and that they react negatively to violations of their learned spatial expectations much as they would to an insult against their learned religious beliefs.

Hall also points to the high incidence of "social problems" (addiction and crime) in densely settled, low-income areas of the city. Yet addiction, crime, and crowding may appear together because of some other factor or factors such as poverty, unemployment, and/or racial discrimination. Moreover, subsequent research that considered such factors found little or no evidence that crowding had any of the negative effects suggested by Hall

(Evans, et al. 2001; Lepore and Evans 1991; Rousseau and Standing 1995).

Urbanites do contend with crowded conditions, such as crammed elevators and subway cars, rambunctious cabdrivers, the frustrations of traffic, and intense competition for parking spaces. People, however, have one distinct advantage over rats: superior adaptability. First, we live and work on many levels, so we are not continually milling together on the ground like rats. Second, we have codes of urban conduct that guide us to wait in line for the bus, to keep to the right when walking, and to alternate whether we merge or stop at red lights when driving. Cities have bicycle, foot, and horse paths connecting parks and open space that make movement safer and more pleasant. Freeways permit faster travel to and from downtowns, while traffic circles, one-way streets, and coordinated traffic lights ease the traffic flow in crowded areas.

Still, what of the fact that some researchers find crowding does heighten aggression in some people? Perhaps an analogy with listening to music may explain the matter. When you listen to music that you like, turning the volume louder enhances the experience. If you don't like that music, however, an increase in volume only makes the experience more unpleasant. For people with a good support system and a high level of life satisfaction, crowding has little effect, except perhaps temporarily affecting one's mood. On the other hand, if people are already in unpleasant circumstances, have aggressive tendencies, or feel alienated or frustrated, then crowding may well generate further negative reactions. The point is that crowding, in and of itself, does not result in pathological behavior; rather, other factors people bring to the situation may have that effect (Bonnes, et al. 1991; Franklin, et al. 2006; Tartaro and Levy 2007).

Finally, in a global context, we see that culture also mediates the experience of city living, influencing how we are affected by population density. For example, Mumbai (Bombay), India, has an extremely high rate of urban crowding but an extremely low homicide rate (National Crime Records Bureau 2010). To cite another example, Turks—whose cultural behavior favors closer interpersonal interaction—do not respond negatively to increased crowding conditions, but given Islamic codes about women in public, they do have coping strategies regarding gender and shared urban space (Mills 2007).

Urban Malaise

A last hypothesis put forth by most of the classical theorists concerned "urban malaise." They suggested that conditions of density aside, the urban environment created loneliness, depression, and anxiety more readily than other types of settlement. Research studies over the past 40 years, however, have found no significant difference in the mental health of urban versus non-urban residents. Instead, such variables as education, income, and self-perceived resources were more closely associated with mental health and depression (Bagby, et al. 2008; Eshbaugh, et al. 2006; Link and Phalen 1995; Roxburgh 2009; Srole 1972).

Also, as suggested earlier, the neighborhood context—such as people's health, social cohesion, or perceptions of problems—is a key factor (Pampalon, et al. 2007). If urban residents are socioeconomically disadvantaged, they are more likely to be mistrusting, especially if their neighborhoods show signs of physical decay and disorder like graffiti, vandalism, abandoned buildings, noise, crime, or drug use (Kruger, et al. 2007; Mair, et al. 2010). In Baltimore, for example, researchers found that neighborhood violent crime had a direct impact on residents' depressive symptoms (Curry, et al. 2008).

Apparently, then, the city, in and of itself, does not create greater psychological distress, but problem neighborhoods do. Elsewhere, the higher population density of urban places may well have positive effects, such as making more people socially accessible to each other. When it comes to city dwellers dealing with their environment, it seems, as the *Urban Living* box on page 146 suggests, that the vast majority do quite well.

Overall, little evidence supports many of the specific claims made by the classical theorists about urban living. The city is clearly not

URBAN LIVING

How City Dwellers Cope—and Cope Well

How is it possible, given the fast pace and obvious stresses of urban life, that city residents can maintain mental health comparable to that of country folks? One explanation offered by experts: The relationship between stress and mental and physical pathology is dependent not so much on the nature of the stress as on the individual's perception of it. The brain has been called a stimulus-reduction system—a means to reduce, in order to comprehend, the nearly infinite number of stimuli that reach the senses at any given moment. It is an aspect of the brain that seems to be tailor-made for life in the city.

An out-of-towner caught in midtown Manhattan at rush hour, for example, may feel under enormous pressure and strain, but New Yorkers, with their stimulus-reduction mechanism operating at full steam, hardly feel any special stress at all. By the same token, the big-city residents may ignore the loud, the profane, the drunk, and the demented—phenomena that might compromise the mental equilibrium of the uninitiated.

Related statistics support such thinking. Diala and Muntaner (2003) found that rural men reported more mood and anxiety disorders than urban men, perhaps a function of diminishing resources (steady, high-paying jobs) or increasing financial strain, particularly among whites, who comprise a majority of rural residents. No differences by place of residence existed among females. The National Center for Health Statistics (2007) conducted a national self-report survey of negative affect items related to anxiety, depression, and stress among city, suburban, and rural residents. The findings showed little difference in the prevalence of negative mood in metropolitan areas (7.7 percent) versus non-metropolitan areas (7.9 percent). A slightly higher prevalence of negative mood, however, occurred among city residents (8 percent) compared to rural residents (7 percent), but this is hardly sufficient to claim that urbanites experience more stress in their lives than those living outside the city.

a heaven, but neither is it the hell that some thought it to be. The city is more tolerant than other types of settlement, is not as impersonal as many thought it was, and does not produce greater rates of malaise or other pathologies. On the basis of what we now know, there is reason for more optimism than that shown by most classical theorists. The reality, in short, is more complex—and more hopeful—than the myths.

New Directions in Urban Sociology

All this research produced a shift in the way that many urbanists approach their subject matter, because the classic hypotheses about the city advanced by Simmel, Wirth, and others wilted under careful scrutiny. By the 1980s, research disproved some theories and required serious modification of others. Emerging from the rubble was something first called "the new urban sociology" (Walton 1981) and now often identified as "critical urban sociology," although that designation is by no means unanimous.

Instead of an emphasis on the role of technology or urban ecology, this newer approach directs attention toward social conflict, inequality, and change as they affect cities, and it does so within a global context. No single theory captures critical urban sociology, although neo-Marxists and conflict theorists predominate. We will explore this important approach in Chapter 7. Before we do so, however, we will first examine its predecessor, the urban ecological approach.

SUMMARY

The context in which urban sociology emerged was one of remarkable change. Indeed, the ferment associated with the Industrial Revolution was responsible for sociologists noticing the city as an object of study in the first place. What have we learned from them?

First, they suggested specific aspects of the city for urban sociological focus, and second, they attempted to analyze the nature of the city in general. In the latter instance, they had both successes and failures. On the positive side, they correctly saw elements of social life in the city not prominent elsewhere. They saw more specialized occupations, more formalized interaction patterns, more rationality, and a more rapid tempo of life. On the negative side, they erred in some of their specific claims about the nature of the city. They were right about the existence of greater tolerance, but they exaggerated the city's impersonality. Also, they apparently were wrong in their generalizations about urban pathology. The context in which these sociologists wrote played a significant role in their misperceptions. Seeing cities growing by millions of inhabitants with seemingly unconquerable problems, they reasoned that the city itself must be the cause of these ills.

Another limitation is the narrowness of all early theory. Marx and Engels saw cross-cultural differences in how civilization evolved in Western compared with Eastern cities, but they concentrated on the economic system as the basis for all attributes of an urban society. Tönnies and Durkheim employed the comparison of oppositional types but did not consider the city in concrete historical settings. Simmel added the social–psychological dimension, although he, too, considered only cities of one time and place. Weber argued for the importance of exploring cities in cross-cultural and historical perspective but wrote little about the modern city (perhaps a subtle way of indicating that he—like all his colleagues except Durkheim—also saw it in a negative light).

Park and Wirth both provided breakthroughs. Park demanded that on-site city research be an integral part of urban sociology, thereby providing the mechanism for getting beyond the surface impressions of the urban environment. Ironically, however, his focus on urban problems and his lack of a comparative historical frame led him to the same negative conclusions about the city as others. Wirth then tried to build a theory of the city by linking the suggestions of his colleagues. A major difficulty was that he built his theory on Park's skewed database and the somewhat misleading evaluations of the European tradition. Wirth's hypothesis was that the city's unique ecological characteristics—large numbers, density, and social heterogeneity—produce a single characteristic lifestyle. Refuting Wirth's hypothesis, Gans argued that sociocultural characteristics, such as class, age, gender, and race, are the real architects of people's lives.

Countering this claim, Fischer replied that Wirth was not all wrong. In his view, the city's ecological traits do affect people's lives, but not in quite the way that Wirth suggested. Rather than producing an effect directly, Fischer argued, large numbers, density, and heterogeneity intensify other characteristics in order to produce pronounced urban lifestyles.

Recent research refuted many of the specific claims made by Wirth and his colleagues. Early work saw the city as the cause of greater impersonality, poorer mental health, and various forms of stressful or pathological behavior. Modern research, however, has revealed that such broad generalizations are false; the neighborhood context is the best indicator of the attitudes and perceptions of its residents. The new urban sociology, which emerged in the wake of the classical urbanists' failing theories, sees the city as existing in a complex historical, cultural, and economic global setting.

CONCLUSION

What we take from the classical tradition is its interest in urban studies per se and its combined model of urban analysis. A useful urban analysis must (1) examine the city in both its social–structural and psychosocial dimensions, (2) study actual cities in historical and comparative perspectives, (3) be aware that no overarching theory of the city can explain urban life, and (4) evaluate cities in terms of the quality of human life. It will be the task of the remaining chapters to do justice to this tradition.

KEY TERMS

cosmopolites (138)
critical mass (140)
ethnic villagers (139)
false consciousness (122)
gemeinschaft (122)
gesellschaft (123)

ideal type (130)
mechanical solidarity (125)
natural areas (137)
organic solidarity (125)
urbanism (136)

INTERNET ACTIVITIES

1. You can find a clear, succinct list that explains classical and contemporary urban sociology theories at *http://stmarys.ca/~evanderveen/wvdv/Urban_sociology/urban_sociology_theories.htm/*.

2. A comprehensive and readable introduction to the Chicago School of Sociology can be found at *http://userpages.umbc.edu/~lutters/pubs/1996_SWLNote96-1_Lutters,Ackerman.pdf*.

CHAPTER 6

SPATIAL PERSPECTIVES
Making Sense of Space

URBAN GEOGRAPHY
    The Location of Cities
    Why Cities Are Where They Are
THE SHAPE OF THE CITY
    The Radiocentric City
    The Gridiron City
URBAN ECOLOGY
    Concentric Zones
    Sectors
    Multiple Nuclei
    Limitations
SOCIAL AREA ANALYSIS AND MAPPING
    GIS Mapping

Limitations
THE LOS ANGELES SCHOOL:
    POSTMODERNISM
    Building Blocks
    Main Arguments
    Limitations
SUMMARY
CONCLUSION
KEY TERMS
INTERNET ACTIVITIES

If you happen to be endowed with topographical curiosity, the hills of San Francisco fill you with an irresistible desire to walk to the top of each one of them. Whoever laid the town out took the conventional checkerboard pattern of streets and without the slightest regard for the laws of gravity planked it down blind on an irregular peninsula that was a confusion of steep slopes and sandhills. The result is exhilarating. Wherever you step out on the street there's a hilltop in one direction or the other. From the top of each hill you get a view and the sight of more hills to the right and left and ahead that offer the prospect of still broader views. The process goes on indefinitely. You can't help making your way painfully to the top of each hill just to see what you can see....

This one is Nob Hill.... Ahead of me the hill rises higher and breaks into a bit of blue sky. Sun shines on a block of white houses at the top. Shiny as a toy fresh from a Christmas tree, a little cable car is crawling up it. Back of me under an indigo blue of mist are shadowed roofs and streets and tall buildings with wisps of fog about them, and beyond, fading off into the foggy sky, stretches the long horizontal of the Bay Bridge.

Better go back now and start about my business. The trouble is that down the hill to the right I've caught sight of accented green roofs and curved gables painted jade green and vermillion. That must be in Chinatown. Of course the thing to do is take a turn through Chinatown on the way down toward the business district....

John Dos Passos, "San Francisco
Looks West"

In a basic sense, cities are things—complex physical entities. Cities exist within geographic and climatic settings that naturally shape them. The hands and minds of human beings, of course, also play a part as people react to a city's physical setting. San Francisco is an excellent example—people started with an exciting geography and a pleasant climate, and then added a host of their own creations (diverse neighborhoods, clattering cable cars, a lively Chinatown, and bridges that span sparkling waters) to produce a particularly enticing urban experience. While San Francisco has its unique features, all cities have a distinct "personality," which is at least partly shaped by the physical layout. This chapter explores that interrelationship between a city and its physical setting.

URBAN GEOGRAPHY

Some cities, like San Francisco, straddle hills. Others, like St. Louis, Tucson, or Oklahoma City, stretch across flat plains. No matter what the topography of the land, however, a city's design reflects its physical environment.

Take, for example, San Francisco's massive neighbor 500 miles to the south—Los Angeles. Originally a Spanish mission outpost, for decades Los Angeles remained a series of scattered communities surrounded by mountains in the relatively flat, near-desert region of California's southwest.

In the 1920s, however, coincident with the rise of the movie industry, Los Angeles began to grow rapidly. As its population surged, the city became a bowl-shaped collection of outlying suburban communities. At first, public transport—electric trains and streetcars—linked the new settlements with Los Angeles. With mass production of the automobile, however, public transportation ridership swiftly declined; commuters preferred the convenience and privacy of driving themselves to and from the city. This heavy reliance on automobiles fostered ever-expanding urban sprawl throughout the region and gave us Los Angeles's incredible freeways. Said Jan Morris,

These remain the city's grandest and most exciting artifacts. Snaky, sinuous, undulating, high on stilts or sunk in cuttings, they are like so many concrete tentacles, winding themselves around each block, each district, burrowing, evading, clambering, clasping every corner of the metropolis as if they are squeezing it all together to make the parts stick. They are inescapable, not just visually, but emotionally. They are always there, generally a few blocks away; they enter everyone's lives, and seem to dominate all arrangements. (2003:230)

As Los Angeles expanded, people settled the mountains themselves, with streets "forever ribbing and probing further into [the] perimeter hills, twisting like rising water ever higher, ever deeper into their canyons, and sometimes bursting through to the deserts beyond" (Morris 2003:229).

Ironically, the city's increasing population, heavy reliance on the automobile, and geography combined to produce an unexpected but monumental environmental problem: smog. Although Los Angeles is by no means the only city beset by this threat to health, its smog problem has been particularly serious, because the surrounding hills trap noxious fumes in the bowl-shaped region where most of the city's people live. In 2010, Los Angeles again had the nation's worst ozone pollution (Huffington Post 2010). Despite its air-quality problems, the Los Angeles area continues to grow—from about 3 million in 1980 to more than 3.8 million in 2010—and the automobile still reigns supreme.

The Location of Cities

Geography and climate, then, provide the physical conditions to which urbanites must adapt. In fact, certain physical characteristics usually determine whether an area even becomes a city at all.

Look at Figure 6–1, which shows the geographical location of the 40 most populous urban areas in North America. All but a few are located on waterways. They are either seaports (Los Angeles, New York, and Vancouver), lakeports (Chicago, Milwaukee, and Toronto), or on major rivers (Cleveland, Memphis, and Montreal). The advantage of such sites for stimulating trade is enormous. Even cities not on important waterways

(Dallas, Denver, Fort Worth, and Phoenix), however, are where they are because, at least initially, there were enough streams and lakes to support their populations.

The sole exception to the waterway thesis is Atlanta. Yet its site, too, was determined by a geographical consideration: In the 1840s, because of its centrality to the rest of the South, Atlanta was selected as the southern terminus of the Western and Atlantic Railroad. Thus, even Atlanta illustrates that environmental considerations play a key role in locating a city. With this in mind, we will consider briefly the sites of five other cities: Houston, Miami, Montreal, Salt Lake City, and Washington, D.C. What products and activities do you associate with each?

Houston. Located near the East Texas oil fields, this city has been booming since the 1950s. Between 1970 and 2011, its population grew by 57 percent, growing from 1.2 to

FIGURE 6–1 Geographical Location of the Most Populous North American Cities, 2010
Source: U.S. Census Bureau, Statistics Canada.

2.1 million. Because of oil—every major oil company has offices in Houston—and cheap shipping of oil via the Gulf of Mexico, the city has the nation's second-busiest port in the country (after New York) and the nation's largest port in international tonnage. Considered by many as the "energy capital of the world," Houston is home to more than 5,000 energy-related companies. It is also home to the largest medical center in the world (52,000 employees) and second only to New York City as home to the headquarters of *Fortune* 500 companies (Houston 2011).

Miami. Although Miami is a port, this city is best known for tourism and as a mecca for retirement. The winter climate is ideal, with temperatures hovering near the 80s, nearly unlimited sun, and endless beaches. "Fun in the Sun" is the city's motto. In recent years, however, Miami has become a major market for specialized goods, primarily because of its large Cuban American community. Because of the Cubans' economic success, the city has become attractive to wealthy Latin Americans. They fly to Miami, stay in or near Little Havana, speak nothing but Spanish, and buy numerous U.S. goods—clothes, computers, stereos—from Cuban merchants at prices much lower than they would pay at home. Such visitors are crucial to maintaining the city's economy (Miami 2011).

Montreal. Built on and around a mountain slope at the junction of the St. Lawrence and Ottawa River systems in the southwestern corner of Quebec, Montreal is North America's fifteenth-largest metropolitan area, containing 3.9 million people (Statistics Canada 2011a). Although Montreal has a strong, diversified industrial base, service dominates its economy. Many national and international service companies, especially in the banking, culture, finance, telecommunications, and transportation sectors, are headquartered there. Montreal also accounts for one-fourth of all corporate research and development expenditures in Canada (twice its share by population). Long, cold winters have prompted an expansive and delightful underground network of shops, restaurants, and theaters

that people enjoy year-round. Montreal also is home to six professional sports franchises, a ballet company, an opera company, and a symphony orchestra (Montreal 2011).

Salt Lake City. Situated at the foot of a mountain range near the forbidding and barren Great Salt Lake in Utah, Salt Lake City might seem an unlikely urban site. The Mormons, however, thought otherwise. Migrating westward in the mid-nineteenth century, looking for a place where they could practice their religion freely, the Mormon leaders saw the Salt Lake region as the place that God had set aside for them. In a sense, the region's remoteness was the key to its founding. As it turned out, the location is more hospitable than it appeared at first glance. Salt Lake City became a point of rest and departure for westward migration, and the salt proved to be a valuable resource. The city became the only area within hundreds of miles able to support a large metropolitan population, numbering well over 1.2 million in 2011 (Salt Lake City 2011).

Washington, D.C. In the capital of the United States, we have a very different case. Its founders did not look on Washington, D.C., as an economic center. The issue was politics—a wish to avoid choosing between Philadelphia and New York as the permanent U.S. capital. In addition, Washington, D.C., represented a symbolic link between two great regions: the North and the South. Once the Potomac River basin (water again!) became the site of the nation's capital city, the emergence of the United States as a world power generated a vast government bureaucracy, hundreds of foreign embassies, countless special interest groups, and a vast array of hotels, restaurants, and national landmarks that make this urban area unique. Its metropolitan population grew from 4.1 million in 1990 to about 5.5 million in 2010 (U.S. Census Bureau 2011c).

Why Cities Are Where They Are

Environmental, economic, and social factors play a role in creating an urban area. On the environmental side, any setting, in order to

Geography has played a large role in Montreal's existence. The junction of the St. Lawrence and Ottawa rivers affected its location choice, and the sloping mountain terrain dictated the layout of its expansion. Its long, cold winters influenced the building of an extensive underground mall of shops, restaurants, and theaters that are as lively as any above-ground complex found elsewhere.

become a city, must fulfill a number of basic conditions.

Environment.   First and foremost, the location must be a *minimally hospitable environment.* It cannot be infested with disease-producing organisms, be subject to extreme heat or cold, or exist on a flood plain. On that last point, the 2008 flooding of more than 400 city blocks in Cedar Rapids, Iowa, of 80 percent of New Orleans in 2005 and major flooding of towns in the Northeast, Midwest, and Mississippi River Valley in 2011 were the results of an unusual congruence of weather conditions (see the *Cityscape* box on page 154).

In addition, any city requires *access to adequate supplies of food, water, and building materials.* This is not to say that cities cannot overcome the limitations of some sites, but settlers' ingenuity and technology must be up to the task. For example, gas and oil heat have made winter survival in northern cities possible for millions, just as air conditioning moderates the extreme heat of southern urban areas. Similarly, water and other resources can be imported. Las Vegas, situated in the Nevada desert, is perhaps the best example of an "impossible" city brought to life by modern technology.

Economics.   Another driving force in situating cities is economics. Port cities, for example, usually thrive as centers of trade and commerce. Alfred Weber (1868–1958), the younger brother of Max Weber, formulated an **industrial location theory** that helps explain the locale of many industrial cities. He suggested that an industry would locate where the transportation costs of both raw materials and the final product would be the lowest. If the raw material, such as metal ore, weighed more, then the processing plant would locate closer to its source; if the final product, such as bottled beer, weighed more, then the processing plant would locate closer to its market.

CITYSCAPE

New Orleans: Paying the Price for Its Location

Its strategic location at the mouth of the Mississippi River allowed New Orleans to emerge as an important break-of-bulk city, making its port the fifth busiest in the country. Farmers in the Midwest send their crops down the river in barges, and the grains are then loaded onto 5,000 ships annually from 60 nations. As a result, the United States is the world's largest exporter of corn, soybeans, and wheat. It is not just agricultural exports, however, that make New Orleans so important. The Mississippi River links into the Ohio, Illinois, and Missouri rivers, and manufacturers from across the Midwest depend on 50,000 inland river barges to carry their products to world export through New Orleans. Leading imports include cocoa beans, coffee, rubber, and steel. In addition, more than 700,000 passengers sail through the port on cruise lines each year (Port of New Orleans 2011). Thus, the devastation to the city in 2005 as a result of Hurricane Katrina had a negative ripple effect on the economy and people far beyond the impacted area.

Moreover, the city's vulnerability to flooding—long known to government officials but never effectively countered—became painfully obvious to even the most casual observer. Although the older part of the city was built on higher ground, as New Orleans expanded, development occurred elsewhere. As a result, major portions of the city are below sea level, protected by levees and seawalls designed to guard against storm surges about 20 feet high. In 2005, however, the damage was done by much higher surges from the Gulf's waters and by the waters of Lake Pontchartrain at the city's northern boundary. This oval-shaped lake is about 40 miles wide from east to west, and it measures about 24 miles from north to south. The heavy rains and winds of Hurricane Katrina were more than the lake's levees could withstand, and in several places, they broke, flooding about 80 percent of the city. The loss of life (1,500 dead), the struggles of the survivors, and the devastation of families, homes, businesses, and personal belongings touched people's hearts everywhere.

More than 800,000 people, mostly black, were forced to relocate, creating one of the greatest scatterings of people in U.S. history. Other cities—most notably Houston, which took in about 200,000 evacuees, giving them housing and health care and offering job fairs—stepped in to offer a place to stay. Since then, some evacuees returned, but many others chose to stay where they were. As a result, New Orleans, which had a 2005 pre-Katrina population of 452,000, dropped 31 percent to 344,000 in 2010, and the black population (those mostly displaced by flooding) declined from two-thirds to 60 percent (Census Bureau 2011a).

Water was the chief reason for the settlement, growth, and destruction of New Orleans. Although still not completely rebuilt, the city's strategic location as a port assures that New Orleans will continue as America's gateway to the global market. The levees and walls protecting the new New Orleans, hopefully, will be much stronger against the forces of nature so that the large bodies of water to the city's north and south cannot again wreak such havoc.

Weber also included cheaper labor and agglomeration—the clustering of support industries in the same area, such as a city—as key elements in the least-cost, maximize-profits decision about where to locate. For example, the availability of cheap labor (as in Southeast Asia today) may override the greater costs of transporting raw materials or finished products over a greater distance. Critics of this theory point out its failure to recognize the many variations in market demand, transportation costs, labor availability, and the wide range of products from manufacturing plants for diverse markets, but it nonetheless offers insights regarding the role of geography (in the locational triangle of raw materials, processing, and market) in the sites of manufacturing cities during North America's industrial age (Puu 2010).

Social. After meeting basic environmental conditions and economic considerations,

social factors come into play. We will look at seven such factors, using the five cities just discussed as illustrations:

1. Some cities are situated at a **natural crossroads** for a region. Montreal, for example, is the most important port on the St. Lawrence River and Seaway, lying between the Atlantic Ocean to the east and the Great Lakes to the west. Other examples are St. Louis and Chicago, with the latter nicknamed "the crossroads of the nation." Such crossroads facilitate the concentration of people, services, and especially, trade goods.

2. Other cities develop because they are located at what economists call **break-of-bulk** points. These are locations where a good—the "bulk"—is transferred from one type of transportation to another—say, from truck to ship. Houston is a break-of-bulk point for oil. In such places, goods often are warehoused for a time or processed in some way

Located at Puget Sound, an inlet of the Pacific Ocean, Seattle is a major seaport and break-of-bulk city, handling more than 1,000 vessels annually. Container ships bring in such imports as wearing apparel, video games, footwear, and motor vehicle parts, while exports consist of inorganic chemicals; beef, pork, and poultry; oilseeds; and industrial equipment.

in order to make the next leg of the trip more economical. When this happens, a city develops a set of subindustries that deal with storing or processing. In Houston, oil to be shipped from the city often is stored in huge tanks before its subsequent refinement into gasoline or heating oil. A smaller city, Buffalo, rose to prominence because, as the western end of the Erie Canal, the city served as the transshipment point for grain sent eastward for the North Central states via Lake Erie and the canal. There, mills processed the grain into flour, which was then shipped by rail to the large East Coast markets (Klein 2005:316).

Furthermore, the break-of-bulk function of cities is an enduring feature. The *Cityscape* box on page 157 describes two cases separated by more than a century. Note the striking similarities of port activity between Charles Dickens's description of 1860 London and Vincent Parrillo's comments about contemporary Seattle.

3. Another major reason for a city's location is access to some valuable *raw material.* Montreal's early history rested heavily on its colonial fur trade. Today, this city remains an important shipping center, handling the millions of gallons of petroleum that are processed each day by Montreal-Est refineries. Similarly, Houston and its refineries are near the East Texas oilfields; San Francisco boomed in the mid-nineteenth century because it was the closest port to the Sierra Nevada gold mines; and Pittsburgh's greatness was largely a result of proximity to coal mines that afforded cheap power for its steel mills.

4. Miami suggests another reason for a city location. Here, we have an **amenity city,** located in a particular place because it provides certain surroundings—sea, surf, sand, and sun—that are not easily available elsewhere. In its recent guise as "Latin America's supermarket," this predominantly Spanish-speaking city boasts a complete array of North American goods for sale. Much the same is true of Orlando (home of Disney World) and many other Florida cities as well. Similarly, Las Vegas offers the attraction of gambling to Westerners, as Atlantic City does to people on the East Coast and Monte Carlo does to Europeans. Other amenity cities are Hot Springs, Arkansas, and Bath, England (both renowned for their hot mineral waters), as well as Innsbruck, Austria (a world-class skiing city).

5. Washington, D.C., is an example of an **administrative or political city,** a city established primarily for governmental purposes, as was Ottawa, Canada's national capital. Two international examples are Canberra, Australia, and Brasilia, Brazil, both constructed in the twentieth century.

6. Closely related historically to the administrative function has been a city's *strategic military location.* That is, many cities began in easily defensible spots (Athens and Quebec City), and others, such as London, began because they offered military access into a whole region.

7. Finally, cities flourish for *religious or educational reasons.* Salt Lake City prospered as the home of Mormonism. In a similar way, Mecca in Saudi Arabia is the fountainhead of Islam, and Jerusalem is a focal point of no fewer than three major world religions: Christianity, Islam, and Judaism. University cities, such as Cambridge in England, Ithaca in New York (home of Cornell University), and Berkeley in California (site of one of the main campuses of the University of California), are cities that achieved prominence for educational reasons.

A combination, then, of geographic and climatic conditions and of social and economic factors explains why cities are where they are. Where many advantages come together, a city typically gains special importance. New York's prominence rests on its location as a natural port, an easily defended island, a gateway to a huge hinterland rich in raw materials, a natural break-of-bulk point, and a crossroads for people.

Finally, if the balance between a city's physical environment and people's social or economic needs and interests shifts, the city must adapt—or else it will decline. History is strewn with the ruins of cities that were unable to adapt, including the ancient Egyptian capital of Luxor and the Mayan city of El Mirador. On the other hand, cities sometimes survive great geographic and/or economic disasters. San Francisco is the best-known U.S. case, having recovered from the calamity of the 1906 earthquake to become one of the most vibrant U.S. cities.

CITYSCAPE

Break-of-Bulk in Two Cities

In the following passage, Charles Dickens describes London's River Thames in early morning, as seen from a small boat traveling downstream.

Nineteenth-Century London

Early as it was, there were plenty of scullers going here and there that morning, and plenty of barges…and we went ahead among many skiffs and wherries, briskly.

Old London Bridge was soon passed, and old Billingsgate market with its oysterboats and Dutchmen, and the White Tower and Traitor's Gate, and we were in among the tiers of shipping. Here, were the Leith, Aberdeen, and Glasgow steamers, loading and unloading goods, and looking immensely high out of the water as we passed alongside; here, were colliers by the score and score, with the coal-whippers plunging off stages on deck as counterweights to measures of coal swinging up, which were then rattled over the side into barges; here, at her moorings, was tomorrow's steamer for Rotterdam…and here tomorrow's for Hamburg, under whose bowsprit we crossed.

In the next passage, Vincent Parrillo describes a similar morning, only this time more than a century later and in a major U.S. port.

Modern Seattle

Even to the casual observer, the Port of Seattle is a busy place, filled with freighters, tugboats, barges, commercial fishing vessels, and pleasure craft. Geographically closer to Asia than any other major U.S. port, its natural deep-water harbor attracts commercial shippers from throughout the Pacific Rim. It is one of the largest U.S. container ports, one of the leading distribution centers on the West Coast, and the top U.S. port in container tonnage exports to Asia (over 6 million metric tons annually). Today ships from Japan, Singapore, and Taiwan are anchored at the docks, each by one of 28 commercial marine terminals.

At these terminals the container cranes transfer auto parts; bamboo baskets; electronic, household, and plastic products; foods; tools; and a variety of other products to an on-dock intermodal rail facility for direct shipment to inland destinations. Elsewhere, toplifts and forklifts transfer shipments to the 1.5 million square feet of warehouse storage space in the Terminal 106 Complex, to other outdoor storage areas, or to the waiting trucks at the 20 loading docks.

Everywhere the eye turns, one sees the bustling activity of workers: Longshoremen, stevedores, crane and forklift operators, grain terminal operators, truckers, railway men, foremen, and supervisors—are all unloading, storing, or loading the imports or exports passing through this port.

Source: Charles Dickens, *Great Expectations* (London: Chapman and Hall, 1860), from Chapter 54; and Vincent N. Parrillo's field research in Seattle.

THE SHAPE OF THE CITY

Once cities begin, what determines the form or physical shape they take? The answer depends on the city's social and economic functions.

To begin, consider that Athens is spread around the natural hilltop of the Acropolis; Edinburgh is similarly sited around a massive, extinct volcanic peak in Scotland; and Paris and Mexico City were initially situated on islands. These examples suggest that defense was one of the prime interests of these city dwellers. Durham, in northern England, provides another example. Founded about 1000 C.E., Durham is situated atop a high, steep peninsula formed by the Wear River. Even if one could get across the river, the sides of the steep ridge are extremely difficult to scale. Naturally protected

The lights of a city such as Toronto at night offer strikingly beautiful visual images while simultaneously illustrating its ongoing life and activities after dark. Toronto's strategic location on the shore of Lake Ontario enhances its economic vitality, making this metropolitan area home to more than 6 million people—one-fourth of Canada's total population.

on three sides, the founders of Durham only had to defend the narrow fourth side, and so here they built their heavily fortified castle.

The Radiocentric City

The importance of defense prompted pre-industrial people to build cities in the form of a great container, protected by natural geographic features (Durham's steep slope) and human constructs, such as walls, moats, castles, or battlements. Urbanists characterize such cities as **radiocentric cities,** because they radiate outward from a common center.

A wonderful example of this urban form is preindustrial Baghdad, Iraq (Figure 6–2). Set within an outer wall that had four fortified gates, the inner core of the city—containing the ruling caliph's palace and the mosque—was further protected by two rings of densely packed residential quarters, where the city's

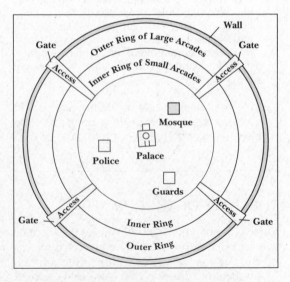

FIGURE 6–2   The Radiocentric City: Baghdad, circa 146-762 C.E.

poor people lived. Along the main access roads leading from the gates to the core, arcades or shops provided easy shopping access for Baghdad's inhabitants.

Not all radiocentric cities, however, have a perfectly radial shape. Ming Peking (see Chapter 9, Figure 9–2) was heavily walled and had a moat for defense, yet it took the shape of a series of rectangles and squares attached to and within one another. These shapes reflect the Chinese cosmology of the 1400s, which led planners to arrange the city on the points of the compass—north, south, east, and west.

Other considerations also encourage cities to develop a radial shape. As any city grows, people want to be as close to the center as possible in order to make travel easier. Because a circle places the most people closest to the center, many cities grow in a ring-like fashion around a central core. As anyone who has ever gazed out an airplane window at night knows, most cities look like huge wheels, with central spokes radiating outward. These spokes—highways and rail lines—suggest another reason for the city's generally radial form. Because the shortest route to the center of a circle is a straight line,

people build access roads to the city as directly as possible. That practice suggests the origin of one of history's best-known sayings: "All roads lead to Rome."

The Gridiron City

Despite the common radial pattern of most of the world's cities, the downtown areas of well-known North American cities—Atlanta, Chicago, Los Angeles, Montreal, New York, Philadelphia, Toronto, and Vancouver—are not of a radiocentric design. Indeed, while radiocentric center cities are the rule in much of the world, that form is the exception in North America.

Closer to home, we find **gridiron cities,** composed of straight streets crossing at right angles to create many regular city blocks. This form is typical of cities built after the Industrial Revolution. Only then did cities place such importance on economic activity, and a city gridiron plan facilitates the movement of people and products throughout the city. This form is also an efficient way to divide land—and to sell it as real estate. Figure 6–3 shows a notable

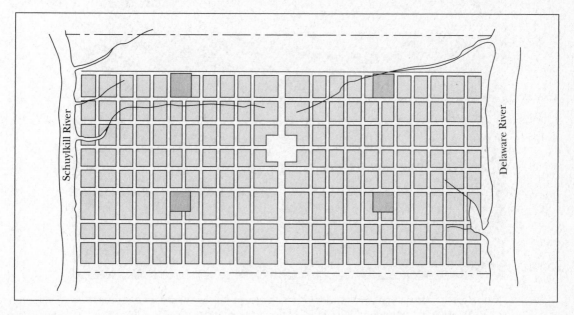

FIGURE 6–3   The Gridiron City: William Penn's Philadelphia Plan, 1682

preindustrial exception: William Penn's 1682 plan for selling lots in Philadelphia.

Grid patterns do not always result from careful planning, however. Typically, when a settlement begins, merchants favor a main-street location that allows people to shop and move from one store to another along the street. Furthermore, open-ended streets serve business well, because they allow room for growth as well as easy access to and from the shopping area. The U.S. and Canadian Midwest and West are full of such "Main Street" towns. If, in time, another major street crosses the original street, then we see the beginnings of a gridiron around "four corners" that may well expand from there.

URBAN ECOLOGY

As we discussed in Chapter 5, Robert Park and his fellow Chicago sociologists used cities as a laboratory to study social life. Their research generated the science of **human ecology,** a term coined by Park that focused on what he viewed as an orderly evolution of urban growth and development:

> There are forces at work within the limits of the urban community…which tend to bring about an orderly and typical grouping of its population and institutions. The science which seeks to isolate these factors and to describe the typical constellations of persons and institutions which the cooperation of these forces produce is what we call human, as distinguished from plant and animal, ecology. (1984:1–2)

Using the ecological approach that studies the relationship between living things and their environment, Park investigated how human beings live in their urban world. He believed that the evolutionary struggle for survival was evident in the everyday *competition for scarce resources,* such as food, clothing, shelter, and land. Emerging from this competition were different clusters of activity that Park called **natural areas:** business districts,

Boston grew from a small, walled, colonial city to an important city of commerce, annexing such adjoining municipalities as Brighton, Charlestown, Dorchester, Roxbury, and West Roxbury between 1868 and 1874. Today, it is a large metropolis, utilizing its waterways to full advantage, both commercially and recreationally.

ethnic neighborhoods, skid rows, and rooming-house areas.

For Park, urban competition is not only economic, it is also about *power*. People compete for control of parks, streets, and ethnic districts—and, above all, for the prestige that comes from living in a fashionable neighborhood or having an impressive occupation.

Beyond competition, Park noted that large-scale *population movements* also influence urban development. Most of the immigrants who came to Park's Chicago and other growing North American cities a century ago had little education and few skills. They were also exceedingly poor. With few options, they poured into overcrowded housing in the center cities and took low-paying jobs in factories. As they did in cities across the continent, immigrants or their descendants later moved, leaving their old neighborhoods to the next poor group to enter the city. The Chicago sociologists called this shifting of population **invasion–succession.**

Concentric Zones

To Park, competition and population movement both shaped and reshaped cities. The more economically successful residents selected the choice city locations for their businesses and homes, leaving the less desirable locations to the less successful. In this process, claimed Park, the city as a whole took on broad, spatial patterns characteristic of an economic hierarchy. In the mid-1920s, one of Park's students, Ernest W. Burgess, suggested that a city develops somewhat the way a tree does—growing outward in a series of concentric rings or zones over time.

Although Burgess assumed that economic competition was central to urban life, he, like Park, also saw other social forces at work. Moving to a suburb, for example, is not just an economic consideration; it also confers prestige, suggesting that people have "made it." Burgess described the city in terms of four main zones, with a fifth commuter's zone outside the city limits (see the right side of Figure 6–4). In his words,

> This chart represents an ideal construction of the tendencies of any town or city to expand radially from its central business district—on the map

"The Loop" (I). Encircling the downtown area there is normally an area in transition, which is being invaded by business and light manufacture (II). A third area (III) is inhabited by the workers in industries who have escaped from the area of deterioration (II) but who desire to live within easy access of their work. Beyond this zone is the "residential area" (IV) of high-class apartment buildings or of exclusive "restricted" districts of single family dwellings. Still farther, out beyond the city limits, is the commuters' zone (V)—suburban areas, or satellite cities—within a thirty- to sixty-minute ride of the central business district. (1984:50; orig. 1925)

Burgess illustrated his model by applying it directly to the Chicago of his day (the left side of Figure 6–4). Once we take the "halving effect" of Lake Michigan into account (the heavy line shows the city's edge by the lake), Burgess's theory did a creditable job in explaining the location of the city's districts. The most valuable land (Zone I) lay within "The Loop" downtown, which was the exclusive preserve of business. In Zone II, the "zone in transition," stood factories and slums, the latter overflowing with down-and-out roomers and ethnic groups of various sorts, including Italians (Little Sicily) and Chinese (Chinatown). Predominantly inhabiting Zone III, the zone of workingmen's homes, were second-generation migrants, the descendants of earlier Chicago immigrants who had escaped the inner city by moving out of the slums. Here, too, was the "two-flat" area, in which two families occupied two-family houses instead of the usual four or more families living in multihousing buildings, as in the inner city. Zone IV was the "residential area," dominated by residential hotels, apartment areas, and most important, single-family homes. In this zone, too, was a relatively wealthy "restricted" residential district, an area that excluded people with "undesirable" ethnic or racial traits.

Soon after the emergence of the Chicago School, two other ecological growth theories achieved prominence. These, the sector and multiple nuclei theories, addressed some of the shortcomings of the Park and Burgess approach.

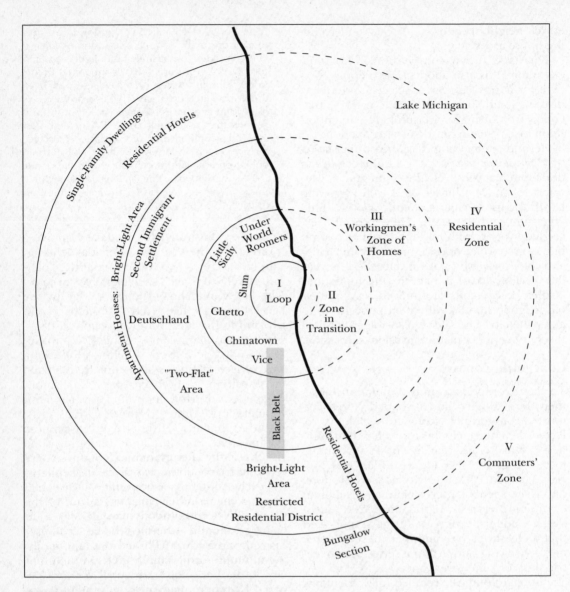

FIGURE 6–4 Chicago's Concentric Zones

Source: From "The Growth of the City," in Robert E. Park and Ernest W. Burgess, eds., *The City.* Copyright © 1967 University of Chicago Press. Reprinted with permission of the University of Chicago Press.

Sectors

Homer Hoyt (1939) noticed that numerous city districts did not conform to the purely concentric model suggested by Burgess. Even in Burgess's Chicago (see Figure 6–4), unusual areas like the "Deutschland Ghetto" (the home of German immigrants) and the "Black Belt" obviously cut across zones. Consequently, Hoyt studied, block by block, the residential patterns of 142 cities in three different time periods—1900, 1915, and 1936—adding an important historical dimension. The scope of

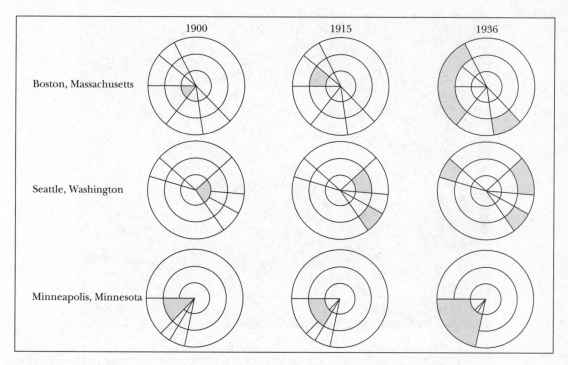

FIGURE 6–5   Shifts in the Location of Fashionable Residential Areas in Three American Cities, 1900–1936. Fashionable areas are indicated by shading.

Source: From Homer Hoyt, *The Structure and Growth of Residential Neighborhoods in American Cities* (Washington, DC: Federal Housing Administration, 1939), p. 115, figure 40.

his study was a major advance over Burgess's work, which was based almost exclusively on Chicago.

First, Hoyt found that high-prestige, fashionable districts formed sectors of varying size. Second, despite a rough concentric shape to the cities, many sectors took on a pie-shaped form rather than resembling an entire ring (Figure 6–5). Third, lower-income districts often abutted and, sometimes, even surrounded fashionable districts. A classic example is Harlem's "Striver's Row" of the 1920s and 1930s, a wealthy, two-block oasis of pristine buildings (West 138th and 139th Streets between Seventh and Eighth Avenues) surrounded by other buildings approaching utter collapse. Fourth, Hoyt found a tendency, as time passed, for sectors to move out of the city radially, along a path begun by the sector in earlier years (Seattle provides a good example).

Fifth, in the later periods, cities revealed two or three fashionable areas in different places, with factors other than competition and population movement influencing this process. Often, the wealthy neighborhoods in many cities stood on "high ground"—Boston's Beacon Hill and San Francisco's Nob Hill and Pacific Heights, for instance—indicating a preference by the wealthy to be "above" the city's poorer residents. Elsewhere, high-prestige sectors located for aesthetic reasons, such as on waterfronts (like Chicago's North Shore), while still others located along main transportation lines that facilitated easy access to the center city (such as Philadelphia's Rittenhouse neighborhood).

Multiple Nuclei

Although Hoyt's study was a major advance over the Burgess model, it was limited by a focus on residential sectors. Hoyt imagined

Paterson, New Jersey—the first planned U.S. industrial city—typifies an old manufacturing city. In classic sector theory patterning, many of its factories lined the railroad tracks, and its fashionable district moved eastward along Broadway to the high ground of Manor Hill. No longer thriving, the city struggles to maintain a solid economic base.

that industry, too, moved radially outward from the center city—upriver or along railroad lines, for instance—but he never investigated this hunch.

Chauncy Harris and Edward Ullman (1945) argued that as the contemporary city grew, it diversified, developing many distinct sectors of activity rather than retaining one center. Modern cities typically have a major central business district (CBD, sector 1 in Figure 6–6), but various historical, cultural, and economic factors specific to a given city generate other districts. For example, wholesale light manufacturing (sector 2 in Figure 6–6) might be near the CBD, with low-income residences (sector 3) in various separate districts nearby. A medium-income residential area (sector 4) might abut the CBD and give way on its outer edge to a high-income residential area (sector 5). Between these two areas might exist a secondary business district

(sector 7) and, farther out, a completely separate residential suburb (sector 8). Heavy manufacturing (sector 6) might lie a relatively large distance from the CBD and evolve an industrial–residential suburb (sector 9) nearby.

Why do multiple nuclei develop? First, certain types of activities require specialized facilities. For example, heavy manufacturing requires a great deal of space. A century ago, space was plentiful downtown. In recent decades, however, space near the CBD has become hard to find and, when it can be found, expensive. Many modern factories also require more floor space on one level. As a result, much heavy manufacturing has moved from the CBD to outlying industrial areas, where land is readily available and taxes are often lower. In Chicago, for example, heavy manufacturing once located in the CBD moved to the southeast, around Gary, Indiana.

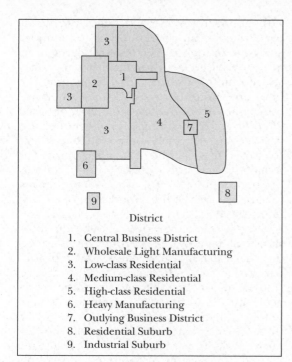

District

1. Central Business District
2. Wholesale Light Manufacturing
3. Low-class Residential
4. Medium-class Residential
5. High-class Residential
6. Heavy Manufacturing
7. Outlying Business District
8. Residential Suburb
9. Industrial Suburb

FIGURE 6–6   The Multiple Nuclei Theory

Source: From Chauncy O. Harris and Edward L. Ullman, "The Nature of Cities," *The Annals 242* (November 1945), American Academy of Political and Social Science.

Second, multiple CBDs can be the result of annexation. As the city absorbs a nearby municipality into its political domain, that preexisting CBD may evolve further as a secondary business district. This is particularly true of the so-called "spread cities," such as Phoenix, that have expanded greatly in the age of the automobile. As it becomes more time-consuming to travel into the central city's CBD for shopping, entertainment, or business-related activities, other CBDs emerge within the boundaries of large, outlying areas in order to accommodate those inconvenienced by a longer commute into the city center.

Perhaps the most important contribution of Harris and Ullman's theory is that it seriously questions the notion that urban land use is predictable at all. Burgess's zonal hypothesis and, to a lesser extent, Hoyt's sector theory both implied certain inevitable patterns of land use. By contrast, Harris and Ullman's multiple nuclei theory suggests that a mix of historical, cultural, and economic situations both shapes and reshapes every city. Even the core CBD might fall into decline, as it has in some smaller cities.

Limitations

Although he based his model on Chicago, Burgess thought his concentric zone hypothesis would describe any city. Do other cities and towns conform to the concentric zone pattern? Certainly, some do. For example, an examination of changes in land use for the Moscow metropolitan area revealed concentric zones of outwardly declining land-use intensity (Ioffe and Nefedova 2001). A longitudinal study (1950–1980) of 318 U.S. metropolitan areas found that such evolving patterns occurred among industrially based, older, larger, more dispersed metropolitan communities in the Northeast (Schwirian, et al. 1990:1143).

Hoyt's sector theory offered a helpful description of urban expansion along major highways and, later, along interstate highways built through a massive federal construction program begun during the 1950s, which contributed to the development of suburbia. Still, it was a descriptive analysis only, as was the multiple nuclei model, which more effectively described spread cities or metropolitan areas with their large complexes of shopping malls as well as office and industrial parks (usually along those major highways).

Critics, however, questioned all three ecological models' suggestion of uniformity within zones and their reliance on concepts of unrestrained competition and large population movements. These vary in their intensity at different locales and time periods and, even then, may or may not play a key role in a city's growth and development. To illustrate, an analysis of Beijing land-use patterns revealed five concentric zones, but each zone had mixed urban functions; most notably, high-income people did not move to the suburbs because of traffic congestion and high-quality schools, hospitals, and hotels still in central cities (Tian, et al. 2010). Other forces—for example, globalization, technological advances in production, communication, and transportation—can impact on how a city's spatial development occurs.

Finally, some critics dismiss the very idea of "urban ecology" as "too biological." That is, the principles of plant and animal ecology are inadequate to explain human activity. People, unlike plants, are thinking creatures who reflect and act creatively on their urban environment. The urban ecological approach pays little attention to the roles played by (1) choice, (2) culture in the city, and (3) community. In other words, this approach ignores important social considerations.

Such criticism has diminished the importance of the urban ecological approach and its various models for urban development over time—and, in fact, has even changed the essence of this field. Today, the field of **ecological sociology,** with its own organizations and journals, includes urban ecologists who use urban design, land-use planning, and policy reform to help communities plan and build neighborhoods that are environmentally sound (Urban Ecology 2011). To understand the unfolding processes of urban growth and vitality, a host of alternative theories and approaches suggest that the forces shaping land use are more complex than the early urban ecologists suspected.

SOCIAL AREA ANALYSIS AND MAPPING

One current technique to describe urban land use is comparing the socioeconomic characteristics of urbanites living in different census tracts. A **census tract** averages about 4,000 residents, and it typically contains relatively homogeneous units with respect to population characteristics, economic status, and living conditions (see the *Cityscape* box on page 167). Using these social attributes, social scientists can classify each census tract and then compare it

with others to create a detailed profile of the larger urban community. For example, analysts can identify the level of segregation in a city based on the clustering of racial and ethnic groups in each census tract, or how one neighborhood differs from another in educational level, income, number of children, type of housing, or whether the mother worked. Such analysis enables social scientists to describe and distinguish the social characteristics that are found among urban neighborhoods, because numerous variations serve as the foundation of a community's social structure.

Social area analysis proved to be a helpful statistical technique, not only for identifying social class, family status, and minority patterns in cities but also for comparative studies measuring changes in these areas over time. In addition, this approach is most helpful in finding relationships between these social characteristics and any other measurable aspect of life, such as crime and mental illness rates or religious and voting behavior.

An increasingly popular way of displaying these findings is through mapping. For example, at its website, the U.S. Census Bureau offers numerous thematic maps to illustrate many of the characteristics listed above. Chapters 10 and 11 include some of these maps to illustrate text material, and at the end of this chapter, you'll find an Internet activity that deals with accessing thematic maps of cities.

GIS Mapping

A particularly valuable research tool is **GIS mapping.** Short for *Geographic Information Systems,* GIS mapping is a computer-based method to gather, transform, manipulate, and analyze information related to the surface of the earth. Called *Geomatics* in Canada, GIS mapping allows us to view, understand, question, interpret, and visualize data in many ways that reveal relationships, patterns, and trends in the form of maps, globes, and charts (GIS.com 2011).

CITYSCAPE

Miami's Little Havana

The center of Little Havana lies along 8th Street in Southwest Miami. It is one of several areas in Miami and its environs in which substantial numbers of Cuban Americans reside. As is typical in areas that served as initial enclaves for a particular group (Chinatown in San Francisco, for example) the current population of Little Havana is older and poorer than other, later Cuban concentrations in the Miami area....

Along 8th Street, for a stretch of several miles, are homes and apartments occupied primarily by Cuban families. Many of the homes have characteristically Cuban features such as decorative Spanish tiles, Catholic shrines in the backyards, and fences enclosing the front yards. There are many Cuban-owned stores, restaurants, and financial institutions catering largely, but not exclusively, to co-ethnics....Some shops offer special wearing apparel such as guayaberas: lightweight, short coats traditionally worn by Cuban men. There are a number of botanicas selling religious goods, including potions for recalling saints and spirits and aerosol cans whose contents are guaranteed to improve one's love life. Many small grocery stores sell Cuban food products and almost all the pharmacies in Little Havana have signs in their windows announcing that they send medicine to Cuba. Local churches offer masses in Spanish and English.

A dozen or more daily and weekly Spanish-language newspapers are available at Little Havana's newsstands or from coin-operated boxes. Some of the newspapers are primarily oriented to news about Cuba and the Cuban population in the United States, whereas others focus on Latin America as a whole. The area is also served by WQBA, one of several Spanish-language radio stations, but the one that has historically claimed to be La Cubanisma (the most Cuban). Little Havana also contains a number of outdoor cafes and outdoor tables, where a mostly elderly male clientele gathers during the day and evening to play cards and dominos under black olive trees. A focal point in Little Havana is Domino Park, where older men play dominos throughout the day, smoke cigars, and talk about the old days in Cuba.

A number of Little Havana's restaurants offer traditional Cuban dishes such as chicken and yellow rice. Some of the restaurants are inconspicuous neighborhood eateries, others are highly ornate. The most famous among the latter is probably the Restaurant Versailles, "the mirrored palace," which was designed to closely resemble several once-popular night spots in Havana....

Walking down Southwest 8th Street gives a former Cuban a feeling of being transported back in time to the Havana of yesterday. Little Havana in Miami is, in many respects, a copy of Havana in Cuba. Murals of the latter, complete with street signs, decorate the walls of restaurants, keeping alive memories of life in Cuba.

Source: From Mark Abrahamson, *Urban Enclaves: Identity and Place in America*, 2nd ed. (New York: Worth Publishers, 2005).

The GIS maps serve many useful and varying purposes for all types of organizations in both the private and public sectors. For example, a GIS map can be a valuable resource in land-use management and planning for future development. (Another Internet activity at the end of this chapter will give you an opportunity to look at land use where you live.)

Limitations

Like the other approaches we've discussed, social area analysis also has its limitations. One problem is that this approach is not theoretical; it merely gives a description of cities' areas. That is, social area analysis cannot predict where groups will settle, or explain why groups settled where they did, in order to aid in planning. By contrast, Park and Burgess noted the ecological forces of competition and population movements that cause concentric rings to develop. Likewise, Harris and Ullman attributed the unique form of each city to historical, cultural, or economic factors as a basis for interpreting findings. Nevertheless, even though social area analysis offers limited insights regarding the possibilities for urban land use, its utility as a systematic measurement of the complexities found in urban communities comes from how it provides us with a fuller understanding of neighborhood characteristics.

THE LOS ANGELES SCHOOL: POSTMODERNISM

Partly as a spin-off from the multiple nuclei theory, but more importantly as a rejection of the Chicago School, a new perspective—dubbed "the Los Angeles School"—emerged in the mid-1980s. Originally focusing on the five-county region of Southern California (Los Angeles, Ventura, San Bernardino, Riverside, and Orange), this perspective has its emphasis on multicentered, dispersed patterns as the new reality of urban growth. Using Los Angeles as their model, proponents argue that the city's multiple realities and its decentralized structure represent the urban future. Such reasoning, with its focus on socially and spatially fragmented patterns, fits into postmodern thinking, which rejects universal truths in favor of more limited interpretations of specific areas.

Los Angeles is a spread city held together more by an intricate freeway system than by a cohesive political system. Critics charge that neither one actually works well. Local government is too fragmented and disorganized, and the densely populated area has the nation's worst traffic congestion, leading to the average driver wasting more than 82 hours each year by sitting in traffic.

Building Blocks

Perhaps the origins of this new perspective lie in the vivid depiction of the Los Angeles area by Rayner Banham (2009; orig. 1973). He identified four basic "ecologies" that differed markedly from those advanced by the Chicago School: (1) *surfurbia* (the beach cities along the coast), (2) *the foothills* (the private enclaves of the privileged in such areas as Beverly Hills and Bel Air), (3) *the plains of Id* (the endless central flatlands), and (4) *autopia* (the freeways that exist as "a single comprehensible place" and "coherent state of mind"). Banham was partly harsh in his description of the "plains of Id," describing them as "gridded with endless streets, peppered endlessly with ticky-tacky houses clustered in indistinguishable neighborhoods, slashed across by endless freeways that have destroyed any community spirit that may have once existed" (p. 161).

Douglas Suisman (1990) insisted that the city's boulevards, not its freeways, are what give form to its structure and communities. As surface streets—rather than the self-contained freeways with their on-off ramps—these boulevards connect different sections of the metropolis, provide an organizational framework for local travel destinations, and serve as a "filter to adjacent residential neighborhoods" (quoted in Dear 2001:13). For Suisman, boulevards are the defining element of the city's public space in its linkage between municipalities.

Edward W. Soja (2000) helped bring a postmodern perspective to this school of thought in his argument that Los Angeles is a decentralized metropolis with a fragmented power structure that is becoming increasingly pliant and disorganized. Although the center may hold as a strategic surveillance point for social control, radiating outward is a complex, highly fragmented mishmash of "wedges" and "citadels," separated by boulevards acting as corridors. With global capitalism serving as an underlying rationale, Soja views Los Angeles as resembling "a gigantic agglomeration of theme parks" (p. 245). Moreover, he suggests that the worldwide future of urbanism will resemble Los Angeles (Miller 2000).

Main Arguments

Michael J. Dear, a leading advocate of the Los Angeles School, shares Soja's belief about the city serving as a prototype for fragmentation and social differentiation in a global economy and a postmodern culture. He also adds that as a consequence of physical sprawl, the city's "decentered politics" is one way that Los Angeles serves as a herald of the future. He describes the Los Angeles region as being "split in many separate fiefdoms, with their leaders in constant battle" (2001:14). With over 100 municipalities in Los Angeles County (total population of nearly 10 million), there are many problems of political representation. These include city–county government disputes, slow-growth/no-growth movements, and the difficulties associated with minority-group political participation. As a result, many alliances—formal and informal, legal and illegal—form to press their claims. Either autocratic—even corrupt—power will result, or there will be "polarization along class, income, racial and ethnic lines" (2001:15).

Proponents of the Los Angeles School reject any depiction of Los Angeles as outside the mainstream of U.S. urban culture because of its widespread urban sprawl, insignificant architecture, and jammed freeways. Instead, they insist, Los Angeles closely resembles other emerging cities with its low-density growth, multiple ethnic enclaves, and multiple urban centers within one region. Moreover, the city contains the same dichotomy as others, with its high concentration of wealth alongside poverty and homelessness. As a result, in contrast to the heritage of the past metropolitan form promoted by the Chicago School, those of the Los Angeles School contend that their approach to urban studies is the accurate depiction of modern urban centers not just on this continent but also elsewhere in the world (Hise, et al. 1996).

Are the postmodernists correct in saying that cities are developing in a way that no longer fits the old logic of urban development advocated by the urban ecologists? Is the evolution of Los Angeles that they describe truly the wave of the future elsewhere? With a projected population increase of 3 million for the Los Angeles region by mid-century (more than all of present-day Chicago), the direction of its ongoing growth and development as the second-largest metropolitan area in the United States is more than just an academic question. Only time will give us the answer, but a new generation of Los Angeles School advocates is emerging, one still interested in interpreting socio-spatial differences among contemporary cities but also seeking to explore how these differences shape reactionary and progressive urban politics (Nicholls 2011).

Limitations

As with other interpretations, this approach also has its critics, who contend that advocates of the Los Angeles School overemphasize the uniqueness, importance, or widespread applicability of the Los Angeles model (Beauregard 2003). Harvey Molotch (2002) says that the Los Angeles analysts assume things are more local than they are, that there have always been cities which differed from the Chicago model of land use, and that demographic distributions in western U.S. cities are but one variation of such nonconformity. Robert J. Sampson (2002) says that neither city—Los Angeles or Chicago—can be reduced to one model, because both have greater internal differentiation than either model allows and because each city actually contains spatial forms and landscape elements of the other. Essentially, all the critics argue for the need to transcend a parochial focus in favor of a theory that transcends time and place. In rebuttal, the analysts of the Los Angeles School say that sufficient evidence exists worldwide to support their position on how to view contemporary urban growth (Dear 2001; Scott 2001).

SUMMARY

People founded cities at particular geographical sites where environmental conditions (water and climate) were favorable and where economic factors would ensure a measure of prosperity. Other human needs—political,

religious, educational, and economic—played a role in locating cities as well. Spatial location of cities also results from their different types—crossroad centers, break-of-bulk points, and amenity, governmental, or religious entities. Industrial location theory suggests that the triangulation of minimized total costs for transportation, labor, and market, in order to maximize profits, will influence the decision about location. In addition, the type of city helps forge a city's basic shape. Radiocentric cities have a tendency to emerge where religious and political forces are of central interest to a population; gridiron cities spring up where economic concerns predominate.

Robert Park and Ernest W. Burgess (the Chicago School) saw competition and population movement as responsible for shaping cities. Burgess's concentric zone model illustrates their ideas. Critics, however, raised questions as to whether a biologically determined competition could explain people's behavior, and they pointed out numerous exceptions to the zonal hypothesis.

Recognizing the difficulties of the Chicago theory, Homer Hoyt suggested that many cities were organized in sectors, and that the prime cause of such sectoring was socioeconomic status. This was a helpful contribution, but like the Chicago model, it ultimately failed to account for the complexity of urban life.

An additional contribution was Harris and Ullman's multiple nuclei theory. This model abandoned any idea of a deterministic pattern to urban development: It held that zones, sectors, and even the CBD were variable, with city form changing over time.

With earlier explanations of urban land use (the concentric zone, sector, and multiple nuclei theories) discredited as too simple, urban ecology now primarily functions as a way to use urban design, land-use planning, and policy reform to help communities plan and build neighborhoods that are environmentally sound.

Social area analysis is an approach distinguished by its lack of theory and explanation for what it reveals, but it provides a detailed description of the existing characteristics of a neighborhood and allows comparisons over time and/or with other neighborhoods. Data from the U.S. Census Bureau can offer such detailed analysis of census tracts, including thematic maps to present visually a number of various socioeconomic indicators. This form and other forms of mapping, particularly GIS mapping, can be of value in many ways, including land-use management and planning.

The Los Angeles School uses a critical spatial perspective and postmodern viewpoint to understand the spread-city phenomenon. Besides more accurately explaining urbanism in Southern California than the urban ecologists could, its emphasis on political fragmentation, multiple urban centers in a region, and a multicultural/multiethnic urban entity calls our attention to the problems of governance and community within a metropolitan area increasingly affected by global capitalism. Advocates insist that Los Angeles is the prototype of the urban future, but critics insist that this claim is not justified.

CONCLUSION

Urban land use is extremely complex. This chapter traced increasingly sophisticated efforts to capture this multifaceted reality. We can be pleased with major advances, particularly in our understanding of how cities in the modern world organize space, but we also need to understand the external forces outside the cities' control that also affect their fortunes and, therefore, their space. It is to this topic that we turn in the next chapter.

KEY TERMS

administrative or political city (156)
amenity city (156)
break-of-bulk (155)
census tract (166)
ecological sociology (166)
GIS mapping (166)
gridiron cities (159)

human ecology (160)
industrial location theory (153)
invasion–succession (161)
natural areas (160)
natural crossroads (155)
radiocentric cities (158)

INTERNET ACTIVITIES

1. At *http://www.socialexplorer.com/pub/maps/map3.aspx?g=0&mapi=SE0012*, Social Explorer enables you to select map menu choices in the upper right corner. Each population map that appears is a social area analysis of the variable you selected. You can click any geographic area to get a closer look.

2. Go to the Guide for Geographic Information Systems *(http://www.gis.com/)* for an introduction into using GIS mapping to present data. Other sublinks at this site will give you numerous real-world examples in many disciplines.

CHAPTER 7

CRITICAL URBAN SOCIOLOGY
The City and Capitalism

URBAN ECONOMICS: THE TRADITIONAL
    PERSPECTIVE
Central Place Theory
The General Pattern of Land Use
Limitations
URBAN POLITICAL ECONOMY
Henri Lefebvre: Redefining the Study
    of Cities
Urban Areas as Themed Environments
David Harvey: The Baltimore Study
Manuel Castells: Updating Marx
Allen Scott: Business Location and
    the Global Economy
John Logan and Harvey Molotch:
    Urban Growth Machines

THE GLOBAL ECONOMY
Deindustrialization
Economic Restructuring
World-Systems Analysis
URBAN POLITICAL ECONOMY:
    FOUR PRINCIPLES
THE URBANIZATION OF POVERTY
The Developing World
The Developed World
SUMMARY
CONCLUSION
KEY TERMS
INTERNET ACTIVITIES

During the early 1970s, an alternative theoretical approach to urban sociology began to take form. In part, this development was a response to what its proponents saw as deficiencies of the Chicago School (described in Chapter 5). It was also a response to the turmoil of the times. The late 1960s and early 1970s were a period of upheaval in both the United States and Europe, prompting a more critical and political outlook on society. Not surprisingly, many scholars began to question the assumption that geography and technology were the main factors shaping urban life.

These "new" urbanists emphasized the distribution of wealth and political power in the city. They noted that the wealthiest people lived on the most desirable land and enjoyed the greatest access to the city's services. Is it any accident, they asked, that the city's best schools are situated in the city's richest neighborhoods? Or that new superhighways tear through old urban neighborhoods, with patent disregard for poor residents, to better serve the city's elite and those who have fled to the wealthy suburbs? Their answer was a resounding "No!" On the contrary, they concluded, "the structure of the city is to be explained by the pursuit of profit" (Hall 1984:32). With the rapid globalization of the economy, many urban scholars turned their attention to how the international economic system was impacting on cities.

Also emerging in refutation to the Chicago School's emphasis on a centralized, core city that dominates a region was the postmodern perspective known as the Los Angeles School (described in Chapter 6). **Postmodernism,** you may recall, rejects the notion of any rational, overarching interpretation of reality and, instead, puts emphasis on the fragmented nature of urban growth, development, and life. Most analysts place the Los Angeles School within the larger framework of political economy models.

This alternative approach, originally called "the new urban sociology" (Gottdiener and Hutchison 2010), has now existed long enough not to be "new," so we will use the term *critical urban sociology*. In truth, however, most of its theoretical arguments are quite old, drawing heavily on the ideas of Karl Marx (1818–1883). What is new is their application to the city and, more specifically, to recent trends, such as globalization of the economy, economic restructuring in the United States, and the proliferation of megacities and new cities.

The heart of this approach, as already mentioned, is a central reliance on *political economy theory* and its application to urban life, in terms of the social structures and processes of change that benefit some groups at the expense of others (Gottdiener and Feagin 1988). Before we examine some of the major aspects of this perspective—now the dominant view in the field—we will review some earlier contributions to political and economic analysis.

URBAN ECONOMICS: THE TRADITIONAL PERSPECTIVE

People familiar with cities often have an image of a vibrant downtown, a place where the action is, where the buildings are taller and the lights brighter. That is, indeed, an accurate image of North American, European, or "Westernized" cities. Approaching a major city at night along a dark highway, one first sees the distant glow of the city lights, even before making out the evening skyline. Barring an electrical blackout, large areas of the center city are never dark, but why is this so? Why shouldn't the "action" be everywhere? Why should the tall buildings be concentrated in a single area?

Central Place Theory

To answer these questions, we should first realize that the city is where everything human comes together. Compared with the fixed life of rural areas or small towns, the city's possibilities are practically limitless. Indeed, the city is the place where the mix of people and ideas makes the creation of new things easy. The city, by its very nature, promotes "interaction and fusion" (Mumford 1991:568; orig. 1961).

Furthermore, as one approaches the center of the city, the level of human activity becomes more intense. The greatest action is, literally, in the center, where people contact each other more frequently. There, in the "downtown," one finds the greatest economic advantages that cities can offer.

The Economic Advantages of Cities. Cities tend to be located where important *goods or services* are available in abundance (Winston–Salem, Raleigh, and Durham, North Carolina, are in the heart of tobacco-producing country) or where goods and services can be obtained easily (New Orleans is near the mouth of the Mississippi River). In either case, a prime location means that cities obtain, produce, and distribute their goods and services more cheaply than smaller settlements can. To ship heating oil to Albany, New York, costs a certain amount, but to transport that oil to the small town of Ticonderoga, 100 miles farther away, adds additional transportation and handling costs.

Second, cities play host to what economists call **agglomeration industries.** Take Detroit, home of the automobile industry. Because the major U.S. car manufacturers have their home bases there, this city also attracts various subindustries to serve them—companies manufacturing car paints or engine pistons, for example. The major automakers actually share these subindustries, which benefits everyone involved, including the customer, who ultimately buys the car for less. Other examples of famous agglomeration industries are the entertainment industry in Los Angeles and Hollywood, meatpacking in Chicago, country music in Nashville, and fashion in New York. In each case, the presence of agglomeration industries keeps production costs lower than they might be in a smaller settlement.

A third economic advantage of cities, particularly those based on a free-enterprise system, is that *competition* among various producers works to keep costs down and quality up for various goods and services. Because so many businesses of the same type exist in cities, no business can charge a great deal more than its competitors for the same product. To do so, in a competitive environment, would simply mean that customers will go elsewhere to find a better deal, with predictable consequences for the company's future. Or, if one business offers poor-quality goods for the same price at which a competitor sells a better product, which firm do you think will prosper?

What about a business in a small town with little competition? There, businesses typically offer less value to their customers, because they know it's too inconvenient and expensive for most local people to go to the city to get the lower price or the better product.

Competition also explains why so many businesses of the same type tend to cluster together in the city, in what we called *natural areas* in Chapter 5. In fact, most cities have entire districts devoted solely to the computer, furniture, camera, automobile, fashion, jewelry, or entertainment businesses. The reasons for such proximity are easy to understand. Businesses of the same type, when located near one another, can (1) know what their competitors are up to simply by walking across the street, (2) provide a single locale where customers can easily engage in comparison shopping, and (3) share agglomeration services, thereby making the products cheaper for everyone.

Fourth, and finally, cities can offer higher-quality products at lower prices because they stand amidst a *greater population*. This means that urban businesses have a larger available work force than their rural counterparts do; thus, other things being equal, urban businesses can hire the more qualified people. Just as important, urban companies benefit from a larger pool of customers.

For these four reasons, the city has marked economic advantages over the hinterland. Once established, a city may operate as a "magnet" or "growth machine," becoming more and more productive as it draws raw materials and people from all around (Molotch 1976; Wilson and Jonas 1999).

Within the city, economic advantages increase as one nears the city center; for this reason, people who stand to benefit from those advantages want to locate near there. This principle points out why we find, at the city's center, a **central business district (CBD)** and why, at the city's center, the action truly is greater, the buildings taller, and the lights brighter.

The Urban Hierarchy. Basic economic advantages also help explain why some cities grow much larger than others. The largest cities are just more centrally located relative to important goods or services. Chicago is a major urban center because of both its location at the southern end of Lake Michigan and its centrality to the nation's population. A century ago, Chicago thrived as the ideal location for shipping goods from the heavily settled Northeast to all other regions of the nation. Similarly, Chicago was a natural stopover for people heading westward. In comparison, Milwaukee, another major Great Lakes port, is less centrally located. Therefore, as Chicago developed into a major city, Milwaukee evolved into a second-tier urban area.

Back in the 1930s, German geographer Walter Christaller (1966; orig. 1933) incorporated this pattern into his **central place theory.** Christaller suggested that the more important a city's economic function to a region, the more its population will increase. In turn, the city's hinterland—smaller cities, towns, and rural areas—becomes dependent on the large city for many goods and services that their smaller populations cannot support. This, in turn, would make the city grow even more.

Christaller also suggested that cities (especially smaller ones) typically space themselves so that they do not cut into each other's markets. In other words, cities emerge at "distance intervals," with each serving a local hinterland. The upstate New York area provides an example: Stretched along the New York State Thruway, at least 75 miles apart, are the major urban areas of Buffalo–Niagara Falls (2010 population: 1.1 million), Rochester (1 million), Syracuse (663,000), Utica–Rome (299,000), and Albany–Schenectady–Troy (871,000).

Over a fairly large geographical region, then, we can expect cities to be distributed by size. Most numerous will be smaller, *local* cities, such as Geneva, New York; next up the scale will be fewer but larger, *regional* cities, such as Rochester, New York; then a smaller number of, large, *national* cities, such as Pittsburgh and Philadelphia; and finally, a very few, very large, *world* cities, such as New York, Paris, and Tokyo. North America's world city, New York, is centrally located within the populous Northeast and affords easy access to the entire United States and Europe. There, one can discover virtually anything from Indonesian restaurants to dozens of Broadway, off-Broadway, off-off-Broadway, and local theater groups. In smaller cities, of course, Indonesian restaurants are usually nowhere to be found, and theatergoers must be content with pre-Broadway trial runs, post-Broadway tours, or small, local theater offerings. This is why, over the last century or two, people have sometimes referred disparagingly to lower-order cities as "one-horse towns." Or, as essayist Alexander Woollcott put it back in the 1930s, "A hick town is one where there is no place to go you shouldn't be" (Answers.com 2011).

The General Pattern of Land Use

> This vertical place is no more an accident than the Himalayas are. The city needs all these tall buildings to contain the tremendous energy there.
>
> Edward Field (1924–1994)

Imagine you are traveling through the countryside toward any North American city. At the beginning of the trip, there are fields and, perhaps, some scattered farms or houses. As you approach the city, built-up residential areas appear, increasing in density as you near the city's center.

A Theoretical Model. Is this pattern typical of the North American cities you know? If you think it is, economist William Alonso (1960, 2012) would say that this perception is no accident, because cities definitely use their land in a patterned way. In building his land-use model, Alonso described the ideal case, assuming that (1) the city existed in a completely flat, featureless place; (2) it had a single CBD; (3) efficient transportation existed in all directions; and (4) every person in the city was motivated by economic self-interest.

Alonso was well aware, however, that in real life, many of these assumptions might not hold. For example, San Francisco exists on hills; the Minneapolis–St. Paul metropolis has two CBDs; Philadelphia's subway system runs only to certain parts of the city; and the Mormons who founded Salt Lake City were hardly motivated by purely economic interests. Similarly, Alonso knew that other factors, such as ethnic relationships, politics, and history, all play a role in urban life. Nevertheless, his model helps us see how *economic concerns* shape a city's land use. Only those who can pay the most will locate in the city's center. This is why the downtown is primarily a business district, with whatever residential property exists there taking the form of smaller apartments typically piled high on a small amount of land.

Overall, Alonso's model suggests a city with two major districts: (1) a CBD in the middle, occupied by businesses of various types (offices, industries, and warehouses), and (2) the surrounding, mostly residential areas. Circling the residential district would be yet other rings, containing businesses that require even more land and where rents are even lower. In such urban fringe areas, we might find cemeteries, golf courses, and farmland. Still farther out, as the population dwindles away, we would begin to find little except farms.

Figure 7–1 summarizes Alonso's model of urban land use. As the figure shows, businesses pay the highest rents to be near the CBD. As the distance from the CBD grows, the number of businesses declines until, at some point, they cease altogether. This means that despite the lower rents, it is not economically feasible to operate a business there, because it requires giving up the trade advantages of location in or near the CBD.

Most residents cannot afford the high rents of the CBD, so they live some distance away. As distance increases, rents continue to drop, but at some point, no matter how low the rent, transportation problems in terms of time and money become so great that virtually no city workers choose to live there. People engaged in agriculture and other land-intensive pursuits can least afford to pay CBD rentals; thus, their businesses are a considerable distance from the CBD.

The Case of the Inner-City Poor. At this point, you may be agreeing with Alonso's

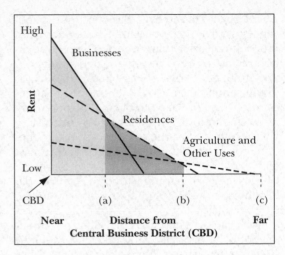

FIGURE 7–1 The Economics of Urban Land Use

general conclusions but wondering why most inner cities in North America also have many poor neighborhoods. If Alonso is correct, poor people, unable to afford high rents, should be living a long distance from the CBD.

Let's take a closer look. With little disposable income, poor people are unable to pay high rents, but they also cannot afford the high costs of travel from a remote area. Therefore, many poor people do pay higher rents than they would farther out so that they can live near the CBD. To do so, however, they live in high-density housing, perhaps sharing an apartment with another family or receiving assistance through a rent subsidy program. Also, the rents in these neighborhoods are set at what the market will bear. If it is an undesirable poor neighborhood, landlords can only charge as much rent as low-income households can afford. If this neighborhood undergoes gentrification, however, with more affluent residents moving in, the rents go much higher, forcing out those who are unable to afford them. Alonso's general conclusion then becomes applicable again.

On the other side of the coin, more affluent families can—and do—accept the higher cost of commuting from outside the CBD. These families do so mostly because they demand a great deal of space, which only a suburban neighborhood within their budgets can provide. And no doubt, many find additional "value" in having few poor people as neighbors.

Limitations

Some scholars question whether free enterprise, in the sense assumed by economic theorists like Alonso and his followers, really exists at all (Todaro and Smith 2011). To them, consumers are too powerless to set the agenda for a society's economic production.

> Unfortunately, the facts of economic life in both the developed and the less developed nations of the world are such as to render much of [this] theory of negligible importance....Consumers as a whole are rarely sovereign about anything, let alone with regard to questions of what goods and services are to be produced, in what quantities and for whom....Producers, whether private or public, have great power in determining market prices and quantities sold. The ideal of competition is typically just that—an "ideal" with little substance in reality....Finally, the invisible hand often acts not to promote the general welfare but rather to lift up those who are already well-off while pushing down the vast majority. (Todaro and Smith 2011:130)

Important non-economic factors also influence urban land use. People in some neighborhoods may actively resist any "undesirables" seeking to move nearby. This resistance often extends beyond personal attitudes, influencing zoning laws and the practices of real-estate agents to keep people from securing housing they may be able to afford. For example, a proposal in late 2006 for affordable, work force housing in Tarpon Springs, in the Tampa Bay region of Florida, touched off widespread resistance and dozens of impassioned letters to the local newspaper. "I am strongly opposed to any building of work force housing, better known as low-income housing," one resident wrote. "Clearly this action would create higher crimes and lower property valuations" (Quoted in Stein 2006:1). So strong was the backlash that the city commission voted to cut the proposed density in half, resulting in no work force housing there.

A third type of criticism points out that Alonso's economic theory applies only to a limited range of cities. For example, the capitalist–industrial city (on which the economic theory is based) is only *one* of at least five major city types that have existed historically. Other types include *regal–ritual* cities (with political and religious concerns at their core), *administrative cities* (with many government activities), *colonial cities* (that manage a colonial region for another nation), and *mercantile cities* (with trade as their principal concern). Of these, only the last operates on economic principles similar to those of the modern Western city. In the other types, people are not making decisions based on the economic principles assumed by Alonso.

None of these criticisms—consumer powerlessness, non-economic factors affecting land use, and its non-universality—means that Alonso's theory is wrong. Clearly, however, it is limited in utility and is but one model of how the free market makes use of land. Let's look at the newer, more dominant economic model, as delineated in critical urban sociology.

URBAN POLITICAL ECONOMY

By the end of the 1960s, an increasing number of social scientists had found that the traditional economic model, as well as conventional theories of urban ecology, no longer accounted for many important changes in cities. In North American cities, one had to look beyond the city itself to understand the dramatic decline in industrial jobs, the movement of millions of people from the cities to the suburbs, the movement from the Snowbelt to the Sunbelt, and the intensifying financial problems of so many cities. Some other model seemed necessary to explain the new urban realities, thus setting the stage for the urban political economy approach.

Several assumptions served as the foundation for this new approach. First, any city exists within the larger political structures of county, state, and nation. Beyond that, international political processes—such as oil prices, trade agreements, and hostilities—can affect urban life on a local level. Second, local economies do not operate independently but, rather, connect to one another and forge state, national, and international economic networks. Most important, the new breed of social scientists discount the notion that "natural processes" shape the physical form and social life of cities and advance their belief that political and economic institutions—including banks, governments, and international corporations—shape urban life.

One key focus is the role of investment decisions in shaping cities. Who makes decisions that direct a city's economy, and for what purposes? In addition, the political economy approach investigates how conflicts—for example, between labor and management, between racial and ethnic populations, and between social classes—shape the physical and social character of cities.

The political economy viewpoint drew together geographers and philosophers, as well as sociologists specializing in the investigation of urban development. Drawing on the ideas of Karl Marx, such thinkers as Henri Lefebvre, David Harvey, Manuel Castells, and Allen Scott argued that urban changes must be understood in light of historical economic and political forces. We now look at each of their contributions.

Henri Lefebvre: Redefining the Study of Cities

French philosopher Henri Lefebvre (1902–1991) sparked the application of the critical perspective to studying the city. Drawing from the writings of Karl Marx and his associate, Friedrich Engels, Lefebvre (1992, 2003) applied the economic categories of capital, labor, profit, wages, class exploitation, and inequality to explain the unevenness of urban development. In doing so, he helped develop many ideas about cities, ideas to which Marx and Engels never devoted much attention. He thus became an influential source of new thinking about the city, suggesting that urban development was as much a product of the capitalist economic system as was any manufactured good.

Two Circuits of Capital.   To advance his concept, Lefebvre made a distinction between two types of investment capital. He identified the commonly studied economic activity—investment to hire workers to manufacture a product to sell at a profit to be used for more investment—as the **primary circuit of capital.** Thus, in a capitalist system, the main flow of money is from investors into materials and labor costs in order to create a manufactured good, the sale of which generates profits for still more manufacturing ventures. This continual circulation of manufacturing capital generates much wealth for investors, but it is also what pumps the national economy. Hence, Lefebvre named this circular money flow the *primary* one.

To examine the unevenness of urban development, Lefebvre identified another important profit-oriented economic activity—real-estate investment—as the **second circuit of capital.** Investment in land, he maintained, almost always leads to profit and serves as an important means for acquiring wealth. One buys property expecting it to appreciate in value or develops land for residential or commercial purposes—both of which yield a profit. The circuit becomes complete when the investor takes that profit and invests it in more land-based projects.

Within a city, he suggested, profit-seeking motives determine the stability, decline, or rejuvenation of various areas. Lefebvre's focus on real-estate investment pushing city growth in certain ways was a turning point that influenced subsequent theories and analyses of the dynamics of urban development.

Space as Part of Social Organization.   Lefebvre made a second important contribution with his assertion that space is more than just a social "container"; it is also closely linked to behavior. In other words, we construct our surroundings to meet particular needs and objectives, and our surroundings, in turn, affect our subsequent behavior. People thus organize their daily lives and actions—whether cultural, economic, educational, or social—within the constraints or opportunities of the built environment. We need to think of planners and developers, then, as important architects of social life. Lefebvre added that comparable social systems organize space in a similar fashion, so edge cities or suburbs in Australia, Canada, and the United States, for example, closely resemble one another.

The Role of Government. Venturing further into territory uncharted by Marx, Lefebvre also considered the actions of government, from the national level down to the local level, to be a critical factor in shaping a city's use of space. Governments are empowered to make various decisions that affect city shape and urban life—decisions that range from condemnations of structures, claims of eminent domain, provision of funding, approving new roads or alterations to roads, supervising urban renewal, and responding to zoning appeals. The federal and state governments also collect taxes from, and distribute resources to, various lower-level political units (states, counties, and municipalities). In addition, the government directly owns a great deal of urban land (fire, police, and government buildings, as well as parks and roads), and it exercises control over the rest (zoning and tax valuation). With all these forms of social control over how space is utilized, governments can strike deals to attract corporations to a certain locale or take many other actions to encourage development, or redevelopment, of an area.

Furthermore, Lefebvre distinguishes between two definitions of space: **abstract space** and **social space.** The first is what businesspeople, investors, and government have in mind when they discuss the dimensions of size, location, and profit. The second is what individuals who live, work, and play in an area think about their environment. Often, Lefebvre claims, government and business leaders talk about abstract space—plans, say, to build a shopping mall or construct a low-income housing project—but pay little attention to the ideas of local people. The resulting conflict, continues Lefebvre, is much the same as, but not identical to, the class conflict discussed by Marx.

These three ideas of Lefebvre—two circuits of capitalism, space as a component of social organization, and the role of government in managing space—were highly influential in charting the course that others would take. Most new theories in urban development trace their origins to this French philosopher, although many later theorists do not agree with all of Lefebvre's arguments.

Urban Areas as Themed Environments

An excellent example of Lefebvre's ideas is found in the recycling of abandoned factories and docks into redeveloped areas that emphasize a heritage and leisure experience (Ward 1998). This transformation of public space into a packaged, themed environment has been a dominant land-use pattern since the 1960s (Gottdiener 2001; Sorkin 1992). At the forefront of such efforts was developer James W. Rouse, who worked to rejuvenate dying downtowns by introducing so-called festival marketplaces: Fanueil Hall in Boston, Harborplace in Baltimore, Market East in Philadelphia, St. Louis Union Station, the South Street Seaport in Manhattan, Riverwalk Marketplace in New Orleans, and Pioneer Place in Portland.

Although these themed public space areas are well known and prosperous, many other cities have also rediscovered their own waterfront areas. Seattle, Cincinnati, Cleveland, Louisville, and Memphis—to name just a few—redeveloped these areas with parks, restaurants, stores, and various activities. Although each city's waterfront view may vary somewhat, one finds a generic similarity existing among all such areas in all cities. Similarly, historic districts—from San Diego's Gaslamp Quarter to Boston's Faneuil Hall marketplace—have their own unique charm, but their redevelopment to lure patrons to their shops, restaurants, and entertainment locales results in a somewhat homogeneous design.

Perhaps, however, the epitome of themed urban space is not in the rebuilding of an old urban environment but, rather, in the building of an artificial city environment as a theme park *away from* the city, such as Disney's Main Street. Built at a cost of $3 billion and opened in 1993, another such entity is CityWalk in Universal City, California.

Originally intended to encourage traffic between Universal Studios' theme park and its Odeon Theatre in order to generate additional profits, it became not just a spectacular success in that regard but its own destination as well for millions of visitors.

Promoted as possessing "all the glitz and excitement of an actual urban boulevard, but with none of the problems associated with real city life...no carjackers, no panhandlers, no grime, no graffiti, no hookers, no muggers—yet also with no mall roof to block out the sunny skies or night time stars," CityWalk claims that, "for once, walking outside in the 'city' is completely safe" (Wayne 2011). Designed by Jon Jerde, the same architect who created the massive Mall of America in Minnesota, CityWalk features outrageous architecture that uses every visual trick imaginable to wow the passing crowds, along with numerous street performers (mimes, magicians, musicians, and entertaining street vendors). In Orlando, Florida, Universal Studios offers a smaller CityWalk combination of shops, restaurants, cinemas, live entertainment, and nightclubs as a gateway between its two theme parks, Universal Studios and Islands of Adventure.

Whatever entertainment value these private themed environments may have, critics warn of their dangers. Michael Sorkin (1992), for example, says that they are not benign imitations but, instead, are manipulative structures designed to maximize behavior control and eliminate the authentic interaction found in traditional public space (see the *Urban Trends* box below). Mark Gottdiener

URBAN TRENDS

If You Build It, They Will Come

The contemporary city appears to be undergoing something of a transformation second only in scale to the onset of industrialisation. All around us are indications and representations of what has been labelled an "urban renaissance," a period that promises good times ahead; times from which the city will emerge as *the* focal point for regenerative social change. Cities...are being re-branded as places to be consumed; as tourist destinations, centres of culture and as places worthy of the "cultured" middle classes. But are such changes any more than purely symbolic? Do they represent a substantive shift in how we as human beings relate to the cities around us? Is the soul of the contemporary city being sold to the consumerist paymaster and, if so, what does this mean for the long-term sustainability of our cities?

...It would not be an exaggeration to suggest that in its latest incarnation, the city is less a place for and of the people and more a unit for the efficient maximisation of culture. Shopping malls, theme parks, art galleries, museums, cinema complexes, designer apartments, casinos, sports stadia, and public spaces of consumption provide us with a mirror of ourselves or at least a mirror of society that has apparently determined what it is we are. Perhaps more worryingly, the effect of consumption on the city is as much symbolic as it is real. Even if some of our cities are struggling to achieve the renaissance that is now considered to be the obligatory norm, they will at least pursue this renaissance at a symbolic level, not least in the hope that if the process of re-branding is believable enough, if you can get people to believe that there is an urban renaissance going on, then real change may follow.

Source: Steven Miles, *Spaces for Consumption* (London: Sage Publications, 2010), pp. 1–2.

believes that in the aftermath of the cold, faceless public space left behind by the modernist era, the forces of capitalism have staged a "vengeful return of meaning and symbolism" to create "material space for the realization of consumer fantasies" through imitation and simulation (2001:34, 70). The problem is that as we buy into a visual theme, we lose our reality, turning our landscape inside out and becoming convinced that all places are the same in the built environment that excludes other forms (Zukin 1993).

David Harvey: The Baltimore Study

Geographer David Harvey (1992; orig. 1973) illustrates Lefebvre's ideas in a Marxist analysis of how the capitalist real-estate system operated in Baltimore, directly shaping many of the city's problems concerning social inequality. He divided Baltimore into real-estate submarkets that included the inner city, white ethnic areas, the low- to moderate-income African American area of West Baltimore,

areas of high turnover, middle-income areas in northeast and southwest Baltimore, and other upper-income areas. Each of these areas revealed a distinct pattern of buying and selling, as reflected in the amount of upfront cash or investment through private loan transactions, bank financing, and government insurance. Each physical environment generated different levels of commitment by community banks, private financial institutions, and government agencies, which, in turn, influenced potential developers, speculators, homeowners, and renters.

Harvey's detailed analysis revealed that urban development is not a monolithic growth process. Instead, it occurs unevenly. This second circuit of capital varies in its investment arrangements from place to place, influenced by different combinations of social factors, profit potential, and conflict. For example, banks showed no interest in lending to the inner-city poor, who, of necessity, financed their housing transactions by cash payment, private loans, and/or government

David Harvey's study disclosed how some Baltimore neighborhoods, with their distinctive row houses, fared better than others because of priorities set by real-estate investors and government programs. His conclusion was that these decisions, more than those by departing industrialists, are closely linked to decaying areas of a city, prompting abandonment and relocation to another area.

programs. White ethnics also had trouble securing bank financing; instead, they financed their housing purchases through community-based savings and loan associations. Both the inner city and white ethnic areas had difficulty obtaining Federal Housing Authority (FHA) or Veterans Administration (VA) insurance, unlike Baltimore's middle-income sections. People in more affluent sections rarely resorted to FHA guarantees, and they made far greater use of commercial and savings banks. Also, unlike residents of poor or working-class neighborhoods, they could repel, with their political and economic power, speculative construction incursions into their own neighborhoods.

Thus, Harvey demonstrated how discrimination by investment capitalists in the housing market affects the dynamics of buying, selling, and neighborhood transition. He also showed the role of government in shaping a city's use of space: West Baltimore improved more than other poor areas in the city did as a result of multiple government renewal programs. Essentially, Harvey's Baltimore study disclosed how the priorities of the second circuit of capital, aided by government programs, are linked directly to decay of the central city and to the suburbanization of the population. Actions by real-estate investors—more so than actions by industrial capitalists, Harvey maintained—led to areas of the city becoming run-down and abandoned.

Urban change, claims Harvey, reflects the changing needs of a capitalist economy. That is, capitalists build a physical city that is appropriate to the city's needs at one point in time only to destroy that physical city later, usually in the course of some crisis. Different segments of the urban population—investors (finance capital), store owners (commerce capital), manufacturers (industrial capital), financial analysts, and even white- or blue-collar workers—have different priorities and goals. Capital interests, seeking to make a profit, and labor, seeking to protect and enhance its standard of living, often engage "in a series of running battles over a variety of issues that relate to the creation, management, and use of the built environment" (Harvey 1992:268).

Unwilling, therefore, to risk their profits by granting too much power to workers, the capitalist class seeks government intervention to secure the type of urban development that serves its narrow interests. This strategy explains widespread urban blight; finance capital has little reason to invest in poor neighborhoods, preferring instead the greater profits to be found in high-rent districts. This reluctance to aid decaying urban areas, claims Harvey, is precisely why government intervention is so important. Public urban renewal projects, however, seem to operate only to restore the area's profitability in order to attract finance and commerce capital once again, and in the process do little for the poor. Harvey's contribution, then, lies in revealing how the actions of finance capital (rather than industrial capital) affect a city's fortunes.

Manuel Castells: Updating Marx

Although influenced by Lefebvre's writings, Manuel Castells initially maintained a more orthodox Marxist approach toward the study of cities. His special contribution (1982, 1985) was extending Marxist analysis beyond the traditional conflict between labor and capital and applying it to distinct urban patterns. He also highlighted the conflict between local government and the working class arising from local administration of various social welfare programs. The federal government funds such programs as needs-based income, housing, and health care benefits for the poor, but local or city governments typically administer them. Thus, city residents seeking these resources often become entangled in conflict with city agencies.

Welfare Capitalism.   Castells views welfare capitalism—that is, the government providing subsidies to workers—as an important social movement affecting urban life. To him, key issues, such as housing, education, mass transportation, health, and welfare, make sense only within the context of disputes arising over their administration by agencies of city government. Such government activity to provide resources to the working class, he says, represents an effort to "extend" capitalism and gives rise to new urban struggles and patterns of conflict unknown in Marx's time.

Changing economic conditions in the 1980s, 1990s, and in recent years lessened the impact of Castells's analysis, as advanced industrialized countries cut back their once-expansive welfare programs. Recessions, aging populations, tax revolts, budget deficits, and fiscal crises all curbed government spending and, in some cases, even led to the dismantling of some welfare programs. In the United States in 2011, the budget deficit crisis and economic realities forced the federal government to find ways to cut billions of dollars from various social welfare programs. With less federal monies coming their way, state and local governments also retrenched in funding their subsidizing programs.

Modes of Development. Examining industrial growth in suburbs, Castells adapted one of Marx's concepts to fit the information age. Whereas Marx had stressed the **mode of production**—the things needed to produce goods and services, such as land, tools, knowledge, wealth, or factories—Castells (1992) introduced the concept of the **mode of development.** The key element in the industrial mode of development, he explained, was discovering and applying new sources of energy. In today's informational mode of development, however, the key element is developing new forms and sources of information. One obvious consequence of this shift is that corporate decisions about location no longer rest on proximity to raw materials or a large, unskilled labor pool, as they once did.

Castells's focus was the differential effect of emerging high-tech businesses on segments of the urban region. Specifically, he found that high-tech production disproportionately occurred in suburban rather than central-city communities. Such companies typically have facilities on the periphery of cities, thereby accelerating the pace of outward movement and sparking the rise of edge cities. Influencing the choice of suburban locations is the need for large-batch production facilities combined

with automated subsidiary plants, access to a freeway system, and the typically suburban locale of research and design centers as well as military installations for testing and marketing defense-related products. Additionally, he contends that real power now exists within the globally integrated network of financial capital and not confined to the global cities themselves (Castells 2000).

Allen Scott: Business Location and the Global Economy

Another geographer, Allen J. Scott (1980, 1988), offers insights regarding the impact of changes in the production process on urban space. His approach is not a comprehensive theory of the built environment, but rather, a study of the relationship between a city's fortunes and the globalization of the economy. Furthermore, in rejecting the urban ecology approach, Scott suggests that the economic interests of powerful transnational corporations—not a biological model of species competition over territory—determine patterns of urban growth.

Horizontal Integration. For most of the twentieth century, until about 1970, cities evolved into metropolitan regions as corporations changed in their economic organization. Once, companies were small entities, with all their functions centralized in one location. Gradually, many industries absorbed or consolidated with competitors, sometimes taking the form of an **oligopoly**—that is, market domination by a few producers. Then, these industries maintained headquarters in a major city, with easy access to banking, marketing, and other necessary services, but they located their production plants, distribution centers, and sales divisions elsewhere, in the locales most advantageous to them. In time, many companies gained control over the manufacture of all parts that went into their final product, as when auto companies manufactured not just the engine, frame, and body of the automobile but also the batteries, headlights, radios, upholstered seats, window glass, and bumpers. Some companies even obtained ownership of raw materials needed for the manufacturing process. With their separate functions thus spatially dispersed, companies maintained a national network of command and control to reduce costs and maximize profits, an economic structure known as **horizontal integration.**

One way to maximize profits is to minimize shipping costs in the total manufacturing process. Not surprisingly, when horizontal integration was predominant, the specialized production facilities were mostly located near the main assembly plant—virtually all auto parts plants, for example, were within 150 miles of Detroit, or "Motor City," the automobile manufacturing center. The close proximity of these subsidiary agglomeration industries not only kept shipping costs low but also created an economically interdependent metropolitan region. As the companies prospered, so, too, did the cities.

Vertical Disintegration. Beginning in the 1970s, large corporations, although still maintaining some horizontal integration (especially of manufacturing, marketing, and administration activities), began to unload their production support companies—a process known as **vertical disintegration.** In other words, instead of manufacturing materials or parts needed for the production process themselves, they awarded contracts to suppliers through a process of competitive bidding. Competitiveness among subcontractors resulted in lower costs by eliminating the overhead expenses of maintaining inventory stocks, which offset concerns about shipping expenses. In addition, the advent of computer-assisted manufacturing enhanced production coordination, enabling companies to keep track of all needs and order "just-in-time" parts more easily.

Once mostly located in the office buildings of cities, many corporate businesses—lured by local tax abatements and other economic incentives—either located or relocated part or all of their operations to suburban campus areas beginning in the late twentieth century. A good example is the Pacific Shores business park in Silicon Valley, Redwood City, California, on the edge of San Francisco Bay.

A significant consequence of vertical disintegration was the creation of many new supplier companies, located where labor and energy costs were lower, either in North America or abroad. Scott sees this last development as the climax of vertical disintegration: the ability of large companies to conduct business on a global scale. In short, many businesses became transnational or multinational, investing their capital and locating their manufacturing, marketing, and administration anywhere in the world that best suited their needs. Suppliers may now be anywhere—perhaps in the non-unionized, low-energy-cost Sunbelt or in extremely low-wage countries of the developing world.

How did this affect older industrial cities? For most, plant closings meant the loss of thousands of jobs, an out-migration of workers and their families seeking jobs elsewhere, and a depressed economy. Loss of an industrial base also adversely affected the city's commercial base, because stores no longer had the same customers as before. In contrast, the Sunbelt exploded in industrial development and population growth. As virtually every northeastern U.S. city steadily shrank in population during the second half of the twentieth century, the fastest-growing cities were those in the Sunbelt (see Chapter 3).

No longer dominated by manufacturing, older cities shifted to providing greater employment opportunities in business services. Most have not fully recovered and are still experiencing population decline. A few cities, however, such as New York, London, and Tokyo, now function as "highly concentrated command posts in the organization of the world economy." They are also important locations of finance, specialized service firms, and innovation sources, and they serve as markets for the products and innovations produced (Sassen 2001:3–4).

New economic realities thus shape the production process and, in turn, affect urban growth patterns—a subject we will now explore further through two sociological approaches, one examining local conditions and the other considering global conditions.

John Logan and Harvey Molotch: Urban Growth Machines

John Logan and Harvey Molotch (2007) employed political economy theory in an effort to identify *who* the central decision makers in North American cities are and determine *why* they do what they do. In concentrating on the battles between pro- and anti-growth factions, their study is essentially an application of Lefebvre's categories of abstract space and social space that we discussed earlier.

Urban growth coalitions—typically made up of bankers, businesspeople, corporate property owners, developers, politicians, and investors—seek to spark population growth, increase the market value of land, and stimulate the city's economy through investment and development. To accomplish these goals, they pressure the city government to create a "good business climate" (cleanliness, safety, tax incentives, low-interest loans, and relocation assistance). They also seek to enhance the image of the city, promoting its attributes, such as cultural and recreational activities, sports teams, landmarks, and nightlife. Their focus on quality of life, however, only extends to what Lefebvre termed "abstract space" issues involving the high profits that accompany urban growth.

In contrast, most local residents have a "social space" view of their community, and they may oppose growth as being against their own best interests. City residents may wish to protect the "character" of their neighborhood, preserve older buildings, limit traffic flow, and maintain parks and other open spaces.

Advocates of urban growth point out its advantages—more jobs, additional tax ratables, increased economic activity—and they are often correct in doing so. What often accompany growth, however, are environmental degradation, higher rents, more crime, greater traffic congestion, and an infrastructure unable to handle an increased population. Tensions in the growth machine materialize as community groups seek to block a proposal or, at least, lessen its negative impact on their community and the environment.

Logan and Molotch also point out how the global economy influences many changes in the city. Today, local political action is less effective than it once was, because the deindustrialization of North American cities has caused the flight of industrial capital. The "new international division of labor" may benefit some people—major corporations and their stockholders reap huge profits from the new global economy—but the loss of jobs hurts ordinary people in cities back home. Thus, local people have less power to oppose the corporate agenda, just as corporations have more power to get their own way.

The question that corporate executives ask is simply, "If we do this, will we make money?" Concerns for the welfare of the worker, the neighborhood, and the city's poor simply take a backseat—if these concerns exist at all. This "profit-bias" results in the relocation of production facilities to developing countries where labor costs are cheaper, thereby undermining the traditional economic base of once-thriving manufacturing regions. Older city plants shut down and skilled workers lose their jobs, setting in motion a ripple effect as multinational corporations centralize their administrative operations in just a few global cities, thus displacing similar functions in other cities and suburbs. Ongoing competition and the disappearance of some companies through **mega-mergers** (acquisitions of companies with assets valued at $1 billion or more by a multibillion-dollar company) help ensure continuance of this process whereby the global economy impacts on local economies.

In the end, urban political economy presents an alternative to what its proponents see as the biased approach of the older urban ecology model. In the newer model, the assumption is that profit making and capitalism are the natural forces shaping cities. Those forces are global in nature and, thus, are mostly beyond the capabilities of cities to influence.

THE GLOBAL ECONOMY

Economic forces always affect cities. As discussed in Chapter 3, for example, the Industrial Revolution redefined urban life and greatly increased the size of city populations. At the midpoint of the twentieth century, the typical North American city was an industrial center. White-ethnic, blue-collar neighborhoods, built around the factories in which residents worked, peppered the urban landscape. In other parts of the city, the middle class resided. Then, in the 1950s and 1960s, the exodus of the middle class—soon followed by many businesses and industries—created a fiscal crisis from which some cities, especially smaller ones, have never recovered.

Deindustrialization

During the 1970s, U.S. manufacturers—in virtually all fields, including steel, auto, clothing, and electronics—made profit-driven decisions to dismantle and disinvest in U.S. operations. To minimize labor costs, they closed factories in the United States and outsourced to Asia and Latin America, dramatically disrupting people's lives and the welfare of many urban communities. For example, Youngstown, Ohio—situated between Pittsburgh, Cleveland, and Chicago—had a robust, blue-collar economy as a center of the steel industry. When its famous Jeannette Blast Furnace shut down in 1978, cutting the heart out of the local economy, 50,000 Youngstown workers lost their jobs, and the city was rocked by economic devastation, from which it has still not fully recovered (Cowie and Heathcott 2003; Linkon and Russo 2003).

Other manufacturers—in appliances and electronics, for instance—quickly followed suit, and by the end of the 1970s, manufacturing in virtually every field was in decline nationwide. This transfer of much economic production to other countries dramatically changed the older cities. Gone were most of the jobs that earlier migrants and immigrants had used as a path toward economic security. Gone, too, were the ties that bound central-city workers to their local employers. Also gone was a sizable portion of the cities' tax base.

The global economy manifests itself in virtually every city. It is practically impossible, for example, to go to any urban locale worldwide as here in Tokyo and not find McDonald's, Burger King, Pizza Hut, KFC, American cigarettes, Coke, or Pepsi. Foreign sales are an important part of all multinational corporate profits.

Economic Restructuring

The 1980s and 1990s bore witness to **economic restructuring** and the globalization of the economy that spawned still other changes in metropolitan regions. Forced to restructure their economies away from manufacturing, North American cities evolved into service centers, specializing in advertising, corporate management, finance, and information processing. In particular, cities expanded those business services required by the finance capitalists heading up investment activity for the global economy (Sassen 2001).

Such changes are evident in the present-day character of the urban labor force. The demand for many of the entry-level factory jobs traditionally held by the urban poor with limited education and skills dropped dramatically, countered by a rising demand for computer-literate workers with verbal and quantitative skills. The reason was that even though some corporate headquarters moved outside the major cities, the latter continued to provide a necessary concentration of services for firms with a world-market orientation requiring access to a support services complex (Sassen 2006:96).

This is an important point. Although the evolution of a global economy prompted a new generation of cynics to sound the death knell for cities, cities still play an essential role in today's world. Ironically, those massive trends of globalization toward the spatial dispersal of economic activities at the metropolitan, national, and global levels contributed to the demand for new forms of territorial centralization of top-level management and control functions. A specialized services complex capable of handling the most advanced and complicated corporate needs is more likely to be in a city rather than a suburban office park (Sassen 2006:97).

World-Systems Analysis

With its macrosocial view, the political economy approach to understanding cities fits nicely into a world-systems perspective. This emphasis views capitalism as evolving through a long, historical process into a single, integrated, worldwide economic and political system. This system operates as a hierarchy so that countries with various levels of economic power constitute (1) the "core," (2) the "semi-periphery," and (3) the "periphery." Within that framework, cities occupy a place in the world urban hierarchy that greatly affects their individual growth patterns (Chase-Dunn and Babones 2006; Wallerstein 2004).

The Hierarchy of Countries. The more economically developed countries—Canada, Japan, the United States, and the nations of Western Europe—constitute the core of this world system and are home to the transnational corporations that dominate the global economy. The headquarters of transnational corporations, located in large cities within affluent countries, carry out high-level decision making that guides the world's economic

forces. Because so many employees are well-paid professionals, these cities benefit by the quality of housing and from the economic and social enterprises that spring up to cater to their tastes.

Large semi-peripheral countries—Argentina, Brazil, China, India, Indonesia, Mexico, and Poland—as well as smaller semi-peripheral countries—Hungary, Israel, South Africa, South Korea, and Taiwan—have close ties with the core nations. These second-tier countries serve as key nodes in the global urban system, as information technology binds their cities together in dense interaction networks. Yet, despite the integration of these cities into cross-border economic networks, they are in the midrange of the global hierarchy, and their countries play a secondary role in global economic matters (Sassen 2002). However, the rapid economic growth of China and Korea in the world economy may soon move them to the level of core countries. Most employees in semi-peripheral

An example of the global economy is the location of manufacturing plants in developing countries. Benefiting in these semi-peripheral or peripheral countries with their cheaper, non-union labor forces and generous tax incentives, companies willingly pay higher shipping costs to escape higher U.S. taxes and expenses for wages, health care, and other employee benefits.

countries are lower middle class, and for the most part, their somewhat lower standard of living brings a less grand variety and quality of activities to the urban scene than are found in cities of the core countries.

Countries in the periphery are the poorer, less-developed countries in Africa, Asia, and Latin America. Jobs in these countries typically pay little and offer little opportunity to advance. These workers are typically rural migrants, living in slums or shantytowns and struggling to survive. The impact of the global economy on the cities of peripheral countries is more negative than positive. A small, affluent elite exists in these cities, but most urban residents live at the lower end of the socio-economic scale, having few of the usual social amenities of a city, which are reserved for tourists or the small, local elite. Integration into the global market encourages informal enterprises within local urban economies, but often at the cost of a serious erosion of wages and employment conditions. Essentially, the major impact of globalization on cities has been a strengthening of income inequality, an increasing vulnerability of their populations to poverty, and large-scale spatial segregation through the peripheral location of the poor (Kaya 2010; Roberts 2005).

Thus, the three tiers of countries in the world system are unequal yet interdependent. The system operates mostly in the interest of the richest nations; it provides far less to the majority of the world's people, who live in less economically developed nations. The quality of urban life in each of the three tiers reflects this world-system hierarchy.

In recent years, many governments and non-profit organizations have taken action against one highly exploitative aspect of the global economy. Many Northern Hemisphere industries, such as apparel and sporting goods, rely on low-wage labor in the third-tier countries of the Southern Hemisphere. Those designers, researchers, executives, and other white-collar employees of these companies live and work in the large cities of the core countries and receive excellent salaries and benefits. In contrast, the workers who actually make the products live in the peripheral countries, where young children and women work long hours for little pay in hot, crowded factories. Often, they are bonded laborers, meaning they have no freedom and are kept in confined areas when not working, receive only minimal amounts of food, and even suffer verbal and physical abuse. Several years ago, some companies, like Adidas and Nike, yielded to public pressure to end their allowing such conditions in their suppliers' factories. Passage of laws in the United States, Canada, Europe, and other countries against importing products made by child labor has reduced—but not eliminated—these practices.

The Role of Cities.   As mentioned earlier, cities serve as important nodes in the global network, linking together money (investment capital), people (human capital), production (industrial capital), and commodities (commercial capital). Instant communications, electronic cash transfers, rapid transportation, and the relative ease of shipping by tankers or cargo jets make cities key elements of the global economy. As such, they are locked in a reciprocal relationship: They help shape the world system, and in turn, the world system shapes them. Today, it is the importance of a city's role in the world system that largely determines its prospects for growth and prosperity (Alderson and Beckfield 2004).

Cities are no longer independent entities whose fortunes rise or fall according to what happens in a limited, local region. The prevailing view is that *place* no longer matters—that modern technology allows firms to locate anywhere, making cities irrelevant to the globalization of economic activity. One expert, however, disagrees. Saskia Sassen argues that cities offer an infrastructure concentration and servicing that are key dynamics in providing the capabilities for global control. Although some components of the financial district—notably in foreign currency markets—may exist in cyberspace, international cities, such as New York, London, Paris, Sydney, Tokyo, and Zurich, are examples of another aspect of the global economy: urban economic cores of banking and service activities. They are "transterritorial centers

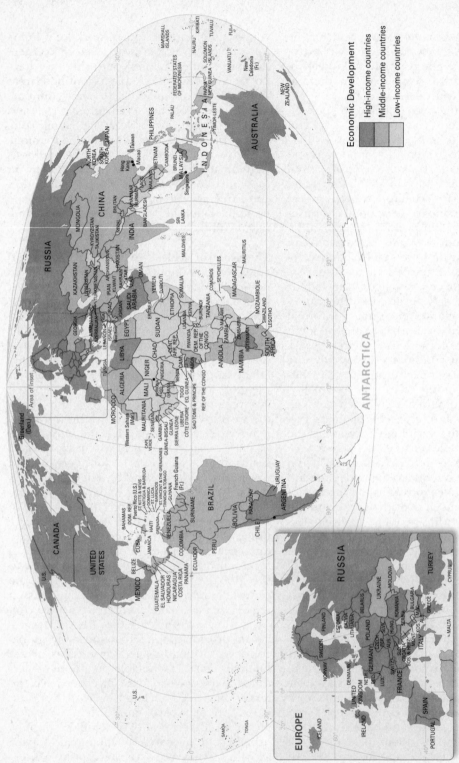

FIGURE 7-2 Economic Development in Global Perspective

Source: From *The United Nations Development Programme* (2006). Used by permission of the United Nations Development Programme.

Nike is Vietnam's single largest private employer, with 130,000 employees. Its production of $700 million worth of footwear ranks it as the third-largest supplier behind China and Indonesia. Also among Vietnam's $6 billion in exports to the U.S. market alone are IKEA housewares and Victoria's Secret lingerie. In the global economy, Vietnam has emerged as a major player.

constituted via intercity electronic networks and various types of economic transactions" within "a specific complex of industries and activities" (Sassen 2006:148). Thus, these cities stand at the apex of the global urban hierarchy, because they are the financial capitals of the nations that dominate the world economy. On a smaller scale, Miami and Toronto—as significant regional sites— illustrate the locational concentration of certain industries and activities embedded in the new international corporate sector. Their financial districts are of recent vintage, and their expansion is a response to the dynamics of globalization.

The place of cities in the world economy, then, is as "command points, global marketplaces, and production sites for the information economy" (Sassen 2006:199). Some intermediate sectors of the economy—the ones not geared to world markets but providing services to the mostly suburbanized middle class—may have left, but cities still provide strategic terrain for operations in a globalized economic system.

URBAN POLITICAL ECONOMY: FOUR PRINCIPLES

Although various urban political economists still emphasize different aspects of economic activity and mix the disciplinary viewpoints of economics, geography, political science, and sociology in one fashion or another, they all essentially agree on four principles as the foundation for studying and analyzing cities and urban life:

1. *A city's form and growth result not from "natural processes" but, rather, from decisions made by people and organizations that control wealth and other key resources.* Rejecting the urban ecology model, urban political economists view cities as benefiting or suffering from investment decisions made by financial and business organizations. To remain competitive, companies will either expand or relocate

Potsdamer Platz, once a no-man's land of weeds and barbed wire between East and West, is the symbolic heart of modern Berlin. The 82-acre development is a cluster of a new mass transit system, sleek corporate high rises, shopping malls, and theaters. The district was developed mainly with global capital from corporations such as Sony, Asea Brown Boveri (an international conglomerate), and DaimlerChrysler for the sites of their European headquarters.

their operations, depending on which action maximizes profits. Thus, broader economic forces and trends, not just local conditions, shape the cities, because advances in transportation and communication technologies allow the geographical mobility of capital and labor, thus freeing businesses from being rooted in a specific locale. When necessary, then, companies will move their corporate offices or production facilities, and such disinvestment in one place and investment in another impact significantly on both localities, affecting economic well-being, labor, and population migration.

2. *Urban forms and urban social arrangements reflect conflicts over the distribution of resources.* Urban life, claim political economists, is an ongoing struggle between rich and poor, powerful and powerless, management and labor, as well as the needs of vast businesses and the desires of local communities. Such ongoing confrontation often brings a sense of paralysis to the people living within today's cities.

3. *Government continues to play an important role in urban life.* Local governments allocate resources and mediate conflicts among various groups that are vying for support. Decisions about zoning, tax incentives, and spending priorities, for example, still have much to do with a city's (a) business locations, (b) housing and resident population types, and (c) public space activities. And, significantly, because cities exist within a larger society, the federal government—with its enormous resources and regulatory powers—is a major influence on urban life, both directly, through its spending programs, and indirectly, through its management of the prime interest rate for loans and its rules governing investors.

4. *Urban growth patterns significantly result from economic restructuring.* The globalization of the economy changed the face of many North American cities, as manufacturing gave way to service industries. Furthermore, corporate mergers and takeovers created

vast conglomerates, in the process eliminating many medium-sized firms and the jobs they provided. Downsizing, by which corporations strive to achieve a leaner, less costly organizational structure, also reduced the number of middle-management positions. Together, these dimensions of economic restructuring dramatically reshaped cities, fostering growth or decline in metropolitan regions throughout North America and around the world.

THE URBANIZATION OF POVERTY

The world's poor once huddled mostly in rural areas, but no longer. Now, they live mostly in cities, and in 2010, one out of four city dwellers lived in slums. Although 22 million people moved out of slums between 2000 and 2010, the actual number of slum dwellers increased, from 777 million in 2000 to 828 million in 2010. This urbanization of poverty creates problems that affect the quality of life for all residents—problems that cities so far have been unable to resolve. Short of drastic action, the situation will only get worse, with UN projections of an additional 6 million annually (UN-Habitat 2011).

The Developing World

In virtually every less-developed country, poverty—once found primarily in the villages of traditional agricultural societies—has moved to its cities (Figure 7–3). Significantly, however, the poverty of the world's poor is not in the same recognizable form that exists in the industrialized countries. This different form of poverty traps these unfortunate people in nations that have solved the first economic problem—the production of material goods—but not yet the second—the sufficient, if not equitable, distribution of the goods their industries produce. Food and consumer goods are not the only areas of deprivation. These cities lack sufficient housing, piped water, sewerage, public transportation, schools, police protection, doctors, hospitals, and other necessary amenities and

defenses of urban life. The *Urban Living* box on page 195 illustrates one profile of urban poverty.

What is intimidating about the urbanization of poverty in less-developed countries is its scale. Between 1950 and 1990, as the first wave of industrialization came to poor, preindustrial countries, their cities expanded by 1 billion inhabitants, both through migration from villages and through natural increase. Expanding slums account for 38 percent of current urban growth, while the city populations are increasing faster than city infrastructure can adapt. Sub-Saharan Africa—including Chad, Niger, and Sierra Leone—has the largest slum population, about 200 million, or about 62 percent of its total urban population. Latin America and the Caribbean have about 111 million (24 percent), Southeastern Asia 89 million (31 percent), and Western Asia 35 million, 25 percent of its total urban population (UN-Habitat 2011).

Already exceeding the total population of cities in industrialized countries, cities in developing countries increase by 5 million new residents every month. These cities cannot now provide for the hundreds of millions already living there, let alone for those yet to come. At present, 884 million people in the world lack access to safe drinking water. In the megacities of Asia, more than two-thirds of the urban poor do not have access to adequate sanitation, as is the case for about three-fifths of urban Africans (World Health Organization 2010). Housing is no problem for most urban poor in less-developed countries, because they had previously built their own shelters in their villages. Most city land already belongs to someone else, however, so they build their makeshift dwellings in the less desirable locales—the lowlands and even wetlands around the city, or on hillsides too steep for ordinary buildings. These shantytowns go by many names: *citas miserias, bustees, bidonvilles, geccondus, favelas,* and *pueblos jovenes*. With a stubbornness and resistance to bureaucratic oppression, the residents struggle to survive, and they do so utilizing a reciprocal exchange system to help one another cope with extreme

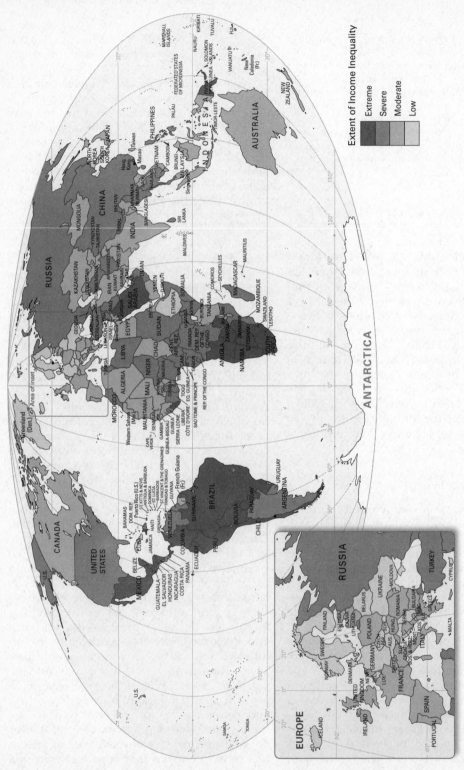

FIGURE 7–3 Prosperity and Stagnation in Global Perspective

Source: From *The United Nations Development Programme* (2006). Used by permission of the United Nations Development Programme.

Extent of Income Inequality

- Extreme
- Severe
- Moderate
- Low

URBAN LIVING

India: A Different Kind of Poverty

India contains about two-fifths of the world's poor, but that statistic does not prepare North Americans to face the reality of poverty there. Many of the country's 1.2 billion people live in conditions far worse than do those we label as "poor" at home. A traveler's first experience of Indian life is sobering and, sometimes, shocking. Arriving in Chennai (Madras), one of India's largest cities, with 4.9 million inhabitants, a visitor immediately recoils from the smell of human sewage that hangs over the city like a malodorous cloud. Untreated sewage also renders much of the region's water unsafe to drink. The sights and sounds of Chennai are strange and intense—as motorbikes, trucks, carts pulled by oxen, and waves of people choke the streets. Along the roads, vendors sit on burlap cloth hawking fruits, vegetables, and cooked food. Seemingly oblivious to the urban chaos all around them, people work, talk, bathe, and sleep in the streets. Tens of millions of homeless people fill the cities of India.

Chennai is also dotted by more than a thousand shanty settlements, containing more than a million people, many of whom have converged on the city from rural villages in search of something better. Shantytowns are clusters of huts constructed of branches, leaves, and discarded material. These dwellings offer little privacy and lack refrigeration, running water, and bathrooms. The visitor from the United States understandably feels uneasy entering such a community, because the poorest sections of our own inner cities seethe with frustration and, often, explode with violence.

Here again, however, India offers a sharp contrast: Its people understand poverty differently than we do. No restless young men hang out at the corner; no drug dealers work the streets; and there is surprisingly little danger. In the United States, poverty often means anger and isolation; in India, even shantytowns are built of strong families—children, parents, and perhaps, elderly grandparents—who extend a smile and a welcome.

In traditional societies like India, ways of life change slowly. To most Indians, life is shaped by *dharma*, the Hindu concept of duty and destiny that encourages them to accept their fate, whatever it may be. Mother Teresa, who won praise for her work among the poorest of India's people, went to the heart of the cultural differences: "Americans have angry poverty," she explained. "In India, there is worse poverty, but it is a happy poverty."

Perhaps we should not describe as "happy" anyone who clings to the edge of survival, but the sting of poverty in India is eased by the strength and support of families and communities, a sense that existence has a purpose, and a worldview that encourages each person to accept whatever life offers. As a result, the visitor comes away from a first encounter with Indian poverty in confusion: "How can people be so poor, and yet apparently content, vibrant, and so joyful?"

Source: Based on UN-Habitat data and John Macionis's field research in Chennai.

poverty. Others live an even worse existence, as homeless city dwellers. Sadly, many of them are the young, as the *Urban Living* box on page 196 reveals.

The Developed World

Unlike the less-developed countries, the more-developed countries of Asia, Europe, and North America have maintained urban

URBAN LIVING

Latin American "Street Children": Living on the Edge

Perhaps the greatest tragedy in Latin American cities is the millions of "street children"— or *meninos de rua*. Like the tip of an iceberg, their presence suggests problems that run far deeper: poverty that stunts the lives of children who labor long hours in factories each day, who work as prostitutes, or who fall victim to hunger and disease. The United Nations International Children's Emergency Children's Relief Fund (UNICEF) estimates that as many as 50 million street children live in Latin America alone, with their greatest numbers in Brazil and Mexico.

The street children are orphans or come from broken or crowded homes where there is not enough to eat—and where physical and sexual abuse is commonplace. About two in five children on the streets are between 6 and 11 years of age (some are younger), and about half are between 12 and 18 years. Most live in and around the cities' sprawling public markets, where it is easy to scavenge for food. A few work at shining shoes, cleaning windshields, or selling anything from candy to their bodies, but most beg or steal to survive. The average age of children at the garbage dump looking for items to reclaim and sell is 10 years. Girls, as well as boys, often become involved in prostitution as early as age 13.

Many cannot resist the temptation of cheap drugs to obliterate their hunger and cold. A few years ago, glue was the drug favored by street kids, but today, solvent and paint thinner are cheaper and easier to come by. A solvent-soaked rag, easily clenched in a palm, is also much more discreet than plastic bags of glue, which police have been known to seize and dump on the children's hair and clothes. All solvents have the desired effect: They stop the hunger pains, and they numb the physical and psychological effects of the brutality of the security forces. Inhaling the fumes produces hallucinations and escape, but the long-term effects are devastating: irreversible brain damage, paralysis, kidney or liver failure, and eventually, death. About 95 percent of street youth in Latin America use drugs on a daily basis, most commonly solvents or shoe glue (Narconon International 2010).

In other countries, the story is much the same. In the eyes of too many people, street children are not even human, so they are dispatched in much the same way that one would step on a cockroach. The statistics are shocking. Violent deaths claim about 45 children in Honduras each month and more than 10 children every week in Guatemala, more than half from gunshot wounds. Authorities often threaten and beat Salvadorian street children with half of their injuries reported from beatings, yet even with these injuries and threats, three-fourths of these children reported feeling safer on the streets than in their own homes. Most Brazilian street children expect to be killed before they are 18 by vigilante death squads. It's a form of social cleansing, ridding the streets of social vermin who lie amid the rubbish or under parked cars, curled up inconspicuously on the concrete until someone comes along and kicks them. And people rarely stop to wonder why they are there in the first place (Honduras Weekly 2008; Toybox 2012).

societies for generations, if not centuries. Although their cities have contained large numbers of poor people for that same period of time, only recently have greater concentrations of the poor clustered in urban areas compared with elsewhere. This pattern is more pronounced in Canada than in the United States.

Canada. In a comparative demographic profile of poverty throughout Canada, the Canadian Council on Social Development reported that images of poverty as a rural phenomenon are out of date. Instead, poverty has an urban dimension, with roughly 7 of every 10 poor Canadians living in an urban area. Canada's three largest cities (Toronto, Montreal, and Vancouver) have the highest proportion of families with income below the low-income cut-off (LICO). Female-headed, single-parent families are more likely to be poor, and the cities with the highest proportion are Winnipeg, Hamilton, and Toronto. Similarly, the rate of poverty among senior citizens is higher among those living in Canada's larger cities (Vancouver, Montreal, Toronto, and Quebec) than in smaller urban areas (Federation of Canadian Municipalities 2010).

United States. Central cities do not house the majority of the U.S. poor. In 2010, 51 percent of the nation's poor lived in metro statistical areas outside principal cities (suburban areas), 16 percent in non-metropolitan areas, and 33 percent in central cities (U.S. Census Bureau 2011d). Central cities, however, do contain the highest concentrations of poverty, and their poverty rate has been above the national average since the early 1970s. Two major reasons account for this concentration of poverty in the centers of large U.S. cities. First, many affluent residents moved to the suburbs, leaving the poor behind. Second, as more jobs moved to the suburbs, employment opportunities for city residents dwindled. Still mired in a recession in 2010, the U.S. poverty rate of 15.1 was its highest since 1994, resulting in many cities reporting a significant increase in family homelessness, with about 636,000 people experiencing homelessness in 2011 (U.S. Census Bureau 2011d; Homelessness Research Institute 2012).

Europe. Many Western European cities are beset with poverty problems, generated in large

Perhaps nowhere in North America is the global economy as visible as in the daily loading and unloading of container shipments onto or off trucks and ships at its seaports, such as here in Baltimore. Many of these goods are finished products on their way to wholesalers, but others are parts destined for assembly in factories of nations other than the ones in which they were manufactured.

URBAN TRENDS

A Bold Initiative

While shelters can provide a clean and safe environment for a homeless family, the shelter system should not be simply a way station until permanent housing is secured. To address the needs of these families, shelters also must provide a variety of services and programs that enable families to build sound, independent living skills, complete their education, and obtain job training before moving to permanent housing. Not shelters, but rather Residential Education Training (RET) Centers—or American Family Inns—are required to deliver such a service intervention plan. Through RET Centers, desperately needed services such as health care, counseling, and substance abuse treatment can be economically and efficiently provided. Educational programs such as living skills workshops for adults or after-school accelerated learning programs for children are immediately accessible and responsive to the needs of parents and children. Homes for the Homeless has developed and has continued to refine the RET Center model over the past five years as a response to the changing characteristics of homeless families.

American Family Inns have proven to be a successful mechanism to start families on a secure path to independent living. *Approximately 94 percent of all families who have participated in the services offered by HFH's RET Centers have maintained their residences once placed in permanent housing.* When compared to New York City's return-to-shelter rate of 50 percent for formerly homeless families, RET Centers offer a successful solution by addressing the severe complexities of the poverty faced by homeless families.

The dramatic changes in the composition and characteristics of homeless families over the last several years highlight the emerging fact that homelessness is not simply a housing issue. Rather, the trends illustrate that homelessness is merely a symptom of a debilitating poverty affecting a very young and vulnerable population. Policymakers and service providers must meet the challenge of this complex issue with bold initiatives such as the RET Center model. Only then will it be possible to break the cycle of poverty and homelessness which is now plaguing the poor urban family.

Source: Excerpted from "A Bold Initiative," in *The Cycle of Family Homelessness: A Social Policy Reader,* copyright @ 1998, Appendix B. Reprinted by permission of The Institute for Children and Poverty.

part by the influx of poor immigrants from developing countries who seek a better life. In fact, two-thirds of the total poor population in the European Union live in six countries: Germany, France, the United Kingdom, Italy, Poland, and Spain. The rural areas of many European countries have a higher level of poverty than the urban areas, especially among Eastern European farmers (United Nations FAO 2010).

Poverty remains a concern in the cities of many advanced economies throughout the world, partially as a result of the uneven costs and benefits of economic globalization. The changing global economy eliminated many low-skill jobs in industrialized nations that once enabled the cities' poor to extricate themselves from poverty. Until innovative policies take aim at causes, not symptoms, of urban poverty and homelessness, they will not go away. See the *Urban Trends* box above for one approach to resolving this problem.

SUMMARY

The traditional economic analysis of cities highlights the advantages of particular locations and the various economic benefits those locations offer over the hinterland. Living in cities allows people to get more goods of higher quality more cheaply. These economic advantages, economists like William Alonso argue, are sufficient to explain recurrent patterns in urban land use: For example, businesses predominate at the center (the CBD), surrounded by residential areas and, farther out, agricultural areas. Even so, this theory may be descriptive only of Western (primarily North American) cities, and it ignores various non-economic forces, such as racial prejudice, that also affect urban land use.

By the 1960s, many social scientists came to the conclusion that the prevailing theories and models could not address changing patterns of urban life. French philosopher Henri Lefebvre was a major influence on the evolving political economy perspective, and he contributed ideas about the primary and secondary circuits of capital, space as a form of social organization, and the role of government. David Harvey's neo-Marxist analysis of Baltimore revealed that finance capital, not industrial capital, was now the key shaper of neighborhood quality. Manuel Castells updated Marx by suggesting welfare capitalism as a new form of class conflict probability and by discussing modes of development, in lieu of modes of production, as the key element in the information age. Allen Scott discussed horizontal integration and vertical disintegration as a basis for understanding business relocation in the global economy. John Logan and Harvey Molotch, drawing on Lefebvre's distinctions between abstract space and social space, examined the tensions arising between advocates of urban growth and residents of the current built environment who may oppose the proposed new use of that space.

Economic restructuring changed older cities from a manufacturing base to a service industries base. We must understand recent urban economic changes in the context of an evolving world system of economic interdependence that places nations in a global hierarchy. This hierarchy consists of the "core" of highly developed countries, the "semi-periphery" of less-developed countries, and the "periphery" of the least-developed countries. Within the ever-expanding global network, cities are locked in a reciprocal relationship, serving as important nodes linking together wealth (investment capital), people (human capital), production (industrial capital), and commodities (commercial capital).

Although critical urban social scientists go in different directions, depending on their disciplinary viewpoints and areas of focus, they agree on four basic principles of political economy. First, decision makers controlling resources—not natural processes—shape the form and growth of the city, because the geographical mobility of capital and workers gives them flexibility to locate where they can maximize profits. Second, conflicts over distribution of resources also shape the form of, and social arrangements in, the city. Third, government continues to play a role in affecting urban patterns. Fourth, economic restructuring is a key influence on patterns of urban growth.

Just as the world is becoming more urbanized, so, too, is poverty. In developing countries, poverty takes a different form than in developed countries, because the equitable distribution of goods does not match the production of material goods. The rapid growth of urban poor—1 billion over the past 40 years, and a projected 2 billion over the next 15 years—creates a serious problem for cities of the developing world in attempting to provide both necessities and amenities for this burgeoning population. Countries of the developed world, such as Canada and the United States, are experiencing greater geographical segregation based on income levels, placing a burden on their cities to cope with large concentrations of the poor. Poverty results in serious problems of homelessness in more-developed countries, while in less-developed countries, the wretched conditions in the many shantytowns mark their housing problem.

CONCLUSION

The economic trends that have produced major changes in the economic and employment opportunities of North American cities will continue. So, too, will the increased integration of poor countries and their cities into the world economy. Globalization is a process that no one can stop or reverse. Therefore, an understanding of global political economy remains essential in any study of cities and urban life. This perspective addresses the rapid changes that are occurring worldwide; thus, it offers a comparative approach that is lacking in competing ethnocentric models focusing only on individual cities located in North America.

Urban political economy, however, has two important limitations. Large-scale concepts, such as Manuel Castells's modes of development, do not fully explain the differences between cities that are in the same mode of development. In other words, global political and economic forces do not fully determine the character of all cities and neighborhoods; local variations do exist. For one thing, individuals do not respond like a ball in a pinball machine, reacting to the force of a flipper by going in another direction. They reflect, interpret, and react on their own. One danger in the political economy approach is ignoring the individual factor—something researchers now realize and are striving to overcome (Tsakalotos 2004).

The viewpoint of urban political economy provides a strong critique of urban ecology. However, it does not deal very extensively, or very deeply, with cases where capitalist cities have been successful at raising the general standard of living for the city as a whole. Nor does it offer much insight regarding the weaknesses of socialist cities in meeting the needs of many of their people.

Perhaps a fuller understanding would emerge from a synthesis of the conventional ecological and political economy approaches that would form a critical dialogue, one that draws from the strengths, yet avoids the limitations, of each. The location and shape of cities, their patterned land-use and social clustering, are important elements that enable us to grasp more fully the cities' essential qualities, but so, too, is the necessity of knowing the macroeconomic forces at play that affect their welfare. This analytical fusion could provide us with an even more sophisticated understanding of our cities.

Meanwhile, despite its limitations, political economy is now a dominant perspective in urban studies, inspiring many scientific investigations of cities throughout the world. These studies examine not only present-day patterns but also the future of cities—a subject we will turn to at the end of this book. Next, however, we will look at urban behavior as it is shaped and influenced by the physical and social environment.

KEY TERMS

abstract space (179)
agglomeration industries (174)
central business district (CBD) (174)
central place theory (175)
economic restructuring (187)
horizontal integration (184)
megamergers (186)
mode of development (183)

mode of production (183)
oligopoly (183)
postmodernism (173)
primary circuit of capital (178)
second circuit of capital (178)
social space (179)
vertical disintegration (184)

INTERNET ACTIVITIES

1. For information on street children in Canada and the United States, go to one or both of the following links: (1) *http://gvnet.com/streetchildren/Canada.htm;* (2) *http://gvnet.com/streetchildren/USA.htm.*

2. The illustrated evolution of the shopping center—from its nineteenth-century predecessors to suburban centers and urban festival marketplaces—is nicely presented at *http://homepage.mac.com/oldtownman/soc/shoppingcenter.html.*

CHAPTER 8

SOCIAL PSYCHOLOGY
The Urban Experience

THE PHYSICAL ENVIRONMENT
  The Image of the City
  Cognitive Mapping
THE SOCIAL ENVIRONMENT:
  GESELLSCHAFT
  The Pedestrian: Watching Your Step
  A World of Strangers
  The City as *Gesellschaft:* A Reassessment
THE SOCIAL ENVIRONMENT:
  GEMEINSCHAFT
  Urban Networks
  Identifying with the City
  The City as *Gemeinschaft:* A Reassessment

THE TEXTURE OF THE CITY
HUMANIZING THE CITY
SOCIAL MOVEMENTS AND CITY LIFE
SUBURBAN LIFE
  The Stereotypes
  The Physical Environment
  The Social Environment
SUMMARY
CONCLUSION
KEY TERMS
INTERNET ACTIVITIES

What makes cities so stimulating? Why do they cause us to react with either high admiration or powerful aversion? Georg Simmel's answer was that the city is a tremendous concentration of buildings, images, and people that intensifies stimulation like no other form of human settlement. Everywhere you turn—around a corner, breaking through a crowd, entering the subway—the city demands a response.

How do we make sense of this coming-at-you-from-all-sides, sometimes in-your-face creation that is the city? Simmel answered that we learn to categorize the city's elements, paying attention to some things while ignoring others. Louis Wirth agreed, suggesting that we mentally "map" the city. Unfortunately, neither theorist said much about how this mapping process works. But, drawing on later research, this chapter sketches the outlines of this process—the characteristic elements of the social psychology of the city.

THE PHYSICAL ENVIRONMENT

We react to the city in two ways—as a physical setting and as a social environment. First, we consider how people perceive their physical surroundings and try to make sense out of them.

The Image of the City

To explore how people made sense of the city's physical complexity, urbanist Kevin Lynch interviewed urbanites in Boston, Jersey City, and Los Angeles. In each city, Lynch showed his respondents a map representing several square miles of the central city and asked them to describe it in their own terms. Most could offer a personal *image of the city* that Lynch defined as the individual's "generalized mental picture of the [city's] external physical world" (1982:4; orig. 1960).

Before we continue, take a moment and think of the city you know best. On a piece of

To a great many people around the world, the New York City skyline is not only easily recognizable but also a symbol of the power and lure of American life. To the residents of Jersey City, living on the opposite shore of the Hudson River, the skyline is such a looming, overpowering presence that many residents mentioned it to Lynch as one of their landmarks.

paper, draw as detailed a map of it as you can, putting in everything of importance that you can recall. This exercise will make the following discussion far more meaningful.

Building an Image. Most of Lynch's respondents developed their image of the city in a similar fashion. First, their images emerged as part of a two-way process: (1) They made distinctions among the various physical parts of the city, and (2) they organized these parts in a personally meaningful way.

For example, Figure 8–1 shows downtown Boston, where the large park known as the Boston Common and Public Garden separates various downtown districts from one another. To the west of the park is the residential Back Bay area, with its characteristic three- and four-story apartment houses. To the north is the wealthier Beacon Hill district, where one finds the State House. To the east and south is most of Boston's central business district, full of high-rise office buildings, retail stores, restaurants, and entertainment facilities. When we say "downtown," we mean the central business district, and when we speak of the deterioration of the downtowns, we mean its loss of these interdependent commercial activities.

To a person living, say, in a small apartment just west of the Garden and the Common, the park area may be the dominant element in an image of the city, because this person may go there frequently for walks, getting to know every bench, fountain, and footpath. This same individual, however, may know little about the rest of downtown.

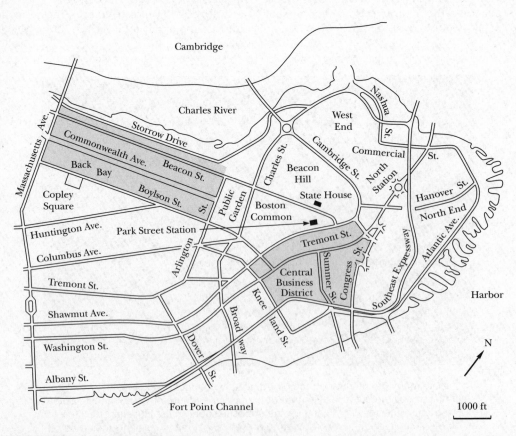

FIGURE 8–1 Downtown Boston

On the other hand, to another Bostonian living nearby, the park may have little significance. Working in the high-rise offices on the east side of the park, this person may have little desire to use the Garden. In this case, the distinct image might be of the downtown buildings, including where the good restaurants are, and of all the shortcuts for getting from one building or street to another.

Common Elements of Images. Lynch discovered that people built their urban images from five common elements. **Paths,** he explains, are "channels along which the observer customarily…moves. They may be streets, walkways, transit lines, canals, railroads" (1982:15). **Edges,** the boundaries between two areas, include shores, walls, wide streets, or breaks between buildings and open space. **Districts** represent medium to large sections of the city. Examples in Boston that people commonly noted were "Back Bay," "Beacon Hill," "the Common," and "the shopping district." **Nodes** stand as points of intense activity, such as a railroad terminal, a square, or a street-corner hangout. Nodes are often the places to which paths lead. Finally, Lynch's subjects built their images around **landmarks**—physical reference points including buildings, signs, stores, domes, gas stations, or hills.

Now, look back at the map you drew a few minutes ago. Were you thinking in terms of Lynch's categories?

Lynch also found that most people incorporate many of the same elements in their own images—that is, what is a path or edge to one person is a path or edge to many others. Looking back at Figure 8–1, virtually every Bostonian recognizes the Charles River as a major edge, separating one large district of the city ("downtown") from another (Cambridge). Similarly, most people also mention "Mass. Ave." to the west and the Southeast Expressway to the east as key edges. Main paths are Beacon Street, "Comm. Ave.," Boylston Street, and Tremont Street. Commonly mentioned nodes include Copley Square (site of the "BPL," the Boston Public Library), North Station (a railroad and subway

terminal), and Park Street Station. Although it is below ground, Park Street Station is another classic example of an urban node: The junction of Boston's three main subway lines is constantly abuzz with activity.

Although Lynch discovered that people in every city appear to use the same elements in constructing their images, he also found that some cities stimulate their residents to conceptualize more complex images than other cities do. In Boston, virtually everyone Lynch interviewed could identify *numerous* paths, edges, nodes, districts, and landmarks. In Jersey City, by contrast, even long-term residents could identify only a few such elements, and they often confessed confusion and uncertainty about what existed in different parts of their own city. They could not identify any element of the city's physical scene that possessed distinguishability; nor did they think the city had a center, but only a collection of various neighborhoods (Lynch 1982:29–31). Perhaps most illustrative of their weak image of their city was the residents' frequent mention of the looming, overpowering New York City skyline to the east as a landmark.

In Los Angeles, Lynch found, residents have an even less of a sharp image for their city because of the great sprawl and uniformity of cross streets, which make it difficult to locate anything with confidence. Although the area studied was comparable in size to those of the other two cities, it included little more than a central business district. Those interviewed, most of whom worked there, could describe only a few landmarks in any specific detail, such as the "ugly" black and gold Richfield Building and the pyramid atop City Hall. The strongest element of all was Pershing Square in the heart of the downtown area. Its well-manicured central lawn—flanked by banana trees and enclosed by a stone wall on which people sat—was a welcome respite from the urban scene of heavily trafficked streets and office buildings surrounding it.

Even so, many Angelenos were uncertain of the precise location of Pershing Square. Moreover, most residents of the city could identify only paths, and they often confused one with another. When asked to describe or symbolize Los Angeles as a whole, residents found it hard to respond, simply describing their city as "spread-out," "spacious," "form-less," or "without centers." This diffused urban image and residents' lack of perceived sense of place are somewhat remindful of the Gertrude Stein line, "There is no there there."

The "Imagability" of Cities. Noting how his respondents differed in their precision about urban images, Lynch suggested that cities differ markedly in terms of *imagability*. This concept is important for two reasons. First, a clear urban image gives people a working knowledge of, and emotional security about, their city. A strong urban image makes ac-quisition of knowledge relatively easy, and it

sets people at ease emotionally. (As the *Urban Living* box below reveals, however, the terror-ist acts of September 11, 2001, make some people feel less secure in cities.) Second, a comprehensible urban environment "height-ens the potential depth and intensity of the human experience" (1982:5). It invites us to experience more, to involve ourselves more in the life of the city. Lynch concluded that imagability is one of the essential aspects of a positive urban environment.

Cognitive Mapping

One of the most intriguing aspects of Lynch's work was his discovery that even people living in the same city construct different mental

URBAN LIVING

Living with Terrorism

In today's world, many of us are aware of the vulnerability of cities to terrorist attacks. Both Masumoto City in 1994 and Tokyo in 1995 fell victim to chemical terrorism, with use of the toxic gas sarin on defense-less civilians in subways. The 2001 attacks on the Pentagon in Washington, D.C., and the twin towers of the World Trade Center in New York City, with their horrific losses of life and mass destruction, still rever-berate in the minds of hundreds of millions of people worldwide. In March 2004, terror-ists in Madrid killed 191 train passengers and wounded more than 1,400 others, while in July 2005, terrorists killed 52 bus and train passengers in London, wounding an addi-tional 700 people. In November 2008, ter-rorists killed 179 people in Mumbai, India.

These and other incidents remind us that urban centers attract terrorists. The large concentrations of people, tall buildings, symbolic monuments, and infrastructure of bridges and tunnels are all tempting targets for those intent on inflicting maximum dam-age and deaths. People once avoided cit-ies for fear of becoming victims of violent crimes. Now, some fear not just being in major cities but even living near one in the event of a biological, chemical, or nuclear attack.

Seeing concrete barricades at many impor-tant locations and undergoing bag searches at concerts, sporting events, and airports are part of our new reality. For some, living or work-ing in tall buildings, or viewing the cityscape from high-perched observation decks, holds little appeal. Others, refusing to allow their lives to be ruled by fear, continue their daily urban routines and lifestyles.

Whether they respond by avoidance or defiance, however, urbanites recognize that their world today is different from the one that existed before September 11, 2001. That realization is also part of the psychology of urban life.

images of their surroundings. Their perceptions of the relationships among space, place, and the physical—even social—features of the natural and built environment in various parts of the city constitute what Lynch called *legibility* (1982:9). Essentially, researchers discover people's interpretations through sketch maps, or hand-drawn renditions of features that are most familiar to them. What one person includes will differ from others. Such differing cognitive mapping occurs because one's interests and personal experiences affect awareness and recollection of some city features and not others. As a result, **mental maps,** as individualized constructs, will (1) mix accurate details with distortions, (2) contain large gaps about unfamiliar sections, and (3) not be fully representative of an area in its entirety.

In the years since Lynch first informed us of these mental maps, many other researchers have used cognitive mapping as a research method to investigate those relationships among place, experience, and community in such places as Panama City, Panama (Powell 2010); Albuquerque, New Mexico (Mendoza 2006); Baltimore (Bembry and Norris 2005); and Los Angeles (Matei et al. 2001). These and other studies have validated the wider application of cognitive mapping for many locales.

The Individuality of Mental Maps.   Figures 8–2 and 8–3 on pages 208–209 present drawings of two people's mental maps of Manhattan. New Jersey suburbanite Beth, who only goes into Manhattan to visit museums or see shows, emphasizes details about the streets and locations of the artistic and cultural centers that draw her to the city's midtown (Figure 8–2). She offers only sketchy information about the Upper West Side or lower Manhattan. By contrast, physical therapist Cara's Manhattan, emphasizes the Upper West Side area where she lives (Figure 8–3). Featured prominently are restaurants, parks, and high-rise apartment buildings, without the need to list streets, given her familiarity with the area. Missing, save for one or two items, are midtown and lower Manhattan.

No one, as suggested above, can re-create the complexity of the whole city, as Cara's map demonstrates. Moreover, everyone's images constantly evolve as urban experiences deepen or as the city changes. A relative newcomer to a city, for example, will typically draw a map of the center city that contains prominent landmarks but almost no detail at all. Often, the few areas noted are misplaced and distorted in size. Yet, for that same person, after living there just a few more months, the city usually comes alive, and she or he can offer far more detail as well as greater geographical accuracy. In short, with time, most people succeed in comprehending the city and using it effectively.

Multiple Urban Realities.   What all this suggests is that there are as many "New Yorks" or "Seattles," for example, as there are people living there. More broadly, each of these active mental maps contributes to the larger urban dynamic that is the full New York City or Seattle.

Mental maps, however, are not completely a matter of individual differences. Cultural and social class differences also affect what people include in their cognitive maps (Frisby 1996). Race plays a key part in how residents understand the city as well. Researchers have found that blacks' perceptions of community undesirability differ from those of whites. Generally, blacks rate most communities as more desirable than whites do, often favoring communities in which they are the numerical minority. Whites often rate mixed-race communities as being less desirable, particularly those with higher proportions of blacks, even when blacks are the numerical minority (Bembry and Norris 2005; Charles 2000; Krysan 2002; Sigelman and Henig 2001).

The city is thus a dynamic, creative, ongoing mixture of perceptions and experiences, as Robert Park explained long ago:

> The city…is something more than a congeries of individual men and of social conveniences—streets, buildings, electric lights, tramways, and telephones…something more, also, than a mere constellation of institutions and administrative devices—courts, hospitals, schools, police, and civil functionaries of various sorts. The city is…a state of mind. (1984:1; orig. 1916)

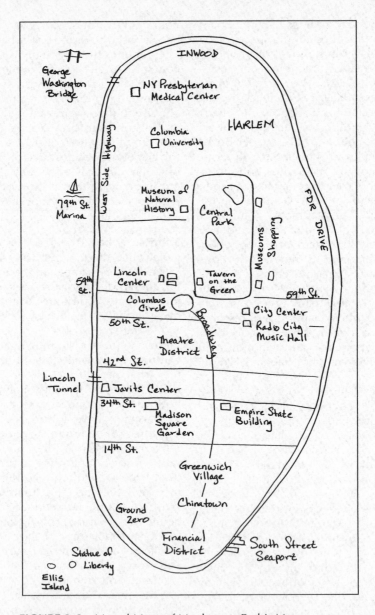

FIGURE 8–2   Mental Maps of Manhattan: Beth's Map

In the *Cityscape* box on page 210, novelist Alfred Kazin describes returning to his old neighborhood in the Brownsville district of New York. Present in his image of the city are all of Lynch's visual categories, complex interpretations of sound and smell, and evidence of his own social background.

THE SOCIAL ENVIRONMENT: *GESELLSCHAFT*

Living in the city demands that we deal with more than just the physical environment. We must also contend with large numbers of *people*, most of whom we don't

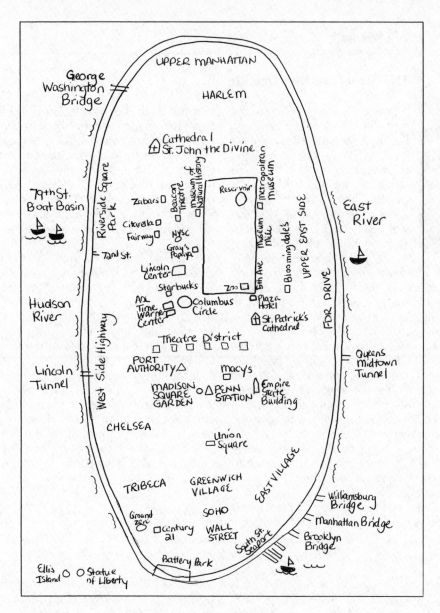

FIGURE 8–3   Mental Maps of Manhattan: Cara's Map

know—and probably don't want to know. How do we cope with what Ferdinand Tönnies (see Chapter 5) called the city's *gesellschaft* characteristics—its vast numbers and characteristic anonymity?

The Pedestrian: Watching Your Step

Standing on the sidewalk during rush hour along Boylston Street in Boston; State Street in Columbus, Ohio; or Kearny Street in San Francisco, anyone can observe the "faceless

CITYSCAPE

The Streets of Brownsville

All my early life lies open to my eye within five city blocks....On Belmont Avenue, Brownville's great open street market, the pushcarts are still lined on each other for blocks, and the din is as deafening, marvelous, and appetizing as ever....When I was a boy, they...reached halfway up the curb to the open stands of the stores; walking down the street was like being whirled around and around in a game of blind man's bluff. But Belmont Avenue is still the merriest street in Brownsville. As soon as I walked into it from Rockaway, caught my first whiff of the herrings and pickles in their great black barrels, heard the familiarly harsh, mocking cries and shouts from the market women—"Oh you darlings! Oh you sweet ones, oh you pretty ones! Storm us! Tear us apart! Devour us!"—I laughed right out loud, it was so good to be back among them....

On my right hand the "Stadium" movie house—the sanctuary every Saturday afternoon of my childhood, the great dark place of all my dream life....

The block: my block. It was on the Chester Street side of our house, between the grocery and the back wall of the old drugstore, that I was hammered into the shape of the streets. Everything beginning at Blake Avenue would always wear for me some delightful strangeness and mildness, simply because it was not of my block, the block, where the clang of your head sounded against the pavement when you fell in a fist fight, and the rows of store lights on each side were pitiless, watching you.

We worked every inch of it, from the cellars and the backyards to the sickening space between the roofs. Any wall, any stoop, any curving metal edge on a billboard sign made a place against which to knock a ball; any bottom rung of a fire escape ladder a goal in basketball; any sewer cover a base....Our life every day was fought out on the pavement and in the gutter, up against the walls of the houses and the glass fronts of the drugstore and the grocery—in and out of...the wheels of passing carts and automobiles, along the iron spikes of the stairway to the cellar, the jagged edge of the open garbage cans....

Source: Alfred Kazin, *A Walker in the City,* reprint ed. (New York: MJF Books, 1997).

crowd" of urbanites going about their daily business. Taking such a detached perspective, the city's people seem almost like sheep—an undifferentiated, robot-like herd.

Is this really so? As most urbanites know, city life is an orderly routine, one that allows people to meet their personal needs while surrounded by an unknown mass of others. People are on the street, of course, for a reason. We move through the city to get to work, to enjoy a restaurant, to meet a friend, to catch a subway, or perhaps, just to take a walk. Simply because the observer cannot perceive such motives is no reason to think they don't exist.

Moreover, pedestrians observe an intricate set of social rules. An unwritten traffic code exists for the sidewalks, just as a written code exists for automobiles using the streets. For example, pedestrian traffic in North American cities sorts itself into two opposing streams, with the dividing line somewhere near the middle of the sidewalk. Within each stream, people "watch their step" in a variety of ways: First, they

As Goffman suggested, pedestrians communally follow a sidewalk traffic code, creating two opposing streams with a dividing line somewhere in the middle of the sidewalk. Within these two streams, they share an intricate set of social rules that enable them to move easily at their own pace, without jostling or colliding with one another.

keep themselves at least slightly aware of obstacles, such as mailboxes, lampposts, or groups stopped on the sidewalk. Second, they casually note the speed of people in front of or behind them, gauging their own speed accordingly in order to avoid collisions. Third, to move faster or slower than the stream, people move to the outside of the lane. Fourth, people utilize various strategies to avoid collisions, perhaps making coughing noises or shifting packages to alert a careless walker about impending contact. Fifth, people scold one another for breaking any of these rules. After someone brushes by, one pedestrian may loudly protest, "Why

don't ya look where you're going?" Such reactions show us that people know the rules for pedestrian behavior and call others to task for any transgressions. In essence, a tacit contract exists among users of public space, who come to trust each other to act like competent pedestrians (Middleton 2010; Wolfinger 1995).

Rules of pedestrian traffic vary from culture to culture, of course. This variety can puzzle—and even intimidate—a traveler, as the next *Urban Living* box on page 212 explains.

Escalators represent another example of cultural variety. In the United States, passengers all pile on together, making passage by anybody behind almost impossible. In most European nations, however, escalator passengers ride on the right side, leaving a lane on the left for anyone wishing to pass. Taking their first ride on a European escalator, North Americans who place themselves on the left-hand side of a ramp are often a bit puzzled to hear people behind them asking them to please move over. Conversely, Europeans riding a North American subway escalator can be quite puzzled at the "rudeness" of locals, who jam up the ramp so that no one can pass.

Finally, even in that most dense and anonymous of urban worlds, the subway, people evolve mechanisms for ordering and personalizing their experience. The second *Urban Living* box on page 212 offers a look at the subway during rush hour.

Together, these examples reveal that street behavior is not nearly as chaotic as it might appear to be at first glance. City dwellers may have to deal with larger numbers of people, often in crowded conditions, but urban life is not necessarily difficult or dehumanizing.

A World of Strangers

Besides coping with the city's sheer numbers, urbanites must also learn to deal with anonymity, living in what Lyn Lofland (1985) calls "a world of strangers." Lofland argues that we look for visual clues in order to classify strangers in much the same way as we make sense of the city's physical environment.

URBAN LIVING

Saigon: Learning to Cross the Street All Over Again

The first morning after we arrived in port, we left the ship early and made our way along the docks toward the center of Ho Chi Minh City—known to an earlier generation as Saigon. After looking us over—a family of U.S. visitors—the government security officers waved us through the security gates without so much as glancing at our papers. But we paused nonetheless, coming face to face with dozens of men crowded just beyond the gate, all operators of cyclos—bicycles with a small carriage attached to the front—which are the Vietnamese equivalent of taxicabs. "No, thanks," I stated firmly, breaking eye contact, and making a firm gesture with my arm. In New York, it is hard enough to find a cab; here, we spent the next 20 minutes fending off persistent drivers who cruised alongside us pleading for our business. The pressure was uncomfortable.

Let's cross the street, I suggested. We turned to the traffic and immediately realized that there were no stop signs or signal lights. In fact, there was no break at all in the steady stream of bicycles, cyclos, motorbikes, and small trucks that rattled along the rough roadway. What to do? Then the answer came, in the form of a tiny woman who walked right next to us and plunged out into the traffic without so much as batting an eye. She simply walked at a steady pace across the street; drivers saw her coming and made room for her. To us, she appeared to part the waves of vehicles as if she had some mysterious power.

We took a deep breath. From several yards back, we walked right into the traffic keeping eyes straight ahead. Amazing! It worked. Such are the rules of the road in Vietnam.

Source: Based on John Macionis' travel to Vietnam.

URBAN LIVING

The Subway at Rush Hour

A crowd of people surged into the Eighth Avenue express at 59th Street. By elbowing other passengers in the back, by pushing and heaving, they forced their bodies into the coaches, making room for themselves where no room had existed before. As the train gathered speed for the long run to 125th Street, the passengers settled down into small private worlds, thus creating the illusion of space between them and their fellow passengers. The worlds were built up behind newspapers and magazines, behind closed eyes or while staring at the varicolored show cards that bordered the coaches.

Source: Ann Petry, *The Street* (Boston: Houghton Mifflin, 1998), p. 27.

Appearance and Location. First, we identify strangers in terms of their *appearance* and their *physical location* within the city. In other words, we give strangers "the once-over," noting their clothing, hairstyle, jewelry, what they're carrying, and how they're walking. We also let location speak for people: For example, in a district of office buildings and expensive restaurants, we expect to find different types of people than we would find in a district full of all-night movie houses or pornographic bookstores.

Lofland concedes such tactics are not uniquely urban. Even in small towns, people judge each other by appearance and by "which side of the tracks" they call home. The point is simply that in big cities, our reliance on clues like appearance and location becomes essential. After all, the odds of running into someone we know in midtown Manhattan or Chicago's downtown "loop" are rather small.

Worth noting is that using spatial location as a clue to people's identities is a modern practice. In preindustrial cities, public spaces, such as the town square, usually had many uses: schooling, religious services, parades, shopping, general loitering, and even executions. In short, because virtually *anybody* might be there, location provided few clues about who strangers were. In part, then, citizens put great stock in appearance, as illustrated in the *Urban Living* box below.

In modern industrial societies, however, the rules change. Dress still plays a part in identifying strangers, but costume is no longer the central clue it once was. Dress codes

URBAN LIVING

Clothes Make the Man

To a degree unknown to moderns, the resident of the preindustrial city literally "donned" his identity. The Roman citizen, for example, expressed the fact of his citizenship by wearing as decreed by law, the white toga. A "gentleman" in the Colonial cities of America was known by his "periwig." ...

Urban elites everywhere struggled to differentiate themselves from their "inferiors" not only by the design of their dress, but by the materials as well. The cap of the medieval Frenchman was made of velvet for the elites, rough cloth for the poor. In Elizabethan England, [Gideon Sjoberg reported that] "Commoners were prohibited by law from wearing clothing fashioned from gold or silver cloth, velvet, furs, and other 'luxury' materials." Hair length also indicated status. Among the Franks, only the elite had long hair....

The clothing of outcaste groups...was often regulated by law.... [T]he Parsi minority in the Persian city of Yezd were forced, until the 1880s, "to twist their turbans instead of folding them, [were] denied various colors, and [were] prohibited rings, umbrellas, and other items."

Occupation, too, was signaled by dress. The lawyers of medieval France, for example, were distinguished by their round caps...and the executioners of the period were forced to wear a special coat of red or gold so that they would be readily recognizable in a crowd....Each of the various types of itinerant peddlers of Peking...wore a distinctive costume as did the clergy of twelfth century Europe and the members of religious sects in numerous preindustrial cities.

Source: Lyn H. Lofland, *A World of Strangers: Order and Action in Urban Public Spaces* (Prospect Heights, IL: Waveland Press, 1985), pp. 45–46.

have relaxed, and people from all walks of life, without fear of censure, wear almost any sort of clothing. Important historical reasons explain this change.

In the preindustrial city, only the wealthy could afford clothes of silk and satin or jewelry made from gold and silver. With the Industrial Revolution, however, mass production made many types of dress much more affordable. Furthermore, even as a rising standard of living allowed more and more people to purchase and display such goods, many affluent people began dressing more casually.

If dress means less to us in modern cities, then, location means more. We recognize that modern cities are composed of numerous distinct districts, such as for business, warehousing, residence, and entertainment. In business districts, we expect to encounter businesspeople, and we expect them to act in a businesslike manner.

For example, Huntington Avenue, which has undergone gentrification along its route in recent years, still marks the boundary between two major districts of Boston (look back at Figure 8–1). On the north side of the street are the nearby upper-middle-class Back Bay and Fenway areas, which include Symphony Hall, the Museum of Fine Arts, and numerous expensive shops and art galleries. Just across the street begins the lower-class, predominantly African American and Puerto Rican Roxbury district, with run-down housing and downscale shops.

To position oneself at the corner of Huntington Avenue and Massachusetts Avenue near Symphony Hall, when the Boston Symphony Orchestra is playing, is a remarkable sociological experience. On one side of the street are men sporting formal black-tie dress and women decked out in ermine and pearls. Yet just 20 feet away are people in threadbare and tattered clothes. Strangers on both sides of the street may stand in fairly close proximity to one another, but each group is well aware that they inhabit two different social worlds.

Of course, such patterns don't mean that some people can't "work the system." We all know that it is possible for us to pass ourselves off as something we are not by manipulating the ways that we dress and act. A narcotics agent may infiltrate a drug ring, for example, and a social scientist may live anonymously in an area, hoping to learn the inside story of people's lives. Sometimes, people intentionally "perform." A sighted person may don dark eyeglasses, hold a sign saying "blind," and beg; sedate, middle-class suburbanites may come into the city to "swing" at night, retiring at evening's end to their normal routine.

Privatizing Public Space. Lofland (1985: 118–23) suggests that another way we reduce the vastness and complexity of a city is to transform areas into private or semi-private space. People can claim a street corner as a hangout; a tavern, such as in television's *Cheers*, can become a club to its regular patrons; and musicians can transform a section of a park into an outdoor performance arena. Such "home territories" are rarely intentional; usually, they result from unplanned, uncoordinated actions that end up spatially segregating certain types of people. The city is full of such patterns: Yuppies appropriate plazas; skid row vagrants lay claim to benches and steam grates; and gay people come to think of a particular neighborhood as "their own." Outsiders entering such spaces soon pick up cues of dress and behavior that indicate they are on semi-private ground.

On a larger scale, whole urban districts can become home territory—or "turf"—to a specific group. Most residential neighborhoods have a dominant character, perhaps based on class, race, ethnicity, and age. Although cities are largely impersonal, they are also (in Robert Park's phrase) "mosaics of small worlds." Within *gesellschaft*, in short, the city reveals many *gemeinschaft*-like subsocieties.

The City as *Gesellschaft:* A Reassessment

Many early urban theorists feared that people could never cope with the city's sheer physical size, its large population, and its anonymity. Yet, we *do* cope. We contend with physical size by creating our personal mental image of the city. We deal with the complexities of street

In a city, many people share public space. Whether in small groups or alone, on a lunch break or resting from sightseeing, they gather wherever there is some sun and a place to sit. Steps and low walls are popular choices, and there, they often engage in that favorite urban pastime of people-watching or enjoy some show, such as this sword-swallower in New York's Washington Square Park.

life by observing codes of behavior and seeking out clues to the identity of strangers. And of course, our own social characteristics place us within some part of the city and make urban life more meaningful.

THE SOCIAL ENVIRONMENT: *GEMEINSCHAFT*

Then, too, the city abounds with personal relationships. Only the most extreme of urban isolates—Jonathan Raban's "marginal man," perhaps—live according to the stereotype of *gesellschaft*. For most, interpersonal bonds provide a basis for social and psychological security in the city.

Urban Networks

The study of interpersonal ties is called *network analysis*. As we shall see, urban networks may or may not involve organized social groups, nor need they be defined by locality.

London Couples.   Examining the relationships of married couples in London, Elizabeth Bott Spillius (2008) uncovered the effects of social class on the urban experience. She found that working-class partners had a strict division of labor, often spent their leisure time separately, and each maintained their own networks. In contrast, tasks among middle-class spouses were shared or interchangeable, and they typically spent their leisure time together and participated in a shared network. Other studies show that strong urban networks form in stable neighborhoods, or around local schools through parenthood, or from a shared sense of group identity (Butler 2008; Robson and Butler 2001; Small 2007). Such findings do not discount the role of class, however.

Washington, D.C., Street-Corner Men.   Eliot Liebow (2003) conducted a famous participant observation study of poor African American men who frequented a street corner—"Tally's Corner"—in Washington, D.C. Most of these men, Liebow found, had believed until their late teens that they would become adult breadwinners and husbands. Driven by this ideal, many married and fathered children. Unfortunately, most of these men had few skills and little education, and they ended up with little more than menial jobs.

Many men came to hate the idea of performing degrading work. In time, many stopped working: Some were fired; some just quit. In any case, the men soon realized they could barely provide for themselves, much less a family. This failure was evident to their wives and children and a deep source of personal pain and family tension. To make matters worse, the government offered to provide public assistance to wives and children—but only if no father was living in the home.

Men crushed by their plight could find some comfort "hanging out" together. At Tally's Corner, people sympathized with each other and didn't ask embarrassing questions. There, a man could forget failure and get by from day to day. Before long, most men were spending more time there than at home. The *Urban Living* box below explains that networks supplied the heart and soul of life on "Tally's Corner."

Neighborhoods. Many urban relationships are set in neighborhoods. Distinguished by physical or social boundaries, neighborhoods contain people who share important social characteristics, such as social class, race, and ethnicity. In a study of Boston's predominantly Italian West End neighborhood in the 1950s, Herbert Gans (1982) suggested that despite the many differences among residents of an urban neighborhood, many *gemeinschaft*-like relations exist. Daily shopping in small grocery

URBAN LIVING

The Networks of Street-Corner Men

[The most important people in a man's network are those] with whom he is "up tight": His "walking buddies," "good" or "best" friends, girl friends, and sometimes real or putative kinsmen. These are the people with whom he is in more or less daily, face-to-face contact, and whom he turns to for emergency aid, comfort or support in time of need or crisis. He gives them and receives from them goods and services in the name of friendship, ostensibly keeping no reckoning. Routinely, he seeks them out and is sought out by them. They serve his need to be with others of his kind, and to be recognized as a discrete, distinctive personality, and he, in turn, serves them the same way. They are both his audience and his fellow actors.

It is with these men and women that he spends his waking, nonworking hours, drinking, dancing, engaging in sex, playing the fool or the wise man, passing the time at the Carry-out or on the street-corner, talking about nothing and everything, about epistemology or . . . about the nature of numbers or how he would "have it made" if he could have a steady job that paid him $60 a week with no layoffs.

So important a part of daily life are these relationships that it seems like no life at all without them. Old Mr. Jenkins climbed out of his sickbed to take up a seat on the Coca-Cola case at the Carry-out for a couple of hours. "I can't stay home and play dead," he explained, "I got to get out and see my friends."

Source: Eliot Liebow, *Tally's Corner,* 2nd ed. (Lanham, MD: Rowman and Littlefield, 2003), pp. 163–64.

stores for fresh meats, fish, and produce provided an opportunity to meet with neighbors and share local news. On Sundays before and after church services, people strolling on the sidewalks and/or visiting friends and neighbors generated frequent social interactions.

At the time of Gans's research, the West End was a low-income, low-rent district adjacent to the elite Beacon Hill area. Traditionally home to immigrants, over the years the West End had been dominated by people of various categories—including Italians, Jews, Poles, and Irish, as well as some artists and bohemians.

Most casual observers of the West End concluded that it was a chaotic slum. Yet living in the area revealed a different—and more accurate—picture. There, Gans found as much *gemeinschaft* as might be found in many non-urban environments. Many had known one another for years, not perhaps personally, but certainly as acquaintances in greeting each other on the street. Moreover, they typically knew something about everyone and that level of familiarity led to their willingness to help their neighbors whenever any kind of emergency occurred. For most residents, then, this forging of strong ties with family, neighbors, and friends resulted in a lifestyle resembling a small town or suburban community.

Other researchers reached similar conclusions after investigating other cities. For example, Gerald Suttles (1974) reported strong interpersonal ties among Italians in Chicago's Addams area, and Joseph Howell (1990) provided a similar description of life in an inner-city Washington, D.C., neighborhood. Finally, a study by Jarrett, et al. (2010) found important extended-kin networks promoting family stability in the face of challenges from living in Chicago low-income neighborhoods. In sum, personal relationships, though hidden to the casual observer, may be every bit as important to low-income urban neighbors as they are to people living in rural communities.

Urban ethnic neighborhoods are often places to find examples of what Lofland calls the privatizing of public space. Here, the street becomes a place to play stickball or wash a parked car, and the sidewalk becomes a site for jump rope or hopscotch games, for stores or street vendors to display their wares, or for people to sit to socialize or watch passersby.

Friendships. Many urban relationships do not involve neighbors. More affluent urbanites especially—many who move from city to city to establish their careers—are not linked to neighborhoods in any traditional sense, but nonetheless have friends. Such people typically forge friendships involving co-workers, people with whom they have lunch or a drink and dinner, or friends they meet more casually—say, at a concert or in the park. The point is that people may not live near each other but still maintain friendships with others who share similar interests (Gibbons and Olk 2003; Whitmeyer 2002).

Industrial technology once broke up the communities of old by offering new opportunities that pulled people away from the towns of their birth. Yet technology also provides new means to stay in touch: The landline telephone served this purpose in the twentieth century, and the cell phone, e-mail, and text messaging heavily reinforce countless relationships in this century.

Scenes. One of the city's hallmarks is its many and diverse places, or **scenes,** where people gather to socialize with friends, meet new ones, and enjoy themselves. In fact, many people *invent* places where they get together. Scenes include bars, clubs, discos, or areas of a city taken over by a group, such as San Francisco's Haight–Ashbury district by hippies in the 1960s or New York's Bryant Park by yuppies in the late 1990s.

Most scenes are part-time. They usually occupy the hours away from work, such as a favorite eatery for lunch, a coffee shop, or a health club/fitness center. Second, to "make the scene" suggests that participants are, in some sense, "on stage," emphasizing only one particular aspect of themselves—their ability to dance or their knowledge of literature, for instance.

Scenes are of four main types (Irwin 1977). Most cities have *lifestyle scenes* that attract writers, musicians, gays, political radicals, and other groups. On summer evenings

Many cities are filled with young adults for whom one of the most popular "scenes" is a bar or club, where they can relax and enjoy themselves with friends, fellow students, or co-workers. Some places attract a particular lifestyle crowd, such as gays, musicians, or writers; others are more open, attracting a wide range of customers.

in Toronto, for example, young people from all over the metropolitan area descend on Yonge Street, and they often remain until the wee hours of the morning. On foot or in cars with stereos blaring, they eat, talk, yell, buy records, and generally hang out up and down a dozen city blocks.

The *local scene* is more exclusive. A local bar, for example, may attract a particular crowd, and it may even discourage "outsiders" from coming in.

The *open scene* is more fluid in terms of clientele, yet it, too, provides the opportunity for personal relationships. Bars without a well-defined clientele fall into this category. Such public drinking places provide opportunities for those present, whether acquainted or not, to engage others in conversational interaction in a setting that promotes the near-obligation to accept these extended overtures of sociability.

Finally, the *specialized scene* involves activities, such as tennis, barbershop harmony, amateur theater, bingo, card playing, chess, skateboarding, and countless others. Like the local scene, these specialized scenes provide a sense of ingroup solidarity with others who share that particular interest. Specialized scenes, however, have a degree of openness and population fluidity that local scenes do not.

Perhaps one of the best-known specialized scenes among college students, especially those attending a city college or university, is the clubs. These typically crowded gathering places have a DJ or band, a dance floor, a bar, and room to sit or stand. For example, in Boston, some of the more popular clubs are Aria, Avalon, Liquor Store, Roxy, and Venu. Other clubs cater to different types of clientele, such as African or Hispanic Americans, or gays. No matter which club, though, people come to hear and dance to the music and, of course, to enjoy some good times with old or new friends.

Temporary Networks. Many urban dwellers use another type of network to make initial or short-term personal contact in the city. Examples of such networks include singles clubs, dating agencies, public ballrooms, call-in radio talk shows, and suicide hot lines.

Sometimes, such networks serve people who are extremely lonely or desperate. Just as frequently, however, they serve people who are quite happy with their lives. People who participate in late-night talk shows, for instance, need not be lonely, after all; they may just be working late, or simply be interested in speaking their mind.

Identifying with the City

The ability to know and identify with an entire city probably ended in the Middle Ages. With the dawning of the modern age, Western cities began a relentless increase in population as well as an expanding division of labor, resulting in the large, diverse cities we find today.

Still, most people have some sense of "knowing" their city, although such knowledge often rests on clichés and stereotypical images that outsiders also may share. Thus, beer has made Milwaukee famous in the same way that sunshine defines Miami and the entertainment industry has elevated Los Angeles and Hollywood. St. Louis has its arch and Toronto its CN Tower (the tallest freestanding structure in the Western Hemisphere). And, while Stratford-on-Avon has its Shakespeare, Hannibal, Missouri, is proud to be the boyhood home of Mark Twain (Samuel Clemens).

In addition, sports teams foster identification with the modern city ("Minneapolis–St. Paul—Home of the Twins, Vikings, and North Stars!"), as do important local events (St. Patrick's Day in Boston, the Rose Parade in Pasadena, Inauguration Day in Washington, D.C., and Mardi Gras in New Orleans). The *Urban Living* box on page 220 examines some of these "urban rituals."

Historical events—both negative and positive—also help to define the urban experience. The San Francisco earthquake of 1906 and the devastating aftermath from Hurricane Katrina in New Orleans in 2005 are examples of costly and tragic events that remain alive in people's minds. The ride of Paul Revere

URBAN LIVING

Great Urban Rituals

Cities, both large and small, have annual events that involve large segments of the population and serve as a means of sharing in an urban experience and, thus, identifying with the city. Here are just a few examples.

Each New Year's Day, weather permitting, about 1 million people line the streets of Philadelphia to watch the Mummers Parade. Thousands of marchers, members of many Mummers clubs—who are capped and caped, in speckled and sequined costumes—literally strut to the music of a distinctive string-band strum. They neither walk nor march; instead, they cakewalk in a distinctive style that is difficult to imitate. It's a colorful, pleasant spectacle and a famous city tradition.

In Boston, the celebration of Patriot's Day (the third Monday in April) commemorates the events in that city that led to the American Revolution (the rides of Paul Revere and William Dawes, the battles at Lexington and Concord). Aside from reenactments of the rides and a traditional parade, the main attraction that day is the Boston Marathon. This oldest race in the United States, a marathon second only in age to the Olympics itself, attracts more than 20,000 runners and more than a half-million enthusiastic spectators along the 26.2-mile route.

Cinco de Mayo festivals celebrate Mexico's victory over French forces in Puebla, Mexico, on May 5, 1862. Though celebrated in many major U.S. cities—including Austin, Chicago, Dallas, Houston, San Antonio, and St. Paul—it is in Los Angeles where hundreds of thousands of people gather in parks and on streets, decorated in the Mexican colors (red, white, and green), to enjoy the crafts, food, music, and dancing.

On Memorial Day weekend, Detroit hosts Movement, an electronic dance music festival. More than 100 artists perform on multiple stages in Hart Plaza in the city's downtown. Held in the birthplace of techno music, the event integrates musical and visual artistry, creativity, diversity, and state-of-the-art technology.

From mid-July to early August, Toronto blazes with the excitement of calypso and elaborate masquerade costumes during the annual Scotiabank Caribbean Festival. This two-week festival is the largest Caribbean festival in North America, attracting over 1 million participants—including hundreds of thousands of American tourists.

Among the many ethnic festivals in New York City, its oldest and most popular one that cuts across ethnic boundaries is the San Gennaro Festival in Little Italy and runs for two weeks in mid-September. The street festivities, which include parades, entertainment, food stands, and a cannoli-eating contest, attract more than 1 million people annually.

Of the thousands of Oktoberfest celebrations in North America, Cincinnati's German heritage celebration is the largest, drawing over 500,000 people each year. Five downtown city blocks are transformed each September into Oktoberfest Zinzinnati, with seven stages offering live entertainment and nearly 100 booths serving German food, wine, and beer.

We cannot end this section without mentioning the rejuvenated Mardi Gras in New Orleans, mostly recovered from Hurricane Katrina in 2005. For about two weeks, dozens of elaborate parades take place through Fat Tuesday, the day before the Christian season of Lent begins. From the parade floats, riders in outrageous costumes throw beads and other trinkets to hundreds of thousands of spectators, many also dressed in costume during this fun-filled time.

through Boston, the signing of the Declaration of Independence in Philadelphia, and the battle at the Alamo in San Antonio are major events still well known many generations later by most of those cities' present-day inhabitants.

The City as *Gemeinschaft*: A Reassessment

A wealth of research supports the conclusion that the vast majority of urbanites are "well-connected" in their cities. On the one hand, most are engaged in a variety of networks, such as families, neighborhoods, friendships, scenes, and even temporary contacts. Similarly, most city residents have a sense of identification with their city. Although they may not always be readily apparent, characteristics of Tönnies's *gemeinschaft*—personal relationships and a sense of belonging—do flourish in the city.

THE TEXTURE OF THE CITY

Most cities convey a unique impression— a look and feel that Gerald Suttles (1984) termed a "texture" and that others call the "soul," "personality," or the "feel" of the city. New York is the "Big Apple," a city of energy and hustle; Boston is relaxed, "cultural," and intellectual; Los Angeles is "laid back," the heart of the "new America"; and New Orleans is "The Big Easy," where life is slower, simpler, and easy-going. These are stereotypical impressions, of course, but many people share them (see the *Cityscape* box on page 222).

To what extent are such images real? Suttles argues that a city's **texture** is grounded in its history, architecture, street names, and even the nicknames for certain parts of town. Together, these elements add up to an objective reality, not just one individual's impression. A visitor to Hollywood, for example, can actually see the footprints and handprints of the stars in the cement in front of Grauman's Chinese Theater, use a map to visit the homes of the stars, and see the huge "Hollywood" sign overlooking the city. And who knows? If you're lucky, you might even end up face to face with a famed actor at a restaurant. Stars,

money, and fame are all part of Hollywood's texture as "Tinsel Town."

Detroit.   The "Motor City" has been battling its negative image of urban decay and high crime for decades. With the decline of the automobile industry in the 1970s, the flight of affluent people to the suburbs, and the collapse of its center-city areas, Detroit gained a reputation as unpleasant and unsafe (consistently listed as one of the nation's worst cities in serious crimes)—a violent cultural wasteland. As both cause and effect, Detroit's population plummeted from 1.8 million in 1950 to 951,000 in 2000, a drop of 52 percent. Between 2000 and 2010, Detroit's population plunged further, down another 237,000 to 714,000, according to the 2010 Census (U.S. Census Bureau 2011c).

How does a city overcome such a loss in both reputation and population? One attempt was to become a more inviting cultural center. A restored Opera House and exhibits at the Henry Ford Museum, Historical Museum, and Museum of African American History do attract many visitors, as does the Institute of Arts, one of the nation's biggest art museums. Another re-urbanization effort, Live Midtown, provides loans and rent allowance to employees and students at Wayne State University, the Henry Ford Health System, and the Detroit Medical Center to encourage them to live in Midtown Detroit through loans and rent allowances.

Another recent innovation is the People Mover—an automated, elevated light-rail system that takes millions of riders on a 2.9-mile loop of downtown Detroit. For just 50 cents, one can easily reach the numerous casinos, offices, restaurants, shops, nightlife, landmarks, and other attractions that are within walking distance of the system's 13 stations and stops. Also, the city's four professional sports teams (NBA Pistons, NFL Lions, NHL Red Wings, and MLB Tigers) attract many living outside the city limits.

Perhaps the best indicator of Detroit's change in its textural image is the symbol of its skyline, the Renaissance Center (nicknamed "RenCen"). One of the world's largest office complexes (5.5 million square feet), its central

CITYSCAPE

The Personality of Cities

Author of the book that inspired the 1959 film *The Young Philadelphians* starring Paul Newman, Richard Powell gave this tongue-in-cheek, provocative commentary on his thoughts about the personalities (textures) of many U.S. cities, one that amuses some and offends others:

Of the major cities of the United States, only nine have distinct and individual personalities. These are New York, Chicago, Philadelphia, Boston, Los Angeles, San Francisco, New Orleans, Charleston, and Savannah....

[Of these,] only San Francisco has a really nice one. The other eight cities often annoy people who have not had the good fortune of being born there. I hope I am not revealing anything top secret when I say that, to many outsiders, Philadelphia and Boston have highly irritating personalities. To many outsiders, these two cities are rather like a pair of sheltered maiden ladies who have become crotchety and eccentric but who happen to be awfully well-heeled.

New York, of course, has a very strong personality. Naturally, as a good Philadelphian, I dislike the place....

Here is a quick review of the personality or lack of personality of other major American cities:

Chicago—Yes, it has personality. It's the neighborhood big shot of the Midwest.

Detroit—No personality. It's just the hot-rod kid of American cities.

Los Angeles—Lots of personality, but of kinds that delight a psychiatrist.

Baltimore—No more personality than one of its own Chincoteague oysters, and just about as retiring.

Cleveland, St. Louis, Cincinnati, Kansas City, Columbus, and Indianapolis—These are the great faceless cities of the Midwest, representing nothing more than the lowest common denominator of many rather interesting small towns.

Pittsburgh—It has no personality. It's merely a pro football player who struck it rich.

Washington—It's not really a city at all. It's just a big international motel whose guests only sign in for overnight.

Milwaukee—A freckle-faced kid peering wistfully through a knothole at the Milwaukee Braves.

Seattle, Rochester (New York), Portland (Oregon), Buffalo, and Minneapolis—All you can say about these is that the name is familiar but you can't place the face.

San Francisco—The most delightful personality of any American city: cultured without being snobbish, cosmopolitan without seeming foreign.

New Orleans—Like Paris, it is one of the few cities with sex appeal. It's a sort of Creole Marilyn Monroe.

Newark and Jersey City—These are nothing but a couple of dead-end kids.

Houston, Dallas, and Fort Worth—They merely pretend to have strong personalities, in the manner of cowboys whooping it up on Saturday night.

Charleston and Savannah—These are lovely old ladies, who sometimes get a bit tiresome in talking about the men who courted them when they were young.

Miami—Just a chromium-plated diner at a crossroads.

Atlanta—It has a split personality, because it can't decide whether to play the role of Scarlett O'Hara or that of Perle Mesta.

Social researchers deflated the myth of urban alienation by documenting the pervasiveness of social networks among virtually all city dwellers, rich and poor alike. One does not need the formal trappings of social organizations to enjoy intimate ties with others. A street corner or public bench can easily serve to create a *gemeinschaft* environment.

tower (the Detroit Marriott) is the tallest all-hotel skyscraper in the Western Hemisphere, with the largest rooftop restaurant as well. This downtown complex of seven interconnected skyscrapers along the Detroit River houses the world headquarters of General Motors. Similarly, the $180 million renovation of the city's most famous grand hotel, the historic, 31-story, Neo-Renaissance-style Book–Cadillac Hotel, has resulted in an upscale, mixed-use Westin Hotel, offices, and luxury condominiums. In addition, Compuware's recently built, $350 million world headquarters houses 4,100 employees and is located only a few blocks from the hotel.

Yet, despite all these textural changes to Detroit, the city still suffers in its image, economic well-being, and quality of life for its residents.

Portland. Portland, Oregon—our case study in Chapter 4—has a strong positive textural image, based on its revitalized downtown, new housing and businesses, and rebuilt waterfront. Visitors take delight in strolling down tree-lined shopping streets, observing the many fountains, and traveling safely on the freely available bicycles. Portland is prospering as one of the vibrant new cities of the West. Still, it effectively controls its land use, despite its 10 percent growth spurt between 2000 and 2010 (Row 2011).

Streetscapes. The "concrete canyons" formed by the tall buildings in midtown Manhattan create a different sense of place in the minds of visitors than, say, the streets of Boston's central business district, where few tall buildings abound, or the streets of San Francisco, with its many steep hills and cable cars.

In short, our senses do not deceive us when we get a different feeling from one city than we get from another. Although urban areas share many common elements, their individuality is quite real.

Ethnic pride parades and street fairs, such as the International Food Festival on Ninth Avenue in New York City, are popular means by which a city not only celebrates its diversity but also provides a rich variety of activities not to be found in any other setting. Regardless of one's own background, such events are a source of interest and enjoyment.

HUMANIZING THE CITY

People have devised ways to humanize life in today's urban environment, just as they did in the towns and villages of the past. Even when struggling with poverty, most people have found ways to maintain positive personal relationships (Curley 2008; Domínguez and Watkins 2003; Henly, et al. 2005). Although some homeless people live on the margins in almost complete isolation, most of the urban poor generate a social network to help themselves cope.

Virginia Schein (1995) conducted in-depth interviews with 30 single mothers receiving public assistance. All were working or had some work experience. She found that for many, a network of family, friends, and teachers provided both emotional support and resources, enabling these women to battle their fears and struggle onward, despite the many hardships in their daily lives. Arlene, a 34-year-old mother of three, had just earned an associate degree in business administration and moved off public assistance benefits to start a job as a customer service representative. Never, she explained, could she have done so without family support:

> I told my sister when I graduated that I owed much of it to her. My sister helped me out with the baby-sitting. She would pick them up [my kids] from day care, feed them supper, and give them baths. Then she would bring them to my house, put them to bed, and wait for me to get home, usually around 9:30. (1995:102)

For others, support came from non-family members, as another woman explained:

> It was like a three-ring circus. I have the [two] children, five classes, driving back and forth. It was quite a struggle to juggle all of that. I realized that I couldn't do this all on my own. I could ask for help and not feel disgraced....
> I realized that there are people out there that care. They helped me. Then it got better. I knew there were people that I could call, that I had the support that I needed, that these people understood what I was going through (1995:99).

Renata, a 37-year-old high school dropout and mother of two teenagers, spoke of the positive support she received from her church:

> I just got tired of trying to fix things and nothing would get fixed. Things would change and I couldn't change them back. I started going to church and I ended up going and going. I started going a year ago and am getting to know a lot of people. I was the type that stayed home all the time. I went to work, came home, went to work, came home. I didn't associate with many people on the block. I had one neighbor on one side and a girlfriend on the other and that was it. Now I go to church every Sunday, I sing in the choir, and I talk to people all day long.
> One woman said, "You look so good, you have a glow, it's your aura. I don't know what

it is but you look so different." A little old lady that lives up the street also said, "You should have started going to church a long time ago—you look good." It all gives me a little more confidence each day. If I can make it this day, then I can make it the next day and the next one and the next one. (1995:102–103)

Carol Stack (1997) stressed the ingenuity of poor African Americans in the inner-city area of a large midwestern city. Most of the men, she learned, were recent migrants from the South whose search for better jobs had resulted, at best, in low-paying, menial work. Most of the women struggled to raise their children with no steady source of income. Despite the odds against them, Stack discovered, these poor people had responded to their plight by constructing a diffuse family structure that allowed them to maintain a stable community and meet everyone's basic needs.

This network was a means to respond to an immediate crisis—people shared clothes, food, and rent money. Each time that help was given, however, a debt was incurred. The helping families and individuals, sure to be in need of assistance themselves at some future point in time, expected that those they had helped would assist them in turn. As these obligations spread, the residents established an extensive network of "cooperation and mutual aid" (1997:28–31). The expanding network became one extended family, a fact suggested by the common practice of referring to the community as "all our kin." Sometimes, fathers of children lived at home, and sometimes, when they could not support their families, they did not. Even then, fathers frequently contributed what they could to the upbringing of their children. When mothers had to work, they turned to their own mothers or to neighbors for help with the children. Thus, an informal day-care system evolved that ensured children always would have the attention of at least one caring adult. Through this reciprocal aid system, people gave what was needed and expected that their kindness would be repaid later on. Or, as one woman put it,

Sometimes I don't have a damn dime in my pocket, not a crying penny to get a box of paper diapers, milk, a loaf of bread. But you have to have help from everybody and anybody, so don't turn no one down when they come round to help. (Stack 1997:32)

In a Harlem neighborhood, Katherine S. Newman (2000) found that the same friends and family support system helps working youth as well as working parents. Living in an extended family household with her grandmother, aunts, uncles, and cousins, teenager Shaquena pooled her Burger Barn earnings with her grandmother's SSI income, one aunt's unemployment insurance, an uncle's wages from working in a police station, and another uncle's car washing earnings, as all shared the household expenses. Shaquena's neighborhood is one in which family and friends visit one another, eat together, and when necessary, borrow from one another. For example, her grandmother might run out of sugar and call Shaquena's aunt who would then bring it right over. Although her grandmother would typically ask a family member first, she also had friends to whom she could turn, and sometimes did. The mutual aid cooperation could cross generations. Shaquena's friend has a grandmother who is friends with her own grandmother, who also keeps a kitchen full of food. So when necessity dictates, she feels comfortable in going upstairs if she needs something, and so the interrelated social network provides the practicalities for survival.

Such a practical arrangement also had an emotional value. The large extended family provided family stability that might otherwise be lacking, such as in the case of Shaquena, whose mother was in and out of jail on drug convictions.

By contrast, those who don't "play fair" by reciprocating are quickly sanctioned, as documented by other researchers, including Doug A. Timmer, et al. (1994), who conducted in-depth interviews of the homeless in Tampa, Denver, and Chicago. As one once-homeless woman explained,

For six months I took [my sister] in my apartment without [the Housing Authority] knowin' about it and helped her out, fed her, bought things for her. We had holidays together. And I threw this in her face three weeks ago and told her, "This is the way it is, you know. I helped you and now you can't help me. Then you can forget about me." So we haven't called each other at all. And I won't call her. 'Til doomsday. I won't call her. Even if she comes lookin' for me, she won't find me. (1994:113)

Through this system of cooperation and mutual support, despite the conditions that hem them in, the people in study after study have invented ways to meet at least their basic needs and to soften the blow of their poverty. Such positive adaptation is a prime example of how people can make their urban experience, even under the harsh conditions of poverty, more humane.

SOCIAL MOVEMENTS AND CITY LIFE

Social movements often begin as informal, though sometimes organized, group actions to initiate or resist social change. Although these movements can begin anywhere—in eighteenth-century coffeehouses or modern universities, for example—they find the most fertile ground within cities. Here, the concentration of large numbers of people facilitates social interaction, enabling like-minded people to find one another and, in that gathering, to organize and initiate a grassroots campaign. Indeed, whether we speak of radical social movements, such as the American and French Revolutions, the "Velvet Revolution" throughout Communist Europe in the late 1980s, or of reform social movements, such as the suffragette, civil rights, and gay rights actions, the stage is almost always in cities.

Consider, for instance, the role played by cities, with their population density, in the 2011 Arab Spring demonstrations. Youthful protestors may have networked through cell phones and the Internet, but it was to the public spaces of major cities that they went to demonstrate. Brought together in those areas, they had face-to-face contact in Tunisia's wide Bourguiba Avenue or in Cairo's Tahrir Square, and it stimulated them further and motivated others to join them despite the risks. Eventually, they succeeded

in their quests, and the televised coverage of such large crowds defying their government inspired people in other Arab countries (Libya, Syria, and Yemen) to demonstrate in their cities and demand government changes.

Local social movements typically involve such issues as traffic safety, elimination of crack houses, drug dealers, and prostitution. Here too, urban design and density enhance the potential strength of a public turnout. Aptly illustrating another form of urban social movements, civic engagement, is Seattle, where, between 1988 and 2002, about 30,000 residents got involved in the development of 37 neighborhood plans. They participated in self-help projects for the common good and built new parks and playgrounds, renovated community facilities, recorded oral histories, created public art, and cultivated community gardens (Diers 2004:19).

SUBURBAN LIFE

Much of the discussion in this chapter has concerned not just those who live in the city but also those who temporarily come to the city—whether as commuters, tourists, patrons at cultural or sports events, or participants at scenes, or in some other capacity. Because the majority of people now live outside the city, however, we should also note some of the social psychology of *suburban* life.

The Stereotypes

When suburban migration became a mass phenomenon in the 1950s, the growing popularity of this lifestyle generated much criticism and caricature. Using the physical homogeneity of the new, Levittown-style subdivisions as their model and often reflecting their own urban bias, sociologists, journalists, and authors offered negative portraits of the supposed boredom and conformity to be found in the suburbs.

The title of David Riesman's essay, "The Suburban Sadness" (1958), easily conveys his feelings. John Keats blasted suburban developments in his best-selling book *The Crack in the Picture Window* (1956), and he named his major characters John and Mary Drone (their neighbors included the Faints and the Amicables) in order to make it absolutely clear that the people of suburbia were as prefabricated as their two-car garages. Numerous other books conveyed similar images, and William H. Whyte's influential *The Organization Man* (2002; orig. 1966)—although a carefully documented study of rootless corporate executives living in Park Forest, Illinois—conveyed another image of suburbanites moving every few years in their quest for success. Malvina Reynolds' 1963 folk song, made popular by Pete Seeger, speaks of suburban homes as "little boxes" that are "ticky tacky" and "all look just the same," as do their inhabitants.

The media helped spread this stereotypical image. TV shows like *The Adventures of Ozzie and Harriet* (1952–1966) epitomized suburban family life. More recently, the film *Edward Scissorhands* (1990) satirized suburban conformity, with its depiction of the men simultaneously leaving for work from their look-alike houses in their similar-looking cars, while the film *Pleasantville* (1998) told of two modern teenagers sucked into their TV set and then forced to live in a 1950s sitcom filled with innocence and naïveté.

All these books, films, and TV shows depicted suburbanites as young, with small children who ate crunchy breakfast cereals. They socialized with each other relentlessly (coffee klatches in the morning, and barbecues in the evening), and they obsessively copied each other in tastes and styles in a demeaning attempt to "keep up with the Joneses." In these stereotypical depictions, suburbanites were portrayed as bland, shallow, and superficial.

Like all stereotypes, some elements of truth existed in these depictions, but they hardly revealed the suburban reality. First, they ignored the diversity of suburbs—the older ones, the industrial ones, and the working-class ones, a topic we will explore in greater depth in Chapter 10. Second, as Herbert Gans (1968) charged, many critics were more interested in exploiting a negative myth than in actually studying the suburbs (as he did for his 1967 participant-observer research in *The Levittowners*). Third, the social dynamics in a

new development, with everyone of a comparable age moving in at the same time, change as the years pass. People age, some move out and younger others move in (creating age diversity in the neighborhood), and the "frontier spirit" of the original "settlers" ebbs.

Some of those old stereotypes remain, supplemented or even surpassed by new ones. The "soccer mom" transporting her children in her gas-guzzling SUV is a common image of today's young suburban mother. The media not only promote such a stereotype but also imprint in the public mind a soap opera quality of lust and frustration in suburban life, such as the 1999 Academy Award–winning film *American Beauty* (1999) and the Emmy Award–winning TV show *Desperate Housewives.* While such plots make for good comedy-drama, most suburban fathers do not desire their teenage daughters' girlfriends, and most suburban wives are not desperate.

The Physical Environment

Just as cities have imagability, so, too, do suburbs. Of course, suburbs may differ from one another in their age of development, typical property values, lot size, and prestige, but they all convey some measure of open space, fresh air, trees, single-family homes, lawns, and quiet streets and neighborhoods. Front lawns are typically for display purposes only; except for mowing the grass, little other activity occurs there. Instead, the backyard is the personal outdoor playground for suburbanites; here, the barbeque and patio, porch deck, swings, gym sets, tree houses, and play area set the stage for leisure activities.

By looking at the physical environment of a suburb, with just a little insight, we can actually answer the question, "What time is this place?" (Lynch 1976). Small houses—Cape Cods or bungalows—built on small lots, perhaps 50 by 75 feet, are likely to be from the 1950s. With subsequent gradations in lot size, you typically find newer and newer homes. As people's tastes changed during the late twentieth century, the size of houses increased, and the inclusion of a family room, fireplace, and greater closet space were deemed to be essential. More recently, the mass construction of **McMansions**—any supersized, large house exceeding 4,000 square feet on too small a lot, leaving little room for yard space—has generated much criticism and local resistance. Considered by critics as "tasteless" and "ostentatious," McMansions nonetheless are an increasing part of the suburban scene, either in new developments or as replacements for older houses torn down to make way for them (Gertner 2005; Nasar, et al. 2007).

Older suburbs, with their smaller lot sizes, are more likely to have sidewalks than newer suburbs are. In fact, an inverse correlation exists between lot size and pedestrian traffic: The larger the former, the less the latter. Streets may be the "rivers of life" in the city, but in the suburbs, they are simply the means to get anywhere; people-watching holds little attraction. The impracticality of bus service in such low-density suburbs makes the car a necessity for adults and the bike a secondary means of transportation for preteens and teens. Parents spend much time and gas in chauffeuring children to school (if not on a school bus route), to after-school athletic programs, or to all kinds of lessons (dance, music, karate, religious).

Few, if any, landmarks exist in the suburbs, and residents rely heavily on mental mapping to get from one locale to another. The visitor, on the other hand, requires specific directions and, even then, often gets confused in reaching that destination. Multiple suburban realities surely exist, but even with the diversity found within and among suburbs, the presence of multiple realities is less intense within any given suburb than within the typical city.

The Social Environment

Gemeinschaft and a comprehensive social network constitute the suburban milieu, not the anonymity and widespread presence of strangers, as in the *gesellschaft* environment of the city. You might not know everyone's name, but a shared sense of community marks most everyday interactions. Moreover, especially in families with school-age children, organized activities (PTA, Little and Junior Leagues, scouting) abound, with parents expected to be active participants. Newest residents, with or without children, often find that a local "welcome wagon" or Newcomers Club initiates contact to integrate them into the community.

Joining a church and participating in its many activities, getting involved in other local programs, and attending block or house parties and cookouts are all part of the interactive neighboring that is common in suburbia. Birthday parties and sleepovers for preteens and early teens, and local high school events for those of that age, are just a few of the many ways that weave young people into the suburban social fabric.

SUMMARY

Living in cities alters our perceptions. The urban experience causes us to react to the city as a physical and social environment, and such reactions represent a social psychology of the city.

We make sense of the city by ordering it. Kevin Lynch observed that we trace the physical landscape, identifying paths, edges, districts, nodes, and landmarks. In part, such distinctions arise from the physical form of the city itself (streets, after all, are "natural" paths). In part, they also arise from our personal needs and creativity (people invent "back street" paths to get from one place to another more quickly). To this basic insight, Lynch contributed a deeper understanding of the process, with the concept of "mental mapping."

A similar ordering occurs as we respond to the city's social aspects. On the one hand, we cope with the city's *gesellschaft* characteristics (large numbers and high density) by inventing rules of behavior for riding the subway, standing in line, or walking in the street. We also size up strangers on the basis of their dress, demeanor, and location in the city. Nevertheless, despite many common strategies, we all react individually to the city. Our social characteristics—whether we are rich or poor, immigrant or native, mainstream or marginal—have much to do with the nature of our urban experience.

On another level, we have developed complex ways of establishing meaningful relationships in the city. Urban networks are a prime example. Personal networks take many forms, including kinship, neighborhood, street-corner friendships, or people frequenting some "scene." Most of us also identify with our city as a whole, merging traits of our particular city (a key industry, a winning sports team, or an important historical event) with our own personal urban experience. All these mechanisms lend a *gemeinschaft*-like character to the urban experience.

Next is the notion of urban texture or city personality. Recent research shows that much truth lies in people's comments that—based on its history, architecture, location, and people—each city "feels" a little different.

Finally, numerous investigations reveal that people, even those facing the most desperate economic conditions, can humanize the city and turn it into a meaningful experience.

Taken together, all these elements of the urban experience provide us with a sense of order and security in this largest of human agglomerations, and they make the city meaningful, usable, and often enjoyable.

A social–psychological examination of suburban life takes us to its stereotypical images, first as a bland locale of superficial conformists promulgated by the media and biased observers, to a more recent one of "soccer moms" on the one hand, to the frustrated and "desperate" people on the other. A certain homogeneity does exist in the various physical elements of a suburb, even though widespread differences in lifestyle exist. A comprehensive network of interaction and organized activities involves youths and adults in numerous ways.

CONCLUSION

The city is a big place. It has more people, more buildings, more paths, more nodes, and more possibilities for interactions and relationships than any other form of settlement. As Georg Simmel argued many years ago, cities demand a great deal of mental work from those who wish to make sense of them. In the end, such extra mental effort may be the unique element that creates the sophistication attributed to urban dwellers. Low-density residence patterns deter pedestrian and bus traffic, and dependence on the car is high. The physical homogeneity and lack of landmarks put the visitor who lacks the detailed mental mapping of suburbanites at a disadvantage in moving about.

KEY TERMS

districts (205)
edges (205)
landmarks (205)
McMansions (228)
mental maps (207)

nodes (205)
paths (205)
scenes (218)
texture (221)

INTERNET ACTIVITIES

1. You can learn more about mental mapping and have a virtual reality, flyover experience at *http://www.mentalmaps.info/*. Once there, click on "Showcase."
2. A vivid example of urban apathy occurred in New York City in April 2010, when a man, stabbed while attempting to help a mugging victim, bled to death on the sidewalk as pedestrians walked past him. Watch the horrific incident and other examples of bystander apathy at *http://www.youtube.com/watch?v=u5_h2v1MJ_M.*

CHAPTER 9

COMPARATIVE URBANISM
The City and Culture

THE CITY AND THE COUNTRYSIDE
  Interdependencies
  Urban Dominance
THE CITY AND CIVILIZATION
  The "Soul" of the City
  The City as the Center of Civilization
  The Civic Culture of the City
THE CITY AND SOCIETAL CULTURE

CASE STUDY: MING PEKING

  Physical Structure
  Symbolism

CASE STUDY: HELLENIC ATHENS

  The Preclassical Period
  The Golden Age
  Behind the Glory
MING PEKING AND ATHENS:
  A COMPARISON

THE CULTURE OF CAPITALISM
  AND THE CITY
  The Capitalist City
  The Industrial Revolution
  Urban Life as Economics
  Assets and Debits

CASE STUDY: COMMUNIST–CAPITALIST
  BEIJING

  Urban Life as Politics
  Economic Reform and
    Environmental Issues
  A Rising Consumerism
SUMMARY
CONCLUSION
KEY TERMS
INTERNET ACTIVITIES

Something rather ironic exists in the title of Louis Wirth's essay "Urbanism as a Way of Life" (1938), which we discussed in Chapter 5. You will recall. Wirth argued that their size, density, and heterogeneity make cities characteristically impersonal, transient, and anonymous. His negative overgeneralizations about cities and their impact on human behavior ignored the role of **culture,** which *is* the urban way of life and often has positive effects on the lives of city dwellers.

In this chapter, we will examine the city and culture from two perspectives. First, we will look at the existence of what Daniel J. Monti calls *civic culture.* That is, in the urban way of life, the many different types of people find an appropriate form of public behavior that enables them, mostly, to get along with one another. Through ceremonies, customs, and codes, they have "worked out a way to be together in public and still carry on their private lives, peaceably and with at least a modicum of predictability" (Monti 1999:103).

Second, *the city is not an entity unto itself.* All cities reflect and intensify the world's cultures. North American culture, with its emphasis on free enterprise and the nuclear family, creates cities with skyscrapers downtown (to maximize trade advantages) and single-family dwellings outside the city center. The culture of the Yoruba (the people who comprise the bulk of the population of Ibadan, Nigeria's second-largest city) emphasizes personalized trade relations, handicrafts, and an extended family, and it generates a city that is quite different in physical layout and social interaction. Cities are, after all, human creations that display the same variety as all human culture, and we can fully understand a city only by exploring the cultural patterns found throughout its larger society.

THE CITY AND THE COUNTRYSIDE

> ...those that are good manners at the court are as ridiculous in the country as the behavior of the country is most mockable at the court.
>
> Shakespeare, *As You Like It*, III, 2

Interdependencies

Shakespeare noted something that everyone knows: Country ways and city ways are often quite different. Yet we must be wary of overgeneralization. For example, in Ibadan, with the city's fields so close by and farmers such a large part of the city's population, it is virtually impossible to distinguish between city ways and country ways (Lawal, et al. 2004). Indeed, in any location, city and country are not independent of each other at all but, rather, have a symbiotic relationship.

Throughout history, the migration of people seeking a better life has transformed city and country alike. To take but one example, during the great expansion of European cities during the nineteenth century, England changed from an almost completely rural society to a nation in which more than three-fourths of the population lived in cities (see Table 9–1). In 50 years, the urban population nearly tripled, as the rural population and the percentage of adult males in agriculture decreased.

The relationship between the city and its countryside involves much more than just the dynamics of migration, however. The resources that each provides create a reciprocal dependence. Because a large proportion of city dwellers (even in Ibadan) engage in

TABLE 9–1   Urban and Rural Population in England and Wales, 1851–1911

Year	Total Urban Population	Total Rural Population	Urban (%)
1851	8,990,809	8,936,800	50.2
1861	10,960,998	9,105,226	54.6
1871	14,041,404	8,670,862	61.8
1881	17,636,646	8,337,793	67.9
1891	20,895,504	8,107,021	72.0
1901	25,058,355	7,469,556	77.0
1911	28,162,936	7,907,556	78.1

Source: Census: England and Wales, 1911, Vol. 1, p. xv, reported in C. M. Law, "The Growth of Urban Population in England and Wales, 1801–1911," pp. 125–43 in *Transactions of the Institute of British Geographers.* Accessed at http://www.jstor.org/stable/621331?seq=2 on April 14, 2012.

specialized occupations other than agriculture, the countryside must supply the city's food. Many of the specialty occupations of the city, such as weaving or steel manufacturing, depend on the countryside's raw materials. Conversely, the countryside obtains many of its goods—the clothes made by weavers, the tractors made with the steel—from the city.

Shakespeare notwithstanding, perhaps the most important link between city and countryside is the reciprocal shaping of lifestyles. Migrants who swell the city's ranks bring to the city their cultural traditions. The result is a living kaleidoscope of human behavior, ranging all the way from groups who devotedly try to continue living as they did in the "old country" (e.g., New York's Hasidic Jews) to the various ethnic Americans (e.g., Asian Americans and Hispanic Americans) who maintain only some of the old ways in their new urban setting.

At the same time, other rural influences, including traditional folk music, art, and literature, continually alter the city's character. For example, at least one radio station in nearly every major U.S. city plays country music exclusively, and "country rock" is a peculiar rural–urban musical blend.

Especially common in North American and European cities (and less so in African cities like Ibadan) is the human cultural hybrid—that is, the urban person who takes a little bit from the numerous, originally rural lifestyles existing in the city and then integrates them into a new lifestyle altogether. Such a person was Mayor Fiorello La Guardia of New York, as described in the *Urban Living* box on page 233. Perhaps it would be fair to say that a little bit of La Guardia exists in most city dwellers today.

This influence works in two ways, however. Just as the city receives much from the countryside, it typically returns the favor, radiating

Intimate, open-air markets are common in many parts of the world. Particularly in developing countries, city life—such as here in Guatemala—is based on kinship and ethnic ties. Typically, the men work their farms or produce their crafts, poultry, and livestock, and the women sell these goods in the marketplace—and often know just about everyone with whom they do business.

URBAN LIVING

Mayor Fiorello La Guardia of New York

To put it sociologically, La Guardia was a marginal man who lived in the edge of many cultures....Tammany Hall may have been the first to exploit the vote-getting value of eating gefilte fish with the Jews, goulash with the Hungarians, sauerbraten with Germans, spaghetti with Italians, and so on indefinitely, but this unorthodox Republican not only dined every bit as shrewdly but also spoke, according to the occasion, in Yiddish, Hungarian, German, Serbian-Croatian, or plain New York English. Half Jewish and half Italian, born in Greenwich Village yet raised in Arizona, married first to a Catholic and then to a Lutheran but himself a Mason and an Episcopalian, Fiorello La Guardia was a Mr. Brotherhood Week all by himself.

Source: Arthur Mann, cited in E. Digby Baltzell, *The Protestant Establishment* (New Brunswick, NJ: Transaction Publishers, 2000), p. 29.

outward an influence far beyond its borders. In fact, many sociologists think that this influence, in modern times, far outstrips the countryside's effect on urban affairs.

Urban Dominance

North American cities have maintained cultural dominance over society far out of proportion to the number of city dwellers ever

By the late eighteenth century, Paris had established urban dominance over all of France in cultural, economic, and political matters. When Napoleon borrowed from ancient Roman tradition to build this massive triumphal arch at the western end of the Champs Elysées, it became a symbol of French patriotism, further strengthening the city's image as the "essence" of what is French.

since the coming of European settlers in the seventeenth century. Moreover, as we described in Chapter 3, supplementing the importance of early eastern settlements—most notably Boston, Charleston, Montreal, Newport, New York, and Philadelphia—were newer cities, as the population moved westward to such places as Chicago, Kansas City, St. Louis, and Toronto. In the Far West, especially following the completion of the transcontinental railroad to San Francisco in 1869, towns and cities continued to stand at the center of social life. Josiah Strong observed this fact in 1885 and commented, "It is the cities and towns which frame state constitutions, make laws, create public opinion, establish social usages and fix standards of morals in the West" (p. 206).

North American growth is thus intertwined with the story of the development of cities. Consistently the centers of an expanding market, the loci of advances in communication, and the sources of leadership in politics, fashion, and the arts, cities have a long linkage with cultural firsts: the first daily newspaper (Philadelphia, 1784), the first stock exchange (New York, 1792), and the first telephone system (Boston, 1877; linked to New York in 1884, to Denver in 1911, and to San Francisco in 1915).

Such a pattern of **urban dominance** over the broader society is hardly limited to North

CITYSCAPE

The Invasion of the City Slickers

An ironic pattern often emerges when city people move to the country to escape the crowds and traffic jams. In seeking to simplify their lives away from the busyness of the city, they soon effect changes in their rural setting that destroy its very nature.

Let's use a hypothetical married couple to illustrate. Bob is a computer graphics designer and Laurie is a freelance book editor. As a dual-career professional couple living in Manhattan, their income is high enough for them to buy a second home in upstate New York. Spending many weekends there, their two children love their mountain retreat as much as they do.

After a few years, Bob and Laurie tire of the long drives on Friday nights out to the country and back to the city on Sundays. They value the quiet pace of life and natural surroundings that their upstate neighbors enjoy every day, unlike the crowding, noise, and hustle and bustle of daily urban life. They begin to think of a change in lifestyle.

Bob's boss agrees to his going to the office only once or twice a week, working from home the rest of the time, and staying in touch via phone, email, and videoconferencing whenever necessary. Because Sue does her work at home, this change gives both of them the flexibility to make their weekend home a full-time one. Moreover, she's tired of her never-ending duties as a Brownie Scout leader, and recently had her car broken into and CD tapes stolen. She is eager to move into their little mountain village where no one locks their doors, and where there is no Brownie troop.

Their first year after the move is mostly a happy one. The flower and vegetable gardens are successful. They hike various trails, take up bird watching, and learn cross-country skiing. Bob enjoys the exercise of splitting wood for the fireplace, by which they spend many cozy evenings.

One problem, though, is the school, which Laurie thinks is not very good. She sees a real

America. We find a description of the same phenomenon in Alexis de Tocqueville's historical account (2004; orig. 1856) of the French Revolution of 1789. Beginning in the 1600s as the feudal system weakened, French life became increasingly centralized in Paris. As a result, when the revolution erupted in Paris, it quickly carried the rest of French society along with it.

Tocqueville noted that in times past, Paris had been "nothing but the largest city in France," but by 1789 things were different and it was no exaggeration to say that Paris "was already France itself" (2004:145). The city controlled the nation's economic, intellectual, and political lifeblood. This urban dominance was also evident as one left Paris for the countryside. Inquiring as to the eighteenth-century political climate of the outlying areas, English observer Arthur Young heard time and again, "We're only a provincial town; we have to see what they'll do in Paris" (Tocqueville 2004:147).

That is exactly what Paris did. One of the remarkable facts of history is that the cultural ideas ("Liberty! Equality! Brotherhood!") that transformed France and much of Western civilization, in conjunction with the American Revolution a decade earlier, were largely city born.

Urban dominance is thus a central pattern of the modern and the historical worlds. Sometimes, however, urban influence is not so welcome, as the people of Grafton County, New Hampshire, have decided. Their views are described in the *Cityscape* box below.

---

need for a new school building, modern playground equipment, and new school buses. In fact, there should a new principal with a more modern approach to education. Both Bob and Laurie are appalled to learn that less than half of the kids who graduate high school go any further in their education. Instead, they join the military or get such small-town jobs as store clerks, farmers, and mechanics. How will their two children get into good colleges from this inferior school? They organize a small group of other recent residents to upgrade education in their community. Some of them plan to get on the school board to make changes, starting with a multimillion-dollar new building.

Bob likes splitting wood so much that he decides to buy a chainsaw so he can cut down some of the trees on his property. He also loves to play golf but the nearest course is more than 20 miles away. He and some of his friends in the education lobby discuss building a nine-hole course. They've found just the place, some land where an old farmer keeps a few dairy cows and no longer works the land. Soon, he'll have to sell the property and they'll grab it. Of course, they admire the local farmers and it's too bad when they quit, but that's life, isn't it?

Some more time passes, as Bob and Laurie settle more fully into their rural lifestyle. However, they also discover other needs. A couple of good restaurants, preferably French and Italian, would make for a nice evening out. Also, the small airport with its infrequent flights, sometimes canceled for lack of sophisticated equipment, really needs an upgrade so Bob doesn't have to drive to those important meetings in Manhattan. More organized activities for the kids are another need. For example, some are suggesting formation of a Brownie troop.

In other words, an influx of upper-middle-class newcomers into a rural town will most likely result in its conversion into a typical suburb. It may remain rustic for a generation, with farms scattered all around and the old-timers gathering at town meetings to voice their opinions. Soon enough, though, higher taxes to pay for the improved facilities and roads will force the local people to move, and as they do, another slice of rural America disappears.

In other instances, urban dominance is understated, as in the case of "Springdale," a small town in upstate New York. With its quiet streets and surrounding rural countryside, it would seem to be a world apart from the city. The appearance is deceiving. Although residents of the town displayed much pride in their traditions of independence and self-sufficiency—values they associated with small-town life—they also recognized that these sentiments were ebbing away. The average Springdaler, wrote sociologists Arthur Vidich and Joseph Bensman,

> sees that the urban and metropolitan society is technically and culturally superior to his own community. He sees this in his everyday life when he confronts the fact that his community cannot provide him with everything he needs: almost everyone goes to the city for shopping and entertainment; large numbers of people are dependent on the radio and television; and everyone realizes that rural life would be drastically altered without cars and refrigerators. (2000:79; orig. 1958)

It may be edge cities and not older cities that impact on many rural landscapes today, but this is merely a newer form of urban dominance. Nor are these the only links that bind the residents of Springdale to the larger urban society. Influencing their lives are outside specialists from organizations such as the state agricultural extension service as well as their own college-trained professionals. Additional organizations that serve to "import" the culture of the urban society include such national organizations as the Odd Fellows and the Kiwanis Club. Perhaps more important, the economic and political life of the town is shaped more by state and federal agencies than by local entities. Taxes, education for the town's children, and the price of local farmers' milk are all increasingly subject to outside forces that are mostly city based. Vidich and Bensman concluded that despite the desires and pretensions of the townspeople, most "plans and decisions that refer directly to the community are made from a distance by invisible agents and institutions" (2000:81). Thus, just as Springdalers now periodically go to the world of the city, the world of the city has subtly transformed, for better or for worse, Springdale and communities like it.

THE CITY AND CIVILIZATION

> Cities have always been the fireplaces of civilization, whence light and heat radiated out into the dark, cold world.
>
> Theodore Parker, nineteenth-century U.S. preacher

The reason for the city's increasing dominance in modern affairs, as we have hinted already, is that everything human—art, music, business, traditions, what we love and hate—converges there. The city does not create a way of life all its own but, rather, provides the setting where any way of life, any cultural tradition, can intensify and re-create itself in a manner not possible in other settings. For example, Socrates, Plato, and Aristotle all lived in Hellenic Athens, where they shared ideas and challenged each other. This simply would not have occurred had they all lived in rural hamlets, cut off from one another.

Nowhere is this process of intensification represented more clearly than in the suggestion that the city encapsulates a whole culture. Throughout history, writers have seen the city as capturing the essence of human civilization. Indeed, Euripides, the classical Greek playwright, maintained, "The first requisite to happiness is birth in a great city." The *Urban Trends* box on page 237 illustrates not only the connections among our most common words about cities and civilization but also the linkage between city and culture as expressed in the writings of some of history's most important urbanists.

Is the city truly synonymous with civilization? To find out, let's examine in more detail the ideas of Oswald Spengler, Lewis Mumford, and Daniel J. Monti.

The "Soul" of the City

Oswald Spengler (1880–1936) was a German philosopher who saw in cities the drama of the rise and fall of civilization. He contended

URBAN TRENDS

The City and Civilization

City Culture

Just as the beginning of Western Civilization is marked by permanent settlement of formerly nomadic peoples...so the beginning of what is distinctly modern in our civilization is best signaled by the growth of great cities. (Louis Wirth, 1938)

The city is...the natural habitat of civilized man. (Robert Park, 1984; orig. 1916)

[The city is] the most precious invention of civilization, second only to language itself in the transmission of culture. (Lewis Mumford, 1991; orig. 1961)

All great Cultures are town-Cultures.... World history is city history. Peoples, states, politics, religion, all arts, and all sciences rest upon one phenomenon...the town. (Oswald Spengler, 2004; orig. 1928)

City Words

In the English language, many of the words connected with the notion of a city are of a positive and complimentary nature. From the Greek word *polis* ("city") emerged the English word *politic*. Synonyms for this word are tactful, diplomatic, prudent, and wise. From the Latin word *civis* ("citizen" or city resident), we get the words *civil* (well mannered), *civilized* (refined behavior), and *civilization* (way of life). Another Latin word, *urbs* ("city"), gave rise to the word *urbane*, describing someone who is suave, polished, or cultured. Such positive connotations reveal the centuries-old belief that city dwellers represented the best in human evolution.

In addition to adjectives, the Greek word *metropolis* gives us a noun in common usage today, and one whose original meaning further implies the positive image of urban life. We gain this insight by breaking the word down into its component parts: *metro* ("mother") *and polis* ("city"). For the ancient Greeks then, the metropolis was not only the center of their everyday lives but also the source of their legacy, the place from which they inherited the knowledge, philosophies, and patterns of living that enabled them to achieve even more.

Understanding word origins and meanings thus help us to understand what people from ages past thought of the city and its people.

---

that cities developed, ultimately dominated a society, and then declined, carrying with them the culture built over generations and centuries. The cyclical element in Spengler's theory (generally considered by contemporary social scientists as too simplistic) is less important for our purposes than his belief that "all great cultures are town-cultures" and that "world history is city history" (Spengler 2004:247; orig. 1928).

Spengler believed strongly that human civilization takes on distinctive qualities in the city. At some point in its development, the "soul" of the city emerges. Spengler also believed that the countryside never has a soul in this sense; it is a "landscape" at most, never a "world." Moreover, he argued, the city has such uniqueness and power that both the peasant and townsman clearly understand the difference between the subordinate environ outside the city and the dominant influence of the city, or as Spangler put it, "The new Soul of the City speaks a new language, which soon becomes tantamount to the language of the culture itself" (2004:248).

Thus, we find the essence of ancient Egypt symbolized by Thebes, ancient Greece by Athens, the Roman Empire by Rome, Islam by Baghdad, and prerevolutionary France by Paris (2004:247). Indeed, Spengler believed that whole periods of European civilization were manifest only in cities. For example, he reminded us that Gothic, Renaissance, and Baroque styles flourished only in the cities nurturing those cultural worlds.

Modern sociologists generally view Spengler's contribution to urban sociology as modest, because few accept his cyclical ideas of historical change. Yet he correctly sensed the connection between city and civilization, an idea developed extensively by a U.S. urbanist whose work we will discuss next.

The City as the Center of Civilization

Lewis Mumford (1895–1990) traced the cultural importance of cities through Western history. Based on historical and comparative evidence, he argued that the city has, indeed, been at the very center of Western civilization from its beginnings.

Mumford believed that of all creatures, only human beings seem to be aware of themselves as fundamentally distinctive. We can think, invent, and wonder about such things as life, death, sex, and god(s). In the course of human evolution, Mumford reasoned, people attached these thoughts to places. The earliest centers of this kind were probably caves and places of burial. These sites were symbolic centers to which wandering groups could return periodically to ponder the mysteries they wished to understand. Thus began civilization. "In the earliest gathering about a grave or a painted symbol, a great stone or a sacred grove, one has the beginning of a succession of civic institutions that range from the temple to the astronomical observatory, from the theater to the university" (Mumford 1991:9; orig. 1961).

As time passed and technology improved, some people began living at these places permanently: The shrine became a camp, then a village, and finally, a town. Mumford (like Spengler) suggests that at a certain point, the cultural ideas, the people, and the place all jelled as the city emerged (see the *Urban Trends* box on page 239).

Thenceforth, the story of civilization became the story of urban history. Yet we must be careful here. We often assume that civilization automatically means progress—that what exists today is somehow a better form of what went before. Neither Spengler nor Mumford meant to suggest this notion of cultural evolution; rather, their idea was that the city was culture "writ large," the living embodiment of a society's or epoch's ideas. Cities did not inevitably progress. In them, as already mentioned, Spengler saw the rise and fall of civilization, and like Max Weber before him (see Chapter 5), Mumford believed that cities better than today's had existed in the past—in Hellenic Athens, for example.

The Civic Culture of the City

Daniel J. Monti rejects the suggestion of some social scientists that cities have become "sinkholes of civic indifference," no longer possessing the cultural or moral vision that once motivated their residents (1999:378). Instead, he argues that cities continue to inspire both a public spirit and a civic mindedness among their inhabitants. Their ability to coexist and cooperate in the everyday routines of public habits and customs is the manifestation of a **civic culture.** With its elements borrowed from other cultures or adapted from earlier times, civic culture helps the many different peoples of a city to get along and make sense of each other's world.

Offering a detailed portrait of a civic culture is a difficult task. First, each city has its own distinctive style, temperament, and public rhythms, so generalizations are misleading. Second, civic culture is not static; it is continually changing and, thus, is hard to pinpoint. Third, some of its elements may be better or less known to certain groups in the city and, therefore, practiced unevenly or not at all in different parts of the city (Monti 1999:103–104).

URBAN TRENDS

The Crystallization of the City

The emergence of the city was more than just an increase in population. Such a concentration and mixture of people generated creativity and advances in virtually all spheres of human activity. Previously scattered and unorganized functions now came together within the city walls and under a centralized control, enabling the harnessing of manpower and, in turn, expanded communication, transportation, and trade. Improved agricultural productivity, advances in architectural design and crafts, and the evolution of the creative arts and sciences all occurred to meet the changing needs of an increasingly complex society. Other early achievements of the city were the creation of the written word, the library, the school, and the university, all of which stimulated further advances in knowledge and technology, reflection and speculation, creativity and discovery—building a cumulative heritage as a springboard for succeeding generations to use to achieve still further progress.

The historic city also had its contradictory elements. Creativity may have flourished but often so too did strict control over residents' lives. For some, the city provided a comfortable lifestyle, but others lived in poverty. The security of living within strong walls that gave protection against outside marauders did not safeguard against dangers in the streets, especially at night. Both sacred and secular power intensified in the city, sometimes competing against one another and at other times existing in blended form. The dynamics of historic city life, then, took on dimensions recognizable to subsequent generations of city dwellers. Also, from its beginnings to the present, the city—with its many activities, diversity, excitement, and promise—has been an attractive lure for a great many people.

Source: Excerpts from "The Crystallization of the City" in *The City in History: Its Origin, Its Transformation, and Its Prospects,* by Lewis Mumford. Copyright © 1961 and renewed 1989 by Lewis Mumford. Reprinted by permission of Houghton Mifflin Harcourt Publishing Company. All rights reserved.

Despite the unevenness of some aspects of civic culture, other parts work well throughout the city, because they are widely shared. These are found in the "ceremonies, customs, and codes for appropriate public behavior" (Monti 1999:103). Essentially, "they are expressions of how persons in that place have worked out a way to be together in public and still carry on their private lives, peaceably and with at least a modicum of predictability" (Monti 1999:103). For example, urbanites typically line up awaiting the arrival of a bus in a single line, not in a cluster. This unspoken, untaught norm of civic culture is quickly learned, enabling strangers to accord one another a mutual respect and an orderly entrance once the bus arrives.

In this and countless other ways, urban public behavior reflects the shared values, norms, and practices of a civic culture that makes it possible for people—different and unknown to one another—to become part of an inclusive community. Essentially minding each other's business in order to behave appropriately in urban public space, rather than focusing only on one's own actions or rituals, city people develop a common view of the world and conceive better ways to be in it together (Monti 1999:104).

The presence of this civic culture does not imply a fairness or equality in the city, but rather a practical existence that works and makes sense to city residents. It may appear to be an inconsistent blend of conservative and

Monti suggests that civic culture in a city includes widely shared codes of appropriate public behavior, which allow strangers to be together and act with a reasonable set of expectations from each other. Such practices as alternate vehicle merging or awaiting a bus in a single line allow fair and orderly movement through unspoken, untaught norms of mutual respect.

liberal practices, but it is effective and visitors benefit from this civic and cultural ethos as well. Though unrealized as an element of our cultural inheritance, the urban way of life has made an important contribution (Monti 1999:379).

THE CITY AND SOCIETAL CULTURE

From Mumford and Spengler we learn that although the city and civilization are not precisely synonymous, the city definitely has a unique power to intensify and symbolize culture. From Monti, we learn the city also generates a civic culture that, to a greater or lesser degree, its residents share and practice. Another aspect of culture is that any city will dynamically and intensely reflect the characteristics of its surrounding culture. Because cultural patterns vary so widely, however, cities may be markedly different from one

another. In the following case studies, we will read about two cities, Peking during the Ming Dynasty (1368–1644 C.E.) and Hellenic Athens of the fifth century B.C.E.—capitals of vastly different civilizations and separated by more than 1,500 years.

CASE STUDY
Ming Peking

Situated on the northern seacoast, China's capital city is centered around the Forbidden City and Tiananmen Square, the world's biggest public square, with an area of 98 acres. Now a city of nearly 20 million people, Beijing (formerly called Peking) has a 3,000-year history and contains fascinating remnants of its glorious past.

Established in northeastern China to protect the country from invaders out of the north, Beijing grew into a city at least several centuries before the birth of Christ. During the thirteenth century C.E., when the Yuan (Mongol) emperor ruled China, Kublai Khan transformed Beijing into a capital city. Soon after the overthrow of the Yuan by the Ming Dynasty in 1368, the Emperor Yung Lo spared no expense in turning the city into a monument to all of Chinese culture and to himself as symbolic head of that culture. It was a massive job, including the transportation of large amounts of marble a distance of 1,500 miles not only to expand the palace but also to upgrade some of the city's roads and bridges (Mote 2003:617–20).

Physical Structure

The design, deliberately created to symbolize everything vital to Chinese life, arranged the whole city on a perfect north–south axis, around which were temples and altars. Perhaps no better example exists of Lewis Mumford's idea about the city as a physical container, for Ming Beijing literally revealed the city within the city, surrounding the all-important core where the emperor lived (Figure 9–1).

The city was about 25 square miles in area and was composed of two major sections, each roughly rectangular in shape. Beijing's southern section, known as the Outer City or Chinese City, contained most of the city's population, probably about 1 million people in the fifteenth century, probably then the largest in the world (Li, et al. 2008:1).

The northern section, however, was of quite another character. Known as the Tartar City or Inner City, this area was surrounded by a massive wall about 50 feet high and just as thick. Indeed, whereas in the West the words for *city* are linked to the words for *civilization* and *politics*, in Chinese the word for *city* literally means "wall," indicating in yet another way that the city was a container of major cultural significance (Murphy 2007:189). All city streets were arranged in a gridiron, with gates through the wall arranged symmetrically.

Centrally located within the walls of the Tartar City was another area, called the Imperial City. Protected by yet another wall, and including about 5 square miles of park-like land, complete with artificially constructed lakes and hills, this was the focus of the political and religious power and splendor of Ming civilization. In the midst of this constructed urban tranquility, and surrounded by a moat and yet another defensive wall, were the palaces and residences—facing south—of the emperor. This was called the Purple City by the Chinese and later dubbed the Forbidden City by Europeans, after their realization that access was gained only through the emperor's personal decree. Just to the north was a large, artificially constructed mound of earth, Coal Hill, on which stood temples that were prominently visible above the city.

Symbolism

Ming Peking was based on elaborate Chinese cosmology, with its temples and altars serving as religious symbols of the sun, earth, and most important, heaven. Chinese astronomers had discovered long before Peking was built that the center of the heavens was the North Star, around which everything revolved. On earth—the human universe—the Chinese believed that everything revolved around the "Son of Heaven," the emperor. As the northernmost major city of China, Peking thus became the emperor's capital. The importance of the north was also evident in the city's location on a north–south axis and by the fact that the emperor could be reached only by traveling north along the Great Processional Way. Even the name of the emperor's city, the Purple City, was chosen because the North Star gave off a purple hue in the night sky (Naquin 2000).

The symbolism did not stop there, however. The colors and height of all buildings had cultural meaning. Peasants, lowly and unimportant, were allowed houses of only one story and could paint their roofs only a dull gray. In the Imperial City, various functionaries couldn't have houses of more than one story, either, but to signify their higher status, they were allowed to paint their roofs green, red, or purple, depending on their role. Only in the Forbidden City itself were buildings

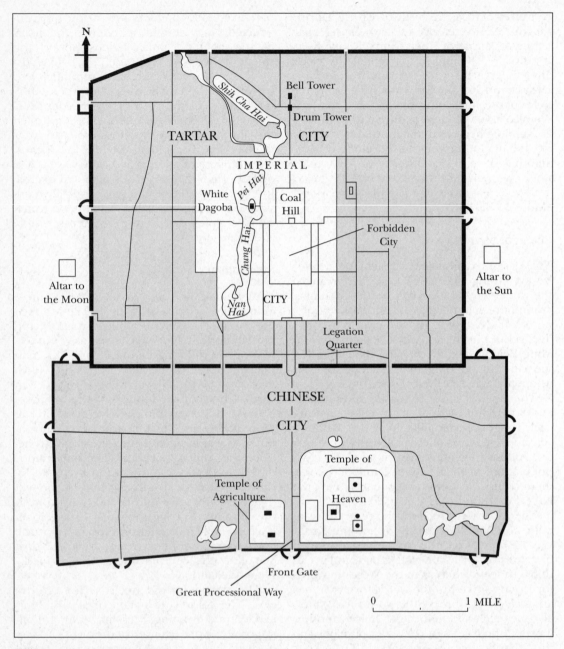

FIGURE 9–1   Ming Peking

Source: From Roderick MacFarquhar, *The Forbidden City* (New York: Newsweek Books, 1972), p. 42.

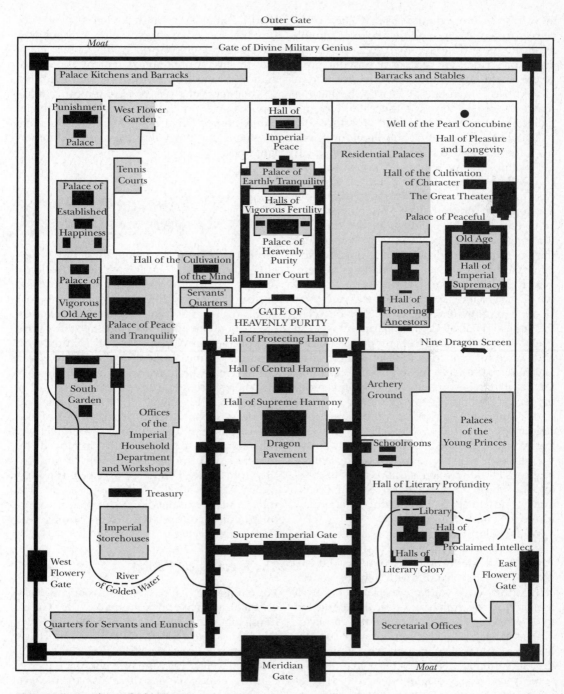

FIGURE 9–2   The Forbidden City

Source: From Roderick MacFarquhar, *The Forbidden City* (New York: Newsweek Books, 1972), p. 73.

allowed to be more than one story. Their roofs were painted a bright golden yellow, symbolizing the life-giving (sun-like) qualities of the emperor's rule. The emperor was the pivot of the world, and ruling from the Forbidden City with the mandate of heaven, he harmonized the world, oversaw the calendar, and maintained order (Beguin and Morel 1997).

It is little wonder that the emperor, given his importance, had everything for the "good life" within a stone's throw. The construction of the Forbidden City was a marvel of urban design, as can be seen by carefully examining the buildings shown in Figure 9–2 on page 243. Note especially the buildings in the center—the emperor's sole preserve. The first group, the buildings immediately to the north of the Supreme Imperial Gate, are buildings of state: The Hall of Supreme Harmony was reserved for special state occasions, such as the New Year's ceremony and the emperor's birthday; the smaller Hall of Central Harmony was the place where the emperor prepared himself and waited for functions; the Hall of Protecting Harmony was for the reception of visitors and for day-to-day governance. The second group of central buildings—to the north of these state buildings—comprised the emperor's residences. Entering by the Gate of Heavenly Purity, one found the Palace of Heavenly Purity, the emperor's quarters; next was the Hall of Vigorous Fertility, which, its name notwithstanding, was where official seals were stored; finally, one found the Palace of Earthly Tranquility, where the empress lived.

Ming Peking is a striking example of the city's ability to intensify culture. Peking was a symbolic world, a whole city built on the cultural themes of harmony with nature, security (city within city), and power. Each "layer of the onion" re-emphasized the whole and led to the vital, omnipotent center—the emperor.

This particular symbolism probably means little to us, but we can imagine what it meant to the city's inhabitants. In a similar manner, our cities transmit and magnify our culture. What is important in our culture is "writ large" in Boston, Birmingham, and Boise. We don't have cities within cities or predominant religious symbolism, like Peking. On the site of the destroyed

World Trade Center twin towers in New York City, however, contractors are presently building the 1,776-foot One World Trade Center, clearly a distinctive symbol and statement about U.S. culture. Flying over North American cities, we see commercial skyscrapers, fast-moving automobiles on superhighways, and private, single-family houses. What might such constructions say about the things that are culturally important to us?

CASE STUDY
Hellenic Athens

Little risk exists of exaggerating the differences between Ming Peking and Hellenic Athens, situated on the rocky northern coast of the Mediterranean. During a period of barely two generations in the fifth century B.C.E., between about 480 and the start of the Peloponnesian War in 431, a civilization took form that Mumford described as "a far richer efflorescence of human genius than history anywhere else records, except perhaps for Renaissance Florence" (1991:167). Imagine an almost simultaneous development of the arts of painting, sculpture, and architecture; the realization of a rationally structured democracy; and the birth of a body of philosophy still at the center of Western thinking today. At the heart of this Golden Age was the city of Athens, leading to an identification of Athenian culture almost synonymous with Greek achievement.

The Preclassical Period

Four migrating tribes settled Athens as early as 2000 B.C.E., and eventually, the Greek peninsula came under the control of feudal overlords who called themselves, perhaps with not the greatest modesty, the *aristoi* (or aristocracy; literally, "the best people"). By the eighth century B.C.E., these overlords were in charge of several hundred independent Greek city-states, or *poli* (the source of our contemporary word *political* and of the urban suffix *-polis*). Over the next two centuries, the city-states grew rich as technology and overseas trade improved and military conquests multiplied.

Ironically, this very success is what led to the aristocrats' downfall. The improvement of trade created a wealthy middle class that began to demand participation in city rule, and the martial victories evolved a warrior class with both the skills and arms to take over the city-states. In a series of *coups d'état* between 660 and 550 B.C.E., they did just that in many trade and maritime city-states, earning in the process the name *tyrannos* (Burn 1970).

Tyrants or not, the preeminence of warriors during this period was to prove fortuitous. Early in the fifth century B.C.E., a series of Persian invasions threatened the Greek peninsula. Together, Athens and her rival city-state, the more militaristic Sparta, finally routed the invaders in 479 B.C.E., setting the stage for what many regard as the city's—and, perhaps, even Western history's—greatest moment.

The Golden Age

In the fifth century B.C.E., the city of Athens (about one mile square) and its surrounding villages had a population of perhaps 350,000 (Waterfield 2006:149). We can best understand Athenian life in the Golden Age as the celebration of human possibilities. "Men come together in the city to live," exclaimed Aristotle in a timeless salute to the human possibilities of city life, and "they remain there in order to live the good life." What was this "good life"? In his famous funeral oration in honor of Athenian victims of the Peloponnesian War, Athenian statesman Pericles conveyed its essence: The Greek ideal, he said, began with the principle of democracy "which favors the many instead of the few."

The Athenian belief in democracy was grounded historically, for the city-states that preceded the Golden Age were independent units. Indeed, so independent were they that

Athens today is strongly shaped by its culture and history. Even the physical environment reveals that social reality, as seen here. Looming above the city from its craggy hilltop site sits the Acropolis—built in the second half of the fifth century B.C.E. as the citadel of ancient Athens. Particularly prominent are the pillars of the Parthenon—the temple of Athena, patron goddess of the city.

one cannot speak of one "nation" even at the apex of Greek culture. Each city-state pursued its own ends and believed that no one had the right to dictate otherwise.

This fierce sense of independence also characterized the Greek citizen. In 600 B.C.E., with dissatisfaction rife, Athens was on the verge of revolution. To avert this, Solon, an aristocrat, was chosen as arbitrator. He immediately proposed a reorganization of the Athenian constitution that allowed all "free citizens" (excluding women, slaves, and foreigners) a place in the city's governing body, the Assembly. He established the People's Council, numbering some 400 members, with the charge of preparing the Assembly's agenda. Members were chosen from the four main Athenian tribes (100 members each), thereby preventing dominance by any one group. Finally, government officials were made accountable to the Assembly for their work each year. Political participation was mandatory for all citizens; without regard to "obscurity of conditions," each was required to take part in the public life of the city.

Athenian democracy was a brilliant innovation, affording all free citizens participation in government. It also allowed the citizen the right to live as one chose within that overarching system. Classical Athens did not stand as a monument to an all-powerful god or to a ruling family but, rather, to all free citizens. In one of the great dramas of the age, Sophocles's *Antigone*, we find this statement (which could well serve as a critique of Ming Peking): "A city that is of one man is no city."

The ideals of human development and versatility were vital to Hellenic civilization. A primary cultural value was that all citizens should strive for refinement (although without extravagance) and pursue individual well-being—a fusion of the well-tutored body, mind, and spirit. Athenians developed the body through constant work, exercise, and sport, including the Olympic Games, in which individuals from different city-states competed for the glory of their state. Continual dialogue provoked the mind; in their leisurely society, citizens often spent much of the day talking about the deeper matters of life. Plato's dialogues between the great philosopher Socrates and his friends are an excellent example.

Athenians even managed their spiritual life differently. For example, no system of formal or mystical religion placed the gods at great distance from the people of the city. In Peking, the priests were "specialists" who were sequestered within the walls of the Forbidden City, but in Athens, the "priest" was just another conscientious layman who made no prophecies and simply executed his religious duties as part of his civic duties. This ideal of participation meant that temples such as the Parthenon were always open to people, who typically marked their religious observances informally and, frequently, outdoors.

Indeed, as Greek civilization entered the Golden Age, the gods themselves became less abstract and more like human beings. They were the objects of jokes, criticism, and bargains, but—all the same—they served as models for human development. The Olympian gods became the symbol of something nobler in human nature, of something within the reach of human endeavor.

A tripartite focus on body, mind, and spirit was the unique combination that formed the crux of Athens's success. By developing serious interests in all three areas, the Athenian indirectly kept any one area from becoming all-absorbing. This focus kept more practical areas of life—politics or economics, for example—in check. Too much politics breeds an overemphasis on power and control; too much economics cultivates an obsession with wealth and material goods. For a brief period, the citizens of Athens avoided these pitfalls.

Behind the Glory

Athens's moment at the pinnacle of urban history was not to last, eventually undermined by the culture's own egocentrism and exploitative practices. The wealth and leisurely pace of Athens during its Golden Age rested, in large measure, on the goods and services of others. During its successful expansion before the fifth century B.C.E., Athens had conquered many other city-states and regions.

From them, Athens extracted tribute in materials, taxes, and people—many of whom became slaves; Waterfield (2006:149) estimates that about one-fourth of the city's population held this unhappy status, as the elite Athenian citizens benefited from the widespread use of such human servants. All women, however, were excluded from citizenship and relegated to household duties and supervision.

Elitism reared its head in yet another, more immediately destructive way. The Athenians refused citizenship to 30,000 foreigners, many of whom, as traders, had become permanent residents. This robbed the citizenry of potentially invigorating new ideas, forcing the foreign population into an exclusive concern with economic matters. Demoralized, these traders devoted their energies to money making and material consumption. In time, they became indifferent to government so long as they were free to make a profit. By the end of the fourth century B.C.E., profit making had become the center of city life, and the older idea that economic activity was simply a means to a more holistic life—so central to the health of the city—began to wane.

Into this setting came the Peloponnesian War, begun in 431 B.C.E. between Athens and Sparta. Soundly defeated, Athens surrendered in 404 B.C.E. Then, in total confusion and in public contradiction of all their democratic ideals, in 399 B.C.E. the Athenians tried Socrates and condemned him to death for "undermining the state by his endless public questionings."

The handwriting was on the wall. In 338 B.C.E., the Athenians put up belated opposition to an invasion force led by Philip of Macedon. Their defeat at the Battle of Chaeronea has been called "the death of the free polis." After that, Athens became a satellite in the Macedonian Empire until the Roman overlords arrived in 148 B.C.E.

MING PEKING AND ATHENS: A COMPARISON

The culture that prevailed in classical Athens was of a character radically different from that of Ming Peking. Without doubt, the cities had certain parallels: substantial inequality; large areas of poor housing; crowded, winding streets; and important central monuments and public buildings. There were all-important differences, however. Chinese civilization rested on a fundamental cultural belief in a god-like emperor, which gave an unmistakable stamp to Peking. Monuments and buildings dwarfed the common individual as they simultaneously magnified the pomp and majesty of the emperor and his elite. Indeed, what clearer indication of a distant, exclusive power structure could there be than a citadel in the form of Peking's Forbidden City?

Athens seemed, overall, to be more humane in character. The Greek cultural ideals citizen participation stamped that city with a human scale, encouraging openness, communication, and development among its free citizens. Such ideals can be seen in all Athens's public buildings—in the theaters (where, not by accident, the audience sat above the performers, not the other way around), in the public forums, in the temples, in the gymnasia, and in the marketplace. These buildings were not monuments to an absolute emperor; rather, Athens was much more a celebration of the "good life," an ideal that was evident despite important failings in practice.

In comparing Hellenic Athens and Ming Peking, we see just how different cities in different cultures can be, but this comparison shows us more: Athenian success at encouraging citizen participation and in developing the very best of human nature by a process of dialogue and growth shows us what the city can be. We are prompted to ask, in other words, how or why one city might be better than another. If we agree, for example, that democracy, equality, and continual mental, bodily, and spiritual development are ideals for which human beings should strive, Athens provides us with a real-life case where those ideals were encouraged. What, then, might we do to encourage the further manifestation of positive cultural values in our own modern-day cities? (See the *Cityscape* box on page 248 for a decidedly negative portrait.)

CITYSCAPE

The Industrial City: 1844

This colossal concentration, this heaping together of two and a half millions of human beings at one point...has raised London to the commercial capital of the world; created the giant docks and assembled the thousand vessels that continually cover the Thames....all this is so vast, so impressive, that a man cannot collect himself, but is lost in the marvel of England's greatness....

But the sacrifices which all this has cost become apparent later. After roaming the streets of the capital a day or two..., after visiting the slums of the metropolis, one realizes for the first time that these Londoners have been forced to sacrifice the best qualities of their human nature, to bring to pass all the marvels of civilization which crowd their city....

The very turmoil of the streets has something repulsive, something against which human nature rebels. The hundreds of thousands of all classes and ranks crowding past each other, are they not all human beings with the same qualities and powers, and with the same interest in being happy? And have they not, in the end, to seek happiness in the same way, by the same means? And still they crowd by one another as though they had nothing in common, nothing to do with one another....

And, however much one may be aware that this isolation of the individual, this narrow self-seeking is the fundamental principle of our society everywhere, it is nowhere so shamelessly barefaced, so self-conscious as just here in the crowding of the great city. The dissolution of mankind into monads, of which each one has a separate principle and a separate purpose, the world of atoms, is here carried out to its utmost extreme. [emphasis added]

...here...people regard each other only as useful objects; each exploits the other, and the end of it all is, that the stronger treads the weaker under foot, and that the powerful few, the capitalists, seize everything for themselves, while to the weak many, the poor, scarcely a bare existence remains.

What is true of London, is true of Manchester, Birmingham and Leeds.... Everywhere barbarous indifference, hard egotism on one hand, and nameless misery on the other, everywhere social warfare...and all so shameless, so openly avowed that one shrinks before the consequences of our social state as they manifest themselves here undisguised, and can only wonder that the whole crazy fabric still hangs together.

Source: Friedrich Engels, *The Condition of the Working Class in England*, edited by David McLellan (New York: Macmillan, 2007), pp. 35–36.

THE CULTURE OF CAPITALISM AND THE CITY

Nineteenth-century London certainly was not like either Ming Peking or Hellenic Athens. Dominated by feverish economic activity, it was the forerunner of the modern city described by U.S. urbanist Louis Wirth in Chapter 5.

Friedrich Engels, however, who first saw London in 1842—the same year he met Karl Marx and began their long collaboration— gave an interpretation radically different from that of Wirth. Whereas Louis Wirth, the Chicago urbanist, imagined he was describing the essential characteristics of all large, modern cities, Engels was aware that he was looking only at a certain cultural setting, a city intensifying the tremendous power of Western industrial capitalism. Note especially the passage in italics in the *Cityscape* box on page 248. What Wirth saw as a consequence of a large, differentiated population, Engels interpreted as cultural forces at work.

Engels was mightily disturbed by what he saw. If Hellenic Athens, with its cultural ideas of developing the whole person, was the city's highest point, surely Engels believed nineteenth-century London to be its lowest point. Yet the characteristics of both cities reflect the dominant ideals and activities of the larger culture. In the same way that Greek culture produced cities in which economic activity was regarded as of decidedly secondary importance, Engels believed that Western culture, under the influence of capitalism, spawned cities where economic gain was an unrestrained obsession.

The Capitalist City

As a means of livelihood, capitalism is very old. A rich capitalist life flourished in the fifth century B.C.E. in Athens, and no doubt, such activity is centuries older. Significant commercial activity aimed at the accumulation of profit also took place on an increasing scale in medieval Europe, especially after the eleventh century C.E.

If capitalism itself was not new, the unparalleled energy with which the spirit of commerce and profit began to assert itself during the sixteenth century C.E. certainly was. Apparently, several factors prompted this change. First, the feudal order of the Middle Ages began to erode as merchants, primarily in cities, gained power. Desiring to broaden their market, these merchants established trade routes among cities all over Europe in the period between 1200 and 1500. Goods began to pour into these cities, and people in the countryside began to get wind that a better life—or at least a life with more material amenities—could be had in cities. Major urban population growth ensued and fueled increased economic vitality (Heilbroner and Milberg 2011).

Gradually, from the sixteenth century onward, the economic interests of life came to dominate Western European cities. Capitalism set the principal cultural theme, with the new order being organized around a rather different set of economic relationships than its feudal predecessor. No longer bound to lords and manors, individual workers could sell their labor to whoever would pay the highest wages. Second, under these conditions, economic activity became increasingly competitive. Because everyone was striving for profits, workers, to get the greatest economic benefits, had to outdo each other in some way. The arrival of industrialization in the mid-eighteenth century greatly enhanced capitalism's hold over Western cities.

The Industrial Revolution

Like capitalism, **industrialism**—the process of manufacturing goods in large quantities for mass consumption—had existed in Western society to a limited degree before the eighteenth century. Only after the adoption of capitalism on a large scale, however, did the influence of industrialism begin to grow, with large-scale industrialism set in motion in England about 1750.

One important reason that English society proved to be so amenable to industrialism was the fondness, particularly evident in the upper middle classes, for engineering and guiding economic activities by the most scientific methods available. If efficient methods were not available, the innovative British invented them. Perhaps the most famous example of an invention that changed the economic order was James Watt's steam engine. This machine, perfected by 1775, had literally hundreds of applications, from textile manufacturing to flour mills to the mass production of the common pin. Its ability to save hand labor and contribute to the mass production of items was nothing short of remarkable, and in little time, entrepreneurs put this invention into widespread use. By 1781, Matthew Boulton, Watt's partner in a steam-engine manufacturing company, was claiming that "the people of London, Birmingham, and Manchester [are] all 'steam mill mad'" (quoted in Mantoux 2006:333). From then on, the Industrial Revolution was in full force. Other inventions, such as Arkwright's spinning jenny and Maudslay's automatic screw machine, revolutionized other areas of production. "The Revolution...fed upon itself. The new techniques...simply destroyed their handicraft competition around the world and thus enormously increased their own markets" (Heilbroner and Milberg 2011:75–77).

For the city dweller, the most important change was the invention of the factory, which gave new structure and purpose to urban life, quickly becoming the primary source of employment. With the domination of the factory, the very symbolism of the city changed. The city in feudal Europe had been, above all, a Christian city, symbolically dominating the region with its Gothic cathedral. (A striking example is Venice, spread out around St. Mark's Cathedral, built in 1176.) The capitalist era, as Mumford remarked, turned the culture of feudalism on its head, transforming "six of the seven deadly sins [gluttony, pride, covetousness, envy, lust, and anger] into cardinal virtues (sloth became perhaps an even greater sin)" (1991:346). The church declined as the focal institution of society: In the place of spires appeared smokestacks, and the public plaza became a growing central business district.

> If capitalism tended to expand the market and turn every part of the city into a negotiable commodity, the change from [small-scale handicraft] to large-scale factory production transformed the industrial towns into dark hives, busily puffing, clanking, screeching, smoking for twelve and fourteen hours a day, sometimes going around the clock. The slavish routine...became the normal environment of the new industrial workers. None of these towns heeded the old saw, "All work and no play makes Jack a dull boy." [They] specialized in producing dull boys. (Mumford 1991:446)

In short, the dominant capitalist cultural theme, in conjunction with industrial mechanization, created a new emphasis in urban

A multistory, mirrored building in Toronto's city center towers above an old stone church. The size and positioning of these buildings suggest dominant cultural themes of the past and present. Today, we see the relative importance of economics and religion in contemporary Western society, which differs from that in previous centuries, when church steeples were the highest visible points in cities.

consciousness. In describing a typical schoolroom in "Coketown," a fictionalized English factory city of the nineteenth century, Charles Dickens explained the main ingredient of this consciousness, presented in the *Urban Living* box on page 251.

Urban Life as Economics

"You are never to fancy!" With this phrase, Dickens summarized what so worried Engels about the capitalist city: It reduced everything

URBAN LIVING

"Nothing but the Facts, Ma'am"— Capitalist–Industrialist Consciousness

"Now, what I want is, Facts. Teach these boys and girls nothing but Facts. Facts alone are wanted in life. Plant nothing else, and root out everything else. You can only form the minds of reasoning animals upon Facts: nothing else will ever be of any service to them. This is the principle on which I bring up my own children, and this is the principle on which I bring up these children. Stick to Facts, Sir!"

The scene was a plain, bare, monotonous vault of a schoolroom, and the speaker's square forefinger emphasized his observations by underscoring every sentence with a line on the schoolmaster's sleeve. The emphasis was helped by the speaker's square wall of a forehead, which had his eyebrows for its base, while his eyes found commodious cellarage in two dark caves, overshadowed by the wall. The emphasis was helped by the speaker's mouth, which was wide, thin, and hard set....

"Thomas Gradgrind, Sir. A man of realities. A man of facts and calculations. A man who proceeds upon the principle that two and two are four, and nothing over, and who is not to be talked into allowing for anything over. Thomas Gradgrind, Sir—peremptorily Thomas—Thomas Gradgrind. With a rule and a pair of scales, and the multiplication table always in his pocket, Sir, ready to weigh and measure any parcel of human nature, and tell you exactly what it comes to. It is a mere question of figures, a case of simple arithmetic...."

"Girl number twenty," said Mr. Gradgrind, squarely pointing with his square forefinger, "I don't know that girl. Who is that girl?"

"Sissy Jupe, Sir," explained number twenty, blushing, standing up, and curtseying.

"Sissy is not a name," said Mr. Gradgrind. "Don't call yourself Sissy. Call yourself Cecilia."

"It's father as calls me Sissy, Sir," returned the young girl in a trembling voice, and with another curtsey.

"Then he has no business to do it," said Mr. Gradgrind. "Tell him he mustn't. Cecilia Jupe. Let me see....

"Give me your definition of a horse."

(Sissy Jupe thrown into the greatest alarm by this demand.)

"Girl number twenty unable to define a horse!" said Mr. Gradgrind, for the general behoof of all the little pitchers. "Girl number twenty possessed of no facts, in reference to one of the commonest of animals! Some boy's definition of a horse. Bitzer, yours...."

"Quadruped. Graminivorous. Forty teeth, namely twenty-four grinders, four eye-teeth, and twelve incisive. Sheds coat in the spring; in marshy countries, sheds hoofs, too. Hoofs hard, but requiring to be shod with iron. Age known by marks in mouth." Thus (and much more) Bitzer.

"Now girl number twenty," said Mr. Gradgrind. "You know what a horse is...."

["But Sir," said Cecilia Jupe, blushing]... "I fancy..."

"Ay, ay, ay! But you mustn't fancy," cried the gentleman, quite elated by coming so happily to his point. "That's it! You are never to fancy!"

Source: Excerpted from Charles Dickens, *Hard Times* (New York: Signet Classics, 2008; orig. 1854), pp. 11–16.

in life to objective facts and quantity. Other aspects of life—subjectivity, quality, art, music, politics, religion, and creative thought—were downplayed or consciously eradicated.

This new consciousness not only transformed how city people acted, it also transformed the physical structure of the city itself, thereby intensifying the capitalist theme even further. Land, once merely a place to live, became real estate:

> If the layout of a town has no relation to human needs and activities other than business, the pattern of the city may be simplified: The ideal layout for the business [person] is that which can be most swiftly reduced to standard monetary units for purchase and sale. The fundamental [urban] unit is no longer the neighborhood...but the individual building lot, whose value can be gauged in terms of front feet: this favors an oblong with narrow frontage and great depth, which provides a minimum amount of light and air to the buildings, particularly the dwellings, that conform to it. Such units turned out equally advantageous for the land surveyor, the real estate speculator, the commercial builder, and the lawyer who drew up the deed of sale. In turn, the lots favored the rectangular building block, which again became the standard unit for extending the city. (Mumford 1991:421–22)

So strong was this pattern in the physical form of the city after the sixteenth century that even cities with mountainous geography, such as San Francisco, which might have benefited from a switchback or zigzag pattern to facilitate moving up and down the terrain, instead used a grid pattern.

Murray Bookchin used even stronger language to suggest the extent to which the modern Western city has been shaped by the industrial–capitalist system:

> Every esthetic urban pattern inherited from the past tends to be sacrificed to the grid system (in modern times, the factory pattern par excellence), which facilitates the most efficient transportation of goods and people. Streams are obliterated, variations in the landscape effaced without the least sensitivity to natural beauty, magnificent stands of trees removed, even treasured architectural and historical monuments demolished, and wherever possible, the terrain is leveled to resemble a factory floor. The angular and curved streets of the medieval city which at every turn delighted the eye with a new and scenic tableau, are replaced by straight monotonous vistas of the same featureless buildings and shops. Lovely squares inherited from the past are reduced to nodal points for traffic, and highways are wantonly carved into vital neighborhoods, dividing and finally subverting them. (1996:90–91)

Assets and Debits

On one level, the capitalist city has unquestionably been successful in generating a higher material standard of living for a larger proportion of its population than any other urban system in history. Useful material goods and technological innovations are omnipresent, and given the "hands-off-the-individual" value that is so central to capitalism, residents of such cities experience a significant degree of political as well as other kinds of freedom. They can vote, come and go as they please, and if they have the money, live where they like.

There are debits as well, however: Millions of poor families live in cities, and many unprofitable districts have fallen into shocking decay. Within such areas, as we will see in later chapters, people suffer incredibly. Similarly, the dominant focus on material goods and technological innovations often means that many people are preoccupied with the newest MP3 or cell phone or the latest car and are less mindful of social and environmental needs that require attention.

Finally, even freedoms have their problematic side. The freedom to accumulate wealth, prestige, and power has meant, over the years, that some individuals in our cities have much more of these limited resources than others. With wealth primarily in the hands of a few (the top 20 percent of U.S. households own 85 percent of all privately held wealth), these people tend to control both the economic and the political spheres of life to such a degree that others are effectively cut off from any true success or representation (Domhoff 2011).

Problems such as these led to a reaction: a second type of modern city, established around and intensifying yet another set of cultural themes, those of communism.

To get a sense of the contemporary communist city, we return to Peking. On October 1, 1949, standing on the Meridian Gate of the old Ming Imperial City (see Figures 9–1 and 9–2), looking out over the millions assembled in Tiananmen Square, Mao Zedung established the People's Republic of China. In 1957, Mao, in an attempt to speed the growth of socialism, moved thousands of peasants into special communes to increase steel production. As a result, steel production nearly tripled, but most of it was impure and useless. Meanwhile, agricultural production plummeted, creating a famine in which more than 32 million people died from food deprivation (Thaxton 2008:5).

To appease the widespread discontent, Mao passed day-to-day control to two political allies. By 1963, however, he began criticizing his allies, and three years later, he launched the Cultural Revolution, supposedly to purge liberals and continue the revolutionary class struggle, but actually a means to regain full power. To accomplish this goal, he gave unbridled power to act to the Red Guard, a youth militia 11 million strong. In the violent turmoil that ensued, about half a million people died, and millions of others were persecuted, including artists, authors, educators, intellectuals, political leaders, and religious officials. During the 10 years of the Cultural Revolution, the Red Guard perpetrated one of the greatest destructions of historical artifacts in human history, devastated minority cultures, and killed hundreds of thousands of minority people, particularly Mongolian Muslims and Tibetan Buddhists. When it finally ended, even traditional Chinese culture had been weakened (Esherick, et al. 2006).

Today, six decades after Mao made that pronouncement of a new country, Peking is a different city—its feudal and imperial past almost completely eradicated, its name reverted back to Beijing (the old name, *Peking*, was a Western transcription of *Beijing*). On the site of the old dynasties has arisen the most important communist city in the world, now that communism no longer dominates Russia and Eastern Europe.

Modern Beijing thus provides us with a final illustration of the consequences of different cultural themes in urban places. The great walls that protected the city and the emperor in the Ming period are gone. In their place is a city-encircling highway, while below ground, the city's modern subway system provides 209 miles of track and averages more than 5 million riders daily. The Forbidden City is now a museum open to everyone, surrounded by great new buildings of state: the Great Hall of the People, the Historical Museum, and the Mausoleum that holds Mao's remains. The many multistoried hotels in Beijing easily dominate the old buildings of the emperor. Replaced, too, are many of the old, sonorous names of the imperial years. For example, the Pavillion of Pleasant Sounds has given way to People's Road and Anti-Imperialist Street.

Beijing in the twenty-first century, however, is significantly different from the "austere" city of the past. Four decades ago, a rigid communist government controlled almost all aspects of life. Everyone dressed alike in dark, uniform-like clothes. Individuals could not own their own businesses and residential relocation—whether from one city to another or from outlying rural areas to the city—was not allowed. Economic stagnation was the norm, and social use of public urban spaces was virtually non-existent, especially at night. By contrast, Beijing today, along with other Chinese cities, has embraced capitalistic enterprise, and city life flourishes with individual enterprises, colorful fashions and consumer goods, nightlife, and a booming economy.

Urban Life as Politics

The Communists vowed to free China from centuries of domination of the many by the few and from exploitation by foreign

Modern Beijing is an energetic city in which capitalism and consumerism flourish, as partly indicated in this view of the Wangfujing shopping street by Oriental Plaza. A lenient government policy toward individual enterprise has generated more spending money, which enables Chinese urbanites to purchase additional goods and enjoy a higher standard of living than in years past.

countries. To do this, they transformed nearly all of Chinese life into an expression of the new political ideas. The job of the state was to provide equally for everyone; the job of the individual was to contribute to the state's success by participating unselfishly in the state-linked neighborhood units, school classes, factories, and party committees. Only by collectivizing everything, the Communists believed, and by constantly reminding everyone about the dangers of backsliding into individualism was true progress to be attained.

The key concept in all this was *tzu-li kengsheng*—"self-reliance" or "regeneration through one's own efforts." In developing this concept, the party divided each city into districts (Beijing has nine), each district into neighborhoods, and each neighborhood into smaller residential areas. Each residential area developed its own "residents' committee" designed to link each individual with the city authorities, and vice versa. It became

the job of these committees to oversee local services—security, fire, and sanitation—and to keep political responsibility uppermost in peoples' minds (Whyte and Parish 1987:21–22).

Study groups developed unceasing political awareness in which all neighborhood residents participated (study groups also existed in schools and factories). The tasks of these groups were (1) to communicate to all citizens the importance of participation in all areas of life; (2) to chastise political troublemakers of all kinds, such as "revisionists," "factionalists," "ultra-Leftists," "capitalists," and "imperialists"; and (3) to examine constantly, through group self-criticism, each individual's performance. The intent was to discourage individualism while encouraging both **groupthink**—conformity to opinions that supposedly reflect group consensus—and control through many eyes of each person's actions. It is difficult to imagine more contrasting views of city life than those outlined above and those held by the people of contemporary Western cities.

Economic Reform and Environmental Issues

With Mao's death in 1976, a great power struggle emerged in Beijing for control of the party—a struggle won by Deng Xiaoping and his followers. The new leaders de-emphasized the more extreme elements of Maoism and moved from a sluggish, Soviet-style, centrally planned economy to a more market-oriented economy, but one still within a rigid political framework of Communist Party control. To this end, the authorities switched to a system of household responsibility in place of the old collectiviza-tion in agriculture, increased the authority of local officials and plant managers in in-dustry, permitted a wide variety of small-scale enterprise in services and light manufactur-ing, and opened the economy to increased foreign trade and investment.

The result has been a quadrupling of the gross domestic product (GDP) since 1978, making China the second-largest economy in the world. China's economic reforms have

China is already the world's leading emitter

of carbon dioxide, and its economic devel-opment—the country has 16 of the 20 most-polluted cities in the world—is affecting its ecosystems:

> Acid rain caused by China's sulfur-dioxide emis-sions severely damages forests and watersheds in Korea and Japan and impairs air quality in the U.S. Every major river system flowing out of China is threatened with one sort of cataclysm or another. The surge in untreated waste and agricultural runoff pouring into the Yellow and China seas has caused frequent fish die-offs, and overfishing is endangering many ocean species. (Leslie 2008)

Many of China's cities are already paralyzed by automobile traffic, but with its car industry now the world's largest and its 100 million cars expected to double in the next decade, the potential impact on climate change is even worse (Chang 2011).

A Rising Consumerism

Visitors to Beijing today find a city alive with energy. In one section of the city—just south of the old Forbidden City—is a shopping section for the capital's citizens. Beneath billboards ad-vertising Toshiba TV sets are department stores filled with goods, with no shortage of lookers and buyers. One reason for this increasing con-sumerism is the additional spending money generated by the new policies encouraging indi-vidual enterprise. For example, in another part of the city is a farmers' market, where workers from a local commune sell surplus vegetables not needed for the commune or for state con-sumption. They are allowed to keep the profits from such transactions. Some young people, selected by the government to go abroad and teach Chinese in a North American college, earn Western salaries—astronomical by Chinese standards. When they return to Beijing, they are allowed to keep the money they have saved and, thus, are able to afford better apartments in new sections of the city and to provide their families with a variety of consumer goods.

All this change—a movement "from Marxism to Mastercard"—has its critics. Many

Modern high-rise buildings in Shanghai tower over the more traditional Chinese housing in the Longtang neighborhood. Rapid economic growth has dramatically changed this city's appearance as China continues its emergence as one of Asia's most vibrant countries. This stark contrast of old and new is a common sight throughout the Asian continent.

powerful Communist Party members see the revolution of Mao being "sold out," and as an indication that the policies of Deng and his successors are not all positive, they cite extensive evidence that corruption now appears in many areas of Chinese life as people scramble for the accoutrements of a consumer society. They charge that the current policies generate self-centeredness and a kind of Western decadence. In fact, theft and prostitution, once virtually non-existent, are now as common as in Western cities. Nonetheless, the open-door policy continues, and China and its cities once again are in the throes of major social change.

SUMMARY

The city does not exist by itself but, rather, as an intricate part of the broader society. Shaping any city's physical and social forms are the cultural values of that society and its history. For example, although some truth exists in the old idea that the ways of the country and of the city are distinct and "ne'er the twain shall meet," research reveals that cities and their countrysides are bound together in a complex interdependence that allows each to have significant influence over the other. Urban dominance, however, makes this mutual influence less than equal. Cities, once the centers for revolutions that spread nationwide, now extend their cultural influence far beyond their borders in such areas as the arts, communication, fashion, and politics.

Cities are not entirely synonymous with civilization. However, they are symbolic centers that concentrate, intensify, and re-create the cultural forces found throughout the society. Spengler envisioned a cyclical rise, dominance, and decline of cities as being reflective of their civilizations. Mumford advanced the concept that cities have always been at the center of civilization. Monti wrote about how each city creates its own civic culture that makes it unique compared to other cities in the same society.

In the cities we compared and contrasted in this chapter—Ming Peking and Hellenic Athens, nineteenth-century industrial–capitalist London and contemporary communist–capitalist Beijing—we found significant differences. These differences attest to the importance of culture in shaping the social and physical environment of the city. Only by studying cities in a comparative manner can we understand this urban variability.

CONCLUSION

If urban variety is so marked, what is left as distinctively urban? What do all the cities we've considered in this chapter have in common? To answer this question, we certainly must go beyond the factors of size, density, and heterogeneity proposed by Louis Wirth. We propose a new definition of the city, one that acknowledges the importance of the cultural dimension Wirth neglected: In comparison with other types of permanent human settlement, *a city is a relatively large, dense settlement that has a civic culture and a complex social structure that greatly reflects, intensifies, and re-creates cultural values and forms.*

A few comments are necessary to clarify this definition. The first set of characteristics—"a large, dense settlement"—is Wirth's; he seems to be quite right about them. The next characteristic—"a complex social structure"—is from V. Gordon Childe (2003). You may recall that Wirth also suggested the city is composed of "socially heterogeneous individuals." By this, he meant that people of different racial, ethnic, and religious backgrounds tend to mingle in the city. Anthropological research has shown that this more accurately describes modern Western cities (to which people of different countries migrate) than it does their non-industrial counterparts, such as Jakarta and Nairobi. Yet even if social heterogeneity is not characteristic of all cities, nearly every urbanist has noted that the city has a more

complex division of labor and a more sophisticated political system (if only to handle the large numbers and density) than do other forms of human settlement. Such complexities are what we mean by "a complex social structure."

Finally, the idea that any city is a reflector, intensifier, and re-creator of cultural values and forms is a direct outgrowth of this chapter. In the final analysis, the nature of any city lies in its unique ability to interpret a particular set of cultural values in a distinctive form. By "cultural values," we mean those shared beliefs and ideas that characterize any social group of long duration. By "form," we mean the typical round of everyday activities and arrangement of urban space that characterize any city. Thus, because the cultural values of the Greeks during Athens's Golden Era (the fifth century B.C.E.) regarded money making as secondary and a holistic life as primary, we found that the daily life of the city was dominated by dialogue, politics, recreation, and ritual. While the Greeks surely went to the *agora* (the market) to trade, they just as frequently went there to talk and relax. Even their buildings reflected this cultural emphasis. The Acropolis, where the most important buildings of Greek civilization (the Parthenon, the Erechtheum, the Propylea, the Temple of Athena Nike) were located, sits on a hill overlooking the rest of the city. The *agora*, lesser in importance, lies at the bottom of the hill.

All this appears to be reversed when we consider the form of contemporary capitalist cities, such as those of North America, where the round of daily activities focuses on the economic. Most people spend the bulk of their day getting, spending, and planning for more of the same. Dialogue, politics, recreation, and ritual come later—in the evenings, on the weekends, or during vacation. The city's physical layout reflects this cultural priority. Streets are arranged on a grid for easy movement and buying and selling, and the most important buildings—or at least those that dominate the skyline of any major North American city—are those of commerce.

In such comparative observations lies a crucial lesson about studying cities: Quite simply, if we don't understand the relationship between the city and culture, we can't properly understand the city. As alluded to in our discussion about the emergence of modern Beijing, however, we also need to consider the role of economic power in dictating quality of life, a subject we turn to next.

KEY TERMS

civic culture (238)
culture (231)
groupthink (254)

industrialism (249)
urban dominance (234)

INTERNET ACTIVITIES

1. Take a virtual tour of the Forbidden City. Go to *http://www.world-heritage-tour.org/asia/china/ming-qing/beijing/forbidden-city/map.html*, and click any photo. Then, click inside the image, and drag left or right to get a full view.

2. At *http://www.commoncensus.org/maps.php* is an intriguing, color-coded map of what viewers consider to be the cultural influence of a nearby city and to what extent that influence extends. You can add your vote to this still-unfolding national map.

CHAPTER 10

STRATIFICATION AND SOCIAL CLASS
Urban and Suburban Lifestyles

SOCIAL STRATIFICATION
    Social Class Distinctions
    Income Distribution Nationwide
    Incomes Within and Outside Cities
    Wealth and Net Worth
    Poverty Nationwide
    Poverty Within and Outside Cities
    A Cautionary Note
URBAN SOCIAL CLASS DIVERSITY
    Upper-Class Urban Neighborhoods
    Middle-Class Urban Neighborhoods
    Working-Class Urban Neighborhoods
    Mixed-Income Urban Neighborhoods

Low-Income Urban Neighborhoods
The Homeless
SUBURBAN SOCIAL CLASS DIVERSITY
    Upper-Income Suburbs
    Middle-Income Suburbs
    Working-Class Suburbs
    Suburban Cosmopolitan Centers
    Minority Suburbs
SUMMARY
CONCLUSION
KEY TERMS
INTERNET ACTIVITIES

What's your stereotype of a person from the city? How about describing someone from the suburbs? Most people find it much easier to answer the second question, because conventional wisdom holds that cities are much more socially diverse than suburbs. Yet, as sociology often shows us, what people think is not necessarily true. Cities in the United States and Canada are home to people of various socioeconomic classes, races, and ethnicities, and exploring any city will reveal neighborhoods with a mix of people as well as many distinctive neighborhoods in which individuals have their own typical lifestyle. The same is true of suburbs. No large city or suburb is accurately described with any single stereotype.

In this chapter, we investigate the diversity found in our cities and suburbs, highlighting the social class differences within them. In Chapter 11, our attention will turn to the importance of race, ethnicity, and gender in creating urban and suburban diversity. These chapters are about social differences, but they are also about social inequality. As we examine the "structure" of the North American city, we shall see that some urbanites experience "the good life" while others contend with a host of problems. These urban problems, including inadequate housing, poor education, and high levels of crime, are the focus of Chapter 12. We begin by investigating how differences in social class create social diversity in both cities and suburbs.

SOCIAL STRATIFICATION

The United States, Canada, and all other countries are stratified societies. In every nation, people are ranked in a social hierarchy that determines their quality of life. The social hierarchy involves access to jobs, income, schooling, and other resources, which, in turn, affects people's choices about where and how to live. Keep in mind that countries are not all the same in terms of social stratification; some have more inequality than others. In addition, within any country, its rural communities, with somewhat more homogeneous populations, typically have fewer social levels than in cities, where people differ more in terms of occupations, incomes, and schooling.

Two classical social theorists—Karl Marx and Max Weber—offered ideas about social stratification that still influence sociological thinking today. Drawing on the work of Marx, social-conflict theorists claim that inequality in wealth and power provides some people with so many greater advantages over others that conflict between social classes is inevitable. Weber agreed with Marx that social stratification caused social conflict, but he saw Marx's two-class view of capitalists and workers as too simplistic and suggested a more complex model. To Weber, economic inequality—the issue so vital to Marx—was certainly important, and he referred to this as *class* position. Weber, however, viewed social class not in terms of two categories but, rather, as a continuum ranging from high to low. He also introduced the concept of *status*, or social prestige, as the second dimension of social stratification, with *power* as the third. With Weber's thinking in mind, most sociologists define **social stratification** as the *hierarchical ranking within a society of various social class groups according to wealth, power, and prestige.*

Following Weber's concepts further, sociologists use the term **socioeconomic status (SES)** to refer to *a composite ranking based on various dimensions of social inequality.* A ranking results from comparison of how many status symbol possessions one accumulates, such as the poshness of one's residence and the expensiveness of one's car, clothing, eating habits, and vacations. Of particular interest is residence, for the ability to live in a particular place—whether voluntarily or involuntarily—is an excellent illustration of social stratification. This is not an issue of city versus suburban living, however, because people in all levels of social class are living in both types of communities.

W. Lloyd Warner and his associates were the first to conduct a comprehensive study of social stratification in the United States with their examination of "Yankee City" in the 1930s. (It was actually Newburyport, Massachusetts, a small town of 17,000.) Combining objective criteria, such as income and occupation, with subjective input, using the **reputational method** in which people compared others to themselves in terms of status, Warner reported the existence of a six-tier class system (upper upper, lower upper, upper middle, lower middle, upper lower, and lower lower). Among his other findings was a significant relationship between an ethnic group's length of residence in the United States and its class status, a pattern that still holds true today for many immigrant groups.

Social Class Distinctions

Since Warner's seminal research, three generations of social scientists have studied the many manifestations of stratification and social class in all types of communities. The paradoxical coexistence of great poverty and wealth that they found in our cities is simply a condensed manifestation of what exists in society itself. Before we look at the social class segregation that we find in our cities

and suburbs, therefore, it would be helpful to describe the general characteristics found among the different layers of social strata in North American society. Although the two countries differ in their definitions of income and poverty levels, what follow are a fairly definitive portrait of U.S. society and a close approximation of Canadian society.

Upper Class.   The main distinction between Warner's upper-upper and lower-upper classes was essentially that of "old money" and "new money"—that is, of either multigenerational, inherited wealth (e.g., Jay Rockefeller, with a 2011 net worth of about $136 million) or first-generation, self-earned wealth (e.g., Bill Gates of Microsoft, with a 2011 net worth of $56 billion). The upper class constitutes about 5 percent of the total population. Whether they have "old" or "new" money, however, creates a social divide between the two levels, and they seldom have membership in the same clubs and organizations.

The high socioeconomic status enjoyed by members of the upper class partly rests, suggested Weber, on social prestige gained through the accumulation of prized status possessions. Among the measurable examples of such conspicuous consumption is a posh residence along with expensive cars, clothing, eating habits, vacations, and other pursuits.

With their great wealth, the upper class live ostentatiously in expensive neighborhoods, enjoy high prestige, and wield considerable political clout. They tend to be a fairly cohesive group, interacting with one another at the "right" social events, belonging to the same clubs and organizations, sending their children to the same private schools, supporting charities and the arts, and vacationing at the same elite resort areas. Upper-class women are in charge of hosting entertainments at home for guests and often do volunteer work for charitable and civic organizations, both locally and nationally; the men often are active in community service organizations (see the *Urban Living* box below).

Middle Class. Constituting about 40–45 percent of society and more diverse both racially and ethnically, this population segment

URBAN LIVING

The "Philadelphia Gentlemen"

E. Digby Baltzell, a sociologist born into the upper class, not only gave an excellent insider's view into the world of the elite, he also provided what is probably the best study of this lifestyle in *Philadelphia Gentlemen* (1989; orig. 1958). Although his in-depth portrait was of the Philadelphia elite, his analysis is applicable to most U.S. cities that have been home to a multigenerational, "old-money" constituency.

He described these "descendants of successful individuals" as a cohesive primary group who grew up together in the same exclusive neighborhoods, attended the same private schools, vacationed in the same restrictive places, and so naturally became friends. Eventually, they intermarried, and in their adult lives, they continued their social bonding by living near one another, belonging to the same churches and clubs, and seeing each other frequently. With a strong sense of group identity and governed by social norms of what is "just not done," they maintained "a distinctive lifestyle and a kind of primary solidarity which [set] them apart from the rest of the population" (Baltzell 1989:7).

In describing the upper-class neighborhood in Philadelphia, Baltzell suggested a three-stage out-migration, which also approximates the pattern in other U.S. cities. From the colonial period through the first half of the nineteenth century, the city's elite lived in what is now the downtown business district; in Philadelphia, this was the area around Independence and Washington Squares. Following the Civil War and until World War I, the upper-upper class shifted away from the increasingly busy, noisy, congested downtown to a quieter residential neighborhood nearby; in Philadelphia, this was about 12 blocks west of the Rittenhouse Square district. In the third stage, following World War I, the elite in small and medium-size cities moved out to the suburbs; those in large cities, however, were able to maintain their upper-income enclaves. In the Philadelphia metropolitan area, the elite continued their westward out-migration to the suburbs. We should also note that throughout all three periods, the city's elite typically maintained at least two residences, one in the city and another in the country (Baltzell 1989:179; orig. 1958).

Source: From E. Digby Baltzell, *Philadelphia Gentlemen: The Making of a National Upper Class* (New Brunswick, NJ: Transaction Publishers, 1989).

is the one most often depicted in films and television and most commonly targeted by advertisers. About half are upper-middle class, earning above-average income, typically in the range of $100,000 to about $200,000 annually. That income enables them to own an expensive co-op or townhouse in the city or a good-sized suburban home, participate in local politics, send their children to universities in preparation for careers in high-prestige occupations and professions, and invest in stocks, bonds, and perhaps, property. Upper-middle-class women may or may not work: Some are in professional careers, while others prefer to be stay-at-home wives and mothers. Many will be active in local charitable, church, or civic organizations, as often are their husbands.

The other half of the middle class work either in less prestigious white-collar occupations, such as office workers, middle managers, and sales clerks, or in highly skilled blue-collar jobs, such as electrical work and carpentry. Their family income is comparable to the national average, about $50,000 to $90,000 annually. Generally, they build up a small nest egg for their retirement, and about half their children graduate from college, often at a state-supported school. To a lesser degree than those of the upper-middle class, the women in this social stratum will also participate in local clubs and organizations, as will the men, who may be active in fraternal organizations as well. Both middle-class groups usually immerse themselves in their children's activities, such as sports programs and scouting.

Working Class.   Sometimes called the lower-middle class, this population segment comprises about one-third of society and yields a family income below the national average, about $30,000 to $50,000 annually. This level of income gives them little means by which to acquire wealth, although about half of working-class families do own their own homes. They are especially vulnerable to financial crisis, however, if they experience unemployment or a serious illness. They are the classic Marxian model of workers in closely supervised jobs with little creativity and over

which they have little control. Furthermore, these jobs offer fewer benefits, such as medical or dental insurance and pension plans, particularly if they are non-union jobs. About a third of the children in these families will go to college. In many working-class families, women only work when single and become full-time homemakers once married. In many instances, however, the high cost of living has obliged these women to work as well. Both genders are likely to restrict their outside activities to church-related or neighborhood association activities. In addition, many men also enjoy participation in fraternal organizations and organized sports for themselves or their children.

Lower Class.   About 20 percent of the population—poor whites as well as poor racial and ethnic minorities—fall into this category. Some are the so-called working poor, who hold low-prestige jobs with low incomes that nonetheless enable them to get by. Located in our inner cities and rural areas, about 40 percent own their own homes. Many have no medical insurance, so a serious illness or long-term unemployment could easily create the need for government assistance. About 12–13 percent of the population receives such welfare assistance. Researchers have found that the men and women living in these poor neighborhoods have distinctly separate social worlds (Liebow 2003; MacLeod 2008). Women are more likely to be involved in organizational activities, usually the church, and interact in more confined areas, whereas men will more often be out and about, congregating with friends to drink, talk, and enjoy sports.

Some urban neighborhoods have such extreme levels of poverty and unemployment that social scientists call them **hyperghettos** (Wacquant 1997). In Canada and the United States, the poverty rate currently hovers around 11–14 percent, but in hyperghettos, more than 40 percent of the residents can live in poverty. The unemployment rate in both countries, normally about 6–7 percent, has been higher in recent years due to the recession, but nothing like unemployment in hyperghettos, which can be as high as 67 percent. Other characteristics of these neighborhoods, which contain mostly rental units, are low levels of education and job skills as well as high levels of single-parent households and social isolation. Because hyperghettos are almost always racial and/or ethnic minority neighborhoods, we will explore this grim social phenomenon more fully in the next chapter.

Before we examine the different social class concentrations in our cities and suburbs, we will first examine, in a larger context, three of the best measurable indicators of social stratification: (1) income, (2) wealth, and (3) poverty.

Income Distribution Nationwide

The disparity between rich and poor is not simply a matter of difference in incomes (a normal fact in any competitive society) but, rather, a difference in the proportionate share of total income that each socioeconomic

group possesses and in how each group's income situation changes from year to year. This information offers helpful insight regarding macrosocial factors relating to poverty.

If family income were distributed equally across the population, each quintile, or 20 percent segment, would receive one-fifth of the total. Of all the industrialized nations, however, the United States has the most unequal distribution of wealth (Philips 2003). As Figure 10–1 on page 265 shows, the top 20 percent of all U.S. households—those earning more than $100,000 in 2010—earned 50.2 percent of all income. That is about as much as the remaining 80 percent of Americans combined! The top two-fifths earned almost three-fourths of all income, leaving the lowest 20 percent of households—those earning less than $20,000—drawing in only 3.3 percent of the total (U.S. Census Bureau 2011d). Among Canadian households, the unequal distribution is also pronounced, though not to the

A fur-coated woman passes a blanketed homeless person on East 51st Street in New York. Not uncommonly, we can find urban scenes like this one where ostentatious displays of affluence contrast with images of poverty. Such visual dichotomy is to be expected as part of the heterogeneity of cities, in which resides a mixture of people of all social classes.

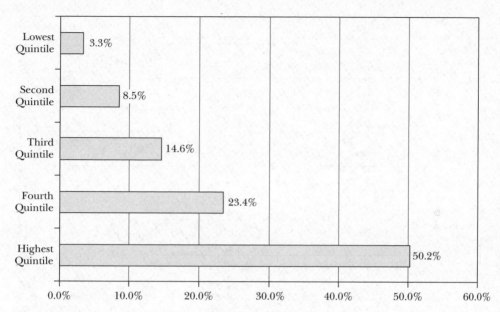

FIGURE 10–1   Household Income, Percentage Share, 2010
Source: U.S. Census Bureau 2011d.

same level of intensity. In 2009, the top 20 percent of all Canadian households earned 39 percent of all income, while the lowest 20 percent of households earned 7 percent of the total (Conference Board of Canada 2011).

Since 1968, the gap between the most affluent Americans and everyone else has been steadily widening, and by 1993, it reached its widest extent since the end of World War II in 1945. It widened still further by 2010 (U.S. Census Bureau 2011d). Similarly, the income gap has widened in Canada over the past 20 years.

Incomes Within and Outside Cities

If we compare income data by residence, we find that in metropolitan areas, those living outside central cities are better off than those living within central cities. Figure 10–2 shows the median income of U.S. households in 2010 in cities, suburban areas, and metropolitan areas. The differences between urban and suburban dwellers in both years give us an initial understanding of the greater financial resources available to many of those living

beyond the city limits. Moreover, the decline of income in suburban areas provides an initial clue into the impact of the Great Recession of 2007–2012 on lost jobs and/or reduced dividend checks from investments and annuities.

Wealth and Net Worth

Two other measures of individual or family economic well-being are wealth and net worth. *Wealth* refers to either (1) marketable assets, such as real estate and other property (boats, cars, furs, and jewelry), bank accounts, and stocks, bonds, and other securities; or (2) financial assets (all of the preceding minus owner-occupied housing). *Net worth* refers to all of one's assets minus all liabilities (what one owes). For example, ownership of a $500,000 home that has a $400,000 mortgage results in a $100,000 net worth, which is quite a difference. Net worth thus is a more accurate indicator of economic well-being. Home ownership, in fact, is the single largest component of individual wealth.

Because home equity is such an important element of wealth, the housing and mortgage

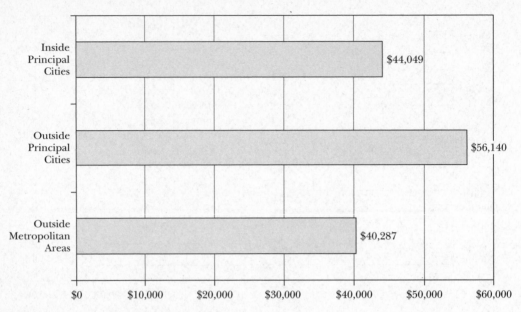

FIGURE 10–2 Median Income, 2010
Source: U.S. Census Bureau 2011d.

crisis of 2007–2012 has been a major factor in creating not just a larger economic crisis but also one that negatively impacted on the wealth of many Americans. Caused by unscrupulous mortgage lenders and brokers, by unregulated transactions in mortgage-backed securities, by millions of job losses, and by buyers who didn't act responsibly, the result was more than 10 million foreclosure filings between 2007 and 2010 (RealtyTrac 2011). Even those homeowners who could afford the higher payments from adjustable rate mortgages suffered, because the homes of tens of millions of families lost value as prices plummeted due to a glut in the market of available homes. As the economic crisis rippled outward, both investors and retirees saw their investments and annuities suffer as well. As a result, nearly two-thirds of American families endured financial damage, with the median family losing one-fifth of its net worth (Federal Reserve Board 2011).

As house values plummeted, Hispanic families were especially hit hard. Between 2005 and 2009, the percentage drop in household wealth was 66 percent for Hispanics, 53 percent for blacks, and 16 percent for whites. The differences primarily result from minority families' net worth primarily vested in home equity. At the same time, wealth disparities *within* the Hispanic community increased, as the top 10 percent of Hispanic households saw their share of all Hispanic household wealth rise from 56 to 72 percent during this period (Pew Hispanic Center 2011b).

As with income, a wealth disparity exists as well. In 2007, the top 1 percent owned 43 percent of total financial wealth and the next wealthiest 19 percent of households held another 50 percent. This left only 7 percent of the total for the remaining 90 percent of the population (Domhoff 2011). Although cities, some more so than others, contain extremely affluent households who are part of this vast holding of wealth, the suburbs contain the majority of these highly prosperous families (Keister 2000).

Poverty Nationwide

In 2010, the poverty threshold for a U.S. family of four was $22,314. The official poverty rate was 15.1 percent—a total of 46.2 million

Americans, the largest number in 52 years. This was up from 14.3 percent in 2009, the third significant annual increase since 2004. The 2009 poverty rates included: non-Hispanic whites, 9.9 percent; blacks, 27.4 percent; Hispanics, 26.6 percent; and Asians, 12.1 percent. Of those living in poverty, 83.5 percent were native-born citizens, 4.1 percent naturalized citizens, and 12.4 percent foreign-born non-citizens (U.S. Census Bureau 2011d).

In Canada, 9.6 percent of its population was classified as being low income after tax in 2009 (Statistics Canada 2011a). Immigrants constituted a higher proportion of those in this category compared to Canadian-born citizens. Length of residence was a factor, as immigrants who had lived in Canada less than five years had a low-income rate 2.5 times that of the Canadian-born. That low-income rate falls fairly quickly with more years spent in Canada, because immigrants improve their language skills, form networks in their new country, and become more familiar with Canadian social and work norms.

Poverty Within and Outside Cities

Poverty data offer an initial understanding of the greater strain put on cities' resources to assist those living below the poverty level. In 2010, more U.S. city residents—19.7 percent, or one in five—lived in poverty compared with those living outside central cities, where the poverty rate was 11.8 percent (one in eight). In non-metropolitan areas, 16.5 percent (one in six) lived in poverty (Figure 10–3). In absolute numbers, this translated to about 19.5 million in central cities, 18.9 million outside central cities, and 7.9 million in non-metropolitan areas (U.S. Census Bureau 2011d).

We can partly explain the higher concentration of poverty in cities by the greater numbers of foreign-born residents. Throughout the history of Canada and the United States, cities have traditionally been home to many poor newcomers struggling to survive and improve their quality of life. That pattern continues today. More than two-fifths of the foreign-born (44 percent) in the United

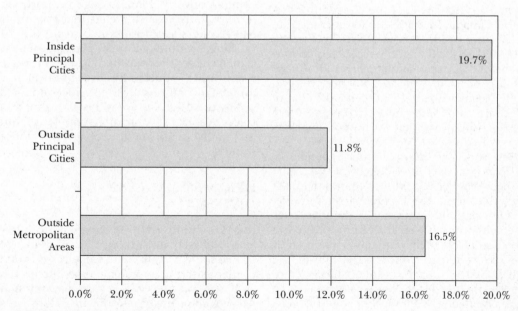

FIGURE 10–3   People in Poverty, Percentage, 2010

Source: U.S. Census Bureau 2011d.

States live in a central city. (Many others have the financial means to live in the suburbs.) Of the 38.2 million foreign-born living in the United States in 2010, 11.3 percent of all naturalized citizens and 26.7 percent of all non-U.S. citizens, much higher than the national figure of 14.4 percent, lived in poverty (U.S. Census Bureau 2011e). Although studies show that the income for most immigrants improves with the passage of time, their early presence—and particularly their large numbers—creates an ethnic underclass that competes with the long-term urban poor for socioeconomic well-being.

In Toronto, for example, between 2001 and 2006, the number of low-income families increased by 7 percent. Higher-poverty neighborhoods (with 25 percent or more low-income families) increased from 30 in 2001 to 32 in 2006 (Figure 10–4). Low-income households are mostly in the inner suburbs—in the former municipalities of East York, Etobicoke, North York, Scarborough, and York. Immigrant families accounted for 57 percent of the total family population living in higher-poverty neighborhoods. As in the United States, the prevalence of low income for immigrants declines the longer they reside in Canada. In 2006, the low-income rate for Toronto residents who arrived in Canada from 2001 to 2006 was 46 percent, compared to rates of 31 percent and 28 percent for those who arrived from 1996 to 2000 and 1991 to 1996, respectively. At 19 percent, the low-income rate for people who arrived before 1991 was equivalent to that of non-immigrants (City of Toronto 2009).

New York City offers another example. In 2010, one out of five residents (20.1 percent) was poor, compared with less than one out of seven Americans (15.1 percent) nationwide. To appreciate the enormity of the first statistic, consider this: If New York City's 1.6 million poor resided in their own municipality, they would constitute the fifth-largest city in the United States; only Houston, Chicago, Los Angeles, and the rest of New York would have a larger population. Even so, New York still had a smaller proportion of poor people than many other major cities, including Miami, Dallas, Houston, Chicago, Minneapolis, Los Angeles, and Boston. Not surprisingly, foreign-born residents are a significant component of the city's poor. New York City is home to 3.1 million foreign-born residents (37 percent of the city's total population). The largest share comes from the Caribbean (26 percent), followed by Asia (24 percent), Europe (20 percent), and Latin America (19 percent) (Roberts 2011b).

A Cautionary Note

It would be a serious mistake to conclude from the foregoing information that the presence of immigrants translates into poor neighborhoods. Actually, hundreds of thousands of immigrants have the educational levels, job skills, and income to settle in middle-class suburban towns rather than in low-income city neighborhoods. It would also be equally wrong to view cities as being primarily the repositories of the poor and less affluent, while viewing suburbs as being essentially the locales of the middle and upper classes. New York City, as mentioned in the previous paragraph, has one in five residents living in poverty. That is a high proportion to be sure, but this also means that four in five New Yorkers are not poor. Instead, they are working-, middle-, or upper-class people. And remember, earlier we cited data that revealed one in nine suburbanites lives in poverty. To understand more fully the socioeconomic diversity in all locales, we will first examine the layers of social stratification among urbanites and then scrutinize the diversity found in suburbs.

URBAN SOCIAL CLASS DIVERSITY

Imagine sitting in Union Square in downtown San Francisco and noting the different types of people who walk by. A well-dressed young woman carrying an attaché case hurries past, as if she is late for her next appointment. An old man, unshaven and in shabby dress, reclines on the grass enjoying the warm sun; occasionally, he removes a brown bag from

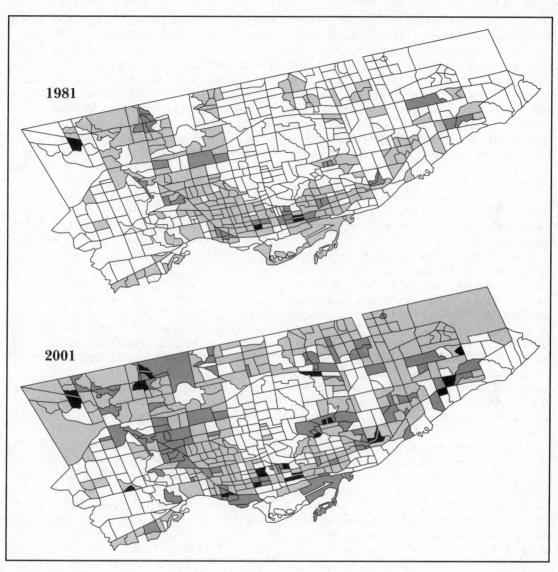

	0 to 12.9
	13 to 25.9
	26 to 39.9
	40 to 72.8

FIGURE 10–4   City of Toronto Family Poverty Rates, 2001 and 2006

Source: City of Toronto 2009.

his coat pocket, unscrews the top of a bottle inside, and raises it for a quick drink. Nearby, four young men in Gap shirts and jeans engage in a serious discussion about the latest violence in Iraq. A short distance away, an African American woman plays a guitar as she offers Christian messages to anyone who will listen. For a moment, she attracts the attention of a group of Chinese American children, 10 or 11 years old, who playfully skip their way through the square. A middle-class couple emerges from Macy's department store carrying a large assortment of packages. They buy ice cream from a street vendor, stroll into the square, and collapse wearily but happily on the soft grass.

Similar scenes play out daily in all the major North American cities. This brief portrait suggests the essence of urban life: tremendous human variety, which is sometimes troubling, sometimes exhilarating, but always interesting. Clearly, urban people in North America lead very diverse lives, and although their lives may touch for a moment in a place like Union Square, different interests, experiences, and life circumstances propel them in different directions. We will now go in a few of those different directions as we explore the different types of social class neighborhoods found in our larger cities.

Upper-Class Urban Neighborhoods

The upper classes typically have several homes and alternate where they live at different times of the year. In the city, they will live in the most fashionable neighborhoods, such as Nob Hill in San Francisco, or in luxury apartments or penthouses in the heart of the city, such as near Lincoln Center and Columbus Circle in Manhattan. Here, they live securely and deliberately segregated from the rest of the population, protected by doormen, security guards, and controlled entrances. Their choice of transportation is mostly likely a door-to-door limousine service, whether to some cultural event (concert, opera, or theater), social event (ball, fundraiser, or private party), or shopping (in exclusive stores, often available by appointment only).

The Upper East Side.   Zip code 10065 is the most prestigious one in New York City, for it encompasses much of Manhattan's Upper East Side, the country's most affluent urban neighborhood, with some of the most expensive real estate in the United States. The Upper East Side runs from 61st Street to 68th Street between Fifth Avenue and the East River. The majestic apartment buildings lining Fifth and Park Avenues offer the ritziest addresses in town—home to advertising and public relations managers, bankers, consultants, doctors, executives, lawyers, management analysts, media stars, and socialites of old wealth alike. Although apartments closer to Fifth or Madison Avenue are generally more expensive and more elegant, the entire Upper East Side neighborhood—all the way along the narrower side streets to the East River—is filled with beautiful buildings, well-maintained parks, and abundant places to eat, drink, and shop.

Separating the two wide residential avenues is the boutique-laden Madison Avenue, the area's shopping hub, where you can find everything from Prada to Picasso. This is the most expensive retail area in the world, with blue-chip art and antiques galleries, jewelry stores, and expensive boutiques and restaurants. The valuable real estate includes such stylish landmarks as The Pierre Hotel, where an available 16-room penthouse listed in 2009 for $70 million, and the renovated Lexington Avenue Barbizon Hotel offered an apartment for $17 million. Nearby are such familiar stores as Henri Bendel, Chanel, Gucci, Tiffany's, and Louis Vuitton, as well as many custom boutiques that devote their entire staff solely to the shopping pleasure of only one client an hour—or day (Cahalan 2008; Huff Post 2011a).

The appeal of this neighborhood extends beyond the elegant living spaces and retail establishments. The Upper East Side is also where you can find such world-class cultural institutions as the Metropolitan Museum of Art, the Guggenheim, and the Whitney, each located on or near New York's magnificent Central Park. Also here are the El Museo del Barrio, the Museum of the City of New York, and the Goethe Institut, a German cultural institution.

One of the biggest draws to the Upper East Side is, of course, Central Park. New York City's most famous green space borders the entire western length of the neighborhood, featuring boathouses, the Central Park Zoo and Children's Zoo, the Reservoir, and the Arsenal Building, the original site of the Museum of Natural History. And for residents with children, this area is a huge draw for its spectacular public and private schools alone. The quiet, refined pace of life spells a perfect place to live or simply a place for nonresidents to escape the "rat race" of more hectic areas in the city.

Although not everyone who lives in the Upper East Side is wealthy, a great many are. According to U.S. Census Bureau, this urban neighborhood has one of the nation's highest per capita incomes. Over one-third of those households in New York City who reported incomes of more than $200,000 lived in the Upper East Side, yet the area contains only 4 percent of all households in New York City.

Other Elite Neighborhoods.   Chicago's Gold Coast is the second-wealthiest urban neighborhood in the United States, after New York's Upper East Side. Located on the city's North Side facing Lake Michigan, this premier residential area is considered to be the "old money" section of town. Luxury high-rise apartment buildings on Lake Shore Drive and rows of century-old, multimillion-dollar mansions reside in quiet contrast to the lively stores, restaurants, and nightspots of Michigan Avenue and Rush and Division Streets. Historical landmarks and preservation districts mark much of this area, including the Astor Street Historic District.

Boston's Beacon Hill is one of the oldest historic districts in the United States, and the

The elite neighborhoods in most North American cities vary according to a city's history and terrain. Some of these residential areas may contain high-rise luxury apartments, century-old mansions, or a combination of the two. Typically, they boast a special ambience at street level and often spectacular views, as here in San Francisco's Pacific Heights.

median household income in this prestigious section easily surpasses that in most other urban neighborhoods nationwide (Higley 2011). Boasting one of the most outstanding and intact collections of mid- to-late-nineteenth-century homes in the country, it features exceptional examples of Federal, Greek Revival, and Victorian architecture. Louisburg Square, known as the heart of Beacon Hill in Boston, has undergone a changing of the guard from the old elite descended from the shipping and merchant banking industries to a new elite of largely self-made millionaires from the high-tech, financial, and other industries. In essence, the old Brahmin monopoly on financial and social power that controlled Louisburg Square has given way to something more open and complex. This change reflects the process of degentrification, in which meritocracy periodically wins out over breeding in forming an elite.

Another elite neighborhood is the Pacific Heights area of San Francisco. This privileged neighborhood, with its median household income well above the average for the city, contains blocks of elegant Victorian mansions and impressive views of the Bay and the Golden Gate Bridge, making the area a perennial favorite with tourists. The nouveau riche of the late 1800s first colonized this neighborhood—loosely bordered by Van Ness and Presidio Avenues and Pine and Vallejo Streets—when the construction of a new cable-car line made the area accessible. That legacy of luxury persists, and the neighborhood remains generally quiet and residential, with the majority of its activity clustered around Fillmore Street. There, shoppers purchase expensive women's clothing and luxury items; visit exquisite gift boutiques, bath-and-body shops, and consignment stores; or stop at a sidewalk cafe to engage in that favorite city pastime: people watching.

Middle-Class Urban Neighborhoods

Most of the middle class live in suburbia, not the city. However, even though the middle-class presence is not as proportionately high in most large cities as it was two generations ago, it is nonetheless a significant reality. Some city census blocks evolve as middle-class neighborhoods through the gentrification process, displacing the lower-income residents who can no longer afford to live there. The impetus for this change began in the 1970s as manufacturing declined in cities and their economies changed to corporate information-processing services, such as financial, legal, and marketing (Sassen 2001).

The rapid growth of the service sector generated well-paying, professional positions that brought young (late twenties to early forties), urban professionals (**yuppies**) to the city not only to work but also to live. While yuppies may be single or married, with or without children, another acronym—**dinks** (dual income, no kids)—came into fashion to describe those young professional couples without children. Then, as a large number of African American college graduates entered the urban labor market, another term—**buppies**—emerged to describe this new group of black, urban professionals (Sassen 2001). The yuppies, dinks, and buppies renovated brownstones and older loft buildings, upgrading the neighborhood. Moreover, their lifestyle prompted the opening of boutiques, fitness centers, specialty stores, new restaurants, coffee shops, bookstores, and other retail establishments, thus completing the gentrification process.

Another lifestyle trend, found in both cities and suburbs, exists among adults born into upper-middle-class households who blend the trappings of their economic success (expensive choices in food, clothing, homes, appliances, and furniture) with socially responsible actions. David Brooks (2001) sees this new social class as a blend of the bourgeois (the successful capitalist middle class) and bohemians (those with unconventional appearance and behavior), which he calls **bobos.** They work hard and emphasize their resumé accomplishments, but they also are comfortable in relaxed, informal activities. They are also into environmentalism and health, favoring recycling; cycling, jogging, and working out; frequenting coffee shops not bars; and living well, but not ostentatiously (see the *Urban Living* box below).

Not all middle-class urban neighborhoods are recently evolved entities. There are also older residential areas in cities that maintain their social-class character, sometimes despite outside forces that threaten their stability. We will look at examples of both types.

Chicago. Identified as low-income neighborhoods in 1990, Logan Square, West Town, the Near West Side, and the Near South Side experienced such significant growth in the 1990s that they are no longer

---

URBAN LIVING

The Bourgeois and Bohemians Merge

The members of this class... grapple with the trade-offs between equality and privilege ("I believe in public schooling, but the private school just seems better for my kids"), between convenience and social responsibility ("These disposable diapers are an incredible waste of resources, but they are so easy"), between rebellion and convention ("I know I did plenty of drugs in high school, but I tell my kids to Just Say No").

But the biggest tension, to put it in the grandest terms, is between worldly success and inner virtue. How do you move ahead in life without letting ambition wither your soul? How do you accumulate the resources you need to do the things you want without becoming a slave to material things?

...These educated elites don't despair in the face of such challenges....When faced with a tension between competing values, they do what any smart privileged person bursting with cultural capital would do. They find a way to have both. They reconcile opposites.

The grand achievement of the educated elites in the 1990s was to create a way of living that lets you be an affluent success and at the same time a free-spirit rebel....Building gourmet companies, like Ben & Jerry's or Nantucket Nectars, they've found a way to be dippy hippies and multinational corporate fat cats. Using William S. Burroughs in ads for Nike sneakers and incorporating Rolling Stones anthems into their marketing campaigns, they've reconciled the antiestablishment style with the corporate imperative....Dressing like Bill Gates in worn chinos on his way to a stockholders' meeting, they've reconciled undergraduate fashion with upper-crust occupations....

When you are amidst the educated upscalers, you can never be sure if you're living in a world of hippies or stockbrokers. In reality you have entered the hybrid world in which everybody is a little of both.

Marx told us that classes inevitably conflict, but sometimes they just blur. The values of the bourgeois mainstream culture and the values of the 1960s counterculture have merged. That culture war has ended, at least within the educated class....The educated elites didn't set out to create this reconciliation. It is the product of millions of individual efforts to have things both ways. But it is now the dominant tone of our age. In the resolution between the culture and the counterculture, it is impossible to tell who co-opted whom, because in reality the bohemians and the bourgeois co-opted each other. They emerge from this process as bourgeois bohemians, or Bobos.

Source: From David Brooks, *Bobos in Paradise: The New Upper Class and How They Got There,* copyright © 2000. Used by permission of Simon & Schuster, Inc.

Many young urban professionals ("yuppies") find much in the city to enjoy. Eating out, shopping, concerts, theater, and clubs are all favorite pastimes. You'll also find many in the parks—biking, jogging, strolling, playing games, or as with this group in New York's Central Park, getting together for ice skating.

low-income neighborhoods (Figure 10–5). Once struggling neighborhoods, they are now among Chicago's most desirable residential areas. This change occurred because each neighborhood became a destination for yuppies. Their arrival spurred further redevelopment, much of it through private developers and not the government. Mostly white, their arrival also coincided with a large exodus of blacks (the Near West Side) and Latinos (West Town). Displacement of low-income minorities did not occur on a significant scale in the Near South Side, because the new development occurred on previously unoccupied land. Logan Square went through a changeover to better-educated, higher-income Latinos (Zielenbach 2005).

The population demographics give strong evidence of a higher social class taking over these neighborhoods. The four communities saw at least a 12 percent increase in residents aged from 25 to 39, with 19 percent or greater

increases in single-person households and sharp drops in the number of children. In addition, there were double-digit increases in the proportion of college graduates (Zielenbach 2005:5–6). This influx of highly educated, upwardly mobile individuals helped drive up the per-capita income and property values, in turn driving out many low-income residents and, thereby, attracting still more middle-class professionals. Although one might argue that these are actually mixed-income neighborhoods, because pockets of low-income households remain, still-developing patterns suggest that this is a temporary phase and that these neighborhoods are evolving into middle-class entities.

Milwaukee.   On the northwest side, 4 miles from the city's downtown, is a culturally diverse, 30-block area known as Sherman Park, the history of which dates back to the 1890s. At that time, the upper class opted to remain closer to the central business district, living

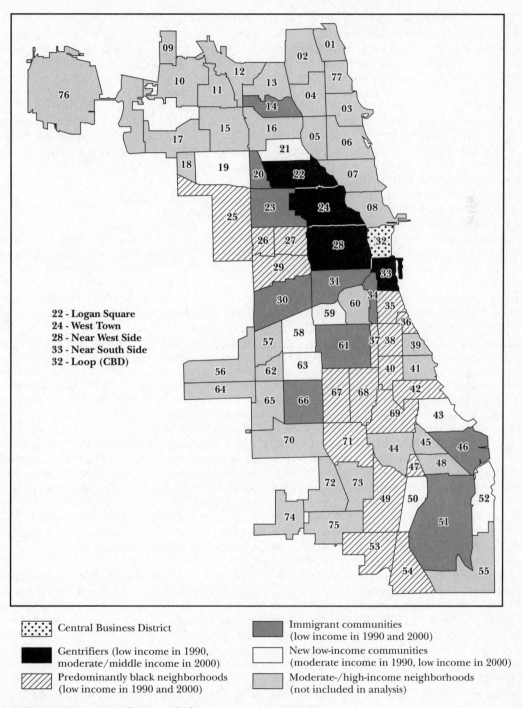

22 - Logan Square
24 - West Town
28 - Near West Side
33 - Near South Side
32 - Loop (CBD)

Central Business District

Gentrifiers (low income in 1990, moderate/middle income in 2000)

Predominantly black neighborhoods (low income in 1990 and 2000)

Immigrant communities (low income in 1990 and 2000)

New low-income communities (moderate income in 1990, low income in 2000)

Moderate-/high-income neighborhoods (not included in analysis)

FIGURE 10–5   Gentrification of Chicago, 1990–2000

Source: The Urban Institute 2005.

on the city's mansion-lined boulevards, but a steady stream of middle-class businesspeople and professionals—usually third- and fourth-generation German Americans—chose this area for building sturdy homes, noted for their ornamentation and high craftsmanship. Ever since, this neighborhood has remained a stable, middle-class residential area.

Today, the neighborhood remains one of Milwaukee's "most vibrant areas" (Curran 2003). Three of its streets have been designated as historic districts, but throughout the neighborhood, that craftsmanship and the variety of architectural styles (bungalows, Arts and Crafts, and Period Revival) have attracted people wanting to live in such fine homes on wide, quiet streets. Property values thus remain high. Most of those living here are long-term residents, however, and everyone knows everyone else.

In the 1970s, when "white flight" was occurring in Milwaukee, as in many cities, the Sherman Park Community Association (SPCA) battled racially discriminatory real-estate practices, landlord neglect, and crime. What was most distinguished about the SPCA was its embrace of racial integration, encouraging blacks and whites to live together. Today, this tight-knit neighborhood retains its racial diversity; a black middle class is now the majority but a stable Jewish community flourishes there as well. Interracial couples also find a high-comfort level here (Borsuk 2007; Curran 2003).

Religious tolerance and integration also mark this neighborhood, which has large numbers of Catholics, Jews, and Protestants. One example is the Sherman Park Area Congregation, formed by clergy from all three faiths, which meets regularly to discuss neighborhood issues in order to reach consensus on how to tackle them.

While the neighborhood maintains residential stability, the stores along its main business thoroughfares—particularly Burleigh Street and Center Street—struggle to compete with suburban stores. Some progress has been made. The Burleigh Street Community Development Corporation, a non-profit coalition of local residents and business professionals, is dedicated to re-energizing the business district. Armed with funding from both

government and private foundations, they replaced the vacant bowling alley and attached restaurant with a new business and community center. The $50 million Wheaton Franciscan–St. Joseph Regional Medical Center is another welcome presence, and so are other new businesses attracted to this neighborhood.

What might have become a changing neighborhood has instead, thanks to the determination of its residents, remained a stable, middle-class urban neighborhood.

Working-Class Urban Neighborhoods

Often, though not always, a city's working-class neighborhoods become distinctive by the ethnic and racial minority groups who predominate. (The East End of Nashville, Tennessee, would be an example of a non-ethnic working-class neighborhood.) The many visual clues—signs, parallel social institutions (churches, clubs, stores, and newspapers), and street activities—give a distinctive sense of place, and they form an important part of the community's social life. The streets in such neighborhoods are, as William H. Whyte (2001; orig. 1980) described, "the rivers of life" of the neighborhood. Here, you will find people meeting and greeting one another, using the stoops and sidewalks as personal social space; the public space of the street becomes, in essence, their front yard. Most importantly, such neighborhoods are a *gemeinschaft* community, with shared values, intimacy, a strong sense of belonging, and a strong support network. They remain what Herbert Gans (1982) called *ethnic villages*.

Newark's Ironbound. This multiethnic, working-class area in the East Ward of Newark, New Jersey, is one such example. It was brought to the attention of millions as supposedly where Tony Soprano grew up (Episode 7) and as the epicenter of the 2005 summer blockbuster *War of the Worlds*. About 4 miles square, it lies between the Passaic River and Newark Liberty International Airport.

The district's name derives from its being surrounded by railroad tracks. Once the industrial center of the city with many factories, forges, and breweries, it was first home to hundreds of impoverished laborers who toiled in the nearby factories during grueling, 72-hour, six-day workweeks. In the 1920s, Portuguese immigrants began to settle in the neighborhood, joining the mixture of blacks, Germans, Irish, Italians, and Polish who were already there.

With a more liberal immigration law passed in 1965, many Portuguese immigrants, driven by political unrest, joined their compatriots as other groups moved out. By the 1970s, most of the factories and breweries in the Ironbound had closed, but more Portuguese arrivals continued to settle here. Economic conditions were worse in their homeland, and here, jobs could be found nearby. Portuguese-speaking Brazilians arrived in the late 1980s and early 1990s, drawn by the low-cost housing, close-knit community, and convenient location. Brazilians now make up half the Portuguese-speaking population in the Ironbound, where initial tensions over cultural differences

between mainland Portuguese and Brazilians have largely disappeared (Lawlor 2004).

Newark, in fact, has the largest Portuguese population of any city in the United States, and the ongoing migration assures that Portuguese is often the first—and, sometimes, the only—language spoken in many Ironbound shops (Alvarez 2009). *Luso-Americano*, the nation's largest Portuguese language newspaper, is published here and has a wide circulation.

The Ironbound is a mix of homes, stores, and industrial buildings, with a vibrant commercial center of shops, ethnic restaurants, cafes, and clubs on Ferry Street, each offering different elements of the European lifestyle. Residents often speak about a strong sense of community, which is easily evident in daily walks and encounters with people they know. The availability of nearby factory jobs and the territorial closeness enticed earlier Portuguese immigrants to settle in the

As with many vibrant, urban ethnic neighborhoods, Newark's Ironbound District serves a dual purpose. Home to first-generation, working-class Americans (Portuguese-speaking, in this case), it also attracts many visitors, of the same or other backgrounds, who partake of its ethnic flavor in the stores and restaurants that line the streets.

Ironbound, who then helped their compatriots to secure work and a place to live.

As in other immigrant neighborhoods, numerous social clubs, each representing a particular locale in the old country, provide assistance to the newcomers and activities to preserve cultural traditions (Lawlor 2004:5). The social clubs also sponsor soccer teams, and the neighborhood parks are usually filled with adults and children playing soccer. In the bars and clubs, soccer is the spectator sport of choice, and when Brazil won the World Cup in 2002, revelers took to the streets in the middle of the night (Lawlor 2004). In fact, World Cup soccer competition remains far more important in the Ironbound than the Super Bowl is. During soccer season, the bars and restaurants are filled with fans rooting for their teams while having lunch or dinner (Stoneback 2005).

Apartment buildings of four or more units comprise about one-fourth of the housing. Demand exceeds the supply, so most tenants are found by word of mouth. Most housing (60 percent) is two- and three-family homes; single-family homes make up the rest. Housing demand has been high since the late 1990s, with 900 new homes built and prices tripling, causing a problem of increased taxes for older residents. The housing boom has led to overcrowding in the Ironbound's schools and the use of classroom trailers; the city plans to build new schools in the neighborhood (Lawlor 2004).

More than 170 restaurants also attract many visitors, but it's not until 9 or 10 P.M. that they fill up with neighborhood residents who follow the Iberian pattern of late dining. On Thursday mornings, the numerous seafood shops are their busiest, as Ironbound regulars line up to buy the fresh seafood that arrives each Wednesday evening from Portugal. From morning to night, this village-within-a-city "throbs with the accents of Portugal, Spain, and Brazil" (Corcoran 2003).

Other Ethnic Villages.   Virtually every U.S. city has one or more ethnic villages, where first-generation Americans cluster and re-create, to some extent, the world they left behind. The old European ethnic neighborhoods are fading, but new ones are taking their place with the concentrations of many African, Asian, and Hispanic immigrants. Of the thousands of examples, here are just a few: Toronto's Little India, found along Gerrard Street East between Greenwood and Coxwell Avenues, offers an active community life and array of ethnic stores. Koreatown, situated principally along Lawrence Avenue ("Seoul Drive") in the Albany Park neighborhood in Chicago's Northwest Side, remains a vibrant community, although other groups are making inroads. The Dominican presence is so strong in New York's Washington Heights neighborhood in upper Manhattan that it is sometimes called "Quisqueya Heights." (*Quisqueya* is the informal nickname of the Dominican Republic.) Two of Miami's better-known, cohesive ethnic neighborhoods are "Little Haiti" in the old neighborhoods of Lemon City, Edison Center, Little River, and Buena Vista East, and "Little Havana" in Miami, located west of Brickell Avenue and along Southwest Eighth Street.

Many working-class neighborhoods have mixed ethnic populations. The urban neighborhood of Ridgewood in the Queens borough of New York City, for instance, is a high-density area known for its brick-and-stone two-story buildings. Once a German and Italian enclave, its newer immigrants are mostly from Central and Eastern Europe (especially Poland) and from Latin America. Archer Heights on Chicago's Southwest Side has mostly brick bungalows and ranches and is home to a large Polish population and a growing Hispanic community. The Excelsior District of San Francisco is primarily a working-class neighborhood of Asian and Latino immigrant families.

Mixed-Income Urban Neighborhoods

Most cities have neighborhoods that contain people from a mixture of income levels. These neighborhoods may result from intervention, such as public housing designed to reduce the concentration of poverty, or from planned gentrification programs or be simply the non-planned result from the social dynamics of people opting to move. Whatever the cause, mixed-income neighborhoods can remain stable in their income diversity, as, indeed, many are. Otherwise, they may be in an early stage of gentrification, with low-income people moving out and higher-income people moving in, or else they are deteriorating, as the middle class moves out and more low-income people move in. The keys to the quality of life in a mixed-income neighborhood, then, are not only household income levels but also the desire and ability of residents to remain there.

Grand Rapids. Located on the western side of Michigan, Grand Rapids is the state's second-largest city, with a population declining from 197,800 in 2000 to 188,000 in 2010. It has a mixed economic base, with the largest employers in construction; transportation equipment; educational, accommodation, and food services. Median family income was $37,625 in 2009, about $8,000 less than the state median. The percentage of city families with incomes below the poverty level in 2009 was 17.2 percent, nearly double the national rate. The city's non-Hispanic white population declined from 67 percent in 2000 to 62 percent in 2010 as population of racial minorities increased, reaching 20 percent black, 16 percent Hispanic, and 2 percent Asian (city-data.com 2012). Hammered by globalization and the recession, Grand Rapids lost tens of thousands of manufacturing jobs since 2000 and is struggling to make a comeback in its furniture industry and others. Grand Valley State University built a downtown campus, and old buildings have been converted into office, retail, and residential space (El Nasser 2006).

An interesting study of 11 stable, mixed-income neighborhoods in Grand Rapids offered insights as to why no significant change in the population occurred over a 10-year period (Thomas, et al. 2004). Unlike other parts of the metropolitan statistical area, these 11 had less vacant housing, lower proportions of families in poverty, and lower family median income. Through focus group interviews in three representative neighborhoods, the researchers identified five stabilizing influences of these

neighborhoods. First, strong religious communities, such as Catholic parishes, kept people in the neighborhoods. Positive feelings about the schools, with the ability of children to walk to local schools, along with strong social networks both between and among neighbors were also important factors. Family connections to the neighborhood and well-organized, professionally staffed neighborhood associations completed the steadying elements.

At the same time, however, the researchers found fragility in these neighborhoods. Respondents were concerned about the increase in rental households, fearing poorly monitored properties and renters who would cause noise, visible blight, and neighborhood change. They were also anxious about the decline in the quality of the public schools and the possible relocation of parochial schools. Many suggested that if the schools declined drastically, so would the neighborhood (Thomas, et al. 2004).

Toronto. The St. Lawrence neighborhood is a different example of a mixed-income area, one that was deliberately created through redevelopment of a large inner-city area previously used for warehousing and industrial activities (De Jong 2000). Now home to about 25,000 residents living in converted warehouses or new structures, it extends from Yonge Street east to Parliament and Queen Streets south to the railroad tracks.

This thriving neighborhood effectively integrates people of all ages and different socioeconomic backgrounds living side by side. Planners achieved this social mix by strategic placement of a range of housing types that included condominium apartments, non-profit cooperatives, private non-profit units, and owner-occupied townhouses. The three-story family townhouses stand on tree-lined interior roads, surrounded by seven- to ten-story apartments on busier streets. This mix nicely blends different levels of affordable housing, ranging from private ownership to rent-geared-to-income apartments (Lewinberg 2011).

Complementing the successful mixture of people and housing types is vibrant economic activity that includes businesses, restaurants,

The revitalized St. Lawrence neighborhood in Toronto is a mixed-income area, successfully integrating people of all ages and socioeconomic levels. What makes this area so successful is its mixture of different housing types in new structures, converted warehouses, and factories with a strategic intermingling of businesses, stores, restaurants, and theaters.

stores, and theaters. Nearby St. Lawrence Market—site of the city's original market and still highly popular—offers a unique shopping destination, as do other businesses on Front Street and the Esplanade. Adding to the mixed use of space and activities are a community center and a social network of civic organizations—a residents' association, a seniors' group, school-based organizations, a community center council, and various other youth and children's organizations.

All this helps reinforce the residents' sense of commitment to stay in the area, a view that is reinforced by their sense of place. Experts further consider this to be a successful neighborhood because its excellent design ensured that the new buildings not only retained the character and scale of the older ones but also followed Toronto's nineteenth-century pattern of alignment along roads in order to encourage street-related activity. That deliberate design, augmented by excellent lighting, provides an active street life in this mixed-use neighborhood, which conveys a sense of safety to pedestrians.

Low-Income Urban Neighborhoods

Typically, we find neighborhoods with high levels of poverty in a city's oldest districts. Many of these communities were once solidly middle-class, or even upper-class, areas that have fallen on hard times. Since these areas of high population density and substandard housing are most often located near the central business district, they came to be called **inner-city neighborhoods,** as well as **ghettos** or **slums.**

For the trapped poor left behind in the inner city, the future is bleak. Lacking the necessary schooling and communication skills required for work in the service and information sectors of the economy, residents may experience unemployment rates as high as 80 percent (Bingham and Zhang 2001).

High rates of substance abuse, single parents, infant mortality, violent crime, and welfare dependency also are common. These "truly disadvantaged" (Wilson 1990) are poor people who rely on welfare assistance and the underground economy in order to survive.

Unlike the immigrant poor of the past, today's poor inner-city residents face social isolation. The exodus of middle- and working-class, two-parent families removes essential role models and reduces community resources. Yet, evidence suggests that carefully planned mixed-income development that provides access to higher quality services is a workable strategy to confront urban poverty (Joseph, et al. 2007).

Chicago. As revealed in an earlier section on middle-class neighborhoods, Chicago experienced significant economic growth since the 1990s to improve many of its low-income neighborhoods. Often, however, the more common pattern in many older cities is the downward economic slide of a community.

To illustrate how a neighborhood declines, we will look at Gage Park, now a low-income Chicago neighborhood that was a moderate-income neighborhood in 1990. Most common here are 80- to 115-year-old bungalows, along with Georgian-style homes from the 1940s, ranches from the 1960s and 1970s, and some more recently built Cape Cods. About 30 percent of the properties are two- and three-family houses (Steele 1998).

An East European and Irish Catholic neighborhood for generations, Gage Park is now about four-fifths Hispanic, and many of the newcomers have difficulty speaking English. Between 1990 and 2000, this neighborhood experienced a 31 percent drop in per capita income and a 10 percent drop in its proportion of high school graduates. In fact, 55 percent of those aged 25 years or older have less than a high school education. Another barometer—the overall index score, which is a composite measure of per capita income, conventional home mortgage purchase rates, and median single-family property values—declined by 52 percent

in relation to the city's overall score (city-data.com 2011; Zielenbach 2005:5).

Los Angeles. One of the poorest and most densely populated neighborhoods in this city is Pico-Union, which gets its name from the key intersection of Pico Boulevard and Union Avenue. Originally developed as a Los Angeles suburb in the early twentieth century, its housing and building types give testimony to that original suburban character. Its nearby location west of the downtown district made it an attractive residential locale for new immigrants, especially Scandinavian Lutherans, Russian Jews, and Greek Orthodox.

As suburbanization extended outward and residents relocated in the mid-twentieth century, Pico-Union became part of the "inner city." The shifting of economic and social resources away from the inner city and to the suburbs resulted in the decline of the physical appearance and service infrastructure of the area. Both housing and commercial buildings became run-down as a result of lack of maintenance. Landlords subdivided the large houses and then rented out those to accommodate the large number of low-income immigrant families. As a result, the neighborhood became a place characterized by overcrowding and substandard housing conditions (UCLA Department of Urban Planning 1998).

Pico-Union is now home to about 45,000 people, mostly Central Americans and Mexicans. Its population is 85 percent Hispanic, 8 percent Asian, 3 percent black, and 3 percent non-Hispanic white (LA Times 2011). As is so typical in immigrant neighborhoods, many community organizations and stores are tailored to the language, culture, and service needs of the population (Zhou 2009).

The number of persons in this neighborhood who are living in poverty (40 percent) is nearly twice that in the entire city. In 2009, median household income was $25,587, compared to $48,617 in Los Angeles as a whole. Educational level offers another stark contrast: In the city overall, about two-thirds have a high school diploma or higher, but in Pico-Union, only about one-third do (city-data.com 2012). Reflecting the low levels of education and the language barrier are the employment patterns and corresponding rates of economic stagnation.

Marred by graffiti and vacant stores, this neighborhood also suffers from a high crime rate. Gang activity is a serious concern, particularly by the 18th Street gang, which is involved in auto theft, drug trafficking, extortion, and murder (Alonzo 2008). Both the police and community organizations attempt to make the area safer and have had some moderate success, but many problems remain.

The Homeless

Most of us encounter homeless people from time to time. Perhaps they are sleeping on benches in parks or bus stations, standing in doorways along skid-row streets, or panhandling on busy walkways. It is all too clear that they inhabit the edges of society, and we usually assume they are cut off from work and family, weeks away from their last job or even their last square meal—a familiar stereotype. The problem is much more complex, however, and no stereotype gives a complete picture of the homeless.

Recent decades have seen a new type of homeless person. Efforts to revitalize cities with new construction on the edges of the central business districts or downtowns destroyed many of the old single-room occupancy hotels (SROs) that once provided housing to people living on the edge of poverty. Between 1970 and 1990, for example, Chicago and New York lost about 70 percent of their SROs, and Los Angeles lost more than half (Koegel, Burnam, and Baumohl 1996; Hoch and Slayton 1990). In addition, the loss of low-cost housing because of urban renewal or rent increases in an area undergoing gentrification forced many out of their neighborhoods, thereby increasing the demand on remaining low-income housing, pushing even those rents beyond what many could afford (Institute for Children and Poverty 2009). Current estimates identify about 26 percent of all homeless as families with children, 72 percent as single adults, and 2 percent as unaccompanied youth. Twenty-six percent are severely mentally ill, while 16 percent are physically disabled and 13 percent are victims of domestic violence (U.S. Conference of Mayors 2011).

Particularly disturbing is the large and growing homeless population of families with children. Each year, more than 800,000 children and youth experience homelessness, and at least one-fifth of them do not attend school (U.S. Department of Education 2010). The average age of the homeless child is six years. One-half of homeless children attend three different schools in one year, and 75 percent perform below grade level in reading. Not surprisingly, they are four times more likely to drop out of school than other children are. Two-thirds of their parents (at least half of them women who fled domestic violence) lack a high school diploma, and 75 percent of them are unemployed. Limited schooling and little work experience are the all-too-typical attributes of the impoverished, but the added factor of homelessness denies these families any stability or community support (Institute for Children and Poverty 2009).

Since 2007, requests for emergency shelter increased for homeless families and decreased slightly for individuals. Despite efforts to adjust to increased demand, in 19 of the 27 survey cities in 2010, emergency shelters were forced to turn away homeless persons because no beds were available (U.S. Conference of Mayors 2011:24).

Clearly, lack of affordable housing is the leading cause of homelessness. The root causes of that inability to pay for a roof over one's head—lack of education, inadequate low-income housing, poverty, and unavailable jobs—are unlikely to go away soon. For many, the images connected with this small, unfortunate segment of a city's population distort their view of the diversity of social class found in the total city population.

SUBURBAN SOCIAL CLASS DIVERSITY

Today's suburbs, particularly those closest to the city, no longer fit the white, middle-class, and family-with-kids stereotype. More and more, suburbs are home to minorities, the working class and poor, and the aged. Suburbs now vary widely in terms of their age and residents' income, racial composition, age, and length of residence.

Upper-Income Suburbs

A century ago, suburban residence symbolized the lifestyle of the well-to-do. Fabulous estates such as Lynnewood Hall—called the "Versailles of America"—clearly distinguished the lifestyle of early suburbanites from the lifestyle of others. The idea was to emulate the country ways of European aristocracy, as Pierre Lorillard II did better than almost anyone. In 1886, Lorillard (heir to a tobacco fortune) inherited some 600,000 acres and, at a cost of $2 million, created a millionaires' colony north of New York. Tuxedo Park was a guarded enclave where the wealthy elite "communed with nature in forty-room 'cottages' with the required ten bedrooms, gardens, stables, and housing for the small army of servants required for entertaining in style" (Conant 2003:4–5).

> At Tuxedo Park Lorillard produced almost a caricature of the Victorian millionaire's mania for exclusiveness. In less than a year, he surrounded seven thousand acres with an eight-foot fence, graded some thirty miles of road, built a complete sewage and water system, a gate house which looked like "a frontispiece of an English novel," a clubhouse staffed with imported English servants, and "twenty-two casement dormered English turreted cottages." On Memorial Day, 1886, special trains brought seven hundred highly selected guests from New York to witness the Park's opening. (Baltzell 1987:122–23)

By offering his club members property within Tuxedo Park for purchase, Lorillard created, as Baltzell suggests, a sort of Levittown for aristocrats. Yet, as streetcar lines and automobiles kept increasing, new housing rippled outward from cities, and with it, a new image of the suburban lifestyle began to take hold among the masses. Its roots were the same— to live "the good life"—but the magnitude of the change ensured that the vision would be watered down.

Today's upper-class suburbs resemble the old aristocratic ones of yesteryear. They include Grosse Pointe Shores near Detroit and South Barrington near Chicago. Families have large houses on large properties, often with swimming pools, and center their social lives on churches or temples and exclusive country clubs, where golf and tennis are favorite leisure activities. This affluent lifestyle is marked by conspicuous consumption, symbols of high social status, and other attributes of class privilege.

The populations in these suburbs tend to be somewhat older, mostly white, and highly educated, with incomes significantly above the state average. Grosse Pointe Shores, for example, within its 1 square mile has a population of 2,500, who have a median age of 48 years, are 92 percent white, and 62 percent are at least college graduates, including 30 percent with advanced degrees. In 2009, the median household income was about $136,000, compared to a Michigan median household income of $45,000. South Barrington is larger, nearly 7 square miles, with a population in 2010 of nearly 4,600 that was 68 percent white and 27 percent Asian. The median household income in 2009 was $200,000 (in Illinois, it was $54,000), and 63 percent were at least college graduates, including 30 percent with advanced degrees (City-Data.com 2012).

Although the older elite suburbs long resisted the entry of racial, ethnic, and religious minorities, the newer affluent suburbs—typically located at the outer suburban edges, such as South Barrington, which is 37 miles from Chicago—accept anyone with the right-sized bank account. A good example of economic elitism prevailing over ethnic prejudice is Beverly Hills, California, where wealthy Arabs and rich Jews live harmoniously as neighbors—a far cry from their counterparts in the Middle East.

Middle-Income Suburbs

Darien, Connecticut, and Levittown, New York, closely resemble the suburban stereotype. Life there centers on the family and child-centered activities.

Here people could live with others like themselves and bring up their children free from the threats and temptations of the city....

Central to all this was the association of middle-class values with a specific understanding of what family life meant in the suburbs. To be middle-class meant more than aspiring to a college education and a white-collar job. It also meant having a family....The family was to be the center of social life. One consequence was an emphasis on family vacations and the active involvement of parents in the lives of their children through organized sports and the local parent–teacher association. (Beauregard 2006:124–25)

In suburbs such as these, few people are poor, and almost everyone has at least finished high school. Once mostly white, these suburbs have become more racially mixed in recent years. Solon, Ohio—profiled in the *Urban Living* box on page 285 —is an example of such communities, where affluent Asians, blacks, and non-Hispanic whites live harmoniously as neighbors.

Working-Class Suburbs

Some working-class suburbs developed in the early twentieth century as a home for both factories and their workers. One such town was the South Gate suburb of Los Angeles. The developer-built and self-built homes, on narrow lots with vegetable gardens and chickens in the backyard, became more standardized and the farm plots abandoned after World War II, as higher wages at the unionized plants changed the town's suburban landscape. Given the residents' limited income, South Gate did not attract major retailers. With only small, mom-and-pop operations like corner grocery stores and service stations, the residents commuted to Los Angeles or other suburbs for most of their shopping, entertainment, and even employment (Nicolaides 2002).

Elsewhere in the United States during the early twentieth century, other working-class, industrial suburbs evolved. Some became more urbanized than others, but all offered blue-collar workers the opportunity to live in their own homes and work nearby. For example,

Flint, Michigan, 2 hours from Detroit; Argo, Illinois, near Chicago; Norwood, Ohio, just outside Cincinnati; and Fairfield, Alabama, on the edge of Birmingham, are but a few of the hundreds of examples for the exodus of industry and workers that began in the early twentieth century and continued for two generations (Taylor 2010; orig. 1915).

Today, some of these older, blue-collar suburbs are suffering from a loss of jobs as industries close or move their factories abroad. With an eroding industrial and commercial tax base, these suburbs are deteriorating physically, and property taxes are on the rise. Not surprisingly, many of the more affluent residents are packing up and moving farther out. There, they hope to find a newer version of their dream home and, perhaps, a lower tax rate. Other working-class suburbs remain healthy, however, and some are even growing. One such town is the Cleveland suburb of North Olmsted, profiled in the *Urban Living* box on page 285.

Suburban Cosmopolitan Centers

In marked contrast to the working-class suburbs (and different even from Darien and Grosse Pointe Shores) are communities like Princeton, New Jersey, home of Princeton University, and Palo Alto, California, home of Stanford University. Composed mainly of academics, professionals, writers, actors, artists, and students, these communities resemble the university areas, bohemian enclaves, and cosmopolite residential neighborhoods of central cities. Their population is usually deeply interested in "high culture," and theaters, music facilities, and elegant, unusual restaurants are found there in abundance.

Minority Suburbs

Minority suburbanization is most pronounced in large metropolitan regions. More than half of all minority groups, including blacks, now reside in the suburbs. In 36 of the 100 largest metro areas, minorities constitute at least 35 percent of the suburban population. For the first time, more than half of blacks (51 percent) in large metro areas live in suburbs. The sharp

URBAN LIVING

Comparing Working-Class and Middle-Class Suburbs

To many people who live in the inner city or rural areas, all suburbs may seem the same. Suburbs differ in many ways, however, as portraits of two suburban Ohio towns close to the city of Cleveland show. The first, North Olmsted, is a working-class suburb. It is located 17 miles to the southwest of Cleveland, has a population of about 33,000 people, and covers about 12 square miles of land. The second, Solon, is a middle-class suburb. It is 17 miles to the southeast of Cleveland and has a far lower population density, with its 23,000 people spread over about 21 square miles.

As you might expect, the cost of housing differs in the two suburbs. In 2009, the median house value in North Olmsted was $153,600, compared to $281,300 in Solon. In Solon, there is much more new housing, with about half of its homes built since 1980. In North Olmstead, by contrast, just 13 percent of all homes were built since 1980. The age of homes matters, because newer homes typically are larger, with bigger rooms, and are more likely to have attached garages and amenities like central air conditioning and, perhaps, even a swimming pool.

By and large, suburbs have a smaller share of minorities than central cities. The middle-class community of Solon, however, has more racial diversity than the working-class community of North Olmstead. In Solon, 80 percent of the people are non-Hispanic whites,

10 percent African American, 9 percent Asian American, 1 percent Hispanic, and 1 percent of two or more races. North Olmsted, by contrast, is 94 percent non-Hispanic white, with African Americans making up just 1 percent of the population, Asian Americans 2 percent, Hispanic Americans 2 percent, and the remaining 1 percent of two or more races.

One of the biggest differences between the populations of these two suburbs involves schooling. Of Solon's adult population, 50 percent have earned at least a bachelor's degree, and 22 percent have a graduate or professional degree. In North Olmstead, just 27 percent of adults have a bachelor's degree, and only 9 percent have a graduate or professional degree. Given this difference, it is no surprise that people in Solon have higher incomes: Median household earnings in Solon for 2009 were $93,254, well above the $54,530 for North Olmsted. Unemployment is typically low in suburbs, but here again, we see a difference: Solon's unemployment rate (1.9 percent) is less that in North Olmstead (3.1 percent).

As this comparison shows, suburbs display their own characteristic diversity, whether by casual observation of differences in property lot sizes and housing structures or by detailed analysis of socioeconomic data. Race and ethnicity thus appear to be less important attributes of differences in social class between the two towns than educational level and income.

Source: Data from www.city-data.com. Accessed May 17, 2012.

rise in black suburbanization mostly rests on the group's increasing percentage of college graduates and their economic progress. In addition, 59 percent of Hispanics and 62 percent of Asians also call suburbia home (Frey 2011).

Most suburbs are now racially diverse and becoming more so all the time. Even so, some suburban communities remain racially segregated, as some African Americans deliberately seek out predominantly black communities.

In the past two decades, many minority Americans, part of a growing middle class, have realized the American Dream by owning a house in suburbia. While some live in integrated neighborhoods, others prefer mostly segregated communities, finding greater comfort for themselves and their children in a homogeneous racial setting.

Examples of these affluent African American suburbs that attract middle-class black families who prefer socializing in a racially homogeneous environment are Rolling Oaks near Miami; Brook Glen, Panola Mill, and Wyndham Park near Atlanta; and Black Jack, Jennings, Normandy, and University City near St. Louis. Similarly, black residents in suburban Prince George's County in Maryland, who comprise 65 percent of the county's total population, find comfort from living in affluent but predominantly black communities or subdivisions. Often, though, black suburbs result from invasion–succession, as minorities enter a community and whites begin to leave. Eventually, their continuing departure results in a segregated black suburban community in many ways analogous to its center-city counterpart, the black ghetto.

Some black suburbs are "spillover" communities, such as Glenarden, Maryland, which is adjacent to Washington, D.C. These suburbs are direct outgrowths of center-city black ghettos that move, over time, beyond the center city. Significant spillover suburbs of blacks presently exist in Cleveland, St. Louis, Chicago, Atlanta, Miami, Los Angeles, and New York, and they are becoming more and more prevalent throughout the country. The income level of spillover communities is high relative to that of other black suburbs, because, like whites who departed from the center cities, blacks moving outward tend to be middle class, wishing to leave poorer neighbors behind.

In contrast, black migration to Compton, California, in Los Angeles County, was not an example of "ghetto sprawl" but rather, at least in part, a manifestation of upwardly mobile suburbanization, fulfilling many blacks' dream of owning their own house (Sides 2006:97, 129). In fact, whether living in a

URBAN LIVING

Life in a Minority Suburb

Robbins, Illinois, is a small, minority suburb in decline. Its steadily declining population, now about 5,300 (94 percent black), dropped by 4,000 since 1970. The town has as many people under age 18 as it does aged 65 or older (12 percent each).

Located 17 miles south of Chicago's Loop, Robbins is one of the oldest incorporated black municipalities in the United States. Largely farmland until 1910, it is characteristic of semi-rural black suburbs that developed during the Great Migration of the early twentieth century. The mostly working-class African Americans who settled here bought lots for as little as $90 each, many building their own houses and living without such amenities as electricity and indoor plumbing.

Outsiders derided the resulting makeshift landscape with its unpaved streets and called it a slum. Yet for the newly transplanted Southerners, Robbins offered numerous advantages: homeownership in a country-like environment; a safe location without risk of violence; a home near available factory jobs; and a tightly knit community. There were also work opportunities for the women, in domestic service or seasonal work in the city's canning and packing industries in Chicago. Moreover, many of the new residents could supplement their low incomes with garden produce and small livestock.

Over the next several decades, as the population increased, residents established a newspaper, the *Robbins Herald*, plus many churches and small stores. Robbins also became a popular recreation spot for black Chicagoans, who crowded its picnic grounds and nightclubs on summer weekends.

Because it was a blue-collar community with almost no commercial tax base, town officials could only undertake modest improvements, given the limited funds to upgrade services. As late as 1950, 22 percent of Robbins homes lacked indoor plumbing, and over 40 percent were considered substandard in 1960. In the 1960s, black developer Edward Starks opened the Golden Acres subdivision, which brought modern, suburban-style houses to the community. Paved streets and sewers came in the 1950s, but these costs—combined with plant layoffs in the 1970s—saddled the suburb with municipal debts. Although Robbins remained one of the few places in greater Chicago where African Americans with very limited resources could afford to buy a home of their own, declining jobs in the area put the local economy into a tailspin.

With a median household income of $23,474 in 2009, other socioeconomic statistics offer little promise of a turn-around anytime soon. Two-thirds of the residents have a high school or higher level of education, but only one in twelve adults has a bachelor's degree or higher. One-fourth are married, one in nine are widowed, one in ten are divorced, and nearly half the eligible population has never married. Nearly one-fourth of its population is unemployed and two-fifths live in poverty, both statistics well above the state average. One hopeful sign is that after more than 10 years of virtually no new construction, more than 70 new buildings have been built since 2006.

Source: From Andrew Wiese, "Robbins, IL," *The Encyclopedia of Chicago* (Chicago: Chicago Historical Society, 2005) and accessed online at city-data.com on May 17, 2012.

predominantly minority suburb or as a minority in an integrated suburb, suburbanization was not something that happened *to* them. Rather, African Americans created their own suburban dream, establishing, through property ownership, new possibilities of equity and economic opportunity (Wiese 2004).

This relationship between social mobility and residential mobility has long been an area of interest to sociologists, dating back to the Chicago School and those sociologists' observations that as the children of immigrants climbed the socioeconomic ladder, they typically moved to better housing in higher-status, suburban residential areas. Native-born blacks were no different. Compton is a minority community today, more than half-Hispanic and two-fifths black. Now an inner suburb of Los Angeles, it suffers from a higher-than-average unemployment, poverty, and crime rates.

Other minority suburbs began that way, such as Kinloch, Missouri (95 percent black in 2010), a small town just outside St. Louis, represent a second type. Often, these isolated communities originally arose as shantytowns outside the city proper, and in recent decades, white suburbs grew up around them. Colonies are poor areas (see the *Urban Living* box on page 287) with deteriorating housing and large numbers of people living below the poverty level (about 54 percent, in Kinloch's case). Only 53 percent of adults age 25 or older have a high school education; none has a college degree. Most work in low-skill jobs, and more than half the population lives in poverty. The outlook for them is as bleak as it is for center-city ghetto residents.

In 2010, 59 percent of all U.S. Hispanics in large metro areas lived in suburbs. Hispanic suburbs experiencing the largest numeric gains in Hispanic residents include those surrounding Riverside, New York, Houston, Miami, Los Angeles, Dallas, Chicago, and Washington, D.C., all areas with long-standing Hispanic populations. Areas with fewer Hispanics overall and therefore experiencing the fastest suburban Hispanic growth rates are in the Southeast, notably Knoxville, Nashville, Charleston, and Charlotte. Such cities now have what are in essence Hispanic suburbs (Frey 2011).

Monterey Park near Los Angeles is an Asian suburb, its population more than 41 percent Chinese American and another 20 percent a mixture of Japanese, Vietnamese, Korean, and other Asian Americans. This is the exception, however, because Asians—a diverse racial category of many cultures—typically move to predominantly white suburbs. As the most affluent U.S. minority group, with a median household income of $64,308 in 2010, more Asians (62 percent) live in suburbia than any other racial or ethnic category (Yen and Nuckols 2012).

The continuing influx of Asian and Hispanic immigrants, together with the tendency of many to settle directly in the suburbs, suggests that suburbs will become more diverse in the years to come. Clearly, the old stereotype about suburbia as a "white cocoon" no longer fits.

SUMMARY

If stereotypes about urbanites contain some truth, they also contain distortions. Research consistently points out the existence of pronounced urban variety—a range of social class lifestyles that defies easy description. This is as true of the suburbs as it is of the center city. Proportionately, more residents in towns within the metropolitan region hold higher socioeconomic status than urban dwellers. If we look more carefully, however, we can find many examples of social class heterogeneity in both locales.

Ever since Marx and Weber offered their analyses about social stratification, sociologists have studied this aspect of community life, beginning with Warner's study of Yankee City in the 1930s and continuing ever since. The middle class is the largest grouping in the United States (about 40–45 percent), followed by the working class (about 33 percent), the lower class (about 20 percent), and the elite upper class (about 5 percent). Each class has distinctive characteristics in wealth, power, prestige, and lifestyles, but not necessarily in choice of urban or suburban residence.

The gap between rich and poor is so pronounced that the United States has the most unequal distribution of wealth of all industrialized countries. The top quintile of the population earns about half of all income, as much as the remaining 80 percent combined, and the top 40 percent earns three-fourths of all income. Canada's unequal income distribution is not as pronounced, but the top 20 percent still earns 41.5 percent of all income.

The median household income is significantly higher in suburbia than in the city, and the poverty rate is significantly higher in the city than in suburbia. While this broad-brush portrait of city–suburb economic contrasts is accurate, sociologists use fine-brush analysis to see the details, intricacies, and inconsistencies of that broader portrait. Rather than upholding the simplistic stereotype of affluent suburbanites and non-affluent urbanites, a much more complex picture exists, as this chapter has illustrated.

Our large cities are mosaics of enclaves containing different social classes: upper-, middle-, working-, and lower-class neighborhoods. There are also mixed-income neighborhoods, some of them stable and others changing upwardly or downwardly. Cities do, indeed, have a high proportion of people living in poverty, but most city residents maintain a higher socioeconomic status. One poverty-struck population segment, the homeless, is a mixture of families and individuals, some of them mentally ill and/or substance abusers. They are a tiny percentage of the urban population, but they do form an indelible part of many people's image of the city.

Suburbs emerged in the late nineteenth century as country estates and small enclaves for the well-to-do—people anxious to escape the immigrant lifestyles and industrial commotion of the inner city. With the invention of the automobile in the twentieth century, however, a working- and middle-class exodus accelerated, especially after World War II. The last three decades have witnessed a marked increase in suburban diversity as increased numbers of the working class and minorities moved to these outlying areas. This migration produced a lifestyle complexity that rivals that of the central city. This complexity and diversity will undoubtedly continue to increase as immigration and decentralization continue.

Suburbs fall into recognizably distinct types. There are exclusive upper-income suburbs, middle-income suburbs, working-class suburbs, minority suburbs, and—increasingly in the South, Southwest, and West—Hispanic suburbs. Social class appears to be more significant than race and ethnicity in suburban settlement patterns as more and more African Americans, Asians, and Latinos move into the newer suburbs. Some suburbs have even developed into true cosmopolitan centers, offering all the goods, services, and entertainment that once drew people to the city's center.

CONCLUSION

Ultimately, what we have learned is that the manifestations of social stratification in North America are found within *both* the city and the suburb. Any simplistic socioeconomic comparison of the two ignores the lifestyle variations existing in each and, really, does a disservice to the many positive attributes that cities possess. Of course, central cities do have their problems, as do some of the older suburbs. In addition to the diversity of social class, this chapter's topic, there is the diversity of race, ethnicity, and gender, to which we will turn in the next chapter.

KEY TERMS

bobos (272)
buppies (272)
dinks (272)
ghettos (280)
hyperghettos (263)
inner-city neighborhoods (280)

reputational method (261)
slums (280)
social stratification (260)
socioeconomic
   status (SES) (260)
yuppies (272)

INTERNET ACTIVITIES

1. At this *New York Times* website, *http://www.nytimes.com/packages/html/national/20050515_CLASS_GRAPHIC/index_01.html,* you will find an interactive graphic on social class and income mobility.

2. An excellent demographic report of suburban diversity, drawing from the 2010 census, can be found at *http://www.brookings.edu/~/media/Files/rc/papers/2011/0504_census_ethnicity_frey/0504_census_ethnicity_frey.pdf.*

CHAPTER 11

RACE, ETHNICITY, AND GENDER
Urban Diversity

CITIES AND IMMIGRANTS
    Ethnic Enclaves and Ethnic Identity
    Ethnic Change
RACIAL AND ETHNIC MINORITIES
    Blacks
    Asians and Pacific Islanders
    Hispanics
    Muslims
    Native Peoples
WOMEN AND URBAN LIFE
    Work
    Urban Space
    The Public Sphere

*CASE STUDY: CHICAGO, "CITY
   OF THE BIG SHOULDERS"*

Early Chicago
The Burning and Rebuilding of Chicago
Jane Addams and Hull House
Chicago in the Early Twentieth Century
The Postwar Period
The Chicago Machine
Ordered Segmentation
Chicago Today
SUMMARY
CONCLUSION
KEY TERMS
INTERNET ACTIVITIES

Everywhere and always, cities have been immigrant-luring magnets. This basic fact explains why so many cities display striking diversity—in people, in neighborhoods, and in ways of life. Indeed, part of the excitement of a city lies in precisely this heterogeneity, the range of urban choices, the countless activities and opportunities. Especially in the major immigrant-receiving nations—Britain, Canada, and the United States—racial and ethnic diversity has long been a common trait of cities. This chapter focuses on social diversity in North America and the ways in which race, ethnicity, and gender continue to play a vital part in shaping urban life.

CITIES AND IMMIGRANTS

In Canada and the United States, destinations for millions of immigrants, cities have long been mosaics of ethnic communities. At times, minorities even became the majority, as in Milwaukee back in 1850, when that city contained 6,000 Germans and 4,000 native-born citizens (Parrillo 2011:108). At the height of the "Great Immigration" between 1880 and 1910, about 1 million immigrants came to these shores annually, and 7 out of 10 settled in cities. Not surprisingly, in most cities in the northeastern United States, foreign-born people comprised from two-thirds to three-fourths of the population.

In recent years, both Canada and the United States have been experiencing unprecedented numbers of immigrant arrivals, particularly from Africa, Asia, and Latin America, bringing ever-greater diversity to the cities. In 2010, as seen in Table 11–1, the cities with the highest percentage of foreign-born residents were Miami (60.6 percent), Toronto (45.7 percent), Los Angeles (41.3 percent), New York (36 percent), Vancouver (39.6 percent), and San Francisco (36.7 percent)—proportions significantly higher than those in 1990, but still far lower than those at the beginning of the twentieth century.

Certainly, the greater presence of immigrants affects cities' economies, but are immigrants a benefit or a problem for cities? That question—whether on a national, state, or local level—is fiercely debated. Between 1990 and 2010, the metropolitan areas with the strongest economic growth were also the ones with the greatest increase in immigrant share of the labor force. Significantly, the immigrant share of economic output closely

TABLE 11–1   Racial/Ethnic Population in Selected Cities, 2010 (percentage)

City	Asian	African American	Hispanic	Foreign Born
Boston	8.9	24.4	17.5	27.0
Chicago	5.5	32.9	28.9	22.6
Dallas	2.9	25.0	42.3	26.5
Detroit	1.1	82.7	6.8	6.4
Houston	6.0	23.7	43.8	28.1
Los Angeles	11.3	9.6	48.5	41.3
Miami	1.0	19.2	70.0	60.6
New York	12.7	25.5	28.6	36.0
Philadelphia	6.3	43.4	12.3	10.0
San Francisco	33.3	6.1	15.1	36.7
Toronto*	32.6	8.4	206	45.7
Vancouver*	39.7	1.1	1.4	39.6
Washington, D.C.	3.5	50.7	9.1	14.6

Note: *Data are from 2006 Canadian Census.

Source: U.S. Census Bureau 2011c; *Immigration in Canada 2006: A Portrait of the Foreign-born Population,* Statistics Canada.

matches the immigrant proportion of the population. For example, immigrants constitute 3 percent of the Pittsburg metro population and contribute 4 percent of economic output, while the 37 percent of immigrants in Miami represent 38 percent of economic output (Fiscal Policy Institute 2009).

Critics argue that some urban centers receive the lion's share of immigrants, and that their concentrated presence strains the community's social fabric and places an economic burden on those areas in education, health, and welfare costs (Swain 2007). George Borjas (2004) maintains that while immigrants in general may enrich the nation, their high numbers and the growing proportion of poorly educated, low-skill workers have negative consequences for lower-skilled native workers.

Ethnic Enclaves and Ethnic Identity

Like the European immigrants of previous generations, the new immigrants create their own ethnic enclaves and distinctive social institutions. These large concentrations of ethnic peoples make cities mosaics of small worlds, abuzz with different sights, sounds, and smells reflected in ethnic celebrations, parades, restaurants, street fairs, stores, and other cultural activities. For some people, however, cities—or at least certain neighborhoods in cities—are to be avoided precisely because of these differences. In contrast, others find this variety to be one of the lures of the city.

The shifting pattern of ethnic and racial immigration underlies much of the complexity of today's cities. Table 11–2 shows that from 1861 to 1960, the vast majority of legal immigrants to the United States were white people from Europe and Canada. During this period, differences between immigrants and people already in this country were mostly ethnic. That is, various whites—say, the Irish, Italians, and East Europeans—differed in cultural traditions but not in race. Since 1960, however, the bulk of legal (and illegal) immigrants have been people of color from Africa, Asia, and Latin America. Racial diversity, as

Park called the city a "mosaic of small worlds," and it still is. In every major city, you can find a patchwork of communities in which the lives of individuals are embedded. Yet even as these different cultures coexist in semi-isolated worlds, they also collide with one another in the city itself, as does this multiethnic group of visitors to New York City's Little Italy.

well as ethnic differences, compounds the problems of acceptance and rejection.

Ethnic Change

A city's spatial structure reflects ethnic subcultures as immigrants arrive and, through a process known as **chain migration,** settle near friends and relatives. A vibrant ethnic community evolves—with leaders, institutions and organizations, stores, clubs, and same-language media—to help newcomers put down roots and "make it." At the same time that this pluralism manifests itself, however, the forces of assimilation also take hold as immigrants seek to be part of their adopted country. Despite

TABLE 11–2   Legal Immigrants to the United States, 1861–2010 (percentage)

Region of Birth	1861–1900	1901–1930	1931–1960	1961–1990	1991–2000	2000–2009
Europe	90	79	58	18	15	13
Canada and Newfoundland	7	11	16	5	2	2
Asia	2	3	5	31	31	34
Latin America	0	5	17	34	38	41
Africa	—	—	1	2	4	7
Other	1	2	3	10	10	3

Source: U.S. Office of Immigration Statistics, 2010.

the challenges of learning a new language and, for some, barriers based on skin color, virtually all immigrants gradually identify more and more with their new country, where they expect to spend the rest of their lives.

Herbert Gans (1982) noted that tight "ethnic villages" built by first-generation European immigrants did not always hold up when members of the second and third generations moved from the "old neighborhood" in the central city to the leafy (and less ethnic) suburbs. Of course, such out-migration makes room for new immigrants, an **invasion–succession** process that refreshes urban pluralism even as assimilation draws others into the mainstream.

New York City.   For most of the nation's history, New York has stood as a symbol of racial and ethnic diversity. More than a generation ago, E. Digby Baltzell noted,

> Even today [New York's] citizenry, almost half of whom are foreign born or the children of foreign born, includes more blacks than most cities in Africa, a greater concentration of Jews than at any other time or place.... More Puerto Ricans than any other city outside of San Juan, more persons of Italian descent than most cities in Italy, and more [Irish] than Dublin. (1987:ix; orig. 1964)

New York still holds first place as the nation's leading destination of immigrants and it is truly a multicultural city (see the *Urban Living* box on page 295). In 2010, about 186,000 immigrants settled in the New York City metropolitan area, compared with about 87,400

coming to the Los Angeles metropolitan region (U.S. Office of Immigration Statistics 2011). Brighton Beach, Brooklyn, is known as "Little Odessa"—a place where tens of thousands of Russians live in the largest Russian immigrant community in the world. New York City also has the largest concentration of Haitians (about 200,000 living mostly in the Brooklyn neighborhoods of La Saline, Flatbush, Bedford–Stuyvesant, Bushwick, and East New York), Dominicans (more than 650,000 living mostly in Washington Heights and southwest Queens), and Asian Indians (more than 192,000, living mostly in Queens).

Today, Lower Manhattan's Chinatown is five times the size it was in 1965, both in physical size and numbers, and is home to about 150,000 people. Chinatown has now all but swallowed up New York's Little Italy, with more than two-thirds of the buildings on the Little Italy stretch of Mulberry Street now being Chinese-owned. More than 1 million Asian Americans live in New York City, nearly half of them Chinese. Asian Indians and Koreans are the next two largest groups. Not surprisingly, New York surpasses all other U.S. cities with the most Asian-owned businesses (about 154,000).

Los Angeles.   Los Angeles grew from 3.5 million in 1990 to nearly 3.8 million in 2010, mostly from foreign immigration. Today, nearly half of all residents in Los Angeles are Hispanic, and two-thirds of these are Mexican Americans. The city now has more people of Mexican ancestry than any other city in the Western Hemisphere except for Mexico City and Guadalajara. Salvadorans

URBAN LIVING

The Multicultural City and Food

Each ethnic group has its own cuisine, and part of the fun of recalling your heritage or of widening your ethnic experiences is to taste the foods associated with other groups. As any urbanite will tell you, one of the great pleasures of the city is to partake in the great variety of foods available during the numerous cultural celebrations or at the many ethnic eateries and restaurants found everywhere. And there is yet another intriguing aspect of eating these ethnic foods, brought on by the invasion-succession process of one group replacing another.

With the decline in arrivals of French, Irish, Italian, Japanese, and Jewish immigrants, and as their children move into professional fields, Asian and Hispanic newcomers are replacing the old chefs in cities throughout North America. The new arrivals learn how to prepare the other culture's foods and take over established locales, popular for their original cuisine. Some of these changes seem an easy transition because of the old countries' proximities and histories. In New York City, for example, it is not unusual to find Bangladeshis running Indian restaurants or Albanians operating Italian restaurants.

However, New York also offers more radical examples. For instance, at Second Avenue and 80th Street, there's a pizza maker who is Tibetan. Down on West 48th Street, a sushi chef at a popular Japanese restaurant is Mexican. At a French restaurant on West 55th Street, the pastry chef is Ecuadorian. A Chinese immigrant from Hong Kong, who learned his culinary art at a famous Jewish restaurant, now has his own place and serves smoked salmon and sturgeon to appreciative Jewish customers. And that wonderful nectar of the old Jewish neighborhoods, the egg cream (a wonderful, frothy drink that blends seltzer, milk, and chocolate) is served in the East Village by an Asian Indian who learned the secret recipe from the previous owner, an Italian, who learned it from the original storeowner, a Jewish immigrant.

So this is the multicultural face of the city: many different peoples serving many different kinds of food, not necessarily from their own homeland. A Central American may well have made that Middle Eastern falafel you get, or your Greek moussaka may be coming your way thanks to the efforts of a Peruvian. The city! Even its ethnic varieties have variety!

Source: Drawn from the experiences of Vincent N. Parrillo, his family, and friends.

---

and Guatemalans are two other heavily represented populations. African Americans comprise 10 percent of the city's population, followed by Asians and Pacific Islanders (particularly Filipinos, Koreans, Chinese, Asian Indians, Japanese, and Vietnamese in descending numerical order) at 11 percent. Also, so many Iranians, perhaps 500,000, live in the city that many expatriates call it "Tehrangeles."

Before moving on to the next section, we should note that Toronto—considered to be the largest *and* most racially/ethnically diverse city—will be profiled in the last chapter.

RACIAL AND ETHNIC MINORITIES

In past generations, cities were home to fewer different groups than they are today. Once, a city might be known primarily for its black, Mexican, Irish, or Italian concentrations, for example, but now, virtually any major North

American city is a multicultural place, with dozens of immigrant groups from all parts of the world.

The early history of people of color in North American cities is primarily the story of people of African descent living in the United States. Their influx into Canada occurred in small numbers during the nineteenth century but increased significantly during the twentieth century as more and more blacks from the Caribbean and the United States moved north. Interestingly, in the United States, most blacks call themselves *African Americans*, but in Canada, blacks refer to themselves as *black Canadians* (Fabbi 2003). Native peoples in both Canada and the United States have seldom lived in the white people's cities, and an Asian presence did not become significant in most locales until the second half of the nineteenth century. The Muslim presence is a more recent social phenomenon.

Blacks

Canada's history with its black population is rather different from that of the United States. Although slavery existed in Canada during the eighteenth century, by the nineteenth century it had ended, and Canada became the destination for tens of thousands of fugitive slaves from the United States (Winks 2000:236–40). Afterward, other U.S. black emigrants settled in Canada, but since the late twentieth century, black immigrants from other countries have surpassed those of U.S. origin. Today, recently arrived immigrants constitute the majority of the more than 300,000 blacks living in Canada. Most live in the metropolitan areas of Toronto, Halifax, Montreal, Vancouver, Calgary, Edmonton, and Ottawa. They are somewhat less likely to have college degrees, and their incomes are generally below the rest of the population (Statistics Canada 2007a).

From the time of the first census in 1790 until the beginning of the twentieth century, about 90 percent of the U.S. black population lived in the South, mostly in rural regions, with just one in four African

Americans living in an urban area. A few southern cities had sizable black populations (ranging from 25 to 50 percent of the total) in the late 1800s, a time when the black population of northeastern cities had yet to reach even 5 percent.

The Lure of the North. The promise of schooling and better work lured black migrants to the North after 1900. By 1910, 10 percent of the African American population lived in the North. Full implementation of the segregationist Jim Crow laws in the South, economic hard times, and the boll weevil's destruction of cotton crops prompted many more to head north during the next decade, raising the northern black population from 850,000 in 1910 to 1.4 million in 1920.

Hostility to labor unions in the North and **de facto segregation** (unequal treatment of people based on social customs and traditions) created a dual society there, just as **de jure segregation** (unequal treatment established by law) had done in the South. Northern blacks were an urban people, however, with some of them poor and others working class or even middle class. Black churches formed the bedrock of the segregated racial community. Economically, African Americans could immediately quadruple their income by moving north, which led to the greatest internal migration in the country's history (Gregory 2007).

The Great Migration. World War I and the restrictive legislation that followed put an end to the Great Immigration from Europe, initiating that Great Migration from the South. As cities such as Chicago, New York, and Boston grew into industrial metropolises, African Americans saw greater opportunity there than in the agricultural South. The **push–pull factors** spurring migration included the decline of southern agriculture as well as farm mechanization on the one hand and northern industries' shortage of labor and active recruitment of black workers from southern states on the other.

During the 1920s, the net black out-migration from the South amounted to almost

1 million people. Slowing during the Great Depression of the 1930s, the massive relocation of blacks once again accelerated when industrial production rose during World War II. Migration remained high until the 1970s, when urban decentralization and minority movement to the South reversed the process.

Black Flight.   When large numbers of whites left the cities in the 1950s and 1960s, many social observers termed the movement *white flight* and offered a variety of reasons, most of them centered on fear (crime, violence, and avoidance of minorities). As Table 11–3 shows, a clear trend of blacks moving out of cities is underway. Except for Boston, Indianapolis, Milwaukee, and Philadelphia, most northern and midwestern cities lost black population,

many of whom either chose to move south for better jobs and living conditions or else moved outward into suburbia.

Yet even in the Sunbelt, 8 of the 13 listed cities also registered a decline between 2000 and 2010. Undoubtedly, one reason for the decline is black suburbanization. New Orleans is a special case: The aftermath of Hurricane Katrina in 2005 forced the mostly black flood victims to relocate elsewhere. Similarly, part of the explanation for some Sunbelt cities gaining in black population is that they were the relocation destination of many New Orleans evacuees.

Black Majority.   In Detroit (83 percent), Baltimore (64), and Atlanta (54), blacks are the majority population, as they also are in

TABLE 11–3   African American Population in Selected U.S. Cities

Region	City	2000	2010	Percentage Change
Northeast	Boston	149,202	150,437	+0.8
	New York	2,129,762	2,088,510	−1.9
	Philadelphia	655,824	661,839	+0.9
	Baltimore	418,951	395,781	−5.5
	Washington, D.C.	343,312	305,125	−11.1
Midwest	Cleveland	243,939	211,672	−13.2
	Detroit	775,772	590,226	−23.9
	Indianapolis	199,412	225,355	+13.0
	Chicago	1,065,009	887,608	−16.7
	Milwaukee	222,933	237,769	+6.7
	St. Louis	178,266	157,160	−11.8
	Kansas City, MO	137,879	137,540	−0.2
South	Atlanta	255,689	226,894	−11.3
	Jacksonville, FL	213,514	252,421	+18.2
	New Orleans	325,947	206,871	−36.5
	Houston	494,496	498,466	+0.8
	Dallas	307,957	298,993	−2.9
	San Antonio	78,120	91,280	+16.8
West	Denver	61,649	61,435	−0.3
	Phoenix	67,416	93,608	+38.9
	San Diego	96,216	87,949	−8.6
	Los Angeles	415,195	365,118	−12.1
	San Jose	31,349	30,242	−3.5
	San Francisco	60,515	48,870	−19.2
	Seattle	47,541	48,316	+1.6

Source: U.S. Census Bureau, *American Factfinder,* 2011.

Gary, Indiana (87); Jackson, Mississippi (79); Birmingham, Alabama (73 percent); Macon, Georgia (68); Memphis, Tennessee (63); Savannah, Georgia (57); Newark, New Jersey (52); and Richmond, Virginia (51) (U.S. Census Bureau 2011b). While it is conceivable that blacks may achieve a majority in a few other major cities as well, the fact that African Americans represent about 14 percent of the total U.S. population makes it statistically improbable that black majorities will appear in most other major cities.

Residential Segregation.   Most African American migrants, like earlier European immigrants, typically settled in the least desirable central-city neighborhoods. For the Europeans, this residential segregation reflected mostly lower resources and group preferences. As these immigrants gained education and income, they assimilated and moved out of these traditional ethnic enclaves. Although many blacks have also done the same, others remain confined and isolated in racial ghettos, particularly in the Northeast and Midwest (St. Clair and Clymer 2000).

Complicating any portrait of racial segregation, however, is the relatively new presence of black immigrants from Africa and the Caribbean. Although race remains a factor, ethnicity also affects residential choice, so any examination of residential segregation requires our consideration of ethnic diversity within race and a group's length of residence in the country. We must also look at the larger picture, at the role of suburban municipalities replacing urban neighborhoods as the units of metropolitan segregation (Farrell 2008).

Between 1870 and 1920, segregation in the cities of the North was slight. By 1965, Karl and Alma Taeuber's classic study of racial segregation revealed a dramatic climb in the segregation index. To measure the relative separation or integration of groups across all neighborhoods, the Taeubers developed what they called an **index of dissimilarity.** Their index ranged from a low of zero (complete

Although racial residential segregation has slowly decreased since 1970, it still remains fairly high among blacks and whites in both cities and suburbs. Most of the 10 most segregated metropolitan areas are in the North, while the 10 least segregated metropolitan areas are in the South. Even so, the 2010 Census showed high segregation levels in Atlanta, Miami, and New Orleans.

integration) to a high of 100 (complete segregation). Overall, in 1960, the average white–black dissimilarity index for 207 large cities was 86.2, which meant that 86.2 percent of whites would have to move to another neighborhood in order to make whites and blacks more evenly distributed across all city neighborhoods.

Since the Taeubers' findings, other researchers have used the index of dissimilarity to track trends in residential segregation. In another classic and influential study, Douglas Massey and Nancy Denton (1993) used the term **hypersegregation** for the intense geographical grouping of racial groups, as found in Fort Lauderdale and Detroit. They assigned five conceptual dimensions to hypersegregation—evenness, exposure, clustering, centralization, and concentration of the population—and if a group scored high in all five areas, it was considered to be hypersegregated. Identifying 29 metropolitan areas as fitting their criteria, they called their study *American Apartheid*, after the infamous racial structuring in old South Africa.

Although racial segregation remains, since the 1970s it has slowly but steadily decreased in the United States. In 1980, the black–white metropolitan segregation index was 73, but by 2010, it dropped to 59. However, although the trend is clearly toward increased diversity in black and white neighborhoods, the average white person in metropolitan America resides in a neighborhood that is 75 percent white, 8 percent black, 11 percent Hispanic, and 5 percent Asian. In contrast, the typical black individual lives in a neighborhood that is only 35 percent white, 46 percent black, 15 percent Hispanic, and 4 percent Asian (Logan and Stults 2011).

Of the 50 metropolitan areas with the largest black populations, those with the highest levels of segregation (in descending order) were Detroit (Figure 11–1), Milwaukee, New York City, Newark, Chicago, Philadelphia, Miami, Cleveland, St. Louis, and Nassau–Suffolk (NY). All but Miami experienced modest declines in segregation since 2000, and some are "Rustbelt" metro areas, where black–white segregation has been particularly resistant to change. Although more moderate than their northern counterparts, southern metro areas also rank high in residential segregation. Despite signs of progress in the South, several cities in this region also display persistent segregation, notably Birmingham, New Orleans, Memphis, and Atlanta (Logan and Stults 2011).

The Truly Disadvantaged.   For the trapped African American poor left behind in the inner city, the future is bleak. Among those lacking the necessary schooling and communication skills required for work in the service and information sectors of the economy, widespread unemployment exists, and these jobless black men are concentrated, clustered, and segregated in small areas of the metropolis (Wagmiller 2007).

Unlike the immigrant poor of the past, today's poor inner-city residents face social isolation. The exodus of middle- and working-class, two-parent black families removes essential role models and reduces community resources. Furthermore, outsiders avoid these neighborhoods, leaving them plagued by massive unemployment, crime, and schools that do not promote achievement. Consequently, area residents—women and children on welfare, school dropouts, single mothers, and aggressive street criminals—live virtually cut off from the larger society.

Besides being isolated, the ghettoized poor have poor-quality schools, limited medical care, and high rates of infant mortality, substance abuse, and violent crime. Current social indicators offer little cause for optimism, because such problems have structural causes that society has yet to overcome.

Asians and Pacific Islanders

Like Hispanics, Asians in North America reflect a wide range of distinctive cultures. They are a highly urban population, with 96 percent living in metropolitan areas in 2010, compared with 81 percent of the total population (Figure 11–2). They are also more likely than Africans and Hispanics to live in suburbia, however, and in fact almost half do so. Most numerous are the Chinese, Filipinos, Asian Indians, Vietnamese, Japanese, and Koreans, typically residing in the larger Canadian and U.S. cities.

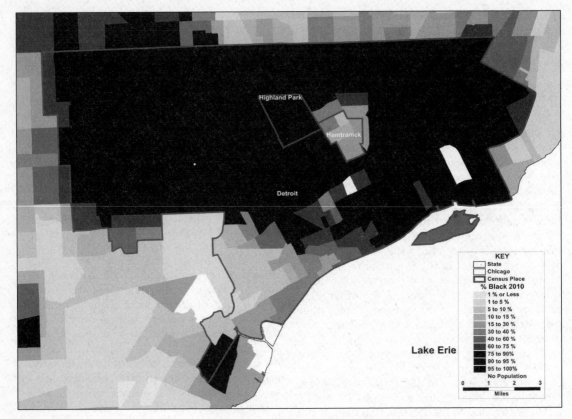

FIGURE 11–1 Percentage of Persons Who Are Black in Detroit, 2010
Source: U.S. Census Bureau.

Chinese. After their initial arrival on the West Coast around 1850, Chinese immigrants gradually moved eastward in both Canada and the United States. Usually, they banded together in low-rent urban enclaves, often situated near transportation hubs (shipping docks or railroad terminals). These areas became the Chinatowns that even today still attract immigrants and, of course, tourists. San Francisco, where one in five residents is Chinese, is home to North America's largest Chinatown, and the second largest is in Vancouver, where Chinese is spoken in 30 percent of the city's households.

Canadians of Chinese origin are the largest ethnic group of non-European origin in Canada, and they are increasing fast, with 30,000 immigrants arriving annually. Numbering more than 1.2 million, they are the fifth largest of any ethnic origin in Canada other than English or French, and 72 percent reside in Toronto and Vancouver. That same percentage—72 percent—constitutes the proportion who are foreign born, with almost 45 percent from the People's Republic of China, 30 percent from Hong Kong, and 10 percent from Taiwan (Statistics Canada 2007b).

Chinese Americans (numbering about 3.4 million and accounting for 1 percent of the total U.S. population) and Chinese Canadians (accounting for 4 percent of all Canadians) currently present a bipolar occupational

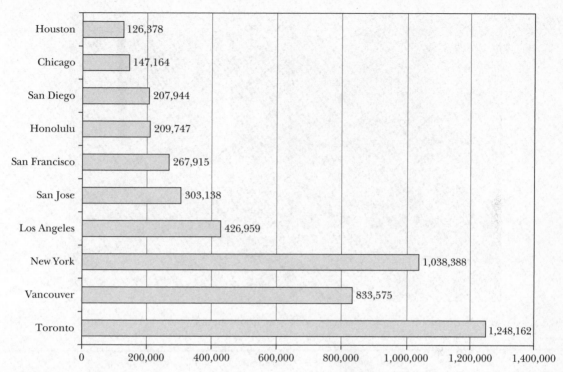

FIGURE 11–2   North American Cities with the Largest Asian Populations, 2010
Source: U.S. Census Bureau.

distribution. About 30 percent are in professional and technical positions, twice the rate among whites. However, the Chinese are also over-represented as low-skilled, low-paid service workers, with about one-fourth in this category. Median family income among Chinese Americans is above the national average, but they are likely to have more wage earners in the family. That fact, rather than a greater proportion of higher-paying positions, accounts for most of the difference.

Filipinos. More than three-fourths of all Canadians of Filipino descent arrived since 1980, and most live in either Toronto or Vancouver. Three in 10 have a college degree, double the ratio for all Canadians, and while 7 in 10 are employed, a rate 10 percentage points higher than the national average, their income is $5,000 lower. About

18 percent of all Filipino children live in low-income families, the same as the national average (Statistics Canada 2007c).

In the United States, Filipinos number around 2.6 million, with their largest concentration in Hawaii, followed by the West and East coast metropolitan areas. More than half arrived since 1980, and the new arrivals tend to have better educational and occupational skills than most of their native-born ethnic cohorts (Parrillo 2011:202).

Asian Indians. The Asian Indian presence in North America has increased dramatically during the past several decades. Census tallies reported about 466,000 Asian Indians in Canada in 2006 and 2.8 million in the United States in 2010, three times the number in 1990. With overpopulation a serious problem in India (one in six of the world's people

Many large North American cities—once principally the locales of European ethnic enclaves—now often teem with thriving Asian and Hispanic neighborhoods and commercial areas reflective of changed migration patterns. Here, traffic creeps along a busy street lined with businesses displaying signs in Chinese and English in the Chinatown district of Toronto, Ontario.

live there!), high migration rates are likely to continue. Asian Indian immigrants also arrive from East Africa and Latin America, particularly from the Caribbean and Guyana, where earlier generations had first gone as indentured plantation laborers. Almost three-fourths of the immigrants are in professional or managerial occupations; the remainder most often run convenience stores, gas stations, and family-managed hotels and motels. Consequently, most Asian Indians settle in large metropolitan areas, most significantly in Chicago; New York; San Jose; Washington, D.C.; and Central New Jersey (U.S. Office of Immigration Statistics 2011).

Two out of three Canadians of Asian Indian origin are foreign born, with about half arriving since 1990. Again, most live in either Toronto or Vancouver, constituting 7 percent of each city's population. About one-fourth have a college degree. Like the Chinese, they have a bipolar occupational distribution,

being more likely than other Canadians to be in manufacturing jobs or in science and technological jobs. While some do well economically, other Asian Indians are more likely than other Canadians to have earnings below the official low-income cutoffs (Statistics Canada 2007d).

Vietnamese. Barely noted by the U.S. Census Bureau in 1970, more than 1.5 million Vietnamese lived in the United States in 2010, and over 160,000 in Canada in 2006. They are the largest Asian group in Texas; but by far, the largest concentration of Vietnamese—some 150,000 people—is in "Little Saigon" in Orange County, California, where the language, signs, shops, offices, and music all convey a distinctly Vietnamese character. San Jose is home to 100,000 Vietnamese Americans, and the Houston–Sugarland–Baytown metro area contains another 211,000 (U.S. Census Bureau 2011b).

Three-fourths of the more than 150,000 Vietnamese in Canada arrived in the past two decades. Almost all live in Ontario, Quebec, British Columbia, or Alberta, mostly in the large metropolitan areas of those provinces. Their average income is $7,000 below the national average, and more than a third live below the unofficial poverty line (Statistics Canada 2007e).

Japanese. With low annual immigration, Japanese Americans represent a steadily declining share of Asian Americans and now number about 763,000. Most are U.S. born and have high educational and income levels, higher even than whites. Outgroup marriage exceeds 50 percent, making Japanese Americans the most structurally assimilated non-white group (Fu 2001; Zia 2001).

Almost all Japanese Canadians live in the provinces of British Columbia, Ontario, and Alberta, with more than half living in either Vancouver or Toronto. More than three-fourths were born in Canada, one in three has a college degree, and their average income per person is about $3,000 higher than the national average. They constitute only 0.3 percent of the total population (Statistics Canada 2007f).

Koreans. More than 1.4 million Koreans now live in the United States, making them the fifth-largest Asian American group. Their rate of self-employment is higher than that in any other racial or ethnic category, and their retail stores can be found in virtually every major city and in many small towns as well. About half buy an existing enterprise, and the rest begin their own business operations. Their higher success rate in both Canada and the United States compared to other ethnic entrepreneurs rests on their high educational achievement and a marketing strategy of scattering themselves throughout the metropolitan areas to work the mainstream market instead of an ethnic enclave (Ley 2006).

Seven of 10 Canadians of Korean origin are foreign born, and like other Asians, most live in Ontario or British Columbia, principally in Toronto or Vancouver. Although Koreans are more than twice as likely as the overall population to have a university degree, the group's average annual income is about $10,000 less per person (Statistics Canada 2007g).

The "Model Minority" Stereotype. Despite their cultural diversity, many Asians have a record of educational achievement, high income, and overall success in Canadian and U.S. metropolitan areas. Dubbed a "model minority" because of their accomplishments, they often display success in a variety of occupational roles. For example, Chinese engineers, Japanese financiers, Filipino nurses, Korean entrepreneurs, and Vietnamese restaurateurs abound, reinforcing this positive stereotype. Yet the reality is not entirely favorable. Not fitting this positive stereotype are many others, often non-citizens, who eke out an existence in low-paying jobs, often work at more than one job, and depend on multiple wage earners in the household (Kwon, et al. 2004).

Hampered by language difficulties, poor education, and weak job skills, many Southeast Asian refugees remain on welfare. Not all Asian students perform well in school. The criminal activities of Asian drug rings, extortion gangs, and youth gangs are often a brutal menace. In short, there is some truth to the "model minority" stereotype, but like other generalizations, it conceals as much as it reveals about a complex category of people.

Hispanics

By far, the fastest-growing non-white category in the United States is Hispanics—Mexicans, Puerto Ricans, Cubans, Central and South Americans, and others of Spanish origin—and they now constitute the nation's largest minority. In most U.S. cities with a population exceeding 100,000, Hispanics outnumber African Americans. These cities include Albuquerque, Dallas, Denver, Houston, Las Vegas, Los Angeles, New York, Phoenix, Salt Lake City, San Diego, San Francisco, and Tucson. In 12 other large U.S. cities, Hispanics are a majority of the population, outnumbering all other categories combined (Table 11–4).

In Canada, the Hispanic presence is not as dramatic, but it is growing significantly and now stands at more than a quarter of a million. About two-thirds are immigrants, and

TABLE 11–4 Hispanic Majorities in Selected Cities of 100,000 or More—Percentage of Total City Population, 2010

Brownsville, TX	93.2	Miami, FL	70.0
Corpus Christi, TX	59.7	Oxnard, CA	73.5
El Monte, CA	69.0	Pomona, CA	70.5
El Paso, TX	80.7	Salinas, CA	75.0
Hialeah, FL	94.7	San Antonio, TX	63.2
Laredo, TX	95.6	Santa Ana, CA	78.2

Source: U.S. Census Bureau, 2011b.

most prefer to live in large cities. In 2006, for example, 33 percent lived in Toronto, 25 percent in Montreal, and 7 percent in Vancouver. The rate of those with college degrees is slightly higher than the national average (17 to 15 percent). The average annual income for all Canadians of Hispanic origin is lower than for non-Hispanic Canadians, and more than one-fourth have incomes below the low-income cutoff, compared with 16 percent of all Canadians (Statistics Canada 2007h).

Many first-generation Hispanic Americans cluster in urban ethnic neighborhoods, repeating a centuries-old pattern of earlier immigrants. Here, they create a community support network through **parallel social institutions** (clubs, churches, organizations, and stores), where they can share the commonality of language and culture.

The U.S. Census Bureau term *Hispanic* wrongly suggests a single category of people. In truth, Hispanics differ in race, cultural background, social class, and length of residence in North America. Some—most often Mexican Americans—live in rural areas, particularly in the U.S. Southwest. Others, such as Cuban Americans not living in Miami, often live in suburbs. In terms of residence, many Central and South Americans have been in North America only for a few years, while others, notably Puerto Ricans and the *Hispanos* of the U.S. Southwest, have lived all their lives on the U.S. mainland. Although Hispanics live in all 50 states and in all Canadian provinces, certain categories of Hispanics tend to cluster in one

geographical area. Florida is home to more than 110,000 Nicaraguans and about two-thirds of all Cubans. More than half of all Puerto Ricans live in the Northeast (primarily New York and New Jersey); California and Texas, by contrast, are home to three-fifths of all Mexican Americans (Pew Hispanic Center 2011a).

Cubans. More than 1 million Cubans have come to the United States since 1960. Although they settled in many regions, their main concentrations were in South Florida, particularly Miami, and in the New York metropolitan area. Often settling in blighted urban areas, the first wave of Cuban refugees possessed the education, motivation, and entrepreneurial skills that enabled them to restore stability to previously declining neighborhoods. While other cities experienced a depressed housing market in the 1960s, Miami experienced an economic boom as Cubans brought a new commercial vigor to the downtown area and vitality to residential neighborhoods.

Today, two of every three Cuban Americans live in Florida, and Miami, dubbed "Little Havana," changed from a resort town to a year-round commercial center, with linkages throughout Latin America. About 856,000 Cuban Americans now live in Miami–Dade County, and their cultural imprint on Miami's skyline, commerce, and texture is obvious (Stepick, et al. 2003).

Puerto Ricans. As U.S. citizens, Puerto Ricans enjoy open migration privileges between their island and the mainland. By 1960, some 900,000 Puerto Ricans lived within the continental United States, with about 600,000 residing in New York City. The center of the New York Puerto Rican community became East Harlem, also known as Spanish Harlem (97th Street to about 125th Street between Third and Fifth Avenues). Until the late 1970s, however, continuous shuttle migration (migrants returning to the island and new arrivals coming to the mainland) inhibited an organized community life. By the late 1970s, however, greater neighborhood organization was evident, as more people put down roots in the city.

More than 4.6 million people living on the mainland United States identify themselves as Puerto Rican. New York City, where most Puerto Ricans once lived, was home to 16 percent in 2010 (U.S. Census Bureau 2011b). New York State's Puerto Rican population—64 percent of the mainland total in 1970—fell to 23 percent in 2010 as a result of out-migration into other states. Primary destination states were Florida (18 percent of the total Puerto Rican population), New Jersey (9 percent), Pennsylvania (8 percent), Massachusetts (6 percent), and Connecticut (5 percent), with California and Illinois at about 4 percent each (U.S. Census Bureau 2011a).

Although 41 percent earned family incomes exceeding $50,000 in 2009, more Puerto Ricans live in poverty than do other Hispanic groups, as shown in Table 11–5. One factor contributing to Puerto Rican poverty is a high level of female-headed families: Females head 28 percent of all Puerto Rican families, compared with 18 percent of Mexican American families. Yet 77 percent of Puerto Ricans aged 25 years and older have graduated from high school, a share that is higher than the 56 percent for Mexican Americans (U.S. Census Bureau 2012:42). Perhaps as educational attainment improves (17 percent of Puerto Ricans have graduated from college), future earnings for this group will also improve.

Mexican Americans. About 32 million Mexican Americans live in the United States, with most living in the West (53 percent) and South (35 percent). Mexican Americans make up 32 percent of the Los Angeles and Houston populations, 25 percent of San Diego, and 21 percent of Chicago (U.S. Census Bureau 2011b). Mexican immigration continues into both rural and urban areas, but most immigrants are settling in urban neighborhoods, although not necessarily in inner cities. About 9 in 10 Mexicans live in metropolitan areas, with half of them inside central cities. In a settlement pattern reminiscent of past German, Irish, Italian, and Jewish immigrants, many Mexicans—particularly those in California and Texas—are segregated in urban neighborhoods, where these ethnic enclaves have the potential to isolate them from the societal mainstream.

Aiding their adjustment is the Mexican American tradition of family support, which continues (although somewhat weakened) in large cities. Today's urbanites tend to follow nuclear family instead of extended-family residence patterns and to have less male dominance, higher rates of intermarriage, and more diverse occupations (Parrillo 2011:292).

Many of the central-city residents are of low socioeconomic status and live in areas where the school dropout rate of Mexican American youths runs as high as 45 percent, with student alienation serving as a major cause. Drug use and gang violence are unfortunate everyday realities (Lichter and Crowley 2002; Mayer 2004; Wayman 2002).

Central and South Americans. An average of 143,000 immigrants from Central and South

TABLE 11–5   Income Levels of Hispanic Americans, 2009–2010

	All Hispanics	Mexicans	Puerto Ricans	Cubans	Central Americans	South Americans
Median family income	$42,074	$40,419	$42,300	$52,113	$41,791	$52,338
Percent of families in poverty	23.2	24.8	25.2	16.8	16.7	10.7
Percent of persons in poverty	25.3	27.7	22.4	17.1	25.2	11.6
Percent of female-headed households	20.6	19.5	26.5	15.9	23.0	16.9

Source: U.S. Census Bureau, 2011d.

America enter the United States each year, more than half of them from Colombia, El Salvador, Guatemala, and Peru (U.S. Office of Immigration Statistics 2011). About 700,000 Central Americans live in the Los Angeles–Long Beach metropolitan area, and more than 200,000 in the Washington, D.C., and Miami areas. New York and Houston each contain more than 150,000 Central Americans. With a population exceeding 1.6 million, Salvadorans constitute the majority of Central Americans in most cities, followed by Guatemalans, who number more than 1 million. From the Caribbean, Dominicans are another significant urban presence, exceeding 1.4 million, with at least half of them living in New York City (Hernández and Rivera-Batiz 2003; U.S. Census Bureau 2011b).

More than 909,000 Colombians reside in the United States. Although they are dispersed throughout the country, sizable Colombian communities exist in New York, Miami, and Los Angeles. Colombians are a mixture of educated professionals and low-skilled peasants seeking a better life in North America's cities.

Residential Segregation. Hispanic residential segregation is less than that for blacks but higher than that for Asian Americans. The degree of segregation varies by ethnic group and social class. Cubans and South Americans are far less segregated than are Dominicans, Central Americans, Puerto Ricans, and Mexicans. See Figure 11–3 on page 307 for a depiction of the heavy Dominican concentration in New York's Washington Heights and of other Hispanics, especially Puerto Ricans, in the Bronx.

Similar to the situation for blacks, the metro areas with the most Hispanics are also the most highly segregated. Highest among these are Los Angeles; New York City; Newark, New Jersey; Philadelphia; Chicago; Santa Ana–Anaheim–Irvine, CA; Boston; and Houston (Logan and Stults 2011). Such residential clustering in ethnic enclaves has historically been common among numerous immigrant populations. The traditional account of minority assimilation holds that acculturation gained

through years spent in the United States—as well as through improved income, English language proficiency, and citizenship—increases geographical and residential mobility into mainstream neighborhoods. Recent research shows this also holds true for Hispanics (South, et al. 2005).

Muslims

More than 500,000 Muslims, mostly post-1980 immigrants and their children, live in Canada. This population is about equally divided between Middle Eastern Muslims from Egypt and Turkey and South Asians from Pakistan, India, Bangladesh, and Indonesia, together with significant numbers from Africa and the Caribbean (Bryant 2001). More than one-third live in and around Montreal and more than one-fifth reside in the Greater Toronto area. Like some Asian groups, they also constitute a bipolar occupation distribution, with 30 percent holding a college degree (double the national average), yet Muslim children are twice as likely to live in low-income families (Statistics Canada 2007i).

For more than 100 years, Muslim immigrants have settled in U.S. cities, and today, about 5 million Muslims live in the United States, nearly 2 million of them black. As in Canada, most have arrived since 1980 and come from many parts of the world: 33 percent from South-Central Asia, 25 percent from Arab countries, 3 percent from Africa, and 2 percent from Europe, with native-born U.S. blacks constituting about 30 percent (Council on American-Islamic Relations 2011). Like other Americans, hundreds of thousands of Muslims are choosing the suburban life over that of the city (Karim 2006; Stewart 2005).

In the early twentieth century, work in the auto industry brought Muslims from many parts of the Middle East to Dearborn, Michigan, outside Detroit. Together with Middle Eastern Christians, these Michigan Muslims today constitute the largest Arab American settlement in the country. Significant concentrations of Muslims can also be found in such large U.S. cities as New York, Chicago, and Los Angeles, as well as in small cities like Paterson, New

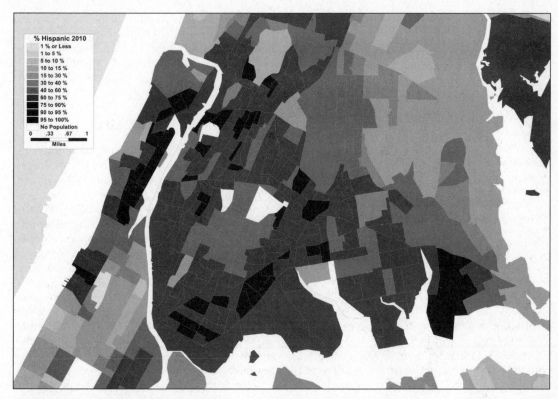

FIGURE 11–3   Percentage of Persons Who Are Latino in Upper Manhattan and the Bronx, New York, 2010

Source: U.S. Census Bureau.

Jersey. Everywhere, it seems, mosques and Islamic organizations, elementary and upper-level Islamic schools, and Muslim stores and businesses have sprung up.

These are difficult times for North American Muslims, particularly those living in cities. Almost all of them follow the non-violent teachings of their religion, but the attacks by Muslim radicals on September 11, 2001, as well as others in Madrid, London, Mumbai, and elsewhere, have heightened prejudices and/or suspicions among non-Muslim urbanites. Muslims were killed in all those attacks as well, but this group finds itself the frequent target of **racial profiling,** both in antiterrorist law enforcement actions and in stereotyping. The howls of protest in 2010–2011 against the attempt to build an Islamic center in New York City near the World Trade Center site illustrate the current difficulties in intergroup relations.

Native Peoples

Throughout most of their history, few native peoples lived in cities, instead residing mostly in rural areas, on or near reservations. In recent decades, however, a steady migration to cities has brought many to urban areas. The 2010 U.S. Census revealed the presence of 2.9 million Native Americans, up significantly from 800,000 in 1970, and that 70 percent live in urbanized areas. About 43 percent of U.S. natives reside in the West and another 31 percent in the South, although several hundred thousand live in various metropolitan areas across the country. Table 11-6 provides

TABLE 11–6   Native American Population in Selected Cities, 2010

Albuquerque	25,087	Omaha	3,391
Boston	2,399	Ottawa	20,590
Calgary	26,575	Philadelphia	6,996
Chicago	13,337	Phoenix	32,366
Cleveland	1,340	Portland, Oregon	5,991
Dallas	8,099	Regina	17,105
Detroit	2,636	San Antonio	11,800
Denver	8,237	San Diego	7,696
Edmonton	52,100	San Francisco	4,024
Houston	14,997	Saskatoon	21,535
Jacksonville	3,270	Seattle	4,809
Los Angeles	28,215	Toronto	26,575
Minneapolis	7,601	Tucson	18,305
Montreal	17,865	Tulsa	20,817
New York	57,512	Vancouver	40,310
Oklahoma City	20,533	Winnipeg	68,385

Source: Statistics Canada and U.S. Census Bureau.

population totals for native peoples living in major Canadian and U.S. cities.

At nearly 1.2 million in 2006, aboriginals constitute 4 percent of the total Canadian population, compared to 1 percent in the United States. They can be one of three officially recognized groups: First Nations (Indians), Inuit (Eskimos), or Métis (a mixture of First Nations and French Canadians). The aboriginals are becoming increasingly urban, with 54 percent living in cities or census metropolitan areas. One-fourth lives in one of nine cities: Calgary, Edmonton, Montreal, Ottawa, Regina, Saskatoon, Toronto, Vancouver, or Winnipeg (Statistics Canada 2008).

As always, migration to cities is prompted by the desire for a better life—most reservations are economically depressed, offering few jobs, little schooling, and insufficient services from the two federal governments. Yet for most natives, the city has not delivered much, even though the situation is somewhat better in Canada. Although not living in ghettos, about three-fourths of urban Native Americans in the United States do live in poorer neighborhoods. Those who lack schooling and job skills generally experience the same poverty they left behind, but now without the tribal support system. Research

suggests that Native Americans who migrate to cities are more likely to earn a higher income than those who remain behind on the reservations, but this is partly a result of their higher educational attainment (Larriviere and Kroncke 2004).

WOMEN AND URBAN LIFE

Women's lives in the city have commonly reflected the gender stratification of the larger society. Before the women's liberation movement, the differentiated roles that men and women played in the home, school, workplace, and community resulted in what Daphne Spain (1992) called **gendered spaces.** By this, she meant how differences in gender status resulted in the organization of space to reflect and reinforce those unequal distinctions. For example, women were once excluded from college altogether, and then secluded in women's colleges before finally being permitted to attend coed schools, at which point the gender stratification system began to change for the better (Spain 1992:4–5).

The workplace also revealed the division of labor, both in terms of occupation and in terms of place. Men and women performed different tasks that split along gender lines—for example, domestic service and teaching for women, compared to medicine and law for men—and they usually worked in segregated spaces. In fact, when women first entered the labor force, their doing factory or clerical work became controversial, because both sexes were occupying the same spaces (Spain 1992:14).

A clear distinction also existed in the use of public and private space. Men had the freedom to use public space at any time, but genteel women did not venture alone onto the streets without a male or female companion (see the *Urban Living* box on page 310). Only prostitutes or poor working women used urban public space, and then only in certain areas of the city. Public space was essentially a male domain; a woman's "place" was the private space of her home.

For the city's middle and upper classes, life in that city home—typically a two- or three-story brownstone or mansion—followed

One dimension in the progression of gender equality is the greater use by women of urban public space. This scene is one such example. This walkway, adjoining New York's East River and going under Manhattan Bridge, provides an unconstrained and safe environment for jogging, strolling, or picture taking. Its lighting and numerous activities and people along its inland edge add to the security.

gender-specific guidelines in the use of physical space. Men rarely ventured into the kitchen, leaving that room to the women and servants. The parlor (a room designated for the reception of guests) and dining room were used by both sexes. After dinner, however, the men "retired" to the study or billiard room for cigars and brandy, while the women "withdrew" to the drawing room for tea and, perhaps, biscuits. That social segregation of private space in one's house extended to the downtown district, where exclusive men's clubs enabled the city's "wheelers and dealers" to dine, drink, socialize, and talk business in a comfortably furnished, male domain.

In the second half of the twentieth century, as women's rights and social interactions increased during society's evolution toward greater gender equality, so, too, did the use of private and public space by women at home, at work, and in the public sphere. Homes became more open, with fewer inside doors shutting off kitchens, dining rooms, and living rooms. Family rooms, shared by all, became common instead of separate men's and women's relaxation areas. With men and women working side by side, adjustments in the work environments occurred, from the obviousness of restrooms to what could or could not be done or displayed in order to avoid what legally came to be defined as a **hostile environment.**

In short, the changing times and values led to greater life opportunities for women in all facets of life, which, in turn, prompted new spatial arrangements in both cities and suburbs. We now turn to these considerations.

Work

As both Canada and the United States industrialized, poor women, mostly from immigrant families, went to work at urban factories in low-skill jobs for low wages. In fact, women

URBAN LIVING

Targets of Street Harassment

Starting at a young age, as many as 80 percent of women around the world face at least occasional unwanted, harassing attention in public places from men they do not know; some women face it daily. The harassment ranges from physically harmless leers, whistles, honks, kissing noises, and nonsexually explicit evaluative comments, to more insulting and threatening behavior like vulgar gestures, sexually charged comments, flashing, and stalking, to illegal actions like public masturbation, sexual touching, assault, and rape. This type of unwanted attention is termed street harassment....

Street harassment and the underlying fear of it escalating into something worse make most women feel unwelcome and unsafe in public at least sometimes, especially when they are alone. It causes women to restrict their time in public alone and to be on guard while there, limiting their access to resources and leadership opportunities. It also reminds them that they live in a society in which,

because they are female, men are allowed to interrupt and bother them at any time in annoying, disrespectful, creepy, and threatening ways, virtually without any consequences.

While public harassment motivated by racism, homophobia, transphobia, or classism—types of deplorable behavior that men can be the target of and sometimes women perpetrate—is recognized as socially unacceptable behavior, men's harassment of women motivated by gender and sexism is not. Instead it is portrayed as complimentary and "only" a trivial annoyance. In reality, like other forms of harassment, street harassment is bullying behavior motivated by power and disrespect, and its negative impact on women can be as extreme as causing them to move neighborhoods, change jobs because of harassers along the commute, and stay home more often than they would otherwise. No country to date has achieved gender equality, and until street harassment is recognized as a serious problem and people work to end it, no country ever will.

Source: From Holly Kearl, *Stop Street Harassment: Making Public Places Safe and Welcoming for Women* (Wesport, CT: Praeger, 2010), pp. 3, 4–5.

---

were the main work force in many textile mills and garment factories.

In the mid-nineteenth century, millions of Irish flocked to North American cities to seek their fortunes. The number of Irish households headed by women was high, approaching 20 percent, often because many husbands died from industrial accidents. In such cases, women commonly expanded their households to include other relatives or boarders in order to help meet living expenses. Then, too, of some 2 million Irish who came to the United States between 1871 and 1910, most were women, unlike the common pattern by which males migrated first.

Many unmarried women migrated to U.S. cities, primarily to seek domestic work as maids or jobs in textile mills. For Irish women, the city was a place of continual hard work but economic security.

Most other immigrant women also sought work in cities. In Chicago, the needs of immigrant women and their families prompted Jane Addams to found Hull House, beginning the U.S. settlement home movement. The case study of Chicago at the end of this chapter looks more closely at her role in improving women's lives.

A different story centers on middle- and upper-class women, usually born to prosperous

Railroad commuters are a familiar part of a large city's work force. Once their ranks were mostly male, but with almost half the labor force now female, so, too, is the proportion of commuters. The greater presence of women has led to changes in the texture of urban space and in services and activities catering to their needs.

U.S. merchants and industrialists. Men placed them on a pedestal, as towers of moral strength and refinement, as if to balance their own competitive world of work. Prevailing values in the nineteenth and early twentieth centuries held that the nature of women was to please and the nature of men was to achieve. By the 1920s, the expanding number of middle-class families only reinforced the notion that a woman's place was as housewife and mother, as keeper of home and hearth (Kerber, et al. 2010).

For the most part, this attitude prevailed among the middle class until World War II, when a labor shortage drew women into the work force, filling factory positions that had been vacated by men who were now in uniform. From 25 percent in 1920, the percentage of working women increased to 36 percent during the early 1940s. A postwar recession and soldiers returning to their former jobs, however, resulted in the firing of 2 million women within 15 months after the war ended. Then, as the suburban decade of the 1950s ensued,

the "Ozzie and Harriet" generation (named after the popular sitcom) resumed the pattern of women's lives being confined to the house.

By 1970, however, change was under way, resulting in part from the increasing costs of a middle-class lifestyle (including the soaring costs of sending children to college) and in part from a wide range of new employment opportunities for women in the city's information and service economy. The dual-career family became the norm. By 2010, the female participation rate in the labor force was 59 percent, compared to 46 percent in 1980. Mothers, too, joined the labor force: In 1975, 45 percent of married mothers of children under age 18 worked for pay; by 2009, that share was 70 percent (U.S. Census Bureau 2012).

Urban Space

A key focus of recent feminist urban research is the extent to which cities use or should use space to meet the needs of women (Miranne and Young 2010). For example, how does the urban environment support the needs of today's working woman? One answer is that a host of specialized services have emerged, providing child care, household cleaning, lawn care, and shopping assistance to the working woman. Moreover, fast food and takeout restaurants, laundries, and dry cleaners carry out tasks for which she often has little time. Large merchandising stores and supermarkets, as well as malls and mini-malls, make shopping efficient by minimizing the time spent going from store to store.

Another issue concerns the allocation of public space. In a male-dominated society, planners typically allocate most open space to male-oriented activities, such as sports, giving little consideration to the needs of women. More attention needs to be given to creating safe environments in order to protect children at play, providing less-constrained places for women to walk or jog, and creating housing that promotes more contact with neighbors, especially for children. Finally, researchers suggest that spatial arrangements should not segregate the sexes, thereby reinforcing traditional ideas about gender; rather, they should allocate space to help all individuals' lives.

The Public Sphere

More women than ever before now hold elected public office; tens of thousands serve as mayors or members of city councils across North America. Among major cities where women have served as mayor are Atlanta, Baltimore, Chicago, Oklahoma City, Phoenix, Portland, San Antonio, San Francisco, San Jose, and Seattle, and in Canada the cities are Edmonton, Mississauga, Ottawa, Quebec City, and Toronto. As women become more active and visible in the public arena, they seek to shape and redirect policies affecting women's daily lives in the city. Many women now participate in decision making, but they have had limited success in putting on the political agenda the key issues that challenge male dominance. As the number of women leaders increases, however, this situation is likely to change.

In concluding this chapter, we present a case study of what was, for a century, the "second city" of the United States—its greatest inland metropolis, Chicago. The development of Chicago illustrates all the issues raised in this chapter. As Robert Park and the University of Chicago sociologists (see Chapter 5) found out, Chicago has been a city in which class, race, ethnicity, and gender have played a central part in people's lives.

CASE STUDY
Chicago, "City of the Big Shoulders"

Hog Butcher for the World,
Tool Maker, Stacker of Wheat,
Player with Railroads and the Nation's
　Freight Handler;
Stormy, husky, brawling,
City of the Big Shoulders:
They tell me you are wicked and I believe
　them, for I have seen your painted women
　under the gas lamps luring the farm boys.
And they tell me you are crooked and
　I answer: Yes, it is true I have seen the
　gunman kill and go free to kill again.
And they tell me you are brutal and my
　reply is: On the faces of women and chil-
　dren I have seen the marks of wanton
　hunger.
And having answered so I turn once more
　to those who sneer at this my city, and
　I give them back the sneer and say to
　them:
Come and show me another city with lifted
　head singing so proud to be alive and
　coarse and strong and cunning.
Flinging magnetic curses amid the toil
　of piling job on job, here is a tall bold
　slugger set vivid against the little soft
　cities;
Fierce as a dog with tongue lapping for
　action, cunning as a savage pitted against
　the wilderness,
　　Bareheaded,
　　Shoveling,
　　Wrecking,
　　Planning,
　　Building, breaking, rebuilding,
Under the smoke, dust all over his mouth,
　laughing with white teeth,

Under the terrible burden of destiny laughing as a young man laughs,
Laughing even as an ignorant fighter laughs
   who has never lost a battle,
Bragging and laughing that under his wrist is
   the pulse, and under his ribs the heart of
   the people,
Laughing!
Laughing the stormy, husky, brawling laugh-
   ter of Youth, half-naked, sweating, proud
   to be Hog Butcher, Tool Maker, Stacker of
   Wheat, Player with Railroads and Freight
   Handler to the Nation.

Carl Sandberg, "Chicago"

Carl Sandberg captures much of the flavor of turn-of-the-century Chicago in this poem he wrote in tribute to the city in 1916. Not everyone, of course, shared his enthusiasm. Visiting Chicago in the 1850s, Swedish novelist Frederika Bremer decried it as "one of the most miserable and ugly cities," a place where people come "to trade, to make money, but not to live" (Bremer, et al. 2007). Rudyard Kipling, visiting the Chicago of the Gay Nineties, was more direct: "Having seen it," he wrote, "I urgently desire never to see it again. It is inhabited by savages" (Kipling 2011:vii).

What is it about Chicago that draws such powerful and divergent responses from observers? Perhaps it is that the most powerful themes in the United States concern wealth, prestige, power, and the drama by which they are gained or lost. Chicago, which rocketed to prominence in barely 50 years, clearly exhibits such themes. This "city of the big shoulders," at once brash and breathtaking, is a vivid magnifier of U.S. wealth and poverty.

Early Chicago

In 1673, the future site of Chicago, where the Chicago River joins Lake Michigan, caught the attention of early explorers Jacques Marquette and Louis Joliet as a possible

Chicago's skyline offers a striking array of architectural styles that enhance its visual appeal. Within the city itself, as in all cities, a population that is also rich in diversity often grapples with problems of housing and crime that affect the quality of life and satisfaction with urban living.

water link between Lake Michigan and the Mississippi River.[1] The area remained under Indian and French control for almost a century, until the English took charge in 1763. Shortly thereafter, it passed into the hands of the new United States of America. Early in the next century, Native Americans vacated the area, and the U.S. Army erected Fort Dearborn amidst a sprinkling of settlers' cabins. Another generation passed before, in the shadow of a fort, the settlement of Chicago began in earnest.

By 1830, a century of spectacular growth was under way. Starting with just 50 persons, the new city (incorporated in 1833) boasted 4,000 residents by 1837. As the Erie Canal stimulated regional trade, Chicago became a boomtown. A building lot that sold for $100 in 1830 brought $15,000 by 1835. The population soared—growing by 50 percent or more between 1840 and 1900. So great was the demand for housing that the city emerged as a center for innovative architectural techniques, a tradition it has maintained. "Balloon frame" housing—assembled quickly with machined lumber rather than heavy timbers—was an early Chicago strategy to provide homes for waves of new arrivals.

The key to the economic success of the city was its position in the growing urban trade network. Chicago was linked to the East by the Great Lakes and the Erie Canal, to the South by river and canal to the Mississippi River, and by midcentury, to the West by railroad. In the 1850s, the McCormick Reaper Company made Chicago a center for farm machinery. The famed stockyards developed during the Civil War, and with the making of steel rails, Chicago also took its place as a manufacturing center. With nearly 100 trains entering and leaving the city daily by 1855, Chicago became the center for the entire Midwest, a break-of-bulk point for goods shipped in all directions.

In the following decades, Chicago's wealth and influence continued to grow. Railroad lines converged on the city from all directions, and water traffic expanded as trade in lumber, grain, and livestock increased dramatically. Factories proliferated, forming new industrial districts. By 1885, the Swift and Armour meatpacking companies employed more than 10,000 workers. Prosperity seemed to be everywhere. As commercial enterprises expanded at the city's center, they displaced the residential facilities, forcing them to move outward to the edge of town.

Many industrialists became rich beyond imagination: Cyrus McCormick (reaper), Henry B. Clarke (hardware), and Archibald Clybourne, Gustavus Swift, and Philip Armour (beef and meat packing) became the city's first elite. As the rich did elsewhere, these men displayed their new wealth with spectacular homes away from the city's center that contrasted sharply with the working people's squalid settlements near Packingtown and other industrial areas. Further enriching the lifestyle of the privileged residents was the opening of an opera house and art gallery in 1850 and, a decade later, of Marshall Field's, the nation's first modern department store.

The Burning and Rebuilding of Chicago

According to Chicago lore, on the night of October 8, 1871, near the corner of 12th and Halsted Streets, Mrs. O'Leary went behind her cottage to milk her cow in her small barn. The cantankerous old cow kicked over her lamp, however, and started the fire that burned down the city of Chicago. Fanned by a stiff southwest wind, the fire swept northward along the lake, consuming 1,700 acres within 24 hours. As with London in 1666 and Atlanta in 1864, the destruction was virtually total. In a day, 100,000 Chicagoans were rendered homeless, and the heart of the city's business district lay in ashes.

Even so, the forces that had created Chicago—the quest for commercial and industrial success—were very much alive.

[1]Much of the history of Chicago that follows is based on Irving Cutler, *Chicago: Metropolis of the Mid-Continent*, 4th ed. (Carbondale, IL: Southern Illinois University Press, 2006).

The new Chicago became more of a "growth machine" than ever before. In 1884, the city opened the age of the urban skyscraper with the construction of a 10-story, steel building. By 1890, Chicago's population passed the 1 million mark. Pushing its borders outward, the nation's second-largest city once again dominated the Midwest.

Jane Addams and Hull House

In 1889, Jane Addams—suffragist, activist, and the first woman to win a Nobel Peace Prize—founded Hull House in an old mansion at the corner of Halsted and Polk Streets amid Chicago's West Side slums. Her house was a refuge for displaced people to "aid in the solution of industrial and social problems which are engendered by the modern conditions of life in a great city" and to help her neighbors "build responsible self-sufficient lives for themselves and their families" (Addams 2011:50).

Immigrant Aid.   Hull House was situated in an ethnically diverse section, astride Italian, Bohemian, Greek, Jewish, Polish, and Russian neighborhoods. To build pride and respect for ethnic heritage, Addams implemented the Hull House Labor Museum, which portrayed the labor of immigrant parents in their native countries and connected it to the jobs held by young adults in Chicago. Unlike most of her contemporaries, Addams recognized the unique problems of African Americans and became a pioneer in the fight against racial discrimination (Addams 2010; orig. 1930).

In *The Spirit of Youth and the City Streets* (2010; orig. 1909), Addams voiced concern over the breakup of the sense of community that had been caused by industrialization, which tended to segregate not only social classes as well as immigrants but also the generations within the same social class. A gifted speaker and writer, she often addressed the issue of respecting diversity in others:

> Possibly another result of our contemptuous attitude toward immigrants who differ from us is our exaggerated acceptance of standardization. Everyone wants to be like his neighbors, which is doubtless an amiable quality, but leading to

one of the chief dangers of democracy—the tyranny of the herd mind. (1930:330)

Through it all, Hull House remained the center of her activism.

> Hull-House expanded to include many buildings. Eventually 70 people experienced collective living and more than 2,000 others crossed its doorway daily. It became a community center for all of Chicago; there was an art museum, a theater, a boys' club, a music school, a coffee house, meeting rooms for discussion clubs, a gymnasium, an employment bureau, a lunchroom, a library, apartments for working women and their children, a kindergarten, and much more. Scholars from the universities, leaders from Chicago society, and international leaders came to observe and learn. (Lundblad 1995:662)

Social Activism.   Addams's social activism included successfully lobbying the Illinois state legislature to pass strong child labor laws as well as laws protecting women. She conceived of and helped create the juvenile court system, set up school playgrounds, demanded enforcement of housing and sanitation laws, worked for woman's suffrage, advocated for the legal protection of immigrants, and much more. Among Hull House firsts were

- The first public swimming pool in Chicago
- The creation of four labor unions (Women Skirt Makers, Women Cloak Makers, Dorcas Federal Labor Union, and Chicago Women's Trade Union League)
- The nation's first private venture capital fund for neighborhood business development
- The first domestic violence court in Chicago, in conjunction with the Chicago Metropolitan Battered Women's Network (Domestic Violence Court Advocacy Program)
- The first infant care facility in a Chicago high school
- The first community-based foster care program of its kind in the country (Neighbor to Neighbor)

Early Feminism.   Equally important, Addams believed that dramatic changes could be made in U.S. society, and to that end, she provided a forum where people of all classes, races, and genders could speak together. An especially important feature of Hull House was its role as a nurturing, fertile arena for women to engage in intellectually stimulating debates with men. With Hull House as a model, scores of settlement houses sprang up in slum neighborhoods of other cities and offered hot meals, education, and other services. Everywhere, settlement houses served as a breeding ground for feminism and activism. At least half the women residents went on to lifelong careers in some branch of social service (Knight 2010).

Jane Addams was a close associate of George Herbert Mead, who gave lectures at Hull House. Her contributions to the founding of the science of sociology and to the first department of sociology at the University of Chicago are pivotal intellectual achievements. The noted educator John Dewey was also an associate and her good friend; Dewey modeled his classes at the Laboratory School, University of Chicago, after the children's activities at Hull House. Clearly, Jane Addams was a major force not only on the Chicago urban scene but at the national and international levels as well. Her achievements, contributions, and humanitarian efforts still shape our lives today.

Chicago in the Early Twentieth Century

> Chicago...offered a world of hope and opportunity to the beginner. It was so new, so raw; everything was in the making...the youth, the illusions, the untrained aspirations of millions of souls....Chicago [at the turn of the century] meant eagerness, hope, desire. It was a city that put vitality into almost every wavering heart. It made the beginner dream.
>
> Theodore Dreiser, *The Genius* 1915

Chicago plunged into the last century with clear title as the "metropolis of the Midwest." The city shot upward as a towering skyline took form. Immigrants from Europe swelled the city's population: Germans, Swedes, Irish, Poles, and Italians. For many, life in Chicago's poorest neighborhoods was often brutal, unsanitary, and exceedingly overcrowded. Over time, however, the dreams of many working-class Chicagoans became a reality. More

and more sons and daughters of immigrants moved outward from the old, crowded neighborhoods into newer, middle-class housing. This outward flow spilled into newly annexed developments on the city's edge.

Success did not come to all, however. African Americans had an especially hard time. Drawn to Chicago in ever-increasing numbers during the early 1900s, blacks settled primarily on the city's South Side. Unlike many others, they experienced little prosperity, and few migrated outward. The black ghetto simply expanded to the north and west of the city. Periodically, too, racial violence erupted. On July 27, 1919, after a confrontation on a local beach, a black youth drowned, leading to five days of rioting in the South Side ghetto. Damage was extensive, and many blacks suffered death and injury at the hands of white mobs.

By the 1920s, when the sociologists of the University of Chicago began studying their city intensively, they found that a complex system of social stratification based on race, ethnicity, occupation, and income shaped the city. Soon, organized crime asserted itself in the form of "gangsters," fed by the public's thirst for alcohol despite Prohibition. Nowhere did guns speak louder than in the smaller city of Cicero, adjacent to Chicago, where Johnny Torrio, Al Capone, and "the mob" had their headquarters. To consolidate his control of the city, Capone launched a campaign of terror on Election Day in April 1924. This represented urban political corruption at its peak of power, and the mob's victory gave gangsters control over much of the city. By 1931, however, the federal government succeeded in convicting Capone on income tax evasion and he spent the rest of his life in prison.

The Great Depression of the 1930s cut deeply into Chicago's economic life. Unemployment soared, construction stalled, and even the city's second World's Fair in 1933 couldn't conceal the widespread social injury. Homeless Chicagoans sleeping in public parks or milling about street corners became commonplace. Only with World War II did the economy finally recover.

The Postwar Period

Post–World War II growth took place largely beyond Chicago's city limits. A familiar pattern changed the social character of Chicago as the more affluent population moved out, leaving behind the growing ranks of minorities and the poor. By 1960, with people demanding more services as the economic base continued to contract, some began speaking about the "death of the city." Chicago fought back under the leadership of its mayor, Richard J. Daley, whose long and controversial record lasted from his election in 1955 until his death in 1976.

The Chicago Machine

An old saying about Chicago held that "the Jews own it, the Irish run it, and the blacks live in it" (Cohen and Taylor 2001:31). This was partly incorrect: White Anglo-Saxon Protestants controlled the greatest wealth in the city, but the Irish controlled the politics of the city for most of its history. Today, however, they face a growing political challenge from blacks and Hispanics, who constituted 62 percent of the city's population in 2010 (U.S. Census Bureau 2011b).

The Chicago political machine of the Democratic Party came to power in the 1930s, later than in many other cities, and did not reach its greatest strength until Richard J. Daley became the undisputed city boss. Political life in Chicago under Daley carried the tone of the immigrant political machines of the late nineteenth century. Its leaders, from block captains to the mayor himself, tried to meet the needs of their constituents, and in return, they expected people's votes.

Daley focused on maintaining the quality of the central business district—the Loop. Centered along State Street, the Loop is the economic heart of the city, of vital concern to the city's powerful business interests. In addition, the city revitalized the lakefront to make Chicago attractive and exciting both to visitors and to Chicagoans themselves. The record of improvements was uneven, however. While all residents of the city benefited to some degree from better lighting, street cleaning, and snow removal, poorer neighborhoods continued to decay.

Chicago also boasts four of the six tallest buildings in the nation—including the Willis Tower, the eighth tallest in the world—yet a commitment to improve housing for the poor was lacking until recently, a topic highlighted in the next chapter. Especially for African Americans, segregation remains all too evident, prompting a greater political voice from the black community (now 32 percent of the population). Hispanics, too, are a growing political force (29 percent of the city's people).

Since Daley's death in 1976, the Irish-dominated machine held on in Chicago, although with considerably less power. Soon after Daley's death, Jane Byrne became the city's first woman mayor, followed by Harold Washington, Chicago's first black mayor, elected in 1983 following a divisive racial campaign. Richard M. Daley, son of the late mayor, served as Chicago's leader from 1989 to 2011. Rahm Emanuel, President Obama's former Chief of Staff, became the city's first Jewish mayor in 2011.

Ordered Segmentation

Race and ethnicity are thus fundamental parts of the social organization of Chicago, as Gerald Suttles (1974) discovered through a participant–observer study of the Addams area on Chicago's West Side. Most observers considered this area, once prime turf for the Capone mob, to be little more than a disorganized slum. Suttles's most important finding was that while some housing was surely dilapidated and many people were poor, the area was far from "disorganized." Rather, Suttles found a marked social order, which he termed **ordered segmentation,** based on race and ethnicity.

How did it work? Back then, four categories—African, Italian, Mexican, and Puerto Rican Americans—made up the bulk of the area's population. Each had its own distinctive way of life, claimed its own "territory," and had its own ideas about all the others who lived nearby. Suttles found the Italians to be closely knit and trusting of one another. African Americans, in contrast, seemed to be alienated from each other, typically distrustful, and very poor. The Mexican Americans and Puerto Ricans fell somewhere in between. They were somewhat better off than the blacks economically and had more of a sense of community.

Contacts across racial and ethnic lines were rare. Most people kept their distance from others who, according to local stereotypes, were different and best avoided. The positive irony here is that such divisiveness allowed most people to establish community ties with those whom they did trust. In other words, by avoiding African Americans, Italians, and Mexican Americans, Puerto Ricans could form a sense of identity and community among themselves, thereby providing some defense against a hostile outside world. Suttles concluded,

> For all its shortcomings…the moral order they have developed includes most, if not all, of their neighbors. Within limits, the residents possess

a way of gaining associates, avoiding enemies, and establishing each others' intentions. In view of the difficulties encountered, the [ordered segmentation] of the Addams Area has provided a decent world within which people can live. (1974:234)

Chicago Today

Until the 2008 recession halted new, large-scale building projects, remarkable changes occurred to Chicago's trademark skyline. High-rise residences with great views sprouted up throughout the downtown area and nearby neighborhoods. In 2005 alone, 4,500 new condo units were built and quickly purchased by young professionals, aging suburban empty nesters, and speculators. Downtown are the 49-story Hyatt Center and the Aqua Building, the tallest in the world to have a woman chief architect. By the lakefront is the Legacy at

In the 1990s, Chicago experienced both a renaissance of its older commercial streets and a building boom along Michigan Avenue at the edge of Lake Michigan. Navy Pier—with its mix of amusements, exhibitions, restaurants, shops, theaters, and touring boats—is a year-round attraction for hundreds of thousands of residents and visitors annually.

Millennium Park, a 72-story luxury condo building.

New theater venues and restaurants in the Loop brought additional vitality to the downtown. Moreover, the city's half-billion-dollar, year-round lakefront playground is the number-one Midwest tourist and leisure destination, attracting nearly 9 million visitors annually. The highlight of this leisure area is the 3,000-foot-long Navy Pier—a mix of year-round entertainment, shops, restaurants, exhibition facilities, and attractions, including a 525-seat Shakespeare Theater, a 440-seat IMAX theater, a 150-foot Ferris wheel, and a stained glass window museum (Toronto Star 2010; Widholm 2005).

Another significant change is in Chicago's population composition. Since 1980, the city's black and white populations have been declining as new immigrants introduce fresh dimensions of social diversity. As recently as the 1970s, most immigrants were Europeans; today, however, the European-born population of Chicago has fallen to less than 8 percent. In their place are Hispanics, whose numbers tripled since 1970 to nearly 779,000 by 2010, and Asians, who total about 147,000 (U.S. Census Bureau 2011b). As mentioned earlier, Chicago has one of the nation's highest levels of black residential segregation (Figure 11–4), but its Hispanic residents are not as intensely segregated (Figure 11–5, below).

In the Chicago of today, neighborhoods that once contained Germans, Poles, and Czechs bustle with African, Filipino, Korean, Mexican, Puerto Rican, and Vietnamese Americans, as well as many other ethnic groups. Within each category, of course, there is greater diversity still. Some new

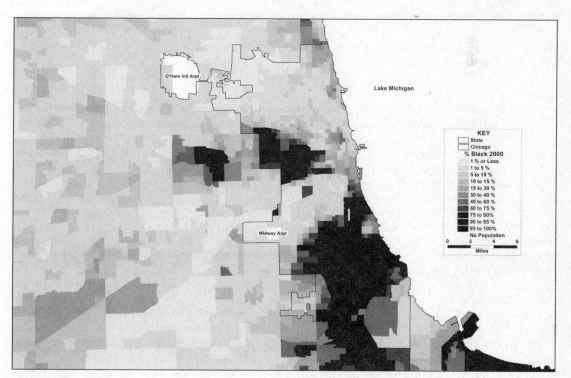

FIGURE 11–4 Percentage of Persons Who Are Black in Chicago, 2010
Source: U.S. Census Bureau.

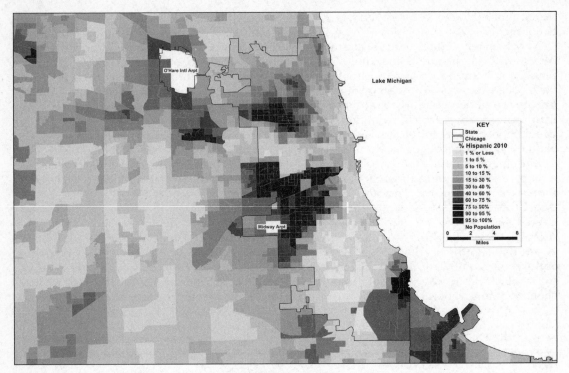

FIGURE 11–5 Percentage of Persons Who Are Latino in Chicago, 2010

Source: U.S. Census Bureau.

immigrants come to Chicago with wealth, extensive schooling, and bilingual fluency. Others, by contrast, are poor. Like immigrants throughout history, they come with little, seeking something more. As one might expect, those with the greatest social advantages tend to spread most widely throughout the city; most of Chicago's new immigrants from India (30,000), for example, are professionals and are widely dispersed. On the other hand, those with the fewest social advantages are re-creating the racial and ethnic enclaves that have existed in Chicago throughout its history, as evident in the clusters of signs marking Mexican, Korean, and Chinese neighborhoods.

Most of the newer racial and ethnic communities in Chicago are still too small to have a marked impact on the political scene. Yet, in the heyday of the Irish-dominated political machine, probably few could have imagined

that the city would ever elect a black or Jewish mayor. As new performers step to the stage in the twenty-first century, the leaders of this large and complex city will need to have big shoulders indeed.

SUMMARY

Cities are marked by social diversity. Throughout history, one characteristic of the city has been its ability to generate more opportunity for its people than rural living can. Seeking this opportunity, billions have streamed into cities. Certainly, this was the wheel driving the Great Immigration to North American cities that occurred between 1880 and 1920. By and large, many people were able to realize their goals. As time passed, many immigrants, and many more of their descendants, moved from poverty into relative affluence.

This was not true for all, however. North American cities also became home to an impoverished class. Historically, the worst-off have been the city's newest arrivals: northern Europeans until 1830, southern and eastern Europeans until 1920, and newer minorities, including African, Asian, Hispanic, and Native peoples, since then.

Women with few privileges typically worked out of necessity. Middle-class women, though, moved in and out of the labor force over time. Today, most women work for pay, a fact that shapes the city by fostering various support services to meet the needs of dual-career families and single parents. Moreover, as women become better represented in decision-making positions, we can expect further changes in how cities use space.

Finally, our case study of the Windy City, Chicago, illustrates all these themes. Since its beginnings as the Midwest's regional center, Chicago (like any other North American city we might have studied) has had a clear-cut stratification system based on differing amounts of wealth, prestige, and power. At the top were such industrialists as the Armours and the McCormicks. At the bottom were, first, poor European immigrants; somewhat later, African Americans; and most recently, immigrants from Latin America and Asia.

Out of the Great Depression of the 1930s arose the Democratic Party machine that reached its culmination in the 21-year administration (1955–1976) of Mayor Richard J. Daley. Like machines elsewhere, this one benefited some people and largely ignored others. Among the latter were various racial and ethnic minorities, such as those who lived in the Addams area on Chicago's West Side. It was here that Jane Addams founded Hull House and centered her highly productive career of social activism. In his later study of this district, Gerald Suttles noted the persistence of racial, ethnic, and territorial divisions, an organization pattern he termed "ordered segmentation." As European immigrants once organized themselves within urban neighborhoods in decades past, so do many of today's immigrants in a city that recently experienced a building boom in new residential, commercial, and leisure space.

CONCLUSION

The larger insight from Suttles's work is that prejudice always works to distinguish an *ingroup* from an *outgroup*. Looking around them, people conclude that "they" simply don't look, think, or act the way "we" do. Such prejudice and the resulting discrimination are at the heart of the disadvantages faced by African Americans, a visible minority based on skin color. Much the same applies to people with a different language, who are also set apart as different and who become easy targets for discrimination. Thus, some of the success experienced by white ethnics is a result of their ability, over time, to "pass"—that is, to assimilate into the dominant urban culture. The same opportunity is not as easily afforded to others with more clearly identifiable differences.

This pattern reminds us that cities do not exist in a cultural vacuum, for the values, norms, and stratification that shape the broader society also shape cities. Thus, the unequal distribution of wealth and power that characterizes North America, as well as structures of prejudice and discrimination, plays out most clearly in our cities.

KEY TERMS

chain migration (293)
de facto segregation (296)
de jure segregation (296)
gendered spaces (308)
hostile environment (309)
hypersegregation (299)

index of dissimilarity (298)
invasion–succession (294)
ordered segmentation (317)
parallel social institutions (304)
push–pull factors (296)
racial profiling (307)

INTERNET ACTIVITIES

1. Go to *http://www.censusscope.org/*, click one of the "Segregation Measures" links, and then one of the three segregation indices. The 1990, 2000, and 2010 data are the dissimilarity indices discussed in this chapter and the change in their percentages over the decades.

2. Go to the U.S. Census Bureau at *http://factfinder2.census.gov/faces/nav/jsf/pages/index.xhtml*. Enter the city or metro area of your choice, click "population groups" underneath, and then click "Go." On the next screen, click "Profile of General Population and Housing Characteristics: 2010." As you scroll down, you will see demographic data about that city or metro area, including Census 2010 information about its racial and ethnic composition.

CHAPTER 12

HOUSING, EDUCATION, CRIME
Confronting Urban Problems

HOUSING: A PLACE TO LIVE
Adequate Housing: Who Has It?
Housing Problems: A Brief History
Public Housing
Deterioration and Abandonment
  in the Inner City
The Great Recession and Foreclosures
The Inner City Today: A Revival?
The New Urbanism

EDUCATION: THE URBAN CHALLENGE
Meeting the "No Child Left Behind"
  Challenge
Magnet Schools

School Vouchers
Charter Schools

CRIME: PERCEPTION AND REALITY
Public Perception of Crime
Explaining High-Crime Areas
Effects of Crime on Everyday Life
What Is the Solution?

SUMMARY

CONCLUSION

KEY TERMS

INTERNET ACTIVITIES

With four out of five North Americans living in cities, we are unquestionably an urban people. Most of us, however, recognize that urban living involves not just opportunities and excitement but also various problems. Indeed, troubles such as poor housing, poor education, and crime seem to be more intense in cities than elsewhere and often serve to convey negative images of the city.

A close look at such problems reveals that they do not exist in isolation. On the contrary, many connections exist among the problems of poverty, poor housing and education, crime, and racial and ethnic tensions. Focusing on any one alone not only hinders understanding but also frustrates any efforts at solutions. Urban problems are part of a "package," partly a product of cities and partly a product of the structure and values of society itself.

Because quality-of-life judgments often rest on the standards found in housing, education, and safety, we will examine them in an urban context. How well do our cities provide housing for everyone, including the poor? How well do they educate our children? How well do they offer safety for all citizens?

HOUSING: A PLACE TO LIVE

Chapter 10 explained that the lifestyles of the urban population are strikingly diverse, a fact that is clearly evident in people's choice of housing. Some urbanites prefer the life of a downtown apartment; others desire the liveliness of row houses in an ethnic neighborhood; still others are drawn to a spacious, single-family suburban home. Of course, housing and neighborhood are not simply matters of personal choice. Differences in income set the range of choices that are available. Also important are past and present economic forces that created the city and the cultural factors that set many of our personal priorities.

Adequate Housing: Who Has It?

To define housing as either "adequate" or "substandard" is, of course, somewhat arbitrary. It is also culturally variable, because even the worst housing in the United States is of far

better quality than that which exists in much of the developing world (see Chapter 13).

Still, we can all agree that housing characterized by structural defects; inadequate plumbing, heating, or sanitation; or lead paint that can be easily ingested by children poses a threat to the health and safety of those who live there. Millions of people do live in such substandard housing, and most of them live in our cities. Because most North Americans never have any direct experience with such housing, we might well be shaken if we were to confront the daily reality of the worst-housed members of our society.

Not surprisingly, the worst housing is concentrated in areas occupied by the poor and minorities who are subject to discrimination—in short, the people with the fewest social choices. Further limiting such people's options are changes in the housing market itself: a steady decline in available, low-rent housing units and a corresponding increase in higher-rent housing units. Reduced government funding for low-income housing, urban renewal, and gentrification has lowered the number of available units even as demand has risen. One unintended consequence was a worsening of homelessness in cities.

Housing Problems: A Brief History

Current housing problems have their roots in the past. Many of the older cities' tenements are nineteenth-century structures in which housing conditions were far worse than they are today despite their greater age. In an examination of conditions in New York in 1870, James D. McCabe, Jr., recorded the following impressions:

> But what shall we say of those who pass their lives in the cellars of [these] wretched buildings...?
> [Most] have but one entrance and that furnishes the only means of ventilation...and...the filth of the streets comes washing down the walls into the room within. The air is always foul. The drains of the houses above pass within a few feet of the floor, and as they are generally in bad condition the filth frequently comes oozing up and poisons the air with its foul odors.

...The poor wretches who seek shelter here are half stupefied by it, and pass the night in this condition instead of in a healthful sleep. Mccabe, Jr., 2010. (2010:405, 406, 409; orig. 1872)

Despite such horrors, government leaders for generations made little effort to regulate housing. For their part, private builders, concerned mainly with profits, did little on their own. Indeed, only the collapse of the U.S. economy in the 1930s forced the government to enact a housing program—part of President Franklin Roosevelt's "New Deal."

A New Deal. Under the Roosevelt administration, the federal government became more involved in everyday life than ever before. Officials argued, first, that inadequate housing was so widespread it amounted to a serious social problem and, second, that only governmental intervention was likely to lead to a solution.

Under the New Deal, federal housing programs had four specific goals. First, government directed federal funds to encourage the construction of new housing. Second, because some 500,000 families had lost their homes because of an inability to pay their mortgage debts (not unlike the current housing crisis), agencies offered assistance to homeowners faced with foreclosure. Third, the Federal Housing Administration (FHA) guaranteed construction loans to increase the housing supply. Fourth, the Public Works Administration, begun in 1938, hired unemployed people to build low-rent public housing in 30 U.S. cities.

Taken together, these programs rapidly improved urban housing. The 1940 housing census, however, revealed that about 40 percent of urban housing in the United States still had at least some serious defect, such as a lack of running water or other inadequate plumbing.

Postwar Programs. All housing construction, public and private, slowed for the duration of World War II. Soon afterward, however, a major housing shortage loomed as military personnel returned home, started families, and launched the "baby boom." This shortage, along with the continued need to improve the overall quality of housing, led the government to devise several new strategies.

One was a broadening of federal mortgage guarantees through the FHA and the Veterans Administration (VA). The latter agency, created under the Servicemen's Readjustment Act of 1944, popularly known as the GI Bill of Rights, provided federally backed loans to military personnel and veterans. These programs greatly enhanced the home-buying ability of moderate-income families. Another major initiative, the Housing Act of 1949, initiated the suburban boom that followed. Its encouragement of new housing and home ownership outside the city relieved the urban population pressure but did little to improve the cities' housing stock.

Another component of the Housing Act of 1949 was **urban renewal,** which provided federal financing for slum clearance and the building of huge public housing projects. It rested on the principle of **eminent domain** that, in recent years, has become highly controversial in its wider application, as discussed in Chapter 7. City governments seized decaying areas, and then sold the properties to private developers who would demolish old buildings and build new ones. Of course, developers sought *profitable* redevelopment, so little of the new construction was affordable to the low-income residents who had previously occupied the neighborhood. Most often, urban renewal projects created new housing for the middle class. A classic example is Boston's once-thriving Italian West End. Declaring it in need of renewal in 1953—despite the fact that the outwardly aging buildings were, on the inside, extremely well kept by residents—the city bought up the area between 1958 and 1960, evicted its residents, and let the developers have a go at renewal.

The obliteration of a still-viable, working-class neighborhood was unlike previous slum clearance programs in that the intent was not to provide better housing for that income stratum. The newly constructed high-rise, luxury apartments in the "new" West End were beyond the reach of virtually all of the area's earlier residents (Vale 2007:273–6). With this pattern repeating itself in many cities throughout the 1960s, critics often charged that urban renewal meant "poor or Negro removal." Many of the displaced poor had no choice but to crowd into other low-grade housing that they could afford, and the resultant overcrowding only hastened the decay of those buildings. Thus, ironically, "slum clearance" actually created more slums.

Urban renewal often made the housing crisis worse in another way: Many redevelopers did not build as many housing units as had been destroyed. A classic example is the demolition of 18 square blocks of slums (7,000 low-income apartments) in New York City to build Lincoln Center for the Performing Arts along with 4,400 new apartments, 4,000 of them luxury apartments (Gratz 2010:204–8).

Public Housing

Public housing has never been that successful in the United States. Our cultural orientation has long viewed private home ownership as the foundation of a virtuous life and a stable social order (Bellush 2000). Therefore, people tend to judge those living in publicly supported rental housing as somehow deficient. Factor in the reality that public housing is almost exclusively the preserve of poor minorities, and we understand the stigma that is attached to housing projects. Instantly, they become ghettos, places to avoid, and out-of-the-way reservations designed to contain an "unwanted" segment of society.

Originally conceived as incorporating exciting housing innovations, too many of these high-rise projects turned into unmitigated human disasters, plagued by crime, low income, overcrowding, and terrible sanitary conditions. Even poor people soon looked on them as residences of last resort. People in almost every major city can tell of such a high-rise housing project nightmare. One of the most infamous is St. Louis's Pruitt–Igoe project, described in the *Cityscape* box below. Some later housing projects—notably Philadelphia's Society Hill—overcame the mistakes of these first programs. Still, the failures far outnumber the successes.

CITYSCAPE

Pruitt–Igoe: Symbol of a Failed National Solution

It sounded so promising in 1951—a public housing project designed to improve the lives of thousands in a badly run-down area of East St. Louis. Taking advantage of the Housing Act of 1949, local officials sought to break through the "collar of slums which [was] threatening to strangle [the] downtown business section" (*Architectural Forum* 1951:129, quoted in Fogelson 2003:344).

Three years later, residents fully occupied the 2,762 apartments in 33 innovative high-rise buildings. By 1959, however, Pruitt–Igoe "had become a community scandal" (Rainwater 2006:8; orig. 1970). Crime, dirt, and accidents were rampant; the project became "a concrete shell where anarchy prevailed" (Green 1977:179). Essentially a concentration of poor, welfare-dependent African American families (57 percent were female-headed households with children), Pruitt–Igoe's population declined as more and more residents could not bear to remain. The history of Pruitt–Igoe came to a dramatic close in 1972, when the St. Louis Housing Authority dynamited the buildings into oblivion. Soon, high-rise housing projects would meet the same fate in other U.S. cities as well.

Since the dynamiting of Pruitt–Igoe in 1972, a similar fate befell other high-rise public housing as city governments attempted to correct past mistakes (not considering social as well as physical factors) with low-rise replacements. This photo shows the implosion of one of three remaining 13-story buildings of the Scudder Homes complex in Newark, New Jersey, in 1996.

Exactly why life in public housing is often so bad is a matter of strong disagreement. Urban critics such as Edward Banfield (1990) suggested that residents themselves are largely to blame, because many do not work, have children they cannot afford, and generally act in irresponsible ways. Architectural critics (as we'll discuss shortly) point to the design of such structures, condemning high-rise buildings as anonymous spaces vulnerable to crime and vandalism (Newman 1996). Others, such as Lee Rainwater (2006), point to the negative influences of concentrated poverty—not to the people themselves—as the fundamental cause of public housing's rather dismal record.

Different Approaches. In the climate of criticism and social reform that characterized the late 1960s, the federal government renewed efforts to ensure a "decent home for every American." The Housing Act of 1968 attempted to place home ownership within reach of more families through loan guarantees and direct subsidies. The basic plan was laudable: Low-income families would pay only 20 percent of their income toward the home, and the government would pick up the rest. Often, however, purchasers ended up with an overpriced house in need of extensive repairs that they could not afford. The result was foreclosure, leaving the "owners" back on the street and the government saddled with 100,000 undesirable houses.

By the early 1970s, the handwriting was on the wall, and the program was cut back after government expenditure of more than $4 billion. "With hindsight," Robert Green concluded, "it can safely be said that private concerns [investors, developers, banks] were given too much rope, and with it, they hung the poor" Robert Green, 1977 (1977:181).

An alternative approach, begun in 1974 and still active, is the Section 8 Program, which provides rent subsidies to low-income tenants in private housing. This assistance program enables tenants to choose where to live instead of forcing them into a public housing project. The program offers subsidies to developers to build or rehabilitate rental housing. Developers then set aside a certain portion of the units for low-income families and—in a subsidy contract with the government—receive 30 percent of the rent from the tenant and the rest from the government. Although Section 8 and other rental assistance programs have increased the stock of low-cost rental housing, the program is severely underfunded. Waiting lists can run into the years, and many local housing authorities frequently close their waiting lists and stop accepting applications because their lists are too long.

Evaluation. Even this brief history makes clear that federally supervised urban housing programs fell well short of their lofty goals. Some specific problems are worth highlighting.

First, because of the deep involvement of private banking and construction industries in renewal programs, for many, profit overshadowed any sense of social responsibility to help the poor. Furthermore, the design of some redevelopment projects was intended for more affluent buyers, at prices out of the reach of those who originally lived there. The original intention of urban housing programs of the 1930s—to improve the housing of the poor—changed into a large-scale program to redevelop the central city in order to restore its economic health. The result was a reduction in the total amount of low-cost housing across urban North America.

A second problem is that given the tendency of investors and developers to pursue profit rather than assist the poor, local residents had little voice in the decision-making process. Herbert Gans studied the redevelopment of Boston's West End, claiming that local residents were unorganized and lacked understanding of the programs that seemed to "attack" them. Thus, for many, renewal was a bitter experience.

A similar fate befell the residents of Poletown, a mostly ethnic but racially integrated, 465-acre neighborhood in Detroit that contained more than 1,300 homes and apartments, 143 businesses, 16 churches, 2 schools, and a hospital. In 1981, anxious to keep a new General Motors (GM) plant and 6,000 jobs in the city, municipal leaders exercised their right of eminent domain to take over Poletown, razed it (at a cost exceeding $200 million), and sold the land to GM (for $8 million) as the location for its new plant. Residents—joined by consumer advocate Ralph Nader and Gray Panthers leader Maggie Kuhn—tried to stop the forced uprooting and destruction of their homes, churches, and businesses, but lost and had to move.

Third, Gans and other critics, such as Jane Jacobs, argued that redevelopers didn't even try to understand that many areas subject to redevelopment were actually healthy, safe neighborhoods. In effect, many development programs reflected the bias of middle-class planners against the lifestyle of low-rent areas. Somehow, such areas just weren't what the planners considered to be "normal."

For example, one common misperception was to judge people congregating on front stoops, street corners, or in local establishments as a bad thing instead of realizing that, in the city, shared public space is actually an ideal locale for social interaction.

At present, we find some promise for public housing, even with budget cutbacks, and will discuss those bright spots in both public and private housing shortly. First, though, we will look at housing troubles in the private sector that also plague the cities.

Deterioration and Abandonment in the Inner City

Beginning in the 1950s, because of outward migration, the decline of manufacturing, and economic globalization, the older central cities fell on hard times. Inner-city neighborhoods lost population and deteriorated sharply, in some cases falling victim to extensive vandalism and arson. Many of the older, industrial inner cities of the Midwest and Northeast soon contained block after block of empty, dilapidated buildings, many burned, as if the area had collapsed under a full-scale bomb attack. These cities contained as many as 2 million abandoned buildings, making them look like urban "ghost towns," with 150,000 additional abandonments yearly well into the 1980s.

During the 1990s, these numbers dropped considerably, thanks to the economic revitalization in many cities and the gentrification process. Still, a recent study revealed a total of 185,000 abandoned residential units in 19 cities with a population of more than 100,000, or an average of 10,000 per city. Detroit had 45,000 abandoned buildings, Philadelphia 27,000, and St. Louis 13,000 (Mallach 2010:4).

Why would people simply walk away from otherwise usable buildings in cities where housing was in short supply? The answer is a complex, vicious circle of decline. Faced with the mounting expenses of taxes, insurance, heating fuel, and repairs because of vandalism, not to mention the loss to the suburbs of middle-income renters, and often constrained by rent control caps, some building owners reduce, or entirely eliminate, routine maintenance and repairs in an effort to retain some profit. If the building eventually represents more costs or trouble than rental income warrants, and they are unable to sell it, some owners simply default on their mortgages or taxes and their property goes into foreclosure. As desperate ex-tenants scatter in search of other housing, vandals and looters seek whatever of value remains (including sinks, bathtubs, and plumbing). First the building, then the block, and eventually the whole neighborhood succumbs to the process. In the end, just hollow buildings remain: giant headstones marking the grave of a now-dead urban neighborhood.

Other developments in the private sector are more encouraging. During recent years, housing in major cities has vastly improved. Although much more needs to be done, notable progress is clearly evident, as we shall now explain.

The Great Recession and Foreclosures

Walking away from one's property, unfortunately, is not just an urban landlord phenomenon. Without question, the past several years of recession have had a disastrous effect on the housing market. Two key factors led to the unraveling of the American Dream.

The South Bronx in the 1980s looked like a war zone, and its violent crime rate made it feel like one. Arson and abandonment led to the loss of 30,000 buildings in the 1970s, leading to a desolate environment for both children and adults. By the mid-1990s, however, urban homesteading and gentrification programs had transformed this area into a safe, pleasant place to live and raise children.

First, millions of people lost their jobs and were unable to pay their mortgages, becoming delinquent on their loan repayments and often facing bank foreclosure. Second, as lack of buyers caused property values to fall about 10 percent, millions of other homeowners owed more on their mortgages than their homes were worth. Unable to sell to recoup their investment, many simply walked away. That double whammy resulted in more than 200,000 foreclosures monthly in 2008–2010 (Quinn 2010:8). Although members of all racial and ethnic groups have been hit hard by the foreclosure crisis, studies show that blacks and Latinos were 70 percent more likely to lose their homes, primarily due to their higher unemployment rates and fewer financial resources to fall back on (Merle 2010).

Although homeowners throughout the country were affected by the housing market crisis, the economic fallout was especially bad in Sunbelt metro regions. Of the 20 metro regions with the highest foreclosure rates in 2010, 19 were located in just three states: Nevada, California, and Florida. In Las Vegas, an astonishing 1 in 10 housing units went through foreclosure. In actual number of foreclosures (in contrast to rate), the three metro regions with the greatest totals were Miami (171,704), Phoenix (124,720), and Riverside (101,210). Nationwide, foreclosure rates were up in 72 percent of 206 U.S. metro areas in 2010 (Florida 2011).

The Inner City Today: A Revival?

> When a city begins to grow and spread outward
> from the edges, the center which was once
> its glory...goes into a period of desolation,
> inhabited at night by the vague ruins of
> men....Nearly every city I know has such a
> dying mother of violence and despair where
> at night the brightness of the street lamps is
> sucked away and policemen walk in pairs. And
> then one day perhaps the city returns and rips
> out the sore and builds a monument to its past.
>
> (John Steinbeck,
> *Travels with Charley*, 1962)

Although the success of public programs has surely been limited, efforts by private

groups to rebuild certain inner-city areas have achieved significant results in recent decades. In particular, two trends deserve attention: urban homesteading and gentrification.

Urban Homesteading. In 1973, burdened with some 1,200 abandoned homes, the city of Wilmington, Delaware, revived the mid-nineteenth-century Homestead Act that gave away land and mules to pioneers if they built on vacant land in the West and lived on it for five years. The city offered buildings it acquired through default of tax payments for a token fee of a few hundred dollars to people who agreed to rehabilitate them and stay there for a minimum of three years. Wilmington's success in restoring tax ratable properties encouraged many other cities to initiate their own homesteading programs, often transferring houses to people at the top of long waiting lists for Section 8 rental housing who were willing to become "urban homesteaders"—pioneers in rebuilding an urban area.

In New York's ravaged South Bronx, where more than 30,000 buildings were abandoned in the 1970s (an average of eight a day) and arsonists set many others ablaze, the neighborhood became known as the "worst slum in America" and the symbol of all that was wrong with cities. However, through a massive city government redevelopment program, a dramatic change occurred in the 1980s. Local citizens' groups and dedicated individuals stood up against seemingly impossible odds to return deteriorating inner-city buildings to life. With little capital to invest, such groups could rely only on their own physical efforts. Their collateral was not future earnings or other property but, rather, their own sweat, giving rise to the term *sweat equity*.

Urban homesteading, however, had only limited success, because too many abandoned homes were deteriorated and vandalized beyond rehabilitation. Others stood amid so much ruin and desolation that they were not worth salvaging. Furthermore, both the cost of repairing the building to meet occupancy code standards and the difficulty of getting rehabilitation loans eliminated most of the urban poor from participating in urban homesteading.

Still, some successes occur. A few years ago in New York City, for example, the Urban Homesteading Assistance Board turned over 167 apartments in the Lower East Side to squatters who had been living there. These squatters had invested time and money into making habitable these buildings abandoned by their owners. More than 800 abandoned buildings that the city acquired through foreclosure are now owned by tenants through low-income cooperatives. Each apartment had to be brought up to housing code standards, serve as the tenants' primary residence, and not be sold for a profit in an effort to bar speculators or absentee landlords (Steinhauer 2002).

Another form of urban homesteading requiring hundreds of hours of sweat equity of incoming homeowners is Habitat for Humanity. Habitat is a non-profit organization that utilizes volunteer labor and some donated materials from area churches and organizations to build new housing for low-income families. Those screened to become homeowners pay interest-free, low-mortgage loans and must work along with the volunteers to build their house. Since its founding in 1976, Habitat has built more than 30,000 houses across the United States and 2,000 in Canada, most in areas of massive urban blight, ultimately transforming many places into attractive, stable neighborhoods. The organization now has more than 1,500 local affiliates throughout Canada and the United States, plus another 550 active affiliates in more than 100 countries, where it has built some 400,000 homes (Habitat for Humanity 2011).

Gentrification. Unlike urban homesteading, which is limited to the reclamation of just a few buildings or blocks at a time, gentrification is a broader process. The word

Habitat for Humanity is a non-profit organization that builds new, low-income family housing. It has built more than 400,000 homes around the world to date through church fundraising, volunteer labor, and donated materials, including this effort for Katrina victims. How do urban homesteading projects, such as Habitat for Humanity and gentrification, offer a solution to problems of urban housing?

gentrification—coined by the wealthy "landed gentry" during the nineteenth century to describe the renovation of run-down London homes—today refers to the movement of more affluent individuals and families back into older, often decaying areas in the city. Virtually every major city in Canada and the United States is experiencing this spreading urban renaissance, following a path taken by Paris and London years earlier.

Today's gentry, like those of the past, are a rather select group of people. They are usually the cosmopolites or unmarried and childless groups, or "yuppies" discussed in Chapters 3 and 5. More to the point, they are people with enough money to buy a brownstone in Manhattan; a Society Hill townhouse in Philadelphia; a brick cottage in the German Village of Columbus, Ohio; or a Victorian house in San Francisco's Haight-Ashbury district or in Toronto's South Parkdale. Sometimes, however, working-class neighborhoods undergo gentrification while retaining their socioeconomic group identity, as in several of Baltimore's rowhouse districts.

Why, though, would middle-class people choose central-city neighborhoods when the trend in the last century was to escape to the suburbs? The reasons vary, but certainly, many find that the central city still has the greatest amount of variety and stimulation. Theaters, music, and chic stores—all flourish in the greatest concentrations downtown. Second, as we noted in Chapter 7, economic restructuring increased the number of administrative and professional jobs available in central cities. The well-paid "gentry" taking these jobs need a place to live and central-city living eases the time and costs of getting to work. Third, as more women enter the work force (59 percent of women were in the labor force in 2010) and two-career couples become common (54 percent of all married couples in 2010), the time needed to maintain a single-family suburban house often makes it too burdensome (U.S. Census Bureau 2012). Fourth, suburban housing is expensive, and while some central-city housing is extremely costly (brownstones in Manhattan often top $3 million), one can

still find bargains, particularly in districts where the average income is low. Fifth, and finally, remember that much central-city housing built from about 1880 to 1910 (except tenements) has a level of craftsmanship and quality—with details like solid oak floors and stained-glass windows—rarely found in today's suburbs.

Political economy theorists see gentrification as a logical inflow of investment capital. Beginning in the 1950s, investment capital moved out of the cities and into the suburbs, where profit rates were higher. Later, with the emergence of a "rent gap" (profits above costs) in the inner city, capital returned in order to make greater profits there, as low-valued property rose in value in gentrifying neighborhoods (Huang 2010; Sze 2010). This return to the inner city certainly contradicts the predictions about an ever-outward migration of the affluent made by Ernest W. Burgess in the 1920s (Chapter 6).

The New Urbanism

Perhaps the best-known critique of public housing came from Jane Jacobs in *The Death and Life of Great American Cities* (1993; orig. 1961), a still-influential book on urban form and function. Critical of conventional planners, Jacobs argued that the creation of housing projects as stand-alone entities was wrong in the first place, and as long as that conceptualization remains, nothing will overcome their stigma and unsafe environment. Instead, planners should seek physical changes that would integrate such places into the surrounding neighborhood so that both the previously isolated projects and the nearby community would benefit.

One of the most encouraging developments in restoring the vitality of older cities has been an approach in urban design called the **New Urbanism,** which includes sociological principles in physical planning. Initially a response to the perceived lack of community in sprawling suburbs, the New Urbanism caused a rethinking of the entire city. Some of the principles of the New Urbanism are walkability, connectivity, mixed use and diversity, mixed housing types, and a traditional neighborhood structure with public space at the center. Today, in both central cities and suburbs, the goal is creating spaces that encourage people to socialize and watch out for each other.

Seaside, Florida, offers one example. Built during the mid-1980s in Florida's Panhandle, this planned community has codes mandating that houses have front porches close to the sidewalk so that residents sitting outside can converse easily with pedestrians. The town boasts corner stores that serve a function more important than simply providing provisions. They are places where friends frequently come to chat with one another over a cup of coffee.

Far more impressive is what architects and planners influenced by the New Urbanism are accomplishing in old, urban, problem-infested neighborhoods.

Columbia Point/Harbor Point. In Boston, a government-funded housing project known as Columbia Point—built in 1953 on a small, swampy peninsula near the first suburbs of Dorchester and Roxbury—long stood as evidence for the insensitivity of urban planners. There, a full mile from the closest subway stop, architects originally laid out 28 bland, institutional-style buildings three and seven stories high. Further, the surrounding water and lack of roads isolated residents even more. With few stores in the area, shopping became a major effort, both more expensive and more time-consuming than for other city residents nearer the mainstream of Boston life.

Eventually, the 1,502-unit development fell victim to the same problems that plagued public housing nationwide. By the 1970s, crime was so rampant in Columbia Point that even ambulances refused to enter the project without a police escort. By 1984, only 350 families wanted to stay when, encouraged by the U.S. Office of Housing and Urban Development, the Boston Housing Authority leased the land for 99 years at $1 a year to a partnership of the remaining tenants and a private developer. Architects for the project decided to redesign Columbia Point, modeling it after some of Boston's active, thriving neighborhoods. Also influencing their design was the New Urbanism idea that cities are enriched by the creation of a "public realm" that highlights amenities such as waterfront views. Architects thus set down a new street pattern, with old-fashioned street lamps and benches, so that all residents would have a view of both the harbor and the Boston skyline, and enjoy the open, shared space of a large, grassy mall placed in the middle of the complex.

Reopened in 1990, what is now called Harbor Point is a mixed-income complex that appeals to people from all ethnic backgrounds and social classes, which ensures the diversity and stability of this revitalized community (Roessner 2000). Housing is now a mixture, with two-thirds market-rate apartments and one-third low-income housing, but with no physical distinctions between the two types of apartment buildings. Moreover, architects designed a variety of building types: blue and gray townhouses with wood clapboard siding as well as red and brown brick apartment houses. They remodeled 10 of old Columbia Point's flat-topped residential buildings with new peaked roofs, decoration, and a reddish stain to make them indistinguishable from the new buildings.

To free Harbor Point completely from the stigma of public housing, they added other visual subtleties, such as rounded and pointed rooftop gables. Still other centrally located amenities were added, including a health club, two outdoor swimming pools, tennis courts, ample parking, buses to and from the city center, and a waterfront trail for biking, jogging, or walking to downtown Boston. Small front yards, front doors and windows directly facing the deliberately narrow streets, and sidewalk activity all combine to create "eyes on the street" and a safe neighborhood (Goody and Chandler 2010).

Many consider Harbor Point to be a success model of urban revitalization. Critics claim that Harbor Point may have residents with mixed incomes but it has the "contrived variety of a planned community" and not the mixed uses that make city neighborhoods "hum" (Kamin 1995). Still, it stands as a successful

The new urbanism design of Harbor Point, which replaced Columbia Point, was modeled after thriving Boston neighborhoods, such as Back Bay. Mixed building types are set close together along narrow streets canted at a 45-degree angle to the water's edge, which opens views of the harbor and Boston skyline to all residents.

alternative to an urban nightmare and offers vivid testimony to the extraordinary transformations that the New Urbanism can achieve.

Water as an Amenity. Just as Harbor Point's architects redesigned its grid to enable all residents to enjoy the view of surrounding water, so, too, has the New Urbanism enabled many cities to rediscover the aesthetics and possibilities for social use of public space at water's edge (Whyte 2001; orig. 1980). Baltimore's Inner Harbor and New York's South Street Seaport are thriving, rebuilt areas enjoyed by tourists and natives alike. Chicago, Cleveland, Cincinnati, Louisville, and many other cities have converted decaying piers and waterfront properties into park areas and mixed-use sites. San Antonio converted what was essentially a narrow and dirty drainage canal into the charming, 2.5-mile cobblestone River Walk—with lush green lawns, flowering shrubs and trees, and a view of paddleboats—where one delights in many interesting shops,

restaurants, and night clubs. Here and at many other renovated water's-edge locales, cities have successfully merged social and commercial activities into a vibrant urban atmosphere.

Replacing High-Rises. As Harbor Point demonstrates, the New Urbanism is transforming public housing, as the "superblocks" of giant high-rises come down, replaced by modest townhouses and low-rise buildings that don't "look like projects." City after city have leveled entire blocks or more of these decaying buildings in crime-ridden slums and replaced them not only with low-rise apartments laid out to promote social interaction, but also with playgrounds, pleasant landscaping, and paths for bicycles and pedestrians.

Many cities have addressed the failure of high-rise public housing by blowing up the buildings. Scudder Homes—seven high-rises built in 1963 in Newark, New Jersey, to house 1,800 low-income families—are now gone, replaced by 150 single-family townhouses. Replacing the 1,206 units in that city's seven hulking, 13-story Stella Wright homes are townhouses for low- and moderate-income residents. In Atlanta, a developer demolished more than 1,000 housing units in Techwood Homes—the first U.S. public housing project, completed in 1935—to build a mixed-income "village," with new stores, community facilities, schools, and apartments. Today, this once predominantly black enclave has been transformed into Centennial Place, a residential complex of 900 units that is host to a variety of races, ethnicities, and income levels.

In Chicago, the Housing Authority demolished the Cabrini–Green high-rise project buildings that once housed as many as 13,000 residents and was notorious for its crime, gangs, and poverty. Its 65 acres now contain 2,000 units of new, low-rise housing units; a new Town Center; a 145,000-square-foot shopping center; new schools; an East Chicago District police headquarters; and a library. Half the housing units are sold at market prices, with another 20 percent reserved as "affordable" units for less-affluent working families, thereby creating a mixed-income site similar to Harbor Point and totally unlike the all-low-income site that Cabrini–Green once was (Lydersen 2011; Saulny 2007).

The designs of all three developments—in Newark, Atlanta, and Chicago—use grid patterns linking them to the surrounding neighborhoods rather than setting them apart, minding Jacobs's recommendation that housing projects be rewoven into the urban fabric. These rebuilding programs seek to achieve two key goals of the New Urbanism. First, don't isolate the poor by themselves but instead, create a mixed-income housing complex to integrate all strata of society. Second, create an environment that is physically attractive and facilitates walking and social interaction, fostering a sense of control and community among residents.

Limitations. As promising as the New Urbanism may be, three major problems prevent it from having a broader impact. First,

in every case noted, there are now fewer low-income housing units than before. As with post–World War II urban renewal, displacement of the poor has also occurred in these redevelopment projects. Of course, one might argue that at least some poor people are better off living in safer and more vibrant communities, but what of the rest who have been displaced?

Second, weaving a housing project into the surrounding area is enormously difficult in the midst of extensive, nightmarish ghettos. If little more than empty lots or bombed-out buildings are nearby, for example, reorganizing a public housing project as an inward-facing enclave may be the only strategy, at least in the short run.

Finally, even at its best, the New Urbanism cannot, by itself, address the extensive poverty that makes public housing such a problem in the first place. For instance, in San Francisco, the Robert Pitts Plaza development project in 1991 replaced a notorious, dangerous high-rise called Yerba Buena Plaza West. This 203-apartment, neo-Victorian complex in no way looked like a public housing development. Its architecture blended in with neighboring apartment buildings and included projecting cornices and pastel shades of blue—a far cry from the high-rise "boxes" so common in public housing. It also contained other amenities, such as an internal rectangular courtyard with lush sod, bushes, and neat lines of trees and also a colorful play set for children in a sand playground.

Three years later, though, broken glass lay everywhere. Gone were the sod and sprinkler heads; gone, too, were the bushes and plants, ripped out by vandals. Profane graffiti covered concrete seating ledges. Bars shielded ground-floor windows following a rash of burglaries suspected to have been committed by residents. Wire mesh covered many other windows, suggesting an escalating sense of fear. The problem was poverty, and all that went with it.

A Comparison. The situation at Robert Pitts Plaza improved for a while once this building complex became part of a larger, 19-block redevelopment area of Yerba Buena and a successful mixture of a wide variety of housing, cultural facilities, and open space. However, in 2011, the U.S. Department of Housing and Urban Development (HUD) gave this development one of its lowest ratings for failing to meet minimum standards for health, safety, and sanitary conditions (Bush 2011).

The lesson to be learned here is that new architecture and even new planning strategies, such as the New Urbanism, don't work if they have limited application. Robert Pitts Plaza reveals that simply replacing high-rise buildings with low-rise buildings, even if those buildings are wonderfully designed, is not enough. A more comprehensive approach is necessary. Harbor Point is a good example for at least the beginnings of connecting low-income housing to its surroundings— through a return to traditional urban forms that promote interaction and a mix of income groups to eliminate public housing's isolation. In short, any successful approach to improving urban life must take account of not only local planning considerations but also broader, structural concerns that include social stratification and the region's economy.

EDUCATION: THE URBAN CHALLENGE

Schools in urban settings face a variety of challenges, which are often more daunting than school districts elsewhere face. These difficulties include overcrowded schools, discipline and violence, high dropout rates, and issues of quality education and student learning outcomes. Moreover, many of these schools since the 1990s have become re-segregated, heavily filled with African and Hispanic American students, reversing an earlier trend of desegregation (Lane and White 2010). Cities also attract large numbers of immigrant families and children with limited English proficiency and a greater concentration of low-income families that, together with a weaker tax revenue base than most suburbs enjoy, place a heavy burden on urban schools to educate, fully and effectively, the students they serve.

Meeting the "No Child Left Behind" Challenge

The controversial No Child Left Behind Act of 2001 dramatically increased the role of the federal government in guaranteeing the quality of public education for all children. Its main provisions are increased funding for poor school districts, higher achievement standards for minority and poor students, and new measures to hold schools accountable for their students' progress. Significantly, it requires the annual administration of standardized tests in reading and math to all students in grades 3 through 8, with the results publicly reported according to income level, race, ethnicity, disability, and limited English proficiency. These results are then compared to an independent benchmark called the National Assessment of Educational Progress (NAEP).

Learning Outcomes. Before this legislation, most urban schools had a policy of **social promotions**—that is, moving children through grades with their age peers regardless of their actual learning achievement. Whatever merit this practice had, it led to a watering-down of course content because of the gradual but steady lowering of general class ability. As a result, it produced graduates deluded into thinking they had received an education when, in reality, many of them lacked even basic skills, requiring colleges to institute non-credit, basic skills courses for freshmen. No more. Published test results will identify schools in which students are not doing well on the tests. Those schools that fall behind may be subject to various "school improvement," "corrective action," or "restructuring" measures imposed by the state.

Of particular concern are the significant differences in scores on standardized achievement tests between urban and suburban students. One of the most common arguments advanced for these different outcomes is the role of social class in providing an advantage (for middle-class suburban students) or a disadvantage (for low-income urban students). Researchers such as anthropologist John Ogbu (2003), however, argue that even black students in affluent suburbs suffer from "academic disengagement," engendered by inappropriate sports and entertainment role models, a lack of parental involvement in their schooling, and a defeatist attitude resulting from a profound distrust of the establishment. Only an approach that reinforces positive study habits, recognizes achievement, and strengthens neighborhood schools as well as the students' resolve against attempts by peers to drag them down will overcome this problem (Ravitch 2010; Whittle 2005).

Language Proficiency. Immigration remains a challenging urban phenomenon, although it affects suburban and rural schools and communities as well. Large concentrations of immigrant children in metropolitan areas strain school resources because the students' language proficiency plays an important role in academic achievement and thus meeting NAEP standards. About 62 percent of all immigrants now choose to live in just 15 metropolitan areas: New York; Los Angeles; Miami; Washington, D.C.; Chicago; San Francisco; Houston; Dallas; Boston; Atlanta; San Diego; San Jose; Philadelphia; Seattle; and Riverside–San Jose, California (U.S. Office of Immigration Statistics 2011:17). Urban schools in these and other cities, therefore, must accommodate a large influx of immigrant pupils, and it is not unusual for a third or more of a school's population to lack proficiency in English (Zhou 2003). This creates the need for hiring a greater number of bilingual or English-as-a-second-language (ESL) teachers, in addition to teachers of regular subjects. The schools must also deal with other cultural adjustment issues, such as clothing, food, religious observances, role behavior, and parents whose own language and educational deficiencies may limit support for at-home study.

Environment. Whether immigrant or native born, many students come from home environments where poverty, family instability, or poor health may limit educational success. Other dangers or obstacles that can work against educators' goals are (1) conflicting values in the student's home or on the street

about the importance of education; (2) the lack of positive, academically successful role models; and (3) the presence of gangs, street crime, drugs, and violence. In 2007, a total of 34 percent of city students, 19 percent of urban fringe students, and 17 percent of town students in public schools reported a street gang presence at school, a fairly constant finding for the past several years (Robers, et al. 2010).

Funding. Further undermining academic achievement in many city schools is the lack of funding. Unlike affluent communities, cities lack the tax base to provide adequate per-student expenditures, even with additional state aid. As a result, students in urban schools are more likely to enter older, dilapidated buildings, where they face overcrowded classrooms with limited supplies, poor discipline, insufficient libraries and labs, and often, a shortage of qualified teachers. So far, the additional funding through the No Child Left Behind Act has not been sufficient to overcome the urban–suburban disparity in school funding.

To illustrate, in 2010 the Detroit education system—faced with a huge financial deficit—closed one-fourth of its 172 schools. School officials in Kansas City, Missouri, shut down even more to avoid bankruptcy by closing 26 of 61 schools. Other cities also struggle with dwindling enrollments as parents move their children from urban to suburban public schools, or into private schools (Wickham 2010). In Ontario a sweeping research report of urban–rural disparities said that public schools in cities of more than 200,000 lack the funding and aid they need to face the challenges of educating children, nearly half of them immigrants (Brown 2008).

Political Clout. Cities actually have limited control over their affairs, whether in education or in other areas, such as mass transit and poverty. Under the one-person, one-vote apportionment to balance legislative district representation, with the majority of the population now living in the suburbs, cities have fewer representatives in state legislatures. Added to the rural–suburban bias against cities is the frequent political split between

Democratic-controlled city governments and Republican-controlled state legislatures, further hindering efforts to solve urban problems.

Cities across the country are struggling to meet the federal government's demand to improve their schools. Some modest gains have occurred, but enormous challenges remain. For example, Chicago has been making a concerted effort to improve its educational system since passage of the Chicago School Reform Act in 1988 (see the *Urban Trends* box below). Notable improvements have occurred since

then, yet even now, fewer than half of its high school students graduate (Vevea and Yednak 2011). Perhaps with continued improvement at the elementary level, as mandated by the No Child Left Behind Act, Chicago and other cities will also see progress at the secondary level. It will take more than wishful thinking, however, to make this a reality.

A deepening dissatisfaction with traditional public schools has engendered several innovations to give parents other options for educating their children, thus providing

URBAN TRENDS

The New Urban Schools

Chicago's experience from 1988 through 2005 demonstrates that large urban school district reform is not only possible—it's powerful. In Chicago, reform has been based on a model that combines strong neighborhood and teacher involvement with school-based, decentralized authority at the local level.

Success in reform efforts has come primarily from activity at the local level and through the implementation of practices developed in the past 50 years by high-performing organizations. The district's central office, while it has provided positive support with union and financial issues, academic standards, training, coaching, and accountability, thus far has been unable to find a way to truly support all schools.

Improvements have been dramatic, but have taken hold only in about half of the low-scoring elementary schools. Close examination of the schools that have made steady and impressive progress on the one hand, and those that have not on the other, reveals clear lessons about what has worked and what has not worked in reform.

About half of the low-scoring public elementary schools in Chicago—181 schools—have made extraordinary gains and have sustained the process of continuous improvement. Three hundred and sixty of Chicago's elementary schools, 82 percent of the total number of elementary schools, had very low results on the 1990 Iowa Test of Basic Skills (ITBS) in reading. Nearly all the schools were in low-income neighborhoods.... [H]alf of these starting scoring at 20 percent and they now have 49 percent of their students at or above the national average on the norm-referenced ITBS—scoring as well as a representative sample of urban, suburban, and rural schools. (Norm-referenced tests are designed so that 50 percent of the students must fall below the national average.) The gains in math in the high gain schools were even better than in reading.

These impressive results may be better than those of any other large urban district between 1990 and 2005.

Source: John Simmons, *Breaking Through: Transforming Urban School Districts* (New York: Teachers College Press, 2006), p. 11.

competition in order to force all schools to do a better job. Three of the most popular programs to improve urban education are magnet schools, school vouchers, and charter schools.

Magnet Schools

Magnet schools—schools offering special programs, originally to attract students from many districts to achieve integration—began as an alternative to mandatory busing, but their success in raising students' scholastic achievement gained them even more popularity. They offer special facilities and programs to promote educational excellence in a particular area, such as computer science, foreign languages, science and mathematics, or the arts. Parents can choose the school that is best suited to a particular student's talents and interests, enabling these advanced programs to attract talented students from beyond traditional neighborhood boundaries. This permits magnet schools to overcome residential segregation patterns to create a more diversified student population. For example, Los Angeles magnet schools are less segregated than non-magnet schools (Straus 2010).

About 20 percent of U.S. students living in or around cities attend one of the nation's more than 3,000 magnet schools (National Center for Education Statistics 2011). Of these schools, however, about 21 percent are partial-site magnet schools (a mixture of traditional and special programs), resulting in desegregated buildings that have racially segregated classrooms. Critics charge that magnet schools are "elitist" in luring the best students and teachers, thereby relegating the majority of students to the "mediocrity" of ordinary city schools, and that they might even worsen stratification among schools by family income. Recent research, however, reveals no significant difference in school districts with or without magnet-school choice (Archbald 2004).

School Vouchers

Another option for choice in some school districts is to give parents a **school voucher** equal to the state's share of the cost to educate a child (usually about 90 percent of the average private school's tuition). Parents can then use this voucher to place their child in a public or private school of their choice. The program is limited at present, because there are not enough private-school spaces to meet demand. In such cases, a lottery usually determines who goes to choice schools. A federal voucher program operates in Washington, D.C., and among the cities utilizing their own school voucher plan are Cleveland, Indianapolis, Milwaukee, and Minneapolis. Critics (including teachers' unions) charge that this approach siphons off much-needed public education funding, thus undermining the nation's commitment to public education, and that it does little to improve central-city schools, where the need is greatest (Gorman 2003; Schemo 2006).

Because many of the private schools are church-affiliated, opponents of vouchers charge that this system violates the First Amendment provision concerning the separation of church and state. At the state level, recent court decisions have given mixed signals on this issue. The supreme courts of Arizona, Ohio, and Wisconsin ruled that voucher programs did not violate the state or federal constitution by including religious schools. In contrast, the supreme courts of Florida, Vermont, and Maine ruled against such schools on constitutional grounds. After years of conflicting lower-court opinions about parents in Cleveland using vouchers at private schools, the U.S. Supreme Court ruled in 2002 that they could do so. Experts believe this ruling may be as significant as the 1954 *Brown* v. *Board of Education* decision on school desegregation, because it gives the green light nationwide to this program (Brokaw 2002). As a possible portent in 2011, Indiana enacted the largest voucher program in the nation, making 60 percent of the state's students eligible within three years (Wolfgang 2011).

Charter Schools

Charter schools—now numbering more than 5,000—are a recent alternative to traditional public schools and, in cities where a voucher plan exists, they are a major beneficiary of such payments. Charters are private schools that operate with less state regulation so that teachers and administrators can try out new teaching strategies. Unlike public schools, however, they are held accountable for achieving educational results. If a school fails to meet the terms of its charter with the local school board or the state, the charter can be revoked and the school closed. In essence, then, a charter school receives greater autonomy to operate in return for greater accountability for student performance. Nationwide, charter schools enrolled 1.9 million students in 2011–2012 (Center for Education Reform 2011).

Authorized in 39 states and the District of Columbia, spaces in charter schools are in high demand, and small class size appears to be a principal reason for this. The average enrollment of charter schools is about half that of traditional public schools. Smaller classes afford teachers the space to be more creative with curriculum and the time to provide more individualized instruction. Whether for the arts- or science-oriented or for the at-risk, these schools provide assistance to students who are otherwise underserved by the public school system (Walberg 2007).

Supporters of charter schools hope that local educators, ministers, parents, community members, school boards, and other sponsors will provide new models of schooling and exert competitive pressures on public schools that will improve the current system of public education. Others, however, fear that charter schools, at best, may be little more than escape valves that relieve pressure for genuine reform of the whole system and, at worst, may add to centrifugal forces that threaten to pull public education apart (Buckley and Schneider 2009).

In fact, some charter schools are no better than their public school counterparts. Critics say that many have weak curricula and teaching, substandard buildings, and a surprising

Magnet schools—such as this one in Schenectady, New York—enable cities to overcome residential segregation patterns by offering special programs and facilities to raise students' scholastic achievement. Despite their success, critics complain that they are expensive, that they have limited appeal, and that their elitism relegates most urban students to "mediocre" schooling.

prevalence of financial abuses. Basic class-room supplies are often lacking, labs and libraries are rare, and staff turnover is high among the low-paid, inexperienced teachers. Also, the segregation of many charter schools along ethnic, racial, and religious lines has created church–state conflicts in conjunction with the voucher controversy (Carnoy, et al. 2005).

Originally designed to provide better schooling for minority students, the single biggest group in charter schools is now non-Hispanic whites (54 percent), compared to 18 percent non-Hispanic blacks and 22 percent Hispanics (Center for Education Reform 2011).

CRIME: PERCEPTION AND REALITY

The problems of poor housing and poor education affect only part of the urban population. Surveys suggest, however, that almost everyone expresses concern about the extent of crime. Often, people living in outlying areas point to fears about personal safety as the primary reason they chose not to live in the city. And many city people conclude that a higher risk of crime is just part of the price one pays for the advantages of urban living. Are such perceptions correct, however? Is crime worse in the city than elsewhere? Is there more crime in bigger cities than in smaller ones? Are visitors to the city more likely than residents of the city to fall victim to crime?

Urban crime gets extensive media attention and influences public perception. Yet the public's fear about crime overlooks the important fact that the U.S. crime rate is much lower than in previous years. The property crime rate (for burglary, motor vehicle theft, and property theft) has dropped 9 percent since 2006, and the violent crime rate (for murder, rape/sexual assault, robbery, and assault) fell 13 percent. In fact, these crime rates are far lower than they were in the 1970s, 1980s, and early 1990s (FBI 2011).

Crime in Canada has dropped steadily for 20 years and in 2010 was at its lowest level since 1973. Its homicide rate was the lowest since 1966, although sexual assaults increased

five percent from 2009, the first increase since 2005. Non-violent crime rates—for theft, break-ins, motor vehicle theft, and DUI—were all lower than in 2009, but drug offenses increased, continuing an upward trend that began in the early 1990s. Among metropolitan areas with populations exceeding 500,000, Toronto and Quebec had the lowest crime rates, while St. John's, Winnipeg, Edmonton, and Vancouver had the highest. A 2009 survey revealed that 93 percent of respondents said they felt safe from becoming a crime victim. Also, 90 percent said that they felt safe walking alone in their neighborhoods at night, in contrast to 63 percent of Americans (Gallup 2010a; Statistics Canada 2011a).

Public Perception of Crime

In a 2010 Gallup poll, 66 percent of respondents thought there was more crime in the United States than in the previous year; 60 percent thought the crime problem was "extremely serious" or "very serious," up from 55 percent in 2009. Yet 49 percent of these same respondents thought that the problem of crime where they lived was declining (Gallup 2010b).

In light of the facts, why do so many think that crime is such a serious problem? Part of the answer lies in more extensive news reporting of violent crime. An ABC News poll revealed that 82 percent of Americans said their perception of crime is based on what they read or see in the news; only 17 percent said that they base their views on personal experience (ABC News 2000). In addition, the frequent "promos" of upcoming violent crime stories, the popularity of "reality-based" crime dramas on broadcast and cable television, and tabloid sensationalism spread the image of crime well beyond the news programs themselves. Various studies have found positive correlations between TV viewing of crime news, crime fiction (e.g., *Law and Order*), and crime non-fiction (e.g., *Cops*) and concerns about crime (Dixon 2008; Grabe 2007; Kort-Butler and Hartshorn 2011).

Another concern is becoming the homicide victim of a stranger, which accounts for 29 percent of all murders. Also, drug- or gang-related shootings sometimes result in stray bullets killing innocent people, even in their homes or blocks away from the source. Most vulnerable are urban black males aged 18–24, who are twice as likely to be victims as are older black males. Although their victimization rates are much lower now than in the late 1980s and early 1990s, they are higher than those in earlier decades (U.S. Bureau of Justice Statistics 2010b).

Attitudes about crime, then, are a mix of facts and fears. To gain a more accurate sense of crime in the city, we need to look at additional statistics.

Crime and City Size. Most violent crimes take place in cities, often growing out of street, school, or social club altercations. Indeed, the negative attitudes of non-city dwellers and their reluctance to enter cities stem in large measure from their fear of becoming an urban crime statistic, but are cities really more dangerous? Table 12–1 compares crime rates in various types of communities.

Note the steady decline of crime rates in mostly all locales. Also note that violent crime rates are higher in large metropolitan areas than in smaller cities outside metropolitan areas and, especially, in rural (non-metropolitan) areas. Such data would seem to support the conclusion that large cities are dangerous places. Property crime rates, however, are higher in those smaller cities than in the metropolitan regions.

Louis Wirth, whose theory of urbanism was central to Chapter 5, might claim that the size, density, and social heterogeneity of cities are to blame. If this were true, however, we would expect the largest metropolitan areas to have the highest crime rates, which is not the case. As Table 12–2 shows, the highest crime rates occur in second-tier cities (those with populations from 500,000 to 999,999) and in smaller, third-tier cities (those with populations under 500,000).

These data point to the conclusion that although cities have higher crime rates than other types of communities, city size, by itself, does not explain crime rate. How else can we explain the fact that New York, the nation's largest city, has less crime per capita than all other U.S. cities with a population of 1 million or more? On a per-capita basis, New York City has at least three times less crime than Albuquerque, Miami, Memphis, New Orleans, Oklahoma City, Phoenix, and Tucson. Put differently, in 2010, New York City ranked 132 out of 400 U.S. cities, and it had a slightly higher crime rate than Lincoln, Nebraska (CQ Press 2011).

Before going further, however, a warning is in order. Crime statistics are notoriously imperfect. For example, many crimes are not discovered, or reported to police, or recorded carefully. All the statistics in Tables 12–1 and 12–2 reflect official police records. Many criminologists argue that a more accurate portrait of crime comes from the National Crime Victimization Survey that utilizes a representative sample of about 38,000 households. By questioning people (rather than police), the victimization survey uncovers many unreported crimes that are missed in

TABLE 12–1   Crime Rates per 1,000 Residents by Type of Community, 1980, 2000, and 2010

	Property Crime			Violent Crime		
	1980	2000	2010	1980	2000	2010
U.S. Total	53	36	25.2	5.8	5.1	4.1
Metropolitan Areas	61	39	30.5	7.0	5.6	4.3
Cities Outside Metro Areas	50	41	36.0	3.5	4.0	4.0
Non-Metropolitan Counties	21	17	16.1	1.8	2.1	2.0

Source: Federal Bureau of Investigation, *Crime in the United States* (2010), accessed online at http://www.fbi.gov/about-us/cjis/ucr/crime-in-the-u.s/2010/crime-in-the-u.s.-2010 on April 16, 2012.

TABLE 12–2   City Size and Crime Rates, 2010

Population Size	Violent Crime	Property Crime
1,000,000 or higher	7.2	31.4
500,000–999,999	8.1	45.9
250,000–499,999	7.6	42.2
100,000–249,999	5.2	38.5
50,000–99,999	3.9	32.3
25,000–49,999	3.3	30.2
10,000–24,999	2.9	28.8
Under 10,000	3.1	32.0
Suburban Areas	2.7	24.2
Non-Metropolitan Counties	2.0	16.5

Source: Federal Bureau of Investigation, 2010.

the crime index and crime rate calculations. While such studies confirm the decline in crime over time, they also suggest that the actual number of crimes may well be twice that of the official statistics.

Furthermore, criminologists agree that as with other problems, the amount of crime varies throughout the urban area. The greatest concentration of offenses occurs in inner-city districts with poverty-stricken, minority populations. In 2008, for example, members of the poorest U.S. households (those with incomes under $7,500) were far more likely to be assaulted or robbed than were those in higher-income households (U.S. Bureau of Justice Statistics 2010b). Urbanists at the University of Chicago first identified this pattern back in the 1940s, and it still holds true for both the inner city and the suburbs.

The Race Issue.   In the United States, discussions of crime almost always raise the issue of race, because many people link crime to non-white minorities. In truth, however, 69 percent of the arrests that police make for serious crimes involve white people (FBI 2011). Even so, relative to population size, African Americans are more likely to be arrested than whites.

Keep in mind, too, that crime is largely intraracial. To illustrate, 65 percent of single-offender violent crimes committed in 2008 by blacks were against black victims, and 67 percent of such crimes committed by whites involved white victims (U.S. Bureau of Justice Statistics 2010b).

Moreover, the crime problem is worst in overwhelmingly black urban ghettos, where homicide is at a crisis level. Blacks are six times more likely to be murdered than whites, and 90 percent of all black victims are killed by blacks. In 2010, blacks killed 2,458 blacks— only 318 fewer than the number of killings of whites by whites, who outnumber blacks by more than six to one (Federal Bureau of Investigation 2011). Nationwide, the leading cause of death for black males between the ages of 15 and 34 is, by far, homicide (National Center for Health Statistics 2011). In New York City, blacks comprise 25 percent of the population but were 67 percent of all homicide victims, with four in five of them killed by other blacks (New York City 2011).

Explaining High-Crime Areas

Why are some communities terrorized by crime? We know that the highest crime rates occur in the poorest sections of cities. Why? Social scientists offer a variety of theories to explain concentrations of urban crime. Four of the main causative explanations, some of them highly controversial, involve (1) cultural patterns, (2) lower intelligence, (3) persistent racial inequality and prolonged poverty, and (4) residential segregation. As we shall see, each position has both advocates and critics.

Cultural Patterns.   Edward Banfield (1990) claimed that crime flourishes in urban areas that are steeped in a lower-class culture, where people share a "present-time orientation," have low aspirations, and generally are morally irresponsible. Under such conditions, he contended, people victimize anyone who seems to be an easy mark, including one another.

Moreover, parents pass on these cultural patterns to their children, which explains the persistence of crime in some neighborhoods for decades. Rather than learning values and skills that ease their way toward success, children too often learn apathy, resignation, and fatalism; indifference toward schooling; a desire for immediate gratification; and a distrust of authority. In such an environment, crime simply thrives. Add to this the fact that high-crime neighborhoods tend to have high levels of single parenting, which means that children have less supervision, especially from fathers.

Critics of such a culture-of-poverty position responded that such cultural patterns should be viewed as the consequences, not the causes, of poverty. Among people who have few opportunities to work; are forced to live in crowded, run-down housing; and must contend with the worst schools a city has to offer, we should not be surprised that crime rates are high. Only structural changes that alleviate societal inequality are likely to bring about changes in the vicious circle of poverty and crime (Stricker 2007).

Lower Intelligence. In perhaps the most controversial effort to explain concentrations of crime and other social problems, Richard Herrnstein and Charles Murray asserted that criminality is concentrated in areas where average intelligence is low. In their book *The Bell Curve*, they suggested that crime—like poverty, welfare dependency, and illegitimacy—is strongly related to low IQ (1996:338–39). Because the more talented people have long since left the inner cities, these researchers continued, the plight of those who are left is worse than ever. And given the cause, even a compassionate public can do little about this problem.

Critics attacked this book on many fronts, suggesting that intelligence tests are unfair to begin with and that it is far from clear what intelligence really is (Fischer, et al. 1996; Willie and Taylor 1995). More specifically, numerous studies have shown that low-income people who test lower on IQ tests and scores typically find their scores improving as they achieve a higher socioeconomic status (Fraser 1995; Sowell 1977:57).

Persistent Racial Inequality and Poverty. Far broader support exists for the idea that the primary problem with crime lies in social structure, that the explanation for high crime rates lies in racial and economic inequalities (Fajnzylber, et al. 2002; Mechtenberg-Berrigan and Kramer 2008; Skrentny 2006).

Insofar as a city concentrates people of highly unequal incomes, those with less than others may see themselves as being unjustly deprived. Therefore, even in the absence of **absolute poverty,** a city with significant **relative poverty** could still breed resentment and crime. In other words, the minority poor may engage in more crime as offenders—and suffer more as victims—because they are heavily represented among the economically deprived (Blau and Blau 1982; Like 2011; Loury 2010; Shihadeh and Steffensmeier 1994).

Many researchers favor **general strain theory** (GST) as a way of understanding the connection between economic/racial inequality and crime. GST focuses on an individual's social environment, one in which a discrepancy exists between aspirations and achievements, between fair and actual outcomes, and with negative stimuli replacing positively valued stimuli (Agnew 1992). The resultant negative relationships and rejections feed alienation, frustration, and anger, all of which could possibly then motivate nonconforming or criminal behavior. Since African Americans disproportionately live in unique social conditions, experiencing qualitatively unique types of strain compared to whites, they may cope with strain and negative emotions through crime (Kaufman, et al. 2008). No universal pattern exists, however, because changing structural conditions (neighborhood demographics, competition, and racial inequality) can lead to differing rates of violence (McCall and Parker 2005).

Other social scientists favor the application of **social disorganization theory** to understand the connection between poverty and crime. The structure of socially integrated neighborhoods fosters an attachment among residents, which in turn prompts their exercise of informal social controls, resulting in safer neighborhoods with less street crime and vandalism (Burchfield 2009). Conversely, a weak social network among neighbors lessens the sense of community, leading to a breakdown in civic engagement and social controls, and in an inability to influence public behavior.

Once that absence of an interrelated social structure occurs, the probability of increased crime in that area is very real (Hipp 2010).

Residential Segregation. A fourth factor noted by social scientists to explain the high rate of African American crime is that residential segregation—from the time of slavery to the present—makes the black situation unique, even though a slow decline in residential segregation of African Americans has occurred since 1980 (see Table 12–3). In some smaller and newer metropolitan areas, their segregation from whites has declined markedly, but in the larger places where most African Americans live, segregation has remained high.

Recall in Chapter 11 our discussion of **hypersegregation**—the extensive segregation existing on many dimensions simultaneously. Although nine less hypersegregated metropolitan areas exist than in 1990, blacks remain especially disadvantaged and hypersegregated in 29 other metropolitan areas. The six most segregated of these are Chicago, Cleveland, Detroit, Milwaukee, Newark, and Philadelphia (Wilkes and Iceland 2004).

Many social scientists reject the notion that black urban crime is simply a product of individual failings, but rather a combination of several factors. William J. Wilson (2010)

TABLE 12–3   Most Segregated Metropolitan Areas, Black and White, 2010

Metropolitan Area	Index of Dissimilarity
1. Detroit–Livonia–Dearborn, MI	79.6
2. Milwaukee–Waukesha–West Allis, WI	79.6
3. New York–White Plains, Wayne, NY-NJ	79.1
4. Newark–Union, NJ	78.0
5. Chicago–Joliet–Naperville, IL	75.9
6. Philadelphia, PA	73.7
7. Miami–Miami Beach–Kendall, FL	73.0
8. Cleveland–Elyria-Mentor, OH	72.6
9. St. Louis, MO-IL	70.6
10. Nassau–Suffolk, New York	69.2

Source: John R. Logan and Brian J. Stults, "The Persistence of Segregation in the Metropolis: New Findings from the 2010 Census," US2010.

suggests that only a holistic public policy approach that recognizes the complex web of structural and cultural factors that create and reinforce racial exclusion and inequality will overcome the problems in inner-city black neighborhoods.

For some, such crime is "an inevitable outgrowth of social conditions created by the coincidence of racial segregation and high rates of black poverty" (Anderson and Massey 2001:334).

Two recent studies examined this relationship between black segregation and violent crime, one examining 201 metropolitan statistical areas (Eitle 2009) and the other 7,622 neighborhoods in 79 cities (Krivo, et al. 2009). The researchers found that black–white segregation far exceeded other variables, such as income inequality and poverty, in explaining intercity variations in the black murder rate.

Effects of Crime on Everyday Life

The toll of crime extends far beyond its immediate victims. For one thing, nothing pulls down property values like a high crime rate (Tita, et al. 2006). Owners lose equity in their investment, face high homeowners' insurance premiums, and lose neighbors or renters who otherwise would provide stability and community role models. If large numbers of people move out and cannot be replaced, owners may well abandon buildings they cannot sell, eroding the city's tax base. The vicious circle grinds on and on.

The fear of crime also reduces our use of public space. As William H. Whyte (2001:59) observed, "Streets are the rivers of life of a city. We come to partake of them, not to escape them." Certainly, in areas where people feel safe, extensive use of streets, parks, plazas, and other public places provides enjoyment for people at all hours of the day and night. Such urban areas contain the social dynamics and all the variety and excitement the city can offer. However, crime (or merely the fear of crime) restricts the use of public spaces. Another vicious circle is thus set in motion, because empty streets, plazas, and subway stations are unprotected and become ever more dangerous. In some communities, "take back the streets" campaigns have had some success, but the sad reality remains that urbanites' enjoyment of public space is more limited than it once was, especially after sunset, in too many areas.

What Is the Solution?

Can high crime rates in urban places be reduced? Is there a way to make our cities safe so that people can walk through a park in the daytime (let alone at night!) without fear? Here, again, a number of proposals are noteworthy, and New York City offers a positive model.

Physical Design. Urban planner Oscar Newman (1996) maintained that building design plays an important part in controlling crime. High-rise apartment blocks,

Newman explained, serve to encourage crime, because they isolate inhabitants from each other, creating many unwatched places where crime can easily occur. Instead, architects could design windows and entries in such a way that the paths of movement and the areas of activity provide inhabitants with continuous, natural surveillance of the street. Such designs create what Newman calls **defensible space,** allowing people to protect their own communities naturally, as they go about their daily lives, rather than relying on security guards and police for protection (see Figure 12–1 below).

To support his argument, Newman compiled crime data from various low-income public housing projects, first in New York and subsequently in other cities. He found that the average crime rate is higher in taller buildings (over six stories) than in lower

FIGURE 12–1 One example of defensible space is this courtyard with only one vehicular entrance route and footpaths and with many windows placed in buildings to overlook it. Such a design creates a sense of shared territorial ownership, creating an environment where the owners feel safe and the potential offender is aware of a substantial risk of scrutiny and apprehension.

Source: From http://tessellarsociety.blogspot.com/2007/05protection-from-crime.html. Reprinted with permission of the author.

A recent form of community policing in order to reduce crime in many North American cities has been the utilization of police officers on bike patrols, such as this multiethnic trio in Los Angeles. Using bicycles provides greater mobility and coverage of territory than covering a beat on foot, yet allows closer observation and interaction than in a car.

ones. Tall buildings with hundreds of living units are worst of all and appear to encourage isolation, stigmatization, apathy, neglect, and withdrawal, first by the residents, then by housing management, and finally, by the municipal agencies that service the project: police, education, parks and recreation, refuse collection, and social services (Newman 1996:28). Furthermore, in larger, taller buildings, crime occurs mostly in public areas—for example, elevators, halls, and lobbies—places that residents cannot easily monitor. Crime in such spaces is far less frequent in low-rise buildings, where residents can more easily supervise their surroundings.

Community Involvement. Improving the physical design of buildings appears to be a partial solution to the problem of urban crime. Regardless of architectural design, however, residents of a building must be motivated to notice and respond to potentially criminal situations. For example, neighborhoods in which a greater sense of community

exists are where greater crime prevention and deterrence occur (Lee and Earnest 2003).

Another crime-fighting strategy is the use of Neighborhood Crime Watch organizations. Through this association, neighbors look out for each other, for community members' families and properties, and they alert the police about any suspicious behavior or crime in progress. Studies have found that this is an effective means to reduce neighborhood crime (Gaspers 2006; Pattavina, Byrne, and Garcia 2006; Sanders 2000).

Get Tough. The term *zero tolerance* became a popular catchphrase in the 1990s in its repeated use by politicians, police leaders, policy makers, and the media (Newburn and Jones 2007). The model for North America was the crackdown by New York City police on all minor offenses; they arrested tens of thousands of people for subway fare evasion and all forms of disorderly behavior, such as drunkenness, urination, graffiti, vandalism, begging, and vagrancy. Under the belief that reduction of minor offenses would reduce all crime and create safer neighborhoods, the mayor and police commissioner pointed to the drop in the violent and property crime rates each year thereafter. New York's success was not lost on leaders in other cities and they adopted similar policies. In the mid-1990s, Canadian federal and provincial governments also adopted zero-tolerance policies (DeKeseredy 2009). Critics argue that crime rates were already dropping prior to this action and that statistics show zero tolerance was not an effective way to reduce crime, and that improvement in police–community relations is more successful (Silverman 2004).

New York City. Officials also enacted stronger community and strategic policing measures as well as a "get tough" approach. **Community policing** is an approach that increases interaction and cooperation between law enforcement agencies and the people and neighborhoods they serve. The focus is not just on responding to crime, but forging a partnership with citizens to identify and resolve problems, assign officers to a specific geographical area on a permanent basis, empower them to speak to neighborhood groups, participate in business and civic events, and otherwise participate positively in community life.

Strategic policing is an aggressive tactic of deploying increased patrols, decoys, and sting operations in locales identified through frequent computer analyses as high-crime areas. New York's success (violent crime dropped almost in half) made it a model for other cities. Homicides, for example, were 536 in 2010, compared to 2,245 in 1990, which is a truly remarkable achievement. As some critics see it, however, "get tough" approaches do little to solve the root causes of crime; rather, they deal only with the consequences.

Ultimately, achieving long-term reductions in crime probably depends on increasing economic opportunity in poor communities. Doing so may involve providing greater mobility for inner-city residents so that they are able to reach jobs on the metropolitan periphery, or providing job training and economic incentives through government to encourage businesses to locate in economically depressed areas. In addition, of course, community efforts at policing the streets, greater involvement by churches and local community groups, and efforts at upgrading neighborhoods, such as that by Habitat for Humanity, all will help. Fortunately, many city leaders recognize these needs and are taking steps to improve living and employment conditions.

SUMMARY

Poor housing, substandard education, and crime are three significant problems that plague our cities. Certainly, there are others, including environmental pollution, inadequate public transportation, and governmental corruption. This chapter highlighted housing, education, and crime, because the progress made so far in these areas offers the promise of more within our lifetimes.

All urban problems closely link to the state of a city's economy and, especially, to the extent of urban poverty. Thus, we can see that urban problems are complex, interrelated issues, such as poverty, crime, and drug abuse, with roots that extend beyond a particular city to society as a whole.

In the 1930s, as part of Franklin Roosevelt's New Deal, the federal government first enacted public housing policies. Financial assistance to homeowners and builders, together with public works programs, quickly improved urban housing. Even so, by 1940, some 40 percent of U.S. urban housing still lacked amenities such as adequate indoor plumbing. The Housing Act of 1949 launched urban renewal programs and initiated the construction of more public housing. Private developers, however, never provided anywhere near as many low-income housing units as were torn down, resulting in the displacement of the poor. Moreover, high-rise public housing stigmatized and isolated the poor and created unsafe neighborhoods. Rent subsidies were a better idea, giving families choices other than public housing.

Rising taxes and increased maintenance costs, coupled with rent levels limited by local policy and the inability of tenants to pay, eventually resulted in hundreds of thousands of landlords abandoning buildings. More recently, urban homesteading, gentrification, and the New Urbanism improved the urban scene. Each approach has limitations, however, and none can solve all the cities' housing problems.

Beset by problems of old buildings in need of repair, limited funding, a growing minority student population with limited English proficiency, a shortage of qualified teachers, and inadequate teaching resources, the nation's urban schools face serious challenges in their efforts to provide a quality education. A deepening dissatisfaction with the failure of urban schools to do their job has led to alternative approaches. Magnet schools, vouchers, and charter schools become more popular each year, but they also have their critics. Charges of elitism, violation of church–state separation, and the siphoning off of much-needed funds for urban public schools are controversies that surround these innovations.

Rates of serious crime are going down (although remaining high among juveniles). Media coverage and the fear of stranger-on-stranger violence, however, have raised public worries about crime. The greatest concentration of crime is in poor inner-city neighborhoods. Various explanations for the existence of high-crime areas highlight cultural patterns, alleged intellectual deficiencies, persistent racial inequality and poverty, and residential segregation.

Crime victimizes everyone by eroding property values, increasing insurance premiums, and generating a climate of fear. Crime also reduces the use of parks, streets, and mass transit, denying urbanites free use of their city.

Trying to build "defensible spaces" is a partial solution to the crime problem, as are "get tough" policies that target vulnerable areas for extra police protection. Yet neither approach can ultimately solve the problem of crime. Strengthening families in order to provide good adult role models for young people, generating jobs for adults, and building a sense of community through churches and other local organizations are also needed.

CONCLUSION

While there is some reason for pessimism and concern, recent decades have witnessed positive signs of improvement in urban life. For example, New York City dramatically curtailed violent crime. Many other cities have also reduced crime, but whether this trend will persist remains to be seen. Similarly, time will tell whether the recent innovations in housing and education improve the quality of life and the life chances for all segments of the cities' population. As cities convert the failed high-rise projects to more livable, mixed-income housing complexes that no longer isolate and stigmatize the poor, they are guided by important lessons learned from the past. What is happening to cities in developing countries, however? Are they learning from Western mistakes, or is their situation even worse? In the next chapter, we will discuss Latin American, African, Middle Eastern, and Asian cities to learn the answers.

KEY TERMS

absolute poverty (344)
charter schools (339)
community policing (348)
defensible space (346)
eminent domain (325)
general strain theory (344)
gentrification (332)
hypersegregation (345)

magnet schools (339)
New Urbanism (332)
relative poverty (344)
school voucher (339)
social disorganization theory (344)
social promotions (336)
strategic policing (348)
urban renewal (325)

INTERNET ACTIVITIES

1. *The Condition of Education* is an annual assessment of educational quality with different special features each year. At *http://nces.ed.gov/programs/coe/analysis/ 2010-section1b.asp*, you will find an analysis of student academic performance in central-city schools.

2. At *http://www.fbi.gov/about-us/cjis/ucr/ucr*, you can access the latest statistics from the Federal Bureau of Investigation in its *Uniform Crime Reports*. Click on a year (not preliminary findings), and explore the data tables for cities, suburbs, and nonmetropolitan regions.

CHAPTER 13

CITIES IN THE DEVELOPING WORLD

LATIN AMERICAN CITIES
    Early Cities
    European Dominance
    Modern Cities
AFRICAN CITIES
    Early Cities
    European Dominance
    Modern Cities
MIDDLE EASTERN CITIES
    Islamic Cities
    European Dominance
    Modern Cities
    New Cities
ASIAN CITIES
    India
    China

Japan
Southeast Asia

COMMON LEGACIES
    Economic Legacies
    Political Legacies

COMMON PROBLEMS
    Spiraling Populations
    Quality of Life
    Environment
    Shantytowns

SUMMARY

CONCLUSION

KEY TERMS

INTERNET ACTIVITIES

When most of us think of large cities, we usually imagine towering New York City or sprawling Los Angeles. The largest city in the Western Hemisphere, however, is São Paolo, Brazil, with a population of about 11 million, and Mexico City follows, with a population of 8.8 million. The 23 million inhabitants of Shanghai easily surpass New York City's 8.4 million, while the 12.3 million people in Mumbai (Bombay) are more than three times the population of Los Angeles (4 million).

These major cities, and many others throughout Africa, Asia, Latin America, and the Middle East, have an urban history unlike that of Canada and the United States. That past explains, in part, their present situation. All of these regions had indigenous cities that fell under the control of colonizers but that eventually gained their political independence. Today, these areas are in the midst of rapid and far-reaching urban transformation and are growing at a startling rate, as vast numbers of people pour into their cities. Furthermore, as explained in Chapter 7, the economic well-being of these cities (as well as of those in Canada and the United States) is linked to a world-systems economic arrangement in which the more-developed countries affect the fortunes of cities in the less-developed countries.

Mexico City symbolizes in many ways the current state of poor cities around the globe. Pouring in are tens of thousands of people who must compete for extremely limited resources. Not surprisingly, those meager resources are not shared equally. Nowhere in sub-Saharan Africa is there a metropolitan area approaching the size of Cairo (at 10.9 million, it is the continent's megacity), but large cities are numerous throughout Africa. Lagos, Nigeria, boasts 10.2 million inhabitants, while Kinshasa, Congo (formerly Zaire), has 8.4 million inhabitants. Bangkok, Thailand, has 6.9 million.

Moreover, **primate cities** (principal cities that are extremely large compared to other cities in the country) dominate a great many countries in the developing world. In many cases, a single city is home to more than half a country's urban population (see the *Urban Trends* box on page 353).

This chapter explores the development of cities throughout the developing world, with an eye to what they have in common, how they vary, and how they compare with Canadian and U.S. cities. This is a formidable task. Africa and Asia are vast continents of striking geographical and cultural contrasts. Africa has more than 1,000 spoken languages, and Asia has four major cultural traditions (in China, India, Japan, and Southeast Asia). Latin America, although it mostly shares a Spanish heritage, nonetheless varies significantly from one country to another in its population composition, resources, and economic development. The Middle East (Western Asia) is a region where countries (and their cities) vary considerably in economic development, political structure, and quality of life. Still, many common elements exist in the global urbanization that we are witnessing.

From the standpoint of world-systems analysis, no developing country is a core nation in the global economy. In Latin America, Mexico, Venezuela, Argentina, Brazil, and Chile are in the semi-periphery; the rest are in the periphery. Most African countries are in the periphery, with Nigeria and South Africa in the semi-periphery. Saudi Arabia and the Asian countries that we feature in this chapter are also in the semi-periphery, except China, which is rapidly emerging as a core nation. Each country's place in the global hierarchy affects the economic well-being of its cities.

Before we look at various parts of the world, we must first remind ourselves of a point made in Chapter 1. Because countries vary widely in how they define "city" or "urban," cross-national comparisons are difficult in any urban study. For our purposes, the populations given in this book are calculated according to each country's definition and so cannot be exactly compared to the populations of cities in other countries.

LATIN AMERICAN CITIES

Today's Latin American cities—Rio de Janeiro, Brazil; Buenos Aires, Argentina; Bogotá, Colombia; Santiago, Chile; Lima, Peru; Mexico City, Mexico—did not exist before the

URBAN TRENDS

The Evolution of Primate Cities

A *primate city* is one that grows in population and influence far beyond other cities in a nation or region. In many poor countries, the largest city may have several times the combined population of the two or three next-largest cities. Primate cities thus resemble, to use Alejandro Portés's metaphor, "gigantic heads on dwarfish bodies" (1977:68), absorbing an enormous portion of the available labor, trade, and population.

The extent of the dominance by a primate city in its own country can be shown using a **primacy ratio,** which is computed through dividing the primate city's population by the population of the second-largest city in the country. The following table shows some examples.

Note that with the exception of four cities, the primacy ratios for most of the largest cities of the developed world are relatively low. This suggests that primacy is linked to more than a good location and established trade patterns. Recent research suggests that primate cities develop more frequently in (1) small countries (Copenhagen and Vienna are clear examples); (2) countries that, for historical reasons, have only one or a few cities with anything approaching modern facilities (certainly true of poor countries around the world); and (3) countries that once were or still are under foreign control either politically or economically (colonial or postcommunist cities, for example).

Selected Developing World Cities in 2010*		Selected Developed World Cities in 2010*	
Monrovia, Liberia	24.7	Budapest, Hungary	8.3
Bangkok, Thailand	18.2	London, England	7.5
Luanda, Angola	15.9	Vienna, Austria	6.6
Conakry, Guinea	14.0	Bucharest, Romania	6.2
Ulan Bator, Mongolia	13.9	Copenhagen, Denmark	4.9
Asmara, Eritrea	11.4	Prague, Czech Republic	3.3
Kigali, Rwanda	11.0	Paris, France	2.6
Lima, Peru	10.8	Tokyo, Japan	2.4
Addis Ababa, Ethiopia	11.8	Moscow, Russia	2.3
Beirut, Lebanon	8.7	Warsaw, Poland	2.3
Lomé, Togo	8.7	Zurich, Switzerland	2.3
Nouakchott, Mauritania	8.3	New York, USA	2.2
Bamako, Mali	8.0	Rome, Italy	2.1
Antananarivo, Madagascar	7.8	Athens, Greece	2.0
N'Djamena, Chad	7.5	Berlin, Germany	1.9

Note: *All ratios computed from populations reported in "Nations of the World," *Britannica Book of the Year* (Chicago: Encyclopedia Britannica, 2011).

ntury. They, and many others, are
ts of **colonization** by Spanish and
e conquerors. Before the founding
of su~ ~ties, however, other complex urban
centers existed. The most outstanding examples were the capitals of the Mayan and Aztec
civilizations in Central America and Mexico
and of the Inca Empire on the western coast of
South America.

Early Cities

Of the many pre-Columbian cities—including
Teotihuacan, the Mayan capital located
in central Mexico, and Cuzco, the Inca
Empire's capital city in southeastern Peru—
perhaps Tenochtitlán offers the most poignant example of an awe-inspiring but lost
city (see the *Cityscape* box below). Originally

CITYSCAPE

The Magnificent City of Tenochtitlán

The Aztecs built Tenochtitlán
into an island metropolis of incredible magnificence. Situated
amid the calm, clear, turquoise
waters of Lake Texcoco and
linked to mainland suburbs by
three great paved causeways,
Tenochtitlán had a population
of about 350,000 by the end of
the fifteenth century. With its
pyramid temples and elegant
palaces—together with its spotless streets, broad
plazas, and exotic gardens—Tenochtitlán was
probably, after Rome, the world's greatest city.

In 1519, the Spaniard Hernan Cortés and his
men gazed with disbelief on this city. Cortés
later described it as "the most beautiful city
in the world," and one of his soldiers, Bernal
Diaz, described the Spanish reaction this way:

> We were amazed.... [I]t was like the enchantments they tell of in the legend of Amadis, on
> account of the great towers and [temples] and
> buildings rising from the water, and all built
> of masonry. And some of our soldiers even
> asked whether the things that we saw were not
> a dream.... I do not know how to describe it,
> seeing things as we did that had never been
> heard of or seen before, not even dreamed
> about. (Stannard 1993:4)

Matching the city's splendor was the cleanliness of its streets, people, and water supply:

> Criss-crossed with a complex network of canals, Tenochtitlán in this respect reminded

the Spanish of an enormous Venice; but it
also had remarkable floating gardens that reminded them of nowhere else on earth. And
while European cities then, and for centuries
afterward, took their drinking water from the
fetid and polluted rivers nearby, Tenochtitlán's
drinking water came from springs deep within
the mainland and was piped into the city by a
huge aqueduct system that amazed Cortés and
his men—just as they were astonished by the
personal cleanliness and hygiene of the color-
fully dressed populace, and by their extrava-
gant (to the Spanish) use of soaps, deodorants,
and breath sweeteners. (Stannard 1993:5)

Commerce was the lifeblood of the city, and
especially impressive to the Spanish visitors
was the enormous so-called Great Market
that sprawled across the city's northern end:

> This area, "with arcades all around," according to Cortés, was the central gathering place
> where "more than sixty thousand people come
> each day to buy and sell, and where every
> kind of merchandise produced in these lands
> is found..." (Stannard 1993:6)

So great was the variety of food, animals and
birds, metals, herbs, clothing, pottery, housewares, sweets, wines, timber, tiles, firewood,
and charcoal for sale, that Diaz wrote,

> Some...among us who had been in many
> parts of the world, in Constantinople, all over
> Italy, and in Rome, said that so large a marketplace and so full of people and so well
> regulated and arranged, they had never beheld
> before. (Stannard 1993:7)

received hospitably, Cortés and his forces encircled Tenochtitlán in April 1521, cut off its food and water for three months, and then entered the city as its conquerors in August. To ensure that the remnants of the proud Aztec Empire never rose again, Cortés utterly demolished Tenochtitlán and, on its rubble, erected a city focused around a completely European culture. He called it *Ciudad Imperial de Mexico*—Mexico City.

During the conquest of the Inca Empire in Peru about a decade later, Francisco Pizarro followed the same pattern. He conquered and destroyed the Inca cities and replaced them with Spanish cities. All over Latin America, newly constructed colonial cities served as administrative centers for local domination and export-oriented trade. Inland settlements such as Mexico City were linked with port cities such as Vera Cruz (Figure 13–1, page 356). Where no important port existed, the Europeans built one: Lima (Peru), Valparaiso (Chile), Buenos Aires (Argentina), and Rio de Janeiro (Brazil) are examples (Figure 13–2, page 357). The "trade" of these cities, however, was a one-way operation, with precious gold, silver, tobacco, and coffee shipped to Spain and Portugal to help these nations become rich and powerful.

European Dominance

The strategic location of most of these cities in relation to the hinterland also allowed colonists to dominate the native population. Ensconced in fortifications on the coast, the Europeans could defend themselves from internal attack and receive supplies from the sea. Such battlements also protected them from an external enemy—pirates—who lusted after the wealth these cities harbored.

One of the most tragic aftermaths of the conquest was the literal decimation of the indigenous population. In scarcely a single century, the native population plummeted from more than 25 million to, perhaps, 1 million. Among the many reasons for this frightening loss of life, foremost were the brutal wars with the colonists and the toll taken by European diseases, such as measles and smallpox,

against which the indigenous people had no biological defense.

Imposing European culture on Latin America had other long-lasting effects. Decreeing a set of principles called the "Laws of the Indies," the Spanish constructed all their new cities along similar patterns, resulting in the breakdown of local cultural patterns. Although local geography and earlier customs brought some variations, most colonial cities were constructed around a grid plan with a central plaza—the *plaza mayor*. At one end of the plaza was an imposing Catholic church. On the other three sides were government offices, residences of the wealthy, and some businesses. Such a design established the dominant institutions of European culture—church, state, elite power, and commerce—in the heart of the city.

Around the city center, in a second district, were the residences of the city's middle class: artisans, government clerks, and small merchants. Farther out still, in a third zone, were the much more dilapidated residences of the city's poor. Finally, on the outskirts were large parcels of land originally called *encomiendas*, given in trust to the local elite by the Spanish government. After independence in the nineteenth century, many of these large parcels of land became part of the equally exclusive *hacienda* system: large farms or ranches run by elites and worked by serfs.

Although physically similar to European cities, these preindustrial colonial cities were even more exclusive, favoring a small and extremely powerful elite of European descent. Under normal circumstances, native Latin Americans could never become members of the elite. Although remnants of pre-Columbian culture remained—particularly in rural communities—the dominance of colonial cities in Latin America ensured the dominance of European culture in most areas of life (Skidmore, et al. 2010).

By the early 1800s, local insurgents, such as Simón Bolivar, mounted frequent challenges to colonial governance. Soon after a series of wars for independence (1816–1825), most Latin American nations gained their freedom. With colonial restrictions removed,

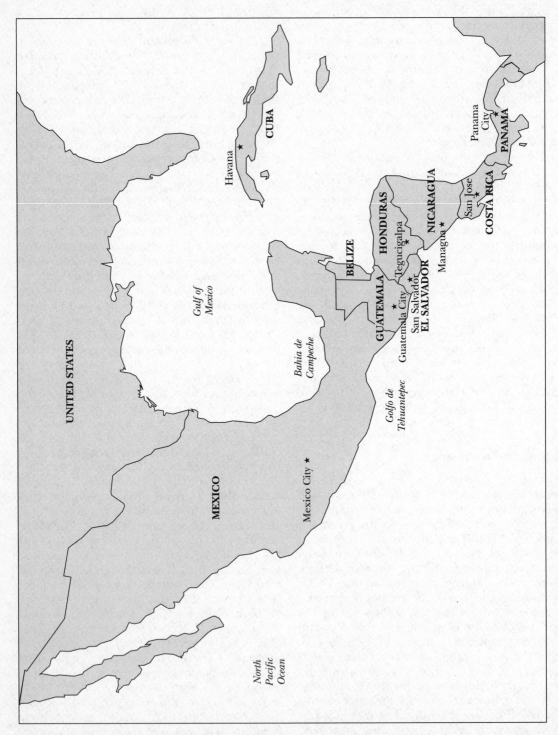

FIGURE 13–1 Map of Major Central American Cities

FIGURE 13–2 Map of Major South American Cities

Throughout Latin America, the Spanish influence manifests itself in both architecture and urban design. One common feature is a large church or cathedral, as well as a government palace, adjacent to or dominating a central plaza in the heart of the old city area. Illustrating this pattern is Murillo Plaza in La Paz, Bolivia.

many Latin American cities began to prosper through trade with cities in England, France, and the United States. By 1900, although the population remained decidedly rural, Mexico City, São Paolo, and Santiago each grew to over a half-million inhabitants, while Buenos Aires and Rio de Janeiro increased to more than a million (Eakin 2007:230). Similar patterns appeared in Montevideo, Caracas, Lima, and Havana. Indeed, by the early twentieth century, these few cities had grown so much that they dominated all the other cities in their respective countries.

Modern Cities

Not all of the growth in Latin American cities resulted from rural migrants seeking greater economic opportunity. Some was attributable to immigration between 1860 and 1930, as Latin America absorbed millions of Jews, Russians, Poles, Italians, Swiss, and Germans. Because of their generally higher level of education and greater familiarity with business, these immigrants soon came to control much

of the medium-scale commerce of many Latin American cities, dominating such areas as construction, small industry, and artisan and craft activities. As a result, immigrants occupied many middle-class jobs at the expense of the impoverished indigenous population also streaming into the cities of Argentina, Brazil, Paraguay, and Uruguay (Eakin 2007:230–35).

Most Latin American cities have not followed the pattern of rapid industrialization typical of Europe, Canada, and the United States. Despite a century and a half of independence, Latin American cities, in terms of wealth and productive capacity, lag far behind the cities of these other regions.

Why? First, most Latin American cities were, from the outset, export-oriented. Their valued products or raw materials—gold, silver, cattle, coal, oil, grains, coffee, fruits, and wool—were sent to other countries; they were not consumed by their own populations. The demand by other nations for these goods did not change after independence, and Latin American cities continued such one-way trading. The problem is that selling raw materials generates far less money than processing and marketing finished products. As a result, Latin American cities generated much less wealth than cities engaged in processing and distributing goods to consumers.

Second, with exports of raw materials as their primary source of wealth, most Latin American cities never developed much of an industrial base. Modern cities without major industries not only develop fewer jobs for their populations, but also cannot compete on numerous levels (skilled labor, investment opportunities) with those cities that have them. Consequently, export-oriented cities simply fall further behind their industrialized counterparts, leading to a worsening gap between "the rich nations" and "the poor nations."

Many urbanists argue that rich nations and their corporations contributed significantly to this problem (Armstrong and McGee 2007; Geisse and Sabatini 1988; Greenfield 1994; Morse and Hardoy 1993). Still seeking raw materials and cheap labor in Latin America, these countries and corporations have thrown their aid and political support to Latin American governments that favored export over local development. Many Latin American business and government elites have become rich "playing ball" in this way, but this pattern has done little for the overall development of their countries. Thus, the old colonial pattern of external domination is preserved in another guise.

Some Latin American countries—particularly Argentina, Brazil, and Mexico—have benefited somewhat by gaining the industrial operations that closed down in postindustrial nations such as the United States. Notably, Brazil has emerged as the world's fifth-largest economic power (behind the United States, China, India, and Russia). Consequently, its largest cities (including São Paolo, Rio de Janeiro, Salvador, Brasilia, Fortaleza, and Belo Horizonte)—although beset by many problems—also stand to benefit by the nation's rapidly growing economic prosperity (Brainard and Martinez-Diaz 2009; Roett 2011). Brazil's hosting the 2016 Olympic Games will further add to its recognition as a country becoming a major player on the world stage.

AFRICAN CITIES

African urbanization is uneven, with most contemporary African cities located either on or near the continent's coastlines (Figure 13–3, page 360). The greater urbanization on Africa's northern coast is a historical legacy of trade, both with Europe and with the Islamic countries of the Middle East. To reach Europe, Africans transported their goods from the interior, crossing the forbidding Sahara Desert and then loading them onto ships that plied the Mediterranean or sailed Europe's western coast. Established during seventeenth- and eighteenth-century European colonization to facilitate exports (including slaves), cities on Africa's western and eastern coasts soon became the most technologically and economically developed settlements on the continent.

Early Cities

Complex civilizations, complete with highly developed urban centers, existed in Africa as early as 3000 B.C.E. One such civilization, Kush, with its core cities of Meroë, Musawarat, and Naga, was centered about 100 miles north of the modern city of Khartoum. Archaeological evidence reveals these Kushite cities, though originally imitators of the ancient cities of Egypt, were also highly sophisticated. By 590 B.C.E., Meroë traded extensively with Saharan and Mediterranean peoples in slaves, gold, ivory, iron, and copper (Wenke 2007). In fact, Meroë's trade in copper was so extensive that great slag heaps from the manufacturing process are still evident in the city's ruins.

Other early African cities, particularly those in the sub-Saharan region, served as capitals of indigenous African empires, as craft or manufacturing centers, or as break-of-bulk points on major trade routes. Gao, in present-day Mali, was built in the seventh century C.E. as the capital of the Songhai Empire. More impressive was Kumbi, capital of the Empire of Ghana around 1000 C.E. Backed by a large army equipped with iron weapons, Kumbi had an estimated population of 30,000, supported by a rural population numbering in the hundreds of thousands. Trade

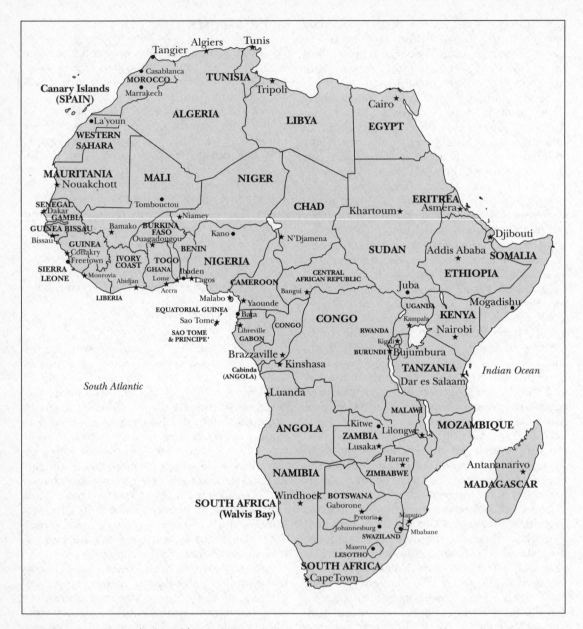

FIGURE 13–3 Map of Major African Cities

in gold and ivory—as well as in salt, kola nuts, slaves, and iron weapons—provided the empire's economic base (Wenke 2007).

In the eighth century C.E., shortly after the establishment of Islam as a major religion, cities based on trade with Arab countries and

the East began to appear throughout Africa, such as Mogadishu in Somalia and Mombasa in Kenya. As exchange became more lucrative, the Muslim traders transformed the North African cities into major shipping centers to Europe. Their trade networks linked

Taroudannt, Morocco, is a city of 30,000 that traces its origins to the eleventh century. Its sixteenth-century, 23-foot, fortified walls are in excellent condition and still define three-fourths of the city's borders. Walled cities once existed on all continents except Antarctica as a defensive measure, and those that remain offer vivid testimony to how cities once defined their boundaries.

these cities to dozens of inland, sub-Saharan cities to the south. One such city was Kano, founded in 999 C.E. Another was the legendary Timbuktu, founded in 1100 C.E. and, with its stone palaces, many-windowed homes, university, and bustling marketplace, became the intellectual capital of western Sudan.

All these early African cities were typical, preindustrial cities with a walled enclosure, narrow and winding streets, and daily life organized around religion and crafts. Residence was often determined by craft—for example, metalsmiths might cluster together—or by tribal or religious affiliation. Rich and poor, commerce and residences, all intermingled within shared city areas.

European Dominance

Slavery has a long history. Ancient Egyptians, Greeks, and Romans, for example, regularly subjugated those they conquered. Among Africans, this practice also stretched far back into the past. An export trade in slaves was fairly modest, amounting to about a few thousand each year until the fifteenth century. Thereafter, the European opening of Africa stimulated the slave trade for the next 400 years, with more than 11.3 million slaves transported across the Atlantic (Lovejoy 2000:15–18). Traders enlisted the aid of a cadre of professional slave traders—Europeans, Muslims, and Africans—to bring the "black gold" to market at Daka in Senegal, Elmina on the coast of Ghana, Zanzibar in Tanzania, and other slave-trade towns established up and down the continent's coasts.

The first European invasion also upset many of the delicate economic, political, and interpersonal linkages of precolonial Africa. The Portuguese demolished the east coast cities and destroyed the trade alliances that had linked them to the Persian Gulf, India, and the Far East. In other parts of Africa, Europeans destroyed many of the political allegiances that had kept African tribes and empires in balance with one another. In the wake of such practices and the slave-trade abductions, much of African society was brought close to collapse.

The character of urban Africa changed radically in the nineteenth century, when Europeans arrived in force. No longer looking for a passage east, and with the slave trade waning, the rapidly industrializing colonizers now eyed Africa with much the same plundering eye that Cortés and Pizarro had cast upon Latin America more than three centuries earlier. With Africa so abundant in raw materials, they swarmed like locusts over the continent, claiming as much land and other wealth as they could. Between 1862 and 1915, Europeans established city after city. Where no previous cities existed, they built them; where indigenous urban centers were in place, they either "Europeanized" them or created "dual cities." In cities like Kano, Ibadan, and Kampala, the Europeans paired the African city with their own new city next to it. The contrast was striking: An African city constructed of mud bricks and organized around its religious life and craft associations would coexist with a European city built of stone and organized around a growing central business district.

In all cities, however, a policy of racial segregation prevailed—a form of **apartheid** (as the practice came to be known in South Africa) by which Europeans dominated the local people. Obviously, such a system imposed tremendous economic, political, and social hardships on Africans while enriching the Europeans. Racism was at its worst in southern Africa. In more northerly parts of the continent, different colonizers and different urban traditions allowed the races some contact and, thus, mitigated the racism somewhat. Thus, although racial tensions remain in West, East, and North Africa, conflict was greatest in the south, in the Republic of South Africa, Namibia, and Zimbabwe, where rigid racial segregation and stratification ended only in the late twentieth century.

Unlike Latin America, where the "Laws of the Indies" produced a continent of similar cities, the presence of many European nations in Africa resulted in a variety of different policies for urban areas. The British, for example, subscribed to a policy of indirect rule, content to let local African leaders maintain their positions as long as they bowed to the colonial government. The French, on the other hand, insisted on the eventual assimilation of Africans into the French way of life. To promote this, they dismantled indigenous governments, taught only French in public schools, and encouraged the local population in identifying totally with French culture.

Modern Cities

During the colonial era, most African cities grew slowly, hampered, like their Latin American counterparts, by one-sided trade policies (exporting raw materials at low prices). Only a few cities—coastal ports or mining cities, for example—grew more swiftly, either because of their location or because of their special wealth.

Nationalist movements in the 1950s led to fights for independence, and Africa became a site of confrontation for competing world ideologies. Siding with the Africans in most cases were leftist or Communist countries, prominent among them the former Soviet Union, China, and later, Cuba. Such countries often equipped local insurgents with arms to fight the colonizers. Furthermore, colonies became too costly to maintain, both economically and politically, giving Europeans second thoughts about the whole business. In the 1960s, a total of 32 former colonies in Africa gained their freedom. In 1960 alone—dubbed the "African Year"—more than 3 million square miles and 53 million of Africa's people saw an end to colonialism (Herskovits 2007). This success only further fueled independence movements, with the result that the retreating colonizers became more and more eager to let go.

In some cases, the rapid withdrawal and newfound freedom often unleashed tribal warfare and a succession of military coups. For example, after the hurried Belgian retreat from the Congo in 1960, that country endured five years of bloody civil war as factions warred for control. The civil war and horrendous slaughter in the mid-1990s between the

Hutu and Tutsi tribes in the former English colony now known as Rwanda is attributable, in part, to the same legacy.

In global perspective, Africa is still the least urbanized continent, but it has the highest rate of increase in urbanization. In 1950, just 15 percent of the African population lived in cities, but by 2010, that proportion had more than doubled to 40 percent. Demographers estimate that by 2050, the number of African urbanites will reach 62 percent (United Nations Population Division 2012).

This increase is the result of both in-migration from the hinterland and natural population increase. Some nations—including Zambia, Zimbabwe, Gambia, Botswana, Kenya, Madagascar, Mauritania, Namibia, and Tanzania—have had success in bringing down fertility rates. Ethiopia, Nigeria, and the Congo, by contrast, have not. Nigeria is presently 1 of 10 countries with more than 100 million people, a level that Ethiopia and the Congo will reach within the next 40 years. Tragically, the AIDS epidemic is worst in sub-Saharan Africa; in 2009, this area accounted for 68 percent of the world's adult HIV infections, and 14.8 million children are orphans due to the death of their parents from AIDS. In Botswana, Lesotho, and Swaziland, between 24 and 26 percent of the population is infected with HIV (UNAIDS and World Health Organization 2010). Despite this tragic epidemic, projections are for a sub-Saharan population growth from 883 million in 2011 to 1.25 billion in 2025 (Population Reference Bureau 2011).

Taken together, these factors help explain why Africa is a continent in severe crisis. Aside from Africa's health crisis, much of its population is starving. Food shortages and chronic malnutrition are unfortunately common in many countries in sub-Saharan Africa. In 2011, East Africa faced its worst drought in 60 years, affecting more than 11 million people. Thousands of desperate people flooded into such cities as Mogadishu, Somalia, looking for food and water. Officials warned that 800,000 children could die of malnutrition throughout Somalia, Ethiopia, Eritrea, and Kenya.

MIDDLE EASTERN CITIES

Chapter 2 highlighted early Middle Eastern cities, including the world's first-known city, Jericho, and Catal Hüyük. Beginning in the fourth millennium B.C.E., the Persian and Egyptian empires dominated but then faded—a process hastened by the invasions of Philip of Macedon, Alexander the Great, and the Romans during the last four centuries before the birth of Christ. All left behind established cities on which more modern ones later flourished. After 300 C.E., the declining fortunes of Rome, plus soil erosion and overgrazing, led to the eclipse of most of them.

Islamic Cities

The prophet Muhammad died in 632 C.E., unleashing a religious movement that swept over all of western Asia, into Europe via Spain and the Balkan states, across some of sub-Saharan Africa, and eventually, as far east as Pakistan, India, Indonesia, and the southern Philippine Islands. As it spread, Islam generated an impressive array of cities. Even as European cities shrunk during the Middle Ages, Islamic cities along the coast of North Africa entered their greatest period. The Muslims, among history's greatest "middlemen," helped assure the success of these cities, as traders utilized their geographical location to become the link between Europe and the Far East and, in the case of North Africa, between Europe and the sub-Saharan region. The inland cities, however, were probably Islam's greatest triumph. For centuries, as nomads and overland traders, the people of the Middle East had learned how to live and prosper across vast distances of inhospitable terrain. As trading centers, they established Mecca, Riyadh, Baghdad, and Tehran, among others (Figure 13–4).

All the Islamic cities had a similar form, as described in the *Cityscape* box on page 365. By and large, the Muslim city reflected the power of the city's royal and religious elites, and many found these to be the most beautiful of all the world's cities. In Robert Byron's writings on his travels in the Middle East during the 1930s, he described Isfahan in

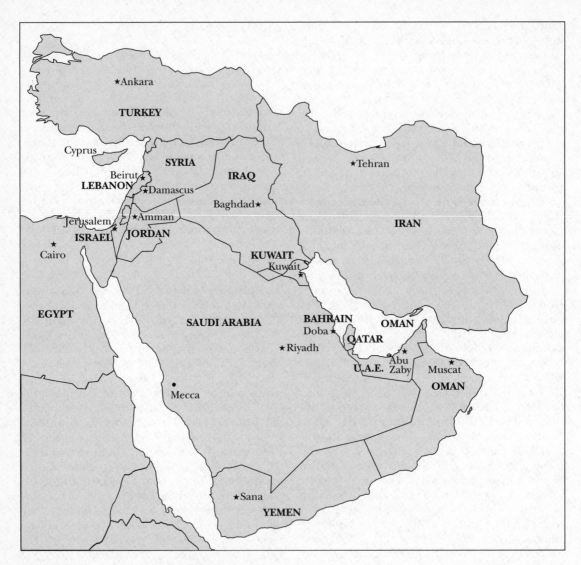

FIGURE 13–4   Map of Major Middle Eastern Cities

Iran as a beautiful array of colors: white tree trunks and canopies; turquoise and yellow domes gleaming in a deep-blue sky, along a river whose muddied silver waters reflected that blue; with pale toffee-colored brick bridges; and nearby pastel lilac mountains. For him, the city made an indelible and positive impression, a treasured memory (Byron 2007:166).

Yet Byron's romanticized image is misleading, for poverty and internal conflict often characterized Islamic cities. Given the division of the city into multiple residential quarters—sixteenth-century Damascus contained no

CITYSCAPE

The Islamic City

In the typical Islamic city, the dominant environmental and cultural elements in the Middle East combined to produce a unique urban place. The surrounding wall, for example, served a dual function, first as a defense against marauders and, equally important, as a barrier to dust-laden winds coming from a variety of directions, depending on the time of day or season of the year. When bush shrubs were planted along the wall, the effect on wind and dust was that of an almost-total barrier, and with strategic planting of vegetation within the settlement, wind and dust could be kept aloft and away from inhabited areas across the whole extent of the settlement.

The main thoroughfares of the city contrasted dramatically with the emptiness and quiet of the desert outside the wall. Here was the hustle and bustle of the Islamic city—its commercial lifeblood of bazaars filled with many vendors shouting their wares to the passing throng. In these wide but noisy and greatly congested streets, all kinds of goods and services were available—animals, fruits, vegetables, arts and crafts, food and drink, fabrics, leather and metal goods, and jewelry and other luxury items. Beyond these heavily used routes on both sides were the residential sections. Their passageways were so narrow that often one could extend arms and simultaneously touch the walls on either side. As people walked onward to the private houses, the clamor of street sounds quickly faded. Cooled by the shade provided by the closely built walls

and dwellings, a pedestrian could easily sense the change not just in temperature and quiet, but also in the more intimate ambiance of the corridor.

Still another contrast beyond the plain, mud-colored walls and exteriors of houses facing the street was the warmly decorated interiors of these houses, even in the more modest ones. Somewhat similar to Roman houses, these houses typically had numerous rooms opening onto a central courtyard and fountain. This private open space—the primary shared living space of the family—was the final line of shelter from the environment. It lay nestled within the structure of the house, located within its own walls, which in turn were situated within the city walls. The close proximity of the other houses to one further protected each of them from the dust and wind outside the city.

Some rooms in the houses were for the use of the women only, and—to preserve further the modesty of Islamic tradition—the layout of the house enabled the entertaining of guests without their unavoidably encountering all household members.

The more recent urban settlements in the Middle East often lack the high degree of unity and atmosphere found in the still-existing, specific features of the older Islamic towns. The flavor of these old urban communities, in complete contrast to the desolation all around them, was at once intimate, intricate, and intense. Thus, cities such as Baghdad, Cairo, Fez, or Tehran—situated in one of the harshest environments in the world—could provide comfortable living conditions for populations running into the hundreds of thousands.

fewer than 70 quarters in the city itself—in-group neighborhood solidarity often led to surging outgroup hostility, particularly when central religious values were at stake:

> [T]he religious minorities (Christians and Jews) inhabited their own separate quarters both because the state wanted to contain (and keep an eye on them) and because minorities naturally sought protection through clustering.... The poorest quarters were frequently on the city periphery...where land prices and housing rents were cheapest, and where much of the city's noxious industries (furnaces, tanneries, slaughterhouses) were located. (Khoury 2004:460)

Islamic cities reached their zenith during the Middle Ages. Thereafter, like their Persian, Egyptian, Greek, and Roman predecessors, they began to slide into decline. Again, the land near the cities became overgrazed and the topsoil depleted, leading to evaporation of precious water supplies and increasing dust and erosion. This, in turn, triggered a loss of timber, a crucial raw material any preindustrial society consumes for heat, artifacts, houses, ships, and tools. City populations plummeted. For instance, in the sixteenth century, Baghdad's population dropped to less than 100,000—one-tenth of its former size. In Syria, Egypt, Iran, and Saudi Arabia, cities were reduced to shadows of what they had been. Even in the largest cities, such as Alexandria and Aleppo (in Syria), trade slowed to a trickle.

European Dominance

Not until the nineteenth century, under European influence, did urban growth begin once more. In the Middle East, Europeans saw untapped markets for their goods, a potential source of raw materials, and in some areas, such as Suez, strategic locations for military affairs.

Located in Abu Dhabi, the capital city of the United Arab Emirates, the majestic Sheikh Zayed mosque is the third-biggest mosque in the world. It is clearly a distinctive architectural landmark, built at a cost of $545 million. Large enough to accommodate 41,000 worshipers, it also houses a library collection that includes rare publications dating back more than 200 years.

The Europeans, however, never viewed the Middle East as the valuable prize that Latin America and Africa were, so they made limited efforts at colonization. Yet trade with outsiders was sufficient to weaken the centuries-long Islamic pattern. Despite efforts by many Muslims to bar non-believers and their way of life (including books, telephones, and automobiles), their world was changing. As European influence spread across the region, new urban patterns emerged. From Cairo to Beirut to Tehran, suburban districts swelled beyond the quarters of the old cities, and new, wider roads were routinely clogged with motor vehicles (Cleveland and Bunton 2009).

The real change, however, went deeper than the physical level. Foreign traders ventured into rural areas to make better deals for agricultural products, thereby passing up the ancient bazaars. Foreign investors opened businesses and factories in Middle Eastern cities and began undercutting the prices of the traditional guilds. This new competition altered the face of the entire region's economy. Where local sheikhs had administered land communally and restricted the open-market sale of goods, now people began to sell land, goods, and skills to the highest bidder. The ultimate cost was a weakening of traditional authority and an erosion of long-established communities. Before long, the earlier, self-sufficient, subsistence economies of Middle Eastern cities evolved into export-oriented ones that were dependent on the economies and needs of Europe and North America. Of course, this process only accelerated with the discovery of the new "black gold" of the region: oil.

Modern Cities

Economic development increased the prominence of coastal cities and undermined the significance of inland urban areas, thereby sparking a major migration to those cities. As in Latin America and Africa, this urban migration taxed the city's capacity to provide for its people. Iran's urban population, for example, increased 11-fold—from nearly 4.7 million in 1950 to 53.1 million in 2010, with 71 percent now living in cities, compared to 28 percent in 1950. The urban population in Syria also grew dramatically during the same time period, going from 1 million to more than 12.5 million, an increase in urban population from 31 to 56 percent (United Nations Population Division 2012). In addition, the free-market economy created in the Middle East, as elsewhere, a relatively large middle class of affluent entrepreneurs, who mostly live in new and exclusive suburbs outside the old cities.

Rapid urban growth also established a primate-city pattern for the entire region. Tehran, for instance, has outdistanced all other Iranian cities in size, market strength, and problems. In similar fashion, Baghdad, Kuwait City, Damascus, Beirut, Amman, and Cairo dominate their countries. As elsewhere in poor regions, some urbanists see the existence of such primate cities as curbing the growth of other cities and creating virtually multiple problems both in those regions and in the primate cities themselves.

In short, contemporary Middle Eastern cities are in a period of intense social change. Most are no longer the pure Islamic-styled cities of the past millennium, yet they are not likely to become fully Westernized either. Like the cities of Latin America and Africa, these cities are forging a new and complex urban tradition. The emphasis here is on the word *complex*. Generalizations about cities within the context of the Arab-Islamic culture would be unrealistic. The countries in which Middle Eastern cities exist include the extremely poor (Sudan, Yemen), charity cases supported by other countries (Egypt, Jordan, Lebanon), the oil rich (Kuwait, Saudi Arabia), the socialist (Syria), and those still showing a colonial imprint (Morocco, Tunisia). Middle Eastern countries and cities thus find their urban development greatly influenced by their economic and political context.

New Cities

Two spectacular new cities have arisen in the United Arab Emirates, located south of the Persian Gulf on the Arabian Peninsula (see Figure 13–4). The capital city, Abu Dhabi—with a population of 666,000 in 2009—has emerged rapidly from a planned urban center in the 1970s into a global city today. A commercial and political center, it is the location of important financial institutions and corporate headquarters of many large companies and multinational corporations. Most impressive is the beautiful Grand Mosque, an architectural landmark with a capacity to hold 41,000 persons. Wide, grid-pattern boulevards form the paths for the more than 60 towering skyscrapers, with still others in the planning stage. The high-rise office and apartment buildings are in the city's central downtown, with two-story villas or low-rise residential buildings in the surrounding suburban area.

Dubai is an even more striking global city. At a cost of $20 billion, this massive, mixed-use urban development, still under construction, includes a downtown district with the world's largest shopping mall (1,200 shops) with such attractions as an aquarium and olympic-sized ice rink. Its downtown contains more skyscrapers exceeding 500 feet, 1,000 feet, and 2,000 feet than any other city in the world. Burj Khalifa Tower (2,717 feet) is the world's tallest building and, outside it, there is the unmatched Dubai Fountain, more than 900 feet long and shooting water more than 500 feet into the air (the equivalent of a 50-story building). A light rail system (the world's longest fully automated metro network) eases movement of the city's 1.5 million residents into and out of the city (Emaar 2011). The worst urban problem in Dubai at present is the ability of its sewage treatment infrastructure to keep up with rapid population growth, but authorities are determined to overcome this problem (Wheeler 2008).

ASIAN CITIES

The richness and complexity of Asian culture force us to be highly selective (Figure 13–5). Of all global regions, Asia provides the greatest challenge, because it encompasses almost 30 percent of the earth's land area and is a region of many sharp contrasts: Japan is an aging, highly industrialized, rich nation, with one of the world's lowest birth rates. China has a rapidly growing economy and the largest

Punctuating the skyline of Dubai, a city with more tall skyscrapers than anywhere else, is Khalifa Tower, the world's tallest building at 2, 717 feet. Its 160 floors contain corporate suites, hotel suites, apartments, and a restaurant. Primary locale of a 2011 *Mission Impossible* film, the building cost $1.5 billion to build and is a showplace for the oil-rich United Arab Emirates.

urban population of any country in the world. Southeast Asia stands out as having no real tradition of indigenous cities at all, yet despite this history, major cities now are growing at a startling rate. After struggling for many years, India is also an economic power now, but it still faces urban problems as serious as those found anywhere in the world. We begin there.

India

Chapter 2 revealed that the Indus Valley region had thriving cities, such as Moenjo-Daro, as early as 2500 B.C.E. And in antiquity, the fabled

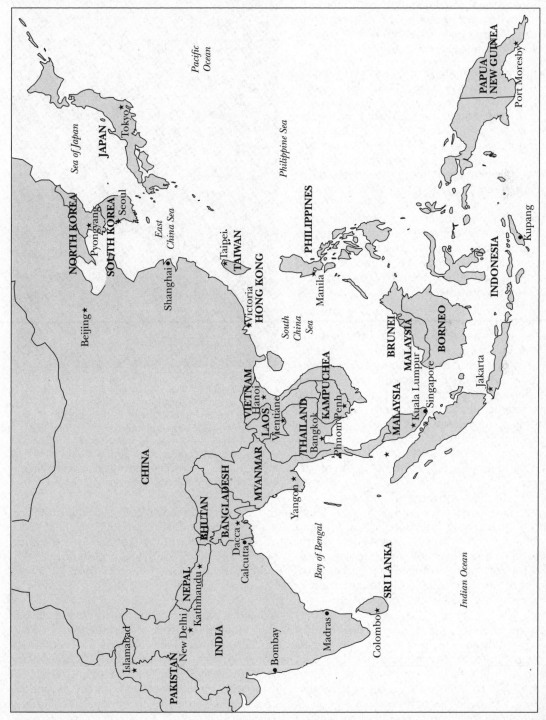

FIGURE 13–5 Map of Major Asian Cities

opulence and beauty of ancient India and China held nearly mythical fascination for Westerners. These myths enticed that most famous of world travelers, Marco Polo, to set out from Venice in 1271 to find an easy route to the East.

European Domination. In the seventeenth century, the British began their colonization of India. As in Latin America and Africa, the cities they founded had a dual purpose: as centers of political control and as bases for economic exploitation. Where cities already existed, like Delhi, the British simply constructed a second settlement next to it—in this case, New Delhi. This pattern of separation was nearly identical to the dual-city African settlements described earlier, resulting in a striking contrast between the indigenous part and the Anglicized part. One typical distinction would be a congested urban center in the old section and carefully planned, often-spacious, sections nearby.

The older area (the original city) typically has a form much like that of the Islamic cities described in the last section. Crowded into a central market or bazaar, numerous small retail shops offer a vast range of goods, including foods, cloths, hardware, and jewelry. Surrounding the marketplace is a residential area strictly divided into quarters, dividing Muslims from Hindus and separating Hindus according to their caste position. Brahmins and other high castes are usually in the best-built residential areas, either in or near the center of the old cities. The laboring castes and the menial outcastes of lowest socioeconomic status occupy the poorest houses, which tend to be located in the outskirts rather than in the center. The British part of the city, on the other hand, is very Western in form, with broad streets, often arranged in a grid pattern. At the center is a trading and manufacturing area, with a railroad leading outward.

Modern Cities. India's rate of population increase (about 1.6 percent annually) leads demographers to project that its 2011 population of 1.24 billion may grow to more than 1.69 billion in 2050, by that time easily surpassing China to become the world's most populous nation. Demographers project that

Like many Asian and Middle Eastern cities, Delhi, a city of about 12.3 million people, suffers from growing pains. India's rapidly rising population increasingly worsens traffic congestion, and many roads cannot cope with the increasing volume. Streets typically are jammed with cars, bicycles, and pedestrians moving at a snail's pace, especially at the intersections.

India's urban areas will gain 159 million more people between 2011 and 2025, and an additional 352 million by 2050, and thus be one of the world's largest urban populations at 0.9 billion (Population Reference Bureau 2011; UN Population Division 2010).

Kolkata (Calcutta). Although Kolkata is favorably located for trade in northeastern India, its land slopes away eastward and westward from the Hooghly River, with its metropolitan area primarily a north–south strip about 3–5 miles wide on either bank. With the exception of the grid pattern in the central area where Europeans formerly lived, the narrow roads have a haphazard character. With Kazi Nazrul Islam Avenue as the only express highway, and few river crossings, Kolkata's transportation system—like its utilities and municipal facilities—is seriously overburdened. Most of the city's heavily used roads are heavily congested. The 17-mile subway system carries an estimated 25 percent of Calcutta's 7 million commuters as an alternative to the limited tram service and buses.

Kolkata operates as a port, shipping coal, iron, jute, manganese, mica, petroleum, and tea from its hinterland. Its river channel, however, enables Kolkata to handle only a small share of India's imports and exports. Although set in one of the poorest and most overpopulated regions of India, Kolkata's artistic, cultural, and intellectual life thrives. Home to three major universities and known as the "cultural capital" of India, Kolkata is unmatched among Indian cities in the volume of people who flock to its art exhibitions, book fairs, and concerts. Never very far away, however, are hundreds of shantytowns (*bustees*), which contain about one-third of the metropolitan area's 15.3 million residents. Worse off still are the hundreds of thousands of Kolkata's homeless who sleep either on the streets or wherever they can find temporary shelter. People dump all manner of human and other refuse into open sewers and, needless to say, disease is widespread.

Mumbai (Bombay). A port city on India's western coast, Mumbai is the most populous city in India and sixth largest in the world. As the commercial and entertainment (including Bollywood) capital of India—as evidenced by its new skyscrapers and opulent hotels—Mumbai provides good incomes for many; it ranked sixth on the 2011 list of "Top Ten Cities for Billionaires" (Brennan 2011). In stark contrast, the outskirts of Mumbai are home to massive slum areas, as depicted in the film *Slumdog Millionaire* (2008). Legions of unskilled newcomers still stream in from the countryside, where life is even worse. Such migration—the primate-city pattern—depletes the rural areas of people and creates continuing problems of extreme poverty, prostitution, and organized crime in the city.

The majority of Mumbai's 12 million residents are concentrated on an island, giving this city one of the highest population densities in the world. Mumbai has another distinction, as India's most culturally and religiously diverse city. More than half its residents are Hindu, with the remainder divided among Muslims, Christians, Parsis, Buddhists, Jains, and Sikhs. To make matters even more complex, Mumbai's people speak three major languages: Marathi, Gujarati, and Hindi.

Now one of the world's top 10 centers of commerce, Mumbai is home to numerous Indian and multinational corporate headquarters, as well as important financial institutions. In manufacturing, the surrounding Black Cotton Soils, India's greatest cotton-growing area, made Mumbai one of the largest cotton textile centers in the country. This industry employs almost half of Mumbai's factory workers. Most others are employed in the production of silk, artificial fibers, chemicals, and glassware or in the dyeing, bleaching, and printing industries.

Outlook. The long-run picture for India's cities may be somewhat brighter. Recent progress has occurred against hunger, and transportation, electricity, and schooling are more widely available than ever before. Some rural areas—notably the Punjab in the north—are self-sufficient, and smaller cities (those under 100,000 people) seem to be faring better for more of their citizens than the major cities like Mumbai, Delhi, Kolkata, and Chennai.

A growing economy has improved living standards since the 1990s, particularly for the 160 million middle-class consumers expected to increase to 267 million by 2016 (*Economic Times* 2011). Capitalizing on its large, growing numbers of educated people skilled in the English language, India has become a major exporter of software services and software workers. Negative factors include the desperate poverty of about 38 percent of the population (380 million) and the impact of the huge and expanding population on an already overburdened environment (Azad India Foundation 2010). Whether the positive trends and hopes can finally eradicate the urban horrors in this country remains to be seen.

China

Like India, China is a land of ancient cities. Beijing (Peking), as profiled in Chapter 9, has long stood as a magnificent center of Chinese culture. Today, some of traditional China remains, but this rapidly modernizing trade nation is now a major economic power.

Foreign Domination. From the mid-nineteenth century until the end of World War II, China was subjected to foreign control, first by Europeans and then by the Japanese. From Shanghai to Canton, Europeans remade parts of Chinese cities. Hotels, parks, tennis courts, and residential areas emerged, all catering to non-Chinese. To oversee European control of the area's economy, each city had a European-style central business district, complete with banks, corporate headquarters, and docks equipped to handle Western ships. As always, the Europeans imagined themselves as on a "civilizing" mission.

Not surprisingly, the Chinese people resented such treatment. Thus, after establishment of the People's Republic in 1949, Mao Zedong and his followers tried to eradicate all aspects of European influence and privilege from China's cities. Moreover, believing that cities, by their very nature, undermined revolutionary ideals, Mao encouraged China's citizens to remain in their rural villages and transform the country from there. More extreme action followed in the 1970s, when the highly regimented and often brutal Maoist system forced perhaps 25 million urbanites from large cities into small towns and rural villages. Despite these efforts, however, China's urban population continued to grow. Although reliable data are hard to come by, only about 10 percent of the Chinese population was urban in 1950, while the urban share increased to 50 percent by 2011 (Population Reference Bureau 2011).

Modern Cities. In the 1970s, China introduced major reforms aimed at curbing population growth and stimulating economic growth in order to help Chinese cities "catch up quick." It allowed cities to introduce private enterprise in an attempt to create a flexible, market-driven economy, but one that remained under centralized, one-party political control. As a result, China is now the world's largest exporter and stands as the second-largest economy in the world after the United States (*CIA World Factbook* 2011). This dramatic change has led to significant changes in the nation's cities.

Special Economic Zones. One radical innovation was the establishment of numerous Special Economic Zones, such as the city of Xiamen in southern China. With a population of about 3.5 million, Xiamen is so liberalized from the old policies that it seems to be almost capitalist. The city is a free-trade zone where China's manufacturers can wheel and deal with their Western counterparts without the restrictiveness that characterized the Mao regime. Chongqing, a city of more than 6 million people, serves as another example. The Beijing government gave the city free rein to make deals with foreign companies, and it encouraged Chongqing's citizens to use their ingenuity to find ways to make the city more productive. Another city, Guangzhou, also with more than 6 million people, is alive with free enterprise. Glittering window displays and neon signs dazzle the eyes on such major shopping streets as Beijing Road. On the side streets, private stalls selling clothes, stir-fried food, and household commodities line block after block.

Hong Kong. Located on the southeastern coast of mainland China just 80 miles southeast of Canton, Hong Kong has 7.1 million residents, giving it a population density of about 18,176 people per square mile, double that of Los Angeles (United Nations Population Division 2012).

Not surprisingly, overcrowding is omnipresent, despite a low birth rate. Shantytowns, which have virtually disappeared from the People's Republic, number nearly 400,000 in Hong Kong, despite determined efforts to provide public housing (Lei 2010). Other, particularly older, housing is bursting at the seams. Even the port itself has become a kind of slum, housing hundreds of thousands of the city's poor on Chinese-style boats called junks. In some areas, one can literally walk

This view across the Huangpu River at the central business district of Shanghai provides a study in contrasts. The foreground offers a glimpse of the "old" city in the architectural style and height of its buildings, while modern skyscrapers on the opposite bank, notably the Shanghai World Financial Center, suggests its importance as a global city with a major influence in commerce.

across much of the harbor by simply stepping from one moored junk to another. On one level, Hong Kong has been and continues to be very successful. It has become the most important trade port on the China coast other than Shanghai, and it has generated an industrial machine that is the envy of much of the world, replacing a number of other major manufacturing points. That industrialization, however, together with high population density, has resulted in such serious air pollution problems that a 2011 directive mandated changes in air quality rules and enactment. Shanghai and Beijing are actually even worse in air pollution (Regus Media Centre 2011).

Japan

Japan is a notable exception to the over-urbanization–underdevelopment pattern so common elsewhere in the non-Western world. Because it was never colonized, Japan was spared the social indignities and exploitation-oriented urban economy so characteristic of many other regions. Thus, the cities and urban life of Japan stand in marked distinction to those in most of Asia.

Early Cities.   The urban roots of Japan extend back to at least the eighth century C.E., when ruling elites established a series of provincial capitals. The *samurai* (a warrior caste) protected these capitals, which were weakly linked to an emperor living in the capital city of Kyoto. Within this feudal structure, local elites kept the citizenry in subjugation over the next few centuries while they warred with each other for control of various regions. At the end of the sixteenth century, a samurai named Ieyasu emerged victorious over the warring elements, and as *shogun* (leader and protector of Japan), he established his capital at the city of Edo (now Tokyo). Ieyasu and

Definitively dominating the skyline of Hong Kong (China), the International Finance Centre offers vivid testimony that it has a major capitalist service economy. Also, it has one of the highest per capita incomes in the world. Not as apparent in this photo is the fact that Hong Kong is one of the most densely populated places in the world, approximately 18,176 persons per square mile.

his successors set about reorganizing the administrative system of Japan, putting greater emphasis on cities. By the eighteenth century, Edo had a population of nearly 1.5 million, making it the largest city in the world (at the time, London had a population of 900,000). Osaka and Kyoto had populations of more than half a million.

Over the centuries, the growth of Japanese cities produced, as it had in Europe and North America, a wealthy and powerful middle class. By the mid-1800s, these merchants controlled the purse strings of the country, and the power of the shogun declined considerably. In less than half a century, Japan became a world power economically, technologically, and militarily. As people flocked to the cities, industrialization proceeded throughout the twentieth century. Japan's lack of the natural resources needed to run its industrial machine, however, as well as its own imperialistic ambitions,

led the country into foreign expansion and, finally, into the disaster of World War II. Its postwar history is impressive.

Modern Cities.   The economic success of contemporary Japanese cities is remarkable. Government–industry cooperation, a strong work ethic, mastery of high technology, and a comparatively small defense allocation (roughly 1 percent of gross domestic product) helped Japan advance with extraordinary rapidity to become one of the most powerful economies in the world. Another reason for Japan's success lies in its unique combination of the spirit of free enterprise and a collective orientation, in which employees hold great loyalty to their companies.

Japan's economic growth, however, has a downside. Exorbitant land costs and expensive housing force urbanites either to live in small-sized dwellings in wall-to-wall lots without any traditional Japanese gardens or to commute long distances by subway or commuter rail lines. The typical commuter, forced to live in a satellite town because of high city housing costs, travels 1 hour and 30 minutes each way to and from work. During rush hour, commuter lines operate at 250 percent of capacity, necessitating the employment of "pushers" to force additional passengers into overcrowded cars. Heavy automobile traffic clogs the city streets, including the express roads built above the streets because of space limitations.

On the positive side, Japan has established an exemplary health care system, and its life expectancy (83 years) is among the world's highest. The Japanese have significantly reduced crime, unemployment (only 5.1 percent in 2010), and slums. They have the strictest air pollution standards in the world, and their high-quality urban lifestyle impresses visitors, who express amazement at the tidiness of urban facilities, the reliability of public transportation, and the quality of restaurants. The thriving central business districts bedazzle the first-time visitor to Japan, even a visitor from the United States or Western Europe; for example, Tokyo's Ginza district, alight at night, makes New York's Great White Way and London's Piccadilly Circus seem tawdry in comparison. Tokyo is a major primate city, twice the size of Yokohama and more than three times that of Osaka and Nagoya. All have industrialized effectively, spreading wealth and opportunity throughout the country. This keeps "overload" on a single city to a minimum.

In contrast to other non-Western countries, Japan's population is shrinking. Its multiyear low birth rate and current **total fertility rate** (the average number of children a woman has during her lifetime) of 1.4 indicate that its 2010 population of 127.3 million may be only 95.2 million by 2050 (Population Reference Bureau 2011). As a result, Japan can provide jobs for its citizens and keep the lid on the massive shortage and pollution problems that bedevil many other cities throughout the world. Because it has the world's most rapidly aging population, however, Japan faces severe economic issues in terms of health care and pension costs, as do all Western nations.

Southeast Asia

Unlike India and China, Southeast Asia has little tradition of large, indigenous cities. Most of its urban areas are the product of Chinese or European influence within the past few centuries. However, the principal cities of the region—Yangon, formerly Rangoon (in Myanmar, formerly Burma), Bangkok (Thailand), Ho Chi Minh City (formerly Saigon, in Vietnam), Manila (Philippines), Jakarta (Indonesia), and Singapore (Republic of Singapore)—essentially reflect the themes we have encountered throughout Asia. A few portraits will illustrate.

Singapore.   Situated at the southern end of the Malay Peninsula, Singapore is a city-state, the largest port in the region and one of the largest in the world. Despite a dearth of natural resources, it prospers as a center of East–West trade. In 2010, Singapore, which is 100 percent urban, had a population of 5.1 million, with about 74 percent Chinese, 13 percent Malayan, and 9 percent Asian Indian. Population density (about 18,600 people per square mile) is thus a problem (*CIA World Factbook* 2011). To reduce congestion and pollution, the government bans cars from the city center during working hours; only those few with an expensive entry permit may drive into the central business district during the day.

As the city's population increased throughout the twentieth century, shantytowns (*kampongs*) and squatter settlements appeared on Singapore's periphery. To alleviate the situation, the government took a novel, if heavy-handed, approach: It ripped up old neighborhoods, constructed thousands of high-rise apartment buildings, and literally forced the city's population into them. Importantly, most residents own their apartments through a government-incentive purchasing program. The process transformed an old Asian city into an ultramodern one. From a distance, today's Singapore appears Western, with a clearly recognizable downtown and apartment high-rises almost as far as the eye can see. The high-rises have absorbed more than four-fifths of the city's population, and each group of well-maintained buildings boasts its own school, parking lot, community center, social facilities center, and lush landscaping.

Singapore thrives with its open-market economy, strong service and manufacturing sectors, and excellent international trading links derived from its history as a **break-of-bulk** port. The economy depends heavily on exports, particularly in consumer electronics, information technology products, and pharmaceuticals. Singapore is emerging as Southeast Asia's financial and high-tech hub (*CIA World Factbook* 2011).

Significantly, Singapore's population growth is under control. Its growth rate of about 0.5 percent a year is much lower than that in almost all other cities of the developing world. Its success in population control is the product of an all-out attack: Singapore's government made contraceptives and abortion readily available, decreased taxes for families with fewer children, increased educational and housing benefits for small families, and raised hospital costs to families for each additional child.

All of this progress comes at a price: Singapore has a highly autocratic government. Rigid social regulations control people's lives. Violators receive harsh punishments, even for minor offenses—littering is punishable by a heavy fine, and drawing graffiti is punishable by caning. Singapore thus is a tightly controlled society, but its citizens accept the regimentation and prosper.

Jakarta. Indonesia, lying along the equator between the Asian mainland and Australia, consists of 17,000 islands, of which only 6,000 are inhabited. As the fourth most populous country in the world, Indonesia is the largest Muslim nation. Nearly 80 percent of the country's total population (growing from 79.5 million in 1950 to 233 million in 2010) resides on the three islands of Java, Madura, and Sumatra. As a primate city, Jakarta, on the island of Java, with its 9.1 million residents has a high population density, but in Java as a whole, the population density is less than one-fourth that in Jakarta (United Nations Population Division 2012).

To reduce the strain on severely crowded areas of the archipelago, Indonesia initiated a voluntary but controversial transmigration program through which poor, landless families in overpopulated areas move to underdeveloped regions and begin new lives with a house, land, and technical assistance. Since the program started in 1950, more than 12 million Indonesians have relocated, half of them without government sponsorship. Violent conflicts with the indigenous populations, resulting in hundreds of deaths, and accelerated deforestation of sensitive rainforest areas, however, have been the unintended consequences.

The Indonesian capital, Jakarta, is a primate city par excellence, with a growing number of high-rise buildings and monumental traffic jams. People migrate to Jakarta for the same reasons they trek to all cities: They want a better life, and the city's booming economy is an attractive lure. One indicator of the potential for improving the quality of life in Jakarta and its hinterland is that between 1985 and 2011, the total fertility rate dropped from 4.1 to 2.3, thereby bringing Indonesia's population more under control.

In 1965, more than 60 percent of Indonesians lived in poverty, but by 2008, that figure was about 13 percent. Indonesia also has made significant improvements in education, health care, nutrition, and housing over the past several decades. Although Indonesia remains a poor country in most respects, its rising levels of education and literacy, combined with falling fertility, may help accelerate socioeconomic development and bring greater prosperity to Jakarta and its people (*CIA World Factbook* 2011).

Bangkok. Like Jakarta, Bangkok is relatively typical of Southeast Asia's cities and serves as the capital of Thailand, a country that was never colonized. Currently with a population of 6.9 million, the city has more people than all the 118 other Thai municipal areas combined. It is also more than 18 times as large as Samut Prakan, the country's second-largest city, making Bangkok one of the premier primate cities of the world.

A few figures illustrate the predominance that such primacy causes in Thai affairs. Bangkok contains more than three-fourths of the nation's telephones and half its cars, consumes over four-fifths of its electricity, holds three-fourths of all commercial bank deposits, and generates two-thirds of the country's construction. All automobile roads, railroads, and airplane routes converge on the city (so much so that to go from one place to another, you have to go through Bangkok, even if it is out of your way). Most Thai universities are in Bangkok, as are all the country's television stations. The city has about 20 daily newspapers (a few other cities have one), and it is the seat of the federal government.

With such advantages, people are drawn to the city by the millions, further strapping its meager resources. A massive "riverboat culture," much like that in Hong Kong, houses many of the city's poor. About 20 percent of the city's population—1.4 million people—live in slum communities. Population density in the inner city is about 11,000 persons per square kilometer, which is less than the 15,270 reported in 1978. Farther out, but still within the city, are about 1,300 persons per square kilometer, and that number is increasing (UN Environment Programme 2009). Bangkok thus is a city of contrasts. Its population growth further intensifies its overcrowding, traffic jams, and pollution, yet the city's cultural, economic, and educational opportunities attract many tourists, business leaders, and students.

Southeast Asia remains one of the least urbanized areas of the world (see Chapter 1, Table 1–2), yet its urban growth rate is incredible. In the past 20 years, Jakarta, Kuala Lumpur (Malaysia), and Hanoi (Vietnam) have tripled their populations. During the same period, Surabaja (Indonesia), Yangon, Manila, and Ho Chi Minh City have doubled theirs. This pattern of over-urbanization is not likely to stop, because natural population increase and in-migration will continue for the foreseeable future. The primate cities cannot keep up with staggering growth, however, nor meet obvious needs. Unlike Singapore, they draw population from the whole geographical spans of their countries. For example, people from all over Thailand (almost 200,000 square miles) flock to Bangkok. As a result, over-urbanization is rampant, causing a scarcity of jobs and services.

COMMON LEGACIES

With the exception of Japan and some parts of Western and Southeast Asia, all of the regions covered in this chapter were colonized. Although the specifics of such colonial control varied—it lasted for a longer period in Latin America than in Africa, and it destroyed indigenous culture more thoroughly in Latin America than in Asia—its legacy has been much the same.

Economic Legacies

Colonization left behind an urban system with an underdeveloped economy. In most instances, it was a process established for the benefit of a ruling elite and the citizenry of the mother country. Most colonial cities specialized in exports, and so they did not generate wealth or opportunities for the bulk of the local population or develop industrial capabilities. Thus, these cities prospered only to a point and remained relatively small. For example, in 1780, a full two centuries after its founding, Buenos Aires was a city of only 25,000, with few roads and virtually no contact with other cities.

Compare this with the postcolonial cities of the United States. Freed of their ties with England, they exploded in population and wealth as they forged links with each other and the westward frontier. When independence came for developing countries in the twentieth century, however, their cities were well behind Western cities in competitive advantage and without the capability to catch up. Despite ongoing efforts, most are still unable to provide enough jobs or wealth for their populations.

Even in areas of the developing world never colonized directly, economic development has been slow. In non-colonial Southeast Asia—Thailand, for example—urban industrial capacities, especially automotive and textiles, have only recently expanded, overcoming the lack of a tradition of vital indigenous cities and previous, disadvantageous export-oriented trade agreements with Western countries. In the non-colonial Middle East, the situation is much the same. Although indigenous cities have long existed, the insular policies of Islam and foreign domination of trade in the last century produced cities unable to provide for the growing needs of their populations. (This situation is dramatically changing in the oil-rich countries.)

Exceptions to this pattern are Singapore, Hong Kong, and Japan. By means of its rigid politics, Singapore controls its population growth and maintains a steadily rising standard of living, as does the more democratic Japan. Yet Japan's history is markedly different: It has a tradition of vital indigenous cities, no colonization, a strong commitment to industrialization that began a century ago, a basically stable political system, and a social structure flexible enough to allow most of its people the chance to improve their standard of living.

A crucial factor in the rapid urbanization of less-developed countries is improved agricultural production. During the 1960s, the so-called "Green Revolution" introduced new, high-yield varieties of rice, oats, corn, and wheat into developing countries, thereby expanding their food supplies to the point of surplus. Just as agricultural advances created a food surplus to enable the creation of early cities, so, too, have modern advances been a catalyst enabling more of the world's rural population to migrate to cities.

Political Legacies

In many areas of the developing world, colonization also left political instability in its wake. The leadership vacuum created by departing colonial powers left each country's rule either to a foreign-trained, native elite or simply "up for grabs" between competing factions. Foreign-trained elites (as in much of Latin America) typically re-created the limited-opportunity social structure of colonial days—advantageous to the few and difficult for the many. Competing factions (in much of Africa) often generated ongoing violence and unrest in urban areas. All these conditions further retarded economic growth. What corporation wants to invest heavily in a city where a coup may cause the loss or nationalization of its entire investment? Ironically, when corporations do invest, another negative reaction often follows. Many regard this type of investment as a contemporary form of colonialism—an alliance between multinational corporations and government elites—and see it as a continuing strategy to exploit the people.

Another political consequence concerns the irrelevance of the arbitrary national boundaries established by the European colonizers in relation to the territorial boundaries of indigenous populations. The Spanish and Portuguese carved up Latin America in terms of what they were able to conquer, without concern for any native group's natural homeland. As a result, many peoples previously separated by political, linguistic, and other cultural factors for centuries became citizens of a single, newly constructed country. Similarly, these arbitrary boundaries separated some groups who, traditionally having shared a given territory, now found their lands split by the European conquerors. European powers enforced a similar but much more severe carving-up process in Africa. When political independence came, many nations had yet one more barrier to their rapid entry into the modern world: a local citizenry divided against itself by an artificial historical boundary. (Many analysts see this situation as still contributing to the political instability in many African nations today.)

COMMON PROBLEMS

The diversity of history, cultural traditions, religion, and politics accounts for the differences of cities in developing countries from those in developed countries. Islamic cities of the Middle East are in many respects radically unlike cities of North America. Equally important, the cities of the developing world—Latin America, Africa, the Middle East, and

Asia—vary tremendously among themselves. No brief formula can ever grasp the diversities existing among La Paz, Kano, Kolkata, and Tokyo; however, these diverse cities do share some common concerns.

Spiraling Populations

Latin America—much more urbanized than Asia or Africa—had a population equal to that of North America as recently as 1950. By 2011, though, the total population in Latin America and the Caribbean had skyrocketed to 596 million, far more than the 346 million people in North America, even though the growth rate in Latin America dropped from 2.0 percent in 1994 to 1.2 percent in 2011. Still, this level of population growth (projected to increase the population to 676 million by 2025) is considerably higher than the annual percentage increases of Canada (0.4) and the United States (0.5). Throughout Latin America and the Caribbean, the total fertility rate was 2.2 in 2011, versus 1.7 in Canada and 2.0 in the United States (Population Reference Bureau 2011).

Should the AIDS epidemic still rampaging across Africa be stopped, population growth (now about 2.4 percent annually) will only increase that much faster, given that continent's 2011 total fertility rate of 4.7, by far the highest in the world (Population Reference Bureau 2011). In 2011, Africa's total population exceeded 1 billion, with projections of an increase to 1.4 billion in 2025. By 2030, more than half of all Africans will be living in cities, and then increase to 60 percent by 2050. As the world's fastest urbanizing continent, Africa will see its cities' population more than triple over the next 40 years (UN Habitat 2010).

As for Asia—where three-fifths of the world's population live—demographers project that its 2011 population of 4.2 billion, at its present total fertility rate of 2.2, will increase by 1.1 percent annually and reach about 4.8 billion by 2025 (see Table 13–1). The growth rate is higher in the Middle East (1.9 percent), where the present total fertility rate of 3.0 will result in its 2011 population of 238 million increasing to 300 million by 2025 (Population Reference Bureau 2011). By 2030, the urban population will reach 73 percent in the Middle East (Western Asia), 53 percent in Asia, 85 percent in Latin America and the Caribbean, and, as previously stated, 50 percent in Africa (United Nations Population Division 2012).

Population totals in less-developed countries will soar further. In most of these nations, one-third or more of the population is under the age of 15, so they have not yet entered their childbearing years. Another factor promoting a strong population increase in the less-developed countries is that scientific advances and technological improvements (vaccinations, better sewage systems, and the like) have brought death rates down sharply. Although this is obviously good news, it also contributes to a bigger overpopulation problem as time goes on.

Quality of Life

As the cities in poor countries swell in size, they often become less able to provide sufficient employment and even basic services in water, sanitation, waste removal, gas, electricity, and police and fire protection. In Latin America alone, where only one city exceeded a million people in 1930, 50 cities reached that level by 2000. Almost all of these Latin

TABLE 13–1   Current and Projected Population Demographics

Region	2011 Population	Total Fertility Rate	Rate of Increase	2025 Population
Africa	1,051,000,000	4.7	2.4	1,444,000,000
Asia	4,216,000,000	2.2	1.1	4,780,000,000
Latin America/Caribbean	596,000,000	2.2	1.2	676,000,000
Middle East	238,000,000	3.0	1.9	300,000,000

Source: Population Reference Bureau, *2011 World Population Data Sheet.* Copyright © 2011. Used with permission.

American cities are surrounded by *cinturones de miseria*, large belts of extreme poverty that often lack even the most basic comforts, infrastructure, and social services. Similarly, in Africa, Asia, and the Middle East, cities struggle with street congestion, overcrowding, inadequate infrastructure, and pollution.

Many of the less-developed countries are extremely poor—so much so that they simply cannot generate the capital they need to solve their cities' problems. Chronic underemployment and unemployment characterize many cities—a legacy of historical dependency on one or two trade goods and the lack of a diversified industrial base. One way that many nations attempt to improve this situation is by encouraging tourism. A mixed blessing, tourism brings the world's richest citizens into contact with its poorest, a contrast only the most myopic tourists fail to see.

Finally, political corruption, crime, and urban violence are everywhere on the rise. Eight of the 10 most dangerous cities in the world in 2012 were in developing countries: Cape Town, South Africa; San Pedro Sula, Honduras; Guatemala City, Guatemala; Baghdad, Iraq; Bogota, Colombia; Ciudad Juárez, Mexico; Mogadishu, Somalia; and Caracas, Venezuela. Rounding out the list were Grozny, Chechnya, Russia, and Rio de Janeiro, Brazil (Urban Titan 2012).

Environment

An urban population impacts on the environment more than a rural population, particularly in terms of energy consumption for electricity, transportation, cooking, and heating. Because cities radiate less heat upward than rural areas do, they create "heat islands" that trap pollutants and affect local weather patterns, generating more rain and thunderstorms. Since they also reduce the infiltration of water and lower the water tables, runoff occurs more rapidly, increasing the likelihood of floods and water pollution downstream (Torrey 2004). In cities experiencing rapid growth without the accompanying expansion

of infrastructure to handle such growth, environmental problems like an inadequate supply of safe water and sanitation, lack of rubbish disposal, air pollution from vehicle exhausts, and industrial pollution have serious health implications. For example, Africa's urban population without access to safe drinking water jumped from close to 30 million in 1990 to well over 55 million in 2008 (UN Environment Programme 2011b).

Toxic pollution is a particular threat to the health of the developing world's urbanites, affecting more than 1 billion of its citizens. The World Bank says that as much as 20 percent of all the health problems in the developing world can be attributed to environmental factors, particularly pollution (CNN 2008). In the 2008 list of the world's dirtiest cities—based on a scientific comparison of air pollution, waste management, water potability, and presence of infectious diseases, among other factors—24 of the 25 dirtiest were in developing countries. Moscow, ranked 14th, was the exception. The cities nearest North America were Port au Prince, Haiti, at number four and Mexico City at number five (Luck 2008).

Shantytowns

One of the major problems accompanying rapid urbanization has been the growth of city slums or squatter settlements and shantytowns on the periphery of the cities, as mentioned throughout this section (see the accompanying the *Urban Living* box on pages 381–382). They have many names: *bidonvilles* ("tin-can cities") in former French African colonies, *bustees* in India, *los villas miserias* ("cities of the miserable") throughout Latin America, and other names elsewhere. They also take many forms: mud and cardboard shacks outside Seoul, Korea; junks moored in Hong Kong harbor; and shacks in Africa and Latin America made from castoff lumber and tin. Their varying names and forms, however, are incidental to one underlying truth: They are the locales of abject poverty, malnutrition, poor sanitation,

URBAN LIVING

Shantytowns Throughout the World

Africa

The hut, only 10-by-10 feet, was made of corrugated metal set on a concrete pad. Armstrong O'Brian, Jr., shared it with three other men. They had no water, so they bought it from a nearby tap owner, and no toilet. The families in his compound, all without sewers or sanitation, shared a single pit latrine. Their electricity, tapped illegally from someone else's wires, powered only one feeble light bulb.

This was Southland, a small shanty community on the western side of Nairobi, Kenya. However, it could have been anywhere in the city, because more than half the city of Nairobi lives like this—1.5 million people stuffed into mud or metal huts, with no services, no toilets, no rights.

Outside, a mound of garbage formed the border between Southland and the adjacent legal neighborhood of Langata. It was perhaps 8 feet tall, 40 feet long, and 10 feet wide, surrounded by a wider watery ooze. Two boys, not more than five or six years old, climbed this Mt. Kenya of trash. They were barefoot, and with each step their toes sank into the muck, sending hundreds of flies scattering from the rancid pile. Perhaps they were playing King of the Hill. No. Once atop the pile, one of the boys lowered his shorts, squatted, and defecated. The flies buzzed hungrily around his legs.

When 20 families—one hundred people or so—share a single latrine, a boy pooping on a garbage pile is perhaps no big thing. But it stood in jarring contrast to something Armstrong had said as we were eating— that he treasured the quality of life in his neighborhood. For Armstrong, Southland wasn't constrained by its material conditions. Instead, the human spirit radiated out from the metal walls and garbage heaps to offer something no legal neighborhood could: freedom.

Asia

In the Bangladesh capital Dhaka, about 3 million people live in slums. The working poor, who are most of the slums' inhabitants, earn their living as construction or factory workers, lorry drivers, rickshaw pullers, or work in informal sectors as domestic helpers or trash pickers.

One shantytown, named No. 2 Pura Basti, is a cluster of tin and bamboo shacks that line narrow cobbled lanes flanked by open gutters. The shacks have electricity, but no running water or gas supply. The women cook food over wood-fired earthen stoves outside their shacks.

Just a few years ago, wells and an intermittent supply from an illegally connected tap to the city's water utility provided the only sources of water for the slum's 500 families. For drinking water, the women and children waited in line for up to two hours to collect a pitcher or bucket of water from a local market or nearby houses where they often had to pay exorbitant prices. Today they use water from wells dug behind their shacks for bathing and washing, but for drinking and cooking, they get "safe" water from the slum's "water point"—two hand pumps that draw water from an underground reservoir that is filled with piped water supplied by Dhaka's water utility.

A few years ago, the Dhaka city corporation, which owns the land, paved the slum's dirt lanes and installed some community toilets. But these basic latrines, which are

(continued)

concrete rings set in the ground without any water or flushing facilities, drain into an open gutter, which in turn is linked to a nearby pond. The area reeks of garbage and human waste. Nearly 200–300 people, carrying pots of water, wait in long queues to use the toilets each morning, and children and the elderly, who cannot make it on time, defecate in the gutters outside their homes.

Latin America

In severely overcrowded Mexico City, one-third of its residents lack such essential services as electricity and sewage facilities. As a result, every day huge amounts of human waste are left in gutters, open ditches, and vacant lots, creating a stench and attracting flies.

With about 400,000 poorly educated, unskilled newcomers to the city every year, unemployment approaches 50 percent, and the shantytowns grow. Most residents are squatters who live anywhere they can: in abandoned boxcars or shacks teetering on hillsides, in public parks, in roadside hovels. About a quarter-million people live illegally in 360 shantytowns built on property they don't own. Or at least, they don't own it yet,

since Mexican law gives squatters property ownership rights after five years' occupancy.

Squatters often live without drainage, with frayed electric cables hooked illegally into the city's electricity grid, and drinking water from buckets or leaky rubber hoses. A fire apparently sparked by illegal electric hook-ups swept through about 100 shacks in "The Last Hope" squatters' camp in an industrial area of downtown Mexico City in 1998. No serious injuries were reported. Most area residents didn't even know the tarpaper shacks had been built between two factories until the squatters' burned possessions were shoveled into the street.

The problem isn't confined to the capital. A fire, also resulting from an illegal electric hookup, swept through a shantytown in Juarez in 2003, killing four women. Another similarly caused fire swept through a public market in Durango in 2004.

Sources: From numerous sources, including Robert Neuwirth, *Shadow Cities: A Billion Squatters, A New Urban World.* London: Routledge, 2004, pp. 3, 5; Mallika Wahab, "Bangladesh Slums Demand Access to Clean Water," *International Journal of Humanities and Peace* 19 (2003):46–47; Chris Hawley, "Trying to Exorcise Mexico's 'Little Devils'," *Arizona Republic* (December 20, 2004); Scott Spoolman and G. Tyler Miller, *Living in the Environment,* 17th ed. (Pacific Grove, CA: Thompson-Brooks/Cole, 2011).

and disease. A quiet determination, strong family ties, and steadfast hope are often their positive counterparts as the inhabitants cling to the edge of survival, but these shantytowns nonetheless constitute the worst side of urban life in the developing world.

SUMMARY

In decades past, social scientists debated whether economic growth was preferable to the preservation of local urban traditions. People taking the preservationist position usually argued, quite convincingly, that "creeping Westernization" by way of industrialization

and foreign-oriented trade was rapidly obliterating ancient urban traditions, which were valuable not only to their peoples but also to the world as examples of the alternative forms that the urban process could take.

Although the preservation argument has lost none of its appeal today, the simple fact is that most cities in the developing world are inundated with so many people that they cannot provide adequately for their populations without major advances in economic vitality and technological efficiency. Already—as we have seen perhaps most dramatically in Kolkata—millions upon millions of the world's urban dwellers are suffering tremendous deprivation. Moreover, some of the large cities in developing nations have become so

Latin American shantytowns, like their African and Asian counterparts, typically exist on the outskirts of cities, such as this inappropriately named "Villa 31," with downtown Buenos Aires in the background. These squatter settlements pose the same health, economic, and psychological problems found in other slum settlements throughout the developing world.

crowded and polluted that they are straining the carrying capacity of their environment.

Once again, the city is literally transforming the world, as it has twice before. In Chapter 2, we spoke of the first and second urban revolutions—the first occurring when people moved into cities in large numbers for the first time, from approximately 8000 to 2000 B.C.E., and the second occurring during the capitalist and industrial revolutions, which began around 1700 C.E. and continued through the first half of the twentieth century. This second urban revolution was responsible for a demographic transition— an unprecedented growth in population, made possible by the city's ability to provide a higher level of income, technological efficiency, and health care than those in rural areas. Now, once again, the city is fostering a demographic transition, only this time with two differences: (1) The greatest population growth is not in the developed world but, rather, in developing countries; and (2) the

magnitude of the change makes the demographic transition of 1700 to 1950 look meager by comparison. This is the third urban revolution. No one ever expected the kind of growth we are seeing now.

Consider this: A generation or two ago, one correctly thought of more-developed countries as the locales of the world's largest metropolitan areas, or **urban agglomerations** as they are sometimes called. No more: Rapid growth and urban migration already have moved numerous developing world cities into this category, as the left-hand column of Table 13–2 shows. The shift to developing world dominance becomes even more pronounced when we consider the longer term (Table 13–2, right-hand column). The only Western city in the top 10 is New York (third only a few years ago), and by 2025, the projections are that it will drop even further, probably not even in the top 10 within 20 years. Next, look at the magnitude of the urban areas in the 2025 column. These

TABLE 13–2   The World's 10 Largest Urban Agglomerations, 2010 and 2025

2010		2025	
Urban Area	Population	Urban Area	Population
Tokyo, Japan	36,930,000	Tokyo, Japan	38,660,000
Delhi, India	21,940,000	Delhi, India	32,940,000
Mexico City, Mexico	20,140,000	Shanghai, China	28,400,000
New York–Newark, USA	20,100,000	Mumbai (Bombay), India	26,560,000
São Paulo, Brazil	19,650,000	Mexico City, Mexico	24,580,000
Shanghai, China	19,550,000	New York–Newark, USA	23,570,000
Mumbai (Bombay), India	19,420,000	São Paulo, Brazil	23,170,000
Beijing, China	15,000,000	Dhaka, Bangladesh	22,910,000
Dhaka, Bangladesh	14,930,000	Beijing, China	22,630,000
Kolkata (Calcutta), India	14,280,000	Karachi, Pakistan	20,190,000

Source: From *World Urbanization Prospects,* 2011 Revision. Copyright © 2012 by the United Nations, Population Division. Adapted with permission.

will truly be **megacities,** unprecedented in human history.

CONCLUSION

This overview of global urbanization offers no single solution for the problems we have examined. Scholars themselves are divided about the causes and the most efficient solutions.

One conclusion, however, seems certain. Whatever is done, most cities of the developing world will continue growing at enormous rates for the foreseeable future. With this growth will come, inevitably, greater problems, including congestion, pollution, and major shortages of basic necessities. As each country copes with its crises, perhaps one solution or a combination of two or more will emerge, thereby providing a means of lightening the load on these overburdened cities.

It is no small task. Millions of poor people in less-developed countries are unable to advance much, because the ever-increasing population does not generate enough additional jobs, housing, or health services to meet the needs. Perhaps the most remarkable contrast in the evolution of developing world cities has been the speed of their growth and modern development—over decades compared with just over a century in Canada and the United States. So-called *over-urbanization* in the developing world may well get much worse before it gets better.

These evolving cities each have their own complex cultural traditions and unique histories. Previously, we discussed how Herbert Gans stressed the primacy of culture over space in detailing the variety of lifestyles *within* a city (Chapter 10), and how cultural values shape a city's physical and social form (Chapter 9). In this chapter, we saw how cities throughout the developing world may share some common legacies and problems but are also different in many ways from one place to another. The expanding global economy and telecommunications networks link these cities more closely to one another than ever before, but they also are evolving through varied patterns of development, with each nation's cities having their own distinct characteristics.

KEY TERMS

apartheid (362)
break-of-bulk (376)
colonization (354)
megacities (384)

primacy ratio (353)
primate cities (352)
total fertility rate (375)
urban agglomerations (383)

INTERNET ACTIVITIES

1. At the International Data Base of the U.S. Census Bureau, you can quickly construct population pyramids for any developed or developing nation to get a quick sense of world population trends. Go to *http://www.census.gov/population/international/data/idb/informationGateway.php.*

2. The United Nations Population Division, at *http://www.un.org/esa/population/unpop.htm,* offers the latest facts on world urbanization prospects (left menu) as well as much other relevant information on the subject.

CHAPTER 14

PLANNING THE URBAN ENVIRONMENT

VISIONS

CITY PLANNING IN WORLD
   HISTORY
   Why Plan?
   Planning in the Industrial Era:
     1800–1900
   The "City Beautiful" Movement

THE NEW TOWNS MOVEMENT
   British New Towns
   New Towns Worldwide
   New Towns in North America
   What Makes New Towns Succeed
     or Fail?

ARCHITECTURAL VISIONS
   The Radiant City
   Broadacre City
   The Arcology
   TRY-2004
   Utopia's Limitations

MORE FOCUSED URBAN PLANNING
   Sidewalks and Neighborhoods
   Squares and Parks
   Placemaking
   Festival Marketplaces

THE REALITIES OF URBAN PLANNING
   Economics and Politics
   The Importance of Values

CASE STUDY: TORONTO, ONTARIO

   The Physical Setting
   History
   Creation of a Metropolitan Government
   Two Phases of Urban Planning
   Toronto Today

SUMMARY

CONCLUSION

KEY TERMS

INTERNET ACTIVITIES

Sometimes, cities work well (Portland, Oregon, and Toronto are frequent examples), and sometimes, they don't (Camden, New Jersey, and Detroit are often cited). Every city, however, struggles with various problems, some cities more so than others. In this chapter, we will introduce the work of individuals who responded to the shortcomings of cities with bold and provocative plans for improvement. Some tackled urban problems at the neighborhood level; others imagined radically transforming the entire city.

Not surprisingly, such plans have been controversial, because they frequently challenged cherished cultural beliefs, clashed with vested economic interests, or just seemed to be too radical. Only by giving all ideas some consideration, however, can we explore the possibilities for a better urban future.

VISIONS

In the late 1800s, what a vision Ebenezer Howard had! Deeply influenced by Edward Bellamy's novel *Looking Backward* (a utopian vision of the year 2000, when all the problems of the city would be solved), Howard dedicated his life to realizing Bellamy's goal in England. As Howard saw it, the industrial city was a virtual nightmare: People streamed to these overcrowded cities, only to experience misery and despair.

Howard agreed that the city had advantages—opportunity, entertainment, and diversity—but he asked why cities should deny people the best of the country—a healthful environment, low population densities, and a sense of freedom. So, he set out to solve this dilemma by creating what he called the "Garden Cities of To-Morrow." In 1898, he wrote,

> The two magnets must be made one. As man and woman by their varied gifts and faculties supplement each other, so should town and country.... The country is the symbol of God's love and care.... All that we are and all that we have comes from it. Our bodies are formed of it; to it they return. We are fed by it, clothed by it, and by it we are warmed and sheltered.... It is the source of all health, all wealth, all knowledge.... Town and country must be married, and out of this joyous union

will spring a new hope, a new life, a new civilization. (2007:48; orig. 1898)

Celebrating the "marriage of town and country," Howard worked out the details of his **garden cities** plan, and he hoped to convince others that his plan was not only desirable but also entirely possible. (The specific outline of his vision is described in the *Urban Trends* box on page 388.)

In 1903, in conjunction with a group of businessmen, he established his first garden city, Letchworth, about 35 miles from London. A second city, Welwyn (pronounced "well-en"), sprang up nearer London in 1919. On balance, both were quite successful, and they continue today as pleasant places to live. Still, until the 1940s, they remained Britain's only attempts at "planned" towns.

The entire history of urban planning is, in many ways, evident in the story of Howard's new towns. To alter established cities would be a massive, expensive, and disruptive undertaking. Cities are not only bricks and mortar. They are people's lives, and they rest on historical traditions, entrenched power relationships, and vested economic interests. Thus, suspicion typically greets plans for urban redesign. And given the consequences of so much *bad* city planning (like urban renewal in the 1970s), suspicion is not altogether a bad thing.

CITY PLANNING IN WORLD HISTORY

Ebenezer Howard was hardly the first to undertake urban planning on a large scale. Moenjo-Daro, a city of the Indus River Valley civilization of 2500 B.C.E., which we discussed in Chapter 2, had streets laid out in a grid pattern, broad thoroughfares, and individual houses designed for comfort and efficiency. Even more impressive were the Mexican cities of Teotihuacan, around 700 C.E., and Tenochtitlán, around 1500 C.E. Both capitals were large and richly symbolic. Expansive plazas, massive temples, and elaborate gardens were central features of these cities. Finally, recall the case study in Chapter 9, in which we discussed the tightly controlled plan of Ming Dynasty Peking. Here, we saw planned city

URBAN TRENDS

Sir Ebenezer Howard's Garden Cities of To-Morrow

Howard's Garden City was to cover about 1,000 acres at the center of a 6,000-acre tract.

Six magnificent boulevards—each 120 feet wide—traverse the city from centre to circumference, dividing it into six equal parts or wards. In the centre is a circular space containing about five and a half acres, laid out as a beautiful and well-watered garden; and, surrounding this garden, each...in its own ample grounds, are the larger public buildings—town hall, principal concert and lecture hall, theatre, library, museum, picture-gallery, and hospital.

The rest of the large space encircled by the "Crystal Palace" is a public park, containing 145 acres, which includes ample recreation grounds within very easy access of all the people. Running all round the Central Park (except where it is intersected by the boulevards) is a wide glass arcade called the "Crystal Palace," opening on to the park. Here manufactured goods are exposed for sale, and here most of that class of shopping which requires the joy of deliberation and selection is done. The space enclosed by the Crystal Palace is, however, a good deal larger than is required for those purposes, and a considerable part of it is used as a Winter Garden—the whole forming a permanent exhibition of a most attractive character, whilst its circular form brings it near to every dweller in the town—the furthest removed inhabitant being within 600 yards.

Passing out of the Crystal Palace on our way to the outer ring of the town, we cross Fifth Avenue—lined, as are all the roads of the town, with trees—fronting which, and looking on to the Crystal Palace, we find a ring of very excellently built houses, each standing in its own ample grounds; and, as we continue our walk, we observe that the houses are for the most part built either in concentric rings, facing the various avenues (as the circular roads are termed), or fronting the boulevards and roads which all converge to the centre of the town.... [T]he population of this little city may be...about 30,000 in the city itself, and about 2,000 in the agricultural estate....

On the outer ring of the town are factories, warehouses, dairies, markets, coal yards, timber yards, etc., all fronting on the circle railway, which encompasses the whole town, and which has sidings connecting it with a main line of railway which passes through the estate. This arrangement enables goods to be loaded direct into trucks from the warehouses and workshops, and so sent by railway to distant markets, or to be taken direct from the trucks into the warehouses or factories; thus not only effecting a very great saving in regard to packing and cartage, and reducing to a minimum loss from breakage, but also, by reducing the traffic on the roads of the town, lessening to a very marked extent the cost of their maintenance. The smoke fiend is kept well within bounds in Garden City; for all machinery is driven by electric energy, with the result that the cost of electricity for lighting and other purposes is greatly reduced.

Source: From Ebenezer Howard, *Garden Cities of To-Morrow,* excerpt from pages 50–56, © 1965 Massachusetts Institute of Technology, by permission of The MIT Press.

within planned city, all connected to convey key themes of China's culture.

Western cities also show a long history of planning. The Greeks planned Hellenic Athens, just as the Romans planned much of the pomp and majesty of Imperial Rome. Even towns of the Middle Ages showed some planning, especially in the walls built for protection and in the various "zones" set aside for specific activities. There were planned markets, squares, residential quarters, and always, the medieval church at the city's center. Still later, during the Renaissance, a veritable boom in urban planning arose, with careful efforts to achieve efficient traffic circulation and to provide fortification against invasion. It was at this time that planners designed the radial boulevards of Paris—roadways as beautiful as they are practical.

Why Plan?

Early city planners sought, first, *to solve specific urban problems.* They planned underground sewage lines for health reasons, walls for protection, parks for leisure hours, and thoroughfares to facilitate movement.

Second, we know that the motives of city planners in Rome, Teotihuacan, Tenochtitlán, and Beijing were also *to glorify those in power.* Thus, the Emperor Augustus and his successors, declared to be gods by the Roman Senate

in the first few decades of the Christian era, were "immortalized" by buildings, parks, plazas, and innumerable statues. City planners had a good reason to glorify the ruling elite: These people, after all, employed them. City planning, in short, often proceeds "from the top down." To ask "Why plan?" then, we also need to keep in mind another question: "For whom are cities planned?"

A third focus of urban planning is often the *glorification of important cultural values.* Ming Dynasty Peking was not only a monument to the all-powerful emperor but also a reminder to everyone of beliefs that were central to the Chinese way of life. Centuries later, during the Renaissance, the residency of the pope was reestablished in Rome. To showcase the Catholic Church as the wealthiest and most important institution in the Western world, Pope Julius decided to replace the old St. Peter's Basilica with the greatest cathedral and piazza in Christendom. The result was the grand Piazza of St. Peter. A long processional way leads the visitor to a massive circular area before the cathedral, which leads to the cathedral itself. The faithful find a powerful religious experience in this setting; everyone is awed by the size and magnificent design of St. Peter's. Both reactions were important to the piazza's designers.

Something different is symbolized in Figure 14–1, which shows Sir Christopher

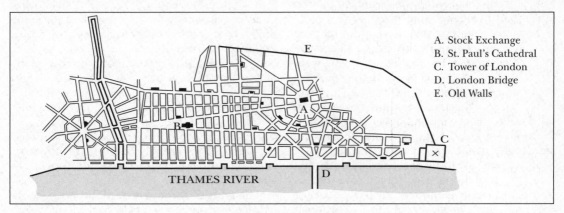

FIGURE 14–1 Sir Christopher Wren's Plan for the Rebuilding of London, 1666

Source: Arthur B. Gallion and Simon Eisner, *The Urban Pattern,* 4th ed. (New York: Van Nostrand, 1980), p. 43. Reprinted by permission of Van Nostrand Reinhold.

Wren's plan for the rebuilding of London after the Great Fire of 1666 (see the case study in Chapter 2). Here, although the magnificent St. Paul's Cathedral (B in Figure 14–1) is a dominant focus, major roads lead not to the cathedral but to the city's stock exchange (A in Figure 14–1). The dominant feature of the plan, which ultimately was not adopted, was the financial and trade element of the city's life. London at the time was fast becoming the most powerful economic center in the world. City planning thus reflected this change.

Three concerns, then, appear again and again in the history of urban design. People plan their cities, or parts of them, in order to (1) solve specific problems, (2) serve the interests of those with wealth and power, and (3) reflect and intensify cultural ideals.

Planning in the Industrial Era: 1800–1900

Ebenezer Howard shared many concerns about the overcrowded industrial cities with the classical sociological theorists—Tönnies, Durkheim, Weber, Marx, Simmel, Park, and Wirth—whom we discussed in Chapter 5. Howard saw little hope for the industrial city, viewing it as a monument to greed and to the interests of the few rather than the many. Effective city planning, he believed, could never exist in cities of such size.

In many ways, Howard was right. Planning on a citywide scale did not exist in early cities. While quite a few industrial towns were built during the 1800s—Manchester and Birmingham in England, as well as Paterson, New Jersey, and Falls River, Massachusetts, in the United States (see Chapter 3) are good examples—by and large the underlying concern was limited to profit and efficiency.

In the early 1600s when the Dutch settled New Amsterdam at the tip of Manhattan Island, street development evolved more or less haphazardly, as in medieval European cities. Two centuries later, though, as the city expanded northward, city leaders in 1811 adopted a rigid, gridiron plan that they applied to the entire island regardless of topography. Profit and efficiency carried the day with the transformation of space into a standardized commodity. "Right-angled houses," reported the city commission, when adopting the gridiron plan, "are the most cheap to build and the most convenient to live in" (Scobey 2003:120).

In the new, trade-dominated city, tradition counted for little. Buildings went up only to be torn down as commercial interests dictated. Builders adopted architectural styles, such as Parisian facades, "for show" and not for their deeper symbolism of a revered historic tradition (Scobey 2003:171–3). With the major (and wonderful) exception of Central Park, the profit motive fundamentally shaped all of New York. Boston Commons, a park in midtown Boston, is another notable exception.

The "City Beautiful" Movement

In the United States, some architects, planners, and civic leaders had other ideas. The first significant innovation in U.S. city planning grew out of the 1893 Chicago World's Fair, which showcased architect Daniel Burnham's "White City" (a vision opposing grimy, sooty, industrial cities). Burnham proposed a city constructed around monumental civic centers built in a neoclassical style, with great public spaces and a network of parks all linked by spacious boulevards. Inspiring a **City Beautiful movement,** Burnham's ideas had considerable influence among urban planners across the country. Scarcely a major city exists without a city hall, courthouse, library, or train station built in imitation of ancient Roman and Greek architecture. Chicago, Cleveland, Detroit, Los Angeles, Minneapolis, St. Louis, San Francisco, and Washington, D.C., all initiated such City Beautiful projects after the fair.

The costs of this movement, however, soon led even advocates to scale back their plans. Moreover, some private interests, especially businesses, resisted compromising their narrow objectives. Before long, the City Beautiful movement simply went away. Any new communities built, whether nineteenth-century frontier towns or twentieth-century suburbs, usually lacked a large-scale plan, instead typically beginning with a nondescript Main Street center and then rippling outward in a gridiron design unless forced to adjust because of elevated terrain.

THE NEW TOWNS MOVEMENT

I will not cease from mental strife,
Nor shall my sword sleep in my hand,
Till we have built Jerusalem
In England's green and pleasant land

William Blake

This stanza by the great English poet and artist William Blake opens Sir Ebenezer Howard's book *Garden Cities of To-Morrow.* Howard's belief that his New Towns movement would solve all of urban society's ills influenced many others both in and beyond his native England.

Before we get further into this section, let's clarify what we mean by *new towns.* In this sense, we are not referring to a new settlement, such as what occurred in the development of the American and Canadian West, when railways decided where to build their station stops and a town would grow around it, or when the discovery of valuable metal ores resulted in a new boomtown. Instead, the sociological concept of a **new town** deals with the large-scale, holistic planning of a mixed-use, self-sufficient community—its physical design of streets and infrastructure; its provision of residential, commercial, educational, recreational, shopping, and service facilities; its center, squares, parks, lakes, and pathways; its blend of employment and leisure activities; and much more.

British New Towns

The devastation of London from repeated Nazi bombings during World War II created a desperate housing shortage and renewed interest in Ebenezer Howard's vision. In 1946,

Britain passed the New Towns Act, providing for government sponsorship of new urban communities to draw population away from London and other cities. One central goal of the New Towns Act was to limit London's increasing sprawl by surrounding the city with a **green belt**—an idea taken directly from Howard.

New communities—complete with industrial, housing, and commercial areas—were built at some distance from larger cities. In all, Great Britain built 34 new towns, with their success in large measure assured because of deep government involvement. The first new communities—called the Mark I towns—adhered closely to Howard's ideas and were modeled after Letchworth and Welwyn. Mostly single-family houses organized in neighborhoods, these communities of about 30,000 residents were completely self-sufficient centers of industry, housing, education, and transportation facilities.

A second wave of new towns—the Mark II group, built in the 1950s and 1960s—deviated rather significantly from Howard's original plan. Typified by Cumbernault, located outside Glasgow, Scotland, these towns reflected the government's concern that small cities of just 30,000 were insufficient to alleviate population problems in the larger cities. A second concern was that too many small towns would consume too much land. Thus, the Mark II towns (those built since the 1960s), with population projections of 80,000, began to sacrifice greenery for density and to emphasize central (rather than neighborhood) shopping and recreational facilities. The most recent new towns are larger still. One example, Milton Keynes, lies 50 miles north of London, with a population of about 185,000 living in its 120 square miles.

Britain's new towns—Howard's "marriage of the city and country"—proved to be eminently successful at providing decent housing and sufficient jobs. On other levels, however, the new towns fell short. With their small number (34) and limited size, they have not had much impact on the large populations of Britain's major cities. Moreover, most of these towns are socially rather cliquish, with the same ethnic and class prejudices that one encounters in most large cities. Some critics claim that homogeneity is a product of the planning process itself, with its emphasis on neighborhoods. As sociologists often note, ingroup solidarity, which neighborhood living facilitates, often creates a corresponding sense of outgroup hostility.

Another problem has been the inflexibility of many new-town plans. Rather than recognizing that cities are dynamic entities that must adjust to changing human needs, many new towns stuck rigidly to their original plans. Often, the result has been a sense of inefficiency and even oppression that, as we will see, crops up again and again in city planning efforts.

New Towns Worldwide

To some degree, early British new towns were anticity. They were small towns, their limited size suggesting a distinct dislike of large urban areas. They were also antigrowth, strictly limiting their population in the belief that more was always less. Bigness meant disorder and destruction of a delicate ecological balance between people and the environment. Several recent new towns, however, take an opposite view. In France, the Netherlands, and Spain, new-town development has attempted to stimulate the growth of an entire urban region. Creating jobs around a cluster of industries, the new communities draw population from the countryside while also luring away people from nearby established cities. In the mid-1960s, for example, to accommodate population growth and "demagnetize" its cities, France developed five new towns near Paris and others near Grenoble, Lille, Marseille, and Rouen, in an effort to collect the population in the immediate area and lessen migration into those older cities.

Sweden.   The Scandinavian countries, particularly Sweden, look on new towns as a form of "suburb control." Like many European and North American cities, Stockholm had a problem with suburban sprawl during the 1950s. In an effort to curb decentralization,

the Swedish government planned a series of satellite cities linked to the central city and to each other by efficient transportation. The five cities, known as the Vallingby Complex, are distinct entities but look to the larger city for goods, many services, and jobs. Each of these small cities has about 10,000 people living in low-density housing within 300 yards of a subway-station/plaza complex.

As in Britain, the Swedes also built higher-density new towns. Instead of low-rise brick buildings that promote a sense of community and allow open space, the newer towns contain physically parallel rows of unattractive, look-alike, concrete-slab buildings with six to eight stories. These drab structures look much like sterile, low-income housing projects in the United States. Not surprisingly, these developments repel the middle class; only impoverished immigrants or low-income natives concentrate in them. Such places can also be found in France, Germany, and Italy, and there, as in Sweden, crime, drugs, and welfare dependency are common.

Australia.   Australia presents us with a different new-town concept, one designed to be the core of a new urban region and home to the national government. Located in the outback (isolated rural area), Canberra is some 180 miles from the seacoast metropolis of Sydney. Settled as early as 1912, Canberra was to be a new, inland city that would not only house the Australian government but also develop the Australian hinterland. This was no simple task. Canberra was far from Australia's normal trade routes, and it had no major resources (mineral deposits or cheap water power) to attract investors. Thus, government and planners were in complete control, which might well have pleased Ebenezer Howard.

The result is a physically beautiful city with a population now exceeding 350,000. Economically, the city has both a lower unemployment rate and higher average weekly earnings than in the rest of Australia. Now home to 25,000 businesses, the city has a diverse economy, although it is undeniably oriented toward the service industries and public administration (Australian Capital Territory

2011). Canberra is essentially an upper- and middle-class city though. Because of the high cost of living, most low-income families simply cannot afford to live there.

Brazil. Brasilia is another planned inland capital city. Conceived in the 1950s as a showcase for a modernizing Brazil, the city is about 600 miles from the coastal megalopolis of Rio de Janeiro. As with Canberra, Brasilia's location helped develop the nation's interior, with the intent of siphoning off population from the country's older cities.

An artificial lake surrounds much of the city and separates it from the suburban towns to the north. The cross-shaped plan of the central city utilizes the North–South Axis, Brasilia's main transportation artery, and the East–West, or Monumental, Axis, lined by federal and civic buildings.

With just 12,000 people in 1957, Brasilia grew to more than 500,000 by 1970 and now exceeds 2.3 million. Expanding faster than anticipated as people streamed into the city looking for construction jobs, Brasilia abandoned or modified many parts of the original plan. As elsewhere in poor nations, migrants unable to find adequate housing constructed their own shelters out of anything they could find. Thus, Brasilia evolved *favelas*, or squatter shantytowns, filled with tens of thousands of working-class and poverty-stricken people and lacking waste removal, water, and electricity. In the early 1970s, however, the government took steps to remove the shanty dwellers from the city by building houses 15 miles away in the newly created satellite town of Ceilândia (a Portuguese acronym for center for eradication of squatters).

New Towns in North America

All the new towns and cities that we've considered so far were government sponsored, with limited involvement of private investors. During the early history of the United

When first conceived and built in the 1950s, Brasilia was a stark example of modern architecture lacking in people-friendly usage—and, for that matter, even people, as few chose to live there. Now its population exceeds 2.3 million, much of its original plan has been scrapped, and squatter settlements ring this "model" city, which today exhibits many of the urban ills found elsewhere.

States, government-planned communities were not unusual and included Williamsburg; Washington, D.C.; Indianapolis; Raleigh, North Carolina; Tallahassee, Florida; and Austin, Texas. Except for one program in the 1930s, however, U.S. new towns for more than 100 years have been almost completely dependent on the ideals, plans, and investments of private businesses. We begin with the privately developed new town that served as the model for both public and private efforts thereafter.

Radburn.   Developed by architect and planner Clarence Stein, Radburn—about 20 miles west of New York City—was a direct attempt to adapt Ebenezer Howard's garden city to the United States. Radburn was laid out using what Stein called "superblocks," each surrounded by a green space. Radburn also attempted to separate pedestrian and automobile traffic completely. The backs of the houses faced the street, and the fronts faced a common green space with unimpeded pathways (underpasses eliminated street crossings) for bikes and pedestrians to go to the town center, school, library, stores, or shared public facilities. Roads only were for access to and from houses, not for walking or playing. In 1929, Geddes Smith described Radburn as follows:

> [It is a] town built to live in—today and tomorrow. A town "for the motor age." A town turned outside-in—without any backdoors. A town where roads and parks fit together like the fingers of your right and left hands. A town in which children need never dodge motor-trucks on their way to school. (quoted in Stein 1972:44)

Like so many new towns, however, Radburn ran into financial difficulties as the years passed, and it was never completed as originally planned. About 670 families live in Radburn today, creating a population of about 3,100 within the New Jersey borough of Fair Lawn.

The Radburn plan has been an inspiration to planners and architects for three generations. It had an impact on the designs of Winnipeg and parts of Calgary in Canada, on parts of Canberra and Melbourne in Australia, as well as in Brazil, Finland, India, Japan, Sweden, and Russia. Its concepts have also been implemented elsewhere in the United States, as the next several sections discuss.

Greenbelt Towns.   During the Great Depression, when millions of Americans were out of work, Rexford Tugwell, Assistant Secretary of Agriculture, persuaded President Franklin Roosevelt to create the Resettlement Administration, with funding through the Emergency Relief Appropriation Act of 1935. One of his main objectives was to provide housing for poor urban dwellers outside the city.

> My idea is to go just outside centers of population, pick up cheap land, build a whole community and entice people into it. Then go back into cities and tear down slums and make parks of them. (quoted in Knepper 2001:14)

The three towns constructed as part of this project were Greenbelt, Maryland (13 miles northeast of Washington, D.C.); Greendale, Wisconsin (7 miles from Milwaukee); and Green Hills, Ohio (5 miles north of Cincinnati). Planners had high hopes that these towns would help solve big-city problems and create the jobs needed to help end the Great Depression.

These hopes soon faded. Unlike new towns in Great Britain, these settlements never attracted their own industry. Built before the age of superhighways, they simply did not provide enough economic incentive for major industry to relocate there. Then, too, soon after the towns were started, World War II intervened, diverting funding to military objectives. And by the time the war was over, the Cold War followed, leading many to charge that government-sponsored towns smacked of "communism." By 1949, government began selling off the new towns to private interests. The Greenbelt Towns became, and remain, more like suburbs of the large nearby cities than like the independent small cities originally envisioned.

After World War II, architects and private developers created more than 100 new

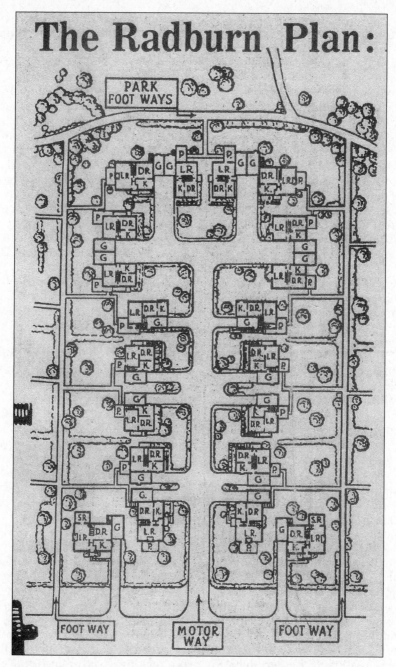

The Radburn Plan:

The Radburn design provided charming, moderate-sized homes grouped on a series of cul-de-sacs, with streets designed for cars only and footways for pedestrians only. No child had to cross a street to get to school or to play. The houses backed on the street, and their fronts faced parks. Shared public spaces—23 acres of parks, two swimming pools, four tennis courts, other recreational facilities, and a community center—were for the use of all 3,000 residents.

urban environments in an attempt to follow Howard's approach. Among them were Baldwin Hills (now part of Los Angeles); Park Forest and Park Forest South near Chicago; Jonathan, Minnesota; and St. Charles, Maryland. However, most of the so-called U.S. garden cities—despite containing elements of Howard's vision, such as shared public space—lack their own industry and so are essentially middle-class suburban developments, not "new towns" as Howard proposed. Nevertheless, all these efforts, from Radburn onwards, foreshadowed the New Urbanism movement discussed in Chapter 12 in designing pleasant, unified neighborhoods and mixed-use urban spaces for families from a range of economic backgrounds.

Reston. Twenty-five miles from downtown Washington, in suburban Virginia, Reston was the brainchild of developer Robert E. Simon, with the town's name made from his initials. Simon planned his "quality urban environment" around two town centers linking seven villages of approximately 10,000 residents each in a beautiful, contemporary design filled with trees, lakes, and pathways. He intended Reston to be economically self-sufficient and diverse, with mixed-income housing (high-rise luxury apartments side by side with single-family homes). Only about one-fourth of its residents live and work in Reston, however, and the rest commute. Home to about 2,000 businesses, the town has 58,000 residents—9 percent black, 11 percent Asian, 10 percent Hispanic, and 68 percent non-Hispanic white.

Reston is mostly an affluent community, with a median family income exceeding $96,000 in 2009. Its housing includes single-family homes, townhouses, condominiums, waterfront homes, homes on the golf courses, and homes that back up to woods and nature paths. The median house or condo values in 2009 were substantially higher than for Virginia. One of Reston's main focal points is Town Center, which includes high-rise offices, a Hyatt Regency hotel, boutiques, national retailers, and restaurants. Town Center has a covered outdoor ice-skating rink that

doubles as a concert and events shelter during the rest of the year (City-Data.com 2011).

Columbia. For Columbia, Maryland, James Rouse, the town's developer, intended to create a people-friendly social and physical environment that would simultaneously allow private venture capital to make a profit in land development and sale (Olsen 2004). To apply the best thinking available in the execution of his city, Rouse employed a host of specialists during the planning phase, including government employees, family counselors, recreationalists, sociologists, economists, educators, health specialists, psychologists, and transportation and communications experts.

Larger than Reston, Columbia—with a current population approximately 97,000—does have low- to moderate-income housing. A racially integrated community (25 percent of its residents are African American), Columbia successfully scattered its several hundred subsidized units throughout the city. Covering more than 27 square miles, the new town is composed of communities of 800–900 homes, each with its own elementary school, neighborhood center and convenience store, swimming pool, and recreational facilities. The plan then groups four neighborhoods into villages (of which there are ten), each with a middle school, meeting hall, supermarket, and some other shops clustered around a small plaza. In the town center are office buildings, large department stores, and a larger shopping center.

Enhancing the town's variety of programs is Howard Community College and Lincoln Technical Institute. Columbia has 5,300 acres of permanent open space, including 144 "tot lots" (children's playgrounds), 225 pedestrian bridges, the 40-acre Symphony Woods, three lakes, 19 ponds, and natural open space areas interlaced with more than 83 miles of pathways for walking, biking, and jogging. A vast network of plazas, picnic areas, public areas, tennis courts, and two par-course fitness trails also exist. In 2010, *Money* magazine ranked Columbia (with nearby Ellicott City) #2 out of the 100 "Best Places to Live in the United States."

Irvine. Also begun in the 1960s, Southern California's Irvine is the largest planned community in North America, covering 46 square miles, and headquarters for more than 100 major corporations. It is also home to a 15,000-acre campus of the University of California. An upper-middle-class city, with a population of 210,000, its median household income in 2009 was approximately $85,000. Its racial-ethnic breakdown is 47 percent non-Hispanic white, 3 percent African American, 37 percent Asian American, and 11 percent Hispanic (City-Data.com 2011).

Celebration. Celebration, in central Florida, is a good example of the New Urbanism. Construction began with the downtown—a lively mix of retail shops, restaurants, offices and apartments, town hall, post office, grocery store, and cinema—situated along a wide promenade circling the lake in the center of town. Most notable is the Art Deco–style movie complex and a cylindrical post office. More than 4,000 people call Celebration their home, with an eventual total population planned to reach approximately 12,000. Oversized porches and verandas encourage old-time neighborhood socializing, and the community is surrounded by a 4,700-acre, protected green belt with miles of walking paths.

A 900-student elementary school and a 1,000-student high school, together with a private Montessori school and Stetson University campus, are part of the community. A 60-acre "health campus"—a cross between a full-service gym and a hospital—enables people to keep in shape downstairs to avoid the medical wards upstairs. Unlike the average "designer suburb," where all the houses carry a similar price tag, Celebration's nearly three dozen $1-million estates coexist with other homes that have a median value of about $706,000, as well as with about 350 rental apartments, to form a social mix not often seen such communities (City-Data.com 2011).

Celebration is clearly an attempt to return to the pedestrian-friendly, compactly built town of the past, as compared with what the New Urbanists describe as the car-dominated, suburban sprawl of freeways, malls, and widely dispersed single-family homes. Admired by many, Celebration also receives criticism from others, who call it a retreat to a dream world of the past that only appeals to a small segment of the population. This mostly white (85 percent), upper-middle-class community, had a $94,000 median household income in 2009, more than twice that of Florida.

Erin Mills, Ontario. The largest planned new town in Canada is located on 8,000 acres within the incorporated city of Mississauga, about 20 miles west of Toronto. Now completing its final building phase, this fast-growing community of about 105,000 residents is a successful blend of residences, industry, and commerce. A planned community, it contains high-rise condominiums, large low-density housing, or medium-density, single-detached town or row houses; a town center; hospital; and an interconnected, tree-lined recreational trail system.

What Makes New Towns Succeed or Fail?

Many new towns have been built worldwide since Ebenezer Howard sounded the clarion call in 1898. Most of those that come into existence, however, do not succeed as the new towns they were intended to be. Why?

One major goal of most new towns was to distribute population more broadly. Howard and his followers thought that the congestion of big cities was destructive of human well-being and that their economic dominance sapped vitality from the rest of the region. Critics point out that new towns don't do much to meet this goal. Even in Britain, after decades of new-town development, barely 1 percent of the population lives in them. Most governments really can't raise the tax money needed to build new towns on a much larger scale. A more realistic idea may be to improve already-existing center cities. New Orleans could have been one such place after the devastation of Hurricane Katrina in 2005, but no master plan evolved.

New towns were also to be centers of employment and economic activity. Here again, however, few of them attracted much industry or other business. The problem is largely economic: At a distance from major cities, new towns present businesses with added costs for materials and transportation. Thus, especially in North America, new towns ended up with a strong suburban flavor—bedroom communities for people who, by and large, work elsewhere.

New towns are the dream of a few—some city planners, a few public officials, architects, builders, and mayors. Many others think these efforts could be more effectively placed elsewhere—in inner-city development, for example, or in the elimination of slum housing.

This is not to ignore the many contributions of the new-town idea. Columbia's developer, James Rouse, and Reston's developer, Robert E. Simon, both demonstrated broad social concern and purpose in undertaking projects of such economic magnitude and social audacity. We might also direct such tribute to Ebenezer Howard, who aspired to so much in his new-town vision. Nevertheless, no one has built "the new Jerusalem." Moreover, the new town is not the magic potion to cure all urban problems.

ARCHITECTURAL VISIONS

An irony marks Ebenezer Howard's ambition—to change all of society by building cities that were small. Some visionaries argue that solving the city's problems will demand not outlying new towns but also completely new *central cities*—more efficient, more humane, and for *everybody*. Here, we examine four large-scale "visions of the street." Each is the work of an architect; each is refreshingly different.

The Radiant City

Among the most important figures of modern architecture, Le Corbusier was also an influential urban planner. In his books *The City of Tomorrow and Its Planning* (1987; orig. 1927) and *The Radiant City* (1967; orig. 1933), Le Corbusier, like Howard, condemned modern cities and outlined a vision of a new urban society. His solution, though, was the opposite of

Howard's. Rejecting widespread decentralization, Le Corbusier saw benefits to concentrating people in tall, architecturally magnificent buildings surrounded by huge open spaces. Such mammoth structures, Le Corbusier reasoned, allowed keeping 95 percent of available land free from any building at all.

A second innovation was eliminating the central business district and population concentration by creating equal densities throughout the city. As he stated, "Flows of people would become much more even across the whole city, instead of strong radical flows into and out of the center which characterize cities today" (Hall and Tewdwr-Jones 2011:51).

Although no such **urban utopia** was ever built, Le Corbusier's influence on city planning was great. One classic example is the Alton West estate in Roehampton, in southwest London, built after World War II. A second example of a Le Corbusier–influenced project is Manhattan's Stuyvesant Town. Red brick buildings stand between wide walkways and lawns in this park-like setting constructed in 1947.

Le Corbusier expressed his vision to its fullest extent in his 1953 design of Chandigarh, the first planned city of India and which calls itself "the city beautiful." Structurally, Chandigarh is a modern city, with a population of 900,000. Each of the city's 49 sectors is a block about 1 square kilometer in size, with markets, shopping centers, and schools to limit people's need to travel. Citywide transportation (buses, auto-rickshaws, and taxicabs) links the sectors. One factor Le Corbusier was unable to control, however, was population density; with 7,900 people per square kilometer, its density is four times what Le Corbusier wished.

Broadacre City

Frank Lloyd Wright, the most famous of all U.S. architects, viewed Le Corbusier's urban vision as a nightmare. Such high-density living should be avoided at all costs, Wright maintained, and he championed instead "organic architecture"—the living union of architectural design with the natural environment.

He reasoned that if homes could be constructed in an "organic" way, why couldn't the same be done for entire cities?

Like both Howard and Le Corbusier, Wright accepted the integral role of modern technology. Unlike them, he was antiurban and sought to increase vastly the amount of space occupied by his utopian city in order to lower greatly its density. He thought that a city, without high-rises or large buildings, might easily spread over 100 square miles, or even more. With automobiles (or even individual, small helicopters), he contended, people could live on their own acres of farmland and still easily reach neighbors and shopping facilities. Broadacre City was a fusion of what Wright saw as the ideals of Jeffersonian democracy (fundamentally, extensive personal freedoms), the North American dream of plenty of land for personal use, and modern technology.

Broadacre City never was more than a dream, of course. The plan met with massive criticism during Wright's lifetime (1867–1959). Critics dismissed Broadacre City as too expensive, too unrestrained, and far too radical. Although stung by the negative reaction, Wright never gave up on his ideas. He rewrote his Broadacre treatise, *The Living City*, for the fourth time at age 90.

The Arcology

One of Wright's students was a young Italian named Paolo Soleri, who both respected and rebelled against his mentor's teaching. He accepted Wright's central notion of organic architecture, but he rejected entirely his teacher's vision of Broadacre City. Siding with Le Corbusier, Soleri advocated a dense concentration of people in an urban area. His vision, however, was even more extreme: a completely self-contained unit housing up to half a million people in a megastructure 300 stories high and occupying just the space of a few city blocks! Soleri called such cities **arcologies,** or architectural ecologies—environmentally safe, architecturally beautiful, and totally efficient.

Soleri's Babel IIB, designed for a population of 520,000, contained underground industrial and commercial areas; the city center at ground level; a public area and a promenade on the first level; a neighborhood and a park (both outdoors) on the second level; gardens, a community area (for recreation), and a living–working area on the third level (about 1,500 feet high!); and housing at the very top. All service facilities—elevators, heating, and exhaust systems—would be contained in the central core of the city.

Structures like these (Soleri designed dozens) are so audacious, even in the history of utopian urban planning, that few take them seriously. Critics dismiss arcologies as gigantic beehives. Soleri counters by claiming they are "miniatures" compared with today's cities. They occupy a fraction of the land, free up the surrounding countryside for enjoyment, and allow that countryside a chance to return to nature. Imagine, he suggests, the population of Los Angeles, which now sprawls over 470 square miles, contained in 10–12 well-dispersed Babels, and everywhere else no freeways, no smog, just beautiful Southern California. No doubt, however, such structures would be astronomically expensive, and no one came forward to finance constructing one. Soleri's vision is partially visualized at Arcosanti, a small experimental town in Arizona.

TRY-2004

A bold proposal for an arcology came from Japan's leading architectural and construction firm, the Shimizu Corporation: a massive, megacity pyramid. Twelve times higher than the Great Pyramid of Giza, it would be the largest structure on Earth. Situated over Tokyo Bay, it would stand over 1.2 miles high, with an area of 3 square miles at the base. The structure would consist of eight layers stacked on top of each other, comprising a total area of 34 square miles. Each layer would consist of smaller pyramids, each roughly the size of the Luxor Hotel in Las Vegas, with layers 1 through 4 devoted to mixed residential and commercial usage and layers 5 through 8 devoted to research centers, leisure facilities, and hotels (Shimz 2011).

Plans include 240,000 housing units to accommodate as many as 750,000 residents, with offices and commercial facilities capable of employing 800,000 people. The housing and offices would be in 80-story skyscrapers, suspended above and below and attached to the pyramid's supporting structure by a mega-truss construction method. Transportation within the city would consist of automated, individual pods that travel rapidly through tubes, as well as escalators and elevators. With Japan's population dropping significantly and the cost to build this hyperstructure with its staggering proportions, it seems unlikely any of us will witness this construction.

Then again, perhaps we should not so casually dismiss this proposal. Moscow planners have approved plans for construction of Crystal Island on Nagatino Peninsula, just 4.5 miles from the Kremlin. A self-contained city, it will soar about 1,500 feet in height, with four times the floor area of the Pentagon. This megastructure, resembling a huge transparent wigwam, will have up to 3,000 hotel rooms and 900 serviced apartments, but it will also contain a cinema, a theater, a museum, shopping malls, a sports complex, and an international school for 500 pupils (Parfitt 2008).

Utopia's Limitations

Each of these planned urban utopias share many of the limitations found in the New Town movement. First, they are financially impractical. Second, many are rigid proposals developed by visionaries who assume that everyone would see the basic logic of their vision and support it. Third, such plans seem to be sociologically naive. As Hall and Tewder-Jone (2011) note, these utopians are all *architects* who believe that altering the physical world will automatically alter the social world as well but, of course, beautiful designs do not necessarily do away with social problems, such as racial prejudice or poverty.

Yet, in the final analysis, society needs utopian thinkers. They are, by their work, natural consciousness raisers. They challenge our thinking about cities, point to obvious problems, and prod us to consider visionary solutions that we "on the street" barely understand.

MORE FOCUSED URBAN PLANNING

The problem with utopian planners is that their schemes are simply too grandiose and impractical. A city is simply *too complex a phenomenon* to be controlled as though it were a programmable computer. Other planners argue that urban planning only works when it is focused on a limited segment of city life—say, a neighborhood or park. We may never be able to manage the city as a whole, but we can handle the urban scene one segment at a time.

Sidewalks and Neighborhoods

Since the 1960s, a more popular trend has been away from large-scale, comprehensive visions. Leading this reaction was Jane Jacobs, author of *The Death and Life of Great American Cities* (1993; orig. 1961). To Jacobs, the greatest value of the city is its diversity: The city's "life" lies in its countless interactions and the multiple uses of its streets, parks, sidewalks, and neighborhoods. Anything that diminishes this quality (as does comprehensive planning, by definition) leads cities to their "death." Urban living is never *planned* in any broad sense. People of the city *invent* their lives as they meet their own needs and solve their own problems.

Consider sidewalks. In any vital city, a sidewalk has uses far beyond easing the passage of pedestrians. Front steps facing the sidewalk are places for neighbors to sit and visit, just as corners are places to "hang out." Second, sidewalk street life serves as a means of public surveillance, through which people come to know each other and to identify strangers. Jacobs pointed out that in areas where street life abounds, crime rates are low. Third, sidewalks are environments where children explore their neighborhood, test themselves, and grasp the rules of urban social life. Finally, street life brings a sense of community to a neighborhood. South Philadelphia, New York's Lower East Side, New Orleans's French Quarter, and San Francisco's Haight–Ashbury district all maintain a positive identity based on their street life.

In general, Jacobs supported local planning initiatives but loathed grandiose designs. What city planners should do, she said, is facilitate diversity and vitality and let local people do the rest. The best planning, then, is sometimes the least planning. The *Urban*

Trends box below outlines Jacobs's suggestions to a city planning board.

Squares and Parks

Of course, not everyone who believes in more focused city planning goes as far as Jacobs. While agreeing that holistic city planning is undesirable, some argue that good planning can be more comprehensive than Jacobs allows.

URBAN TRENDS

Jane Jacobs: Planning for Vitality

Consider, for a moment, the kind of goals at which city planning must begin to aim, if the object is to plan for city vitality.

Planning for vitality must stimulate and catalyze the greatest possible range and quantity of diversity among uses and among people throughout each district of a big city; this is the underlying foundation of city economic strength, social vitality and magnetism. To do this, planners must diagnose, in specific places, what is lacking to generate diversity, and then aim at helping to supply the lacks as best they can be supplied.

Planning for vitality must promote continuous networks of local street neighborhoods, whose users and informal proprietors can count to the utmost in keeping the public spaces of the city safe, in handling strangers so they are an asset rather than a menace, in keeping casual public tabs on children in places that are public.

Planning for vitality must combat the destructive presence of border vacuums [vacant land at the edges], and it must help promote people's identification with city

districts that are large enough, and are varied and rich enough in inner and outer contacts to deal with the tough, inescapable, practical problems of big-city life.

Planning for vitality must aim at unslumming the slums, by creating conditions aimed at persuading a high proportion of the indigenous residents, whoever they may be, to stay put by choice over time, so there will be a steadily growing diversity among people and a continuity of community both for old residents and for newcomers who assimilate into it.

Planning for vitality must convert the self-destruction of diversity and other cataclysmic uses of money into constructive forces, by hampering the opportunities for destructiveness on the one hand, and on the other hand by stimulating more city territory into possessing a good economic environment for other people's plans.

Planning for vitality must aim at clarifying the visual order of cities, and it must do so by both promoting and illuminating functional order, rather than by obstructing or denying it.

Source: Jane Jacobs, *The Death and Life of Great American Cities* (New York: Random House, 1993), pp. 531–32.

August Heckscher spent two years studying cities such as Omaha, Dallas, Cincinnati, Buffalo, Rochester, and Milwaukee. To him, the vitality of a city was fundamentally a matter of how well that city organized its space:

> Each city is a place of its own, its uniqueness determined in large measure by patterns created by the alternation of structure and void, of buildings and spaces between. The large green spaces, parks and parkways, river banks and waterfronts, give to a city a coherence that allows the urban dweller to have a feeling of the whole.... What is expressed in open spaces is the essential quality of urban life—its casualness and variety, its ability to crystallize community feeling. (1978:4)

In cities dominated by economic concerns, such as those in North America, Heckscher highlights the value of squares, parks, architecture, and artwork to urban life. These prompt people to remember that there are "other things" to city life. Squares provide small, natural meeting places as well as settings for more formal occasions, such as political rallies and concerts. They provide a vital physical and psychological break in the city's structure. New Orleans's Jackson Square, located in the French Quarter, is one such vital square. Others include Fountain Square in Cincinnati, Union Square in San Francisco, City Hall Square in Toronto, Rittenhouse Square in Philadelphia, and Washington Square in New York.

Parks are equally important. Sara Miller (2003) speaks for many in celebrating the first U.S. urban park, New York's Central Park, 843 acres on the upper half of Manhattan Island, which preserves a bit of country in the city. Although perhaps not as well known as Central Park, a similar public space is found in virtually every major North American city, and there, residents delight in recreation and informal activities of all kinds. Atlanta has Piedmont Park (185 acres), Chicago has Grant Park (305 acres), and San Diego has Balboa Park (1,158 acres). There is Schenley Park in Pittsburgh (456 acres), Stanley Park in Vancouver (1,000 acres), and Griffith Park in Los Angeles (4,063 acres). Phoenix boasts the largest U.S. city park, South Mountain Park (16,283 acres), while Philadelphia has the largest pre-automobile city park, Fairmount Park (4,079 acres).

In a study of urban spaces, William H. Whyte found that many people simply thrive on the streets. Observing the Seagram Plaza in midtown Manhattan, he wrote that "On a good day, there would be a hundred and fifty people sitting, sunbathing, picnicking and schmoozing—idly gossiping, talking 'nothing talk'" (2001:14; orig., 1980). Moreover, claims Whyte,

> [People] go to the lively places where there are many people. And they go there by choice, not to escape the city but to partake of it.... The multiplier effect is tremendous. It is not just the number of people using these small urban places, but the larger number who pass by and enjoy them vicariously, or the even larger number who feel better about the city center for knowledge of them. For a city such places are priceless, whatever the costs. (2001:100–101)

Placemaking

Building on the ideas of Jane Jacobs ("eyes on the street") and William H. Whyte (essential elements for creating social life in public spaces), in 1975 the Project for Public Spaces (PPS) launched a multifaceted approach to the design, planning, and management of public spaces, called **placemaking.** Essentially, this involves learning the needs and aspirations of the people who live, work, and play in a particular space, and then using that information to create a common vision for that place.

The advantage of grassroots involvement is that it helps prevent developers and planners from creating "traffic-dominated streets, little-used parks and plazas, and isolated, underperforming development projects" (PPS 2011). The collective vision of people and planners provides a perspective that views a place in its entirety (social and physical) rather than focusing on isolated fragments of the whole. PPS seeks to spark a re-examination of everyday settings and experiences to find the potential for something better in parks, downtowns, waterfronts, plazas, neighborhoods,

The Project for Public Spaces (PPS), a non-profit organization, suggested the conversion of New York's Astor Place from a void between two neighborhoods to one that instead supports and showcases the best that the city can offer. Note the change in street design that increases the pedestrian area and adds sidewalk amenities.

streets, markets, campuses, and public buildings (PPS 2011).

The PPS premise about streets is quite simple: If you plan for cars and traffic, you get more cars and traffic, but if you design your community around people, you get more people. The quality of great streets includes their identity and image, amenities, clustered activity points of interest, walkable space, attractive edge uses, diverse choices, and diverse user groups with no one group or use dominating (PPS 2007). (The photo essay on pages 403–406 offers some PPS visualizations of improved street designs.)

One notable PPS project was the transformation of New York's Times Square. Hired by the Times Square Alliance (one of the BIDs discussed in Chapter 3), the PPS examined the district through systematic observation techniques such as time-lapse film analysis, activity mapping, tracking, and user surveys. Some of the issues revealed were the lack of

West Broadway in New York City offers a dreary streetscape with little foot traffic, but the bottom photo reveals how, with narrower streets and wider sidewalks, it could become a more dynamic locale. Its spaces, safer and better defined, could generate more activity within a more visually pleasing environment.

amenities in the square, severe pedestrian overcrowding, and a cluttered ground surface or "streetscape schlock" (Times Square Alliance 2011). PPS recommendations included a reconfiguration of streets to accommodate foot traffic better and reduce the negative effects of traffic, numerous amenities to improve the pedestrian experience, and new public space programming such as performances and markets.

The temporary improvements in the Times Square "Bowtie" (where Seventh Avenue crosses Broadway between 42nd and 47th Streets) were so successful in safety and traffic flow that the city administration made them permanent. Vehicles can no longer travel on Broadway between those streets; those lanes now are blue-painted pedestrian plazas, with chairs and sidewalk cafes, and the reduced vehicular traffic has resulted in a 40 percent decrease in pollutants. Bleachers containing 27 ruby-red structural-glass steps at 47th Street provide seating for about 1,000 people and a picture-perfect panoramic view that has enthralled visitors for more than a century (Huff Post 2011b; Dunlap 2008).

New York's Kenmare Square serves as a crossroad of several dynamic neighborhoods: Little Italy, Bowery, Chinatown, and Soho. Its stark appearance could be transformed by a few simple placemaking steps: wider sidewalks and extended "bubble corners," clearly marked pedestrian paths, a transitional area for the joining streets, and sidewalk amenities.

Festival Marketplaces

Later in his life, James Rouse, the creator of Columbia, Maryland, shifted his attention to midsized projects of urban regeneration.

Most of these efforts at placemaking were spectacularly successful. They are neither comprehensive, all-encompassing visions like Columbia nor small-scale, local efforts

Grand Street in New York City could also be more than just a nondescript street that serves primarily as a place for car storage and little else. With a street and sidewalk design that encourages social interaction, it can become much more valuable neighborhood space both for the stores and residents.

like those championed by Jane Jacobs. While such planning takes account of the needs of the whole city, it targets a small portion of the city's space. The most well-known of Rouse's midsized "festival market-place" efforts are the Faneuil Hall complex in Boston, New York's South Street Seaport, Philadelphia's Market East, Baltimore's Harborplace, Union Station in St. Louis, Pioneer Place in Portland, the Riverview Marketplace of New Orleans, and the Grand Avenue Mall in Milwaukee.

All of these projects reclaimed portions of deteriorating central cities in the 1970s and 1980s. Rouse was concerned that Americans had lived so long with grim, congested, and worn-out inner cities and with sprawling and cluttered outer cities that they subconsciously accepted such conditions as both inevitable and unavoidable. He worried that people no longer realized cities could be beautiful, humane, and truly responsive to the needs and yearnings of their people (Olsen 2004).

So, Rouse set to work. Before he began, the Faneuil Hall area of Boston had become as tawdry as one could imagine. The site of the city center in Revolutionary War days, the area abounded with old, dilapidated warehouses that abutted on the harbor. No one lived there, and only a few businesses remained. With a generous spirit, one would have called the locale "down and out."

Today, it is transformed. The old warehouses were outwardly maintained, but the inner cores were thoroughly modernized. Faneuil Hall was revamped in the same manner. Inside, food shops run its football-field length. On either side of the Hall are pedestrian areas with benches, outdoor eating areas, and places where street musicians play. The refurbished old warehouses on either side are now the home of high-quality shops. On any summer day, the place is teeming with people—locals, tourists, and visitors from the suburbs. Looking at the project from the vantage point of one of the high-rises in the area or from the harbor, one sees how Rouse's vision works: The new buildings mimic or harmoniously blend with the old buildings of the area. Perhaps most important, the businesses in the project are profitable, and the success of the Faneuil Hall project subsequently stimulated development throughout Boston's downtown. Much the same happy story applies to his other urban projects.

Critics charge that Rouse's successes pander to the wealthier elements of urban areas and do little for the poor. Some truth lies in this accusation, but Rouse's changes helped turn around one stunning problem by replacing collapsing inner-city districts with thriving, vibrant urban places.

THE REALITIES OF URBAN PLANNING

Whatever philosophical stance one ultimately takes about urban planning, shaping the city always forces us to contend with traditions, vested interests, and environmental conditions. Such realities operate both as barriers and as opportunities.

Economics and Politics

Radical alterations in the urban landscape rarely get far off the ground. Ebenezer Howard could establish only two garden cities, and even with government support, the British new-town effort remains limited. In the United States, Stein's Radburn, New Jersey, fell victim to financial troubles, while Columbia and Reston went through dire straits for the same reason. Partially because of expense (and partially because of its audacity), Frank Lloyd Wright's Broadacre City never even began. The stark reality is that in a free-market economy, urban planning rarely strays very far from the interests of business.

Local politics, too, swirls around city planning, as interest groups contend with each other to achieve their various goals. Sometimes, the complexities of even small-scale projects lead to challenges that intimidate elected officials who fear alienating voters.

The Importance of Values

In the final analysis, urban planning is always a question of values: Which ones and whose are the key issues? We noted previously that city planning reflects cultural values. In Catholic Rome, planning glorified the Church; in monarchic France, planning celebrated the king; in New York City, planning augmented the pursuit of the almighty dollar.

Values also saturate, explicitly or implicitly, the work of urban planners. In a review of Jane Jacobs's *Death and Life of Great American Cities*, Herbert Gans (1962) pointed out that Jacobs is a typical product of her society. She complained that, too often, city planning was not left up to the people. What could be more

Western, more North American, Gans asks, than a complaint that we need more emphasis on the individual, and that we should make way for local initiative?

Similarly, because most of us are deeply committed to the values of individuality and personal initiative, we are put off by all-inclusive planning that seems to demand submission to the group. Indeed, perhaps the characteristic element of North American urban planning has been the lack of comprehensive planning. From the 1600s onward, most U.S. and Canadian cities developed with very limited intervention by any governmental agency. There are notable exceptions, such as Portland, Oregon, and Toronto. Mainly, though, the national governments have no overall plans or policies for their cities, because the residents don't want them. If private investors like Jim Rouse can't make our cities better, then most people seem content to live with the consequences.

Current interest among many scholars and practitioners lies in private, market-based programs to address urban economic and social ills, in the belief that many areas of civic and commercial life do not require government involvement (Beito, et al. 2009). Examples abound of the non-government sector effectively providing for roads and bridges, education, housing, social welfare, land-use planning, commercial law, and even policing and criminal prosecutions. The private, self-governing enclaves and large-scale industrial communities with complex physical infrastructure and services, such as Chicago's Manufacturing District, challenge the orthodoxy that government alone can improve community life and indicate that the private sector can play a greater role in urban planning and policy.

Some Canadian and U.S. cities, however, illustrate the vitality wrought by good government planning. Among them are Portland, San Francisco, Seattle, and Vancouver—locales frequently cited in public opinion polls as among the "best" cities. Another city fulfilling all of these qualifications is Toronto, where planning successfully addresses the challenges of urban diversity and urban sprawl. We examine Toronto as a

model of good urban planning in our final case study.

Toronto is a Great Lakes port and, through the St. Lawrence Seaway, an ocean port as well. With more than 5.5 million people living in the region, Toronto is the most populous metropolitan area in Canada. About one in six Canadians live there, and the city attracts one-fourth of all newcomers to Canada, with an average of 55,000 new immigrants each year (Toronto 2011). The Toronto region has the nation's major concentration of industrial jobs and serves as the commercial and financial center of Canada. The central area, downtown Toronto, is the predominant regional center, encompassing major government, financial, medical, and education services.

Toronto attracts a large number of immigrants from the developing world and has an increasing number of people requiring welfare assistance, but its school system and financial stability are stronger than those of many U.S. cities in a similar situation. Although Toronto faces suburban and edge city development as do other cities, its central city remains strong, the region's growth patterns are not wasteful of environmental resources, and the transportation systems are more efficient, with greater reliance on mass transit. What makes Toronto more successful in these areas than its sister cities elsewhere? The answer lies in a metropolitan approach to governance and policy making that enables Toronto to address spatial development and quality-of-life issues in a more comprehensive manner and with greater resources at its disposal, as we will discuss shortly.

The Physical Setting

Situated on the northern shore of Lake Ontario, Toronto is almost entirely flat, except at approximately 3–4 miles inland, where the land sharply rises about 40 feet at the shoreline elevation of the former glacial Lake Iroquois. Streets are in a grid design, except for the diagonal roads along the shoreline. Railroad tracks and an expressway separate the lakefront from the downtown area. The central business areas are around Bloor, Queen, and Yonge streets, while the central financial district is south of the old city hall, in the vicinity of King and Bay streets. The CN Tower (1,815 feet) dominates the city skyline—along with the Toronto-Dominion Centre, Commerce Court, and First Canadian Place—all of which are more than 50 stories high.

Situated north of the central business district is a fashionable shopping area. The Ontario Parliament Buildings and the University of Toronto rise south of Bloor Street, in a section with tall shade trees and grassy areas known for its park-like atmosphere. One of the most attractive residential areas in Toronto is Rosedale, an older neighborhood of distinguished homes set on winding, tree-lined streets close to the downtown center, which itself contains many attractive streets of modest, well-designed houses.

History

Inhabited first by the Seneca and later by the Mississauga Indians, the area was originally a trading post in the seventeenth century because of its strategic location at the crossing of ancient Indian trails going west to the Mississippi and north to Lake Simcoe and the vast wilderness beyond. The French built three small forts there in the eighteenth century, all of them subsequently destroyed after the English defeated the French in 1759. During and after the U.S. War for Independence, about 40,000 loyalists fled the United States and settled in this region.

In 1787, Lord Dorchester, the Canadian governor-in-chief, peacefully negotiated the purchase of 250,000 acres from three Indian chiefs for the future capital of Ontario. Its name was changed from Toronto to York in 1795, and U.S. forces temporarily occupied the small settlement of about 700 residents during the War of 1812. By 1834, the population grew to 9,000 and restored its original name.

The coming of the Grand Trunk and Great Western railways in the 1850s sparked rapid development. As a break-of-bulk port city, Toronto flourished, shipping agricultural products, minerals, and timber from the surrounding region. Industrialization further spurred growth, as the city and its environs soon produced more than half of Canada's manufactured goods. Through annexation of adjacent villages and towns, the city doubled in area by 1900, and then doubled again by 1920. In 1930, the metropolitan area included the central city, four towns (Leaside, Mimico, New Toronto, and Weston), three villages (Forest Hill, Long Branch, and Swansea), and five townships (Etobicoke, East York, North York, Scarborough, and York).

Creation of a Metropolitan Government

The Great Depression of the 1930s caused severe financial problems for the city that remained until the end of World War II in 1945. Already lacking the financial means to provide water and sewage systems to outlying areas, Toronto saw its municipal burden increase further with a rapid rise in population. After investigating various options, the Ottawa Municipal Board in 1953 recommended that the 13 municipalities (named in the previous paragraph) create a federated form of government unique in North America. Passage that year of the Municipality of Metropolitan Toronto Act united the metropolitan area, and the 25-member Council of Metropolitan Toronto began its task of finding ways to deal with such common concerns as revenues, education, transportation, and urban growth. This combined form of government offered greater credit than each individual municipality had, thereby enhancing financing for various public projects. A significant feature of this metropolitan system was that council members were the elected mayors, aldermen, or controllers of each municipality, which ensured good communication and a high level of coordination between the central body and the local municipalities.

The Metropolitan Council worked well. It authorized construction of new schools and renovation of older ones, and it also introduced a regional system of parks in an attempt to control future development. It greatly improved transportation by upgrading or building new roads and expressways and by constructing an excellent subway and a new airport terminal building. As a result, Toronto's transit system now consists of a grid network of streetcars, buses, three underground rapid-transit lines, and a light-rail transit system that together account for two-thirds of all trips to the central city. This transportation network is integrated with large concentrations of office employment and new housing located along the rapid transit lines and brings workers from the surrounding regions to the downtown area.

In 1967, the Corporation of Metropolitan Toronto reorganized, reducing its 13 municipalities to 6 and increasing the number of seats on the council from 25 to 33. The Council also considerably extended its responsibilities in education and social services and added others, such as ambulance and library services, urban renewal, and waste disposal. Also, the reorganized council resolved many of its difficult problems by creating more effective water and sewage systems.

In 1998, the six municipalities comprising Metropolitan Toronto—East York, Etobicoke, North York, Scarborough, York, and the former City of Toronto—and its regional government were amalgamated into a single City of Toronto. At the same time, the city's responsibilities, revenues, and property tax base were reformed, all without disruption of city services to residents and businesses. Although the new Toronto government centralized its administration, the city still maintained community councils to deal with purely neighborhood matters, and its various local civic and social services remain in local communities.

This reorganization enabled Toronto to consolidate resources and develop a coordinated plan for the growth of both its urban and suburban schools. The Toronto region thus avoided many of the problems that plagued nearby Detroit in the areas of crime, education, and social services, because it evenly controlled use of space and distribution of resources.

Two Phases of Urban Planning

Beginning in the 1950s and into the early 1970s, Toronto's urban planning reflected an all-out, pro-development attitude and adherence to the principles of modernist planning. This approach emphasized intense specialization of land use, massive infrastructure (particularly urban expressways), and redevelopment of older areas (Filion 1995).

City officials identified a number of districts as blighted and then obliterated them to make room for expressways, public housing projects, private high-rise apartment developments, or an expansion of downtown's commercial functions. With little regard for existing neighborhoods in these designated areas, the wrecking ball and bulldozer razed some of the city's architectural gems and destroyed communities in such places as Alexandra Park, Rusholme Road on the east side, St. Jamestown, and Regent Park. These old neighborhoods were seen as an inconvenience between two modernist sectors: the suburbs and a rapidly redeveloping central business district (Caulfield 1994:7).

Alexandra Park exemplifies the outcome of the modernist planning approach also found in many other North American cities. Once it was an area of mixed use, consisting of old residential houses and commercial activities linked with the rest of the city. With the demolition of the neighborhood in the 1960s to build a public housing project, the area became an isolated, virtually impenetrable ghetto (Caulfield 1994:11–13).

Toronto officials and local developers continued to raze prominent architectural landmarks and stable working-class neighborhoods, replacing them with modern, "efficient" structures, until local activist groups began to fight city hall's urban renewal plans. The reformers pointed to the decay of U.S. inner cities and argued that Toronto could avoid their mistakes if it remained "people-oriented" and emphasized neighborhood preservation. Their arguments were persuasive; they succeeded in preserving such areas as Rusholme Road on the west side, Old City Hall, Toronto Island, Church of the Holy Trinity, Union Station, and Trefann Court. This "cultural resistance," suggests Caulfield, played an important role in the introduction of the second phase of planning: postmodern inner-city development. Postmodern urbanism is a celebration of traditional urban form and of social and cultural heterogeneity (Caulfield 1994:97).

From the late 1960s onward, the postmodernist movement—overlapping the modernist movement for a few years before emerging as the dominant force—found sufficient support in Toronto's Metropolitan Council to halt modernist redevelopment of most inner-city neighborhoods. Echoing the antimodernist perspectives of Jane Jacobs and Lewis Mumford, planners began emphasizing the benefits of a diversified, small-grained urban texture and the importance of preserving older buildings. Ironically, the preservation and upgrading of the built environment led to the loss of its social diversity, as middle- and upper-income people—seeking easy downtown access and a more stimulating environment than was available in the suburbs—displaced the working-class and ethnic populations previously there (Bell 2011).

Now, at last, eyes have turned back to Alexandra Park. After staff and consultants met with local residents, Toronto Community Housing officials in 2010 announced an ambitious revitalization plan. Beginning in 2012, more than 300 drab co-op townhouse and apartment units are being demolished and replaced with mixed-income housing. Another 473 existing units will be renovated and to come are a new underground parking garage, commercial and retail space, and improved green space. Adjacent to the site will be about 1,500 new condo units and a dozen townhouses. Zero displacement will occur, as the first housing units will be built on parking lots and open space, enabling people to move directly from their old units to the new. Then, the old units will be torn down, and the process would thus continue over a 15-year period (Donovan 2011).

Toronto Today

As a result of its planning reforms and metropolitan governance, Toronto has emerged into a dynamic city with the safest urban environment in North America. It is, as Jane Jacobs once remarked, "a city that works." It is Canada's top tourist destination, the financial center of Canada, and the third-largest financial center in North America. The city has the most fiber-optic telecommunications cable of any city in North America. It also contains the continent's largest continuous underground pedestrian system, connecting 1,200 stores and restaurants, 50 office towers, 6 major hotels, and several entertainment centers (Toronto 2011).

Toronto is also one of the world's most multicultural cities, attracting one-fourth of all Canada's immigrants. Not surprisingly, then, half the city's residents are immigrants, a much higher proportion than for most major cities in North America. With the exception of Oceania (the countries of the Pacific and South Pacific), every part of the world has sent at least 10,000 emigrants to Toronto in recent years. The 2006 Census identified more than 200 distinct ethnic origin residents. Nearly half the city's residents (47 percent) were visible minorities, up from 43 percent in 2001. South Asians (12 percent) now exceed the Chinese population (11.4 percent) as the largest visible minority group, with blacks at 8.4 percent. Between 2001 and 2006, the fastest growing visible minority group was Latin Americans. The postwar suburbs of North York, Scarborough, and York have become the main immigrant settlement areas as the central city, as mentioned earlier, attracts mostly middle- and upper-income residents.

Toronto is also an important cultural center, with a rich fare of ballet, concerts, films, opera, and theater offerings. In fact, it is the third-largest English-language theater center after London and New York. It is home to the Toronto Symphony Orchestra, three major theaters, and many small experimental theaters, as well as the Art Gallery of Ontario, the Royal Ontario Museum, the Ontario Science Centre, and a zoo. Often called "Hollywood North," it ranks third in TV and film production. Its institutions of higher learning include the Ontario College of Art, Ryerson Polytechnical Institute, the University of Toronto, and York University. The Toronto Blue Jays (baseball), Maple Leafs (ice hockey), Raptors (basketball), Argonauts (football), and Toronto FC (soccer) are professional sports teams that add to the city's excitement and vitality. Like any vibrant city, Toronto also offers an appealing array of restaurants, boutiques, movie theaters, festivals, exhibits, and recreational and social activities (Toronto 2011).

Toronto is not entirely free of problems. Increased traffic congestion, a shortage of affordable housing, and a need by half its residents for grocery stores within a half-mile radius are three of its main concerns (Connor 2010). To address these and other issues, the city seeks to implement its Official Plan—a vision of how Toronto will change and grow—by setting priorities for social, environmental, and economic development (see the *Cityscape* box on pages 412–413). The plan's aim is

---

CITYSCAPE

Toronto Plans Its Future

Following are introductory excerpts from an official master plan—developed, publicly discussed, and adopted in 2002 and revised in 2007—in which the city of Toronto designed its evolution over the next 30 years.

Building a successful Toronto means that we have to make sustainable choices about how we grow. We have to see connections and understand the consequences of our choices. We have to integrate environmental, social and economic perspectives in our decision making. We have to meet the needs of today without compromising the ability of future generations to meet their needs.

There is no such thing as an isolated or purely local decision. Each of us makes choices every day about where to live, work, play, shop and how to travel. They seem like small choices, but together and over time the consequences of these choices can affect everyone's quality of life. That's why planning matters....

This Plan is about the basics of successful city-building. Holistic and integrated thinking is a fundamental requirement for planning a modern city like Toronto. Integrated thinking means seeing, understanding and accounting for all the connections as we go about our decision making. Sometimes it means thinking differently about solutions. Always it means searching for outcomes that demonstrate integration, balance and interdependence and that earn social, environmental and economic rewards....

Toronto cannot plan in isolation or expect to stand alone in dealing with the effects of urban growth. Our view of the quality of urban life tends to be based on the local conditions in our own neighbourhoods. These conditions are in turn affected by events happening in the larger region. The quality of the air, water, services and region-wide transport systems all affect the quality of life in our neighbourhood, where we work and where we play. The way in which growth and change are managed in Toronto must mesh with that of our neighbours because we are integrally linked in many ways....

Building a successful city means making choices that improve our quality of life. As our City grows and matures, we can create a more beautiful environment, healthy and vibrant communities and greater prosperity....

In order to remain economically competitive in today's global economy, a city must be more than functional. It has to work well, but it also must be beautiful, vibrant, safe,

to (1) protect the best of what it has, (2) invest in areas that are aging and need revitalizing, (3) ensure that new development is consistent with the existing character of the area, and (4) convert former industrial lands into uses that fit the surrounding neighborhoods and add to community vitality (Toronto 2011). Facing its future, Toronto's leaders recognize that good, people-oriented planning is essential to its continued vitality as "a city that works."

SUMMARY

Ancient, medieval, and modern cities usually evolved through the planning of their physical layout and structure, if not in their entirety then certainly at least in part. Such planning addressed urban problems (protection, water supply, sanitation, traffic, and leisure activities), glorified the ruling elite (statues,

and inclusive. Great cities do not happen by accident—they are designed and orchestrated so that individual private and public developments work together to create cohesive blocks, neighbourhoods and districts. Good urban design is not just an aesthetic overlay, but an essential ingredient of city-building. Good urban design is good business and good social policy.

Civic pride is infectious. The City and the private sector should work together as partners in creating a great city and achieving Toronto's architectural and urban design potential. The City can play its part by organizing, designing, maintaining and improving the streets, parks and public buildings. The private sector can do its part by building the structures and landscapes that define and support these public places. This Plan demands that both the public and private sectors commit to high quality architecture, landscape architecture and urban design, consistent with energy efficient standards.

Beautiful, comfortable, safe and accessible streets, parks, open spaces and public buildings are a key shared asset. These public spaces draw people together, creating strong social bonds at the neighbourhood, city and regional level. They convey our public image to the world and unite us as a city. They set the stage for our festivals, parades and civic life as well as for daily casual contact. Public space creates communities.

This Plan recognizes how important good design is in creating a great city. Great cities are judged by the look and quality of their squares, parks, streets and public spaces and the buildings which frame and define them. People flock to the world's great cities not just to enjoy the culture, but to wander the streets, to explore their parks and plazas, to enjoy the street life, to shop and to people watch. The same characteristics and qualities that make these cities great places to visit also make them great places to live. What do these places share in common? All are very urban, high density, mixed use, mixed income, transit and pedestrian oriented vibrant places.

Great cities not only have great buildings—but the buildings work together to create great streets, plazas, parks and public places. Great cities inspire and astonish. Whether it's a bustling shopping street lined by vibrant shop windows and sidewalk cafes, an intimate, residential, tree-lined street, or a public plaza in the central business district—everywhere you look there is evidence that the place has been designed. The buildings, both public and private, work together to create the "walls" for the city's great outdoor "rooms."

Source: City of Toronto, *Toronto Official Plan* (October 2009). Accessed online at http://www.toronto.ca/planning/official_plan/pdf_chapter1-5/chapters1_5_dec2010.pdf on April 16, 2012.

buildings, plazas, and parks), and reflected cultural ideals (the scale of religious or commercial structures or the direction of processional routes).

In the late nineteenth century, two urban visionaries influenced many architects and planners. David Burnam's work at the 1893 World's Fair in Chicago inspired the City Beautiful movement throughout the United States. In England, Ebenezer Howard gave action to his concept of "garden cities" by building Letchworth and Welwyn in the early twentieth century. An early example in the United States of a planned new town is Radburn, New Jersey; though never completed, it served as a model for other new towns worldwide. As centers of residence, employment, and leisure activities, new towns have been more successful in countries with a strong tradition of central government planning than they have been in the United States, with their greater emphasis on individualism and home rule.

Architectural visions of a new central city—such as Le Corbusier's "radiant city," Wright's "broadacre city," and Shimizu's "TRY-2004"—are impractical utopias, but they do challenge our thinking about cities and prod us to consider bolder solutions to the cities' ills. The rebuilding of New Orleans provided a unique opportunity for a complete makeover of the city's design to improve the quality of life there, but no bold initiatives took place. Instead, the emphasis was more in line with Jacobs' thought to let the people in neighborhoods decide for themselves.

Elsewhere, urban planners typically focus on smaller sections of the city—its neighborhoods, open spaces, water edges, and historic sections—to revitalize tourist, leisure, and economy activities while making the city a more attractive locale. Economics, politics, and values are extremely significant factors in influencing what does or does not happen in urban planning. Although most cities attempt to control their destinies through good government planning, Toronto serves as a particularly impressive model with a comprehensive plan for its future.

CONCLUSION

Can we honestly say that one type of city planning has been spectacularly more effective than any other? Our review suggests a number of conclusions.

First, all the evidence suggests that changing a city's physical form does not automatically reshape social life. In new towns the world over—from Ebenezer Howard's Letchworth to James Rouse's Columbia to Lucio Costa's Brasilia—new structures have become home to many old problems, including harmful prejudices, class antagonism, and environmental pollution. Changing the city physically, while sometimes necessary, appears not to be sufficient in itself to realize the idealistic environment envisioned by planners. The best planning blends good sociology with dramatic architecture.

Second, all the planning experiments of the last century have fallen short of their goals. New towns have not solved the problems of large cities, nor have they solved many of their own troubles. Utopian designs intrigue us but offer few real solutions. Finally, small-scale efforts, such as those proposed by Jane Jacobs, August Heckscher, William H. Whyte, and James Rouse, are helpful but often leave the larger problems of the city, such as unemployment and poverty, untouched.

Third, we always must realize that urban planning occurs within a framework of certain unbending realities. Economic and political considerations limit the scope of any plan. If it costs too much, it won't be done. If sponsored by the rich, it probably won't be much help to the poor. What some people want, others are sure to resist. Urban planners, if they are to have any chance to work their craft, must become skillful politicians.

Surely, planning is vital to the future of our cities, but we must merge two often-contradictory forces—the planners' desire to shape the urban environment and a free people's need to choose. We must also overcome the tendency to think in purely local terms and, instead, recognize the need for a regional, integrated view of metropolitan regions. Cities and suburbs do not exist independently of one another. Their fates are inextricably linked, for many of the issues and problems that affect the quality of life transcend municipal boundaries. Furthermore, to ensure the vitality of cities in the twenty-first century, planners and the public need to gain an understanding of both the problems and the possibilities of urban life—and, yes, even try to learn from some of the utopian thinkers of the past.

As cities struggle to define their futures, people must ask some hard questions of themselves and of their leaders. Why should we plan in the first place? What are the issues that planners can address better than the people themselves? Whom does any plan really benefit? Guiding the discussion that such questions provoke, we also suggest, must be a fundamental commitment to the health and welfare of all people who live in the city. With such a dedication—as is evident today in the urban life of Toronto's people—it is possible that, in time, we will generate a vision of the street that perhaps all citizens can share.

KEY TERMS

arcologies (399)
City Beautiful movement (390)
garden cities (387)
green belt (391)

new town (391)
placemaking (402)
urban utopia (398)

INTERNET ACTIVITIES

1. The Project for Public Spaces offers a set of interesting slides on how to plan and improve public spaces (with numerous before and after examples) at *http://www.slideshare.net/metroplanning/project-for-public-spaces-streets-as-places.*
2. If you would like to see an example of architectural design that ignores the social environment (much like 1970s urban renewal did), go to *http://digitalurban.com/2008/01/virtual-purdue-future-city-animation.html,* and play the short animated video of a futuristic Turkish city. As you watch, observe how the attractions of a city—walkability, proximity of diverse activities, people watching, public transit, and action—are noticeably missing. Hopefully, this will never be a city of the future.

GLOSSARY

absolute poverty The lack of sufficient resources to secure the basic necessities of life.

abstract space What developers, investors, and government consider in terms of the dimensions of size, location, and profit, rather than the ideas of local people.

administrative or political city A city established primarily for governmental purposes, such as a national capital.

agglomeration industries Interdependent economic enterprises located close to one another that provide some element in the creation and distribution of a product.

amenity city A city primarily known for its specialized recreational opportunities, such as beaches, gambling, mineral springs, or skiing.

apartheid A formal policy of racial segregation that once existed in South Africa, which Massey and Denton applied to the United States because of intense residential segregation patterns.

arcologies Self-contained urban megastructures designed to be environmentally safe, architecturally beautiful, and totally efficient.

bobos Slang term for those living a lifestyle mixture of the bourgeoisie and the bohemians.

boomers Edge cities located at the intersection of two major highways and almost always centered on a mall.

bourgeoisie A term referring to the middle class, such as shopkeepers, traders, bureaucrats, government officials, and people engaged in commercial ventures.

break-of-bulk A strategic geographic location that facilitates the transfer of goods from one form of transportation to another, such as truck to ship.

buppies Slang term for black, young (late twenties to early forties) professionals.

census tract A U.S. Census Bureau population unit of about 4,000 residents who are relatively homogeneous in socioeconomic status and living conditions.

central business district (CBD) A concentration of commercial activity within a city that includes banking, entertainment, offices, restaurants, retail stores, and public transit.

central place theory Christaller's thesis that the more important a city's economic function is to a region, the more its population will increase.

chain migration The pattern of migrants settling near family or friends.

charter schools Schools that operate with less state regulation so that teachers and administrators can try out new teaching strategies.

City Beautiful movement Popular nineteenth-century idea of building cities around neoclassical civic centers, with great public spaces and parks linked by spacious boulevards.

city-states A sociopolitical organization that controls surrounding regions, including a number of other towns, villages, and rural lands.

civic culture Ability of city dwellers to coexist and cooperate in the everyday routines of public habits and customs.

colonization When a dominant group or country establishes control over another country or area, often for purposes of exploitation.

common-interest developments (CIDs) A form of gated community requiring membership in a self-governing homeowners' association that has extensive regulatory power over residents.

community policing An approach that increases interaction and cooperation between law enforcement agencies and the people and neighborhoods they serve.

combined statistical area (CSA) The U.S. Census Bureau term for a megalopolis, or overlapping of metropolitan regions.

cosmic calendar An imaginative concept to examine the entire history of our planet compressed into a single calendar year.

cosmopolites Highly educated urban sophisticates who choose to live in the city because of its wide range of activities, experiences, and social contacts.

critical mass An amount or level of population needed to support other activities, such as churches, hospitals, or shopping centers.

culture The basic beliefs, values, and technology that characterize a city in a particular historical era.

de facto segregation Unequal treatment of people based on social customs and traditions.

de jure segregation Unequal treatment established by law.

decentralization The outward migration of people and business from the central city to outlying suburban regions.

defensible space Physical design that promotes safety through ongoing natural surveillance.

dinks Slang term for couples with dual income, no kids.

districts Medium to large sections of the city, reinforced by physical clues to convey a sense of "being in" them.

division of labor The way that different tasks are apportioned to different people in a given society.

ecological sociology A subfield of sociology that focuses on urban design, land-use planning, and policy reform to create environmentally sound development.

economic restructuring When companies or cities move away from manufacturing as their primary economic activity and evolve into more service-oriented activities.

edge city A new, sprawling, middle-class, automobile-dependent center, typically located at the fringe of an older urban area.

edges Boundaries, either barriers or seams, that exist between two areas.

eminent domain The legal right of government to seize private property for public use, provided that the owner receives compensation at fair market value.

environmental sociology The study of the reciprocal interactions between the physical environment, social organization, and social behavior.

ethnic villagers Migrants who sustain rural life patterns in the city, cluster in a local area, emphasize traditional religious beliefs and family ties, and display suspicion of outsiders. That area is considered an "ethnic village."

exurbs New residential areas that develop on the metropolitan fringe.

false consciousness A misinterpretation of reality by accepting the dominant group's views and not realizing one's situation is the result of exploitation.

garden cities Based on Howard's vision, eco-friendly pedestrian villages that attempt to blend the best of the city and the country by utilizing shared public space.

gated communities Residential neighborhoods that restrict entry to residents and their guests.

gemeinschaft Tönnies' depiction of one form of social life as a community, much like that of a small country village, where all share a common view of life.

gendered spaces How differences in gender status result in the organization of space to reflect and reinforce those unequal distinctions.

general strain theory (GST) A way of understanding the connection between discrepancies between aspirations and achievement, between fair and actual outcomes, and of negative stimuli replacing positively valued stimuli.

gentrification The renovation of a run-down neighborhood and the influx of people from a higher socioeconomic level.

gesellschaft Tönnies' depiction of another form of social life as an association, much like that of a large city, where people do not necessarily share a common view of life.

ghettos Segregated neighborhoods with high unemployment and poverty rates.

GIS mapping A computer-based methodology to gather, transform, manipulate, and analyze information related to the surface of the Earth.

global city Also called a world city, it is one that occupies an influential position in the global economic system, attracting global investments and exercising considerable economic power worldwide.

globalization The development of an increasingly integrated global economy marked by connectivity and interdependence of the world's businesses and markets.

green belt An area surrounding a city or town where no development is permitted.

greenfields A master-planned city, usually by one developer on wooded or farmland acres.

gridiron cities Cities in which the physical layout contains straight streets crossing at right angles to create regular city blocks.

groupthink Conformity to opinions that supposedly reflect group consensus.

hierarchical power structure The levels of power within a society.

horizontal integration When companies gain control over the manufacture of all parts that went into their final product, sometimes even the raw materials.

hostile environment A setting in which members of a particular group are made uncomfortable because of comments made, images displayed, or other inappropriate behavior.

human ecology A term coined by Robert Park, reflecting his concept about the orderly evolution of urban growth and development.

hyperghettos Segregated neighborhoods with extreme levels of poverty and unemployment.

hypersegregation An intense grouping of a racial group within a specific geographical area.

ideal type A model constructed from real-world observation that highlights the crucial elements of some social phenomenon.

index of dissimilarity A measurement tool for determining the level of segregation in a neighborhood.

industrial location theory Explanation that industry would locate where the transportation costs of both raw materials and the final product would be the lowest.

industrial parks Areas zoned for a cluster of manufacturing entities on campus-like settings.

industrialism The process of manufacturing goods in large quantities for mass consumption.

inner-city neighborhoods High-density, low-income areas with substandard housing located near the central business district.

invasion–succession The ecological process in which one group or activity replaces another in a particular area.

landmarks Physical reference points, including buildings, signs, stores, domes, gas stations, or hills.

lifestyle communities Gated communities for those who want separate, private services and amenities within a homogeneous, predictable environment.

magnet schools Schools offering special programs to attract students from many districts to achieve integration.

McMansions Any supersized, large house exceeding 4,000 square feet on too small a lot, leaving little room for yard space.

mechanical solidarity Social bonds that are constructed on likeness, on common belief and custom, and on common ritual and symbol.

megacity A metropolitan area that constitutes its own megalopolis, because the population within its municipal boundary number at least 10 million people.

megalopolis When two or more metropolitan areas expand so that they intermingle with one another to form a continuous or almost continuous urban complex.

megamerger The acquisition of a company with assets valued at $1 billion or more by a multibillion-dollar company.

megaregion The overlapping of two or more metropolitan areas, previously called a megalopolis.

mental maps Individualized constructs of an area based on personal experience, interests, and knowledge of the socially recognized "important areas" of the city.

metropolitan area A large population center and its adjacent communities, with which it has a high degree of economic and social integration.

metropolitan statistical area (MSA) At least one city with 50,000 or more inhabitants, its county, and any surrounding urban counties from which a large proportion of inhabitants are attracted as commuters.

mode of development Castells's notion of the processing and transmission of information as the fundamental resource of productivity and power.

mode of production The things needed to produce goods and services, such as land, tools, knowledge, wealth, or factories.

natural areas Places that evolve as unplanned clusters with specialized activities.

natural crossroads A strategic geographical location that facilitates the concentration of people and services, especially trade.

new cities Sprawling, middle-class, auto-dependent center, often located on the fringe of an older urban area; also called "edge cities."

new towns Large-scale, holistic planning of a mixed-use, self-sufficient communities.

New Urbanism Incorporates sociological principles in physical design, such as walkability, mixed building types and activities, and social interaction.

nodes Anchor points of strategic activity, such as a major transit station or square.

oligopoly Market domination by a few producers.

ordered segmentation Suttles's term for the social organization found within a slum community.

organic solidarity A complex division of labor, in which many different people specialize in many different occupations and depend on one another to meet various needs.

parallel social institutions A minority-group, community support network of clubs, churches, organizations, stores, and media to share the commonality of language and culture.

paths Streets, walkways, transit lines, canals, and railroads along which the observer moves.

placemaking A multifaceted approach to the design, planning, and management of public space that involve those who live, work, and play in that particular space.

political fragmentation The splintered governance structure of numerous local municipalities in a metropolitan region.

postmodernism A reaction against the assumed certainty that rational, objective efforts can explain reality and, instead, an insistence that there are multiple interpretations based on concrete experiences, not abstract principles.

prestige communities Gated communities that are status-oriented enclaves emphasizing exclusion and image, with the gates symbolizing the eminent status of their residents.

primacy ratio The extent of the dominance of a country's primate city, computed by dividing its population by the population of the second-largest city.

primary circuit of capital Lefebvre's identification of investment to hire workers to manufacture a product to sell at a profit to be used for more investment.

primate cities Principal cities that are extremely large in comparison with other cities in the country.

productive surplus The production of a food surplus to enable some people to engage in pursuits other than farming, such as arts, crafts, and science.

push–pull factors Combination of factors that drive one from the homeland and lure that migrant to another locale.

racial profiling Targeting individuals of a specific group on the assumption they are more likely to commit illegal acts than are individuals of other groups.

radiocentric cities Cities in which the physical layout expands outward in all directions from a common center.

regal/ritual city A city with political and/or religious concerns at its core.

relative poverty The lack of resources of some people in comparison to others who have more.

reputational method Subjective input in which people compare others to themselves in terms of status.

scenes Places where people gather to socialize with friends or meet new ones, and to enjoy themselves.

school voucher Giving parents an option by applying the state's share of the cost for educating a child to the school of their choice.

second circuit of capital Lefebvre's identification of real-estate investment as almost always leading to profit as an important means of acquiring wealth.

security-zone communities Gated communities with a fortress mentality of protection and the exclusion of people deemed to be a threat to the residents' safety and quality of life.

slums Low-income neighborhoods with substandard housing.

smart growth Comprehensive land-use planning to revitalize and build compact and environmentally sensitive communities.

social disorganization theory Explains how weak social network lessens a sense of community and ability to influence public behavior, thereby increasing the likelihood of crime.

social impact analysis The study to determine the likely consequences of a project before it is executed.

social power The ability to achieve one's goals and to shape events.

social promotions Moving children through grades with their age peers regardless of their actual learning achievement.

social space What individuals who live, work, and play in an area think about their environment.

social stratification The hierarchical ranking within a society of various social class groups according to wealth, power, and prestige.

socioeconomic status (SES) A composite ranking based of various dimensions of social inequality, such as income, education, and occupation.

sprawl Spread-out or low-density residential development beyond the edge of services and employment.

strategic policing An aggressive tactic of deploying increased patrols, decoys, and sting operations in locales identified as high-crime areas.

sunbelt expansion The growth of population, commerce, and industry in the South and West.

texture The impression that cities convey to the beholder; also called "soul" or "personality."

total fertility rate The average number of children a woman has during her lifetime.

uptowns Edge cities built on top of preautomobile settlements.

urban agglomerations A city with continuous spread around it encompassing a few other towns and outgrowths, based on the core town; a metropolitan area.

urban cluster A combination of contiguous urban areas that extend across city, county, or state boundary lines.

urban dominance A central pattern of the historical and modern world in which the city radiates its influence far beyond its borders.

urban ecology Analysis of how people and activities spread out within an urban area.

urban explosion Ever-greater numbers of people moving into the city.

urban geography A focus on the significance of a city's location and natural resources.

urban implosion Ever-greater numbers of people moving out from the city to surrounding regions.

urban political economy Critical urban sociology perspective; adherents are generally neo-Marxists, but regardless of their ideological orientation, they focus on investment decisions and economic trends that determine a city's fortunes.

urban renewal   A federally funded program to demolish old buildings in decaying areas of a city and build new ones in their place.

urban utopia   An idealized city in which the inhabitants are content because everything works perfectly.

urbanism   The culture or way of life of city dwellers.

urbanization   The changes resulting from people moving into cities and other densely populated areas.

vertical disintegration   When large companies unload their production support companies.

world-systems analysis   An approach suggesting that the economic well-being of most cities is heavily dependent on their placement within this world hierarchy.

yuppies   Slang term for young (late twenties to early forties) urban professionals.

REFERENCES

ABBOTT, CARL, AND JOY MARGHEIM. 2008. "Imagining Portland's Urban Growth Boundary: Planning Regulation as Cultural Icon." *Journal of the American Planning Association* 74: 196–208.

ABC NEWS. 2000. "Crime Fears Linger." Accessed at http://www.abcnews.go.com/sections/politics/DailyNews/poll000607.html on September 23, 2002.

ABRAHAMSON, MARK. 2004. *Global Cities*. New York: Oxford University Press.

ADDAMS, JANE. 2010a. *The Spirit of Youth and the City Streets*. New York: General Books; originally published 1909.

———. 2010b. *The Second Twenty Years at Hull House*. New York: General Books; originally published 1930.

———. 2011. *Twenty Years at Hull House*. Readaclassic. com; originally published 1910.

AGNEW, ROBERT. 1992. "Foundation for a General Strain Theory of Crime and Delinquency." *Criminology* 30: 47–87.

ALDERSON, ARTHUR S., AND JASON BECKWITH. 2004. "Power and Position in the World City System." *American Journal of Sociology* 109: 811–51.

ALEXANDER WOOLLCOTT. 2011. *Answers.com*. Accessed at http://www.answers.com/topic/alexander-woollcott on July 14, 2011.

ALONSO, WILLIAM. 1960. "A Theory of the Urban Land Market." Accessed at http://www.scribd.com/doc/6485508/A-Theory-of-the-Urban-Land-Market-Alonso on July 14, 2011.

ALONZO, ALEX. 2008. "18th Street: Gang in Los Angeles." Accessed at http://www.streetgangs.com/hispanic/18thstreet on July 25, 2011.

ALVAREZ, LIZETTE. 2009. "The Ironbound: Importing a Slice of Portugal." *New York Times*, December 24, p. MB3.

AMERICA 2050. 2011. "Urban Growth in the Northeast Megaregion." Accessed at http://www.america2050.org/northeast.html on August 13, 2011.

AMERICAN LUNG ASSOCIATION. 2011. *State of the Air 2011*. Accessed at http://www.stateoftheair.org/2011/assets/SOTA2011.pdf on August 12, 2011.

ANDERSON, ELIJAH, AND DOUGLAS S. MASSEY. 2001. *Problem of the Century: Racial Stratification in the United States*. New York: Russell Sage Foundation.

ANJEC. 2011. "Urban/Developed Communities." *Association of New Jersey Environmental Commissions*. Accessed at http://www.anjec.org/UrbanDevComm.htm on August 16, 2011.

ARCHBALD, DOUGLAS A. 2004. "School Choice, Magnet Schools, and the Liberation Model: An Empirical Study." *Sociology of Education* 77 (October): 283–310.

ARMSTRONG, WARWICK, AND T. G. MC GEE. 2007. *Theatres of Accumulation: Studies in Asian and Latin American Urbanization*. New York: Routledge.

ATKINSON, ROWLAND, AND SARAH BLANDY, eds. 2006. *Gated Communities: International Perspectives*. New York: Routledge.

ATLANTA REGIONAL COUNCIL. 2007. *Regional Snapshot: Land Development in the Atlanta Region*. Accessed at http://www.atlantaregional.com on July 20, 2008.

AUSTIN, ALFREDO LOPEZ, AND LEONARDO LOPEZ LUJAN. 2006. *Mexico's Indigenous Past*. Norman: University of Oklahoma Press.

AUSTRALIAN CAPITAL TERRITORY. 2011. "Canberra's Economy." Accessed at http://www.business.act.gov.au/investing_in_canberra/canberras_economy on August 7, 2011.

AZAD INDIA FOUNDATION. 2010. "Poverty in India." Accessed at http://azadindia.org/social-issues/poverty-in-india.html on August 3, 2011.

BAGBY, R. MICHAEL, LENA C. QUILTY, AND ANDREW C. RYDER. 2008. "Personality and Depression." *Canadian Journal of Psychiatry* 53: 14–25.

BAGLI, CHARLES V. 2011. "Downtown's Rebirth, 10 Years and $24 Billion Later." *New York Times*, September 11, pp. NJ1, NJ4.

BALTZELL, E. DIGBY. 1987. *The Protestant Establishment*. New Haven, CT: Yale University Press; originally published 1964.

———. 1989. *Philadelphia Gentlemen: The Making of a National Upper Class*. New Brunswick, NJ: Transaction Publishers; originally published 1958.

BANFIELD, EDWARD C. 1970. *The Unheavenly City*. Boston: Little, Brown.

———. 1990. *The Unheavenly City Revisited*. Long Grove, IL: Waveland Press.

BANHAM, RAYNER. 2009. *Los Angeles: The Architecture of Four Ecologies*, 2nd ed. Berkeley: University of California Press; originally published 1973.

BANZHAF, H. SPENCER, WALLACE E. OATES, AND JAMES N. SANCHIRICO. 2010. "Success and Design of Local Referenda for Land Conservation." *Journal of Policy Analysis and Management* 29: 769–98.

BARNETT, JONATHAN. 2002. "Turning Edge Cities into Real Cities." *Planning* 68 (November): 10–13.

BEAUREGARD, ROBERT A. 2003. "City of Superlatives." *City & Community* 2 (September): 183–99.

———. 2006. *When America Became Suburban.* South Minneapolis, MN: University of Minnesota Press.

BEGUIN, GILES, AND DOMINQUE MOREL. 1997. *The Forbidden City: Heart of Imperial China.* London: Thames and Hudson, Ltd.

BEITO, DAVID T., PETER GORDON, AND ALEXANDER TABARROK, eds. 2009. *The Voluntary City: Choice, Community, and Civil Society.* Oakland, CA: Independent Institute.

BELL, BRANDON. 2011. *Perspectives on Urban Toronto.* Raleigh, NC: Lulu.

BELL, WENDELL, AND MARION BOAT. 1957. "Urban Neighborhoods and Informal Social Relations." *American Journal of Sociology* 62: 391–98.

BELLAH, ROBERT N., RICHARD MADSEN, WILLIAM M. SULLIVAN, ANN SWIDLER, AND STEVEN M. TIPTON. 1985. *Habits of the Heart: Individualism and Commitment in American Life.* New York: Harper & Row.

BELLUSH, JEWEL. 2000. *Urban Renewal: People, Politics, and Planning.* Garden City, NY: Doubleday.

BEMBRY, JAMES X., AND DONALD F. NORRIS. 2005. "An Exploratory Study of Neighborhood Choices among Moving to Opportunity Participants in Baltimore, Maryland." *Journal of Sociology and Social Welfare* 32 (December): 93–107.

BENTHAM, MARTIN. 2011. "Foreign-Born Workers Take One in Five Jobs." *Evening Standard* (May 26).

BERMAN, DAVID. 1997. "Shopping on the Edge." *Canadian Business,* October 31, pp. 72–79.

BINGHAM, RICHARD, AND ZHONGCAI ZHANG. 2001. *The Economies of Central-City Neighborhoods.* Boulder, CO: Westview Press.

BLAKELY, EDWARD J., AND MARY GAIL SNYDER. 1999. *Fortress America: Gated Communities in the United States,* New Ed. Washington, D.C.: Brookings Institution Press.

BLAU, JUDITH R., AND PETER M. BLAU. 1982. "The Cost of Inequality: Metropolitan Structure and Criminal Violence." *Sociological Quarterly* 27: 114–29.

BONNES, MIRILIA, MARINO BONAIUTO, AND ANNA PAOLA. 1991. "Crowding and Residential Satisfaction in the Urban Environment: A Contextual Approach." *Environment and Behavior* 23 (September): 531–52.

BOOKCHIN, MURRAY. 1996. *The Limits of the City,* 2nd rev. ed. Toronto: Black Rose Books.

BORJAS, GEORGE J. 2004. "The Economic Consequences of Immigration." *Journal of Catholic Social Thought* 1: 137–52.

BORSUK, ALAN. 2007. "A Toast to Sherman Park." Accessed at http://www.jsonline.com/realestate/29288129.html on July 25, 2011.

BOUMA-DOFF, WENDA. 2007. "Involuntary Isolation: Ethnic Preferences and Residential Segregation." *Journal of Urban Affairs* 29: 289–309.

BRAINARD, LAEL, AND LEONARDO MARTINEZ-DIAZ. 2009. *Brazil as an Economic Superpower? Understanding Brazil's Changing Role in the Global Economy.* Washington, D.C.: Brookings Institution Press.

BRASWELL, GEOFFREY E., ed. 2004. *The Maya and Teotihuacan: Reinterpreting Early Classic Interaction.* Austin, TX: University of Texas Press.

BREAN, HENRY. 2012. "Low Snowpack Signals Water Crisis at Lake Mead." *Las Vegas Review-Journal,* January 23, p. 1.

BREMER, FREDERIKA, ADOLPH BENSON, AND CARRIE CATT. 2007. *America of the Fifties: Letters of Fredrika Bremer.* Carlisle, MA: Applewood Books.

BRENNAN, MORGAN. 2011. "Moscow Leads Cities with the Most Billionaires." *Forbes* (May 17). Accessed at http://www.forbes.com/2011/05/17/cities-with-most-billionaires.html on August 3, 2011.

Britannica Book of the Year. 2011. Chicago: Encyclopedia Britannica.

BROKAW, TOM. 2002. *NBC Nightly News,* June 27.

BROOKINGS INSTITUTION. 2003. *Back to Prosperity: A Competitive Agenda for Renewing Pennsylvania.* Washington, D.C.: Brookings Institution Press.

BROOKS, DAVID. 2001. *Bobos in Paradise: The New Upper Class and How They Got There.* New York: Simon & Schuster.

BROOKS, VAN WYCK. 2005. *The Flowering of New England, 1815–1875.* New York: AMS Press, Inc.; originally published 1936.

BROWN, LOUISE. 2008. "Urban Schools Shortchanged: Report." *Toronto Star* (April 4), p. A08.

BRUCE, J. M. 1970. "Intergenerational Occupational Mobility and Visiting with Kin and Friend." *Social Forces* 49: 117–27.

BRYANT, M. DARROL. 2001. "Some Notes on Muslims in Canada and the US." Accessed at http://www.renaissance.com.pk/Seprefl2y1.html on September 1, 2011.

BUCKLEY, JACK, AND MARK SCHNEIDER. 2009. *Charter Schools: Hope or Hype?* Princeton, NJ: Princeton University Press.

BULMER, MARTIN. 1986. *The Chicago School of Sociology.* Chicago: University of Chicago Press.

BURCHELL, ROBERT, ANTHONY DOWNS, SAHAN MUKHERJI, AND BARBARA MCCANN. 2005. *Sprawl Costs: Economic Impacts of Unchecked Development.* Washington, D.C.: Island Press.

BURCHFIELD, KERI B. 2009. "Attachment as a Source of Informal Control in Urban Neighborhoods." *Journal of Criminal Justice* 37: 45–54.

BURN, A. R. 1970. *Greece and Rome.* Glenview, IL: Scott, Foresman.

BUSH, LARRY. 2011. "San Francisco: Delay Housing Enforcement." *CitiReport.* Accessed at http://www.citireport.com/2011/03/sf-delay-housing-enforcement/ on July 28, 2011.

BUTLER, TIM. 2007. "Re-urbanizing London Docklands: Gentrification, Suburbanization or New Urbanism?" *International Journal of Urban and Regional Research* 31 (December): 759–81.

———. 2008. "In the City But Not of the City?" *International Journal of Social Research Methodology* 11 (April): 141–49.

BUTLER, TIM, AND LEES, LORETTA. 2006. "Super-gentrification in Barnsbury, London: Globalisation and Gentrifying Elites at the Neighbourhood Level." *Transactions of the Institute of British Geographers* NS31, 467–87.

BYRON, ROBERT. 2007. *The Road to Oxiana*. New York: Oxford University Press.

CAHALAN, SUSANNAH. 2008. "Code of Honor: New in-the-Money ZIP Beats Our 10021." *New York Post*, May 12, p. 3.

CALHOUN, CRAIG, ed. 2007. *Sociology in America: A History*. Chicago: University of Chicago Press.

CALHOUN, JOHN B. 1962. "Population Density and Social Pathology." *Scientific American* 206: 139–48.

CALLOW, ALEXANDER B., JR. 1982. *American Urban History: An Interpretive Reader with Commentaries*, 3rd ed. New York: Oxford University Press.

CARCOPINO, JEROME. 2008. *Daily Life in Ancient Rome: The People and City at the Height of the Empire*. New Haven, CT: Carcopino Press.

CARNOY, MARTIN, REBECCA JACOBSEN, LAWRENCE MISHEL, AND RICHARD ROTHSTEIN. 2005. *The Charter School Dust-Up: Examining the Evidence on Enrollment and Achievement*. New York: Teachers College Press.

CARP, BENJAMIN. 2009. *Rebels Rising: Cities and the American Revolution*. New York: Oxford University Press.

CARTER, J. SCOTT, LALA CARR STEELMEN, LYNN M. MULKEY, AND CASEY BORCH. 2005. "When the Rubber Meets the Road: Effects of Urban and Regional Residence on Principle and Implementation Measures of Racial Tolerance." *Social Science Research* 34 (June): 408–25.

CASTELLS, MANUEL. 1982. *City, Class, and Power*. New York: Palgrave Macmillan.

———. 1985. *The City and the Grass Roots*. Berkeley: University of California Press.

———. 1992. *The Informational City*. Malden, MA: Wiley-Blackwell.

———. 2000. *The Rise of the Network Society*. Malden, MA: Wiley-Blackwell.

CASTLEDEN, RODNEY. 2005. *The Mycenaeans*. New York: Routledge.

CAULFIELD, JON. 1994. *City Form and Everyday Life: Toronto's Gentrification and Critical Social Practice*. Toronto: University of Toronto Press.

CENTER FOR EDUCATION REFORM. 2011. "2011-2012 National Charter School and Enrollment Statistics." Accessed at http://www.edreform.com on April 14, 2012.

CENTRAL INTELLIGENCE AGENCY. 2011. *World Factbook*. Accessed at https://www.cia.gov/library/publications/the-world-factbook/ on August 4, 2011.

CHANG, BAO. 2011. "Automobile Ownership to Exceed 100m by Year's End." *China Daily* (July 23). Accessed at http://www.chinadaily.com.cn/cndy/2011-07/23/content_12966765.htm on July 23, 2011.

CHAPMAN, DAVID W., AND JOHN R. LOMBARD. 2006. "Determinants of Neighborhood Satisfaction in Fee-Based Gated and Nongated Communities." *Urban Affairs Review* 41 (July): 769–99.

CHARLES, CAMILLE Z. 2000. "Neighborhood Racial-Composition Preferences: Evidence from a Multiethnic Metropolis." *Social Problems* 47: 379–98.

CHASE-DUNN, CHRISTOPHER, AND SALVATORE J. BABONES. 2006. *Global Social Change: Historical and Comparative Perspectives*. Baltimore: Johns Hopkins University Press.

CHESAPEAKE BAY FOUNDATION. 2011. *Water Quality Issues: Land Use*. Accessed at http://www.cbf.org/page.aspx?pid=611 on August 15, 2011.

CHESAPEAKE ECO-CHECK. 2011. *Chesapeake Bay Health Report Card: 2010*. Accessed at http://www.eco-check.org/reportcard/chesapeake/2010/overview on August 15, 2011.

CHILDE, V. GORDON. 2003. *Man Makes Himself*. Philadelphia: Coronet Books.

CHOWDHURY, DEBASISH ROY. 2007. "Right Moves Being Made on Wealth Disparity." *China Daily*, October 16. Accessed at http://www.chinadaily.com.cn/opinion/2007-10/16/content_6728538.htm on April 14, 2012.

CHRISTALLER, WALTER. 1966. *Central Places in Southern Germany*. Englewood Cliffs, NJ: Prentice Hall; originally published 1933.

CITY OF NEW YORK. 2011. "NYC Statistics." Accessed at http://www.nycgo.com/articles/nyc-statistics-page on August 14, 2011.

CITY OF PORTLAND. 2011. "Elements of Vitality: Results of the Downtown Plan." Accessed at http://www.portlandonline.com on April 7, 2012.

CITY OF SPOKANE PLANNING SERVICES DEPARTMENT. 2011. "Long Range Planning." Accessed at http://www.spokaneplanning.org/longrange.html on August 16, 2011.

CITY OF TORONTO. 2009. *Profile of Low Income in the City of Toronto*. Accessed at http://www.toronto.ca/demographics/pdf/poverty_profile_2010.pdf on April 14, 2012.

CITY-DATA.COM. 2011. Accessed on July 25, 2011.

CLAGHORN, KATE HOLLADAY. 2011. "The Foreign Immigrant in New York City." Accessed at http://www.tenant.net/Community/LES/clag1.html on August 13, 2011.

CLEVELAND, WILLIAM L., AND MARTIN BUNTON. 2009. *A History of the Modern Middle East*, 4th ed. Boulder, CO: Westview Press.

CNN. 2008. "Developing Cities and Pollution." Accessed at http://www.cnn.com/2008/WORLD/asiapcf/03/09/eco.cities/index.html on July 28, 2008.

COHEN, ADAM, AND ELIZABETH TAYLOR. 2001. *American Pharaoh: Mayor Richard J. Daley*. Boston: Back Bay Books.

COMMUNITY ASSOCIATIONS INSTITUTE. 2011. "Industry Data: National Statistics." Accessed at http://www.caionline.org/info/research/Pages/default.aspx about/facts.cfm on April 7, 2011.

CONANT, JENNET. 2003. *Tuxedo Park*. New York: Simon & Schuster.

CONFERENCE BOARD OF CANADA. 2011. "Hot Topic: Canada Inequality." Accessed at http://www.conferenceboard.ca/hcp/hot-topics/canInequality.aspx on July 24, 2011.

CONLIN, MICHELLE. 2008. "Suddenly It's Cool to Take the Bus." *Business Week*, April 23. Accessed at http://www.businessweek.com/magazine/content/08_18/b4082000049320.htm on April 7, 2012.

CONNOR, KEVIN. 2010. "Great City, But Still With Its Problems." *Toronto Sun*, October 5. Accessed at http://www.torontosun.com/news/torontoandgta/2010/10/04/15579776.html on August 8, 2011.

CORCORAN, DAVID. 2003. "Restaurants: Unbound in Ironbound, *New York Times,* July 20, p. NJ10.

COUNCIL ON AMERICAN-ISLAMIC RELATIONS. 2011. Accessed at http://www.cair.com/Home.aspx on April 14, 2012.

COWIE, JEFFERSON, AND JOSEPH HEATHCOTT. 2003. *Beyond the Ruins: The Meanings of Deindustrialization.* Ithaca, NY: Cornell University Press.

CQ PRESS. 2011. "City Crime Rankings 2010-2011." Accessed at http://os.cqpress.com/citycrime/2010/citycrime2010-2011.htm on July 29, 2011.

CURLEY, ALEXANDRA M. 2008. "A New Place, a NEW Network? Social Capital Effects of Residential Relocation for Poor Women." Pp. 85–103 in *Networked Urbanism,* edited by Taja Blokland and Mike Savage. Burlington, VT: Ashgate Publishing.

CURRAN, DAN. 2003. "Sherman Park Still One of Milwaukee's Most Vibrant Areas." Accessed at http://www.onmilwaukee.com/visitors/articles/shermanpark.html on June 23, 2008.

CURRY, AARON, CARL LATKIN, AND MELISSA DAVEY-ROTHWELL. 2008. "Pathways to Depression: The Impact of Neighborhood Crime on Inner-City Residents in Baltimore, Maryland, USA." *Social Science & Medicine* 67 (July): 23–30.

CURTIS WHITE, KATHERINE J., AND AVERY M. GUEST. 2003. "Community Lost or Transformed? Urbanization and Social Ties." *City & Community* 2 (September): 239–59.

DANA, RICHARD HENRY. 2001. *Two Years Before the Mast.* New York: Random House Modern Library; originally published 1862.

DE JONG, IAIN. 2000. "Devolution Hits Housing in Canada." *Shelterforce Online.* Accessed at http://www.nhi.org/online/issues/113/dejong.html on July 25, 2011.

DEAR, MICHAEL J. 2001. *The Postmodern Urban Condition.* Malden, MA: Wiley-Blackwell.

DE KESEREDY, WALTER S. 2009. "Canadian Crime Control in the New Millennium: The Influence of Neo-Conservative US Policies and Practices." *Police Practice and Research* 10: 305–16.

DEMOGRAPHIA. 2011. "New York (Manhattan) Wards: Population & Density 1800-1910." Accessed at http://www.demographia.com/db-nyc-ward1800.htm on August 13, 2011.

DIALA, CHAMBERLAIN C., AND CARLES MUNTANER. 2003. "Mood and Anxiety Disorders Among Rural, Urban, and Metropolitan Residents in the United States." *Community Mental Health Journal* 39: 239–52.

DICKENS, CHARLES. 1853. *Bleak House.* London: Chapman and Hall.

———. 1860. *Great Expectations.* London: Chapman and Hall.

———. 2008. *Hard Times.* New York: Signet Classics; originally published 1854.

———. 2010. *American Notes.* New York: General Books; originally published 1842.

DIERS, JIM. 2004. *Neighbor Power: Building Community the Seattle Way.* Seattle: University of Washington Press.

DILLON, DAVIS. 2003. "Addison Circle Park Gives Suburb a Hub." *Dallas News,* December 17, p. E14.

DIXON, TRAVIS L. 2008. "Crime News and Racialized Beliefs: Understanding the Relationship between Local News and Perceptions of African Americans and Crime." *Journal of Communication* 58 (March): 106–25.

DOMHOFF, G. WILLIAM. 2011. "Wealth, Income, and Power." Accessed at http://sociology.ucsc.edu/whorulesamerica/power/wealth.html on July 23, 2011.

DOMÍNGUEZ, SILVIA, AND CELESTE WATKINS. 2003. "Creating Networks for Survival and Mobility: Social Capital among African-American and Latin-American Low-Income Mothers." *Social Problems* 50 (February): 111–35.

DONOVAN, VINCENT. 2011. "Alexandra Park Community Yearns for a Facelift." *The Star* (May 23). Accessed at http://www.thestar.com/news/article/995831 on August 8, 2011.

DOS PASSOS, JOHN. 1969. "San Francisco Looks West." Pp. 484–89 in *City Life,* edited by Oscar Shoenfeld and Helen MacLean. New York: Grossman; originally published 1944.

DOSS, KELLY R., AND WILLIAM T. MARKHAM. 2004. "The Sprawl Problem in Guilford County." Accessed at http://nc.sierraclub.org/piedmont/excom/sprawl_guilford_2004.pdf on August 16, 2011.

DOUGLAS, GEORGE H. 2004. *Skyscrapers: A Social History of the Very Tall Building in America.* Jefferson, NC: McFarland & Company.

DOWNS, TONY. 2011. "Next Office Building Boom Still Years Away." (May 1). Accessed at http://nreionline.com/property/office/real_estate_next_office_building/ on August 13, 2011.

DUANY, ANDRES, JEFF SPECK, AND MIKE LYDON. 2009. *The Smart Growth Manual.* New York: McGraw-Hill.

DUESTERBERG, THOMAS J., AND ERNEST H. PREEG. 2004. *U.S. Manufacturing: The Engine for Growth in a Global Economy.* Westport, CT: Praeger.

DUNLAP, DAVID W. 2008. "Atop the New TKTS Booth, Ruby-Red Stairs with a View of the Great White Way." *New York Times,* October 17, p. 29.

DURKHEIM, EMILE. 1997. *The Division of Labor in Society.* New York: Free Press; originally published 1893.

EAKIN, MARSHALL C. 2007. *The History of Latin America: Collision of Cultures.* New York: Palgrave Macmillan.

ECONOMIC TIMES. 2011. "India's Middle Class Population to Touch 267 Million in 5 Years," February 6. Accessed at http://articles.economictimes.indiatimes.com/2011-02-06/news/ on August 3, 2011.

ECONOMIST. 2011. "Greening the Concrete Jungle," September 3. Accessed at http://www.economist.com/node/21528272 on September 5, 2011.

EIESLAND, NANCY L. 2000. *A Particular Place: Urban Restructuring and Religious Ecology in a Southern Exurb.* New Brunswick, NJ: Rutgers University Press.

EITLE, DAVID. 2009. "Dimensions of Racial Segregation, Hypersegregation, and Black Homicide Rates." *Journal of Criminal Justice* 37: 28–36.

EL NASSER, HAYA. 2006. "Mich. Pulling Itself out of Slump." *USA Today,* April 25, p. A3.

ELLEN, INGRID GOULD, AMY E SCHWARTZ, AND IOAN VOICU. 2007. "The Impact of Business Improvement

District on Property Values: Evidence from New York City." *Brookings-Wharton Papers on Urban Affairs* 8: 1–31.

EMAAR. 2011. "Downtown Dubai." Accessed at http://www.emaar.com/index.aspx?page=emaaruae-downtownburj on August 7, 2011.

ENGELS, FRIEDRICH. 2009. *The Condition of the Working Class in England,* trans. by Florence Kelly Wischenewetsky. Springfield, MA: Seven Treasures Publications; originally published 1844.

ESHBAUGH, ELAINE M., JACQUES LEMPERS, AND GAYLE L. LUZE. 2006. "Objective and Self-Perceived Resources as Predictors of Depression among Urban and Non-Urban Adolescent Mothers." *Journal of Youth and Adolescence* 35 (October): 839–47.

ESHERICK, JOSEPH W., PAUL G. PICKOWICZ, AND ANDREW G. WALDER, eds. 2006. *China's Cultural Revolution as History.* Stanford, CA: Stanford University Press.

EVANS, GARY W., SUSAN SAEGERT, AND REBECCA HARRIS. 2001. "Residential Density and Psychological Health among Children in Low-Income Families." *Environment and Behavior* 33 (March): 165–80.

FABBI, NADINE. 2003. *Early Black Canadian History.* Accessed at http://www.k12studycanada.org/files/EarlyBlackCanadianHistory.pdf on August 31, 2011.

FAJNZYLBER, PABLO, DANIEL LEDERMAN, AND NORMAN LOAYZA. 2002. "Inequality and Violent Crime." *The Journal of Law & Economics* 45 (April): 1–40.

FARGANIS, JAMES. 2007. *Readings in Social Theory: The Classic Tradition to Post-Modernism,* 5th ed. New York: McGraw-Hill.

FARRELL, CHAD R. 2008. "Bifurcation, Fragmentation, or Integration? The Racial and Geographic Structure of US Metropolitan Segregation, 1990–2000." *Urban Studies* 45 (March): 467–99.

FEDERAL BUREAU OF INVESTIGATION. 2011. *Crime in the United States—2010.* Accessed at http://www.fbi.gov/about-us/cjis/ucr/crime-in-the-u.s/2010/crime-in-the-u.s.-2010 on April 14, 2012.

FEDERAL RESERVE BOARD. 2011. "Surveying the Aftermath of the Storm: Changes in Family Finances from 2007 to 2009," 2011–17 (March).

FEDERATION OF CANADIAN MUNICIPALITIES. 2010. *Mending Canada's Frayed Social Safety Net: The Role of Municipal Governments.* Ottawa: FCM.

FILION, PIERRE. 1995. "City Form and Everyday Life: Toronto's Gentrification and Critical Social Practice." *Journal of the American Planning Association* 61 (Spring): 281–82.

FISCAL POLICY INSTITUTE. 2009. "Immigrants and the Economy." New York: Fiscal Policy Institute.

FISCHER, CLAUDE S. 1975. "Toward a Subcultural Theory of Urbanism." *American Journal of Sociology* 80: 1319–41.

———. 1995. "The Subcultural Theory of Urbanism: A Twentieth-Year Assessment." *American Journal of Sociology* 102 (November): 543–77.

FISCHER, CLAUDE S. et al. 1996. *Inequality by Design: Cracking the Bell Curve Myth.* Princeton, NJ: Princeton University Press.

FLORIDA, RICHARD. 2008. *Who's Your City? How the Creative Economy Is Making Where to Live the Most Important Decision of Your Life.* New York: Basic Books.

———. 2011. "Foreclosures Still Concentrated in Sunbelt Cities." *The Atlantic,* January 28. Accessed at http://www.theatlantic.com/business/ on September 5, 2011.

FOGELSON, ROBERT M. 2003. *Downtown: Its Rise and Fall, 1880–1950.* New Haven, CT: Yale University Press.

FORTUNE. 2011. "Global 500." Accessed at http://money.cnn.com/magazines/fortune/global500/2010/countries/US.html on June 7, 2011.

FRANKLIN, TRAVIS W., CORTNEY A. FRANKLIN, AND TRAVIS C. PRATT. 2006. "Examining the Empirical Relationship between Prison Crowding and Inmate Misconduct: A Meta-Analysis of Conflicting Research." *Journal of Criminal Justice* 34 (July–August): 401–12.

FRASER, STEVEN. 1995. *The Bell Curve Wars: Race, Intelligence, and the Future of America.* New York: Basic Books.

FREY, WILLIAM H. 2011. "Melting Pot Cities and Suburbs: Racial and Ethnic Change in Metro America in the 2000s." Washington, D.C.: Brookings. Accessed at http://www.brookings.edu/~/media/Files/rc/papers/2011/0504_census_ethnicity_frey/0504_census_ethnicity_frey.pdf on April 14, 2012.

FRISBY, CRAIG L. 1996. "The Use of Multidimensional Scaling in the Cognitive Mapping of Cultural Difference Judgments." *School Psychology Review* 25: 77–93.

FU, VINCENT K. 2001. "Racial Intermarriage Pairings." *Demography* 38: 147–59.

GALLUP. 2010a. "Nearly 4 in 10 Americans Still Fear Walking Alone at Night," November 5. Accessed at http://www.gallup.com/poll/144272/Nearly-Americans-Fear-Walking-Alone-Night.aspx on July 29, 2011.

———. 2010b. "Americans Still Perceive Crime as on the Rise," November 18. Accessed at http://www.gallup.com/poll/144827/Americans-Perceive-Crime-Rise.aspx on July 29, 2011.

GANS, HERBERT. 1962. "City Planning and Urban Realities." *Commentary* 33: 170–75.

———. 1967. *The Levittowners.* New York: Penguin.

———. 1968. "Urbanism and Suburbanism as Ways of Life: A Re-evaluation of Definitions." Pp. 170–95 in *Metropolis Center and Symbol of Our Time,* edited by Philip Kasinitz. New York: New York University Press, 1995.

———. 1982. *The Urban Villagers: Group and Class in the Life of Italian Americans.* New York: Free Press; originally published 1962.

———. 1991. "Urbanism and Suburbanism as Ways of Life: A Re-evaluation of Definitions." Pp. 51–69 in *People, Plans, and Policies: Essays on Poverty, Racism, and Other National Urban Problems.* New York: Columbia University Press.

GARDNER, AMY. 2008. "Plan to Remake Tysons Corner Envisions Dense Urban Center." *Washington Post,* May 29, p. A1.

GARREAU, JOEL. 1991. *Edge City.* New York: Doubleday Anchor.

GASPERS, KAREN. 2006. "Keeping an Eye on One Another." *Family Safety & Health* 64: 10–12.

GEISSE, G., AND F. SABATINI. 1988. "Latin American Cities and Their Poor." Pp. 322–27 in *The Metropolitan Era,* edited by M. Dogan and J. Kasarda. Newbury Park, CA: Sage.

GERTNER, JON. 2005. "Chasing Ground." *New York Times Magazine*, October 16, p. 46.

GIBBONS, DEBORAH, AND PAUL M. OLK. 2003. "Individual and Structural Origins of Friendship and Social Position Among Professionals." *Journal of Personality & Social Psychology* 84: 340–51.

GIOVANNINI, JOSEPH. 1983. "I Love New York and L.A., Too." *New York Times Magazine*, September 11, pp. 145, 147–49.

GIS.COM. 2011. "What is GIS?" Accessed at http://www.gis.com/content/what-gis on July 6, 2011.

GLAAB, CHARLES N., AND A. THEODORE BROWN. 1983. *A History of Urban America*, 3rd ed. New York: Macmillan.

GOLDBERGER, PAUL. 1989. *City Observed*. New York: Vintage.

GOODY, JOAN, AND ROBERT CHANDLER. 2010. *Building Type Basics for Housing*, 2nd ed. New York: Wiley.

GORMAN, S. 2003. "Labor Pain." *Washington Monthly* 35 (September): 20.

GOTTDIENER, MARK. 2001. *The Theming of America*, 2nd ed. Boulder, CO: Westview Press.

GOTTDIENER, MARK, AND JOE FEAGIN. 1988. "The Paradigm Shift in Urban Sociology." *Urban Affairs Quarterly* 24: 163–87.

GOTTDIENER, MARK, AND RAY HUTCHISON. 2010. *The New Urban Sociology*, 4th ed. Boulder, CO: Westview Press.

GOTTMANN, JEAN. 1966. *Megalopolis*, 3rd ed. Cambridge, MA: MIT Press.

GRABE, MARIA ELIZABETH, AND DAN G. DREW. 2007. "Crime Cultivation: Comparisons across Media Genres and Channels." *Journal of Broadcasting and Electronic Media* 51: 147–71.

GRATZ, ROBERTA BRANDES. 2010. *The Battle for Gotham: New York in the Shadow of Robert Moses and Jane Jacobs*. New York: Nation Books.

GRAY, ROBERT. 1997. *A History of London*. New York: Barnes & Noble Books.

GREEN, ROBERT L. 1977. *The Urban Challenge: Poverty and Race*. Chicago: Follett.

GREENFIELD, GERALD M. 1994. *Latin American Urbanization*. Westport, CT: Greenwood Publishing Group.

GREER, SCOTT. 1998. *The Emerging City: Myth and Reality*. New Brunswick, NJ: Transaction Publishers; originally published 1962.

GREGOR, ALISON. 2012. "10 Superexclusive Gated Communities." Accessed at http://realestate.msn.com/ on April 7, 2012.

GREGOR, EDWARD J., AND MARY GAIL SNYDER. 1999. *Fortress America: Gated Communities in the United States*, new ed. Washington, D.C.: Brookings Institution Press.

GREGORY, JAMES N. 2007. *The Southern Diaspora: How the Great Migrations of Black and White Southerners Transformed America*. Chapel Hill: University of North Carolina Press.

GUEST, AVERY M., JANE K. COVER, ROSS L. MATSEUDA, AND CHARIS E. KUBRIN. 2006. "Neighborhood Context and Neighboring Ties." *City & Community* 5 (December): 363–85.

HABITAT FOR HUMANITY. 2011. *Habitat for Humanity Fact Sheet*. Accessed at http://www.habitat.org/how/factsheet.aspx on July 28, 2011.

HAGLER, YOAV. 2009. "Defining US Megaregions." *Regional Plan Association*. Accessed at http://www.america2050.org/ on September 5, 2011.

HALL, EDWARD. 1990. *The Hidden Dimension*. Chapter 13, pp. 165–180. New York: Anchor; originally published 1966.

HALL, PETER. 1984. "Geography." Pp. 21–36 in *Cities of the Mind*, edited by Lloyd Rodwin and Robert M. Hollister. New York: Plenum.

HALL, PETER, AND MARK TEWDWR-JONE. 2011. *Urban and Regional Planning*, 5th ed. London: Routledge.

HAMBLIN, DORA JANE. 1973. *The First Cities*. New York: Little, Brown.

HAMNETT, CHRIS. 2003. *Unequal City: London in the Global Arena*. London: Routledge.

———. 2009. "City Centre Gentrification: Loft Conversions in London's City Fringe." *Urban Policy and Research* 27 (September): 277–87.

HANFF, HELENE. 1995. *Apple of My Eye*. Kingston, RI: Moyer Bell Ltd.

HARGREAVES, STEVE. 2011. "Gas Prices Push Consumers to the Train." *CNN Money*, May 12. Accessed at http://money.cnn.com/2011/05/12/news/economy/gas_prices_public_transit/index.htm on August 16, 2011.

HARRIS, CHAUNCEY D., AND EDWARD L. ULLMAN. 1945. "The Nature of Cities." *Annals* 242: 7–17.

HARVEY, DAVID. 1992. *The Condition of Postmodernity*. New York: Wiley-Blackwell.

HAWLEY, CHRIS. 2004. "Trying to Exorcise Mexico's 'Little Devils'." *Arizona Republic*, December 20. Accessed at http://www.azcentral.com/specials/special03/articles/1220electricity.html on August 9, 2005.

HEATHER, PETER. 2007. *The Fall of the Roman Empire: A New History of Rome and the Barbarians*. New York: Oxford University Press.

HECKSCHER, AUGUST. 1978. *Open Spaces: The Life of American Cities*. New York: Harper & Row.

HEILBRONER, ROBERT L., AND WILLIAM S. MILBERG. 2011. *The Making of Economic Society*, 13th ed. Englewood Cliffs, NJ: Prentice Hall.

HEILPRIN, JOHN. 2005. "Groups: Sprawl Threatens Plants, Animals." *Associated Press*, January 11.

HENLY, JULIA R., SANDRA K. DANZIGER, AND SHIRA OFFER. 2005. "The Contribution of Social Support to the Material Well-Being of Low Income Families." *Journal of Marriage and Family* 67: 122–40.

HERNÁNDEZ, RAMONA, AND FRANCISCO L. RIVERA-BATIZ. 2003. *Dominicans in the United States: A Socioeconomic Profile, 2000*. New York: CUNY Dominican Studies Institute.

HERRNSTEIN, RICHARD J., AND CHARLES MURRAY. 1996. *The Bell Curve: The Reshaping of American Life by Differences in Intelligence*. New York: Free Press.

HERSKOVITS, MELVILLE J. 2007. *The Human Factor in Changing Africa*. Whitefish, MT: Kessinger Publishing.

HESS, BETH B., ELIZABETH W. MARKSON, AND PETER J. STEIN. 1996. *Sociology*, 5th ed. Boston: Allyn & Bacon.

HEVESI, DENNIS. 2005. "The Boom Spreads: This House Is Valued at." *New York Times*, August 7, p. RE1.

HIGH LINE. 2011. Accessed at http://www.thehighline.org/ on August 14, 2011.

HIGLEY, STEPHEN R. 2011. "High Income Urban Neighborhoods." Accessed at http://higley1000.com/ on July 25, 2011.

HIPP, JOHN R. 2010. "A Dynamic View of Neighborhoods: The Reciprocal Relationship between Crime and Neighborhood Structural Characteristics." *Social Problems* 57: 205–30.

HISE, GREG, MICHAEL J. DEAR, AND ERIC H. SCHOCKMAN, eds. 1996. *Rethinking Los Angeles.* Thousand Oaks, CA: Sage Publications.

HOCH, CHARLES, AND ROBERT A. SLAYTON. 1990. *New Homeless and Old: Community and the Skid Row Hotel.* Philadelphia: Temple University Press.

HÖFLICH, JOACHIM R. 2006. "The Mobile Phone and the Dynamic between Private and Public Communication: Results of an International Exploratory Study." *Knowledge, Technology, & Policy* 19 (Summer): 58–68.

HOHENBERG, PAUL M., AND LYNN HOLLEN LEES. 1996. *The Making of Urban Europe, 1000–1950,* 2nd ed. Cambridge, MA: Harvard University Press.

HOLMAN, JAMES. 2008. "Portland Area Population Projected to Hit 3.85 Million by 2060." *Oregon Environmental Times,* June 7, p. 1.

HOLMES, GEORGE, ed. 2002. *The Oxford History of Medieval Europe.* New York: Oxford University Press.

HOMELESSNESS RESEARCH INSTITUTE. 2012. *The State of Homelessness in America 2012.* Washington, D.C.: National Alliance to End Homelessness.

HONDURAS WEEKLY. 2008. "A Case for Honduran Street Children and Their Survival against the Odds," October 8. Accessed at http://hondurasweekly.com/ on July 17, 2011.

HOUSTON. 2011. Accessed at http://www.houstontx.gov/abouthouston/houstonfacts.html on July 6, 2011.

HOWARD, EBENEZER. 2007. *Garden Cities of To-Morrow.* New York: Routledge; originally published 1898.

HOWELL, JOSEPH T. 1990. *Hard Living on Clay Street: Portraits of Blue-Collar Families.* Long Grove, IL: Waveland Press.

HOYT, HOMER. 1939. *The Structure and Growth of Residential Neighborhoods in American Cities.* Washington, D.C.: Federal Housing Administration.

HUANG, WEISHAN. 2010. "Immigration and Gentrification: A Case Study of Cultural Restructuring in Flushing, Queens." *Diversities* 12: 56–69.

HUFFINGTON POST. 2010. "Los Angeles Tops Nation in Air Pollution." *Huff Post Lost Angeles.* Accessed at http://www.huffingtonpost.com/2010/04/28/los-angeles-tops-nation-i_n_555249.html on July 5, 2011.

———. 2011a. "Upper East Side." *Huff Post New York.* Accessed at http://www.dnainfo.com/20110713/uppereast-side/hotel-once-home-famous-single-ladies-could-become-landmark on July 25, 2011.

———. 2011b. "Bloomberg: Times Square Pedestrian Plaza Improving Air Quality." Accessed at http://www.huffingtonpost.com/2011/04/13/bloomberg-times-square-pe_n_848806.html on August 10, 2011.

HUMAN RIGHTS WATCH 2008. "Street Children." Accessed at http://www.hrw.org/children/street.htm on June 16, 2008.

IOFFE, GRIGORY, AND TATYANA NEFEDOVA. 2001. "Land Use Changes in the Environs of Moscow." *Area* 33: 273–86.

INNOVATION NJ. 2011. "NJ Ranks 4th in Innovative Companies." Accessed at http://innovationnj.net/page_id=409 on June 7, 2011.

INSTITUTE FOR CHILDREN AND POVERTY. 2009. *Pushed Out: The Hidden Costs of Gentrification* (Spring). Accessed at http://www.icphusa.org/PDF/reports/ICPReport_Pushed Out.pdf on July 26, 2011.

IRWIN, JOHN. 1977. *Scenes.* Beverly Hills, CA: Sage.

ISBELL, WILLIAM H., AND HELAINE SILVERMAN, eds. 2006. *Andean Archaeology III: North and South.* New York: Springer.

JACOBS, JANE. 1993. *The Death and Life of Great American Cities.* New York: Random House; originally published 1961.

JARRETT, ROBIN L., STEPHANIE R. JEFFERSON, AND JENELL N. KELLY. 2010. "Finding Community in Family: Neighborhood Effects and African American Kin Networks." *Journal of Comparative Family Studies* 41: 299–328.

JOSEPH, MARK L., ROBERT J. CHASKIN, AND HENRY S. WEBBER. 2007. "The Theoretical Basis for Addressing Poverty through Mixed-Income Development." *Urban Affairs Review* 42 (January): 369–409.

JUBILEE LINE EXTENSION. 1997. "Archaeological Excavation at London Bridge." Accessed at http://www.jle.lul.co.uk/arch/index.htm on August 5, 2005.

JUN, MYUNG-JIN. 2004. "The Effects of Portland's Urban Growth Boundary on Urban Development Patterns and Commuting." *Urban Studies* 41 (June): 1333–48.

KAMIN, BLAIR. 1995. "Unifying Cities." *Chicago Tribune,* June 19, p. B1.

KARIM, JAMILLAH. 2006. "Ethnic Borders in American Muslim Communities." Pp. 121–48 in *Constructing Borders/Crossing Boundaries: Race, Ethnicity, and Immigration,* edited by Caroline Brettell. Lanham, MD: Lexington Books.

KAUFMAN, JOANNE M., CESAR J. REBELLON, SHEROD THAXTON, AND ROBERT AGNEW. 2008. "A General Strain Theory of Racial Differences in Criminal Offending." *The Australian and New Zealand Journal of Criminology* 41 (December): 421–37.

KAYA, YUNUS. 2010. "Globalization and Industrialization in 64 Developing Countries, 1980–2003." *Social Forces* 88: 1153–82.

KAZIN, ALFRED. 1997. *A Walker in the City,* reprint ed. New York: MJF Books.

KEATS, JOHN. 1956. *The Crack in the Picture Window.* New York: Ballantine Books.

KEISTER, LISA A. 2000. *Wealth in America: Trends in Wealth Inequality.* New York: Cambridge University Press.

KELLY, JOHN. 2005. *The Great Mortality: An Intimate History of the Black Death, The Most Devastating Plague of All Time.* New York: HarperCollins.

KEMP, BARRY J. 2006. *Ancient Egypt: Anatomy of a Civilization,* 2nd ed. New York: Routledge.

KERBER, LINDA K. JANE SHERRON DE HART, AND CORNELIA H. DAYTON. 2010. *Women's America: Refocusing the Past,* 7th ed. New York: Oxford University Press.

KEYES, RALPH. 1999. *The Wit and Wisdom of Oscar Wilde.* New York: Gramercy Books, Random House.

KHOURY, PHILIP S. 2004. "Syrian Urban Politics in Transition." Pp. 429–65 in *The Modern Middle East,* edited by Albert Hourani, Philip S. Khoury, and Mary C. Wilson. London: I.B. Tauris and Company.

KIPLING, RUDYARD. 2011. *From Sea to Sea and Other Sketches: Letters of Travel.* New York: Cambridge University Press; originally published 1899.

KLEIN, MILTON M. 2005. *The Empire State: A History of New York.* Ithaca, NY: Cornell University Press.

KNEPPER, CATHY D. 2001. *Greenbelt, Maryland: A Living Legacy of the New Deal.* Baltimore, MD: The Johns Hopkins University Press.

KNIGHT, LOUISE W. 2010. *Jane Addams: Spirit in Action.* New York: W.W. Norton & Company.

KOBELL, RONA. 2011. "Privatizing the Chesapeake." *Reason* 43: 31–37.

KOEGEL, PAUL, M. AUDREY BURNAM, AND JIM BAUMOHL. 1996. "The Causes of Homelessness." Pp. 24–33 in *Homelessness in America,* edited by Jim Baumohl. Westport, CT: Oryx Press.

KORT-BUTLER, LISA A., AND HARTSHORN, KELLEY J. SITTNER. 2011. "Watching the Detectives: Crime Programming, Fear of Crime, and Attitudes about the Criminal Justice System." *Sociological Quarterly* 52: 36–55.

KOWINSKI, WILLIAM SEVERINI. 2002. *The Malling of America.* Philadelphia: Xlibris.

KRAUSS, CLIFFORD. 2008. "Gas Prices Send Surge of Riders to Mass Transit." *New York Times,* May 10, pp. A1, A15.

KRIVO, LAUREN, RUTH PETERSON, AND DANIELLE KUHL. 2009. "Segregation, Racial Structure, and Neighborhood Violent Crime." *American Journal of Sociology* 114: 1765–1802.

KRUGER, DANIEL J., THOMAS M. REISCHL, AND GILBERT C. GEE. 2007. "Neighborhood Social Conditions Mediate the Association between Physical Deterioration and Mental Health." *American Journal of Community Psychology* 40: 261–71.

KRYSAN, MARIA. 2002. "Community Undesirability in Black and White: Examining Racial Residential Patterns through Community Perceptions." *Social Problems* 49: 521–43.

KUNSTLER, JAMES. 1996. "Home from Nowhere." *Atlantic* (September): 43–66.

KWON, HEE-KYUNG, VIRGINIA S. ZUIKER, AND JEAN W. BAUER. 2004. "Factors Associated with the Poverty Status of Asian Immigrant Householders by Citizenship Status." *Journal of Family and Economic Issues* 25 (Spring): 101–20.

LANE, GINNY G. AND AMY E. WHITE. 2010. "The Roots of Resegregation: Analysis and Implications." *Race, Gender & Class* 17: 81–101.

LARRIVIERE, JAMES B., AND CHARLES O. KRONCKE. 2004. "A Human Capital Approach to American Indian Earnings: The Effects of Place of Residence and Migration." *The Social Science Journal* 41: 209–24.

LASEN, AMPARO. 2003. *A Comparative Study of Mobile Phone Use in Public Places in London, Madrid and Paris,* Digital World Research Centre, University of Surrey.

LAWAL, NIKE S., MATTHEW N. O. SADIKU, AND ADE DOPAMU, eds. 2004. *Understanding Yoruba Life and Culture.* Trenton, NJ: Africa World Press.

LAWLOR, JULIA. 2004. "The Ironbound: A Home Away From Home for Immigrants." *New York Times,* January 11, Section 11, p. 5.

LE, PHUONG. 2011. "Puget Sound Oysters Affected by Pollution in Washington State," July 10. Accessed at http://www.huffingtonpost.com/2011/07/10/ on August 15, 2011.

LE CORBUSIER. 1967. *The Radiant City.* New York: Grossman–Orion; originally published 1933.

———. 1987. *The City of Tomorrow and Its Planning.* Mineola, NY: Dover Publications; originally published 1927.

LEE, MATTHEW, AND TERRI L. EARNEST. 2003. "Perceived Community Cohesion and Perceived Risk of Victimization: A Cross-National Analysis." *Justice Quarterly* 20: 131–57.

LEFEBVRE, HENRI. 1992. *The Production of Space.* Malden, MA: Wiley-Blackwell.

———. 2003. *The Urban Revolution.* Minneapolis, MN: University of Minnesota Press; originally published 1970.

LEI, FU. 2010. "Shantytowns Face Hard Home Truths." *China Daily,* December 13. Accessed at http://www.chinadaily.com.cn/usa/2010-12/13/content_11692723.htm on August 4, 2011.

LEPORE, STEPHEN J., AND GARY W. EVANS. 1991. "Social Hassles and Psychological Health in the Context of Chronic Crowding." *Journal of Health and Social Behavior* 32 (December): 357–67.

LESLIE, JACQUES. 2008. "China's Pollution Nightmare Is Now Everyone's Pollution Nightmare." *Christian Science Monitor,* March 19, p. 9.

LEVITT, DAVID M. 2011. "1st NYC Office Building Boom since '80s," May 23. Accessed at http://www.newsday.com/classifieds/real-estate/1st-nyc-office-building-boom-since-80s-1.2894818 on August 13, 2011.

LEVY, CLAIRE. 2008. "Urban Sprawl Drives Up the Cost of Living." *Denver Post,* August 10. Accessed at http://www.denverpost.com/opinion/ci_10132477 on August 15, 2011.

LEWINBERG, FRANK. 2011. "The St. Lawrence Neighbourhood: A Lesson for the Future." Accessed at http://archives.chbooks.com/online_books/eastwest/068.html on July 25, 2011.

LEY, DAVID. 2006. "Explaining Variations in Business Performance Among Immigrant Entrepreneurs in Western Canada." *Journal of Ethnic and Migration Studies* 32 (July): 743–64.

LI, LILLIAM M., ALISON DRAY-NOVEY, AND HAILI KONG. 2008. *Beijing: From Imperial Capital to Olympic City.* New York: Palgrave Macmillan.

LICHTER, DANIEL T., AND MARTHA L. CROWLEY. 2002. "Poverty in America: Beyond Welfare Reform." *Population Bulletin* 57 (June).

LIEBOW, ELIOT. 2003. *Tally's Corner,* 2nd ed. Lanham, MD: Rowman & Littlefield.

LIKE, TOYA Z. 2011. "Urban Inequality and Racial Differences in Risk for Violent Victimization." *Crime & Delinquency* 57 (May): 432–57.

LINK, BRUCE G., AND JO C. PHELAN. 1995. "Social Conditions as Fundamental Causes of Disease," *Journal of Health and Social Behavior*, Extra Issue: 80–94.

LINKON, SHERRY LEE, AND JOHN RUSSO. 2003. *Steeltown USA: Work and Memory in Youngstown*. Lawrence: University Press of Kansas.

LIVERANI, MARIO. 2006. *Uruk: The First City*. London: Equinox Publishing.

LOFLAND, LYN. 1985. *A World of Strangers: Order and Action in Urban Public Spaces*. Prospect Heights, IL: Waveland Press.

LOGAN, JOHN, AND HARVEY MOLOTCH. 2007. *Urban Fortunes: The Political Economy of Place*, 2nd ed. Berkeley: University of California Press.

LOGAN, JOHN R., AND BRIAN J. STULTS. 2011. "The Persistence of Segregation in the Metropolis: New Findings from the 2010 Census." *US 2010 Project*. Accessed at http://www.s4.brown.edu/us2010/Data/Report/report2.pdf on April 20, 2012.

LONDON & PARTNERS. 2011a. "Overseas Visitors to London Spend More Than £8.6 Billion in 2010 as Capital Bucks UK Trend." Accessed at http://www.londonandpartners.com/media-centre/press-releases/2011/ on June 1, 2011.

———. 2011b. "London Remains Top City in Europe for International Investment." Loc. cit.

LOS ANGELES TIMES. 2011. "Pico-Union." Accessed at http://projects.latimes.com/mapping-la/neighborhoods/neighborhood/pico-union/ on July 25, 2011.

LOURY, GLENN C. 2010. "Crime, Inequality & Justice." *Daedalus* 139 (Summer): 134–40.

LOVEJOY, PAUL E. 2000. *Transformations in Slavery: A History of Slavery in Africa*. New York: Cambridge University Press.

LUCK, TIFFANY M. 2008. "The World's Dirtiest Cities." *Forbes Magazine*. Accessed at http://www.forbes.com/2008/02/26/pollution-baku-oil-biz-logistics-cx_tl_0226dirtycities.html on December 13, 2008.

LUNDBLAD, KAREN SHAFER. 1995. "Jane Addams and Social Reform: A Role Model for the 1990s." *Social Work* 40 (September): 661–69.

LYDERSEN, KARI. 2011. "Cabrini-Green to Exit with Poetry and Lights." *New York Times*, March 26, p. A25.

LYNCH, KEVIN. 1976. *What Time Is This Place?* Cambridge, MA: MIT Press.

———. 1982. *The Image of the City*. Cambridge, MA: MIT Press; originally published 1960.

MACIONIS, JOHN J. 2008. *Sociology*, 12th ed. Upper Saddle River, NJ: Prentice Hall.

MACIVER, ROBERT. 2011. "The Great Emptiness." Pp. 48–55 in *The Pursuit of Happiness*. New York: Literary Licensing; originally published 1962.

MACLEOD, JAY. 2008. *Ain't No Makin' It*, 3rd ed. Boulder, CO: Westview Press.

MAGEE, PETER. 2005. *Excavations at Tepe Yahya, Iran, 1967–1975: The Iron Age Settlement*. Cambridge, MA: Peabody Museum Press.

MAIR, CHRISTINA, ANA V. DIEZ-ROUX, AND JEFFREY D. MORENOFF. 2010. "Neighborhood Stressors and Social Support as Predictors of Depressive Symptoms in the Chicago Community Adult Health Study." *Health & Place* 16: 811–9.

MAIR, CHRISTINE A., AND R. V. THIVIERGE-RIKARD. 2010. "The Strength of Strong Ties for Older Rural Adults; Regional Distinctions in the Relationship between Social Interaction and Subjective Well-Being." *International Journal of Aging and Human Development* 70: 119–43.

MALLACH, ALAN. 2010. *Bringing Buildings Back: From Abandoned Properties to Community Assets*, 2nd ed. New Brunswick, NJ: Rutgers University Press.

MANTOUX, PAUL. 2006. *The Industrial Revolution in the Eighteenth Century*. New York: Routledge.

MARX, KARL, AND FRIEDRICH ENGELS. 1976. *The German Ideology*. New York: International Publishers; originally published 1846.

MASSEY, DOUGLAS S., AND NANCY A. DENTON. 1993. *American Apartheid: Segregation and the Making of the Underclass*. Cambridge, MA: Harvard University Press.

MATARRESE, LYNNE. 2005. *History of Levittown, New York*. New York: Levittown Historical Society.

MATEI, SORIN, SANDRA J. BALL-ROKEACH, AND JACK L. QIU. 2001. "Fear and Misperception of Los Angeles Urban Space: A Spatial-Statistical Study of Communication-Shaped Mental Maps." *Communication Research* 28 (August): 429–63.

MATHER, MARK, KELVIN POLLARD, AND LINDA A. JACOBSEN. July 2011. "First Results from the 2010 Census." Washington, D.C.: Population Reference Bureau.

MAYER, MIRA. 2004. "The Dropout Rates of Mexican Students in Two California Cities." *Research for Educational Reform* 9: 14–24.

MCCABE, JAMES D., JR. 2010. *Lights and Shadows of New York Life*. Minneapolis, MN: Filiquarian Publishing; originally published 1872.

MCCALL, PATRICIA L, AND KAREN F. PARKER. 2005. "A Dynamic Model of Racial Competition, Racial Inequality, and Interracial Violence." *Sociological Inquiry* 75: 273–93.

MCKENZIE, EVAN. 2011. "Beyond Privatopia: Rethinking Residential Private Government." New York: Urban Institute.

MECHTENBERG, JERRY, AND RONALD C. KRAMER. 2008. "State Crime and Christian Resistance: The Prophetic Criminality of Philip Berrigan and Elizabeth McAlister." *Contemporary Justice Review* 11 (September): 249–70.

MENDOZA, CRISTOBAL. 2006. "Transnational Spaces Through Local Places, Mexican Immigrants in Albuquerque." *Journal of Anthropological Research* 62 (Winter): 539–61.

MERLE, RENAE. 2010. "Minorities Hit Harder by Foreclosure Crisis." *Washington Post*, June 19, p. A12.

MERTON, ROBERT K. 1968. *Social Theory and Social Structure*. New York: Free Press.

METROPOLITAN WASHINGTON AIRPORTS AUTHORITY. 2011. "Dulles Metrorail Project Overview." Accessed at http://www.dullesmetro.com/about/index.cfm on August 17, 2011.

MIAMI. 2011. Accessed at http://www.miamigov.com on July 6, 2011.

Middleton, Jennie. 2010. "Sense and the City: Exploring the Embodied Geographies of Urban Walking." *Social & Cultural Geography* 11 (September): 575–96.

Miller, D. W. 2000. "The New Urban Studies." *Chronicle of Higher Education*, August 18, pp. A15–16.

Miller, Sara Cedar. 2003. *Central Park, An American Masterpiece: A Comprehensive History of the Nation's First Urban Park.* New York: Harry N. Abrams Publishing.

Mills, Amy. 2007. "Gender and Mahalle (Neighborhood) Space in Istanbul." *Gender, Place and Culture* 14 (June): 335–54.

Miranne, Kristine B., and Alma H. Young, eds. 2010. *Gendering the City.* Lanham, MD: Rowan & Littlefield.

MNS. 2011. "Manhattan Rental Market Report." Accessed at http://www.mns.com/manhattan_rental_market_report on August 13, 2011.

Molotch, Harvey. 1976. "The City as a Growth Machine." *American Journal of Sociology* 82: 309–33.

———. 2002. "School's Out: A Response to Michael Dear." *City & Community* 1 (March): 39–43.

Money. 2010. "Best Places to Live." Accessed at http://money.cnn.com/magazines/moneymag/bplive/2010/top100/ on August 7, 2011.

Mongabay. 2011. "The Poorest and Wealthiest Places in the United States." Accessed at http://wealth.mongabay.com/tables/100_income_zip_codes.html on August 14, 2011.

Monti, Daniel J. 1999. *The American City: A Social and Cultural History.* New York: Blackwell.

Montreal. 2011. Accessed at http://ville.montreal.qc.ca/ on July 6, 2011.

Morgan, Kathleen, Scott Morgan, and Rachel Boba. 2011. *City Crime Rankings 2011–2012.* Washington, D.C.: CQ Press.

Morris, David. 2008. *Self-Reliant Cities: Energy and the Transformation of Urban America.* Accessed at http://www.ilsr.org/pubs/selfreliantcities.pdf on June 4, 2011.

Morris, Jan. 2003. *The World: Travels 1950–2000.* New York: W.W. Norton & Company.

Morse, Richard J., and Jorge E. Hardoy, eds. 1993. *Rethinking the Latin American City.* Washington, D.C.: Woodrow Wilson Center.

Mote, F. W. 2003. *Imperial China 900–1800.* Cambridge, MA: Harvard University Press.

Muller, Thomas. 1994. *Immigrants and the American City.* New York: NYU Press.

Mumford, Lewis. 1991. *The City in History: Its Origins, Its Transformations, and Its Prospects,* New ed. New York: Penguin Books; originally published 1961.

Murphy, Rhodes. 2007. "City as a Mirror of Society." Pp. 186–204 in *The City in Cultural Context,* edited by John A. Agnew, John Mercer, and David E. Sophen. New York: Routledge.

Naquin, Susan. 2000. *Peking: Temples and City Life, 1400–1900.* Berkeley: University of California Press.

Narconon International. 2010. "Narconon Programs Helping Traumatized Street Children in Latin America," September 27. Accessed at http://drugfree.narconon.org/2010/09/27/ on April 14, 2012.

Nasar, Jack L., Jennifer S. Evans-Cowley, and Vicente Mantero. 2007. "McMansions: The Extent and Regulation of Super-Sized Houses." *Journal of Urban Design* 12: 339–58.

National Center for Education Statistics. 2009. *Digest of Education Statistics,* Table 100.

———. 2011. *The Condition of Education 2011,* Indicator 27. Accessed at http://nces.ed.gov/programs/coe/pdf/coe_cps.pdf on July 28, 2011.

National Center for Health Statistics. December 7, 2011. "Deaths: Final Data for 2008." *National Vital Statistics Reports* 59 (10).

National Crime Records Bureau. 2010. *Crime in India 2009.* New Delhi, India: Ministry of Home Affairs.

Neuwirth, Robert. 2004. *Shadow Cities: A Billion Squatters, A New Urban World.* London: Routledge.

Newburn, Tim, and Trevor Jones. 2007. "Symbolizing Crime Control: Reflections on Zero Tolerance." *Theoretical Criminology* 11: 221–43.

New York City. 2011. "Murder in New York City 2010." Accessed at http://www.nyc.gov/html/nypd/downloads/pdf/analysis_and_planning/2010_murder_in_nyc.pdf on July 30, 2011.

New York City Department of City Planning. 2006. *New York City Population Projections by Age/Sex & Borough 2000–2030.* Accessed at http://www.nyc.gov/html/dcp/pdf/census/projections_report.pdf on August 13, 2011.

New York City Economic Development Council. 2011a. "The New Industrial NYC." Accessed at http://www.nycedc.com on August 14, 2011.

———. 2011b. "Economic Snapshot: A Summary of New York City's Economy." Accessed at http://www.nycedc.com on August 13, 2011.

New York City Office of The Mayor. 2011. "Announce New Nightly Program to Accelerate the Constructions Approval Process and Spur Economic Development Citywide." Press Release, May 3.

New York Times. 1983. "St. Louis Reports 3 Attacks, and Nobody 'Gets Involved'." August 18, p. D16.

New York Times. 1984. "Caller Reported an Attack During Assault on Woman." December 3, p. B10.

Newman, Katherine S. 2000. *No Shame in my Game: The Working Poor in the Inner City.* New York: Vintage.

Newman, Oscar. 1996. *Creating Defensible Space.* Washington, D.C.: U.S. Department of Housing and Urban Development.

News24.com. 2003. "Girl Raped on Busy Street," March 6. Accessed at http://www.news24.com/News24/World/News/on July 17, 2005.

Nicholas, David. 2003. *Urban Europe, 1100–1700.* New York: Palgrave Macmillan.

Nicolaides, Becky M. 2002. *My Blue Heaven: Life and Politics in the Working-Class Suburbs of Los Angeles, 1920–1965.* Chicago: University of Chicago Press.

Nicholls, Walter J. 2011. "The Los Angeles School: Difference, Politics, City." *International Journal of Urban & Regional Research* 35: 189–206.

Ogbu, John. 2003. *Black Students in an Affluent Suburb: A Study of Academic Disengagement.* Mahwah, NJ: Lawrence Erlbaum.

O'HANLON, SEAMUS AND CHRIS HAMNETT. 2009. "Deindustrialisation, Gentrification and the Re-invention of the Inner City: London and Melbourne, c.1960–2008." *Urban Policy and Research* 27 (September): 211–16.

OLSEN, JOSHUA. 2004. *Better Places, Better Lives: A Biography of James Rouse.* Washington, D.C.: Urban land Institute.

OREGON BREWERS GUILD. 2011. Accessed at http://www .oregonbeer.org/portland-metro/ on April 7, 2012.

PAMPALON, ROBERT, DENIS HAMEL, MARIA DE KONINCK, AND MARIE-JEANNE DISANT. 2007. "Perception of Place and Health: Differences between Neighbour-hoods in the Québec City Region." *Social Science & Medicine* 65 (July): 95–111.

PARFITT, TOM. 2008. "Moscow Rises to Foster's Space-Age Vision." *The Guardian,* January 4. Accessed at http://www.guardian.co.uk/world/2008/jan/04/ architecture.uk on August 8, 2011.

PARK, ROBERT E. 1964. *Race and Cultures.* In *The Early Sociology of Race and Ethnicity,* Vol. VI., edited by Kenneth. Thompson, NY: Routledge, 2005.

———. 1984. "The City: Suggestions for the Investigation of Human Behavior in the Urban Environment." Pp. 1–46 in *The City,* reprinted, edited by Robert E. Park and Eugene W. Burgess. Chicago: University of Chicago Press; originally published 1916.

PARRILLO, VINCENT N. 2011. *Strangers to These Shores,* 10th ed. Boston: Allyn and Bacon.

PASTERNAK, JUDY. 1998. " 'Edge City' Is Attempting to Build a Center." *Los Angeles Times,* January 1, p. 5.

PATTAVINA, APRIL, JAMES M. BYRNE, AND LUIS GAR-CIA. 2006. "An Examination of Citizen Involvement in Crime Prevention in High-Risk Versus Low-to-Moderate-Risk Neighborhoods." *Crime & Delinquency* 52: 203–31.

PETERS, ARNO. 2002. *Hammond Compact Peter's World Atlas.* Union, NJ: Hammond World Atlas Corporation.

PETRY, ANN. 1998. *The Street.* Boston: Houghton Mifflin; originally published 1946.

PEW HISPANIC CENTER. 2011a. "Demography." Accessed at http://pewhispanic.org/topics/?TopicID=1 on April 14, 2012.

———. 2011b. "The Toll of the Great Recession," July 26. Accessed at http://pewhispanic.org/reports/ report.php?ReportID=145 on September 5, 2011.

PHILIPS, KEVIN. 2003. *Wealth and Democracy: A Political History of the American Rich.* New York: Broadway Books.

PIIPARINEN, RICHEY. 2011. "The Cleveland Comeback: Version 5.0." Accessed at http://rustwire.com/2011/ 04/04/the-cleveland-comeback-version-5-0/ on August 13, 2011.

PISELLI, FORTUNATA. 2007. "Communities, Places, and Social Networks." *American Behavioral Scientist* 50 (March): 867–78.

PLOEGER, NANCY. March 15, 2002. "Six Months Later." New York: Manhattan Chamber of Commerce.

POPULATION REFERENCE BUREAU. 2011. *2011 World Population Data Sheet.* Washington, D.C.: Population Reference Bureau.

PORT OF NEW ORLEANS. 2011. Accessed at http://www .portno.com/pno_pages/about_overview.htm on July 7, 2011.

PORTÉS, ALEJANDRO. 1977. "Urban Latin America: The Political Condition from Above and Below." Pp. 59–70 in *Third World Urbanization,* edited by Janet Abu-Lughod and Richard Hay, Jr. Chicago: Maaroufa.

POSSEHL, GREGORY L. 2003. *The Indus Civilization: A Contemporary Perspective.* Lanham, MD: AltaMira Press.

POUNDS, NORMAN. 2005. *The Medieval City.* Westport, CT: Greenwood Press.

POWELL, KIMBERLY. 2010. "Making Sense of Place: Mapping as a Multisensory Research Method." *Qualitative Inquiry* 16 (7): 539–55.

POWELL, RICHARD. 2006. *The Philadelphians,* 50th anv. ed. Medford, NJ: Plexus Publishing.

PROJECT FOR PUBLIC SPACES. 2007. "Streets as Places." Accessed at http://www.slideshare.net/ metroplanning/project-for-public-spaces-streets-as-places on April 20, 2012.

———. 2011. Accessed at http://www.pps.org/ on August 10, 2011.

PUTNAM, ROBERT D. 2001. *Bowling Alone: The Collapse and Revival of the American Community.* New York: Simon & Schuster.

PUU, TÖNU. 2010. *Mathematical Location and Land Use Theory: An Introduction,* 2nd ed. New York: Springer.

QUINN, JAMES. 2010. "US Home Seizures by Banks Close to Record." *Daily Telegraph,* August 13, p. 8.

RABAN, JONATHAN. 1998. *Soft City,* reprint ed. London: Harvill Press.

RAINWATER, LEE. 2006. *Behind Ghetto Walls: Black Families in a Federal Slum.* New Brunswick, NJ: Aldine Transaction; originally published 1970.

RAMSDEN, EDMUND. 2011. "From Rodent Utopia to Urban Hell." *Journal of the History of Science in Society* 102 (December): 659–88.

RAVITCH, DIANE. 2010. *The Death and Life of the Great American School System.* New York: Basic Books.

REALTYTRAC. 2011. "National Real Estate Trends." Accessed at http://www.realtytrac.com/trendcenter/ trend.html on July 24, 2011.

REGIONAL PLAN ASSOCIATION. 2011. "America 2050: A Prospectus." Accessed at http://www.america2050 .org/pdf/America2050prospectus.pdf on June 7, 2008.

REGUS MEDIA CENTRE. 2011. "Poor Air Quality Threatens Hong Kong's Competitive Edge," May 31. Accessed at http://www.regus.presscentre.com/Press-Releases/ on August 4, 2011.

REUTERS. 2007. "Iron Age and Roman Discoveries at Olympic Site," November 28. Accessed at http:// uk.reuters.com/article/2007/11/28/uk-britain-olympics-romans-idUKL2868027820071128 on May 26, 2011.

RICE, MICHAEL. 2004. *Egypt's Making: The Origins of Ancient Egypt 5000–2000 BC,* 2nd ed. New York: Routledge.

RIESMAN, DAVID. 1958. "The Suburban Sadness." Pp. 375–408 in *The Suburban Community,* edited by William Dobriner. New York: G.P. Putnam's Sons.

Riis, Jacob. 1957. *How the Other Half Lives.* New York: Hill and Wang; originally published 1890.

Robers, Simone, Jijun Zhang, and Jennifer Truman. 2010. *Indicators of School Crime and Safety: 2010* (NCES 2011-002/NCJ 230812). National Center for Education Statistics, U.S. Department of Education, and Bureau of Justice Statistics, Washington, D.C.

Roberts, Bryan R. 2005. "Globalization and Latin American Cities." *International Journal of Urban and Regional Research* 29: 110–23.

Roberts, Sam. 2009. "N.Y. Poverty Data Paint Mixed Picture." *New York Times,* September 29, p. A31.

———. 2010a. "Census Data Shows, in New Ways, How the Recession Hit New Yorkers." *New York Times,* September 29, p. A22.

———. 2010b. "In Harlem, Blacks Are No Longer a Majority." *New York Times,* January 6, p. A16.

———. 2011a. "Slower Racial Change Found in Census of City." *New York Times,* July 29, p. A22.

———. 2011b. "As Effects of Recession Linger, Growth in City's Poverty Rate Outpaces the Nation's." *New York Times,* September 22, p. A23.

Robson, Garry, and Tim Butler. 2001. "Coming to Terms with London: Middle-Class Communities in a Global City." *International Journal of Urban & Regional Research* 25 (March): 70–86.

Rodriguez, Clara E. 1996. "The Puerto Rican Community in the South Bronx: View from Within and Without." P. 507, in *Sociology,* 5th ed., edited by Beth B. Hess, Elizabeth W. Markson, and Peter J. Stein. Boston: Allyn and Bacon.

Roessner, Jane. 2000. *A Decent Place to Live: From Columbia Point to Harbor Point.* Boston: Northeastern University Press.

Roett, Riordan. 2011. *The New Brazil,* rev. ed. Washington, D.C.: Brookings Institution Press.

Romig, Kevin. 2005. "The Upper Sonoran Lifestyle: Gated Communities in Scottsdale, Arizona." *City & Community* 4 (March): 67–86.

Rousseau, Francois, and Lionel Standing. 1995. "Zero Effect of Crowding on Arousal and Performance: On 'Proving' the Null Hypothesis." *Perceptual and Motor Skills* 81 (August): 72–74.

Row, D. K. 2011. "Interpreting Oregon's Population Shift from the 2010 Census," April 11. Accessed at http://www.oregonlive.com/pacific-northwest-news/index.ssf/2011/ on July 19, 2011.

Roxburgh, Susan. 2009. "Untangling Inequalities: Gender, Race and Socioeconomic Differences in Depression." *Sociological Forum* 24: 357–81.

Sagan, Carl. 2005. *The Dragons of Eden.* New York: Black Dog & Leventhal Publishers.

St. Claire, Clyde, and robert clymer. 2000. "Racial Residential Segregation by Socioeconomic Status." *Social Science Quarterly* 81: 701–15.

Salt Lake City. 2011. Accessed http://www.saltlakecityutah.org/salt_lake_demographics.htm on July 6, 2011.

Sampson, Robert J. 2002. "Studying Modern Chicago." *City & Community* 1: 45–48.

Samuelson, Robert J. 2011. "The Jobs Mismatch." *Washington Post,* June 20, p. A17.

Sanchez, Thomas W., Robert E. Lang, and Dawn M. Dhavale. 2005. "Security Versus Status?" *Journal of Planning Education and Research* 24: 281–91.

Sandburg, Carl. 1944. *Chicago Poems.* New York: Harcourt Brace Jovanovich.

Sanders, Jerry. 2000. "Racial and Ethnic Minorities in San Diego, United States." *Policing and Society* 10: 131–41.

Sassen, Saskia. 2001. *The Global City: New York, Tokyo, and London,* 2nd ed. Princeton: Princeton, NJ University Press; originally published 1991.

———. 2002. *Global Networks: Linked Cities.* London: Brunner-Routledge.

———. 2006. *Cities in a World Economy,* 3rd ed. Thousand Oaks, CA: Pine Forge Press.

Saulny, Susan. 2007. "At Housing Project, Both Fear and Renewal." *New York Times,* March 17, p. A20.

Schein, Virginia E. 1995. *Working from the Margins: Voices of Mothers in Poverty.* Ithaca, NY: Cornell University Press.

Schemo, Diana Jean. 2006. "Federal Program on Vouchers Draws Strong Minority Support." *New York Times,* April 6, pp. A1, A20.

Schomp, Virginia. 2005. *Ancient Mesopotamia: The Sumerians, Babylonians, and Assyrians.* New York: Franklin Watts.

Schrank, David, Tim Lomax, and Shawn Turner. 2010. *The 2010 Urban Mobility Report.* Accessed at http://tti.tamu.edu/documents/mobility_report_2010.pdf on August 16, 2011.

Schwirian, Kent P., F. Martin Hankins, and Carol A. Ventresca. 1990. "The Residential Decentralization of Social Status Groups in American Metropolitan Communities, 1950–1980." *Social Forces* 68: 1143–63.

Schultz, David. 2011. "New Potomac River Bridge? Don't Count on It." WAMU 88.5, June 2. Accessed at http://wamu.org/news/11/06/02/new_potomac_river_bridges_dont_count_on_it.php on August 16, 2011.

Scobey, David M. 2003. *Empire City: The Making and Meaning of the New York City Landscape.* Philadelphia: Temple University Press.

Scott, Allen J. 1980. *The Urban Land Nexus and the State.* London: Pion.

———. 1988. *Metropolis.* Berkeley: University of California Press.

———. 2001. *From Chicago to L.A.: Making Sense of Urban Theory.* Thousand Oaks, CA: Sage Publications.

Shihadeh, Edward S., and Darrell J. Steffensmeier. 1994. "Economic Inequality, Family Disruption, and Urban Black Violence: Cities as Units of Stratification and Social Control." *Social Forces* 73 (December): 729–51.

Shimz Corporation. 2011. "TRY 2004: The 'Pyramid City in the Air' Concept." Accessed at http://www.shimz.co.jp/english/theme/dream/try.html on August 8, 2011.

Sides, Josh. 2006. *L.A. City Limits: African American Los Angeles from the Great Depression to the Present.* Berkeley: University of California Press.

SIEMENS. 2011. *U.S. and Canada Green Cities Index.* Accessed at http://www.siemens.com on September 5, 2011.

SIGELMAN, LEE, AND JEFFREY R. HENIG. 2001. "Crossing the Great Divide: Race and Preferences for Living in the City Versus the Suburb." *Urban Affairs Review* 37: 3–18.

SILVERMAN, ELI B. 2004. " 'Zero Tolerance' in Police Activity." *Inchiesta* 34: 18–22.

SIMMEL, GEORG. 1964. "The Metropolis and Mental Life." Pp. 409–24 in *The Sociology of Georg Simmel,* edited by K. Wolff. New York: Free Press; originally published 1905.

SISKIND, PETER. 2006. "Suburban Growth and Its Discontents." Pp. 161–82 in *The New Suburban History,* edited by Kevin M. Kruse and Thomas J. Sugrue. Chicago: University of Chicago Press.

SJOBERG, GIDEON. 1965. *The Preindustrial City.* New York: Free Press.

SKIDMORE, THOMAS E., PETER H. SMITH, AND JAMES N. GREEN. 2010. *Modern Latin America,* 7th ed. New York: Oxford University Press.

SKRENTNY, JOHN D. 2006. "Law and the American State." *Annual Review of Sociology* 32: 213–44.

SMALL, MARIO LUIS. 2007. "Racial Differences in Networks: Do Neighborhood Conditions Matter?" *Social Science Quarterly* 88 (June): 320–43.

SOJA, EDWARD W. 2000. *Postmetropolis: Critical Studies of Cities and Regions.* New York: Wiley–Blackwell.

SORKIN, MICHAEL, ed. 1992. *Variations on a Theme Park: The New American City and the End of Public Space.* New York: The Noonday Press, Farrar, Strauss and Giroux.

SOUTH, SCOTT J., KYLE CROWDER, AND ERICK CHAVEZ. 2005. "Geographic Mobility and Spatial Assimilation among U.S. Latino Immigrants." *International Migration Review* 39 (Fall): 577–607.

SOUTHERN CALIFORNIA ASSOCIATION OF GOVERNMENTS. 2008. *Final 2008 Regional Transportation Plan: Making the Connections.* Accessed at http://www.scag.ca.gov/rtp2008/final.htm on July 21, 2008.

SOWELL, THOMAS. 1977. "New Light on Black I.Q." *New York Times Magazine,* March 27, p. 57.

SPAIN, DAPHNE. 1992. *Gendered Spaces.* Chapel Hill: University of North Carolina Press.

SPECTORSKY, A. C. 1957. *The Exurbanites.* New York: Berkley.

SPENGLER, OSWALD. 2004. *The Decline of the West.* New York: Vintage; originally published 1928.

SPILLIUS, ELIZABETH BOTT. 2008. *Family and Social Network,* 2nd ed. New York: Routledge.

SROLE, LEO. 1972. "Urbanization and Mental Health: Some Reformulations." *American Scientist* 60: 576–83.

STACK, CAROL. 1997. *All Our Kin: Strategies for Survival in a Black Community.* New York: Basic Books.

STANNARD, DAVID E. 1993. *American Holocaust: The Conquest of the New World.* New York: Oxford University Press.

STARK, ANDREW. 2002. *Conflict of Interest in American Public Life.* Cambridge, MA: Harvard University Press.

STARK, MIRIAM T. 2006. *Archaeology of Asia.* Malden, MA: Blackwell.

STATISTICS CANADA. 2007a. "The African Community in Canada." *Profiles of Ethnic Communities in Canada.* Ottawa: Minister of Industry.

———. 2007b. "The Chinese Community in Canada." *Profiles of Ethnic Communities in Canada.* Ottawa: Minister of Industry.

———. 2007c. "The Filipino Community in Canada." *Profiles of Ethnic Communities in Canada.* Ottawa: Minister of Industry.

———. 2007d. "The East Indian Community in Canada." *Profiles of Ethnic Communities in Canada.* Ottawa: Minister of Industry.

———. 2007e. "The Vietnamese Community in Canada." *Profiles of Ethnic Communities in Canada.* Ottawa: Minister of Industry.

———. 2007f. "The Japanese Community in Canada." *Profiles of Ethnic Communities in Canada.* Ottawa: Minister of Industry.

———. 2007g. "The Korean Community in Canada." *Profiles of Ethnic Communities in Canada.* Ottawa: Minister of Industry.

———. 2007h. "The Latin American Community in Canada." *Profiles of Ethnic Communities in Canada.* Ottawa: Minister of Industry.

———. 2007i. "The Arab Community in Canada." *Profiles of Ethnic Communities in Canada.* Ottawa: Minister of Industry.

———. 2008. *Aboriginal Peoples in Canada in 2006: Inuit, Métis, and First Nations, 2006 Census.* Ottawa: Minister of Industry.

———. 2011a. "Income of Canadians." Accessed at http://www.statcan.gc.ca/daily-quotidien/110615/dq110615b-eng.htm on July 24, 2011.

———. 2011b. Accessed at http://www.statcan.gc.ca on August 12, 2011.

STEELE, JEFFREY. 1998. "Profile: Gage Park." *Chicago Tribune,* July 24, p. 16.

STEFFENS, LINCOLN. 2009. *The Shame of the Cities.* Charleston, SC: BiblioBazaar; originally published 1904.

STEIN, CLARENCE. 1972. *Toward New Towns for America.* Cambridge, MA: MIT Press.

STEIN, ROBIN. 2006. "Furor over 'Work Force Housing.'" *North Pinellas Times,* December 5, p. 1.

STEINBECK, JOHN. 1962. *Travels with Charley: In Search of America.* New York: Franklin Watts.

STEINHAUER, JENNIFER. 2002. "Once Vilified, Squatters Will Inherit 11 Buildings." *New York Times,* August 20, p. A1.

STEPICK, ALEX, GUILLERMO GRENIER, MAX CASTRO, AND MARVIN DUNN. 2003. *This Land Is Our Land: Immigrants and Power in Miami.* Berkeley: University of California Press.

STIFFLER, LISA. 2011. "Scientists Zero In on Culprits behind Puget Sound Water Problems." *Crosscut News,* June 6. Accessed at http://crosscut.com/2011/06/06/puget-sound/20978/ on August 15, 2011.

STILL, BAYRD. 1999. *Mirror for Gotham: New York as Seen by Contemporaries from Dutch Days to the Present,* 2nd ed. New York: Fordham University Press.

STEWART, NIKITA. 2005. "Muslims Find Room to Grow in D.C.'s Outer Suburbs." *The Washington Post,* August 1, p. A1.

STONEBACK, DIANE. 2005. "Ironbound Ambiance: Historic District in Newark, N.J., Is Packed with the Tasty, the Spicy and All Good Things Portuguese." *Allentown Morning Call,* June 26, p. F1.

STRAUS, RYANE MCAULIFFE. 2010. "Measuring Multi-Ethnic Desegregation." *Education and Urban Society* 42: 223–42.

STRICKER, FRANK. 2007. *Why America Lost the War on Poverty—And How to Win It.* Chapel Hill: University of North Carolina Press.

SUISMAN, DOUGLAS R. 1990. *Los Angeles Boulevard: 8 X-Rays of the Body Politic.* Princeton, NJ: Princeton Architectural Press.

SUTTLES, GERALD. 1974. *The Social Order of the Slum.* Chicago: University of Chicago Press.

———. 1984. "The Cumulative Texture of Local Urban Culture." *American Journal of Sociology* 90: 283–304.

SWAIN, CAROL M., ed. 2007. *Debating Immigration.* New York: Cambridge University Press.

SYDENSTRICKER–NETO, JOHN. 2011. *Environmental Sociology.* Accessed at http://www.socialresearchmethods .net/ Gallery/Neto/Envsoc1.html on August 16, 2011.

SZE, LENA. 2010. "Chinatown Then and Neoliberal Now: Gentrification Consciousness and the Ethnic-Specific Museum." *Identities: Global Studies in Culture and Power* 17 (5) (September): 510–29.

TAEUBER, KARL, AND ALMA TAEUBER. 2009. *Residential Segregation and Neighborhood Change.* Piscataway, NJ: Aldine Transaction; originally published 1965.

TALEN, EMILY. 2006. "Neighborhood-Level Social Diversity." *Journal of the American Planning Association* 72: 431–46.

TAMMEMAGI, HANS. 2008. "Progressive Portland: A Model for Smart Growth with Many Lessons for Vancouver." *Vancouver Sun,* October 21, p. B1.

TARTARO, CHRISTINE, AND MARISSA P. LEVY. 2007. "Density, Inmate Assaults, and Direct Supervision Jails." *Criminal Justice Policy Review* 18 (December): 395–417.

TAYLOR, GRAHAM ROMEYN. 2010. *Satellite Cities: A Study of Industrial Suburbs.* New York: General Books; originally published 1915.

TEAFORD, JON C. 2006. *The Metropolitan Revolution: The Rise of Post-Urban America.* New York: Columbia University Press.

THAXTON, RALPH A., JR. 2008. *Catastrophe and Contention in Rural China.* New York: Cambridge University Press.

THILL, JEAN-CLAUDE, AND DANIEL Z. SUI. 1993. "Mental Maps and Fuzziness in Space Preferences." *The Professional Geographer* 45 (August): 264–76.

THOMAS, JUNE, JOHN SCHWEITZER, AND JULIA DARNTON. 2004. *Mixed-Income Neighborhoods in Grand Rapids: A Summary of Findings.* East Lansing: Michigan State University.

THORP, ROBERT L. 2006. *China in the Early Bronze Age: Shang Civilization.* Philadelphia: University of Pennsylvania Press.

TIAN, GUANGJIN, JIANGUO WU, AND ZHIFENG YANG. 2010. "Spatial Pattern of Urban Functions in the Beijing Metropolitan Region." *Habitat International* 34 (April): 249–55.

TIMES SQUARE ALLIANCE. 2011. "Times Square Bowtie." Accessed at http://www.timessquarenyc.org/facts/ bowtie.html on August 10, 2011.

TIMMER, DOUG A., D. STANLEY EITZEN, AND KATHRYN D. TALLEY. 1994. *Paths to Homelessness: Extreme Poverty and the Housing Crisis.* Boulder, CO: Westview Press.

TITA, GEORGE E., TRICIA L. PETRAS, AND ROBERT T. GREENBAUM. 2006. "Crime and Residential Choice: A Neighborhood Level Analysis of the Impact of Crime on Housing Prices." *Journal of Quantitative Criminology* 22 (4) (December): 299–317.

TOCQUEVILLE, ALEXIS DE. 2004. *The Old Regime and the French Revolution,* Vol. 1. Chicago: University of Chicago Press; originally published 1856.

TODARO, MICHAEL P., AND STEPHEN C. SMITH. 2011. *Economic Development,* 11th ed. Upper Saddle River, NJ: Prentice Hall.

TÖNNIES, FERDINAND. 2003. *Community and Society.* Mineola, NY: Dover Publications; originally published 1887.

TORONTO. 2011. Accessed at http://www.toronto.ca/ toronto_facts/diversity on August 8, 2011.

TORONTO STAR. 2010. "Windy City Blows Us Away: Waterfront and Parks Make Chicago Seem a Century Ahead of Toronto," August 21, p. T1.

TORREY, BARBARA BOYLE. 2004. "Urbanization: An Environmental Force to be Reckoned With." Washington, D.C.: Population Reference Bureau.

TOYBOX. 2011. "Street Children Facts." Accessed at http://www.toybox.org.uk/street_children_facts .html on July 17, 2011.

TRIMET. 2011. *Facts About TriMet.* Accessed at http:// trimet.org/pdfs/publications/factsheet.pdf on September 5, 2011.

TSAKALOTOS, EUCLID. 2004. "Homo Economicus, Political Economy, and Socialism." *Science & Society* 68: 137–60.

UCLA DEPARTMENT OF URBAN PLANNING. 1998. *The Byzantine-Latino Quarter.* Accessed at http:// www.sppsr.ucla. edu/blq/home.html on July 11, 2005.

UNAIDS AND WORLD HEALTH ORGANIZATION. 2010. *UNAIDS Report on the Global AIDS Epidemic: 2010.* Geneva: UNAIDS.

UN-HABITAT. 2010. *State of African Cities 2010.* Accessed at http://www.unhabitat.org/documents/SOAC10/ SOAC-PR1-en.pdf on April 16, 2012.

———. 2011. *State of the World's Cities 2010/11.* Accessed at http://www.unhabitat.org on July 15, 2011.

UNITED NATIONS ENVIRONMENT PROGRAMME. 2009. *Bangkok Assessment Report on Climate Change.* Accessed at http://www.unep.org/dewa/pdf/BKK_ assessment_report2009.pdf on April 16, 2012.

———. 2011a. "Street Children by Country." Accessed at http://www.yapi.org/street/ on July 17, 2011.

———. 2011b. "Fast Pace of African Urbanization Affecting Water Supplies and Sanitation." Accessed at http://www.unep.org/Documents.Multilingual/ Default.asp?DocumentID=664&ArticleID=8666&l=en on August 6, 2011.

UNITED NATIONS FOOD AND AGRICULTURE ORGANIZATION. 2010. *Poverty in Europe.* Accessed at http://www.fao.org/docs/eims/upload/263500/ Poverty in Europe1.pdf on April 16, 2012.

United Nations Population Division. 2012. *World Urbanization Prospects: 2011 Revision.* Accessed at http://www.esa.un.org/unpd/wup/index.htm on April 16, 2012.

University of Virginia Library. 2011. *Letter to Dr. Benjamin Rush, September 23, 1800.* Accessed at http://etext.virginia.edu/toc/modeng/public/JefLett.html on June 2, 2011.

Urban Ecology. 2011. Accessed at http://www.urbanecology.org/mission.htm on July 6, 2011.

Urban Institute. 2005. "Understanding Community Change: A Look at Low-Income Chicago Neighborhoods in the 1990s." Accessed at http://www.urban.org/uploadedPDF/311151_understanding_community_change.pdf on April 14, 2012.

Urban Titan. 2011. "The Most Dangerous Cities in the World." Accessed at http://urbantitan.com/the-10-most-dangerous-cities-in-the-world-in-2012/ on April 16, 2012.

U.S. Bureau of Justice Statistics. 2011a. *Homicide Trends in the United States, 1980-2008: Annual Rates for 2009 and 2010.* Accessed at http://bjs.ojp.usdoj.gov/content/pub/pdf/htus8008.pdf on April 21, 2012.

———. 2011b. *Criminal Victimization in the United States, 2008 Statistical Tables.* Accessed at http://bjs.ojp.usdoj.gov/index.cfm?ty=pbdetail&iid=2218 on April 21, 2012.

U.S. Census Bureau. 2009. *Characteristics of the Foreign-Born Population by Nativity and U.S. Citizenship Status,* Table 1.13.

———. 2010a. *Current Population Survey: Annual Social and Economic Supplement,* Table POV41.

———. 2010b. *Nativity Status and Citizenship in the United States: 2009,* October, ACSBR/09-16.

———. 2011a. *Profile of General Population and Housing Characteristics: 2010.*

———. 2011b. *American Factfinder 2.* Accessed at http://factfinder2.census.gov/faces/nav/jsf/pages/index.xhtml on April 14, 2012.

———. 2011c. "U.S. Census Bureau Delivers Michigan's 2010 Census Population Totals." Accessed at http://www.census.gov/newsroom/releases/archives/2010_census/cb11-cn106.html on July 19, 2011.

———. 2011d. *Income, Poverty, and Health Insurance Coverage in the United States, 2010.* Washington, D.C: U.S. Government Printing Office.

———. 2012. *Statistical Abstract of the United States: 2012.* Washington, DC: U.S. Government Printing Office.

U.S. conference of mayors. 2011. *Hunger and Homelessness Survey.* Accessed at http://www.usmayors.org on April 14, 2012.

U.S. department of education. 2010. *Education for Homeless Children and Youths.* Accessed at http://www.ed.gov/programs/homeless/ index.html on July 26, 2011.

U.S. Department of Housing and Urban Development. 2011. *American Housing Survey,* Table 2-8, p. 25. Accessed at http://www.census.gov/prod/2011pubs/h150-09.pdf on April 7, 2012.

U.S. Environmental Protection Agency. 2001. "Threats to Wetlands." Accessed at http://www.epa.gov/owow/wetlands/pdf/threats.pdf on April 7, 2012.

U.S. Geological Survey. 2006. "Flood Hazards—A National Threat." Accessed at http://pubs.usgs.gov/fs/2006/3026/2006-3026.pdf on April 7, 2012.

U.S. Office of Immigration Statistics. 2011. *2010 Yearbook of Immigration Statistics.* Washington, D.C.: U.S. Government Printing Office.

Vale, Lawrence J. 2007. *From the Puritans to the Projects: Public Housing and Public Neighbors.* Cambridge, MA: Harvard University Press.

Vesselinov, Elena. 2008. "Members Only: Gated Communities and Residential Segregation in the Metropolitan United States." *Sociological Forum* 23 (September): 536–65.

Vevea, Rebecca, and Crystal Yednak. 2011. "New School Board Tackles Familiar Worries." *New York Times,* April 29, p. A23.

Vidich, Arthur, and Joseph Bensman. 2000. *Small Town in Mass Society,* rev. ed. Champaign, IL: University of Illinois Press; originally published 1958.

Wacquant, Loïc J. D. 1997. "Three Pernicious Premises in the Study of the American Ghetto." *International Journal of Urban & Regional Research* 21: 341–53.

Wagmiller, Robert L. 2007. "Race and the Spatial Segregation of Jobless Men in Urban America." *Demography* 44 (August): 539–62.

Wahab, Mallika. 2003. "Bangladesh Slums Demand Access to Clean Water." *International Journal of Humanities and Peace* 19: 46–47.

Walberg, Herbert J. 2007. *School Choice: The Findings.* Washington, D.C.: Cato Institute.

Waldinger, Roger, and Michael I. Lichter. 2003. *How the Other Half Works: Immigration and the Social Organization of Labor.* Berkeley: University of California Press.

Wallerstein, Immanuel. 2004. *World-Systems Analysis: An Introduction.* Durham, NC: Duke University Press.

Walton, John. 1981. "The New Urban Sociology." *International Social Science Journal* 33: 374–90.

Ward, Steven V. 1998. *Selling Places: The Marketing and Promotion of Towns and Cities 1850–2000.* London: Spon Press, Taylor & Francis Group.

Warner, Sam Bass, Jr. 1978. *Streetcar Suburbs,* 2nd ed. Cambridge, MA: Harvard University Press/MIT Press.

Washington Post. 2009. "Where the Money Will Go to Transform Tysons Corner," November 7, p. A22.

Waterfield, Robin. 2006. *Athens: A History, From Ancient Ideal to Modern City.* New York: Basic Books.

Wayman, Jeffrey C. 2002. "Student Perceptions of Teacher Ethnic Bias: A Comparison of Mexican American and Non-Latino White Dropouts and Students." *High School Journal* 85: 27–37.

Wayne, Gary. 2011. *The Universal CityWalk.* Accessed at http://www.seeing-stars.com/Shop/CityWalk.shtml on July 14, 2011.

Webb, Mary, and Jackie Tee, eds. 2011. *Jane's Urban Transport Systems 2011–2012.* Surrey, UK: Jane's Information Group.

WEBER, MAX. 1968. *The City.* New York: Free Press; originally published 1921.

WENKE, ROBERT J. 2007. *Patterns in Prehistory: Humankind's First Three Million Years,* 5th ed. New York: Oxford University Press.

WHEELER, JULIA. 2008. "Raw Sewage Threat to Booming Dubai." *BBC News,* October 13. Accessed at http://news.bbc.co.uk/2/hi/middle_east/7663883.stm on August 7, 2011.

WHITFORD, JOSH. 2006. *The New Old Economy: Networks, Institutions, and the Organizational Transformation of American Manufacturing.* New York: Oxford University Press.

WHITMEYER, JOSEPH M. 2002. "A Deductive Approach to Friendship Networks." *Journal of Mathematical Sociology* 26: 147–65.

WHITTLE, CHRIS. 2005. *Crash Course.* New York: Penguin Riverhead.

WHYTE, MARTIN K., AND WILLIAM L. PARISH. 1987. *Urban Life in Contemporary China,* reprint ed. Chicago: University of Chicago Press.

WHYTE, WILLIAM FOOTE. 1993. *Street Corner Society,* 3rd ed. Chicago: University of Chicago Press; originally published 1943.

———. 2001. *The Social Life of Small Urban Spaces.* New York: Project for Public Spaces; originally published 1980.

———. 2002. *The Organization Man.* Philadelphia: University of Pennsylvania Press; originally published 1966.

WICKHAM, DEWAYNE. 2010. "Fixing Education Is More Important than Revamping Health Care." *USA Today,* March 23, p. A21.

WIDHOLM, PAULA. 2005. "Chicago Is Back on the Upswing." *National Real Estate Investor* 47 (Fall): 34–38.

WIESE, ANDREW. 2004. *Places of their Own: African American Suburbanization in the Twentieth Century.* Chicago: University of Chicago Press.

———. 2005. "Robbins, IL." *The Encyclopedia of Chicago.* Chicago: Chicago Historical Society.

WILKES, RIMA, AND JOHN ICELAND. 2004. "Hypersegregation in the Twenty-First Century." *Demography* 41: 23–36.

WILLIAMS, TIMOTHY. 2008. "Mixed Feelings as Change Overtakes 125th Street." *New York Times,* June 13, p. B1.

WILLIE, CHARLES, AND HOWARD TAYLOR. 1995. "The Bell Curve Debate." Panel discussion at Eastern Sociological Society annual meeting, Philadelphia, March.

WILSON, DAVID, AND ANDREW E. G. JONAS. 1999. *The Urban Growth Machine.* Albany: SUNY Press.

WILSON, THOMAS C. 1991. "Urbanism, Migration, and Tolerance: A Reassessment." *American Sociological Review* 56 (February): 117–23.

WILSON, WILLIAM J. 1990. *The Truly Disadvantaged,* reprint ed. Chicago: University of Chicago Press.

———. 2010. "Why Both Social Structure and Culture Matter in a Holistic Analysis of Inner-City Poverty." *Annals of the American Academy of Political and Social Science* 629: 200–19.

WILSON-DOENGER, GEORJEANNA. 2000. "An Exploration of Sense of Community and Fear of Crime in Gated Communities." *Environment & Behavior* 32: 597–611.

WINKS, ROBIN W. 2000. *The Blacks in Canada: A History,* 2nd ed. Montreal: McGill–Queen's University Press.

WIRTH, LOUIS. 1938. "Urbanism as a Way of Life." *American Journal of Sociology* 44 (July): 1–24.

———. 1964. *On Cities and Social Life.* Chicago: University of Chicago Press.

WIRTH, LOUIS, AND ALBERT J. REISS. 1981. *On Cities and Social Life: Selected Papers.* Chicago: University of Chicago Press.

WOLBRECHT, CHRISTINA, KAREN BECKWITH, AND LISA BALDEZ, eds. 2008. *Political Women and American Democracy.* New York: Cambridge University Press.

WOLFE, TOM. 1998. "Atlanta's Edge Cities." *A Man in Full.* New York: Farrar, Straus and Giroux.

WOLFINGER, NICHOLAS H. 1995. "Passing Moments: Some Social Dynamics of Pedestrian Interaction." *Journal of Contemporary Ethnography* 24 (October): 323–40.

WOLFGANG, BEN. 2011. "States Leaving Feds Behind on School Reforms." *Washington Times,* April 29, p. 3.

WOLINSKY, JULIAN. 2004. "What Follows the Millennium?" *Railway Age* 205 (July): 27–29.

WORLD HEALTH ORGANIZATION. 2010. *Progress on Sanitation and Drinking Water: 2010 Update.* Geneva: World Health Organization.

YELP.COM. 2011. "Tower City Center." Accessed at http://www.yelp.com/biz/tower-city-center-cleveland on August 13, 2011.

YEN, HOPE, AND BEN NUCKOLS. 2012. "Urban Chinatowns Wan as Asians Head to Suburbs." *Huff Post DC,* January 19. Accessed at http://www.huffingtonpost.com/2012/01/19/urban-chinatowns-decline_n_1217122.html on April 14, 2012.

ZHOU, MIN. 2003. "Urban Education: Challenges in Educating Culturally Diverse Children." *Teachers College Record* 105 (May): 208–25.

———. 2009. "How Neighbourhoods Matter for Immigrant Children: The Formation of Educational Resources in Chinatown, Koreatown, and Pico Union, Los Angeles." *Journal of Ethnic & Migration Studies* 35 (August): 1153–79.

ZIA, HELEN. 2001. *Asian American Dreams: The Emergence of an American People.* New York: Farrar, Straus and Giroux.

ZIELENBACH, SEAN. 2005. "Understanding Community Change: A Look at Low-Income Chicago Neighborhoods in the 1990s." *Neighborhood Change in America.* Washington, D.C.: The Urban Institute. Accessed at http://www.urban.org/publications/311151.html on July 25, 2011.

ZUKIN, SHARON. 1993. *Landscapes of Power: From Detroit to Disney World.* Berkeley: University of California Press.

PHOTO CREDITS

INDEX

Note: The letters 'f' and 't' followed by locators refer to the figures and tables cited in the text

A

absolute poverty, 344, 416
abstract space, 179, 416
Addams, Jane, 315–16
Adidas, 189
administrative cities, 177, 416. *See also* political cities
administrative function, 3
Africa, 359–68, 381
African Americans
  buppies, 272
  in Chicago, 62–53, 106, 315–16
  crime and, 352–55
  in Detroit (2010), 300f
  migration from south to north, 63
  poverty rates, 266–67
  in selected U.S. Cities, 297t
  in suburbs, 284–88
African cities, 360f
agglomeration industries, 174, 184, 416
agglomerations, urban, 74, 229, 383, 384t, 419
aging in place, 19
agricultural revolution, 25
AIDS, 363
Akron, Ohio, 19
Alexander the Great, 33, 363
All Our Kin (Stack), 225
Alonso, William, 175–77
amenity cities, 156, 416
American Beauty (film), 227
American Dream, minorities, 286f
American Express, 82
American Family Inns, 198
American Psychologist, 128
America's Technology Highway, 71
Anderson, Elijah, 345
Anderson, Nels, 139
The Annals (Tacitus), 46
annexations, 63
anonymity, 142, 209, 211. *See also* impersonality in the city
Antigone (Sophocles), 246
antisocial behavior, 137, 144. *See also* impersonality in the city
An-Yang, China, 35
apartheid, 362, 416. *See also* segregation
apathy, 128
Apple of My Eye (Hanff), 76
archeological discoveries. *See also* historical perspectives
  Caral, Peru, 10, 24
  Catal Hüyük, Turkey, 27–30
  Egyptian cities, 32–33

  Indus region, 33–35
  Jericho, Israel, 26–27
  London, 10–11
  New York, 11
  Uruk, Mesopotamia, 31
arcologies, 399, 416
Arcosanti, Arizona, 399
Aristides, Aelius, 38
Aristotle, 12, 13, 20
Armour, Philip, 314, 321
Asia Minor, 28f–29f
Asian cities, 369f
Asian Indians, 294–95, 301–2
Asians, 284, 285, 288, 299–3
As You Like It (Shakespeare), 231
Athens, Greece, 2157, 244–47, 245f, 257, 389
Atlanta, Georgia, 15f
  black population, 286, 297–8
  Centennial Place, 335
  central business district, 15f
  edge cities of, 99–100, 106
  location of, 151
  Piedmont Park, 402
  spaghetti junction, 93f
  sprawl, 89, 92–93
  transit solutions, 99
Atlanta's Edge Cities (Wolfe), 100
Atlanta Regional Council, 89
Augustus (emperor), 389
Austin, Texas, 18, 99, 220, 394
Aztecs, 354

B

Babel IIB, 399
Bacon, Roger, 48
Baghdad, Iraq, 158
Baltimore, Maryland
  black population in, 63, 297t
  crime, 145
  declining population, 19
  gentrification, 332
  globalization, 197f
  growth and expansion, 58–59, 60
  Harborplace, 179, 406
  Harvey's study, 181–82, 199
  mental health, 145
  neighborhoods of, 181f
  seaport, 197 ll
  shopping centers in, 67
Baltzell, E. Digby, 262, 283, 294
Banfield, Edward C., 72, 327, 34
Bangkok, Thailand, 376–77

Banham, Rayner, 169
Baricevic, Frank, 128
Beacon Hill, 163, 271–72
Beijing, China, 253–58, 389. *See also* Ming Peking, China
  Oriental Plaza, 254f
Bellah, Robert N., 110
Bellamy, Edward, 387
The Bell Curve (Herrnstein and Murray), 344
Bell South, 98
Ben & Jerry's, 273
Bensman, Joseph, 236
Benson, Simon, 114
Berlin, Germany, 192f
  mass transit system, 192f
BIDs (Business Improvement Districts), 83
big box stores, 89, 116
birth rate, 44
Black Plague, 44, 48–49
blacks
  buppies, 272
  in Chicago, 63, 106, 315–16, 319f
  crime and, 343–45
  migration from south to north, 63
  poverty rates, 266–67
  in suburbs, 284–88
  in urban areas, 296–99
Blakely, Edward J., 108, 109
Blake, William, 391
Blau, Judith, 344
Blau, Paul, 344
Bleak House (Dickens), 15
bobos, 272–73, 416
Bobos in Paradise: The New Upper Class and How They Got There (Brooks), 273
Bookchin, Murray, 252
boomer cities, 102, 105f, 416
Borjas, George, 293
Boston
  Downtown, 204f
  Harbor point, 334f
Boston Commons, 390
BosWash megalopolis, 69. *See also* megalopolis, megaregion
Bott, Elizabeth, 215
Boulton, Matthew, 249
bourgeoisie, 44, 416
boweries, 77
Brasilia, Brazil, 6, 393f, 414
Breaking Through: Transforming Urban School Districts (Simmons), 338
break-of-bulk points, 155, 157, 409, 416
Bremer, Frederika, 313

Broadacre City, 398–99, 407
Brooks, David, 272–73
Brownsville, New York, 208
Brown, Theodore, 62
Brown v. Board of Education, 339
bubonic plague, 49
Buffalo, New York, 75
buppies, 272, 416
Burchell, Robert, 95
Burgess, Ernest W., 161–63, 165, 168, 332
Burleigh Street Community Development Corporation, 276
Burnam, David, 414
Burnham, Daniel, 390
Burroughs, William S., 273
Business Improvement Districts (BIDs), 83
Byron, Robert, 363–64

C

Caesar, Julius, 46
Calhoun, John B., 144
Callow, Alexander B., Jr., 56
Cambridge Shopping Centres, 106
Canada. *See also* Montreal, Canada; Toronto, Canada
    crime in, 341
    edge cities, 99, 106, 179
    gated communities, 109
    geomatics, 166
    immigration, 13, 292–94
    megalopolis of, 68
    migration from farms to cities, 62
    poverty in, 197
    racial and ethnic minorities, 292–94, 296, 300–2
    social stratification in, 9
    sprawl in, 92–93
Canadian Council on Social Development, 197
Canberra, Australia, 392
capitalism
    crime and, 343–44
    culture and, 248–53
    Industrial Revolution and, 44
    Marxist views of, 122
    in North America, 260
    urban development and, 178–79, 181
    welfare capitalism, 182–83
    world-systems analysis, 187–89
Capone, Al, 316
Caral, Peru, 10, 24
Carcassonne, France, 43f
Castells, Manuel, 178, 182–83, 199
Catal Hüyük, 27f
CBD (central business district), 15f, 164–65, 174, 176f, 204–5, 416
Celebration, Florida, 397
cell phones, 143f, 226
Celtic tribes, 46–47
census tracts, 106, 166, 416
Central American cities, 356f

central business district (CBD), 15f, 164–65, 174, 176f, 204–5, 416
Central Park, 76, 78, 271, 388, 402
central place theory, 173–74, 416
Cephren (pharaoh), 33
chain migration, 293, 416
Chan Chan, Peru, 36
Chandigarh, India, 398
Charleston, South Carolina, 56, 58, 60, 222, 234, 288
charter schools, 339–41, 416
Chattanooga, Tennessee, 96
Cheng-chou, China, 35
Chennai, India, 195
Cheops (pharaoh), 33
Chesapeake Bay Foundation, 91
Chicago, Illinois
    Addams area, 220
    black population, 63, 106, 315–16, 319f
    Cabrini-Green, 335
    case study, 312–20
    concentric zones, 161, 162f
    crime rate, 343
    crossroads location, 151, 155
    edge cities, 106
    Gage Park neighborhood, 281
    gated communities, 109
    gentrification of, 275f
    Gold Coast, 271–72
    green roofs, 99
    gridiron city, 159
    growth and expansion, 63, 132, 311–12, 314
    Hispanics, 317, 319, 320f, 321
    historical perspectives, 313–14
    Hull House, 315–16
    Navy Pier, 318f
    organized crime, 316
    politics, 316–17
    population in, 69
    sectors, 161
    skyscrapers, 61
    skyline, 313f
    sociology of, 133–34
    South Barrington, 283
    urban schools, 338
Chicago School, 161, 168–70, 173, 288, 338
Chicago Urban League, 133
Childe, V. Gordon, 257
Chinatown, migration pattern, 302f
Chinese cities
    Beijing, 253–56
    historical perspectives, 372–73
    Ming Peking, 159, 240–48, 257
    urban empires, 35–37
Chinese immigrants, 300–1
Chongqing, China, 372
Christaller, Walter, 175. *See also* central place theory
CIDs (common-interest developments), 111–13, 117, 416. *See also* gated communities
Cincinnati, Ohio, 63, 89, 179, 220, 284, 334, 394

City Beautiful movement, 390–91, 416
city-data.com, 279, 283, 285, 396, 397
city dwellers, 137f, 141f, 146, 223f
city, emergence of, 239
city slickers, 234–35
The City of Tomorrow and Its Planning (Le Corbusier), 398
city planning. *See* urban planning
city-states, 30–31, 38, 416
CityWalk, 179–80
civic culture, 238–39, 240f, 257, 416
civilization and cities, 236–40
Civil War, 60, 78
Clarke, Henry B., 314
class differences. *See* social stratification
Claudius (emperor), 41, 46
Cleveland, Ohio, 62, 74–75, 99, 151, 186, 284
clothing, 213
Clybourne, Archibald, 314
Colonial Era, 56–57, 77, 362
colonization, 49, 354, 359, 367, 370, 377, 416
Columbia, Maryland, 113, 303, 333, 396, 414
combined statistical area (CSA), 67
common-interest developments (CIDs), 111–13, 117, 416. *See also* gated communities
communism, 132, 253–57
community policing, 347f, 348, 416
community, sense of, 110–11
commute distances, 92–93. *See also* traffic
competition, 160–61, 170, 174
Compton, California, 286, 288
concentric zones, 161
The Condition of the Working Class in England (Engels), 120
conurbation, 3
consolidated statistical area (CSA). *See* megalopolis
Cortés, Heman, 354–55
cosmic calendar, 24, 416
cosmopolites, 138, 139–40, 332, 416
Costa, Lúcia, 414
Council of Metropolitan Toronto, 409
Cowley, Abraham, 141
The Crack in the Picture Window (Keats), 226–27
Cressey, Paul, 139
Crete, 38
crime, 3, 20, 66, 128, 144, 166, 221, 341–48, 375
    city size, 343t
    rates per 1,000 residents by type of community, 342t
critical mass, 140, 416
critical urban sociology. *See also* urban sociology
    Baltimore study, 181–82
    capitalism and, 182–83, 188
    economics and, 173–85
    focus of, 14
    globalization and, 64, 173, 187, 189

political economy and, 177–78
urban growth and, 185–86
welfare capitalism, 182–83
crossroads, natural, 155, 156, 222, 418
crowded conditions, 144–45, 211, 316
Crusades, 40
Crystal Island, 400
Cubans, 304
Cultural Revolution, 253–56
Culture, 231
Beijing, China, 253–56
capitalism and, 248–53
civic, 238–39, 240, 257, 416
civilization and cities, 236–40
defined, 15, 416
Hellenic Athens, 2, 236, 238, 240,
244–46, 248–49, 257, 389
immigration and, 62–63
Ming Peking, 240–44
thriving cities and, 48
urban/rural tensions, 231–34
Cuzco, Peru, 36, 354
*The Cycle of Family Homelessness: A Social
Policy Reader*, 198
Czech Republic, Church of Our
Lady, 14f

D

Daley, Richard J., 317
Dallas, Texas, 69, 92, 102, 109, 151, 303,
337, 402
Dana, Richard Henry, 6, 7
Dear, Michael J., 169, 170
The Death and Life of Great American Cities
(Jacobs), 332, 400–1
decentralization
defined, 64, 417
of inner city populations, 19, 64–68
Le Corbusier and, 398
migration and, 293
New York City, 79
in Sweden, 392
trend of, 19
de facto segregation, 296, 416
defensible space, 346f, 349, 417
Delhi, India, 370, 371
traffic congestion, 370f
deindustrialization, 186
de jure segregation, 296, 417
demographic transition, 44, 53, 383
density of population, 137, 144–45
Denton, Nancy, 299
Denver, Colorado, 99, 106, 151, 225, 303
design life, 89
Desperate Housewives (TV), 227
de Tocqueville, Alexis, 235
Detroit, Michigan
abandoned buildings in, 329
agglomeration industries, 174, 184
black population, 63, 297–98, 299,
300f
City Beautiful movement, 390
declining population, 18

economic ranking, 75
education system, 337
environmental initiatives, 99
horizontal integration, 183
Muslim population, 306–7
Poletown, 328
revitalization of, 220, 221, 223
resource distribution, 410
Dewey, John, 316
Diala, Chamberlain C., 146
Dickens, Charles, 15, 45, 63, 157, 250–51
"Die Stadt" (Weber), 129–30
dinks, 272, 417
Disney's Main Street, 179
districts, 205, 417
diversity
homeless people, 282
low-income neighborhoods, 280–82
middle-class neighborhoods,
272–73, 276
mixed-income neighborhoods, 278–80
and population size, 136
suburban social class, 282–88
upper-class neighborhoods, 270–72
working-class neighborhoods, 276–78
division of labor, 25, 417
domestication of plants, 10, 25
Dorchester, Lord, 409
Doré, Gustave, 49
Dos Passos, John, 150
Downs, Anthony, 74
downsizing, 193
Dreiser, Theodore, 316
dress codes, 213–14
Dubai, Khalifa Tower, 368f
Durham, England, 157
Durkheim, Emile, 122, 125–26, 129–30,
131–32, 133, 135, 136, 147, 390

E

Eade, John, 50
early cities, 36–38, 57f, 354–55
ecological perspectives, 13, 160–66
ecological sociology, 166, 417
economics. *See also* globalization
central place theory, 173–75
colonization effects, 377–78
free enterprise and, 174–75, 177
global development, 188f
importance of, 15
and politics, 407
restructuring, 187, 192–93, 417
in siting cities, 151–52
Special Economic Zones, 372
as urban defining criteria, 3
edge cities. 105f. *See also* new cities
characteristics of, 100–1, 105–6, 179
defined, 418
emergence of, 74, 100–1, 117
examples of, 106–7
types of, 102–5
Edge City (Garreau), 100
edges, 205, 417

education, 336–41
Edward Scissorhands (film), 227
Edward the Confessor (king), 47
Egyptian cities, 32–33
Eiesland, Nancy, 99, 100, 101
Eliot, T.S., 1–2, 3
Elizabeth I, 48
El Museo del Barrio, 271
emergence of cities, 12–13, 24–25
Emergency Relief Appropriation
Act, 394
eminent domain, 96–97, 325
Engels, Friedrich, 49, 120–21, 122–23,
131–32, 178, 248–49, 250
England, 231
urban and rural population, 231t
environmental concerns
China, 255–56
in developing world, 380
garden cities, 387–88, 391, 396, 417
green belts, 391, 417
natural areas, 96, 137, 160–61,
174, 418
physical surroundings, 203–8
sprawl, 91–96
environmental sociology, 95, 417
Erie Canal, 58
Erin Mills, Ontario, 397
escalators, 211
Ethelred (king), 47
ethnic differences, 293–94. *See also*
minorities
ethnic food, 295
ethnic villages, 138, 139, 276, 278,
294, 417
Euripides, 236
Europe. *See also* London, England; Paris,
France
evolution of cities, 10–12. *See also*
megaregions
The Exurbanites (Spectorsky), 99
exurbs, 99–101, 417. *See also* suburbs

F

factories, 276–77
false consciousness, 122, 417
Family Disorganization (Mowner), 139
Federal Bureau of Investigation
(FBI), 71
Federal Housing Administration
(FHA), 325
feudalism, 40–41, 43–44
Field, Edward, 175
Filipino immigrants, 301
first cities, chronologies, 37f
The First Cities (Hamblin), 30
first urban revolution, 30–31
Fischer, Claude, 40, 147, 344. *See also*
subcultural theory of urbanism
flooding, 92
food
in multicultural city, 295
surplus, 25, 26, 34, 36

free enterprise, 174, 177
friendships, 218
functional nature, 3

G

The Gang (Thrasher), 139
Gans, Herbert, 138–39, 140, 216, 217,
    227, 276, 294, 328, 407
garden cities, 387, 396, 414
Garden Cities of To-morrow (Howard),
    387–88
Gardner, Carol Brooks, 108
Garreau, Joel, 74, 100, 102, 106–7
gated communities, 108–11, 108f,
    117, 417. *See also* common-interest
    developments (CIDs)
Gates, Bill, 261, 273
gemeinschaft, 122–26, 123f, 132, 144,
    215–23, 228, 276, 417
Gemeinschaft and Gesellschaft (Tönnes),
    121–25
gender differences, 308–11. *See also*
    women
gendered spaces, 308, 417
General Electric, 73
General Motors, 328
general strain theory (GST), 349, 417
The Genius (Drieser), 316
Genovese, Kitty, 128
gentrification, 74, 278–79, 282, 324,
    329–32, 417
geographical perspectives. *See also* urban
    geography
  central place theory, 173–75
  economics and, 173
  Houston, Texas, 151–52
  location of cities, 151–52
  Los Angeles, 12, 168–70
  Los Angeles, California, 150
  Miami, Florida, 152
  Montreal, Canada, 152
  New Orleans, Louisiana, 154
  New York City, 13, 152, 198
  Salt Lake City, Nevada, 152
  San Francisco, California, 150
  siting factors, 152–57
  Washington, D.C., 152
Geographic Information Systems (GIS),
    166–67, 417
geomatics, 166
gesellschaft, 122–26, 132, 134, 144, 209,
    214–15, 228, 417
ghettos, 280, 286, 298, 326, 335, 343,
    417. *See also* shantytowns; slums
GI Bill of Rights, 325
GIS (Geographic Information Systems),
    166–67, 417
Glaab, Charles N., 62
global cities, 7, 428
global economy, 187f, 188f,
    191f, 197f
  economic development, 190f, 194f
globalization, 64. *See also* economics
  Baltimore, Maryland, 197f

critical urban sociology and, 173, 183,
    187, 189, 191–92, 198, 200
defined, 417
deindustrialization and, 187
economic restructuring, 189, 191
Grand Rapids, Michigan, 279
Los Angeles, California, 174
Miami, Florida, 191
New York City, 185, 189
postindustrial cities and, 73
Toronto, Canada, 191
urban growth and, 185, 193
world-systems analysis, 187–89
Goethe Institut, 271
The Gold Coast and the Slum
    (Zorbaugh), 139
Gottdiener, Mark, 179
Gottman, Jean, 69, 70
governments, 177–79, 181–83, 192. *See
    also* zoning
Grafton County, New Hampshire, 235
Grand Central Terminal, 82
Grand Rapids, Michigan, 279
Grand Trunk and Great Western
    railways, 409
Greater London Council, 47, 51
Great Expectations (Dickens), 157
Great Fire of London, 49, 390
Great Migration, 62–63, 62f, 287,
    296–97
Greece, 2–3, 12, 38, 40, 246–47,
    257, 390
green belts, 394–96, 417
greenbelt towns, 394–96
Greendale, Wisconsin, 394
greenfields, 102, 417
Green Hills, Ohio, 394
Green, Robert, 327
Greensboro, North Carolina, 93–94
gridiron cities, 159–60, 159f, 241,
    390–91, 417
Grosse Point Shores, Michigan, 283
groupthink, 254, 417
growth versus sprawl, 87, 95
Guangzhou, China, 372
Guatemala, open air markets, 232f
Guggenheim Museum, 271

H

Habitat for Humanity, 331, 348
Hall, Edward, 144
Hamblin, Dora Jane, 30
Hamilton, Alexander, 59
Hanff, Helene, 76
Hard Times (Dickens), 251
Harold (king), 47
Harris, Chauncy, 164–65
Harvey, David, 181–82. *See also* Baltimore
    study
Hayner, Norman, 139
Heckscher, August, 115, 412, 414
Hell's Kitchen, 79
Henry Ford Museum, 221
Henry VIII, 48

Herrnstein, Richard, 344
Hester Street (film), 210
heterogeneity, 137–38
Hewlett-Packard, 116
hierarchical power structure, 25–26, 417
hierarchy of countries, 188–91
Hispanics
  in Boston, 308
  in Chicago, 281, 306
  in gated communities, 109
  heterogeneity, 138
  in ethnic villages, 278–89
  income, 305t
  life style, youngsters, 219
  in Los Angeles, 303, 305, 306, 308
  more than 100,000 (2010), 304t
  in New York City, 76, 306
  in Ohio, 284
  population statistics, 83–84, 304t, 305t
  poverty and, 266–67
  in suburbs, 285, 288, 289
  in Upper Manhattan and the
    Bronx, 307f
  in urban areas, 303–6
  wealth, 266
historical perspectives. *See also* archeo-
    logical discoveries; Colonial Era;
    Industrial Revolution
  African cities, 359–63
  Chicago, 312–20
  Chinese cities, 372–73
  city-states, 31–32
  early city characteristics, 36–38
  Egyptian cities, 31–33
  emergence of cities, 12–13, 25–26
  housing, 324–28
  Indian cities, 368–71
  Japanese cities, 373–75
  Latin American cities, 358–59
  Middle Eastern Cities, 363–68
  North American cities, 56–64
  permanent settlements, 25–26
  Rome, Italy, 38–40, 41, 389
  Southeast Asia, 375–77
  Toronto, Canada, 409–10
  urban empires, 30–35
  urbanization, 6, 7, 8t, 19, 43–45, 62–63
  urban planning, 400–4
Hitler, Adolf, 50
The Hobo (Anderson), 139
Ho Chi Minh City, Vietnam, 212
Höflich, Joachim, 17
Hollywood, California, 140, 174,
    219, 221
home equity, 265–66
"Home From Nowhere" (Kunstler), 89
homelessness, 198, 264f, 282, 324
Homelessness Research Institute, 197
homeowner's associations, 111
Homes for the Homeless, 198
Honduras Weekly, 196
Hong Kong, China, 372–73
  International Finance Centre, 374f
horizontal integration, 183–84, 417
hostile environments, 309, 417
Hotel Life (Hayner), 139

housing, 19, 193, 198, 324–29,
    331–35, 341
    low-income, 331f
Housing Act of 1968, 327
Houston, Texas
    break-of-bulk point, 155
    gated communities, 109
    growth and expansion, 69, 151–52,
        151f
    Hispanics in, 288, 303–306
    Hurricane Katrina and, 154
    immigration to, 292t, 337
    poverty, 268
    raw material access, 155
Howard Community College, 396
Howard, Ebenezer, 387–88, 390, 391,
    392, 394, 397–98, 414
Howell, Joseph, 217
How the Other Half Lives (Riis), 79
Hoyt, Homer, 162–63, 165
Hull House, 315–16
human ecology, 171, 417
hunting and gathering societies, 25–26
Hurricane Katrina, 92, 154, 397
Hyatt Center, 318
hyperghettos, 263, 417
hypersegregation, 299, 345, 418

I

Ibadan, Nigeria, 231, 232
ideal type, 130, 418
ignored stranger, 129f
imagability of cities, 206
immigration
    Asians, 284, 285, 295, 299–3
    to Canada, 13, 300–3
    Chicago, 312–13
    Hispanics, 303–6
    legal immigrants (U.S), 294t
    London, 50, 51
    Los Angeles, California, 294–5
    Muslims, 306–7
    Newark, New Jersey, 276–78
    New York City, 62–63, 78, 79, 294
    poverty and, 268–69, 279
    U.S. and Canada, 13, 292–93
    women, 388–10
impersonality in the city, 142–44
income, 265–68, 272–75, 280–86, 305t,
    327–28. *See also* poverty
    Hispanic Americans, 305t
    households, 265f
    median, 266f
index of dissimilarity, 298, 418
India, 195, 368–71
Indus region, 33–35
industrialism, 249–50, 418
industrial location theory, 170, 418
industrial parks, 65–66, 418
Industrial Revolution, 49f
    city growth in, 12, 13, 44, 186
    clothing and, 213
    gridiron cities and, 159
    industrialism in, 250

in London, 49
in North America, 59–60
sociology and, 122
urban planning in, 383
inequality, 9
information technology, 188
inner cities. *See also* poverty
    decentralization of, 19, 64–68
    defined, 418
    deterioration and abandonment,
        328–30
    fighting in, 347
    neighborhoods, 280
    poverty in, 195, 285–88, 299
    revitalization of, 330–36
Institute for Children and Poverty, 282
Intel, 116
invasion-succession, 13, 161, 286,
    294, 418
Ironbound area, 276–78
Irvine, California, 397
Isfahan, Iran, 363–64
Islamic cities, 363–66

J

Jacobs, Jane, 72, 115, 328, 332, 400–2,
    411, 414
Jakarta, Indonesia, 376
James, Duke of York, 77
Japanese cities, 374–75
Japanese immigrants, 303
Jeannette Blast Furnace, 186
Jefferson, Thomas, 60
Jerde, Jon, 180
Jericho, Israel, 26–27, 363
Jersey City, New Jersey, 203f, 205
Johnson, Samuel, 45, 52
Joliet, Louis, 313

K

Kazin, Alfred, 208–10
Keats, John, 226
Kelo v. *City of New London*, 97
Kipling, Rudyard, 313
Kistiakowski, Bogdan, 133
Kiwanis Club, 236
Kolkata (Calcutta), India, 370–71
Koreans, 294–95
Krivo, Lauren, 345
Kuhn, Maggie, 328
Kunstler, James Howard, 89
Kush civilization, 359–61
Kyoto, Japan, 373–74

L

La Guardia, Fiorello, 232–33
Lake Mead, 92
landmarks, 203, 418
land-use, 94–99, 165–67, 175–77, 176f,
    179–80

Las Vegas, Nevada, 90f, 92, 153
    spread-city phenomenon, 90f
Latin America, 196, 352–59, 358f, 382
Latinos. *See* Hispanics
Le Corbusier, 398–99, 414
Lefebvre, Henri, 178–79, 181, 182, 185
L'Enfant, Pierre, 59
Letchworth, England, 387, 414
Levitt, Abraham, 66–67
The Levittowners (Gans), 227
Levittown, New York, 66–67, 227
Liangzhu, China, 35
Liebow, Eliot, 215, 216
lifestyle communities, 109–10, 418
Lincoln Technical Institute, 396
Little Havana, 167
The Living City (Wright), 399
location of cities. *See* geographical
    perspectives
Lofland, Lyn, 211–13, 217
Logan, John, 185–86
London, England, 16f, 51f
    archeological discoveries, 10–11
    break-of-bulk point, 157
    case study, 45–52
    Great Fire, 49, 390
    industrialization and colonization, 49,
        248–49
    Medieval era, 47–48
    modern era, 49–52
    population, 44, 48
    rebuilding of, 389f
    Renaissance era, 48–49
    Roman influence on, 39, 46–47
    social class, 215
    social stratification in, 248
    Wren Sir Christopher's Plan, 389f
Looking Backward (Bellamy), 387
Lorillard, Pierre II, 283
Los Angeles, California, 103f
    Baldwin Hills, 396
    black population, 286
    Cinco de Mayo, 220
    City Beautiful movement, 390
    community policing, 347f
    crime, 347f
    edge cities, 102
    gated communities, 109
    gentrification of, 98
    geographical perspectives, 12–13,
        150–51, 168
    globalization and, 203
    gridiron city, 159
    Griffith Park, 402
    growth and expansion, 150–51
    Hispanics in, 284, 292,
        303, 305
    Hollywood, 140, 174, 219, 221
    imagability of, 206
    immigration, 294, 303–5, 337
    Kevin Lynch study, 203
    map, 103f
    Monterey Park, 288
    Pico-Union neighborhood, 281
    poverty in, 268, 281–82
    South Gate suburb, 284–88

Los Angeles, California (*Continued*)
    sprawl, 92
    sunbelt city, 69
    traffic congestion, 168f
Los Angeles School, 168–70, 173
lower class, 263–64, 288–89
Lynch, Kevin, 203–6

M

Machu Picchu, 11f
Macionis, John, 195, 212
MacIver, Robert, 110
magnet schools, 339, 418
Mall of America, 180
Manchester, England, 120–21
Manhattan
    Beth's Map, 208f, 209f
    recession, impact on, 80
A Man in Full (Wolf), 100
Mann, Arthur, 233
mapping, 166–68, 206–11
Mark I and Mark II towns, 391
Marquette, Jacques, 313–4
Marshall Field's, 314
Marx, Karl, 49, 122–23, 131–33, 136,
    146–47, 173, 178–79, 182, 260
Massachusetts Institute of Technology
    (MIT), 71
Massey, Douglas, 299, 345
mass transit, 67, 93f, 98f, 114–16
Mather, Cotton, 56, 72, 85
McCabe, James D., Jr., 324
McCall, Tom, 114
McCormick, Cyrus, 314
McCormick Reaper Company, 314
McKay, Henry, 139
McKenzie, Evan, 112, 113
McMansions, 228, 418
Mead, George Herbert, 316
mechanical solidarity, 125, 418
medieval cities, 41–42, 42f, 47–48
megacities, 2, 7, 8t, 19t, 173, 193,
    384, 418
megalopolis, 6, 69–60, 73, 393, 418
Megalopolis (Gottman), 70
Megamergers, 186, 418
megaregions, 6, 69–71
    defined, 418
    evolution, 69
    Northeast assets, 69–71, 80
    in U.S., 71f
    sprawl, 87
Menes *See* pharaoh
mental health, 145–46
mental maps, 207–9, 418
Merton, Robert, 138
Mesoamerica, 35–36
Mesopotamia, 31–33
Metropolis, 237
    racial segregation, 345t
metropolitan area, 6–7, 418
Metropolitan Museum of Art, 270–71
metropolitan statistical areas (MSA), 67,
    80, 418

Metropolitan Toronto Act, 409
Mexican Americans, 305
Miami, Florida
    amenity city, 156
    blacks in, 286, 299
    crime, 342
    ethnic villages, 278
    gated communities, 109
    globalization and, 191
    growth and expansion, 152
    Hispanics in, 292–93, 304–6
    immigration to, 292, 337
    Little Havana, 167, 304
    poverty in, 286
Middle Ages, 13, 40, 44, 249
middle class, 262–63, 272–74, 276, 280
Middle Eastern cities, 363–68, 364f. *See
    also* Islamic cities
migration
    chain, 293, 416
    from farms to cities, 62, 296
    from south to north, 63, 296–7
    to suburbs, 284–87
    tolerance and, 142
Miller, Sara, 402
Milton Keynes, England, 391
Milwaukee, Wisconsin, 18, 151, 175, 219,
    274–76, 292, 402
Ming Peking, China, 159, 240–48, 257.
    See also Beijing, China
    Forbidden City, 243f
Minneapolis, 163f
minorities
    Asians, 299–3. *See also specific industries*
    Blacks. *See* blacks
    in Canada, 303, 296, 300–4, 308–10
    crime and, 343–45
    Hispanics. *See* Hispanics
    London, 50
    model, 303
    Muslims, 306–7
    Native Peoples, 308
    New Orleans, Louisiana, 154
    New York City, 84
    post-Civil War U.S., 78
    urban experience and, 215–16
mixed-income neighborhoods, 274,
    279, 289
mobile phones, 17, 128
model minorities, 303
mode of development, 183, 418
mode of production, 183, 418
Moenjo-Daro, Indus region, 33–34, 34f,
    37, 368–69, 387
Molotch, Harvey, 170, 185–86
money, 126
Monterey Park, California, 288
Monti, Daniel J., 231, 238–39
Montreal, Canada, 153f
    annexations, 63
    colonial era, 56–57, 234
    crossroads location, 156
    gridiron city, 159
    growth and expansion, 58–59, 62, 69
    Hispanics in, 304
    immigration to, 296, 304

location, 151
    poverty in, 197
    raw material access, 155
More, Sir Thomas, 48
Morris, Jan, 150
Mowner, Ernest, 139
MSA (metropolitan statistical areas), 67,
    80, 418
Muhammad, 363
multiple nuclei theory, 165f, 168, 170
Mumbai, India, 145, 311
Mumford, Lewis, 22, 25, 116, 238–41,
    244, 250, 252, 411
Muntaner, Carles, 146
Murray, Charles, 344
Museum of New York, 271
Muslims, 306–7, 370–71

N

Nader, Ralph, 328
Nantucket Nectars, 273
National Assessment of Educational
    Progress (NAEP), 336
National Center for Education
    Statistics, 339
National Center for Health Statistics,
    146, 343
National Road, 58
National Wildlife Federation, 92
Native Peoples, 308t
natural areas, 96, 137, 160, 174, 418
natural crossroads, 155, 418
NatureServe, 92
Neighborhood Crime Watch
    organization, 347
net worth, 265–66
New Amsterdam, 56, 77, 390
Newark, New Jersey, 276–78, 327f,
    334–35
    ethnic neighborhoods, 277f
new cities
    characteristics, 102
    defined, 418
    Islamic countries, 367–68
    growth of, 101–2
    Portland, example as, 223
    types, 102–6
    urban sociology, 173
New Communities Program, 391. *See also*
    Mark I and Mark II towns
New Deal, 325
New London, Connecticut, 97
Newman, Katherine S., 225
Newman, Oscar, 346
Newman, Paul, 222
New Orleans, Louisiana, 61, 92, 153–54,
    342, 401–2, 414
    Katrina, impact on, 154
new towns
    in Britain, 391–2
    defined, 391, 418
    in North America, 393–97
    success and failure, 397–98
    worldwide, 392–93

New Towns Act, 391
New Urbanism, 332–36, 396–97, 418
New York City, New York, 104f
  agglomeration industries, 174
  apathy in, 128
  archeological discoveries, 11
  area map, 104f
  Asian population, 302
  black population, 63, 286, 296
  case study, 75–84
  Central Park, 76, 78, 271, 274f,
    390, 402
  colonial era, 56–57, 77, 233
  compact growth, 95
  crime, 342, 346, 348
  decentralization and, 79
  edge cities, 102, 106
  exurbs, 99–101
  first U.S. capital, 77
  Freedom Tower, 81
  gated communities, 108–9
  gentrification, 286
  geographical perspectives, 12, 146,
    151, 174
  global city, 7
  globalization, 185, 189
  Grand Street, 406f
  green roofs, 99
  gridiron city, 159
  growth and expansion, 58–59, 60–62,
    68, 77, 236
  Hispanics in, 303–6, 307f
  homeless, 198, 264f
  housing, 324–25
  immigration to, 62–63, 78–79, 278,
    288, 292–3, 294, 337
  International Food Festival, 224f
  Kenmare Square, 405f
  Little Italy, 293f
  location of, 12
  magnet schools, 340f
  map of area, 104f
  mass transit, 62
  megalopolis, 70
  mental maps of, 207–8
  minorities in, 84
  modern era, 80–84
  Muslims in, 307
  New Amsterdam, 56–57, 390
  as New Amsterdam, 56–57, 77
  PATH transit hub, 80
  personality of, 221
  politics, 232–33
  population statistics, 19, 78t, 80–81
  post-Civil War, 78–80
  poverty in, 76, 271
  revitalization of, 80–84, 406
  San Gennaro Festival, 220
  Seagram Plaza, 402
  skyline, 203f
  South Bronx, 82, 329f, 330
  stress in, 146
  sword-swallower, 215f
  technological advances, 61
  tenements, 63
  Tuxedo Park, 283

  unemployment in, 84
  Upper East Side, 270–71
  urban hierarchy, 175
  Washington Square, 402
  West Broadway, 404f
New York Mercantile Exchange, 82
New York Public Library, 83
New York Stock Exchange, 77
Nike, 116, 189, 191f, 273
No Child Left Behind Act of 2001,
  336–38
nodes, 205, 418
nomads versus settlers, 25
Nordstrom's, 116
North America. *See also* Mesoamerica
  capitalism in, 260
  colonial era, 56–57
  great metropolis era, 60–63
  growth and expansion, 58–60
  modern era changes, 64–71
  postindustrial cities, 71–74
  urban concentrations, 73f
  urban dominance, 233–34
North American Cities, 59t
  Asian Populations (2010), 301f
  geographical location, 151f
North Olmstead, Ohio, 285

O

Odd Fellows, 236
Ogbu, John, 336–37
Olaf (king), 47
oligopolies, 183, 418
Olympic Games, 46
ordered segmentation, 317–18, 418
organic solidarity, 125, 418
The Organization Man (Whyte), 227
organized crime, 63, 316, 371
Oshawa Centre, 106–7
Ottawa Municipal Board, 409
Our Town (Wilder), 124
outsourcing, 73

P

Palo Alto, California, 284
parallel social institutions, 304, 418
Paris, France, 235, 238
  urban dominance, 233f
Parker, Theodore, 236
Park, Robert, 133–36, 160, 170, 207,
  237, 312. *See also* human ecology
Parrillo, Vincent, 57, 157, 292
Pasternak, Judy, 107
Paterson, New Jersey, 59, 396, 390
  first planned U.S. industrial city, 164f
paths, 205, 418
pedestrians, 210–11
  social rules, 211f
Penn, William, 159–60. *See also*
  Gridiron city
Pericles, 245
permanent settlements, 25–26, 36–37

Petry, Ann, 212
*Philadelphia Gentlemen: The Making
  of a National Upper Class*
  (Baltzell), 262
The Philadelphian (Powell), 222
Philadelphia, Pennsylvania
  black population, 63
  capital city of U.S., 57–58, 152
  CID restrictions, 112
  colonial era, 56, 234
  declining population, 18, 69
  gay community, 140
  gridiron city, 159
  growth and expansion, 58–59, 78
  Hispanics in, 306
  housing, 326, 329, 332
  immigration to, 337
  mass transit, 60, 175
  as megalopolis, 7, 70
  national city, 175
  parks and squares, 406
  personality of, 222
  upper class, 262
  urban rituals, 220
Philip of Macedon, 247, 363
Phoenix, Arizona
  crime, 342
  gated communities, 109
  Hispanics in, 303
  housing market crisis, 330
  light-rail system, 98f
  location of, 151
  sprawl, 89, 165
  sunbelt city, 19, 69
phone usage, 17, 234
physical surroundings, 203–7,
  227–28, 347
Pizarro, Francisco, 355
Placemaking, 402–5, 418
*Placing London: From Imperial Capital to
  Global City* (Eade), 50
Plato, 236, 246
Pleasantville (film), 227
policing, 348
political "bosses," 63
political cities, 156, 416
political economy
  Castells theories, 182–83
  defined, 419–20
  focus of, 14
  gentrification and, 332
  Harvey theories, 181–82. *See also*
    Baltimore study
  Lefebvre theories, 178–79, 181,
    182, 185
  limitations of, 200
  Logan and Molotch theories,
    185–86
  principles of, 191–93
  Scott theories, 183–85
  themed environments, 179–81
  urban life and, 173
  world-systems analysis and, 187–89,
    193–96
political fragmentation, 90,
  171, 418

population. *See also* population statistics; urbanization
changes in (2000-2010), 68f
current and projected, 379t
demographic transition, 44–45
density, 137–38, 144–45
in developing world, 383
distribution, 45f
heterogeneity of, 137–38
increases in, 4–6
largest world cities, 352–53
of London, 44, 46
in megacities, 8t
movement of, 159–61
projection, urban areas, 5f
racial/ethnicity, 292t
size and diversity, 136
30 largest U.S. Cities (2000–2010), 18t
world, 4t
population statistics
African Americans, 292t, 297t
Asians, 301f
crime, 343t
early East Coast cities, 58t
European cities, 44t
Hispanics, 305t, 307f, 320f
New York City, 78t, 80–81
North American cities, 65t
Northern U.S. cities, 64t
primate cities, 353
racial/ethnic, 297t
rate of change, 64, 71f
selected East Coast Cities, 58t
selected European Cities (1700-2010), 44t
selected Metropolitan Areas, 65t
selected Northern U.S. Cities, 64t
ten largest U.S. Cities in 2010 compared to 1950, 69t
urban agglomerations, 384t
as urban defining criteria, 3–4
U.S. cities, 19, 71
world cities, 2, 8, 25
world countries, 4t, 45f
Portland, Oregon, 96, 113–17, 223, 408
Portland Trail Blazers, 116
postindustrial cities, 71–74
postmodernism, 13, 14, 168–70, 173, 418
Portland
Tom McCall Waterfront Park, 115f
poverty. *See also* inner cities
absolute, 344, 416
African American rates of, 268
in Canada, 197, 267
in Chicago, 273–74
data, 266–68
in developing world, 193–95, 380–82
distance from CBD and, 176–77
Hispanics and, 267
in Houston, 268
hyperghettos, 263, 417
immigration and, 267–68, 277
in London, 49
in Los Angeles, 268, 281–82
lower-class neighborhoods, 280–81, 298–9

in megacities, 2–3
in Miami, 286
mutual support and, 224–26. *See also* income
in New York City, 75, 268
percentage in 2010, 267f
public housing and, 326, 327
relative, 344, 419
social stratification and, 9
in Toronto, 197, 279–80
urbanization of, 193–97
Powell, Richard, 222
Powell's City of Books, 116
preindustrial cities, 57f
prestige communities, 110, 419
primacy ratio, 353, 419
primary circuit of capital, 178, 419
primate cities, 352–53, 367, 419
Princeton, New Jersey, 284
Privatopia (McKenzie), 112
productive surplus, 26, 419
The Professional Thief (Sutherland), 139
The Project for Public Spaces (PPS), 403f
Pruitt-Igoe, 326, 327f
The Protestant Establishment (Mann), 233
public behavior, 239–40
public harassment, 310
public housing, 326–28, 333
public space, 309 ill, 311f
privatization of, 217f
young adults, 218f
Public Works Administration, 325
Puerto Ricans, 304–5
push-pull factors, 296, 419

Q

quality of life, 20–22, 63–64, 379–80
Quebec City-Windsor megaregion, 69

R

Raban, Jonathan, 215
racial minorities. *See* minorities
racial profiling, 307, 419
racial residential segregation, 298f
Radburn, New Jersey, 394, 395f, 414
The Radiant City (Le Corbusier), 398
radiocentric cities, 158f, 419
Radio City Music Hall, 76
Rainwater, Lee, 327
Raleigh, Sir Walter, 48
Ramses II (pharaoh), 33
recession 1990, 80
Residential Education Training (RET) Centers, 198
regal/ritual cities, 36, 419
Regional Plan Association, 95
relative poverty, 344, 419
Renaissance cities, 40–43, 53, 389–90
reputational method, 261, 419
Residential Education Training Centers (RET), 198

Reston, Virginia, 396
RET (Residential Education Training Centers), 198
retirement areas. *See* Sunbelt cities
Revere, Paul, 219–21
revitalization of cities
Chattanooga, Tennessee, 96
Detroit, Michigan, 221–23
inner cities, 330–32
New York City, 80–84, 411
North America, 72–74
Portland, Oregon, 223
San Antonio, Texas, 97f
Suisun, California, 96
Revolutionary War, 57–58, 77
Reynolds, Malvina, 227
Riesman, David, 226
Riis, Jacob, 78, 79
rituals in cities, 220
Ritz-Carlton Hotel, 74, 82
Robbins, Illinois, 287
blue-collar community, 287
Rockefeller, Jay, 261
Rolling Stones, 273
Rome, Italy, 38–40, 46–47, 389, 407
great wall, 46f
imperial days, 39f
Roosevelt, Franklin D., 325, 394
Rouse, James, 115, 179, 396, 398, 405–7, 408, 414
rural/urban tensions, 60, 63, 233–36
Rush, Benjamin, 60

S

Sagan, Carl, 24
Saigon, Vietnam, 212
Saks Fifth Avenue, 116
Salt Lake City, Utah, 151
Sampson, Robert J., 170
San Antonio, Texas, 18, 69, 97f, 221, 334
Sandberg, Carl, 313
San Francisco, California
changes in, 6–7, 10
Chinatown, 133, 167, 300
City Beautiful movement, 390
diversity, 272
earthquake, 156, 219
Excelsior District, 278
geography, 150, 175, 222
gridiron layout, 252
Haight-Ashbury, 218, 332, 401
Hispanics in, 292, 303
immigration to, 292, 337
Pacific Heights, 271–72, 271f
pedestrians, 209–10
personality, 218
raw material access, 156
Robert Pitts Plaza, 335
Union Square, 402
urban planning, 405
"San Francisco Looks West" (Dos Passos), 150
Sassen, Saskia, 45, 185, 189
scenes, 218–19, 419

Schaumburg, Illinois, 107
Schein, Virginia, 224
school vouchers, 339, 419
Scott, Allen, 183–85
Seagram Plaza, 402
Seattle, Washington
    break-of-bulk point, 156
    edge cities, 106
    mass transit, 99
    seaport, 155
    sectors, 163f
    social movements, 226
    sprawl, 91
    themed environments, 179
    urban planning, 408
second circuit of capital, 178, 181, 419
second urban revolution, 43–45
Section 8 Program, 327, 330
sector theory, 165
security-zone communities, 109, 419
Seeger, Pete, 227
segregation, 296, 298–99, 306, 309, 319,
    345, 345. *See also* apartheid
sense of community, 110–11
September 11, 2001, 80. *See also* New
    York City, New York
Servicemen's Readjustment Act of
    1944, 325
SES (socioeconomic status), 260
settlers versus nomads, 26
sexual harassment, 310
Shakespeare, William, 48, 231, 232
The Shame of the Cities (Steffens),
    133, 134
Shanghai
    modern high-rise buildings, 256
    World Financial Center, 373f
shantytowns, 20–21, 189, 193, 288,
    380–82, 393. *See also* ghettos; slums
    India, 195
    Latin America, 383f
shapes of cities, 157–58
Shaw, Clifford, 139
Sherman Park Community Association
    (SPCA), 276
Shimizu Corporation, 399
shopping malls, 67, 87, 102
Silicon Valley, 184f
Simmel, Georg, 122, 126–38, 144, 147,
    203, 229
Simon, Robert E., 396
Singapore, Republic of Singapore, 375
single-room occupancy hotels
    (SROs), 282
skyscrapers, 61
slavery, 361
slums, 280–81, 419. *See also* ghettos;
    shantytowns
Small, Albion W., 133
smart growth, 94–97, 419
sprawl versus smart growth, 95t
Smart Growth America, 92
Smith, Geddes, 394
smog, 150
snowbelt cities, 72f
Snyder, Mary Gail, 108, 109

social area analysis and mapping,
    166–68
social disorganization theory, 344, 419
Social Factors in Juvenile Delinquency
    (Shaw and McKay), 139
social impact analysis, 94, 419
social movements, 226
social power, 9, 50, 419
social promotions, 336, 419
social psychology
    gemeinschaft, 215–21
    humanizing cities, 224–26
    of physical environment, 227–28
    of social environment, 215–21
    social movements, 226
    of suburbs, 226–27
    texture of cities, 221, 222, 229
    urban experience and, 14–15
social space, 179, 419
social stratification, 9, 260, 268, 288,
    419. *See also* diversity
social structure, 6, 257
socioeconomic status (SES), 261f
Socrates, 236, 246, 247
Soja, Edward W., 169
Soleri, Paolo, 399
Solon, Ohio, 246, 284, 285
Sophocles, 246
Sorkin, Michael, 179
soul of cities, 236–38
South America, 357f
South Barrington, Illinois, 283
South Bronx, New York, 82, 329f, 330
Southeast Asian cities, 375–77
*Spaces for Consumption (*Miles), 180
Spain, Daphne, 308
spatial behavior, 144
spatial patterns, 149–71
SPCA (Sherman Park Community As-
    sociation), 276
Special Economic Zones, 372
Spectorsky, A.C., 99
Spengler, Oswald, 236–37, 240, 256
spillover communities, 286
The Spirit of Youth and the City Streets (Ad-
    dams), 315
Spokane, Washington, 94
sprawl. *See also* suburbs
    consequences of, 91–94
    defined, 419
    open space, 96
    overview, 87–90
    Phoenix, Arizona, 89, 165
    Portland, Oregon, 109
    traffic and, 92–93, 97–98
*Sprawl Costs: Economic Impacts of
    Unchecked Development* (Burchell et
    al.), 88
sprawl versus smart growth, 95t
Springdale, New York, 236
squatters, 20–21
SROs (single-room occupancy
    hotels), 282
Stack, Carol, 225
Stamp Act, 77
Stark, Andrew, 110

Steffens, Lincoln, 133, 134
Steinbeck, John, 330
Stein, Clarence, 394
stereotypes, 226–27
St. Joseph Regional Medical
    Center, 276
St. Louis, Missouri
    abandoned buildings, 329
    blacks in, 286–87, 299
    crime, 128, 134
    crossroads location, 155
    gated communities, 108
    geography, 150
    Pruitt-Igoe project, 326–27
    Union Station, 406
Stockholm, Sweden, 392
*Stop Street Harassment: Making Public
    Places Safe and Welcoming for Women*
    (Kearl), 310
strangers, 211–13
strategic policing, 348, 419
The Street (Petry), 212
streetcars, 61, 66f
street children, 196
Street Corner Society (Whyte), 142
stress and urban life, 146
Strong, Josiah, 234
subcultural theory of urbanism, 140
suburbs, 61–63, 65–68, 70, 86–118,
    226–28, 282–88. *See also* exurbs;
    sprawl
subways, 212
Suisman, Douglas, 169
Suisun, California, 96
Sumer, 31–33
Sunbelt cities, 18, 72, 84, 90, 297
sunbelt expansion, 64, 68–69, 419
Sutherland, Edwin H., 139
Suttles, Gerald, 217, 221, 317
Swift, Gustavus, 314

T

Tacitus (Roman historian), 46
Taeuber, Karl, 298
Talen, Emily, 143
Tally's Corner (Liebow), 216
Taroudannt, Morocco, 361f
Tarpon Springs, Florida, 177
The Taxi Dance Hall (Cressey), 139
Teaford, Jon, 99
technological developments, 17, 60,
    61, 66
tenements, 63
Tenochtitlán, 354–55, 387, 389
Teotihuacan, Mexico, 36–37, 354,
    387, 389
terrorism, 206
texture of cities, 221, 222, 419
"The City: Suggestions for the Investiga-
    tion of Human Behavior in the
    Urban Environment" (Park), 133
"The Invasion of the City Slickers"
    (Perrin), 234–5
themed environments, 179–80

"The Metropolis and Mental Life" (Simmel), 126
theorists' views, city, 131t
"The Suburban Sadness" (Riesman), 226
Thomas, June, 279
Thrasher, Frederich, 139
Times Square, 83f, 135f
Time Warner, 82–83
Timmer, Doug A., 225
tolerance, 141
To Rome (Aristides), 38
Toronto, Canada
  Alexandra Park, 410
  annexations, 63
  blacks in, 272
  Caribana Festival, 220
  case study, 408–12
  City Hall Square, 402
  Council of Metropolitan Toronto, 67–68
  crime, 341
  ethnic villages, 278
  family poverty rates (2001, 2006), 269f
  future plans, 412–13
  gated communities, 109
  gentrification, 331
  globalization and, 189–90
  gridiron city, 159
  growth and expansion, 58, 62, 64
  Hispanics in, 304
  historical perspectives, 409–10
  immigration to, 300–1, 306
  lifestyle scenes, 218
  location of, 151
  mass transit, 67
  multistory, mirrored building, 250f
  native peoples in, 308
  postindustrial, 71
  poverty in, 196, 267–68
  St. Lawrence neighborhood, 279–80
  urban planning, 387–88, 412–13
Torrio, Johnny, 316
total fertility rate, 375, 419
traffic, 92–93, 97–98
TRY-2004, 399–400
Tutankhamun (pharaoh), 33
Tuxedo Park, 283–84
Tweed, William "Boss," 79
Two Years Before the Mast (Dana), 6, 7
typhoid epidemics, 64
Tysons Corner, Virginia, 101f, 102

U

Ullman, Edward, 164–65, 168
unemployment, 50, 84
UN-Habitat, 193
The Unheavenly City (Banfield), 72
United Nations International Children's Emergency Relief Fund (UNICEF), 196
United Nations Population Division, 3
University of California, 156
University of Chicago, 133–36
upper class, 261–62, 270–72, 308–9

uptowns, 102, 419
urban agglomerations, 6, 383, 384t, 419
urban cluster, 3, 419
urban development and growth, 178–79, 181–84, 226, 250–53
urban dominance, 233–36, 419
urban ecology, 12, 160–65, 191, 419
urban empires
  Americas, 35–36
  China, 35
  Crete and Greece, 38
  Egyptian cities, 32–33
  Indus region, 33–34
  Medieval cities, 40–43
  Mesopotamia, 31–32
  Middle Ages effect on, 40
  Renaissance cities, 43
  Rome, 38–40, 41
Urban Enclaves: Identity and Place in America (Abrahamson), 167
urban explosion, 64, 419
urban geography, 12, 150–51, 419. *See also* geographical perspectives
urban growth boundaries, 96, 114–17
urban implosion versus urban explosion, 64, 419
urbanism, 9, 136, 140–41, 332–36, 418, 420
"Urbanism as a Way of Life" (Wirth), 136, 231
urbanization. *See also* population; population statistics
  in Africa, 362
  decentralization, 19, 64–69
  defined, 4, 6, 420
  England, nineteenth century, 231
  global perspectives, 3, 6t, 9t, 19–20
  historical perspectives, 6f, 8t, 18t, 45–46, 61–62
  origins of, 24
  of poverty, 193–98
  process of, 4
  versus urbanism, 140
Urban League, 133
Urban Mobility Report, 92
The Urban Neighborhood (Keller), 278
urban networks, 215–21
urban planning
  architectural visions, 398–400
  economics and politics, 407–8
  historical perspectives, 387–91
  mid-size developments, 405
  new towns movement, 391–400
  sidewalks and neighborhoods, 400–1
  squares and parks, 401–2
  Toronto, Canada, 410–11, 412–13
  values and, 407–8
urban political economy. *See* political economy
urban redevelopment. *See* revitalization of cities
urban renewal, 179, 282, 324–25, 326, 335, 410
urban/rural tensions, 60, 62, 231–33
urban sociology. *See also* critical urban sociology
  analytic criteria, 148

defined, 12
Emile Durkheim, 125–26
European tradition, 122–32
Georg Simmel, 126–27, 129
Karl Marx and Friedrich Engels, 122–24
Max Weber, 129–30
modern research, 141–47
in North America, 132–40
urban utopias, 398, 400, 420
Uruk, Mesopotamia, 31
U.S. Bureau of Transportation Statistics, 92
U.S. and Canada Green Cities Index, 99
U.S. Census Bureau, 4, 67–68
U.S. Geological Survey, 92

V

Vancouver, British Columbia, 64, 98–99
vertical disintegration, 184–85, 420
Vidich, Arthur, 236
Vietnamese immigrants, 302–3

W

Waldinger, Roger, 75
A Walker in the City (Kazin), 210
Wal-Mart, 89
Walton, John, 146
Warner, W. Lloyd, 260–64
War of the Worlds (film), 276
Washington, D.C.
  administrative city, 156
  blacks in, 63, 292
  City Beautiful movement, 390
  edge cities, 106, 107
  government-planned communities, 394
  growth and expansion, 18
  immigration to, 306, 337
  interpersonal networks, 217
  location of, 152
  megalopolis, 7, 70
  school vouchers, 339
  street-corner men, 215–16
  terrorism, 206
Washington, George, 77
Watt, James, 249
wealth, 265–66
Weber, Alfred, 153–54
Weber, Max, 129–30, 153, 238, 260
welfare capitalism, 182–83
Wells Fargo Bank, 116
Welwyn, England, 387
Western and Atlantic Railroad, 151
Westminster Abbey, 47
wetlands, 91–92
white flight, 276
Whitney Museum, 271
Whyte, William F., 142, 227, 334
Whyte, William H., 115, 276, 345, 402, 414
Wiese, Andrew, 287
Wilde, Oscar, 48

Wilder, Thornton, 124
William the Conqueror, 47
Wilmington, Delaware, 330
Wirth, Louis, 136–44, 146–47, 231, 237, 248, 257, 342, 382, 390
Wolfe, Tom, 100
women, 308–11
working class, 263, 284, 296, 393
world cities, 45
A World of Strangers (Lofland), 211
world-systems analysis, 8, 187–89, 352, 420
World Trade Center, 80, 81f, 206

Wren, Sir Christopher, 3, 389–90
Wright, Frank Lloyd, 398

X

Xiaoping, Deng, 255

Y

Yerba Buena, California, 6, 335
Young, Arthur, 235

The Young Philadelphians (film), 222
Youngstown, Ohio, 186
yuppies, 72, 74, 214, 272, 274, 332, 420

Z

Zedong, Mao, 253, 372
zoning, 90, 96, 111, 117. *See also* governments
Zorbaugh, Harvey, 139
Zukin, Sharon, 181